Microsoft®
Windows 2000
Beta Training Kit

Microsoft Press

PUBLISHED BY
Microsoft Press
A Division of Microsoft Corporation
One Microsoft Way
Redmond, Washington 98052-6399

Library of Congress Cataloging-in-Publication Data
Microsoft Windows 2000 Beta Training Kit / Microsoft Corporation.
     p. cm.
  ISBN 0-7356-0644-7
   1. Microsoft Windows (Computer file). 2. Microsoft Windows NT.
  3. Operating systems (Computers). I. Microsoft Corporation.
  QA76.76.O63M52413225 1999
  005.4'469--dc21   99-17058
                                        CIP

Printed and bound in the United States of America.

1 2 3 4 5 6 7 8 9 WCWC   4 3 2 1 0 9

Distributed in Canada by ITP Nelson, a division of Thomson Canada Limited.

A CIP catalogue record for this book is available from the British Library.

Microsoft Press books are available through booksellers and distributors worldwide. For further information about international editions, contact your local Microsoft Corporation office or contact Microsoft Press International directly at fax (425) 936-7329. Visit our Web site at mspress.microsoft.com.

For Microsoft (Original Instructor-Led Course Content)
Project Lead: Gerry Lang
Program Manager: Rodney Miller
Instructional Designers: Jeanette Decker (Write Stuff), Jim Toland (Computerprep, Inc.)
FYI Technology Services (Program Manager): Paul Adare
Editor: Lynette Skinner (Write Stuff)

For Microsoft Press
Program Manager: Jeff Madden
Project Editor: Michael Bolinger

Author: Rick Wallace

Contents

About This Book

Welcome to *Microsoft Windows 2000 Beta Training Kit*. This kit introduces you to the Windows 2000 family of products and prepares you to install, configure, administer, and support Microsoft Windows 2000 Professional and Microsoft Windows 2000 Server.

This kit introduces the various tools for administering and configuring Windows 2000 including the Microsoft Management Console, the Task Scheduler, Control Panel, and the registry. You will learn about the network protocols and services that ship with Windows 2000. This kit concentrates on Transmission Control Protocol/Internet Protocol (TCP/IP), the network protocol of choice for Windows 2000. It also emphasizes the Domain Name System (DNS), which is an Internet and TCP/IP standard name service, and is required for Windows 2000 domains and Active Directory. Active Directory integrates the Internet concept of a namespace with Windows 2000 directory services. Active Directory uses DNS as its domain naming and location service so Windows 2000 domain names are also DNS names. In fact, the core unit of logical structure in Active Directory is the domain.

This course also supports the Microsoft Certified Systems Engineer program.

Note For more information on becoming a Microsoft Certified Systems Engineer, see the section titled "The Microsoft Certified Professional Program" later in this introduction.

Each chapter in this book is divided into lessons. Many lessons include hands-on practices that allow you to demonstrate a particular concept or skill. Each chapter ends with a set of review questions to test your knowledge of the chapter material. The "Getting Started" section of this chapter provides important setup instructions that describe the hardware and software requirements to complete the procedures in this course. It also provides information about the networking configuration necessary to complete some of the hands-on procedures. Read through this section thoroughly before you start the lessons.

Intended Audience

Anyone who wants to learn more about Windows 2000 will find this book useful. This book was developed for information system (IS) professionals who need to design, plan, implement, and support Windows 2000.

Prerequisites

- A knowledge of the fundamentals of current networking technology is required.

- At least 6 months of experience supporting a network or successful completion of the *Networking Essentials, Hands-On Self-Paced Training for Supporting Local and Wide Area Networks* course is recommended.

Features of This Book

Each chapter opens with a "Before You Begin" section, which prepares you for completing the chapter.

▶   Each chapter is divided into lessons. Many step-by-step practices are provided for you to perform on your test machine to learn the different facets of administering a Windows 2000 network. These practices are placed at the end of lessons and consist of one or more exercises or procedures. Each procedure is marked with a triangle as shown in the margin next to this paragraph.

Some additional procedures are placed outside the practices in the general text material to outline techniques in a more general way or to present procedures that can't be carried out with the minimum hardware configuration required for this Training Kit. You will find the minimum hardware requirements for this Training Kit listed later under "Hardware Requirements" in the Getting Started section of this chapter.

Important   The additional procedures that are not included within the practice sections are intended as general information to advance your knowledge of Windows 2000. Because many of the practices build upon procedures you do in earlier practices, if you work through the additional procedures in the general text of the book you may alter the state of your test machine and may not be able to carry out subsequent practices exactly as they are presented.

The "Review" section at the end of the chapter allows you to test what you have learned in the chapter.

Appendix A, "Questions and Answers," contains all of the book's review and practice questions and corresponding answers.

Notes

Notes appear throughout the lessons.

- Notes marked **Tip** contain explanations of possible results or alternative methods.
- Notes marked **Important** contain information that is essential to completing a task.
- Notes marked **Note** contain supplemental information.
- Notes marked **Caution** contain warnings about possible loss of data.

Conventions

- Hands-on procedures that you may follow are presented in numbered lists of steps (1, 2, and so on). A triangular bullet (▶) indicates the beginning of a procedure.

- The word *select* is used for highlighting folders, file names, text boxes, menu bars, and option buttons, and for selecting options in a dialog box.

- The word *click* is used for carrying out a command from a menu or dialog box.

Notational Conventions

- Characters or commands that you type appear in **bold lowercase** type.

- *Italic* in syntax statements indicates placeholders for variable information. *Italic* is also used for book titles.

- Names of files and folders appear in title caps, except when you are to type them directly. Unless otherwise indicated, you can use all lowercase letters when you type a file name in a dialog box or at a command prompt.

- File name extensions appear in all uppercase.

- Acronyms appear in all uppercase.

- Monospace type represents code samples, examples of screen text, or entries that you might type at a command prompt or in initialization files.

- Square brackets [ ] are used in syntax statements to enclose optional items. For example, [*filename*] in command syntax indicates that you can choose to type a file name with the command. Type only the information within the brackets, not the brackets themselves.

- Braces { } are used in syntax statements to enclose required items. Type only the information within the braces, not the braces themselves.

- Icons represent specific sections in the book as follows:

Icon	Represents
	A hands-on practice. You should perform the practice to give yourself an opportunity to use the skills being presented in the lesson.
	Chapter review questions. These questions at the end of each chapter allow you to test what you have learned in the lessons. You will find the answers to the review questions in Appendix A, "Questions and Answers," at the end of the book.

Keyboard Conventions

- A plus sign (+) between two key names means that you must press those keys at the same time. For example, "Press Alt+Tab" means that you hold down Alt while you press Tab.

- A comma (,) between two or more key names means that you must press each of the keys consecutively, not together. For example, "Press Alt, F, X" means that you press and release each key in sequence. "Press Alt+W, L" means that you first press Alt and W together, and then release them and press L.

- You can choose menu commands with the keyboard. Press the Alt key to activate the menu bar, and then sequentially press the keys that correspond to the highlighted or underlined letter of the menu name and the command name. For some commands, you can also press a key combination listed on the menu.

- You can select or clear check boxes or option buttons in dialog boxes with the keyboard. Press the Alt key, and then press the key that corresponds to the underlined letter of the option name. Or you can press Tab until the option is highlighted, and then press the Spacebar to select or clear the check box or option button.

Chapter and Appendix Overview

This self-paced training course combines notes, hands-on practices, and review questions to teach you how to install, configure, administer, and support Windows 2000. The course is designed to be completed from beginning to end. If you choose not to complete the book from beginning to end, see the "Before You Begin" section in each chapter. Hands-on practices that require preliminary work from preceding chapters refer to the appropriate chapters.

The book is divided into the following chapters:

- The "About This Book" section you are now reading contains a self-paced training overview and introduces the components of this training. Read this section thoroughly to get the greatest educational value from this self-paced training and to plan which lessons you will complete.

- Chapter 1, "Introduction to Windows 2000," explains the Microsoft Windows 2000 family of products, which includes Windows 2000 Professional, Windows 2000 Server, Windows 2000 Advanced Server, and Windows 2000 Datacenter Server. This chapter presents the features and benefits of using Windows 2000. It provides an overview of workgroups, domains, and domain trees, and explains the logon process and the Windows 2000 Security dialog box.

- Chapter 2, "Installing Windows 2000," reviews the Windows 2000 installation process and provides a hands-on lab in which you install Windows 2000 Server. It also presents troubleshooting solutions to some common problems that may occur during the installation process.

- Chapter 3, "Examining the Windows 2000 Architecture," presents an overview of the Windows 2000 architecture. Understanding the Windows 2000 architecture and system components helps you to better understand Windows 2000 installation, configuration, customization, optimization, and support. This chapter also presents Windows 2000 processing and the Windows 2000 memory model.

- Chapter 4, "Using Microsoft Management Console and Task Scheduler," introduces one of the primary administrative tools that you use to manage Windows 2000, the Microsoft Management Console (MMC). MMC provides a standardized method to create, save, and open administrative tools. MMC does not provide management functions itself, but it is the program that hosts management applications used to perform administrative tasks.

- Chapter 5, "Using Windows Control Panel," introduces the Windows 2000 Control Panel. Control Panel is another of the primary administrative tools that you use to manage Windows 2000. It contains programs that you use to configure hardware settings by using hardware profiles; display properties, including multiple displays; and system settings, such as virtual memory settings and user and system environment variables.

- Chapter 6, "Using the Registry," presents an overview of the registry and Registry Editor. The registry is a hierarchical database that Microsoft Windows 2000 uses to store system configuration information. Registry Editor is the tool you use to view and modify the registry.

- Chapter 7, "Managing Disks," presents an overview of Microsoft Windows 2000 Disk Management. The tool used to manage disks in Windows 2000 is the Disk Management snap-in. It provides shortcut menus to show you which tasks you can perform and includes wizards to guide you through creating partitions and volumes and upgrading disks.

- Chapter 8, "Installing and Configuring Network Protocols," presents the skills and knowledge necessary to configure TCP/IP and to install other network protocols, including NWLink, NetBIOS Enhanced User Interface (NetBEUI), and Data Link Control (DLC). This chapter also discusses the process for configuring network bindings, which are links that enable communication between network adapter cards, protocols, and services.

- Chapter 9, "Configuring the DHCP Service," introduces the Dynamic Host Configuration Protocol (DHCP) Service in Microsoft Windows 2000. DHCP centralizes and manages the allocation of TCP/IP configuration information by assigning Internet Protocol (IP) addresses automatically to computers that are configured as DHCP clients. This chapter presents the skills and knowledge necessary to install and configure the DHCP Service. It also discusses the DHCP lease process.

- Chapter 10, "Configuring the Windows Internet Name Service," introduces the purpose and function of the Windows Internet Name Service (WINS), as well as name registration. It also explains WINS server and client configuration, support for non-WINS clients, and DHCP server for WINS configuration.

- Chapter 11, "Configuring the DNS Service," introduces DNS and name resolution. DNS is a distributed database that is used in TCP/IP networks to translate computer names to IP addresses. It also presents the skills and knowledge necessary to install and configure the DNS Service, to configure DNS clients, and to troubleshoot the DNS Service.

- Chapter 12, "Implementing Active Directory," introduces Active Directory. Active Directory integrates the Internet concept of a namespace with Windows 2000 directory services. Active Directory uses DNS as its domain naming and location service so Windows 2000 domain names are also DNS names. In fact, the core unit of logical structure in Active Directory is the domain. This chapter presents the skills and knowledge necessary to plan and install Active Directory.

- Chapter 13, "Setting Up User Accounts," introduces user accounts. User accounts provide users with the ability to log on to a domain to gain access to network resources or to log on at a computer to gain access to resources on that computer. This chapter explains how to plan your user accounts. It also presents the skills and knowledge necessary to create domain and local user accounts and to set properties for them.

- Chapter 14, "Setting Up Groups," introduces groups. A group is a collection of user accounts. This chapter explains how grouping user accounts simplifies user account administration. It also presents the skills and knowledge necessary to implement groups.

- Chapter 15, "Setting Up and Configuring Network Printers," presents the skill and knowledge necessary to add and configure network printers. Network printers allow users to print over the network. This chapter also discusses how to troubleshoot common printing problems that are associated with setting up network printers.

- Chapter 16, "Securing Resources with NTFS Permissions," introduces NT File System (NTFS) folder and file permissions. It presents the skills and knowledge necessary to assign these permissions to user accounts and groups. It also explains how moving or copying files and folders affects these permissions and explains how to troubleshoot common resource access problems.

- Chapter 17, "Administering Shared Folders," explains how to share file resources. When a folder is shared, users can connect to the folder over the network and gain access to the files that it contains. However, to gain access to the files, users must have permissions to access the shared folders. This chapter also explains how to secure shared folders with permissions and how to provide access to them.

- Chapter 18, "Administering Active Directory," continues where Chapter 12, "Implementing Active Directory," left off. Active Directory is the Microsoft directory service. It stores information about resources on the network and provides the services that make these resources easy to locate, use, and manage. Each resource is represented as an object in the directory. This chapter explains how to create, locate, control access to, and delegate administrative control of Active Directory objects.

- Chapter 19, "Administering User Accounts," extends your knowledge of user accounts beyond creating user accounts for new users. It explains how to use and create local, mandatory, and remote user profiles; how to modify existing user accounts; and how to plan and use home directories on a client computer or on a file server.

- Chapter 20, "Auditing Resources and Events," explains the basics of auditing, which is the process of tracking activities on a computer. In addition, this chapter helps you understand what you need to consider before you set up an audit policy, how to set up auditing on resources, and how to maintain security logs.

- Chapter 21, "Implementing Group Policy," introduces you to group policies, which are another method for defining a user's desktop environment, and which are typically set for the entire domain or network to enforce corporate policies. This chapter teaches you what group policies are and helps you understand the different types of group policies.

- Chapter 22, "Administering Network Printers," presents the skills and knowledge necessary to administer printers. The tasks involved with administering network printers consist of managing printers, managing documents, and troubleshooting printers. This chapter also introduces the Manage Printers permission, and the tasks that require you to have the Manage Printers permission.

- Chapter 23, "Managing Data Storage," introduces data storage management on NTFS-formatted volumes. It provides the skills and knowledge necessary for you to use disk compression, disk quotas, and disk defragmentation. Disk compression allows you to store more data on a disk. Disk quotas allow you to control how much space a user can use on a disk. Defragmenting a disk allows your system to access files and save files and folders more efficiently.

- Chapter 24, "Backing Up and Restoring Data," introduces you to backing up and restoring data, which enables you to ensure that network data, such as Active Directory, is not lost. Windows 2000 provides the Windows Backup tool to allow you to back up your data.

- Chapter 25, "Implementing Disaster Protection," introduces techniques available in Microsoft Windows 2000 for preventing and recovering from computer disasters. Computer disasters include any event that renders a computer unable to start. Disaster protection is a term that describes efforts by support professionals to prevent computer disasters and to minimize downtime in the event of system failure. This chapter discusses using an uninterruptible power supply (UPS), implementing fault tolerance using redundant array of independent disks (RAID), and using Automatic System Recovery (ASR).

- Chapter 26, "Monitoring Access to Network Resources," explains how to use the Shared Folders snap-in. You use the Shared Folders snap-in to view and create shares, to view sessions and open files, and to disconnect users from your shared folders.

- Chapter 27, "The Windows 2000 Boot Process," introduces you to the Microsoft Windows 2000 boot process. It explains the Intel-based boot process and the Alpha-based boot process. It also explains the Boot.ini file and how to create a Windows boot disk for an Intel-based computer.

- Appendix A, "Questions and Answers," lists all of the practice questions and review questions from the book, and provides the suggested answer.

- Appendix B, "Computing the Number of Client Access Licenses," provides a worksheet for you to use to calculate the number of Client Access Licenses (CALs) you need to buy and whether you should use Per Seat or Per Server licensing.

- Appendix C, "Creating Setup Disks," explains how to create the four Windows 2000 Server Setup disks. Unless your computer supports booting from a CD-ROM drive, you must have the four Windows 2000 Server Setup disks to complete the installation of Windows 2000 Server.

- Appendix D, "Managing Backup Tapes," provides strategies for rotating and archiving tapes. It also helps you determine the number of tapes required for your backup strategy.

Getting Started

This self-paced training course contains hands-on practices to help you learn about Windows 2000.

Some practices and some exercises within practices are marked as optional. To complete these, you must have two networked computers or be connected to a larger network. Both computers must be capable of running Windows 2000. If you have only one machine, read through the steps and familiarize yourself with the procedure as best you can.

Caution   Several exercises may require you to make changes to your server. This may have undesirable results if you are connected to a larger network. Check with your network administrator before attempting these exercises.

Hardware Requirements

Each computer must have the following minimum configuration. All hardware should be on the Microsoft Windows 2000 Hardware Compatibility List (HCL). You'll find this list in the HCL.TXT file in the \Support directory of the Windows 2000 installation CD-ROM.

- Pentium 166
- 64 MB of RAM
- 2-GB hard disk
- 12X CD-ROM drive
- SVGA monitor capable of 800X600 resolution (1024X768 recommended)
- Microsoft Mouse or compatible pointing device

Software Requirements

The following software is required to complete the procedures in this course:

- Windows 2000 Server Beta 3

Setup Instructions

Set up your computer according to the manufacturer's instructions.

For the exercises that require networked computers, you need to make sure the computers can communicate with each other. The first computer will be designated as a primary domain controller, and will be assigned the computer account name Server1 and the domain name microsoft.com. This computer will act as a domain controller in microsoft.com.

The second computer will act as a stand-alone server for most of the optional practices in this course.

Caution   If your computers are part of a larger network, you *must* verify with your network administrator that the computer names, domain name, and other information used in setting up Windows 2000 as described in Chapter 2 do not conflict with network operations. If they do conflict, ask your network administrator to provide alternative values and use those values in all of the exercises in this book.

The installation of Windows 2000 is part of this kit and is covered in Chapter 2. If you are installing two computers, follow the same instructions on both computers.

The Microsoft Certified Professional Program

The Microsoft Certified Professional (MCP) program provides the best method to prove your command of current Microsoft products and technologies. Microsoft, an industry leader in certification, is on the forefront of testing methodology. Our exams and corresponding certifications are developed to validate your mastery of critical competencies as you design and develop, or implement and support, solutions with Microsoft products and technologies. Computer professionals who become Microsoft certified are recognized as experts and are sought after industry-wide.

The Microsoft Certified Professional program offers six certifications, based on specific areas of technical expertise:

- **Microsoft Certified Professional (MCP).** Demonstrated in-depth knowledge of at least one Microsoft operating system. Candidates may pass additional Microsoft certification exams to further qualify their skills with Microsoft BackOffice products, development tools, or desktop programs.

- **Microsoft Certified Professional + Internet.** MCPs with a specialty in the Internet are qualified to plan security, install and configure server products, manage server resources, extend servers to run CGI scripts or ISAPI scripts, monitor and analyze performance, and troubleshoot problems.

- **Microsoft Certified Systems Engineer (MCSE).** Qualified to effectively plan, implement, maintain, and support information systems in a wide range of computing environments with Microsoft Windows 95, Microsoft Windows 98, Microsoft Windows NT, and the Microsoft BackOffice integrated family of server software.

- **Microsoft Certified Systems Engineer + Internet (MCSE + Internet).** MCSEs with an advanced qualification to enhance, deploy, and manage sophisticated intranet and Internet solutions that include a browser, proxy server, host servers, database, and messaging and commerce components. In addition, an MCSE+Internet-certified professional is able to manage and analyze Web sites.

- **Microsoft Certified Solution Developer (MCSD).** Qualified to design and develop custom business solutions with Microsoft development tools, technologies, and platforms, including Microsoft Office and Microsoft BackOffice.

- **Microsoft Certified Trainer (MCT).** Instructionally and technically qualified to deliver Microsoft Official Curriculum through a Microsoft Authorized Technical Education Center (ATEC).

Microsoft Certification Benefits

Microsoft certification, one of the most comprehensive certification programs available for assessing and maintaining software-related skills, is a valuable measure of an individual's knowledge and expertise. Microsoft certification is awarded to individuals who have successfully demonstrated their ability to perform specific tasks and implement solutions with Microsoft products. Not only does this provide an objective measure for employers to consider, it also provides guidance for what an individual should know to be proficient. And as with any skills-assessment and benchmarking measure, certification brings a variety of benefits to the individual and to employers and organizations.

Microsoft Certification Benefits for Individuals

As a Microsoft Certified Professional, you receive many benefits:

- Industry recognition of your knowledge and proficiency with Microsoft products and technologies
- Access to technical and product information directly from Microsoft through a secured area of the MCP Web Site
- Logos to enable you to identify your Microsoft Certified Professional status to colleagues or clients
- Invitations to Microsoft conferences, technical training sessions, and special events
- A Microsoft Certified Professional certificate
- Subscription to Microsoft Certified Professional Magazine (North America only), a career and professional development magazine

Additional benefits, depending on your certification and geography, include the following:

- A complimentary one-year subscription to the Microsoft TechNet Technical Information Network, providing valuable information on monthly CD-ROMs.
- A one-year subscription to the Microsoft Beta Evaluation program. This benefit provides you with up to 12 free monthly CD-ROMs containing beta software (English only) for many of Microsoft's newest software products.

Microsoft Certification Benefits for Employers and Organizations

Through certification, computer professionals can maximize the return on investment in Microsoft technology. Research shows that Microsoft certification provides organizations with the following:

- Excellent return on training and certification investments by providing a standard method of determining training needs and measuring results
- Increased customer satisfaction and decreased support costs through improved service, increased productivity, and greater technical self-sufficiency
- Reliable benchmark for hiring, promoting, and career planning
- Recognition and rewards for productive employees by validating their expertise

- Retraining options for existing employees so they can work effectively with new technologies
- Assurance of quality when outsourcing computer services

To learn more about how certification can help your company, see the following backgrounders, white papers, and case studies available on

http://www.microsoft.com/train_cert/cert/bus_bene.htm:

- The Microsoft Certified Professional Program Corporate Backgrounder (mcpback.exe 50K)
- A white paper (mcsdwp.doc 158K) that evaluates the Microsoft Certified Solution Developer certification
- A white paper (mcsestud.doc 161K) that evaluates the Microsoft Certified Systems Engineer certification
- Jackson Hole High School Case Study (jhhs.doc 180K)
- Lyondel Case Study (lyondel.doc 21K)
- Stellcom Case Study (stellcom.doc 132K)

Requirements for Becoming a Microsoft Certified Professional

The certification requirements differ for each certification and are specific to the products and job functions addressed by the certification.

To become a Microsoft Certified Professional, you must pass rigorous certification exams that provide a valid and reliable measure of technical proficiency and expertise. These exams are designed to test your expertise and ability to perform a role or task with a product, and are developed with the input of professionals in the industry. Questions in the exams reflect how Microsoft products are used in actual organizations, giving them "real-world" relevance.

Microsoft Certified Product Specialists are required to pass one operating system exam. Candidates may pass additional Microsoft certification exams to further qualify their skills with Microsoft BackOffice products, development tools, or desktop applications.

Microsoft Certified Professionals + Internet are required to pass the prescribed Microsoft Windows NT Server 4.0, TCP/IP, and Microsoft Internet Information System exam series.

Microsoft Certified Systems Engineers are required to pass a series of core Microsoft Windows operating system and networking exams, and BackOffice technology elective exams.

Microsoft Certified Solution Developers are required to pass two core Microsoft Windows operating system technology exams and two BackOffice technology elective exams.

Microsoft Certified Trainers are required to meet instructional and technical requirements specific to each Microsoft Official Curriculum course they are certified to deliver. In the United States and Canada, call Microsoft at (800) 636-7544 for more information on becoming a Microsoft Certified Trainer. Outside the United States and Canada, contact your local Microsoft subsidiary.

Technical Training for Computer Professionals

Technical training is available in a variety of ways, with instructor-led classes, online instruction, or self-paced training available at thousands of locations worldwide.

Self-Paced Training

For motivated learners who are ready for the challenge, self-paced instruction is the most flexible, cost-effective way to increase your knowledge and skills.

A full-line of self-paced print- and computer-based training materials is available directly from the source—Microsoft Press. Microsoft Official Curriculum courseware kits from Microsoft Press are designed for advanced computer system professionals and are available from Microsoft Press and the Microsoft Developer Division. Self-paced training kits from Microsoft Press feature print-based instructional materials, along with CD-ROM-based product software, multimedia presentations, lab exercises, and practice files. The Mastering Series provides in-depth, interactive training on CD-ROM for experienced developers. They're both great ways to prepare for Microsoft Certified Professional (MCP) exams.

Online Training

For a more flexible alternative to instructor-led classes, turn to online instruction. It's as near as the Internet and it's ready whenever you are. Learn at your own pace and on your own schedule in a virtual classroom, often with easy access to an online instructor. Without ever leaving your desk, you can gain the expertise you need. Online instruction covers a variety of Microsoft products and technologies. It includes options ranging from Microsoft Official Curriculum to choices available nowhere else. It's training on demand, with access to learning resources 24 hours a day.

Online training is available through Microsoft Authorized Technical Education Centers.

Authorized Technical Education Centers

Authorized Technical Education Centers (ATECs) are the best source for instructor-led training that can help you prepare to become a Microsoft Certified

Professional. The Microsoft ATEC program is a worldwide network of qualified technical training organizations that provide authorized delivery of Microsoft Official Curriculum courses by Microsoft Certified Trainers to computer professionals.

For a listing of ATEC locations in the United States and Canada, call the Microsoft fax service at (800) 727-3351. Outside the United States and Canada, call the fax service at (206) 635-2233.

Technical Support

Every effort has been made to ensure the accuracy of this book. If you have comments, questions, or ideas regarding this book, please send them to Microsoft Press using either of the following methods:

E-mail

tkinput@microsoft.com

Postal Mail

Microsoft Press
Attn: Microsoft Windows 2000 Beta Training Kit Editor
One Microsoft Way
Redmond, WA 98052-6399

Microsoft Press provides corrections for books through the World Wide Web at the following address:

http://mspress.microsoft.com/support/

Please note that product support is not offered through the above mail addresses. For further information regarding Microsoft software support options, please connect to http://www.microsoft.com/support/ or call Microsoft Support Network Sales at (800) 936-3500.

For information about ordering the full version of any Microsoft software, please call Microsoft Sales at (800) 426-9400 or visit www.microsoft.com.

C H A P T E R   1

Introduction to Windows 2000

About This Chapter

This chapter presents an overview of the Microsoft Windows 2000 operating system. The information contained in this chapter is based on an early-release beta version of Windows 2000.

Before You Begin

There are no special requirements to complete this chapter.

Lesson 1: Features and Benefits of Windows 2000

This lesson introduces you to the family of Windows 2000 products. It explains the renaming of the Microsoft Windows NT version 5.0 operating system, some of the key differences between these products, and the environment for which each product is designed.

After this lesson, you will be able to

- Identify the key features of Windows 2000, including features that are specific to Windows 2000 Professional and to Windows 2000 Server.

Estimated lesson time: 15 minutes

Overview of Windows 2000

Windows 2000 is a multipurpose operating system with integrated support for client/server and peer-to-peer networks. It incorporates technologies that reduce the total cost of ownership and provides for scalability from a small network to a large enterprise network. *Total cost of ownership (TCO)* is the total amount of money and time associated with purchasing computer hardware and software, and deploying, configuring, and maintaining the hardware and software. TCO includes hardware and software updates, training, maintenance and administration, and technical support. One other major factor in TCO is lost productivity. Lost productivity can occur because of many factors, including user errors, hardware problems, or software upgrades and retraining.

If you have been using any of the earlier Windows NT 5.0 betas, you may be surprised to learn that Microsoft is renaming the Windows NT 5.0 product line to Windows 2000. While the self-paced training kit and the Beta 3 release of Windows 2000 may still contain references to Windows NT Workstation 5.0 and Windows NT Server 5.0, this training kit focuses on the following two versions of the new Windows 2000 operating system:

- **Windows 2000 Professional.**   This product is a high-performance, secure-network client computer and corporate desktop operating system that includes the best features of Microsoft Windows 98, while significantly extending the manageability, reliability, security, and performance of Windows NT Workstation 4.0. This product will be the main Microsoft desktop operating system for businesses of all sizes.

- **Windows 2000 Server.**   This product is a file, print, and applications server, as well as a Web-server platform, that contains all of the features of Windows 2000 Professional plus many new server-specific functions. This product will be ideal for small- to medium-sized enterprise application deployments, Web servers, workgroups, and branch offices.

The Windows 2000 line of products will also include the following two products:

- **Windows 2000 Advanced Server (formerly Windows NT Server 5.0 Enterprise Edition).**   This product will be a more powerful departmental and application server, and it will also provide rich network operating system (NOS) and Internet services. This product is beyond the scope of this training kit; features unique to Advanced Server will not be covered in this kit.

- **Windows 2000 Datacenter Server.**   This new product will be the most powerful and functional server operating system ever offered by Microsoft. It is optimized for large data warehouses, econometric analysis, large-scale simulations in science and engineering, and server consolidation projects. This product is outside the scope of this kit; features unique to Datacenter Server will not be covered in this kit.

Table 1.1 describes the features and benefits of Windows 2000.

Table 1.1   Features and Benefits of Windows 2000

Feature	Benefit
Lower total cost of ownership	Reduces the cost of running and administering a network by providing automatic installation and upgrading of applications and by simplifying the setup and configuration of client computers.
	Reduces the amount of calls to support by providing the familiar Microsoft Windows interface for users and administrators, including wizards, interactive help, and more.
	Reduces the need for administrators to travel to desktop computers to upgrade the operating system.
Security	Authenticates users before they gain access to resources or data on a computer or the network.
	Provides local and network security and auditing for files, folders, printers, and other resources.
Directory service	Stores information about network resources, such as user accounts, applications, print resources, and security information.

(continued)

Feature	Benefit
Directory service	Provides the services that permit users to gain access to resources throughout the entire Windows 2000 network and to locate users, computers, and other resources. Also enables administrators to manage and secure these resources.
	Windows 2000 Server. Stores and manages Active Directory information. *Active Directory* is the Windows 2000 directory service. The Directory is the database that stores information about network resources, such as computers and printers, and the directory services make this information available to users and applications. Active Directory also provides administrators with the capability to control access to resources. (For more information on Active Directory, see Chapter 12, "Implementing Active Directory."
Performance and scalability	Supports symmetric multiprocessing (SMP) on computers that are configured with multiple microprocessors. Also supports multitasking for system processes and programs.
	Windows 2000 Server. Supports up to four microprocessors with support for additional microprocessors available from computer manufacturers. Configured as a file, print, and applications server.
	Windows 2000 Professional. Supports up to two microprocessors.
Networking and communication services	Provides built-in support for the most popular network protocols, including TCP/IP and network client utilities.
	Provides connectivity with Novell NetWare, UNIX, and AppleTalk.
	Provides Dial-Up Networking, which lets mobile users connect to a computer running Windows 2000.
	Windows 2000 Server. Supports 256 simultaneous inbound dial-up sessions.
	Windows 2000 Professional. Supports one inbound dial-up networking session.

(continued)

Internet integration	Integrates users' desktops with the Internet, thereby removing the distinction between the local computer and the Internet. Users can securely browse the network, intranet, and Internet for resources, as well as send and receive e-mail messages. **Windows 2000 Server.** Includes Microsoft Internet Information Services (IIS), which is a secure Web-server platform to host Internet and intranet Web sites on network servers. **Windows 2000 Professional.** Provides a personal Web server, which enables users to host a personal Web site.
Integrated administration tools	Provides the means to create customized tools to manage local and remote computers with a single standard interface. Provides the means to incorporate third-party administrative tools into the standard interface.
Hardware support	Supports *universal serial bus (USB)*, an external bus standard that eliminates many constraints of earlier computer peripherals. Supports Plug and Play hardware, which Windows 2000 automatically detects, installs, and configures.

Lesson Summary

In this lesson, you learned that Windows 2000 consists of a family of four separate products. In the earlier betas of Windows NT 5.0, three of the Windows 2000 products used the same naming conventions that were used by earlier Windows NT products. These products are being renamed as follows: Windows 2000 Professional (formerly Windows NT Workstation 5.0), Windows 2000 Server (formerly Windows NT Server 5.0), Windows 2000 Advanced Server (formerly Windows NT Server 5.0, Enterprise Edition). The fourth product, Windows 2000 Datacenter Server, is new and will be ideal for large data warehouses, econometric analysis, large-scale simulations in science and engineering, and server consolidation projects. Features unique to Advanced Server and Datacenter Server are not covered in this training kit.

Lesson 2: Windows 2000
Workgroups, Domains, and Domain Trees

Windows 2000 supports secure network environments in which users are able to share common resources, regardless of network size. The two types of networks that Windows 2000 supports are workgroups and domains.

After this lesson, you will be able to

- Identify the key characteristics of workgroups, domains, and domain trees.

Estimated lesson time: 15 minutes

Windows 2000 Workgroups

A *Windows 2000 workgroup* is a logical grouping of networked computers that share resources, such as files and printers. A workgroup is referred to as a *peer-to-peer network* because all computers in the workgroup can share resources as equals, or as peers, without a dedicated server. Each computer in the workgroup, running either Windows 2000 Server or Windows 2000 Professional, maintains a local security database, as shown in Figure 1.1. A *local security database* is a list of user accounts and resource security information for the computer it is on. Therefore, the administration of user accounts and resource security in a workgroup is decentralized.

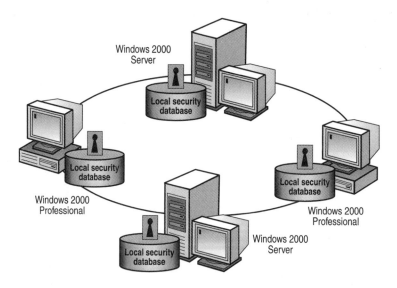

Figure 1.1   An example of a Windows 2000 workgroup

Because workgroups have decentralized administration and security

- A user must have a user account on *each* computer to which he or she wants to gain access.

- Any changes to user accounts, such as changing a user's password or adding a new user account, must be made on each computer in the workgroup. If you forget to add a new user account to one of the computers in your workgroup, the new user will not be able to log on to that computer and will be unable to access resources on it.

A Windows 2000 workgroup provides the following advantages:

- A workgroup does not require a computer running Windows 2000 Server to hold centralized security information.

- A workgroup is simple to design and implement. A workgroup does not require the extensive planning and administration that a domain requires.

- A workgroup is convenient for a limited number of computers in close proximity. A workgroup becomes impractical in environments with more than 10 computers.

Note   In a workgroup, a computer running Windows 2000 Server is called a *stand-alone server*.

Windows 2000 Domains

A *Windows 2000 domain* is a logical grouping of network computers that share a central directory database (see Figure 1.2). A *directory database* contains user accounts and security information for the domain. This directory database is known as the Directory and is the database portion of Active Directory, which is the Windows 2000 directory service.

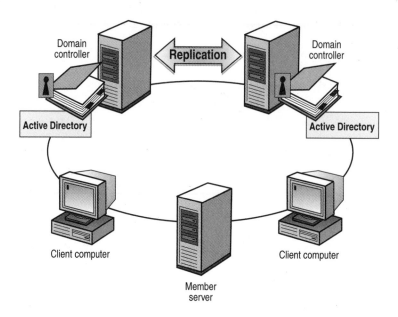

Figure 1.2   A Windows 2000 domain

In a domain, the Directory resides on computers that are configured as domain controllers. A *domain controller* is a server that manages all security-related aspects of user/domain interactions. Security and administration are centralized.

Note   You can only designate a computer running Windows 2000 Server as a domain controller.

A domain does not refer to a single location or specific type of network configuration. The computers in a domain can share physical proximity on a small local area network (LAN) or can be located in different corners of the world, communicating over any number of physical connections, including dial-up lines, Integrated Services Digital Network (ISDN) lines, fiber lines, Ethernet lines, token ring connections, frame relay connections, satellite connections, and leased lines.

The benefits of a domain are as follows:

- A domain provides centralized administration because all user information is stored centrally.

- A domain provides a single logon process for users to gain access to network resources, such as file, print, and application resources for which they have permissions. In other words, a user can log on to one computer and use resources on another computer in the network as long as he or she has appropriate privileges to the resource.

- A domain provides scalability so that you can create very large networks.

A typical Windows 2000 domain will have the following types of computers:

- **Domain controllers running Windows 2000 Server.**   Each domain controller stores and maintains a copy of the Directory. In a domain, you create a user account once, which Windows 2000 records in the Directory. When a user logs on to a computer in the domain, a domain controller checks the Directory for the user name, password, and logon restrictions to authenticate the user. When there are multiple domain controllers, they periodically replicate their Directory information.

- **Member servers running Windows 2000 Server.**   A member server is a server that is not configured as a domain controller. A member server does not store Directory information and cannot authenticate users. Member servers provide shared resources such as shared folders or printers.

- **Client computers running Windows 2000 Professional.**   Client computers run a user's desktop environment and allow the user to gain access to resources in the domain.

Domain Trees

A *domain tree* refers to a hierarchical grouping of domains, as shown in Figure 1.3. You can join domains by adding one or more child domains to an existing parent domain.

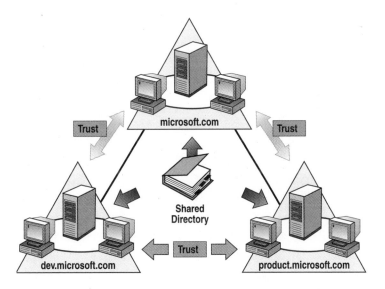

Figure 1.3   A domain tree

All domains in a tree share information and resources to function as a single unit. There is only one Directory in a domain tree, but each domain maintains a portion of the Directory that contains the user account information for the users in that domain. Within a tree, a user who logs on in one domain can use resources in another domain, as long as the user has the appropriate permissions.

The following are key characteristics of a domain tree:

- **Contiguous namespace.**   All domains in a tree must share a contiguous namespace. A *namespace* is a set of naming rules that provides the hierarchical structure, or path, of the tree. The child domains share the namespace of the parent domain. As shown in Figure 1.3, the domain names of the child domains, dev.microsoft.com and product.microsoft.com, include the name of the root domain, microsoft.com. The Windows 2000 namespace uses the Domain Name System (DNS) naming scheme, which provides the hierarchical structure for the tree. A domain tree name should map to a company's registered Internet name.

- **Shared directory.**   Windows 2000 combines the Directory information from all domains into a single directory, which makes the information of each domain globally accessible. In addition, each domain automatically provides a subset of its domain information in Active Directory to an index, which resides on domain controllers. Users search this index to locate other users, computers, resources, and applications throughout the domain tree.

- **Two-way transitive trusts.**   Domains in a tree are connected by a *two-way transitive trust*, which means that each domain in a tree trusts the authority of other domains to authenticate its own users. Therefore, because a parent domain trusts each of its child domains, the child domains implicitly trust each other. These trust relationships make all resources in each tree available to all other domains in the tree. Therefore, a user who logs on to his or her domain can gain access to resources in any domain in the tree.

Note   You can combine domain trees to form a forest. A *domain forest* is a collection of two or more domain trees that do *not* share a contiguous namespace.

Lesson Summary

In this lesson you learned about Windows 2000 workgroups, domains, and domain trees. A Windows 2000 workgroup is a logical grouping of networked computers that share resources, such as files and printers. Workgroups are referred to as peer-to-peer networks because all computers in the workgroup can share resources as equals (peers), without a dedicated server. Security and administration are not centralized in a workgroup because each computer maintains a list of user accounts and resource security information for that computer.

A Windows 2000 domain is a logical grouping of network computers that share a central directory database that contains user accounts and security information for the domain. This directory database is known as the Directory and is the database portion of Active Directory, which is the Windows 2000 directory service. In a domain, security and administration are centralized because the Directory resides on domain controllers, which manage all security-related aspects of user/domain interactions.

A domain tree is a hierarchical grouping of domains. You can join domains by adding one or more child domains to an existing parent domain. All domains in a tree share information and resources to function as a single unit. There is only one Directory in a domain tree, but each domain maintains a portion of the Directory that contains the user account information for the users in that domain. Within a tree, a user who logs on in one domain can use resources in another domain, as long as the user has the appropriate permissions.

Lesson 3: Logging On to Windows 2000

This lesson explains the Enter Password dialog box that you use to log on to Windows 2000. It also explains how Windows 2000 authenticates a user during the logon process to verify the identity of the user. This mandatory process ensures that only valid users can gain access to resources and data on a computer or the network.

After this lesson, you will be able to

- Identify the features of the Enter Password dialog box.
- Identify how Windows 2000 authenticates a user when the user logs on to a domain or logs on locally.

Estimated lesson time: 10 minutes

Logging On to a Domain

To log on to a computer running Windows 2000, a user provides a user name and password. Windows 2000 authenticates the user during the logon process to verify the identity of the user. Only valid users can gain access to resources and data on a computer or the network. Windows 2000 authenticates users who either log on to the domain or log on locally to the computer at which they are seated.

When a user starts a computer running Windows 2000, the user is prompted to press Ctrl+Alt+Delete to log on. Windows 2000 then displays the Enter Password dialog box.

Table 1.2 describes the options in the Enter Password dialog box.

Table 1.2   Enter Password Dialog Box Options

Option	Description
User name	A unique user logon name that is assigned by an administrator. To log on to a domain with the user name, the user account must reside in the Directory.
Password	The password that is assigned to the user account. Users must enter a password to prove their identity.
	Passwords are case sensitive. The password appears on the screen as asterisks (*) to protect it from onlookers. To prevent unauthorized access to resources and data, users must keep passwords secret.

(continued)

Log on to	Determines whether a user logs on to a domain or logs on locally to that computer. A user can click the down arrow at the end of the field to choose one of the following:
	A domain name. The user must select the domain that contains his or her user account. This list contains all of the domains in a domain tree.
	The computer name. The user must select the name of the computer that he or she wants to log on to. The user must have the log on locally user right for the computer. The option to log on locally is not available on a domain controller.
Log on using dial-up connection	Permits a user to connect to a domain server by using dial-up networking. Dial-up networking allows a user to log on and perform work from a remote location.
Shutdown	Closes all files, saves all operating system data, and prepares the computer so that a user can safely turn it off. On a computer running Windows 2000 Server, the Shutdown button is unavailable. This prevents an unauthorized person from using this dialog box to shut down the server. To shut down a server, a user must be able to log on to it.
Options	Toggles on and off the Log On To option and the Log On Using Dial-up Connection option. The Options button appears only if the computer is a member of a domain.

Logging On Locally to the Computer

A user can log on locally to either of the following:

- A computer that is a member of a workgroup.
- A computer that is a member of a domain but is not a domain controller. The user selects the computer name in the Log On To box in the Enter Password dialog box.

Note   Domain controllers do not maintain a local security database. Therefore, local user accounts are not available on domain controllers, and a user cannot log on locally to a domain controller.

Windows 2000 Authentication Process

To gain access to a computer running Windows 2000 or to any resource on that computer, a user must provide a user name and password.

How Windows 2000 authenticates a user varies, based on whether the user is logging on to a domain or logging on locally to a computer (see Figure 1.4).

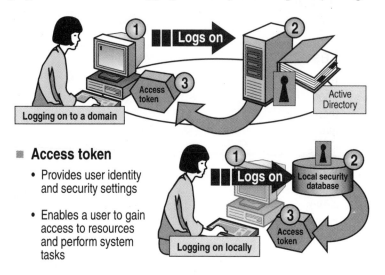

- **Access token**
  - Provides user identity and security settings

  - Enables a user to gain access to resources and perform system tasks

Figure 1.4   Windows 2000 Authentication Process at Logon

The steps in the authentication process are as follows:

1. The user logs on by providing logon information, such as ***user name*** and ***password***.

   - If the user is logging on to a domain, Windows 2000 forwards this information to a domain controller.

   - If the user is logging on locally, Windows 2000 forwards this information to the security subsystem of that local computer.

2. Windows 2000 compares the logon information with the user information that is stored in the appropriate database.

   - If the user is logging on to a domain, the domain controller contains a copy of the directory that Windows 2000 uses to validate the logon information.

   - If the user is logging on locally, the security subsystem of the local computer contains the local security database that Windows 2000 uses to validate the logon information.

3. If the information matches and the user account is valid, Windows 2000 creates an access token for the user. An *access token* is the user's identification for the computers in the domain or for that local computer, and it contains the user's security settings. These security settings allow the user to gain access to the appropriate resources and to perform specific system tasks.

Note   In addition to the logon process, any time a user makes a connection to a computer, that computer authenticates the user and returns an access token. This authentication process is invisible to the user.

Lesson Summary

In this lesson you learned that when a user starts a computer running Windows 2000, the user is prompted to press Ctrl+Alt+Delete to log on. Windows 2000 then displays the Enter Password dialog box, and the user must enter a valid user name and password to log on. You also learned about the various options available in the Enter Password dialog box.

When a user logs on, he or she can log on to the local computer, or, if the computer is a member of a domain, the user can log on to the domain. The authentication process for logging on locally and logging on to a domain is similar. However, when a user logs on locally, the authentication is done by the local computer; and when a user logs on to a domain, the authentication must be done by a domain controller. If the user is logging on locally, the security subsystem of the local computer contains the local security database that Windows 2000 uses to validate the logon information. If the user is logging on to a domain, a domain controller contains a copy of the Directory that Windows 2000 uses to validate the logon information.

Lesson 4: The Windows 2000 Security Dialog Box

This lesson explains the options and functionality of the Security dialog box.

After this lesson, you will be able to

- Identify the features of the Windows 2000 Security dialog box.

Estimated lesson time: 5 minutes

Using the Security Dialog Box

The Windows 2000 Security dialog box provides information such as the user account currently logged on and the domain or computer to which the user is logged on. This information is important for users with multiple user accounts, such as a user who has a regular user account as well as a user account with administrative privileges.

You access the Windows 2000 Security dialog box by pressing Ctrl+Alt+Delete. Table 1.3 describes the Windows 2000 Security dialog box options.

Table 1.3   The Windows 2000 Security Dialog Box Options

Option	Description
Lock Workstation	Allows you to secure the computer without logging off. All programs remain running. You should lock your computer when you leave for a short period of time.
	The user who locks the computer can unlock it by pressing Ctrl+Alt+Delete and entering the valid password.
	An administrator can also unlock a locked computer, logging off the current user.
Log Off	Allows you to log off as the current user and close all running programs, but leaves Windows 2000 running.
Shutdown	Allows you to close all files, save all operating system data, and prepare the computer so that you can safely turn it off.
Change Password	Allows you to change your user account password. You must know the old password to create a new one. This is the only way you can change your own password.
	Administrators can also change your password.
Task Manager	Provides a list of the current programs that are running, a summary of overall CPU and memory usage, as well as a quick view of how each program, program component, or system process is using the CPU and memory resources.
	You can also use Task Manager to switch between programs and to stop a program that is not responding.
Cancel	Closes the Windows 2000 Security dialog box.

Lesson Summary

In this lesson you learned that you access the Windows 2000 Security dialog box by pressing Ctrl+Alt+Delete, and that this dialog box provides information such as the user account currently logged on and the domain or computer to which the user is logged on. You also learned that you can use the Windows 2000 Security dialog box to lock your computer, to change your password, to log off your computer while leaving Windows 2000 running, to shut down your computer, and to access Task Manager.

Review

Here are some questions to help you determine if you have learned enough to move on to the next chapter. If you have difficulty answering these questions, please go back and review the material in this chapter before beginning the next chapter. The answers for these questions are located in Appendix A, "Questions and Answers."

1. What is the major difference between a workgroup and a domain?

2. What is Active Directory and what does it provide?

3. What information must a user provide when he or she logs on to a computer in a domain?

4. What happens when a user logs on to a domain?

5. How would you use the Windows 2000 Security dialog box?

C H A P T E R   2

Installing Windows 2000

About This Chapter

This chapter prepares you to install Microsoft Windows 2000. The information contained in this chapter is based on an early-release beta version of Windows 2000.

Before You Begin

To complete this chapter, you must have

- A computer that meets the minimum hardware requirements listed in "Hardware Requirements," on page xxxiii.
- A Beta 3 version of Windows 2000 software on CD and disk.

Lesson 1: Getting Started

When you install Windows 2000, the Windows 2000 Setup program asks you to provide information about how you want to install and configure the operating system. Good preparation helps you avoid problems during and after the installation.

After this lesson, you will be able to

- Prepare to install Microsoft Windows 2000 version Beta 3 by completing pre-installation tasks such as identifying the hardware requirements and the required installation information.

Estimated lesson time: 30 minutes

Preinstallation Tasks

Before you start the installation, complete the following preinstallation tasks:

- Identify the hardware requirements to install Windows 2000 Server and Windows 2000 Professional, and make sure that your hardware meets these requirements.
- Determine whether your hardware is on the Hardware Compatibility List (HCL).
- Determine how you want to partition the hard disk on which you are going to install Windows 2000.
- Choose a file system for the installation partition.
- Choose a licensing mode for a computer running Windows 2000 Server.
- Identify whether your computer will join a domain or a workgroup.
- Complete a checklist of preinstallation tasks to help ensure a successful installation.

Hardware Requirements

You must know the minimum hardware requirements for installing and operating Windows 2000 Server and Windows 2000 Professional to determine whether your hardware meets these requirements (see Figure 2.1 and Table 2.1). Make sure that your hardware meets or exceeds these hardware requirements.

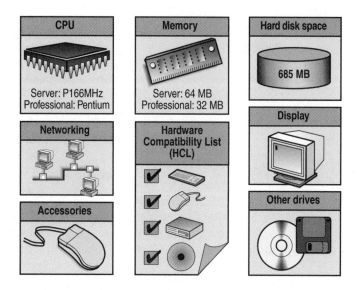

Figure 2.1   Hardware requirements

Table 2.1   Windows 2000 Hardware Requirements

Component	Windows 2000 Server requirements	Windows 2000 Professional requirements
CPU	Pentium 166 megahertz (MHz) or higher or Digital Alpha based	Pentium (or higher) recommended or Digital Alpha based.
Memory	64 megabytes (MB) for servers supporting one to five clients (128 MB or higher recommended for most network environments)	32 MB (64 MB recommended)
	For Alpha-based computers: 96 MB (128 MB recommended)	For Alpha-based computers: 48 MB (96 MB recommended)
Hard disk space	One or more hard disks with a minimum of about 685 MB (1 GB recommended) on the partition that will contain the system files	One or more hard disks with a minimum of about 500 MB (1 GB recommended) on the partition that will contain the system files
	For Alpha-based computers: a minimum of about 367 MB (1 GB recommended)	For Alpha-based computers: a minimum of about 351 MB (1 GB recommended)
Networking	One or more network adapter cards	Network adapter card
Display	Video display adapter and monitor with video graphics adapter (VGA) resolution or higher	Video display adapter and monitor with video graphics adapter (VGA) resolution or higher
Other drives	CD-ROM drive, 12X or faster recommended (not required for installing Windows 2000 over a network)	CD-ROM drive, 12X or faster recommended (not required for installing Windows 2000 over a network)
Accessories	Keyboard and mouse or other pointing device	Keyboard and mouse or other pointing device

Hardware Compatibility List

Before you install Windows 2000, verify that your hardware is on the Windows 2000 Hardware Compatibility List (HCL). Microsoft provides tested drivers for only those devices that are included on this list. Using hardware that is not listed on the HCL might cause problems during and after installation.

For a copy of the HCL, see the Hcl.txt file in the Support folder on the Windows 2000 CD-ROM.

You will also find the most recent versions of the HCL for released operating systems on the Internet at the Microsoft Web site (http://www.microsoft.com).

Note   Microsoft supports only those devices that are listed on the HCL. If you have hardware that is not on this list, contact the hardware manufacturer to determine if there is a manufacturer-supported Windows 2000 driver for the component.

Disk Partitions

The Windows 2000 Setup program examines the hard disk to determine its existing configuration. Setup then allows you to install Windows 2000 on an existing partition or create a new partition on which to install Windows 2000.

New Partition or Existing Partition

Depending on the state of the hard disk, you can choose one of the following options during the installation:

- If the hard disk is unpartitioned, you must create and size the Windows 2000 partition.
- If the hard disk has partitions and has enough unpartitioned disk space, you can create the Windows 2000 partition by using the unpartitioned space.
- If the hard disk has an existing partition that is large enough, you can install Windows 2000 on that partition. Installing on an existing partition will overwrite any existing data.
- If the hard disk has an existing partition, you can delete it to create more unpartitioned disk space to use to create the Windows 2000 partition.

Remaining Free Hard Disk Space

Although you can use Setup to create other partitions, you should create and size only the partition on which you will install Windows 2000. After you install Windows 2000, use the Disk Management administrative tool to partition any remaining unpartitioned space on the hard disk.

Size of the Installation Partition

Microsoft recommends that you install Windows 2000 on a 1 GB or larger partition. Although Windows 2000 requires a minimum of about 500 MB of disk space for installation, using a larger installation partition provides flexibility in the future. Then, if required, you can install updates to Windows 2000, operating system tools, or other files that are required by Windows 2000.

File Systems

After you create the installation partition, Setup prompts you to select the file system with which to format the partition. Windows 2000 supports three file systems: Windows 2000 file system (NTFS), file allocation table (FAT), and FAT32. Figure 2.2 summarizes some of the features of these file systems.

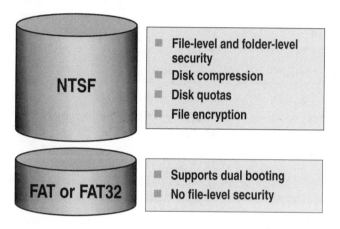

Figure 2.2   Summary of file systems features

NTFS

Use NTFS when the partition on which Windows 2000 will reside requires any of the following features:

- **File and folder-level security.**   NTFS allows you to control access to files and folders. For additional information, see Chapter 16, "Securing Resources with NTFS Permissions."

- **Disk compression.**   NTFS compresses files to store more data on the partition. For additional information, see Chapter 23, "Managing Data Storage."

- **Disk quotas.**   NTFS allows you to control disk usage on a per-user basis. For additional information, see Chapter 23, "Managing Data Storage."

- **Encryption.**   NTFS allows you to encrypt file data on the physical hard disk.

Windows 2000 and Windows NT are the only operating systems that can access data on a local hard disk that is formatted with NTFS.

Important   If you plan to promote a server to a domain controller, format the installation partition with NTFS.

FAT and FAT32

FAT and FAT32 allow access by, and compatibility with, other operating systems. To dual boot Windows 2000 and another operating system, format the system partition with either FAT or FAT32.

Setup determines whether to format the hard disk with FAT or FAT32 based on the size of the installation partition.

Partition size	Format
Smaller than 2 GB	Setup formats the partition as FAT
Larger than 2 GB	Setup formats the partition as FAT32

FAT and FAT32 do not offer many of the features that are supported by NTFS, for example file-level security. Therefore, in most situations, you should format the hard disk with NTFS. The only reason to use FAT or FAT32 is for dual booting. If you are setting up a computer for dual booting, you would only have to format the system partition as FAT or FAT32. For example, if drive C is the system partition, you could format drive C as FAT or FAT32 and format drive D as NTFS. However, Microsoft does not recommend dual booting a server.

Licensing

In addition to the license that is required to install and run Windows 2000 Server and the license that is required to install and run an operating system on each client computer, you also need to license each client connection to the server.

Client Access License

A Client Access License (CAL) gives client computers the right to connect to computers running Windows 2000 Server so that the client computers can connect to network services, shared folders, and print resources. When you install Windows 2000 Server, you must choose a CAL mode: Per Seat or Per Server.

The following services do not require Client Access Licenses:

- Anonymous or authenticated access to Windows 2000 Server with Microsoft Internet Information Services version 4.0 (IIS) or a Web-server application that provides Hypertext Transfer Protocol (HTTP) sharing of Hypertext Markup Language (HTML) files.
- Telnet and File Transfer Protocol (FTP) connections.

Note   If your company uses Microsoft BackOffice products, you must also have licenses for the BackOffice products. A Windows 2000 license does not cover BackOffice products.

Per Seat Licensing

The Per Seat licensing mode requires a separate CAL for each client computer that is used to access Windows 2000 Server for basic network services. After a client computer has a CAL, it can be used to access any computer running Windows 2000 Server on the enterprise network. Per Seat licensing is often more economical for large networks where client computers will be used to connect to more than one server.

Per Server Licensing

With Per Server licensing, CALs are assigned to a particular server. Each CAL allows one connection per client computer to the server for basic network services. You must have at least as many CALs that are dedicated to the server as the maximum number of client computers that will be used to concurrently connect to that server at any time.

Per Server licensing is preferred by small companies with only one computer running Windows 2000 Server. It is also useful for Internet or remote-access servers where client computers might not be licensed as Windows 2000 network client computers. In this situation, Per Server licensing allows you to specify a maximum number of concurrent server connections and reject any additional logon attempts.

Important   If you are unsure which licensing mode to use, choose Per Server because you can change, only once, from Per Server to Per Seat licensing at no additional cost (by double-clicking the Licensing icon in Control Panel). It is not necessary to notify Microsoft to make this change. This is a one-way conversion; you cannot convert from Per Seat to Per Server.

For help in determining the number of Client Access Licenses that you need to buy, see Appendix B, "Computing the Number of Client Access Licenses."

Domain or Workgroup Membership

During installation, you must choose the type of network security group that you want the computer to join: a domain or a workgroup (see Figure 2.3).

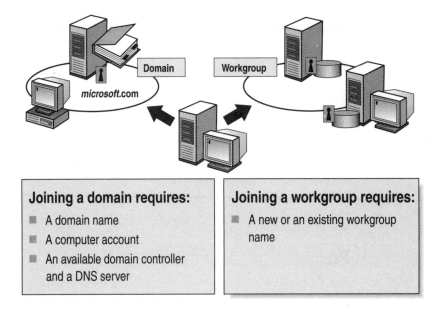

Figure 2.3   Domain or workgroup membership

Joining a Domain

During installation, you can add the computer on which you are installing Windows 2000 to an existing domain. Adding a computer to a domain is referred to as *joining a domain*. If you are installing Windows 2000 Server, the computer is added as a member server. A computer running Windows 2000 Server that is a member of a domain, and is not a domain controller, is called a *member server.*

Joining a domain during installation requires the following:

- **A domain name.**   Ask the domain administrator for the Domain Name System (DNS) name for the domain that you want to join. An example of a DNS-compatible domain name is *microsoft*.com, where *microsoft* is the name of your organization's DNS identity.

- **A computer account.**   Before a computer can join a domain, you must create a computer account in the domain. You can ask a domain administrator to create the computer account before installation, or, if you have administrative privileges for the domain, you can create the computer account during installation. If you create the computer account during installation, Setup prompts you for a name and password of a user account with authority to add domain computer accounts.

- **An available domain controller and a server running the DNS Service (called the *DNS server*).**   At least one domain controller in the domain that you are joining and one DNS server must be online when you install a computer in the domain.

Note   You can join a domain during installation or after installation.

Joining a Workgroup

During installation, you can add the computer on which you are installing Windows 2000 to an existing workgroup. Adding a computer to a workgroup is referred to as *joining a workgroup*. If you are installing Windows 2000 Server, the computer is added as a stand-alone server. A computer running Windows 2000 Server that is not a member of a domain is called a *stand-alone server*.

If you join a workgroup as a stand-alone server during installation, you must assign a workgroup name to your computer. The workgroup name that you assign can be the name of an existing workgroup or the name of a new workgroup that you create during installation.

Preinstallation Tasks Summary

The following is a preinstallation checklist that you can use to make sure you have all the necessary information available before you begin the installation process.

Task	✔
Verify that your components meet the minimum hardware requirements.	☐
Verify that all of your hardware is listed on the HCL.	☐
Verify that the hard disk on which you will install Windows 2000 has a minimum of 500 MB of free disk space, and preferably 1 GB.	☐
Select the file system for the Windows 2000 partition. Unless you need to dual boot operating systems or have clients running operating systems other than Windows NT or Windows 2000 that need to access information on this computer, format all partitions with NTFS.	☐
Determine whether to use Per Server or Per Seat licensing. If you select Per Server licensing, note the number of Client Access Licenses that were purchased for the server.	☐
Determine the name of the domain or workgroup that you will join. If you join a domain, be sure that you write down the DNS name for the domain. Also, determine the name of the computer before installation.	☐
Create a computer account in the domain that you are joining. You can create a computer account during the installation if you have administrative privileges in the domain.	☐
Create a password for the Administrator account.	☐

Lesson Summary

This lesson identified the preinstallation tasks you must understand and complete before you install Windows 2000. The first task is to identify the hardware requirements for installing Windows 2000 Server and Windows 2000 Professional and to ensure that your hardware meets these requirements. You learned about the Windows 2000 hardware compatibility list and that it is important that your hardware be on the HCL so that it is compatible with Windows 2000. After you have determined that your hardware is on the HCL, you must determine how you want to partition the hard disk on which you are going to install Windows 2000. You must also determine whether you are going to format the partition as NTFS so that you can have better security and a richer feature set or as FAT or FAT32 so that other operating systems can access the data on the installation partition.

You learned about Client Access Licenses (CALs) and that a CAL gives client computers the right to connect to computers running Windows 2000 Server. With Per Seat licensing mode a separate CAL is required for each client computer that accesses a Windows 2000 Server. When a client computer has a CAL, it can be used to access any computer running Windows 2000 Server on the enterprise network. With Per Server licensing, CALs are assigned to a particular server. Each CAL allows one connection per client computer to the server, and you must have at least as many CALs that are dedicated to the server as the maximum number of client computers that will be used to concurrently connect to that server at any time.

You also learned that during installation your computer must join a domain or a workgroup. If your computer is the first one installed on the network, or if for some other reason there is no domain available for your computer to join, you can have the computer join a workgroup and then have the computer join a domain after the installation. This lesson also provided a checklist of preinstallation tasks that you can complete to help ensure a successful installation of Windows 2000.

Lesson 2: Installing Windows 2000 from a CD-ROM

In this lesson you will learn about the four-stage process of installing Windows 2000 from a CD-ROM. These four stages are as follows: run the Setup program, run the Setup wizard, install Windows NT networking, and complete the Setup program. After you learn about these four stages, you will install Windows 2000 on your computer.

After this lesson, you will be able to
- Install Windows 2000 Server from a CD-ROM.

Estimated lesson time: 90 minutes

The Windows 2000 Setup Program

Installing Windows 2000 is a four-stage process that begins by running the Setup program and then uses a wizard and informational screens to complete the installation (see Figure 2.4).

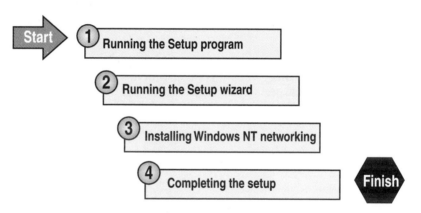

Figure 2.4   Windows 2000 installation steps

Installing Windows 2000 from a CD-ROM on to a clean hard disk consists of these four stages:

1. Run the Setup program.

   The Setup program prepares the hard disk for later stages of the installation and copies the necessary files to run the Setup wizard.

2. Run the Setup wizard.

   The Setup wizard requests setup information about the computer, which includes names, passwords, licensing modes, and so on.

3. Install Windows NT networking.

After gathering information about the computer, the Setup wizard prompts you for networking information and then installs the networking components so that the computer can communicate with other computers on the network.

4. Complete the Setup program.

   To complete the installation, Setup copies files to the hard disk and configures the computer. The system restarts after installation is complete.

Running the Setup Program

To start Setup, use the Setup boot disks. Insert the disk labeled Setup Disk 1 into drive A, and then turn on, or restart, the computer. If your computer supports booting from a CD-ROM drive, you can also start the installation by using the Windows 2000 CD-ROM.

The following steps describe running the Setup program on a clean disk drive (see Figure 2.5):

1. After the computer starts, a minimal version of Windows 2000 is copied into memory. This version of Windows 2000 starts the Setup program.

2. Setup restarts the computer and then starts the text-based version of Setup. This version of Setup prompts you to read and accept a licensing agreement.

3. Setup prompts you to select the partition on which to install Windows 2000. You can select an existing partition or create a new partition by using unpartitioned space on the hard disk.

4. After you create the installation partition, Setup prompts you to select a file system for the new partition. Then, Setup formats the partition with the selected file system.

5. After formatting the Windows 2000 partition, Setup copies files to the hard disk and saves configuration information.

6. Setup restarts the computer and then starts the Windows 2000 Setup wizard. By default, the Windows 2000 operating system files are installed in the C:\Winnt folder.

Note   For instructions on how to create the Windows 2000 Setup boot disks, see Appendix C, "Creating Setup Disks."

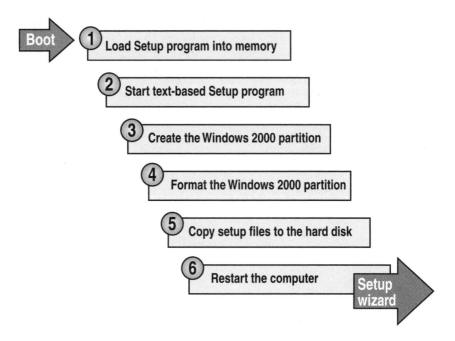

Figure 2.5   Steps in the Setup program

Running the Setup Wizard

The graphical user interface (GUI)-based Windows 2000 Setup wizard leads you through the next stage of the installation process. It gathers information about you, your organization, and your computer.

After installing Windows 2000 security features and installing and configuring devices, the Windows 2000 Setup wizard asks you to provide the following information:

- **Regional settings.**   Customize language, locale, and keyboard settings. You can configure Windows 2000 to use multiple languages and regional settings.
- **Name and organization.**   Enter the name of the person and the organization to which this copy of Windows 2000 is licensed.
- **Licensing mode.**   Select Per Server or Per Seat licensing. If you select Per Server, you must enter the number of Client Access Licenses that were purchased for this server. Each connection requires a Client Access License.
- **Computer name.**   Enter a computer name of up to 15 characters. The computer name must be different from other computer, workgroup, or domain names on the network. The Windows 2000 Setup wizard displays a default name, using the organization name that you entered earlier in the setup process.

- **Password for Administrator account.** Specify a password for the Administrator user account, which the Windows 2000 Setup wizard creates during installation. The Administrator account provides administrative privileges that are required to manage the computer.
- **Windows 2000 optional components.** Add or remove additional components during the installation of Windows 2000 Server.

Additional Component	Description
Certificate Services	Allows you to create and/or request X.509 digital certificates for authentication. Certificates provide a verifiable means of identifying users on nonsecure networks (such as the Internet), as well as provide the information necessary to conduct secure private communications.
Internet Information Services (IIS)	Includes FTP and Web servers, the administrative interface for IIS, common IIS components, and documentation.
Message Queuing Services	Installs Microsoft Message Queuing (MSMQ) Routing Server or Client. MSMQ provides developers with a simplified asynchronous programming model and built-in transactional support so your message queues can participate in Microsoft Transaction Server (MTS) transactions.
Microsoft Indexing Service	Installs Index Server system files, which enables comprehensive and dynamic full-text searches of data stored on the computer or network.
Networking Options	Includes the Dynamic Host Configuration Protocol (DHCP) Service, the DNS Service, Transmission Control Protocol/Internet Protocol (TCP/IP) print server, file and print services, and other networking components.
Remote Installation Services	Provides the ability to remotely install Windows 2000 Professional on remote boot-enabled client computers.
Terminal Services	Includes components and administration tools that allow this computer to host Windows-based terminals and Microsoft Windows NT Server Terminal Server Edition client computers.
Transaction Server	Installs the DCOM-based MTS Transaction Manager, which enables the user to create transactional components. Includes support for data transactions over the network.

Note IIS and Transaction Server are selected by default.

- **Display settings.**   Configure the size of the desktop area (screen resolution), the number of display colors, and the refresh frequency. If you modify the default settings, you must test the new settings before you continue the setup process. You can also configure the display settings after you install Windows 2000.

- **Time and date.**   Select the appropriate time zone, and adjust the date and time settings, if necessary.

After you complete this stage in the installation, the Windows 2000 Setup wizard starts to install the Windows networking components.

Installing Windows Networking Components

After gathering information about your computer, the Windows 2000 Setup wizard guides you through installing the Windows networking components (see Figure 2.6).

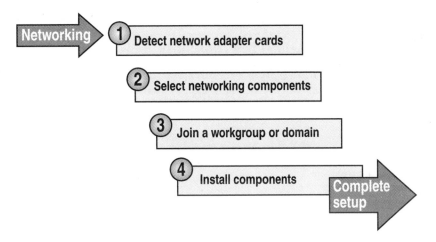

Figure 2.6   Installing Windows networking components

The following list describes the steps in installing Windows 2000 Networking:

1. **Detect network adapter cards.**   The Windows 2000 Setup wizard detects and configures any network adapter cards that are installed on the computer. After configuring network adapters, it locates a server running the DHCP Service (DHCP server) on the network.

2. **Select networking components.**   Choose to install networking components with typical or customized settings. The typical installation includes the following options:

   - **Client for Microsoft Networks.**   This component allows your computer to gain access to network resources.

- **File and Printer Sharing for Microsoft Networks.** This component allows other computers to gain access to file and print resources on your computer.

- **TCP/IP.** This protocol is the default networking protocol that allows your computer to communicate over local area networks (LANs) and wide area networks (WANs).

You can install other clients, services, and network protocols (such as NetBIOS Enhanced User Interface [NetBEUI], AppleTalk, and NWLink IPX/SPX/NetBIOS-compatible transport) now or anytime after you install Windows 2000.

3. **Join a workgroup or domain.** If you create a computer account in the domain for your computer during the installation, the Windows 2000 Setup wizard prompts you for the name and password.

4. **Install components.** The Windows 2000 Setup wizard installs and configures the Windows networking components that you selected.

Completing the Installation

After installing the networking components, the Windows 2000 Setup wizard automatically starts the fourth step in the installation process (see Figure 2.7).

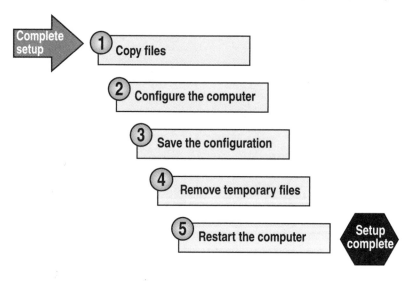

Figure 2.7   The final steps in completing the installation

The following list describes the tasks involved in completing the installation stage:

1. **Copy files.** Setup copies any remaining files, such as accessories and bitmaps.

2. **Configure the computer.**   Setup applies the configuration settings that you specified in the Windows 2000 Setup wizard.

3. **Save the configuration.**   Setup saves your configuration settings to the local hard disk. The next time that you start Windows 2000, the computer will use this configuration automatically.

4. **Remove temporary files.**   To save hard disk space, Setup deletes any files that it installed for use only during installation.

5. **Restart the computer.**   After completing the preceding steps, Setup restarts the computer. This finishes the installation of a stand-alone or member server from a CD-ROM.

Practice: Installing Windows 2000 from a CD-ROM

In this practice, you install the Beta 3 version of Windows 2000 Server on a computer with no formatted partitions. During installation, you use the Windows 2000 Server Setup program to create a partition on your hard disk on which you install Windows 2000 Server as a stand-alone server in a workgroup.

Note   If your computer is configured with an El Torito–compatible CD-ROM drive, you can install Windows 2000 without using the Setup disks. You can run the Setup program by restarting the computer with the CD-ROM inserted in the CD-ROM drive and then skip to step 4 on the next page.

▶   **To begin the initialization phase of Windows 2000 Server Setup**

1. Insert the disk labeled Windows 2000 Server Setup Disk 1 into drive A, and then turn on, or restart, the computer.

   After the computer starts, Windows 2000 Setup displays a brief message that your system configuration is being checked, and then the Windows 2000 Setup screen appears.

   Notice that the gray bar at the bottom of the screen indicates that Setup is loading Windows 2000 Executive, which is a minimal version of the Windows NT kernel.

2. When prompted, insert Setup Disk 2 into drive A, and then press Enter.

   Notice that Setup indicates that it is loading software components to support your computer's motherboard, bus, and mass media hardware. Setup also loads the Windows 2000 Setup program files.

3. When prompted, insert Setup Disk 3 into drive A, and then press Enter.

   Notice that Setup indicates that it is loading additional software components for your computer's mass media hardware and current file system. Setup might pause several times during this process.

Setup initializes Windows 2000 Executive and loads the rest of the Windows 2000 Setup program.

Setup displays the Windows 2000 Server Setup screen, informing you that you are about to install a beta version of Windows 2000.

4. When prompted, insert Setup Disk 4 into drive A, and then press Enter.

5. Read the Setup Notification message, and then press Enter to continue.

Setup displays the Welcome To Setup screen.

Notice that, in addition to the initial installation of Windows 2000, you can use Windows 2000 Setup to repair or recover a damaged Windows 2000 installation.

▶ **To begin the installation phase of Windows 2000 Server Setup**

1. Read the Welcome To Setup message, and then press Enter to begin the installation phase of Windows 2000 Setup.

Setup displays the Windows 2000 Setup screen, prompting you to insert the Windows 2000 Server Beta 3 CD-ROM into the CD-ROM drive. If your computer is configured with an El Torito–compatible CD-ROM drive and you restarted your computer with the Windows 2000 Server Beta 3 CD-ROM in the CD-ROM drive, you will not get this message.

2. Insert the Windows 2000 Server Beta 3 CD-ROM into the CD-ROM drive on your computer, and then press Enter.

Setup displays the License Agreement screen.

3. Read the license agreement, pressing Page Down to scroll down the screen.

4. Select I accept the agreement by pressing F8.

Setup displays the Windows 2000 Server Setup screen, prompting you to select an area of free space or an existing partition on which to install Windows 2000. This stage of setup provides a way for you to create and delete partitions on your hard disk.

Notice that the hard disk that is listed on this screen contains an existing unformatted partition.

5. Make sure that the C: Unpartitioned Space partition is selected, and then type **C**

Setup displays the Windows 2000 Setup screen, confirming that you've chosen to create a new partition in the unpartitioned space and informing you of the minimum and maximum sizes of the partition you might create.

6. Specify the size of the partition you want to create, and then press Enter to continue.

Note Although you can create additional partitions from the remaining unpartitioned space, it is recommended that you perform additional partitioning tasks after you install Windows 2000. To partition hard disks after installation, use the Disk Management snap-in.

Setup displays the Windows 2000 Setup screen, showing the new partition as unformatted.

7. Select the partition and press Enter.

    You are prompted to select a file system for the partition.

    If you are installing another operating system, such as Microsoft Windows 98, in a dual-boot configuration on the same computer, which file system should you choose? Why?

8. Use the arrow keys to select Format The Partition Using The NTFS File System, and then press Enter.

    The Setup program formats the partition with the NTFS file system. After it formats the partition, Setup examines the hard disk for physical errors that might cause Setup to fail and then copies files to the hard disk. This process will take several minutes.

    Setup displays the Windows 2000 Server Setup screen. A red status bar counts down the 15-second delay before Setup restarts the computer.

9. Remove the Setup disk from drive A, and then remove the CD-ROM from the CD-ROM drive.

    Important If your computer supports booting from the CD-ROM drive and you do not remove the Windows 2000 Server Beta 3 CD-ROM before Setup restarts the computer, the computer will boot from the Windows 2000 Server CD-ROM. This will cause Setup to start again from the beginning. If this happens, remove the CD-ROM and then restart the computer.

    It may take a few minutes, but Setup will display the Insert Disk message, prompting you to insert the Windows 2000 Server (Beta 3) CD-ROM into the CD-ROM drive.

10. Insert the Windows 2000 Server Beta 3 CD-ROM into the CD-ROM drive, wait for about 10 seconds, and then press Enter.

    Setup copies additional files and then restarts your machine and loads the Windows 2000 Setup wizard.

▶   **To complete the gathering information phase of Windows 2000 Server Setup**

1. On the Welcome to the Windows 2000 Setup Wizard page, click Next to begin gathering information about your computer.

Setup configures NTFS folder and file permissions for the operating system files, detects the hardware devices in the computer, and then installs and configures device drivers to support the detected hardware. This process will take several minutes.

2. On the Regional Settings page, make sure that the system locale, user locale, and keyboard layout are correct for your language and location, and then click Next.

Note   You can modify regional settings after you install Windows 2000 by using Regional Settings in Control Panel.

Setup displays the Personalize Your Software page, prompting you for your name and organization name. Setup uses your organization name to generate the default computer name. Many applications that you install later will use this information for product registration and document identification.

3. In the Name box, type your name, in the Organization box, type the name of your company or organization, and then click Next.

Setup displays the Licensing Modes page, prompting you to select a licensing mode. By default, the Per Server licensing mode is selected. Setup prompts you to enter the number of licenses that you have purchased for this server.

Which licensing mode should you select if users in your organization require frequent access to multiple servers? Why?

4. Click Per Server For, enter **30** for the number of concurrent connections, and then click Next.

Important   Per Server For and 30 concurrent connections are suggested values to be used in this lab. You should use a legal number of concurrent connections based on the actual licenses that you own. You can also choose to use Per Seat instead of Per Server For.

Setup displays the Computer Name And Administrator Password page.

Notice that Setup uses your organization name to generate a suggested name for the computer.

5. In the Computer Name box, type **Server1**

Important   Windows 2000 displays the computer name in all capital letters, no matter how you type it in.

If your computer is on a network, check with the network administrator before assigning a name to your computer. Throughout the rest of this self-paced training kit, the labs will refer to Server1. If you do not name your computer Server1, everywhere the materials reference Server1, you will have to substitute the name of your server.

6. In the Administrator Password box and the Confirm Password box, type **password** and then click Next.

Important   For the labs in this self-paced training kit, you will use *password* for the Administrator account. You should always use a complex password for the Administrator account (one that others cannot easily guess). Microsoft recommends mixing uppercase and lowercase letters, numbers, and symbols (for example, Lp6*g9).

Setup displays the Windows 2000 Components page, indicating which Windows 2000 system components Setup will install.

Note   You can install additional components after you install Windows 2000 by using Add/Remove Programs in Control Panel.

---

7. Click Next to continue installing Windows 2000.

Setup displays the Desktop Area And Colors page, prompting you to select the display settings for your computer and monitor. Setup selects a default resolution that is compatible with the video adapter that Setup has detected. You can change the default settings now or at any time after you install Windows 2000.

The following table describes the options that you can configure on the Desktop Area And Colors page.

Option	Description
Color Palette	The number of colors. Typically, higher color depths produce more detailed and realistic graphics.
Desktop Area	Drag the slider to specify the screen size that you want. Typically, a larger desktop area will shrink the size of the user interface elements and produce more usable desktop space.
	Select 800 by 600 for a good balance between readability and usable desktop area.
Refresh Frequency	The refresh frequency supported by your monitor. Typically, higher refresh frequencies produce crisper displays.

Warning   If you do not know the refresh frequency that your monitor supports with the color palette and desktop area that you selected, do not change the default setting. Setting the refresh frequency too high might damage your monitor.

---

8. If you did not change the default display settings, go to step 10.

9. If you changed the default display settings, click Test to test the settings for your video adapter, and then click OK to begin the test.

A multicolor test bitmap appears for five seconds, allowing you to evaluate your selected display settings.

Setup displays the Testing Mode dialog box, asking if the bitmap was displayed correctly.

10. If you see the test bitmap, click Yes.

11. Click Next to confirm the video settings.

12. On the Date And Time Settings page, confirm that these settings are correct for your location.

Important   Windows 2000 services perform many tasks that depend on the computer's time and date settings to be completed successfully. Please be sure to select the correct time zone for your location to avoid problems in later labs.

---

13. Under Time Zone, select the time zone for your location.

14. Select the Automatically Adjust Clock For Daylight Saving Changes check box if you want Windows 2000 to automatically change the time on your computer for daylight savings time changes, and then click Next.

Note   If you have configured your computer for dual booting with another operating system that can also adjust your clock for daylight savings time changes, enable this feature for only one operating system. Enable this feature for the operating system that you use most frequently so that the daylight savings time adjustment will occur only once.

Setup displays the Networking Settings page, and starts installing networking components.

▶   **To complete the installing Windows Networking Components phase of Windows 2000 Server Setup**

1. On the Networking Settings page, make sure that Typical Settings is selected, and then click Next to begin installing Windows networking components.

   This setting installs networking components that are used to gain access to and share resources on a network and configures TCP/IP to automatically obtain an Internet Protocol (IP) address from a DHCP server on the network.

   Setup displays the Domain Membership page, prompting you to join either a workgroup or a domain.

   In this lab, you are installing Windows 2000 Server as a stand-alone server in a workgroup. In a later lab, you will create and join a new Windows 2000 domain.

2. On the Domain Membership page, make sure that No, This Computer Is Not On A Network, Or Is On A Network Without A Domain is selected, that the workgroup name is WORKGROUP, and then click Next.

Setup displays the Installing Components page, displaying the status as Setup installs and configures the remaining operating system components according to the options that you specified. This process will take several minutes.

Setup then displays the Completing Setup page, displaying the status as Setup finishes copying files, making and saving configuration changes, and deleting temporary files.

Setup displays the Completing the Windows 2000 Setup Wizard page.

3. Remove the Windows 2000 Server CD-ROM from the CD-ROM drive.

4. After you have removed the CD-ROM, click Finish to continue setting up Windows 2000 Server.

Important   If your computer supports booting from the CD-ROM drive and you do not remove the Windows 2000 Server Beta 3 CD-ROM soon after Setup restarts the computer, the computer will boot from the Windows 2000 Server CD-ROM. This will cause Setup to restart. If this happens, remove the CD-ROM and then restart the computer.

---

5. If Setup displays a Windows 2000 Server Setup dialog box, indicating that one or more errors occurred during Setup, click Yes to view the System Setup log and record the error.

Setup displays the System Setup Log window, displaying any errors that occurred during Setup.

6. Click Close to close the System Setup Log window and continue setting up Windows 2000 Server.

Windows 2000 restarts and runs the newly installed version of Windows 2000 Server.

▶ **To complete the hardware installation phase of Windows 2000 Server Setup**

1. Log on by pressing Ctrl+Alt+Delete.

2. In the Enter Password dialog box, in the User Name box, type **Administrator** and in the Password box, type **password**

3. Click OK.

If Windows 2000 detects hardware that was not detected during Setup, the Found New Hardware wizard is displayed, indicating that Windows 2000 is installing the appropriate drivers.

4. If the Found New Hardware wizard appears, verify that the Restart The Computer When I Click Finish check box is cleared and then click Finish to complete the Found New Hardware wizard.

Windows 2000 displays the Microsoft Windows 2000 Configure Server dialog box. From this dialog box, you can register your copy of Windows 2000 Server online or start the Internet Connection wizard.

5. Minimize the Microsoft Windows 2000 Configure Server dialog box.

   You have now completed the Windows 2000 Server installation and are logged on as Administrator.

Lesson Summary

In this lesson you learned that installing Windows 2000 Server is a four-stage process. You learned the tasks that are completed during each of these four stages, and then you installed Windows 2000 Server from a CD-ROM. During installation you formatted your installation partition as NTFS and had the computer join the default workgroup.

Lesson 3: Installing Windows 2000 over the Network

In addition to installing from a CD-ROM, you can install Windows 2000 over the network. This lesson will demonstrate the similarities and differences between installing from a CD-ROM and installing over the network. The major difference is the location of the source files needed to install Windows 2000. This lesson also lists the requirements for a network installation.

After this lesson, you will be able to

- Identify the steps for completing a network installation of Windows 2000.

Estimated lesson time: 10 minutes

Preparing for a Network Installation

In a network installation, the Windows 2000 installation files reside in a shared location on a network file server, which is called a *distribution server*. From the computer on which you want to install Windows 2000 (the target computer), you connect to the distribution server and then run the Setup program.

The requirements for a network installation are shown in Figure 2.8 and are explained in more detail in the list below.

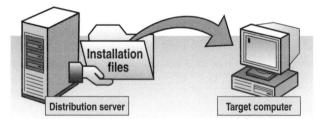

Requirements for a network installation:

- Distribution server
- FAT partition on the target computer
- Network client

Figure 2.8   Requirements for a network installation

- **Locate a distribution server.**   The distribution server contains the installation files from the I386 (or Alpha) folder on the Windows 2000 CD-ROM.

These files reside in a common network location in a *shared folder.* This shared folder allows computers on the network to gain access to the installation files. Contact a network administrator to obtain the path to the installation files on the distribution server.

Note   Once you have created or located a distribution server, you can use the over-the-network installation method to concurrently install Windows 2000 on multiple computers.

- **Create a FAT partition on the target computer.**   The target computer requires a formatted partition on which to copy the installation files. Create a 500-MB (1-GB or larger recommended) partition and format it with the FAT file system.
- **Install a network client.**   A network client is software that allows the target computer to connect to the distribution server. On a computer without an operating system, you must boot from a client disk that includes a network client that enables the target computer to connect to the distribution server.

Installing over the Network

The Windows 2000 Setup program copies the installation files to the target computer and creates the Setup boot disks. After Setup copies the installation files, you start the installation on the target computer by booting from the Setup boot disks. From this point on, you install Windows 2000 in the same way as installing from a CD-ROM.

The following steps describe the process for installing Windows 2000 over the network (see Figure 2.9):

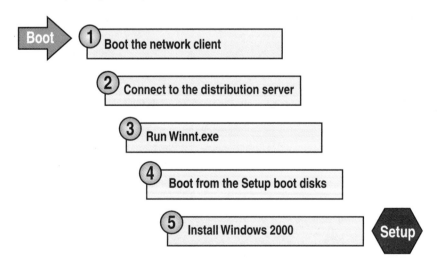

Figure 2.9   Installing Windows 2000 over the network

1. On the target computer, boot from the network client.

2. Connect to the distribution server. After you start the network client on the target computer, connect to the shared folder on the distribution server that contains the Windows 2000 installation files.

3. Run Winnt.exe to start the Setup program. Winnt.exe resides in the shared folder on the distribution server. When you run Winnt.exe from the shared folder, it performs the following steps:

   - Creates four Windows 2000 Setup boot disks using drive A on the target computer. This step requires four blank formatted disks.

   - Creates the Win_nt.~ls temporary folder on the target computer.

   - Copies the Windows 2000 installation files from the shared folder on the distribution server to the Win_nt.~ls folder on the target computer.

4. Boot the target computer from the Setup boot disks. After copying the files to the target computer, the Setup program prompts you to restart the target computer by using the first Setup boot disk.

5. Install Windows 2000. After you restart the target computer with the Setup boot disk, the Windows 2000 Setup program guides you through the normal Windows 2000 installation process.

Modifying the Setup Process

You can modify a server-based installation by changing how Winnt.exe runs the setup process. Table 2.2 describes the switches that you can use with Winnt.exe to control Setup.

Table 2.2   Available Switches for Winnt.exe

Switch	Description
/a	Enables accessibility options.
/e	Specifies the command to be executed at the end of GUI setup.
/I[:]inffile	Specifies the filename (no path) of the setup information file. The default is DOSNET.INF.
/r	Specifies optional directory to be installed.
/rx	Specifies optional directory to be copied.
/s[:]sourcepath	Specifies the source location of Windows 2000 files. Must be a full path of the form x:\[path] or \\server\share\[path].
/t[:]tempdrive	Specifies a drive to contain temporary setup files. If not specified, setup will attempt to locate a drive for you.
/u	Unattended operation and optional script file (requires /s).

Lesson Summary

In this lesson you learned that the main difference between an over-the-network installation and an installation from CD-ROM is the location of the source files. Once you connect to the share containing the source files and start Winnt.exe, the installation proceeds like an installation from CD-ROM. You also learned the switches available for Winnt.exe to modify the installation process.

Lesson 4: Troubleshooting Windows 2000 Installations

Your installation of Windows 2000 should complete without any problems. However, this lesson covers some common issues that you might encounter during installation.

After this lesson, you will be able to

- Troubleshoot Windows 2000 installations.

Estimated lesson time: 5 minutes

Resolving Common Problems

Table 2.3 lists some of these common installation problems and offers solutions to resolve them.

Table 2.3   Troubleshooting Tips

Problem	Solution
Media Errors	If you are installing from a CD-ROM, use a different CD-ROM. To request a replacement CD-ROM, contact Microsoft or your vendor.
Nonsupported CD-ROM drive	Replace the CD-ROM drive with one that is supported, or if that is not possible, try another method of installing, such as installing over the network, and then after you have completed the installation, you can add the adapter card driver for the CD-ROM drive if it is available.
Insufficient disk space	Use the Setup program to create a partition by using existing free space on the hard disk.
	Delete and create partitions as needed to create a partition that is large enough for installation.
	Reformat an existing partition to create more space.
Failure of dependency service to start	In the Windows 2000 Setup wizard, return to the Network Settings dialog box and verify that you installed the correct protocol and network adapter. Verify that the network adapter has the proper configuration settings, such as transceiver type, and that the local computer name is unique on the network.

(continued)

Problem	Solution
Inability to connect to the domain controller	Verify that the domain name is correct.
	Verify that the server running the DNS Service and the domain controller are both running and online. If you cannot locate a domain controller, install into a workgroup and then join the domain after installation.
	Verify that the network adapter card and protocol settings are set correctly.
	If you are reinstalling Windows 2000 and using the same computer name, delete and then recreate the computer account.
Failure of Windows 2000 to install or start	Verify that Windows 2000 is detecting all of the hardware and that all of the hardware is on the HCL.

Lesson Summary

In this lesson you learned some common problems that you may encounter when installing Windows 2000. Installation problems could be caused by bad media, in which case you will have to get a new CD-ROM to be able to install. You may also encounter problems with your installation if your hardware is not on the HCL. If your CD-ROM drive is not on the HCL, you can swap it out for a supported drive or install over the network and add the driver to support the CD-ROM drive if it is available.

If you failed to complete your preinstallation tasks and there is not enough room on any of the partitions to install Windows 2000, you can create a new partition from unused space on the hard disk, if the space is available; you can delete some existing partitions so that you can create one large enough to install Windows 2000; or you can format an existing partition to provide enough space to install Windows 2000.

You also learned some tips to try in case you cannot connect to the domain controller. If you cannot connect to the domain controller, you can complete the installation by having the computer join a workgroup. After you have completed the installation and determined what is preventing you from connecting to the domain controller, you can have the computer join the domain.

Review

Here are some questions to help you determine if you have learned enough to move on to the next chapter. If you have difficulty answering these questions, please go back and review the material in this chapter before beginning the next chapter. The answers for these questions are located in Appendix A, "Questions and Answers."

1. Your company has decided to install Windows 2000 Professional on all new computers that are purchased for desktop users. What should you do before you purchase new computers to ensure that Windows 2000 can be installed and run without difficulty?

2. You are attempting to install Windows 2000 Professional from a CD-ROM; however, you have discovered that your computer does not support booting from the CD-ROM drive. How can you install Windows 2000?

3. You are installing Windows 2000 Server on a computer that will be a member server in an existing Windows 2000 domain. You want to add the computer to the domain during installation. What information do you need, and what computers must be available on the network, before you run the Setup program?

4. You are using a CD-ROM to install Windows 2000 Server on a computer that was previously running another operating system. How should you configure the hard disk to simplify the installation process?

5. You are installing Windows 2000 over the network. Before you install to a client computer, what must you do?

CHAPTER 3

Examining the Windows 2000 Architecture

About This Chapter

Now that you have installed Microsoft Windows 2000, you need to understand how it works. This chapter presents an overview of the Microsoft Windows 2000 operating system architecture. Understanding the Windows 2000 architecture and the interrelationships among system components provides the broad perspective you need to support the operating system. Knowledge of the system architecture will help you to better understand Windows 2000 installation, configuration, customization, and optimization. It will also help you identify system performance problems as they occur. The information contained in this chapter is based on an early-release beta version of Windows 2000.

Before You Begin

There are no special requirements to complete this chapter.

Lesson 1: Overview of Windows 2000 Architecture

Windows 2000 is a modular operating system. That is, it is a collection of small, self-contained software components that work together to perform operating system tasks. Each component provides a set of functions that act as an interface to the rest of the system.

After this lesson, you will be able to

- Identify the layers and layer components in the Windows 2000 operating system architecture.

Estimated lesson time: 20 minutes

Windows 2000 Layers, Subsystems, and Managers

The Windows 2000 architecture contains two major layers: *user mode* and *kernel mode,* as illustrated in Figure 3.1. This lesson provides an overview of the Windows 2000 architecture layers and their respective components.

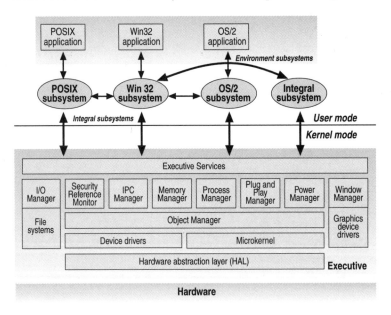

Figure 3.1   Windows 2000 architecture layers

User Mode

Windows 2000 has two different types of user mode components: *environment subsystems* and *integral subsystems.*

Environment Subsystems

One of the features of Windows 2000 is the ability to run applications written for different operating systems. Windows 2000 accomplishes this through the use of environment subsystems. Environment subsystems emulate different operating systems by presenting the application programming interfaces (APIs) that the applications expect to be available. The environment subsystems accept the API calls made by the application, convert the API calls into a format understood by Windows 2000, and then pass the converted API to the Executive Services for processing.

Table 3.1 lists the environment subsystems included with Windows 2000.

Table 3.1   Windows 2000 Environment Subsystems

Environment subsystem	Function
Windows 2000 32-bit Windows-based subsystem (Win32)	Responsible for controlling Win32-based applications, as well as for providing an environment for Win16 and Microsoft MS-DOS-based applications.
	Controls all screen-oriented input/output (I/O) between subsystems. This ensures a consistent user interface, regardless of the application that a user runs.
OS/2 subsystem	Provides a set of APIs for 16-bit, character mode OS/2 applications.
POSIX subsystem	Provides APIs for POSIX-based applications.

The environment subsystems and the applications that run within them are subject to the following limitations and restrictions:

- They have no direct access to hardware.
- They have no direct access to device drivers.
- They are limited to an assigned address space.
- They are forced to use hard disk space as virtual random access memory (RAM) whenever the system needs memory.
- They run at a lower priority level than kernel mode processes.
- Because they run at a lower priority level than the kernel-mode processes, they have less access to central processing unit (CPU) cycles than processes that run in kernel mode.

Integral Subsystems

Many different integral subsystems perform essential operating system functions. In Figure 3.1, there is a generic subsystem on the far right of the figure labeled integral subsystem. This integral subsystem represents any of the various integral subsystems. To introduce you to some of the more important integral subsystems, Table 3.2 lists some examples.

Table 3.2   Windows 2000 Integral Subsystems

Integral subsystem	Function
Security subsystem	Tracks rights and permissions associated with user accounts.
	Tracks which system resources are audited.
	Accepts user logon requests.
	Initiates logon authentication.
Workstation service	Networking integral subsystem that provides an API to access the network redirector. Allows a user sitting at a computer running Windows 2000 to access the network.
Server service	Networking integral subsystem that provides an API to access the network server. Allows a computer running Windows 2000 to provide network resources.

Kernel Mode

The kernel-mode layer has access to system data and hardware. Kernel mode provides direct access to memory and executes in an isolated memory area. Kernel mode consists of four components.

Windows 2000 Executive

This component performs most of the input/output (I/O) and object management, including security. It does not perform screen and keyboard I/O; the Microsoft Win32 subsystem performs these functions. The Windows 2000 Executive contains the Windows 2000 kernel-mode components. Each of these components provides the following two distinct sets of services and routines:

- **System services.** These are available to both the user-mode subsystems and to other Executive components.

- **Internal routines.** These are available only to other components within the Executive.

The Executive consists of the kernel-mode components listed in Table 3.3.

Table 3.3   Components of the Executive

Component	Function
I/O Manager	Manages input from, and the delivery of output to, different devices. The components that make up the I/O Manager include the following:

(continued)

	File systems. Accept the oriented I/O requests and translate these requests into device-specific calls. The network redirector and the network server are both implemented as file system drivers.
	Device drivers. Low-level drivers that directly manipulate hardware in order to accept input or to write output.
	Cache Manager. Improves disk I/O by storing disk reads in system memory. Cache Manager also improves write performance by caching write requests and writes to disk in the background.
Security Reference Monitor	Enforces security policies on the local computer.
Interprocess Communication (IPC) Manager	Manages communications between clients and servers, for example, between an environment sub-system (which would be acting like a client request-ing information) and an Executive Services compo-nent (which would be acting like a server and satis-fying the request for information). The IPC Manager consists of the following two components:
	Local Procedure Call (LPC) facility. Manages communications when clients and servers exist on the same computer.
	Remote Procedure Call (RPC) facility. Manages communications when clients and servers exist on separate computers.
Virtual Memory Manager (VMM)	Implements and controls *virtual memory*, a memory management system that provides a private address space for each process and protects the address space for each process. The VMM also controls demand paging. *Demand paging* allows the use of disk space as a storage area in order to move code and data in and out of physical RAM.
Process Manager	Creates and terminates processes and threads. (A *process* is a program or part of a program and is defined in more detail in Lesson 2. A *thread* is a specific set of commands within a program.) It also suspends and resumes threads, and stores and retrieves information about processes and threads.
Plug and Play Manager	Maintains central control of the Plug and Play process. Communicates with device drivers, direct-ing the drivers to add and start devices.
Power Manager	Controls power management APIs, coordinates power events, and generates power management requests.

(continued)

Component	Function
Window Manager and Graphical Device Interface (GDI)	These two components, implemented as a single device driver named Win32k.sys, manage the display system. They perform the following functions:
	Window Manager. Controls window displays and manages screen output. This component is also responsible for receiving input from devices such as the keyboard and the mouse and then passing messages to applications that are receiving input.
	GDI. Contains the functions that are required for drawing and manipulating graphics.
Object Manager	Creates, manages, and deletes objects that represent operating system resources, such as processes, threads, and data structures.

Device Drivers

This component translates driver calls into hardware manipulation.

Microkernel

This component manages the microprocessor only. The kernel coordinates all I/O functions and synchronizes the activities of the Executive Services.

Hardware Abstraction Layer (HAL)

This component virtualizes, or hides, the hardware interface details, making Windows 2000 more portable across different hardware architectures. The HAL contains the hardware-specific code that handles I/O interfaces, interrupt controllers, and multiprocessor communication mechanisms. This layer allows Windows 2000 to run on both Intel-based and Alpha-based systems without having to maintain two separate versions of Windows 2000 Executive.

Lesson Summary

This lesson introduced you to the Windows 2000 architecture. Windows 2000 architecture contains two major layers: user mode and kernel mode. User mode has two different types of components: environment subsystems which allow Windows 2000 to run applications written for different operating systems and integral subsystems that perform essential operating system functions. The kernel-mode layer has access to system data and hardware, provides direct access to memory, and executes in an isolated memory area.

Lesson 2: Windows 2000 Processing

Windows 2000 is a multithreaded, multitasking operating system capable of running on computer systems with multiple microprocessors.

After this lesson, you will be able to

- Identify Windows 2000 processing concepts.

Estimated lesson time: 15 minutes

Multithreaded

The capacity for a single process to run more than one thread is referred to as *multithreaded*. For example, in a word processing application thread 1 might accept input from the keyboard while thread 2 checks the spelling as the user types. In a single-threaded process, the thread 1 processes and then stops so that thread 2 can process. When thread 2 stops processing, thread 3 can process. Contrast that with a multithreaded process in which all three threads can process simultaneously. (See Figure 3.2.)

Single-threaded process

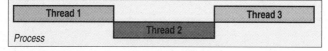

Multithreaded process

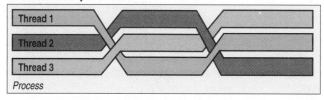

Figure 3.2   Single- and multithreaded processes

A *process* consists of an executable program that undertakes a coherent sequence of steps. A *program* consists of the following items:

- The initial code and data
- A private memory address space
- System resources, such as files, communication ports, and windows resources
- One or more threads

A *thread* is the actual component of a process that is executing at any given time. A process must contain at least one thread before it can do any work. Each thread runs in the address space allocated to the process and makes use of system resources assigned to the process. A thread consists of the following components:

- A unique identifier assigned by the system, which is called a *client ID*.
- Register contents that represent the state of the microprocessor.
- One stack for the thread to use while executing in user mode and one stack for executing in kernel mode. (A *stack* is a region of reserved memory in which programs store status data.)
- A storage space used by subsystems, dynamic-link libraries (DLLs), and run-time libraries.

Windows 2000 can execute multiple threads of a multithreaded process at the same time.

Multitasking

Developers can write applications so that processes contain one or more threads of execution. In a single-threaded process, one thread must finish executing before the process can accomplish another task. Multithreaded processes can run more than one thread of execution concurrently. This allows the process to accomplish two or more tasks simultaneously. This process is called *multitasking*.

While one microprocessor can only execute a single thread at a time, a multitasking operating system can run multiple programs. To the user, this gives the appearance of executing multiple threads concurrently. Windows 2000 uses a multitasking process called *context switching,* which operates in the following manner:

1. A thread executes until the operating system interrupts it or until the thread must wait for available resources.
2. The system saves the context of the thread.
3. The system loads the context for another thread, and then that thread begins to execute.

This process repeats as long as threads are waiting to execute.

Preemptive Multitasking

In a *preemptive multitasking* system, the operating system controls access to the microprocessor. The operating system interrupts, or *preempts*, the thread for one of two reasons:

- The thread runs for a preset amount of time, which is called a *quantum*. At the end of this preset amount of time, the operating system interrupts the thread, so that another thread can have access to the microprocessor.

- If another thread with a higher priority is ready to execute, the operating system interrupts the thread that is currently executing to allow the higher priority thread access to the microprocessor.

The Windows 2000 kernel controls the execution of threads.

Process and Thread Priorities

The Windows 2000 kernel controls access to the microprocessor through the use of *priority levels*. There are 32 different priority levels in Windows 2000, numbered 0 to 31. The levels are divided as follows:

- Levels 0–15 are used for user-mode components.
- Levels 16–31 are reserved for kernel-mode components.

The Windows 2000 kernel assigns each process a *base priority level*. The kernel also assigns a base priority level to threads that execute within that process. The base priority assignment for a process is a single level; for example, level 4. The base priority for a thread ranges from two levels below to two levels above the base priority level of the process to which it belongs. In this example, the thread might be assigned a priority from level 2 through level 6.

Threads have an additional priority level, known as a dynamic priority level. The *dynamic priority level* begins at the assigned base level and ranges upward, depending on thread activity. The kernel controls this dynamic priority level.

The kernel might raise a thread's dynamic priority level if it is accepting user input, and the kernel might lower the dynamic priority level if a thread is compute bound. For example, when you recalculate a complex spreadsheet, the thread for this process is compute bound while it does the recalculation, so the kernel might assign it a lower priority. These continuous adjustments to the threads' dynamic priority levels ensure appropriate thread access to the microprocessor.

Multiprocessing

A *multiprocessing* operating system is capable of using two or more microprocessors. There are two distinct types of multiprocessing systems: asymmetric and symmetric.

Asymmetric Multiprocessing

An *asymmetric multiprocessing* operating system assigns processes to a particular microprocessor. When a process starts, it executes on the assigned microprocessor, regardless of other activities on the other microprocessors in the system. Asymmetric multiprocessing is often inefficient, because the system cannot use idle microprocessors to help complete a process.

Symmetric Multiprocessing

Windows 2000 is a symmetric multiprocessing system. *Symmetric multiprocessing (SMP)* systems run both operating system processes and application processes on any available microprocessor. This ensures that the system uses all the available microprocessor resources, which speeds processing time.

Windows 2000 combines SMP capabilities with multitasking capabilities. If the system has more threads waiting for execution than it has available microprocessors to execute them, the Windows 2000 kernel schedules each microprocessor's time across all of the waiting threads. Some processes always run on the first microprocessor. These include the majority of the kernel-mode processes.

Lesson Summary

In this lesson you learned that Windows 2000 is a multithreaded, multitasking operating system capable of running on computer systems with multiple microprocessors. A multithreaded process can run more than one thread at a time, allowing the process to accomplish two or more tasks simultaneously. This process is called multitasking.

In a preemptive multitasking system, the operating system controls access to the microprocessor, and it can interrupt, or preempt, a thread. You also learned that the Windows 2000 kernel controls access to the microprocessor through the use of priority levels. There are 32 different priority levels in Windows 2000, numbered 0 to 31, and the Windows 2000 kernel can raise or lower the priority level of a thread.

A multiprocessing operating system is capable of using two or more microprocessors, and there are two distinct types of multiprocessing systems: asymmetric and symmetric. An asymmetric multiprocessing operating system assigns processes to a particular microprocessor, while a symmetric multiprocessing system runs both operating system processes and application processes on any available microprocessor. Windows 2000 is a symmetric operating system. This ensures that the system uses all the available microprocessor resources, which speeds processing time.

Lesson 3: The Windows 2000 Memory Model

This lesson provides an overview of the Windows 2000 memory model and describes some of the advantages to using this model.

After this lesson, you will be able to

- Describe the Windows 2000 memory model.

Estimated lesson time: 15 minutes

Introduction to the Windows 2000 Memory Model

The Windows 2000 memory model is based on a flat, linear, 32-bit address space. Windows 2000 uses a *virtual memory management* system to manage memory. This system provides several advantages, including the following:

- The ability to run more applications concurrently than would normally be possible using the amount of physical memory installed in the computer.

- The protection of memory resources. Virtual memory management helps prevent situations where one process interferes with the memory space for another process.

Physical memory refers to the RAM hardware chips inside your computer. *Virtual memory* refers to the way that an operating system makes this physical memory available to an application.

Windows 2000 represents each memory byte, both physical and virtual, with a unique address. The amount of physical RAM installed in the computer limits the number of physical addresses that are available. However, the number of virtual addresses is limited only by the number of bits in the virtual address. Windows 2000, which uses a 32-bit virtual address scheme, has 4 gigabytes (GB) worth of virtual addresses available for use.

The Virtual Memory Manager (VMM) manages memory. The VMM has two specific roles:

- It maintains a memory-mapping table. This table tracks the list of virtual addresses that belong to each process and where the actual data referenced by these virtual addresses resides (see Figure 3.3). When a thread requests access to memory, it requests a virtual address space. VMM uses the virtual address requested by the thread to locate the corresponding physical address. It then transfers the data requested by the thread.

- It moves memory contents to and from disk when required. This process is referred to as *paging*.

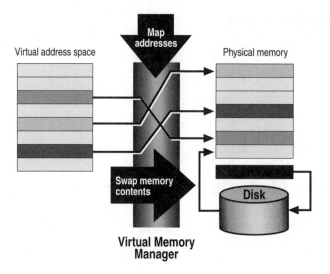

Figure 3.3   Virtual Memory Manager

Virtual Address Space

A *virtual address* is the address space that an application uses to reference memory. When a process is launched in Windows 2000, VMM presents the process with 4 GB of virtual address space (see Figure 3.4).

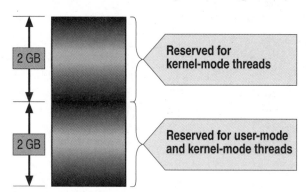

Figure 3.4   Virtual address space

This 4 GB of virtual address space is divided as follows:

- The upper 2 GB is reserved for kernel-mode threads only. The lower portion of this upper 2 GB area is mapped directly by the hardware. Access to this lower portion is extremely fast.

- The lower 2 GB is available to both user-mode and kernel-mode threads. VMM can move it to disk if required. Windows 2000 divides the upper portion into a paged and a non-paged pool. Addresses in the paged pool can be swapped out to disk, but those in the non-paged pool must remain in physical memory. The size of each page is 4 KB.

Paging

The process of moving data in and out of physical memory is called *paging*. When physical memory becomes full and a thread needs access to code or data not currently in physical memory, VMM moves some pages from physical memory to a storage area on disk called a *pagefile* (see Figure 3.5). VMM loads the code or data requested by the thread into the area of physical memory that is released by VMM.

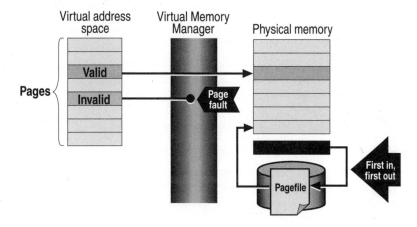

Figure 3.5   Paging

The virtual address space assigned to a process is divided up into either *valid pages* or *invalid pages*. Valid pages are those pages that are located in physical memory and are available to the process. Invalid pages are those pages that do not exist in physical memory. They are not available to the process or are stored on disk.

When a thread requests access to an invalid page, the microprocessor issues a *page fault*. VMM intercepts, or *traps,* the page fault, locates the required page, and then loads it from disk into a free page frame in physical memory. Conversely, to free up physical memory, VMM takes the contents of certain pages and transfers them to disk.

VMM performs three tasks as part of the paging process:

- It determines which pages to remove from physical memory, when memory is full. VMM keeps track of the pages currently in memory for each process. This group of pages is referred to as a process's *working set*. VMM uses a local first in, first out replacement policy to decide which pages to move out of physical memory. The data that has been in physical memory the longest period of time is the first to be removed. When a thread generates a page fault, VMM examines the working set for the thread's process and then moves to disk the page that has resided in physical memory for the longest period of time.

- It brings pages from disk into physical memory, a process called *fetching*. VMM also uses a method known as demand paging with clustering. *Demand paging with clustering* means that when a page fault is triggered, VMM loads the needed page into memory, plus some of the pages that surround it. This helps to reduce the number of page faults that are generated.

- It determines where to place pages retrieved from disk. If physical memory is not full, VMM loads the data into the first free page. If physical memory is full, VMM determines which page or pages to move to disk to make room in physical memory for the pages retrieved from disk.

Lesson Summary

In this lesson you learned that the Windows 2000 memory model is based on a flat, linear, 32-bit address space. Windows 2000 uses a virtual memory management system to manage memory, which provides several advantages, including the ability to run more applications concurrently than would normally be possible using the amount of physical memory installed in the computer.

The Virtual Memory Manager (VMM) manages memory and also maintains a memory-mapping table. This table tracks the list of virtual addresses that belong to each process and where the actual data referenced by these virtual addresses resides. The VMM moves memory contents to and from disk when required. This process is referred to as paging.

Review

Here are some questions to help you determine if you have learned enough to move on to the next chapter. If you have difficulty answering these questions, please go back and review the material in this chapter before beginning the next chapter. The answers for these questions are located in Appendix A, "Questions and Answers."

1. What environment subsystems ship with Windows 2000? Which of these subsystems is responsible for controlling screen-oriented I/O?

2. What component of the Windows 2000 architecture provides portability across multiple hardware platforms?

3. Why is a symmetric multiprocessing operating system more efficient than an asymmetric multiprocessing operating system?

4. What is a page fault?

5. What does the term *working set* mean?

CHAPTER 4

Using Microsoft Management Console and Task Scheduler

About This Chapter

The primary administrative tools that you use to manage Microsoft Windows 2000 are the Microsoft Management Console (MMC), the Task Scheduler, and Control Panel. This chapter presents an overview of the MMC and the Task Scheduler. Chapter 5, "Using Windows Control Panel," discusses Control Panel.

Before You Begin

To complete this chapter, you must have

- A computer that meets the minimum hardware requirements listed in "Hardware Requirements," on page xxxiii.
- Installed the Windows 2000 Server software on the computer.
- Configured the computer as a stand-alone server in a workgroup.

Lesson 1: Introducing the Microsoft Management Console

This lesson introduces the Microsoft Management Console, the MMC. It defines MMC consoles, console trees, details panes, snap-ins, and extensions. The lesson also covers the differences between Author mode and User mode. This lesson discusses the .MSC file extension assigned to the MMC consoles you create and the My Administrative Tools folder where the MMC consoles you create are stored as files. The My Administrative Tools folder is accessible from the Programs menu and offers easy access to the MMC consoles that you create.

After this lesson, you will be able to

- Describe the function and components of Microsoft Management Console (MMC), including snap-ins, console options, and modes.

Estimated lesson time: 20 minutes

MMC Consoles

One of the primary administrative tools that you use to manage Windows 2000 is the Microsoft Management Console (MMC). The MMC provides a standardized method to create, save, and open administrative tools, which are called MMC consoles. The MMC does not provide management functions itself, but it is the program that hosts management applications called *snap-ins,* which you use to perform one or more administrative tasks.

The MMC allows you to do the following:

- Perform most of your administrative tasks by using only the MMC. Being able to use one interface saves time instead of having to use numerous interfaces.
- Centralize administration. You can use MMC consoles to perform the majority of your administrative tasks from one computer.
- Use most snap-ins for remote administration. Not all snap-ins are available for remote administration, so Windows 2000 prompts you with a dialog box when you can use the snap-in for remote administration.

Note   Third-party vendors can design their administrative tools as snap-ins for use in MMC consoles.

MMC consoles contain one or more snap-ins. Consoles are saved as files and have a .MSC extension. All the settings for the snap-ins contained in the console are saved and are restored when the file is opened, even if the console file is opened on a different computer or network.

You configure MMC consoles to hold snap-ins to perform specific tasks. Console options determine how an MMC console operates. By using console options, you can create MMC consoles for other administrators to use from their own computers to perform very specific tasks.

Console Tree and Details Pane

Every MMC console has a console tree. A *console tree* displays the hierarchical organization of the snap-ins that are contained within that MMC console. As you can see in Figure 4.1, this MMC console contains the Disk Defragmenter snap-in and the Device Manager On Local Computer snap-in.

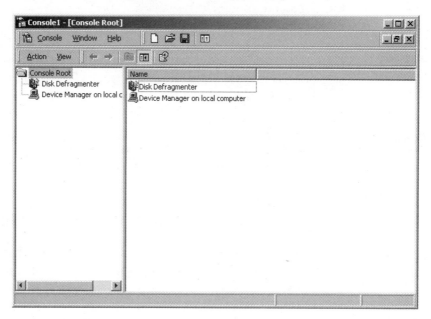

Figure 4.1   MMC consoles

The console tree organizes snap-ins that are part of an MMC console. This allows you to easily locate a specific snap-in. Items that you add to the console tree appear under the console root. The *details pane* lists the contents of the active snap-in.

Every MMC console contains the Action menu and View menu. The choices on these menus vary, depending on the current selection in the console tree.

My Administrative Tools

By default, Windows 2000 saves custom MMC console files (with a .MSC extension) in the My Administrative Tools folder. The My Administrative Tools folder does not exist when you first install Windows 2000, but Windows 2000 creates it for you when you first save a custom console. Windows 2000 creates a separate My Administrative Tools folder for each user. Do not confuse My Administrative Tools with Administrative Tools. Administrative Tools is the same on all computers and contains preconfigured MMC consoles. To use your custom MMC consoles, click Start, point to the Programs menu, click My Administrative Tools, and click your custom MMC console.

Snap-Ins

Snap-ins are applications that are designed to work in MMC. Use snap-ins to perform administrative tasks. There are two types of snap-ins: stand-alone snap-ins and extension snap-ins.

Stand-Alone Snap-Ins

Stand-alone snap-ins are usually referred to simply as snap-ins. Use stand-alone snap-ins to perform Windows 2000 administrative tasks. Each snap-in provides one function or a related set of functions. Windows 2000 Server comes with standard snap-ins. Windows 2000 Professional includes a smaller set of standard snap-ins.

Extension Snap-Ins

Extension snap-ins are usually referred to as *extensions*. They are snap-ins that provide additional administrative functionality to another snap-in. The following are characteristics of extensions:

- Extensions are designed to work with one or more stand-alone snap-ins, based on the function of the stand-alone snap-in. For example, the Group Policy Editor extension is available in the Active Directory Manager snap-in; however, it is not available in the Disk Defragmenter snap-in, because Group Policy Editor does not relate to the administrative task of disk defragmentation.

- When you add an extension, Windows 2000 displays only extensions that are compatible with the stand-alone snap-in. Windows 2000 places the extensions into the appropriate location within the stand-alone snap-in.

- When you add a snap-in to a console, MMC adds all available extensions by default. You can remove any extension from the snap-in.

- You can add an extension to multiple snap-ins.

Figure 4.2 demonstrates the concept of snap-ins and extensions. A toolbox holds a drill. You can use a drill with its standard drill bit. You can perform additional functions with different drill bits. The same is true for snap-ins and extensions.

Some stand-alone snap-ins can use extensions that provide additional functionality, for example Computer Management. However, some snap-ins, like Event Viewer, can act as a snap-in or an extension.

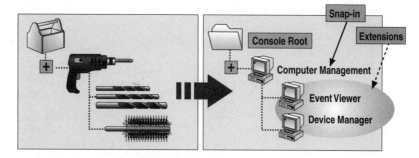

- **Snap-ins are administrative tools.**
- **Extensions provide additional functionality to snap-ins.**
  - Extensions are preassigned to snap-ins.
  - Multiple snap-ins may use the same extensions.

Figure 4.2   Snap-ins and extensions

Console Options

Use console options to determine how each MMC console operates by selecting the appropriate *console mode*. The console mode determines the MMC console functionality for the person who is using a saved MMC console. The two available console modes are *Author mode* and *User mode*.

Author Mode

When you save an MMC console in Author mode, you enable full access to all MMC functionality, which includes modifying the MMC console. Save the MMC console using Author mode to allow those using it to do the following:

- Add or remove snap-ins.
- Create new windows.
- View all portions of the console tree.
- Save MMC consoles.

Note   By default, all new MMC consoles are saved in Author mode.

User Mode

Usually, if you plan to distribute an MMC console to other administrators, save the MMC console in User mode. When you set an MMC console to User mode, users cannot add snap-ins to, remove snap-ins from, or save the MMC console.

There are three types of User modes, which allow different levels of access and functionality. Table 4.1 describes when to use each User mode.

Table 4.1   MMC Console User Modes

Use	When
Full Access	You want to allow users to navigate between snap-ins, open new windows, and gain access to all portions of the console tree.
Delegated Access, Multiple Windows	You do not want to allow users to open new windows or gain access to a portion of the console tree. You do want to allow users to view multiple windows in the console.
Delegated Access, Single Window	You do not want to allow users to open new windows or gain access to a portion of the console tree. You want to allow users to view only one window in the console.

Lesson Summary

In this lesson you learned that one of the primary administrative tools that you use to manage Windows 2000 is the Microsoft Management Console. The MMC provides a standardized method to create, save, and open administrative tools, which are called MMC consoles. MMC consoles hold one or more management applications called snap-ins, which you use to perform administrative tasks. By default, Windows 2000 saves custom MMC console files (with a .MSC extension) in the My Administrative Tools folder. The My Administrative Tools folder does not exist when you first install Windows 2000, but Windows 2000 creates it for you the first time you save a custom console.

You learned that every MMC console has a console tree. The console tree displays the hierarchical organization of the snap-ins that are contained within that MMC console. This allows you to easily locate a specific snap-in. The details pane lists the contents of the active snap-in. You also learned that there are two types of snap-ins: stand-alone snap-ins and extension snap-ins. A stand-alone snap-in is usually referred to simply as a snap-in and provides one function or a related set of functions. An extension snap-in is usually referred to as an extension, and it provides additional administrative functionality to a snap-in. An extension is designed to work with one or more stand-alone snap-ins, based on the function of the stand-alone snap-in.

Finally, in this lesson you learned about console options. You use console options to determine how each MMC console operates by selecting the appropriate console mode. The two available console modes are Author mode and User mode. When you save an MMC console in Author mode, you enable full access to all MMC functionality, which includes modifying the MMC console. You save the MMC console using Author mode to allow those using it to add or remove snap-ins, create new windows, view all portions of the console tree, and save MMC consoles. Usually, if you plan to distribute an MMC console to other administrators, save the MMC console in User mode. When you set an MMC console to User mode, users cannot add snap-ins to, remove snap-ins from, or save the MMC console.

Lesson 2: Using MMC Consoles

This lesson introduces the two types of MMC consoles: preconfigured consoles and custom consoles. It explains how you can use preconfigured consoles and how you can create, use, and modify custom MMC consoles. Finally, this lesson explains how you can use MMC consoles for remote administration.

After this lesson, you will be able to

- Use preconfigured MMC consoles.
- Create and use customized MMC consoles.
- Create custom MMC consoles for remote administration.

Estimated lesson time: 40 minutes

Types of MMC Consoles

You will use MMC consoles to perform the majority of Windows 2000 administrative tasks. There are two types of MMC consoles: preconfigured and custom. Preconfigured MMC consoles contain commonly used snap-ins, and they appear on the Administrative Tools menu. You create custom MMC consoles to perform a unique set of administrative tasks. You can use preconfigured and custom MMC consoles for remote administration.

Preconfigured MMC Consoles

Preconfigured MMC consoles contain snap-ins that you use to perform the most common administrative tasks. Windows 2000 installs a number of preconfigured MMC consoles during installation. Preconfigured MMC consoles

- Contain only one snap-in that provides the functionality to perform a related set of administrative tasks.
- Function in User mode. Because preconfigured MMC consoles are in User mode, you cannot modify them, save them, or add additional snap-ins. However, when you create custom consoles, you can add as many preconfigured consoles as you want as snap-ins to your custom console.
- Vary, depending on the operating system that the computer is running and the installed Windows 2000 components. Windows 2000 Server and Windows 2000 Professional have different preconfigured MMC consoles.
- Might be added by Windows 2000 when you install additional components. Optional Windows 2000 components might include additional preconfigured MMC consoles that Windows 2000 adds when you install a component. For example, when you install the Domain Name System (DNS) service, Windows 2000 also installs the DNS Management console.

Note To select preconfigured MMC consoles, click the Start button, point to Programs, and then click Administrative Tools.

Custom MMC Consoles

You can use many of the preconfigured MMC consoles for administrative tasks. However, there will be times when you need to create your own custom MMC consoles. Although you can't modify preconfigured consoles, you can combine multiple preconfigured snap-ins with third-party snap-ins provided by independent software vendors (ISVs) that perform related tasks to create custom MMC consoles. You can then do the following:

- Save the custom MMC consoles to use again.
- Distribute the custom MMC consoles to other administrators.
- Use the custom MMC consoles from any computer to centralize and unify administrative tasks.

Creating custom MMC consoles allows you to meet your administrative requirements by combining snap-ins that you use to perform common administrative tasks. By creating a custom MMC console, you do not have to switch between different programs or different preconfigured MMC consoles because all of the snap-ins that you need to perform your job are located in the custom MMC console.

▶ **To start MMC with an empty console open**

1. Click the Start button.
2. Click Run.
3. Type **mmc** in the Open box, and then click OK.

   An MMC console window opens, titled Console 1 and containing a window titled Console Root. This is an empty MMC console and you must decide what to do.

   The following table describes when to use the different commands on the Console menu.

Use this command	When
New	You want to create a new custom MMC console.
Open	You want to use a saved MMC console.
Save or Save As	You want to use the MMC console later.
Add/Remove Snap-In	You want to add or remove one or more snap-ins and their associated extensions to or from an MMC console.
Options	You want to configure the console mode and create a custom MMC console.

4. Close MMC.

Using MMC Consoles for Remote Administration

When you create custom MMC consoles, you can set up a snap-in for remote administration. Remote administration allows you to perform administrative tasks from any location. For example, you can use a computer running Windows 2000 Professional to perform administrative tasks on a computer running Windows 2000 Server. You cannot use all snap-ins for remote administration; the design of each snap-in dictates if you can use it for remote administration.

To perform remote administration

- You can use snap-ins from computers running either Windows 2000 Server or Windows 2000 Professional.
- You must use specific snap-ins that are designed for remote administration. If the snap-in is available for remote administration, Windows 2000 prompts you to choose the target computer to administer.

Practice: Using Microsoft Management Console

In this practice, you use one of the preconfigured MMC consoles that ships with Windows 2000 Server. Then you create a customized MMC console.

After completing this practice, you will be able to

- Use preconfigured consoles and customize a console.
- Organize and add Microsoft Management Console (MMC) snap-ins.

Exercise 1: Using a Preconfigured MMC Console

In this exercise, you use one of the preconfigured MMC consoles that ships with Windows 2000 Server.

▶ **To use a preconfigured MMC Console**

1. Log on as Administrator.
2. Click the Start button, point to Programs, point to Administrative Tools, and then click Event Viewer.

    Windows 2000 displays the Event Viewer console, which gives you access to the contents of the event log files on your computer. You use Event Viewer to monitor various hardware and software activities.

    Looking at the console tree, what three logs are listed?

    Can you add snap-ins to this console? Why or why not?

3. Close Event Viewer.

Exercise 2: Creating a Customized MMC Console

In this exercise, you create and customize an MMC console. You use this console to confirm the last time that your computer was started. You also add a snap-in with extensions.

▶   **To create a customized console**

1. Click the Start button, and then click Run.

2. In the Open box, type **mmc** and then click OK.

   MMC starts and displays an empty console.

3. Maximize the Console1 window by clicking the Maximize button.

4. Maximize the Console Root window by clicking the Maximize button.

5. To view the currently configured options, click Options on the Console menu.

   MMC displays the Options dialog box with the User tab active.

   What are the default user options?

6. Click the Console tab.

   The Console tab allows you to configure the console mode.

   How does a console that is saved in User mode differ from one that is saved in Author mode?

7. In the Console Mode box, make sure that Author Mode is selected, and then click OK.

8. On the Console menu, click Save As.

   MMC displays the Save As dialog box.

   What is the default folder for customized consoles? What is the advantage of saving files in this folder?

9. In the File name box, type **All Events** and then click Save.

   The name of your console appears in the MMC title bar.

   To confirm that the console was saved in the correct location, close and then open the console as explained in the following steps.

10. On the Console menu, click Exit.

    You have now created and saved a customized console named All Events.

11. Click the Start button, point to Programs, point to My Administrative Tools, and then click All Events.

Windows 2000 opens the All Events console that you saved previously.

▶ **To add the Event Viewer snap-in to a console**

1. On the Console menu, click Add/Remove Snap-In.

   MMC displays the Add/Remove Snap-In dialog box with the Standalone tab active. Notice that there are currently no loaded snap-ins. You will add a snap-in to the console root.

2. In the Add/Remove Snap-In dialog box, click Add.

   MMC displays the Add Standalone Snap-In dialog box, as shown in Figure 4.3.

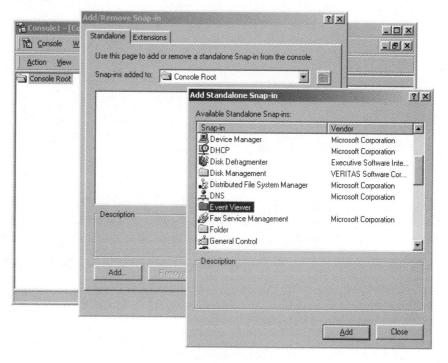

Figure 4.3   Add Standalone Snap-In dialog box

Notice the available snap-ins. MMC allows you to add one or more snap-ins to a console, enabling you to create your own customized management tools.

3. In the Add Standalone Snap-In dialog box, select Event Viewer, and then click Add.

   MMC displays the Select Computer dialog box, allowing you to specify which computer you want to administer.

Notice that you can add Event Viewer for the local computer on which you are working, or if your local computer is part of a network, you can also add Event Viewer for a remote computer.

To add Event Viewer for a remote computer, you would click Another computer, and then click Browse. In the Select Computer dialog box, you would click the remote computer for which you would like to add Event Viewer, and then click OK.

In this lab, you will add Event Viewer for your computer, the local computer.

4. In the Select Computer dialog box, make sure that Local Computer is selected, and then click Finish.

5. In the Add Standalone Snap-In dialog box, click Close; and in the Add/Remove Snap-In dialog box, click OK.

Event Viewer (Local) now appears in the console tree.

Tip   To see the entire folder name, drag the border between the console panes to the right.

▶   **To determine the last time that the computer was started**

1. In the console tree of the All Events console, expand the Event Viewer (Local) folder, and then click System Log.

   MMC displays the most recent system events in the details pane.

2. Double-click the most recent information event listed as eventlog in the Source column.

   The EventLog service started as part of your system startup. The date and time represents the approximate time that your system was started. Make a note of the date and time.

3. To close the Event On Local Computer Properties dialog box, click OK.

4. On the Console menu, click Exit to close the All Events console.

   A Microsoft Management Console dialog box appears, asking if you want to save the console settings to All Events.

5. Click No.

▶   **To remove extensions from a snap-in**

1. Click the Start button, and then click Run.

2. In the Open box, type **mmc** and then click OK.

   MMC displays an empty console.

3. Maximize the Console1 and Console Root windows.

4. On the Console menu, click Add/Remove Snap-In.

   MMC displays the Add/Remove Snap-In dialog box with the Standalone tab active. You will add a snap-in to the console root.

5. Click Add.

   All snap-ins that are listed here are stand-alone snap-ins.

6. In the Add Standalone Snap-In dialog box, in the Available Standalone Snap-Ins box, click Computer Management, and then click Add.

   MMC displays the Select Computer dialog box, allowing you to specify which computer you want to administer. In this procedure, you will add the Computer Management snap-in for your own computer.

7. Verify that Local Computer is selected, and then click Finish.

8. Click Close.

   Computer Management appears in the list of snap-ins that have been added.

9. In the Add/Remove Snap-In dialog box, click OK.

   MMC displays the Computer Management snap-in in the console tree below Console Root. Console Root acts as a container for several categories of administrative functions.

10. Expand Computer Management and review the available functions, and then expand System Tools.

Note   Do not use any of the tools at this point.

Notice that several extensions are available, including Device Manager and System Information. You can restrict the functionality of a snap-in by removing extensions.

11. On the Console menu, click Add/Remove Snap-In.

    MMC displays the Add/Remove Snap-In dialog box with the Standalone tab active.

12. Click Computer Management (Local), and then click the Extensions tab.

    MMC displays a list of available extensions for the Computer Management snap-in.

    What determines which extensions MMC displays in this dialog box?

13. Clear the Add All Extensions check box, and then in the Available Extensions box, clear the Device Manager Extension check box and the System Information Extension check box.

14. Click OK.

MMC displays the console window again.

15. Expand Computer Management and then expand System Tools to confirm that Device Manager and System Information have been removed.

Note   Do not use any of the tools at this point.

When should you remove extensions from a console?

16. Close the console.

MMC displays a message, prompting for confirmation to save console settings.

17. Click No.

Lesson Summary

In this lesson you learned that you can use MMC consoles to perform the majority of Windows 2000 administrative tasks. You learned that there are two types of MMC consoles: preconfigured and custom. The preconfigured MMC consoles contain commonly used snap-ins, and they can be easily accessed through the Administrative Tools menu. In the practice portion of this lesson, you viewed the preconfigured MMC consoles and started the preconfigured MMC console containing Event Viewer.

You also learned that you can create custom MMC consoles to perform a unique set of administrative tasks. Once you create customized MMC consoles, they can be accessed through the My Administrative Tools menu. In the practice portion of this lesson, you created two customized MMC consoles. The first console contained the Event Viewer snap-in, which you used to determine the last time your computer was started. The second custom MMC console you created contained the Computer Management snap-in. After you created the second customized console, you learned how to restrict the functionality of a console by removing two of the extensions normally available with the Computer Management snap-in. Finally, in this lesson you learned how to create custom MMC consoles for remote administration.

Lesson 3: Using Task Scheduler

Use Task Scheduler to schedule programs and batch files to run once, at regular intervals, or at specific times. You can use Task Scheduler to schedule any script, program, or document to start at a specified time and interval or when certain operating system events occur. You can use Task Scheduler to complete many administrative tasks for you.

After this lesson, you will be able to
- Use Task Scheduler to schedule tasks.

Estimated lesson time: 25 minutes

Introduction to Task Scheduler

Windows 2000 saves scheduled tasks in the Scheduled Tasks folder, which is in the Control Panel folder in My Computer. In addition, you can access Scheduled Tasks on another computer by browsing that computer's resources using My Network Places. This allows you to move tasks from one computer to another. For example, you can create task files for maintenance and then add them to a user's computer as needed.

Use Task Scheduler to

- Run maintenance utilities at specific intervals.
- Run programs when there is less demand for computer resources.

Options

Use the Scheduled Task wizard to schedule tasks. You access the wizard in the Scheduled Tasks folder by double-clicking Add Scheduled Task. Table 4.2 describes the options that you can configure in the Scheduled Task wizard.

Table 4.2   Scheduled Task Wizard Options

Option	Description
Program To Run	The applications to schedule. Select the applications to schedule from a list of applications that are registered with Windows 2000, or click Browse to specify any program or batch file.
Task Name	A descriptive name for the task.
Frequency	How often Windows 2000 will perform the task. You can select daily, weekly, monthly, one time only, when the computer starts, and when you log on.
Time And Date	The start time and start date for the task to occur. If applicable, you can enter the days on which to repeat the task.

(continued)

Option	Description
Name And Password	A user name and password. You can enter your user name and password or another user name and password to have the application run under the security settings for that user account.
	If the user account that you used to log on does not have the rights that are required by the scheduled task, you can use another user account that does have the required rights. For example, you can run a scheduled backup by using a user account that has the required rights to back up data but does not have other administrative privileges.
Advanced Properties	Select this check box if you want the wizard to display the Advanced Properties dialog box so that you can configure additional properties after you click Finish.

Advanced Properties

In addition to the options that are available in the Scheduled Task wizard, you can set several additional options for tasks. You can change options that you set with the Scheduled Task wizard or set additional advanced options by configuring advanced properties for the task.

Table 4.3 describes the tabs in the Advanced Properties dialog box for the scheduled task.

Table 4.3   Scheduled Task Wizard Advanced Options

Tab	Description
Task	Change the scheduled task or change the user account that is used to run the task. You can also turn the task on and off.
Schedule	Set and display multiple schedules for the same task. You can set the date, time, and number of repeat occurrences for the task. For example, you can set up a task to run every Friday at 10:00 PM.
Settings	Set options that affect when a task starts or stops, such as how long a backup can take, if the computer can be in use, or if the computer can be running on batteries when it runs the task.
Security	Change the list of users and groups that have permission to perform the task, or change the permissions for a specific user or group.

Practice: Using Task Scheduler

After completing this practice, you will be able to

- Schedule tasks to start automatically.
- Configure Task Scheduler options.

In this practice, you schedule Address Book to start at a predetermined time. You can use this as a reminder to review address information. You also configure Task Scheduler options.

▶ **To schedule a task to start automatically**

1. Double-click My Computer, double-click Control Panel, and then double-click Scheduled Tasks.

   Windows 2000 opens the Scheduled Tasks folder. Because no tasks are currently scheduled, only the Add Scheduled Task entry appears.

2. Double-click Add Scheduled Task.

   The Scheduled Task wizard appears.

3. Click Next.

   Windows 2000 displays a list of currently installed programs. To schedule a program that is not registered with Windows 2000, you would click the Browse button to locate the program.

4. Click Browse.

   The Select Program To Schedule page appears.

5. Double-click Program Files, and then double-click Windows 2000.

6. Double-click Accessories, and then double-click WordPad.

7. In the Name box, type **Launch WordPad** as shown in Figure 4.4.

   The Name box allows you to enter a description that is more intuitive than the program name. Windows 2000 displays this name in the Scheduled Tasks folder when you finish the wizard.

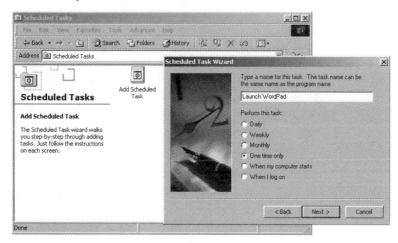

Figure 4.4   Using the Scheduled Task wizard

8. Click One Time Only, and then click Next.

9. In the Start Time box, set the time to four minutes after the current system time and make a note of this time.

   To confirm the current system time, look at the taskbar. Do not change the entry in the Start Date box.

10. Click Next.

    The wizard requires you to enter the name and password of a user account. When Task Scheduler runs the scheduled task, the program receives all of the rights and permissions of the user account that you enter here. The program is also bound by any restrictions on the user account. Notice that your user name, SERVER1\Administrator, is already filled in as the default. (If your computer name is not Server1, Server1 will be replaced by your computer's name.) You must type the correct password for the user account in both password boxes before you can continue.

    You will schedule the console to run with your administrative privileges.

11. In both the Enter The Password box and the Confirm Password box, type **password**

12. Click Next.

    Do not check the box to open the Advanced Properties dialog box for this task. You will review these properties in the next procedure.

13. Click Finish.

    Notice that the wizard added the task to the list of scheduled tasks.

14. To confirm that you scheduled the task successfully, wait for the time that you configured in step 9. WordPad will start.

15. Close WordPad.

▶   **To configure advanced Task Scheduler options**

1. In the Scheduled Tasks folder, double-click Launch WordPad.

   Windows 2000 displays the Launch WordPad dialog box. Notice the tabs and review the options on the tabs. These are the same options that are available if you select the check box for setting advanced options on the last page of the Scheduled Task wizard. Do not change any of the settings.

2. Click the Settings tab.

   Review the options that are available on the Settings tab.

3. Select the Delete The Task If It Is Not Scheduled To Run Again check box.

4. Click the Schedule tab, and then set the start time for two minutes after the current system time.

   Make a note of this time.

5. Click OK.

To confirm that you scheduled the task successfully, wait for the time that you set in step 4 of this procedure. WordPad will start.

6. Close WordPad.

Notice that the scheduled event is no longer in the Scheduled Tasks folder. The option to automatically delete a task after it finishes is useful for cleaning up after tasks that only need to run once.

7. Close the Scheduled Tasks folder.

8. Log off Windows 2000.

Lesson Summary

In this lesson you learned that you can use the Task Scheduler to schedule programs and batch files to run once, at regular intervals, at specific times, or when certain operating system events occur. Windows 2000 saves scheduled tasks in the Scheduled Tasks folder, which is in the Control Panel folder in My Computer. Once you have scheduled a task to run, you can modify any of the options or advanced features for the task, including the program to be run.

In addition, you learned that you can access Scheduled Tasks on another computer by browsing that computer's resources using My Network Places. This allows you to move tasks from one computer to another. For example, you can create task files for maintenance and then add them to a user's computer as needed. In the practice portion of this lesson, you used the Scheduled Task wizard to schedule WordPad to launch at a specified time.

Review

Here are some questions to help you determine if you have learned enough to move on to the next chapter. If you have difficulty answering these questions, please go back and review the material in this chapter before beginning the next chapter. The answers for these questions are located in Appendix A, "Questions and Answers."

1. When and why would you use an extension?

2. You need to create a custom MMC console for an administrator who only needs to use the Computer Management and Active Directory Manager snap-ins. The administrator

   - Must not be able to add any additional snap-ins.
   - Needs full access to all snap-ins.
   - Must be able to navigate between snap-ins.

   What console mode would you use to configure the custom MMC console?

3. Why do you create custom MMC consoles?

4. What do you need to do to remotely administer a computer running Windows 2000 Server from a computer running Windows 2000 Professional?

5. You need to schedule a maintenance utility to run once a week on a computer running Windows 2000 Server. What do you use to accomplish this?

CHAPTER 5

Using Windows Control Panel

About This Chapter

Microsoft Windows 2000 stores configuration information in two locations: the registry and Active Directory. Modifications to the registry or Active Directory change the configuration of the Windows 2000 environment. You use the following tools to modify the registry or Active Directory:

- Microsoft Management Console
- Control Panel
- Registry Editor

Control Panel contains applications that you use to customize selected aspects of the hardware and software configuration for a computer.

Before You Begin

To complete this chapter, you must have

- A computer that meets the minimum hardware requirements listed in "Hardware Requirements," on page xxxiii.
- Installed the Windows 2000 Server software on the computer.
- Configured the computer as a stand-alone server in a workgroup.

Lesson 1: Configuring Hardware Settings

You use Control Panel to configure hardware settings. You use some Control Panel programs to manage user-specific settings and others to manage settings that apply regardless of the user who logs on. This lesson introduces the Control Panel programs that you use to configure hardware devices or services. You configure hardware settings by creating and configuring hardware profiles.

After this lesson, you will be able to
- Manage hardware profiles.

Estimated lesson time: 10 minutes

Understanding Hardware Profiles

A *hardware profile* stores configuration settings for a set of devices and services. Windows 2000 can store different hardware profiles to meet the user's different needs. For example, a portable computer can use different hardware configurations depending on whether it is docked or undocked. A portable-computer user can create a hardware profile for each state (docked and undocked), and choose the appropriate profile when starting Windows 2000.

Creating or Modifying a Hardware Profile

To create or modify a hardware profile, in Control Panel, double-click the System icon, and then click the Hardware tab. Click Hardware Profiles to view the Available Hardware Profiles list (see Figure 5.1).

Tip   To open the System dialog box from the desktop, right-click My Computer, and then click Properties.

Windows 2000 creates an initial profile during installation, which is listed as Profile 1 (Current). You can create a new profile with the same configuration as another profile. To create a new profile, in the Hardware Profiles dialog box, in the Available Hardware Profiles list, select the profile that you want to copy, and then click Copy.

The order of the profiles in the Available Hardware Profiles list determines the default order at startup. The first profile in the list becomes the default profile. To change the order of the profiles, use the Up Arrow and Down Arrow buttons.

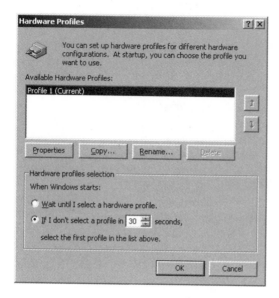

Figure 5.1   Available Hardware Profiles list

Activating a Hardware Profile

If there are two or more profiles in the Available Hardware Profiles list, Windows 2000 prompts the user to make a selection during startup. You can configure the time that the computer waits before starting the default configuration. To adjust this time delay, click If I Don't Select A Profile under Hardware Profiles Selection.

You can configure Windows 2000 to start the default profile by setting the number of seconds in the If I Don't Select A Profile option to 0. To override the default, press Spacebar during the system prompt.

When using hardware profiles, be careful not to disable one of the boot devices with the Devices program in Control Panel. If you disable a required boot device, Windows 2000 might not start. It is a good idea to make a copy of the default profile, and then make changes to the new profile. This way, you can use the default profile again if a problem occurs.

Viewing Hardware Profile Properties

To view the properties for a hardware profile, in the Available Hardware Profiles list, select a profile, and then click Properties. This displays the Properties dialog box for the profile.

If Windows 2000 identifies your computer as a portable unit, the This Is A Portable Computer check box is selected. If Windows 2000 determines that your portable computer is docked, it automatically selects that option. You cannot change this docked option setting after Windows 2000 selects it.

Lesson Summary

You use the System icon in Control Panel to configure hardware devices or services by creating and configuring hardware profiles. A hardware profile stores configuration settings for a set of devices and services. During installation, Windows 2000 automatically creates an initial profile, but you can create additional profiles. To create a new profile, in the Hardware Profiles dialog box, in the Available Hardware Profiles list, select the profile that you want to copy and then click Copy. To view the properties for a hardware profile, in the Available Hardware Profiles list, select a profile and then click Properties. This displays the Properties dialog box for the profile.

The order of the profiles in the Available Hardware Profiles list determines the default order at startup. The first profile in the list becomes the default profile. To change the order of the profiles, use the Up Arrow and Down Arrow buttons. If there are two or more profiles in the Available Hardware Profiles list, Windows 2000 prompts you to make a selection during startup.

Lesson 2: Configuring the Display

Users with permission to load and unload device drivers can also install and test video drivers. Windows 2000 can change video resolutions dynamically without restarting the system.

After this lesson, you will be able to
- Use Control Panel to configure the display.

Estimated lesson time: 25 minutes

Setting Display Properties

To view or modify the display properties, in Control Panel, double-click the Display icon, and then click the Settings tab. Configurable display options include the number of colors, video resolution, font size, and refresh frequency, as shown in Figure 5.2.

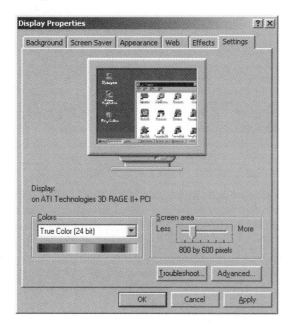

Figure 5.2   Settings tab of the Display Properties dialog box

Table 5.1 describes the options available on the Settings tab for configuring the display settings.

Table 5.1   Settings Tab Options for Configuring the Display

Option	Description
Colors	Lists color depths for the display adapter
Screen Area	Allows you to set the resolution for the display adapter
Troubleshoot	Opens the Windows Display Troubleshooter to aid in diagnosing display problems
Advanced	Opens the Properties dialog box for the display adapter, as described next

To open the Properties dialog box for the display adapter, click Advanced. Table 5.2 describes the display adapter options.

Table 5.2   Display Adapter Advanced Options

Tab	Option	Description
General	Display	Provides small, large, or other display font option. The other option lets you choose any custom font size you want.
	Compatibility	The action that Windows 2000 should take when you make changes to display settings. After you change the color settings, you must choose to do one of the following: ■ Restart the computer before applying the new color settings. ■ Apply the new color settings without restarting. ■ Ask me before applying the new color settings.
Adapter	Adapter Type	The manufacturer and model number of the installed adapter. The Properties button tells you additional information including device status, resource settings, and any conflicting devices.
	Adapter Information	Additional information about the display adapter, such as video chip type, DAC (digital-to-analog converter) type, memory size, and bios.
	List All Modes	Displays all compatible modes for your display adapter and lets you select resolution, color depth, and refresh frequency in one step.
	Test	Tests the display adapter configuration settings.

Monitor	Monitor Type	The manufacturer and model number of the monitor currently installed.
	Monitor Settings	Configures the refresh rate frequency. This option only applies to high-resolution drivers. Do not select a refresh rate/screen resolution combination that is unsupported by the monitor. If you are unsure, refer to your monitor documentation, or select the lowest refresh rate option.
Troubleshooting	Hardware Acceleration	Lets you progressively decrease your display hardware's acceleration features to help you isolate and eliminate display problems.
Color Management		Chooses the color profile for your monitor.

Using Multiple Displays

Windows 2000 adds support for multiple display configurations. Multiple displays allow you to extend your desktop across more than one monitor, as shown in Figure 5.3. Windows 2000 supports extending your display across a maximum of nine monitors.

- **Use of multiple displays extends the desktop across a maximum of nine monitors.**
- **Multiple displays must use Peripheral Component Interconnect (PCI) or Accelerated Graphics Port (AGP) devices.**
- **Hardware requirements for primary (main) and secondary displays differ.**

Figure 5.3   Multiple displays

Important   You must use Peripheral Component Interconnect (PCI) or Accelerated Graphics Port (AGP) devices when configuring multiple displays.

If one of the display adapters is built into the motherboard, note these additional considerations:

- The motherboard adapter always becomes the secondary adapter. It must be multiple-display compatible.

- You must set up Windows 2000 before installing another adapter. Windows 2000 Setup will disable the motherboard adapter if it detects another adapter. Some systems completely disable the onboard adapter upon detecting an add-in adapter. If you are unable to override this detection in the basic input/output system (BIOS), you cannot use the motherboard adapter with multiple displays.

Typically, the system BIOS selects the primary display based on PCI slot order. However, on some computers, the BIOS allows the user to select the primary display device.

You cannot stop the primary display. This is an important consideration for laptop computers with docking stations. For example, some docking stations contain a display adapter; these often disable, or turn off, a laptop's built-in display. Multiple display support will not function on these configurations unless you attach multiple adapters to the docking station.

Configuring Multiple Displays

You must configure each display in a multiple display environment. Windows 2000 displays a number icon to represent each monitor, as shown in Figure 5.4.

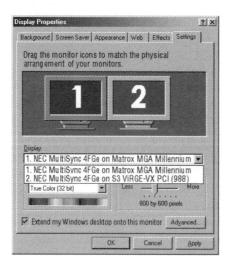

Figure 5.4   Using Control Panel to configure multiple displays

▶ **To configure your display in a multiple display environment**

1. In Control Panel, click Display.

2. In the Display Properties dialog box, click the Settings tab.

   The numbers inside the monitor icons indicate the displays for the computer. Display 1 is the primary display; displays 2 through 9 are secondary displays.

3. Click the monitor icon for the primary display device.

4. Select the display adapter for the primary display, and then select the color depth and resolution.

5. Click the monitor icon for the secondary display device.

6. Select the display adapter for the secondary display, and then select the Extend My Windows Desktop Onto This Monitor check box.

7. Select the color depth and resolution for the secondary display.

8. Repeat steps 5–7 for each additional display.

Windows 2000 uses the virtual desktop concept to determine the relationship of each display. The virtual desktop uses coordinates to track the position of each individual display desktop.

The coordinates of the top-left corner of the primary display always remain 0,0. Windows 2000 sets secondary display coordinates so that all the displays adjoin each other on the virtual desktop. This allows the system to maintain the illusion of a single, large desktop where users can cross from one monitor to another without losing track of the mouse.

To change the display positions on the virtual desktop, on the Settings tab, drag the display representations to the desired position. The positions of the icons dictate the coordinates and the relative positions of the displays to one another.

Troubleshooting Multiple Displays

If you encounter problems with multiple displays, use the troubleshooting guidelines in Table 5.3 to help resolve those problems.

Table 5.3   Troubleshooting Tips for Multiple Displays

Problem	Solution
You cannot see any output on the secondary displays.	Activate the device in the Display Properties dialog box.
	Confirm that you chose the correct video driver.
	Restart the computer to confirm that the secondary display initialized. If not, check the status of the video adapter in Device Manager.

(continued)

Problem	Solution
	Switch the order of the adapters in the slots. (The primary adapter must qualify as a secondary adapter.)
The Extend My Windows Desktop Onto This Monitor check box is unavailable.	Select the secondary display rather than the primary one in the Display Properties dialog box.
	Confirm that the secondary display adapter is supported.
	Confirm that Windows 2000 can detect the secondary display.
An application fails to display on the secondary display.	Run the application on the primary display.
	Run the application in full-screen mode (Microsoft MS-DOS) or maximized (Microsoft Windows).
	Disable the secondary display to determine whether the problem is specific to multiple display support.

Lesson Summary

In this lesson you learned that users with permission to load and unload device drivers can also install and test video drivers. With Windows 2000, you can change video resolutions dynamically without restarting the system.

You learned that you use the Display icon in Control Panel to view or modify display properties, such as the number of colors, video resolution, font size, and refresh frequency. You also learned that Windows 2000 supports multiple displays, with up to a maximum of nine monitors, and that you must configure each display. The lesson concluded with a section on troubleshooting multiple displays.

Lesson 3: Configuring Operating System Settings

You use certain Control Panel programs to configure operating system settings. The System Properties dialog box allows you to configure performance options, paging file settings, environment variables, and startup and recovery settings.

The Control Panel programs that you use to configure the operating system settings affect the operating system environment regardless of the user who is logged on to the computer.

After this lesson, you will be able to

- Use Control Panel to configure the operating system.

Estimated lesson time: 30 minutes

Performance Options

The first Control Panel program that allows you to configure operating system settings is accessed through System Properties. To view operating system performance configuration options, double-click the System icon in Control Panel, click the advanced tab in the System Properties dialog box, and then click Performance Options. The Performance Options dialog box is shown in Figure 5.5.

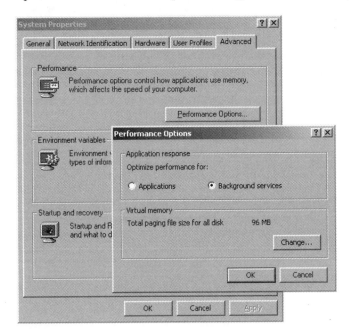

Figure 5.5   Performance Options dialog box

The options in this dialog box allow you to adjust the *Application Response*, which is the priority of foreground applications versus background applications, and Virtual Memory.

Application Response

Windows 2000 uses the Application Response settings to distribute microprocessor resources between running programs. Selecting Applications assigns more resources to the foreground application (the active program that is responding to user input), while selecting Background Services assigns an equal amount of resources to all programs.

Virtual Memory

For virtual memory, Windows 2000 uses a process called *demand paging* to exchange data between random access memory (RAM) and paging files. When you install Windows 2000, Setup creates a virtual-memory paging file, Pagefile.sys, on the partition where you installed Windows 2000.

The minimum paging file size is 2 MB. The default paging file size for both Windows 2000 Server and Windows 2000 Workstation is equal to the lessor of the total amount of RAM plus 12 MB or the amount of available disk space.

Typically, you can leave the size of the paging file set to the default value. In some circumstances, such as when you run a large number of applications simultaneously, you might find it advantageous to use a larger paging file or multiple paging files.

To configure the paging file, in the Performance Options dialog box, click Change. The Virtual Memory dialog box identifies the drives on which the paging files reside and allows you to modify the paging file size for the selected drive and the registry size (see Figure 5.6).

Paging files never decrease below the initial size that was set during installation. Unused space in the paging file remains available to the internal Windows 2000 Virtual Memory Manager (VMM).

If you set the size of the initial paging file significantly below the recommended size, Windows 2000 displays the Limited Virtual Memory box message at logon. The message directs you to the System program in Control Panel to create a paging file or to increase the initial paging file size. Only users with administrative rights can log on and use System to correct this problem.

As needed, a paging file grows from its initial size to the maximum configured size. When the paging file reaches the maximum size, system performance might degrade if you place additional demands on the system by running more applications.

When you restart a computer running Windows 2000, the system resizes all paging files to the initial size.

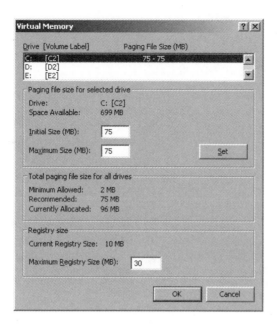

Figure 5.6 Configuring the paging file

Enhancing Performance

There are several things that you can do to enhance your system's performance. First, if your computer has multiple hard disks, create a paging file for each disk. Distributing information across multiple paging files improves performance because the hard disk controller can read from and write to multiple hard disks simultaneously. When attempting to write to the paging file, VMM tries to write the page data to the paging file on the disk that is the least busy.

Second, you can enhance your system's performance by moving the paging file off the drive that contains the Windows 2000 *systemroot* folder (by default, the \Winnt folder). Moving the paging file off the drive containing the boot partition avoids competition between the various reading and writing requests. If you place a paging file on the Windows 2000 system partition to facilitate the recovery feature which is discussed in the "Recovery" section later in this chapter, you can still increase performance by creating multiple paging files. Because the VMM alternates write operations between paging files, the paging file on the boot partition is accessed less frequently.

Third, you can enhance your system's performance by setting the initial size of the paging file to the value displayed in the Maximum Size box in the Virtual Memory dialog box. This eliminates the time required to enlarge the file from the initial size to the maximum size.

Note When applying new settings, be sure to click Set before clicking OK.

Environment Variables

Environment variables define the system and user environment information, and they contain information such as a drive, path, or file name. Environment variables provide information that Windows 2000 uses to control various applications. For example, the TEMP environment variable specifies where an application places its temporary files.

Click Environment Variables on the Advanced tab of the System Properties dialog box to display the system and user environment variables that are currently in effect (see Figure 5.7).

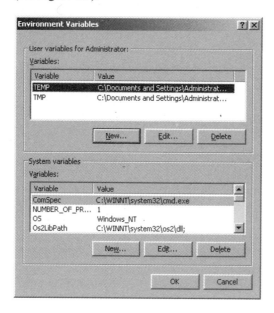

Figure 5.7 Setting environment variables

System Environment Variables

System environment variables apply to the entire system. Consequently, these variables affect all system users. During installation, Setup configures the default system environment variables, including the path to the Windows 2000 files. Only an administrator can add, modify, or remove a system environment variable.

User Environment Variables

The user environment variables differ for each user of a particular computer. The user environment variables include any user-defined settings (such as a desktop pattern) and any variables defined by applications (such as the path to the location of the application files). Users can add, modify, or remove their user environment variables in the System Properties dialog box.

How Windows 2000 Sets Environment Variables

Windows 2000 sets environment variables in the following order:

1. By default, Windows 2000 searches the Autoexec.bat file, if it exists, and sets any environment variables.

2. Next the system environment variables are set. If there are any system environment variables that conflict with environment variables set from the search of the Autoexec.bat file, the system environment variables override them.

3. Finally the user environment variables are set. If there are any user environment variables that conflict with environment variables set from the search of the Autoexec.bat file or from the system environment variables, the user environment variables override them.

For example, if you add the line SET TMP=C:\ in Autoexec.bat, and a TMP=X:\TEMP user variable is set, the user environment variable setting (X:\TEMP) overrides the prior setting C:\.

Note   You can prevent Windows 2000 from searching the Autoexec.bat file by editing the registry and setting the value of the ParseAutoexec entry to 0. The ParseAutoexec entry is located in the registry under the following subkey:

\HKEY_CURRENT_USER\SOFTWARE\Microsoft\Windows NT\CurrentVersion\Winlogon

---

Startup and Recovery Settings

The System program also controls the startup and recovery settings for a computer. In addition to using Control Panel to access the System Program, you can right-click My Computer, click Properties, click the Advanced tab of the System Properties dialog box, and then click Startup And Recovery.

The Startup And Recovery dialog box contains two groups of information, as shown in Figure 5.8. The System Startup options control the behavior of the boot loader menu. The Recovery options control the actions that Windows 2000 performs in the event of a stop error. A *stop error* is a severe error that causes Windows 2000 to stop all processes. Stop errors are also known as *fatal system errors* or *blue screen errors*.

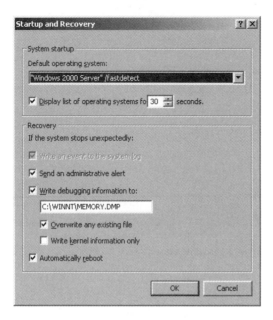

Figure 5.8   Startup and recovery settings

System Startup

When you first turn on the computer, the system displays a boot menu, which lists the available operating systems. By default, the system chooses one of the operating systems and displays a countdown timer. If you do not choose another operating system, the system starts the preselected operating system when the countdown timer reaches zero or when you press Enter. Modify the options under System Startup to determine which operating system is preselected, how long the countdown timer runs, and whether to display the boot menu.

Recovery

The four recovery options that Windows 2000 provides to assist the user in the event of a stop error are described in Table 5.4.

Important   You must be logged on as a member of the Administrators group to set recovery options.

Table 5.4   Recovery Options

Option	Additional information
Write An Event To The System Log	Select this check box to have Windows 2000 write an event to the system log when a system stops unexpectedly.

Send An Administrative Alert	Select this check box to send an administrative alert to administrators when the system stops unexpectedly.
Write Debugging Information To	Select this check box to write debugging information to a specified file name. This provides information that helps Microsoft support engineers solve reported problems.
Automatically Reboot	Select this check box to have Windows 2000 reboot whenever the system stops unexpectedly.

The following requirements must be met for the Write Debugging Information To recovery option to work:

- A paging file must be on the system partition (the partition that contains the *systemroot* folder).
- The paging file must be at least 1 MB larger than the amount of physical RAM in your computer.
- You must have enough disk space to write the file in the location you specify. To overwrite an existing file, select the Overwrite Any Existing File check box.

Practice: Using Control Panel to Change Operating System Settings

After completing this practice, you will be able to

- Configure the boot delay.
- Change the paging file size.

Before working on this practice, you should have completed the preceding lessons of this chapter so that you are familiar with Control Panel.

For more information about setting up Windows 2000, see the Release Notes document, Relnotes.doc, located in the root directory of the Windows 2000 Server CD-ROM.

Exercise 1: Decreasing the Boot Delay

In this exercise, you decrease the boot delay by changing the number of seconds before the default operating system loads.

▶ **To decrease the boot delay**

1. Log on as Administrator.
2. In Control Panel, double-click the System icon.

    The System Properties dialog box appears.

What is an alternate method for accessing the System Properties dialog box?

3. On the Advanced tab, click Startup And Recovery.

   The Startup And Recovery dialog box appears.

   What is the default operating system?

   How long will the countdown timer run before automatically starting the default operating system?

4. In the Display List Of Operating Systems For box, for the number of seconds, type **0** and then click OK.

   You are returned to the System Properties dialog box.

5. Click OK to close the System Properties dialog box.

6. Restart the computer.

   Does the boot loader menu appear?

   Why might you not want the boot loader menu to appear?

7. Log on as Administrator.

8. Return to the Startup And Recovery dialog box, change the boot delay setting to 15 seconds, and click OK. Leave the System Properties dialog box open.

Exercise 2: Changing the Paging File Size

In this exercise, you use the System Properties dialog box to change the size of the Windows 2000 paging file.

▶   **To change the paging file size**

1. On the Advanced tab, click Performance Options.

   The Performance Options dialog box appears.

2. Click Change.

   The Virtual Memory dialog box appears.

3. In the Drive box, click the drive that contains your paging file, if necessary.

4. In the Initial Size box, increase the value by 10, and then click Set.

   Why would you want to increase the initial size of the paging file?

5. Click OK to close the Virtual Memory dialog box.

6. Click OK to close the Performance Options dialog box.

7. Click OK to close the System Properties dialog box.

   The System Settings Change dialog box appears, indicating that you must restart your computer before the changes take effect.

Exercise 3: Adding a System Environment Variable

In this exercise, you use the System Properties dialog box to add a new system environment variable. You then test the new variable by using it at the command prompt.

▶ **To add a system environment variable**

1. In the System Properties dialog box, on the Advanced tab, click Environment Variables.

   The Environment Variables dialog box appears.

2. Under System variables, click New.

   The New System Variable dialog box appears.

3. In the Variable Name box, type **Ntdir**

4. In the Variable Value box, type the path to the Winnt directory on your computer, for example, C:\Winnt.

   If you are not sure of the path to Winnt, use Windows Explorer to locate the Winnt directory.

5. Click OK.

   You are returned to the Environment Variables dialog box.

6. Click OK to close the dialog box, and then click OK to close the System Properties dialog box.

7. Close Control Panel.

▶ **To test the new variable**

1. From the Start menu, point to Programs and select Command Prompt.

2. At the command prompt, type **set | more** and then press Enter.

   The list of current environment variables is displayed.

   Is Ntdir listed as an environment variable?

3. Press Spacebar to display the remaining environment variables.

4. Type **c:** and then press Enter to switch to the drive on which you installed Windows 2000. (Adjust the drive letter if necessary.)

5. Type **cd** and then press Enter if you are not already in the root directory.

6. Type **cd %ntdir%** and then press Enter.

What happens?

7. Close the command prompt.

Lesson Summary

In this lesson you learned that you use the System Properties dialog box to configure performance options, paging file settings, environment variables, and startup and recovery settings. To configure operating system performance options, in the System Properties dialog box, click the Advanced tab and then click Performance Options. The options in this dialog box allow you to adjust the Application Response, which is the priority of foreground applications versus background applications, and Virtual Memory.

To configure environment variables, click Environment Variables on the Advanced tab of the System Properties dialog box to display the system and user environment variables that are currently in effect. Environment variables define the system and user environment information, and they contain information such as a drive, path, or file name. Environment variables provide information that Windows 2000 uses to control various applications.

Windows 2000 sets the environment by first searching the Autoexec.bat file, if it exists, and setting any environment variables. Next the system environment variables are set. If there are any conflicts with the environment variables set from the search of the Autoexec.bat file, the system environment variables override them. Finally the user environment variables are set. If there are any conflicts with environment variables set from the search of the Autoexec.bat file or from the system environment variables, the user environment variables override them.

To configure startup and recovery settings, click Startup And Recovery on the Advanced tab of the System Properties dialog box. The System Startup options control the behavior of the boot loader menu. You modify the options under System Startup to determine which operating system is preselected, how long the countdown timer runs, and whether the boot menu is displayed. The Recovery options control the actions that Windows 2000 performs in the event of a stop error. A stop error is a severe error that causes Windows 2000 to stop all processes. Stop errors are also known as fatal system errors or blue screen errors.

The Control Panel programs that you use to configure the operating system settings affect the operating system environment regardless of the user who is logged on to the computer.

Lesson 4: Installing Hardware Automatically

Windows 2000 supports both Plug and Play and non–Plug and Play hardware. This lesson introduces you to the automatic hardware installation features of Windows 2000.

After this lesson, you will be able to

- Describe how to install hardware automatically.

Estimated lesson time: 15 minutes

Installing Plug and Play Hardware

With most Plug and Play hardware, you simply connect the device to the computer, and Windows 2000 automatically configures the new settings. However, you might occasionally need to initiate automatic installation for some Plug and Play hardware. You do this with the Add/Remove Hardware wizard.

Installing Non–Plug and Play Hardware

For non–Plug and Play hardware, Windows 2000 often identifies the hardware and automatically installs and configures it. For non–Plug and Play hardware that Windows 2000 does not identify, install, and configure, you initiate the automatic installation of the hardware with the Add/Remove Hardware wizard.

▶ **For automatic hardware installations**

1. Initiate automatic hardware installation.

   Windows 2000 queries the hardware about the hardware resources that it requires and the settings for those resources. A *hardware resource* allows a hardware device to communicate directly with the operating system. Windows 2000 can resolve conflicts between Plug and Play hardware for hardware resources.

2. Confirm the automatic hardware installation.

   Once Windows 2000 finishes the installation, you should verify correct installation and configure the hardware.

Using the Add/Remove Hardware Wizard

Use the Add/Remove Hardware wizard to initiate automatic hardware installation. You also use the wizard for undetected hardware devices—both Plug and Play devices and non–Plug and Play devices.

▶ **To start the Add/Remove Hardware wizard**

1. In Control Panel, double-click Add/Remove Hardware Wizard.

2. Click Next to close the welcome page.

3. Select Add/Troubleshoot A Device, and then click Next.

    Windows searches for new devices.

After the Add/Remove Hardware wizard starts, it searches for any new Plug and Play hardware, and then installs any it finds. If the wizard cannot find a new device, it displays the Choose A Hardware Device screen, shown in Figure 5.9. If there are no new hardware devices discovered, Windows 2000 prompts you to select one of the installed devices to troubleshoot it.

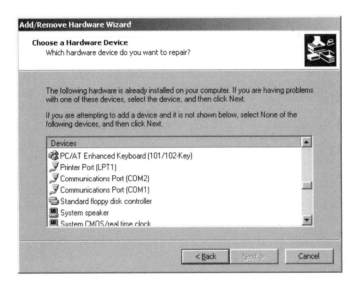

Figure 5.9   Troubleshooting with the Add/Remove Hardware wizard

Confirming Hardware Installation

After installing hardware, you should confirm the installation by using the Device Manager.

▶ **To start the Device Manager**

1. Double-click the System icon in Control Panel.

2. Click the Hardware tab, and then click Device Manager.

    This allows you to view the installed hardware, as shown in Figure 5.10.

Windows 2000 uses icons in the right pane of the Computer Management window to identify each installed hardware device. If Windows 2000 does not have an icon for the device type, it displays a question mark for the device type.

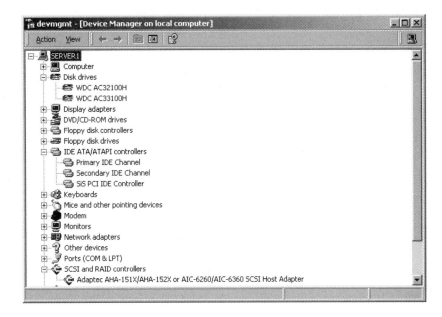

Figure 5.10   Device Manager showing devices listed by type

Expand the device tree to locate the newly installed hardware device. The device icon indicates whether the hardware device is operating properly. You can use the information in Table 5.5 to determine the hardware status.

Table 5.5   Device Manager Hardware Status

Icon	Hardware status
Normal icon	Hardware is operating properly.
Stop sign on icon	Windows 2000 disabled the hardware device due to hardware conflicts. To correct this, right-click the device icon, and then click Properties. Set the hardware resources manually according to what is available in the system.
Exclamation point on icon	The hardware device is incorrectly configured or its drivers are missing.

Lesson Summary

Windows 2000 supports both Plug and Play and non–Plug and Play hardware. In this lesson you learned that with most Plug and Play hardware, you connect the device to the computer, and Windows 2000 automatically configures the new settings. For non–Plug and Play hardware, Windows 2000 often identifies the hardware and automatically installs and configures it. For the occasional Plug and Play hardware device and for any non–Plug and Play hardware that Windows 2000 does not identify, install, and configure, you initiate automatic hardware installation with the Add/Remove Hardware wizard.

Lesson 5: Installing Hardware Manually

Occasionally, Windows 2000 5.0 fails to automatically detect a hardware device. When this occurs, you must manually install the hardware device. You might also have to manually install a hardware device if the device requires a specific hardware resource. You manually install these devices to ensure that they have the necessary resources.

To manually install hardware, first determine which hardware resource is required by the hardware device. Next, you must determine the available hardware resources. In some cases, you will have to change hardware resources. Finally, you might have to troubleshoot any problems you encounter.

After this lesson, you will be able to

- Describe how to install hardware manually.

Estimated lesson time: 10 minutes

Determining Which Hardware Resources Are Required

When installing new hardware, you need to know what resources the hardware can use. You can reference the product documentation to determine the resources that a hardware device requires. Table 5.6 describes the resources that hardware devices use to communicate with an operating system.

Table 5.6   Hardware Device Resources

Resource	Description
Interrupts	Hardware devices use interrupts to send messages. The microprocessor knows this as an interrupt request (IRQ). The microprocessor uses this information to determine which device needs its attention and the type of attention that it needs. Windows 2000 provides 16 IRQs, numbered 0–15; these IRQs are assigned to devices. For example, Windows 2000 assigns IRQ 1 to the keyboard.
Input/output (I/O) ports	I/O ports are a section of memory that a hardware device uses to communicate with the operating system. When a microprocessor receives an IRQ, the operating system checks the I/O port address to retrieve additional information about what the hardware device wants it to do. An I/O port is represented as a hexadecimal number.

Direct memory access (DMA)	DMAs are channels that allow a hardware device, such as a floppy disk drive, to access memory directly, without interrupting the microprocessor. DMA channels speed up access to memory. Windows 2000 has eight DMA channels, numbered 0–7.
Memory	Many hardware devices, such as a network adapter card, use onboard memory or reserve system memory. This reserved memory is unavailable for use by other devices or Windows 2000.

Determining Available Hardware Resources

After you determine which resources a hardware device requires, you can look for an available resource. Device Manager provides a list of all hardware resources and their availability, as shown in Figure 5.11.

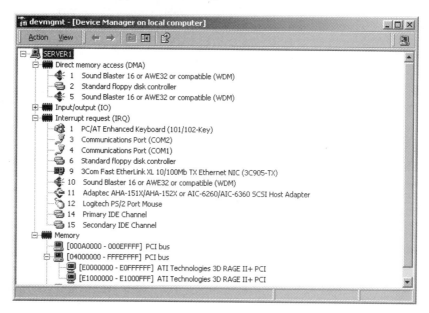

Figure 5.11   Device Manager showing resources listed by connection

▶ **To view the hardware resources lists**

1. From the System Properties dialog box, click the Hardware tab, and then click Device Manager.

2. From the View menu, select Resources By Connection.

   The Device Manager displays the resources that are currently in use (for example, IRQs).

3. To view a list of resources for another type of hardware resource, click the type of hardware resource that you want to see on the View menu.

Once you know which hardware resources are available, you can install the hardware manually with the Add/Remove Hardware wizard.

Note   If you select a hardware resource during manual installation, you might need to configure the hardware device so that it can use the resource. For example, for a network adapter to use IRQ 5, you might have to set a jumper on the adapter and configure Windows 2000 so that it recognizes that the adapter now uses IRQ 5.

Changing Hardware Resource Assignments

You might need to change hardware resource assignments. For example, a hardware device might require a specific resource presently in use by another device. You might also encounter two hardware devices requesting the same hardware resource, resulting in a conflict.

To change a resource setting, use the Resources tab in the device's Properties dialog box.

▶   **To access the Resources tab**

1. From the Hardware tab of the System Properties dialog box, click Device Manager.
2. Expand the device list, right-click the specific device, and then click Properties.
3. In the Properties dialog box for the device, click the Resources tab.

From this point, follow the same procedures that you used to choose a hardware resource during a manual installation.

Note   Changing the resource assignments for non–Plug and Play devices in Device Manager does *not* change the resources used by that device. You only use Device Manager to instruct the operating system on device configuration. To change the resources used by a non–Plug and Play device, consult the device documentation to see whether switches or jumpers must be configured on the device.

Tip   When you change a hardware resource, print the content of Device Manager. This will provide you with a record of the hardware configuration. If you encounter problems, you can use the printout to verify the hardware resource assignments.

Lesson Summary

In this lesson you learned about installing hardware manually. If Windows 2000 fails to automatically detect a hardware device, or if a hardware device requires a specific hardware resource, you might have to manually install these devices. You learned that when you manually install hardware, you must determine any resources required by that hardware device. Hardware resources include interrupts, I/O ports, and memory. You can reference the product documentation to determine any resources that a device requires. You also must determine which hardware resources are available. You learned that the Device Manager snap-in provides a list of all hardware resources and their availability.

You also learned that you might need to change hardware resource assignments. For example, a hardware device might require a specific resource presently in use by another device. You learned that to change a hardware resource, you also use Device Manager. To view or change the hardware resources used by a device, in the Device Manager snap-in, expand the relevant device category in the right pane, right-click the specific device, and then click Properties. In the Device Properties dialog box, click the Resources tab to view the current resources being used and click Change Setting to make changes to the resources in use.

Review

Here are some questions to help you determine if you have learned enough to move on to the next chapter. If you have difficulty answering these questions, please go back and review the material in this chapter before beginning the next chapter. The answers for these questions are located in Appendix A, "Questions and Answers."

1. What should you do if you cannot see any output on the secondary display?

2. You have configured recovery options on a computer running Windows 2000 Server to write debugging information to a file if a stop error occurs. You notice, however, that the file is not being created. What could be causing this problem?

3. How can you optimize virtual memory performance?

4. You installed a new network card in your computer, but it does not seem to be working. Describe how you would troubleshoot this problem.

CHAPTER 6

Using the Registry

About This Chapter

The Microsoft Windows 2000 operating system stores system configuration information in a hierarchical database called the registry. This chapter presents an overview of the registry and introduces Registry Editor. Registry Editor is a tool that allows you to view and modify the registry.

Before You Begin

To complete this chapter, you must have

- A computer that meets the minimum hardware requirements listed in "Hardware Requirements," on page xxxiii.
- Installed the Windows 2000 Server software on the computer.
- Configured the computer as a stand-alone server in a workgroup.

Lesson 1: Overview of the Registry

Microsoft Windows 2000 stores hardware and software settings centrally in a hierarchical database called the *registry*. The registry replaces many of the .INI, .SYS, and .COM configuration files used in earlier versions of Microsoft Windows. The registry controls the Windows 2000 operating system by providing the appropriate initialization information to start applications and load components, such as device drivers and network protocols.

After this lesson, you will be able to

- Identify the purpose of the registry.
- Define the hierarchical structure of the registry.

Estimated lesson time: 30 minutes

Purpose of the Registry

The registry contains a variety of different types of data, including the following:

- The hardware installed on the computer, including the central processing unit (CPU), bus type, pointing device or mouse, and keyboard.
- Installed device drivers.
- Installed applications.
- Installed network protocols.
- Network adapter card settings. Examples include the interrupt request (IRQ) number, memory base address, input/output (I/O) port base address, I/O channel ready, and transceiver type.

The registry structure provides a secure set of records. The data in the registry is read, updated, or modified by many of the Windows 2000 components.

The components that access and store data in the registry include those shown in Figure 6.1 and explained in Table 6.1.

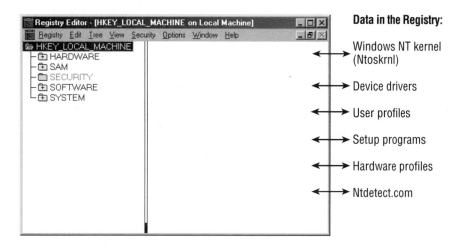

Figure 6.1   Registry Editor

Table 6.1   Components That Use the Registry

Component	Description
Windows NT kernel	During startup, the Windows NT kernel (Ntoskrnl.exe) reads information from the registry, including the device drivers to load and the order in which they should be loaded. The kernel writes information about itself to the registry, such as version number.
Device drivers	Device drivers receive configuration parameters from the registry. They also write information to the registry. A device driver informs the registry which system resources it is using, such as hardware interrupts or direct memory access (DMA) channels. Device drivers also report discovered configuration data.
Setup programs	During setup of a hardware device or application, a setup program can add new configuration data to the registry. It can also query the registry to determine whether required components have been installed.
Ntdetect.com	During system startup, on Intel-based computers, Ntdetect.com performs hardware detection. This dynamic hardware configuration data is stored in the registry.

(continued)

Component	Description
	Reduced-instruction-set-computing (RISC)-based computers extract the data from the computer firmware.
Hardware profiles	Computers with two or more hardware configurations use hardware profiles. When Windows 2000 starts, the user selects a hardware profile and Windows 2000 configures the system accordingly.
User Profiles	Windows 2000 creates and maintains user work environment settings in a user profile. When a user logs on, the system caches the profile in the registry. Windows 2000 first writes user configuration changes to the registry and then to the user profile.

The Hierarchical Structure of the Registry

The registry is organized in a hierarchical structure similar to the hierarchical structure of folders and files on a disk. Figure 6.2 shows the hierarchical structure of the registry as displayed by one of the registry editing tools included with Windows 2000.

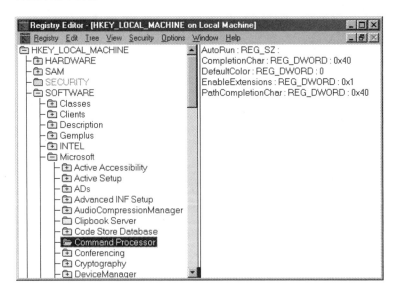

Figure 6.2   Registry Editor displaying the hierarchical structure of the registry

Table 6.2 describes the components that make up the hierarchical structure of the registry.

Table 6.2   Components That Make Up the Registry

Component	Description
Subtree	A subtree (or subtree key) is analogous to the root folder of a disk. The Windows 2000 registry has two subtrees: HKEY_LOCAL_MACHINE and HKEY_USERS. However, to make the information in the registry easier to find and view, there are five predefined subtrees that can be seen in the editor: HKEY_LOCAL_MACHINE HKEY_USERS HKEY_CURRENT_USER HKEY_CLASSES_ROOT HKEY_CURRENT_CONFIG
Keys	Keys are analogous to folders and subfolders. Keys correspond to hardware or software objects and groups of objects. Subkeys are keys within higher-level keys.
Entries	Keys contain one or more entries. An entry has three parts: name, data type, and value (or configuration parameter).
Hive	A hive is a discrete body of keys, subkeys, and entries. Each hive has a corresponding registry file and .LOG file located in *systemroot* System32\Config. Windows 2000 uses the .LOG file to record changes and ensure the integrity of the registry.
Data types	Each entry's value is expressed as one of these data types: ▪ **REG_DWORD.** One value; must be a string of 1–8 hexadecimal digits. ▪ **REG_SZ.** One value; Windows 2000 interprets it as a string to store. ▪ **REG_EXPAND_SZ.** Similar to REG_SZ, except the text can contain a replaceable variable; for example, in the string *systemroot* Ntvdm.exe, Windows 2000 replaces the *systemroot* environmental variable with the path to the Windows 2000 System32 folder. ▪ **REG_BINARY.** Only one value; it must be a string of hexadecimal digits; Windows 2000 interprets each pair as a byte value. ▪ **REG_MULTI_SZ.** Multiple values allowed; Windows 2000 interprets each string as a component of MULTI_SZ separate entries. ▪ **REG_FULL_RESOURCE_DESCRIPTOR.** Stores a resource list for hardware components or drivers. You cannot add or modify an entry with this data type.

Registry Subtrees

Understanding the purpose of each subtree can help you to locate specific keys and values in the registry. The following five subtrees or subtree keys are displayed in the Registry Editor (see Figure 6.3).

- **HKEY_LOCAL_MACHINE.** Contains all configuration data for the local computer, including hardware and operating system data such as bus type, system memory, device drivers, and startup control data. Applications, device drivers, and the operating system use this data to set the computer configuration. The data in this subtree remains constant regardless of the user.

- **HKEY_USERS.** Contains two subkeys:
  - **DEFAULT.** Contains the system default settings (system default profile) used to display the CTRL+ALT+DEL logon screen, and the security identifier (SID) of the current user.
  - **HKEY_CURRENT_USER.** Is a child of HKEY_USERS.

- **HKEY_CURRENT_USER.** Contains data about the current user. Retrieves a copy of each user account used to log on to the computer from the Ntuser.dat file and stores it in the *systemroot*\Profiles*username* key. This subkey points to the same data contained in HKEY_USERS*SID_currently_logged_ on_user*. This subtree takes precedence over HKEY_LOCAL_MACHINE for duplicated values.

- **HKEY_CLASSES_ROOT.** Contains software configuration data: object linking and embedding (OLE) and file-class association data. This subtree points to the Classes subkey under HKEY_LOCAL_MACHINE\SOFTWARE.

- **HKEY_CURRENT_CONFIG.** Contains data on the active hardware profile extracted from the SOFTWARE and SYSTEM hives. This information is used to configure settings such as the device drivers to load and the display resolution to use.

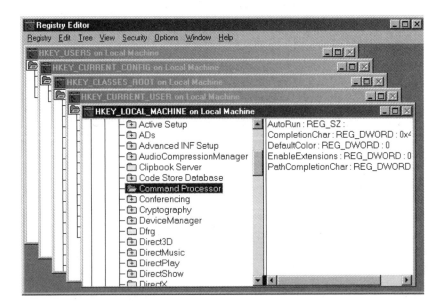

Figure 6.3   Registry subtrees

Note   One version of the registry editor, Regedit.exe, displays a sixth subtree, HKEY_DYN_DATA. This is a subtree of the Windows 95 and Windows 98 operating systems but is not used by the Windows 2000 operating system.

The HKEY_LOCAL_MACHINE Subtree

HKEY_LOCAL_MACHINE provides a good example of the subtrees in the registry for two reasons:

- The structure of all subtrees is similar.

- HKEY_LOCAL_MACHINE contains information specific to the local computer and is always the same, regardless of the user who is logged on.

The HKEY_LOCAL_MACHINE root key has five subkeys. These five subkeys are explained in Table 6.3.

Table 6.3   HKEY_LOCAL_MACHINE Subkeys

Subkey	Description
HARDWARE	The type and state of physical devices attached to the computer. This subkey is volatile, meaning that Windows 2000 builds it from information gathered during startup. Because the values for this subkey are volatile, this subkey does not map to a file on the disk. Applications query this subkey to determine the type and state of physical devices attached to the computer.
SAM	The directory database for the computer. The SAM hive maps to the SAM and Sam.log files in the *systemroot*\System32\Config directory. Applications that query SAM must use the appropriate application programming interfaces (APIs). This hive is a pointer to the same one accessible under HKEY_LOCAL_MACHINE\SECURITY\SAM.
SECURITY	The security information for the local computer. The SECURITY hive maps to the Security and Security.log files in the *systemroot*\System32\Config directory. Applications cannot modify the keys contained in the SECURITY subkey. Instead, applications must query security information by using the security APIs.
SOFTWARE	Information about the local computer software that is independent of per-user configuration information. This hive maps to the Software and Software.log files in the *systemroot*\System32\Config directory. It also contains file associations and OLE information.
SYSTEM	Information about system devices and services. When you install or configure device drivers or services, they add or modify information under this hive. The SYSTEM hive maps to the System and System.log files in the *systemroot*\System32\Config directory. The registry keeps a backup of the data in the SYSTEM hive in the System.alt file.

Lesson Summary

In this lesson you learned that the Microsoft Windows 2000 operating system stores hardware and software settings in the registry. The registry is a hierarchical database and replaces many of the .INI, .SYS, and .COM configuration files used in earlier versions of Microsoft Windows. The registry contains a variety of different types of data, including the hardware installed on the computer, as well as the installed device drivers, applications, and network protocols. The registry also provides the appropriate initialization information to start applications and load components, such as device drivers and network protocols.

The registry structure provides a secure set of records, and the data in the registry can be read, updated, or modified by many of the Windows 2000 components. There are a number of components that make up the hierarchical structure of the registry. First, subtrees (or subtree keys) are analogous to the root folder of a disk. The Windows 2000 registry has two subtrees: HKEY_LOCAL_MACHINE and HKEY_USERS. However, to make the information in the registry easier to find and view, there are five predefined subtrees that can be seen in the editor: HKEY_LOCAL_MACHINE, HKEY_USERS, HKEY_CURRENT_USER, HKEY_CLASSES_ROOT, and HKEY_CURRENT_CONFIG. The other components of the registry include keys, entries, hives, and data types.

Lesson 2: Using Registry Editor

Most users of Windows 2000 never need to access the registry. However, management of the registry is an important part of the system administrator's job and includes viewing, editing, backing up, and restoring the registry. You use Registry Editor to view and change the registry configuration.

After this lesson, you will be able to

- Edit the registry with Registry Editor.

Estimated lesson time: 40 minutes

Regedt32.exe

Setup installs Registry Editor (Regedt32.exe) in the *systemroot*\System32 directory during installation. However, since most users do not need to use Registry Editor, it does not appear on the Start menu. You start Registry Editor by using Run on the Start menu.

Note   Setup also installs a second Registry Editor (Regedit.exe). Regedit.exe does not have a security menu or a read-only mode and does not support REG_EXPAND_SZ or REG_MULTI_SZ, so it is not the recommended Registry Editor for Windows 2000.

Although Registry Editor allows you to perform manual edits on the registry, it is intended for troubleshooting and problem resolution. You should make most configuration changes through either Control Panel or Administrative Tools. However, there are some configuration settings that can only be made directly through the registry.

Caution   Using Registry Editor incorrectly can cause serious, system-wide problems that could require reinstallation of Windows 2000. When using Registry Editor to view data, save a backup copy of the registry file before viewing, and select Read Only Mode on the Options menu to prevent accidental updating or deleting of configuration data.

Registry Editor saves data automatically as you make entries or corrections. New registry data takes effect immediately.

You can find some of the most useful Registry Editor commands on the Registry menu and the View menu in Registry Editor. Table 6.4 describes the commands on these menus.

Table 6.4   Registry Editor Commands

Command	Description
Find Key	Searches the registry for a specific key. Key names appear in the left pane of Registry Editor. The search begins at the currently selected key and parses all descendant keys for the specified key name. The search is local to the subtree in which the search begins. For example, a search for a key in the HKEY_LOCAL_MACHINE subtree does not include keys under HKEY_CURRENT_USER.
Save Key	Saves part of the registry in binary format. It saves the currently selected key and all subkeys. You can then use this file with the Restore command to reload a set of values after testing a change.
Restore	Loads the data in the selected file under the currently selected key. If the selected key was saved in the data file, the Registry Editor will overwrite the key with the values in the file.
Save Subtree As	Saves the selected key and all subkeys in a text file. You can then use a text editor to search for a specific value or key that was added or modified. Note that you cannot convert this text file back to registry data.
Select Computer	Opens the registry on a remote computer. Windows 2000 Server restricts remote access to the Administrators group, but Windows 2000 Workstation allows remote access by any valid user account. To modify remote access permissions for either operating system, create this registry key: HKEY_LOCAL_MACHINE\SYSTEM\CurrentControlSet\Control\SecurePipeServers\winreg, of type REG_DWORD, with a value of 1. Permissions on this key define who can have remote access to the registry.

Practice: Using Registry Editor

In this practice you use Registry Editor to view the information in the registry. You determine information such as the BIOS, the processor on your computer, and the version of the operating system. You use Registry Editor's Find Key command to search the registry for a specific word with key names. You modify the registry by adding a value to it, and you save a subtree as a file so that you can use an editor, like Notepad, to search the file.

Exercise 1: Exploring the Registry

In this exercise, you use Registry Editor to view information in the registry.

▶ **To view information in the registry**

1. Ensure that you are logged on as Administrator.
2. Start Registry Editor (Regedt32.exe).
3. On the Options menu, click Read Only Mode to place a check mark to the left of the option.

4. On the View menu, ensure that Tree And Data is checked.

5. Maximize the Registry Editor window, and then maximize the window titled HKEY_LOCAL_MACHINE On Local Machine.

6. Double-click the HARDWARE\DESCRIPTION\System subkey to expand it, and then answer the following questions:

   What is the basic input/output system (BIOS) version of your computer and its date?

   What is the computer type of your local machine according to the Identifier entry?

7. Expand the SOFTWARE\Microsoft\Windows NT\CurrentVersion subkey, and then fill in the following information.

Software configuration	Value and string
Current build number	
Current version	
Registered organization	
Registered owner	

Exercise 2: Using the Find Key

In this exercise, you use the Registry Editor's Find Key command to search the registry to find a specific word in the key names in the registry.

▶ **To use the find key**

1. Click the HKEY_LOCAL_MACHINE subkey to ensure that the entire subtree is searched.

2. On the View menu, click Find Key.

   The Find dialog box appears.

3. In the Find What box, type **serial**

   Click Find Next and wait for the first matching entry to appear.

4. Continue clicking Find Next until a Warning dialog box appears, indicating that Registry Editor cannot find the desired key.

   Notice that this key appears in multiple locations in the registry.

5. Click OK to close the Warning dialog box.

   Note You might experience a long pause after you click OK before you are able to continue with the next step. This is a limitation of some early-release beta versions of Windows 2000 Server.

6. Click Cancel to close the Find dialog box.

Exercise 3: Modifying the Registry

In this exercise, you add a value to the registry.

► **To add a value to the registry**

1. On the Options menu, click Read Only Mode.

   This will turn off Read Only Mode, which was enabled in Exercise 1.

2. On the Window menu, click HKEY_CURRENT_USER On Local Machine.

   The HKEY_CURRENT_USER window appears in the Registry Editor.

3. In the left pane of the Registry Editor window, click Environment.

   The values in the Environment key appear in the right pane of the Registry Editor window.

4. On the Edit menu, click Add Value.

Note If Add Value is unavailable, make sure Read Only Mode is not selected on the Options menu. If you are having problems deselecting Read Only Mode, exit Registry Editor and then restart it.

   The Add Value dialog box appears.

5. In the Value Name box, type **test**

6. In the Data Type list, click REG_EXPAND_SZ, and then click OK.

   The String Editor dialog box appears.

7. In the String box, type **%windir%\system32** and then click OK.

   test : REG_EXPAND_SZ : %windir%\system32 appears in the right pane of the Registry Editor window.

8. Minimize the Registry Editor window.

► **To verify the new registry value**

1. Right-click My Computer, and then click Properties.

   The System Properties dialog box appears.

2. Click the Advanced tab, and then click Environment Variables.

   The Environment Variables dialog box appears.

   Does the test variable appear in the User Variables For Administrator list?

   What value has been assigned to the test variable? Why?

3. Close the Environment Variables dialog box, and then close the System Properties dialog box.

Exercise 4: Saving a Subtree as a File

In this exercise you save a subtree as a file. Saving a subtree as a file allows you to use Notepad or some other editor to search the file. The file can also be stored or printed as a record of the contents of the subtree and may come in handy for troubleshooting a problem should something accidentally get changed in the registry.

▶   **To save a subtree as a file**

1. Restore the Registry Editor window.
2. On the Window menu, click HKEY_LOCAL_MACHINE On Local Machine.
3. Click HKEY_LOCAL_MACHINE\SOFTWARE.
4. On the Registry menu, click Save Subtree As.

   The Save As dialog box appears.
5. In the Save In box, click Desktop.
6. In the File Name box, type **Software.txt** and then click Save.

Note   You might experience a long delay while Registry Editor saves the subtree. This is a limitation of some early-release beta versions of Windows 2000 Server.

---

7. Exit Registry Editor.
8. On your desktop, double-click Software.

   Notepad opens the Software file.
9. On the Edit menu, click Find.

   The Find dialog box appears.
10. In the Find What box, type **CurrentBuildNumber** and then click Find Next.
11. Click Cancel to close the Find dialog box.
12. Scroll down (if necessary) to see the data for CurrentBuildNumber.

    What is this value's data?

13. Close Notepad.

Lesson Summary

In this lesson you learned that you use Registry Editor (Regedt32.exe) to view and change the registry configuration. However, you also learned that Registry Editor is primarily intended for troubleshooting. For most configuration changes, you should use either Control Panel or Administrative Tools, not Registry Editor. You also learned that there are some configuration settings that can only be made directly through the registry, and for these you use Registry Editor.

You learned that you find some of the most useful Registry Editor commands on the Registry menu and the View menu. These commands include Find Key, which allows you to search the registry for a specific key. The Save Key command allows you to save part of the registry in binary format. The Save Subtree As command allows you to save the selected key and all subkeys in a text file, and the Select Computer command allows you to open the registry on a remote computer.

Review

Here are some questions to help you determine if you have learned enough to move on to the next chapter. If you have difficulty answering these questions, please go back and review the material in this chapter before beginning the next chapter. The answers for these questions are located in Appendix A, "Questions and Answers."

1. What is the registry and what does it do?

2. What is a hive?

3. What is the recommended editor for viewing and modifying the registry?

4. What option should you turn on when you are viewing the contents of the registry? Why?

CHAPTER 7

Managing Disks

About This Chapter

This chapter presents an overview of Microsoft Windows 2000 disk management. You can create a custom MMC and add the Disk Management snap-in to it. The Disk Management snap-in is also included in the preconfigured Computer Management MMC on the Administrative Tools menu. The Disk Management snap-in provides shortcut menus to show you which tasks you can perform on the selected object, and it includes wizards to guide you through creating partitions and volumes and upgrading disks.

Before You Begin

To complete this chapter, you must have

- A computer that meets the minimum hardware requirements listed in "Hardware Requirements," on page xxxiii.
- Installed the Windows 2000 Server software on the computer.
- Configured the computer as a stand-alone server in a workgroup.

Lesson 1: Introduction to Disk Management

If you have free space on your hard disk, you need to partition and format it so that you can store data on that part of the disk. In addition, if you have more than one hard disk, each disk will also have to be partitioned and formatted so that you can store data on it.

After this lesson, you will be able to

- Describe disk management concepts.

Estimated lesson time: 25 minutes

Tasks in Setting Up a Hard Disk

Whether you are setting up the remaining free space on a hard disk on which you installed Windows 2000 or setting up a new hard disk, you need to be aware of the tasks that are involved. Before you can store data on a new hard disk, you must perform the following tasks to prepare the disk:

1. Initialize the disk with a storage type. Initialization defines the fundamental structure of a hard disk. Windows 2000 supports the following two types of disk storage: basic storage and dynamic storage.

2. Create partitions on a basic disk or create volumes on a dynamic disk.

3. Format the disk. After you create a partition or volume, you must format it with a specific file system—Windows NT file system (NTFS), file allocation table (FAT), or FAT32. The file system that you choose affects disk operations. This includes how you control user access to data, how data is stored, hard disk capacity, and which operating systems can gain access to the data on the hard disk.

Before you can decide how to perform the tasks in setting up a hard disk, you must understand the storage types, partition types, and volume types available in Windows 2000.

Storage Types

Windows 2000 supports the following two types of disk storage: basic storage and dynamic storage. A physical disk must be either basic or dynamic; you cannot use both storage types on one disk. You can, however, use both types of disk storage in a multidisk system.

Basic Storage

The traditional industry standard is *basic storage*. It dictates the division of a hard disk into partitions (see Figure 7.1). A *partition* is a portion of the disk that functions as a physically separate unit of storage. Windows 2000 recognizes primary and extended partitions. A disk that is initialized for basic storage is called a *basic disk*. A basic disk can contain primary partitions, extended partitions, and logical drives. New disks added to a computer running Windows 2000 are basic disks.

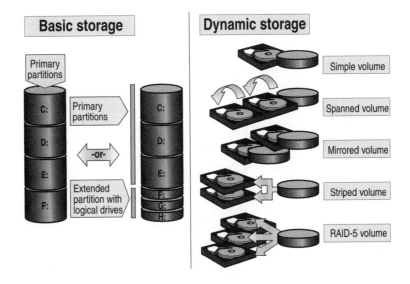

Figure 7.1   Basic and dynamic storage types

Since basic storage is the traditional industry standard, all versions of Microsoft Windows, MS-DOS, Windows NT, and Windows 2000 support basic storage. For Windows 2000, basic storage is the default, so all disks are basic disks until you convert them to dynamic storage.

Dynamic Storage

Only Windows 2000 supports *dynamic storage,* which is a standard that creates a single partition that includes the entire disk. A disk that you initialize for dynamic storage is a *dynamic disk.*

You divide dynamic disks into volumes, which can consist of a portion, or portions, of one or more physical disks. A dynamic disk can contain simple volumes, spanned volumes, mirrored volumes, striped volumes, and redundant array of inexpensive disks (RAID)-5 volumes. You create a dynamic disk by upgrading a basic disk.

Dynamic storage does not have the restrictions of basic storage; for example, you can size and resize a dynamic disk without restarting Windows 2000.

Note Removable storage devices contain primary partitions only. You cannot create extended partitions, logical drives, or dynamic volumes on removable storage devices. You cannot mark a primary partition on a removable storage device as active.

Partition Types (Basic Disks)

You can divide a basic disk into primary and extended partitions. Partitions function as physically separate storage units. This allows you to separate different types of information, such as user data on one partition and applications on another. A basic disk can contain up to four primary partitions, or up to three primary partitions and one extended partition, for a maximum of four partitions, and only one partition can be an extended partition, as shown in Figure 7.2.

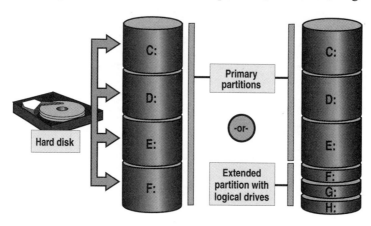

Figure 7.2   Partition types

Primary Partitions

Windows 2000 can use the parts of a disk called *primary partitions* to start the computer. Only a primary partition can be marked as the active partition. The active partition is where the hardware looks for the boot files to start the operating system. Only one partition on a single hard disk can be active at a time. Multiple primary partitions allow you to isolate different operating systems or types of data. To dual boot Windows 2000 with Microsoft Windows 95 or MS-DOS, the active partition must be formatted as FAT because Windows 95 cannot read a partition formatted as FAT32 or NTFS. To dual boot with Microsoft Windows 95 OSR2 (a later release of Windows 95 that contained enhancements to Windows 95, such as the ability to read partitions formatted with FAT32) or Windows 98, the active partition must be formatted as FAT or FAT32.

Extended Partitions

An *extended partition* is created from free space. There can be only one extended partition on a hard disk, so it is important to include all remaining free space in the extended partition. Unlike primary partitions, you do not format extended partitions or assign drive letters to them. You divide extended partitions into segments. Each segment is a logical drive. You assign a drive letter to each logical drive and format it with a file system.

Note   The Windows 2000 *system partition* is the active partition that contains the hardware-specific files required to load the operating system. The Windows 2000 *boot partition* is the primary partition or logical drive where the operating system files are installed. The boot partition and the system partition can be the same partition. However, the system partition must be on the active partition, typically drive C, while the boot partition could be on another primary partition or on an extended partition.

Volume Types (Dynamic Disks)

You can convert basic disks to dynamic storage and then create Windows 2000 volumes. Consider which volume type best suits your needs for efficient use of disk space, performance, and fault tolerance. *Fault tolerance* is the ability of a computer or operating system to respond to a catastrophic event without loss of data. In Windows 2000, mirrored volumes and RAID-5 volumes are fault tolerant.

Simple Volume

A s*imple volume* contains disk space from a single disk and is not fault tolerant. Simple volumes can be mirrored to provide fault tolerance.

Spanned Volume

A *spanned volume* includes disk space from multiple disks (up to 32). Windows 2000 writes data to a spanned volume on the first disk, completely filling the space, and continues in this manner through each disk that you include in the spanned volume. A spanned volume is not fault tolerant. If any disk in a spanned volume fails, the data in the entire volume is lost.

Mirrored Volume

A *mirrored volume* consists of two identical copies of a simple volume, each on a separate hard disk. Mirrored volumes provide fault tolerance in the event of hard disk failure.

Striped Volume

A s*triped volume* combines areas of free space from multiple hard disks, up to 32, into one logical volume. In a striped volume, Windows 2000 optimizes performance by adding data to all disks at the same rate. If a disk in a striped volume fails, the data in the entire volume is lost.

RAID-5 Volume

A *RAID-5 volume* is a fault-tolerant striped volume. Windows 2000 adds a parity-information stripe to each disk partition in the volume. Windows 2000 uses the parity-information stripe to reconstruct data when a physical disk fails. A minimum of three hard disks is required in a RAID-5 volume.

Creating multiple partitions or volumes on a single hard disk allows you to efficiently organize data for tasks such as backing up. For example, partition one-third of a hard disk for the operating system, one-third for applications, and one-third for data. Then, when you back up your data, you can back up the entire partition instead of just a specific folder.

File Systems

Windows 2000 supports the NTFS, FAT, and FAT32 file systems. Use NTFS when you require a partition to have file- and folder-level security, disk compression, disk quotas, or encryption. Only Windows 2000 and Windows NT can access data on a local hard disk that is formatted NTFS. If you plan to promote a server to a domain controller, format the installation partition with NTFS.

FAT and FAT32 allow access by, and compatibility with, other operating systems. To dual boot Windows 2000 and another operating system, format the system partition with either FAT or FAT32. FAT and FAT32 do not offer many of the features that are supported by NTFS, for example file-level security. Therefore, in most situations, you should format the hard disk with NTFS. The only reason to use FAT or FAT32 is for dual booting.

Note   For a review of file systems, see Chapter 2, "Installing Windows 2000."

Disk Management Snap-In

Use the Disk Management snap-in to configure and manage your network storage space.

The Disk Management snap-in can display your storage system in either a graphical view or a list view. You can modify the display to suit your preferences by using the commands on the View menu.

Lesson Summary

Before you can store data on a new hard disk, you must use the Disk Management snap-in to initialize the disk with a storage type. Windows 2000 supports basic storage and dynamic storage. A basic disk can contain primary partitions, extended partitions, and logical drives. All versions of Microsoft

Windows, MS-DOS, and Windows 2000 support basic storage. For Windows 2000, basic storage is the default, so all disks are basic disks until you convert them to dynamic storage.

Dynamic storage creates a single partition that includes the entire disk. You divide dynamic disks into volumes, which can consist of a portion, or portions, of one or more physical disks. A dynamic disk can contain simple volumes, spanned volumes, mirrored volumes, striped volumes, and RAID-5 volumes. Dynamic storage does not have the restrictions of basic storage; for example, you can size and resize a dynamic disk without restarting Windows 2000.

After you create partitions on a basic disk or create volumes on a dynamic disk, you must format the partition or volume with a specific file system. Windows 2000 supports NTFS, FAT, or FAT32. The file system that you choose affects disk operations. This includes how you control user access to data, how data is stored, how much hard disk capacity you have, and which operating systems can gain access to the data on the hard disk. Use the Disk Management snap-in to configure and manage your network storage space.

Lesson 2: Common Disk Management Tasks

The Disk Management snap-in provides a central location for disk information and management tasks, such as creating and deleting partitions and volumes. With the proper permissions, you can manage disks locally and on remote computers.

In addition to monitoring disk information, some of the other disk management tasks that you might need to perform include adding and removing hard disks and changing the disk storage type.

This lesson introduces the following disk management tasks:

- Working with simple volumes
- Working with spanned volumes
- Working with striped volumes
- Adding disks
- Changing storage type
- Viewing and updating information
- Managing disks on a remote computer

After this lesson, you will be able to

- Identify common disk management tasks.
- Create and configure a dynamic disk.

Estimated lesson time: 50 minutes

Working with Simple Volumes

A simple volume contains disk space from a single disk. You can extend a simple volume to include unallocated space on the same disk. A simple volume is not fault tolerant; however, you can mirror a simple volume.

You can create a simple volume and format it with NTFS, FAT, or FAT32 (see Figure 7.3). You can extend a simple volume only if it is formatted with NTFS.

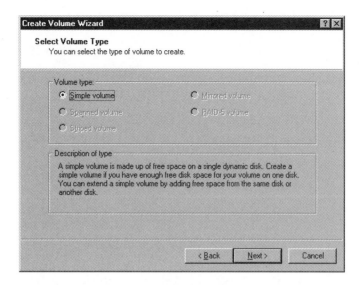

Figure 7.3   Creating a simple volume

▶   **To create a simple volume**

1. Select Disk Management in the Storage section of the Computer Management snap-in.

2. On the dynamic disk where you want to create the volume, right-click the unallocated space, and then click Create Volume. This launches the Create Volume wizard.

3. In the Create Volume wizard, click Next.

4. Click Simple Volume, and then follow the instructions on your screen.

To extend an NTFS simple volume, right-click the simple volume that you want to extend, click Extend Volume, and then follow the instructions on your screen. When you extend a simple volume to another disk, it becomes a spanned volume.

Working with Spanned Volumes

A spanned volume consists of disk space from multiple disks; spanned volumes enable you to use the total available free space on multiple disks more effectively. You can create spanned volumes only on dynamic disks, and you need at least two dynamic disks to create a spanned volume. Spanned volumes cannot be part of a mirror volume or striped volume and are not fault tolerant. Figure 7.4 introduces some of the important concepts for combining free space to create spanned volumes, to extend spanned volumes, and to delete spanned volumes.

- ▪ **Combining free space**
  - Spanned volumes combine space from 2 – 32 disks
  - Data is written to one disk until full
- ▪ **Extending and deleting**
  - Only NTFS-spanned volumes can be extended
  - Deleting any part of a spanned volume deletes the entire volume

Figure 7.4   Creating, extending, and deleting spanned volumes

Combining Free Space to Create a Spanned Volume

You create spanned volumes by combining various sized areas of free space from 2 to 32 disks into one large logical volume. The areas of free space that comprise a spanned volume can be different sizes. Windows 2000 organizes spanned volumes so that data is stored in the space on one disk until it is full, and then, starting at the beginning of the next disk, data is stored in the space on the second disk. Windows 2000 continues this process in the same way on each subsequent disk up to a maximum of 32 disks.

By deleting smaller volumes and combining them into one spanned volume, you can free drive letters for other uses and create a large volume for file system use.

Extending and Deleting

You can extend existing spanned volumes formatted with NTFS by adding free space. Disk Management formats the new area without affecting any existing files on the original volume. You cannot extend volumes formatted with FAT or FAT32.

You can extend spanned volumes on dynamic disks onto a maximum of 32 dynamic disks. After a volume is extended onto multiple disks (spanned), it cannot be part of a mirror volume or a striped volume. After a spanned volume is extended, no portion of it can be deleted without deleting the entire spanned volume. You cannot extend a system volume or a boot volume.

Working with Striped Volumes

Striped volumes offer the best performance of all the Windows 2000 Server disk management strategies. In a striped volume, data is written evenly across all physical disks in 64-kilobyte (KB) units, as shown in Figure 7.5. Because all the hard disks that belong to the striped volume perform the same functions as a single hard disk, Windows 2000 can issue and process concurrent input/output (I/O) commands on all hard disks simultaneously. In this way, striped volumes can increase the speed of system I/O.

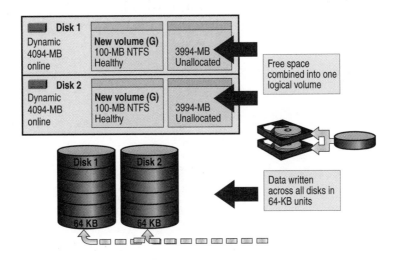

Figure 7.5   Benefits of working with striped volumes

You create striped volumes by combining areas of free space from multiple disks (from 2 to 32) into one logical volume. With a striped volume, Windows 2000 writes data to multiple disks, similar to spanned volumes. However, on a striped volume, Windows 2000 writes files across all disks so that data is added to all disks at the same rate. Like spanned volumes, striped volumes do not provide fault tolerance. If a disk in a striped volume fails, the data in the entire volume is lost.

You need at least two dynamic disks to create a striped volume. You can create a striped volume onto a maximum of 32 disks. You cannot extend or mirror striped volumes.

▶ **To create a striped volume**

1. In Disk Management, on the dynamic disk where you want to create the striped volume, right-click the unallocated space, and then click Create Volume. This launches the Create Volume wizard.

2. In the Create Volume wizard, click Next, click Striped Volume, and then follow the instructions on your screen.

Adding Disks

When you install new disks in a computer running Windows 2000, they are added as basic storage.

Adding New Disks

To add a new disk, install or attach the new physical disk (or disks), and then click Rescan Disks on the Action menu of the Disk Management snap-in, as shown in Figure 7.6. You must use Rescan Disks every time that you remove or add disks to a computer.

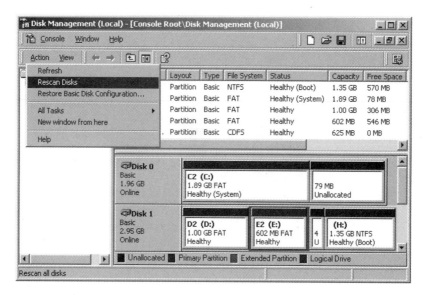

Figure 7.6   Adding disks using the Disk Management snap-in

It should not be necessary to restart the computer when you add a new disk to your computer. However, you might need to restart the computer if Disk Management does not detect the new disk after you run Rescan Disks.

Adding Disks That You Removed from Another Computer

If you want to uninstall or remove a disk from one computer and then install the disk in a different computer the process is different.

▶   **To add a disk that has been removed from another computer**

1. Remove the disk from the original computer and install the disk in the new computer.

2. Open Disk Management.

   Disk Management displays the new disk labeled as Foreign.

3. Right-click the new disk, and then click Import Foreign Disk. A wizard provides on-screen instructions.

Adding Multiple Disks That You Removed from Another Computer

If you want to uninstall or remove multiple disks from one computer and then install the disks in a different computer, the process is much the same as doing so for a single disk.

▶ **To add multiple inherited disks**

1. Remove the disks from the original computer and install them in the new computer.

2. Open Disk Management.

3. Right-click any of the new disks, and then click Add Disk. The disks appear as a group.

4. To specify the disks from the group that you want to add, click Select Disk. However, if you do not have any dynamic disks installed, all of the disks are added regardless of the disks that you select.

When you move a dynamic disk to your computer from another computer running Windows 2000, you can see and use any existing volumes on that disk. However, if a volume on a foreign disk extends to multiple disks, and you do not move all the disks for that volume, Disk Management will not show the portion of the volume that resides on the foreign disk.

Changing Storage Type

You can upgrade a disk from basic storage to dynamic storage at any time, with no loss of data. When you upgrade a basic disk to a dynamic disk, any existing partitions on the basic disk become simple volumes. Any existing mirrored, striped, or spanned volume sets created with Windows NT 4.0 become dynamic mirrored, striped, or spanned volumes, respectively. A Windows NT 4.0 stripe set with parity converts to a RAID-5 volume.

Any disks to be upgraded must contain at least 1 MB of unallocated space for the upgrade to succeed. Before you upgrade disks, close any programs that are running on those disks.

Table 7.1 shows the results of converting a disk from basic storage to dynamic storage.

Table 7.1 Basic Disk and Dynamic Disk Organization

Basic disk organization	Dynamic disk organization
System partition	Simple volume
Boot partition	Simple volume
Primary partition	Simple volume

(continued)

Basic disk organization	Dynamic disk organization
Extended partition	Simple volume for each logical drive and any remaining unallocated space
Logical drive	Simple volume
Volume set	Spanned volume
Stripe set	Striped volume
Mirror set	Mirrored volume
Stripe set with parity	RAID-5 volume

Note   You should always back up the data on a disk before converting the storage type.

Upgrading Basic Disks to Dynamic Disks

To upgrade a basic disk to a dynamic disk, right-click the basic disk that you want to upgrade, and then click Upgrade To Dynamic Disk. A wizard provides on-screen instructions. The upgrade process requires that you restart your computer.

After you upgrade a basic disk to a dynamic disk, you can create volumes with improved capabilities on the disk. After you upgrade a disk to dynamic storage, it cannot contain partitions or logical drives. Only Windows 2000 can access dynamic disks.

Reverting to a Basic Disk from a Dynamic Disk

You must remove all volumes from the dynamic disk before you can change it back to a basic disk. To change a dynamic disk back to a basic disk, right-click the dynamic disk that you want to change back to a basic disk, and then click Revert To Basic Disk.

Caution   Converting a dynamic disk to a basic disk causes all data to be lost.

Viewing and Updating Information

The Properties dialog box for a selected disk or volume provides a concise view of all of the pertinent properties.

Disk Properties

To view disk properties in Disk Management, right-click the name of a disk in the Graphical View window (don't click one of its volumes), and then click Properties. Table 7.2 describes the information displayed in the Properties dialog box for a disk.

Table 7.2   Properties Dialog Box for a Disk

Category	Description
Disk	The number for the disk in the system, for example, Disk 0, Disk 1, Disk 2, and so on
Type	Type of storage (basic, dynamic, or removable)
Status	Online, offline, foreign, or unknown
Capacity	The total capacity for the disk
Unallocated Space	The amount of available free space
Device Type	Integrated device electronics (IDE), small computer standard interface (SCSI), or enhanced IDE (EIDE), as well as the IDE channel (primary or secondary) on which the disk resides
Hardware Vendor	The hardware vendor for the disk and the disk type
Adapter Name	The type of controller to which the disk is attached
Volumes Contained On This Disk	The volumes that exist on the disk and their total capacity

Volume Properties

To view volume properties in Disk Management, right-click a volume in the Graphical View window or in the Volume List window, and then click Properties. Table 7.3 describes the tabs in the Properties dialog box for a volume.

Table 7.3   Properties Dialog Box for a Volume

Tab	Description
General	Lists the volume label, type, file system, and used and free space. Click Disk Cleanup to delete unnecessary files. NTFS volumes list two options, Compress Drive To Save Disk Space and Index Drive For Fast File Searching.
Tools	Provides a single location from which you can perform volume error-checking, backup, and defragmentation tasks.
Web Sharing	Used to share specified folders through Internet Information Services (IIS). This tab only appears if IIS is installed on Windows 2000 Server, or if Personal Web Server is installed on Windows 2000 Professional.
Sharing	Used to set network-shared volume parameters and permissions.
Hardware	Used to check properties of and troubleshoot the physical disks installed on the system.
Security	Used to set NTFS access permissions. This tab is only available for NTFS version 4.0 and 5.0 volumes (Windows 2000 uses NTFS version 5.0).
Quota	Used to set user quotas for NTFS 5.0 volumes.

Refresh and Rescan

When you are working with Disk Management, you might need to update the information in the display. The two commands for updating the display are Refresh and Rescan.

Refresh updates drive letter, file system, volume, and removable media information, and determines whether unreadable volumes are now readable. To update drive letter, file system, and volume information, click Action and then click Refresh.

Rescan Disks updates hardware information. When Disk Management rescans disks, it scans all attached disks for disk configuration changes. It also updates information on removable media, CD-ROM drives, basic volumes, file systems, and drive letters. Rescanning disks can take several minutes, depending on the number of hardware devices installed. To update disk information, click Action, and then click Rescan Disks.

Managing Disks on a Remote Computer

As a member of the Administrators group or the Server Operators group, you can manage disks on a computer running Windows 2000 that is a member of the domain or a trusted domain from any other computer running Windows 2000 in the network.

To manage one computer from another computer—remote management—create a Microsoft Management Console (MMC) that is focused on the remote computer.

▶   **To manage disks on a remote computer**

1. Click Start, click Run, type **mmc** and then click OK.

2. On the Console menu, click Add/Remove Snap-In.

3. Click Add.

4. Click Disk Management, and then click OK.

5. In the Choose Computer dialog box shown in Figure 7.7, click Another Computer, and then type the name of the computer.

6. Click Finish.

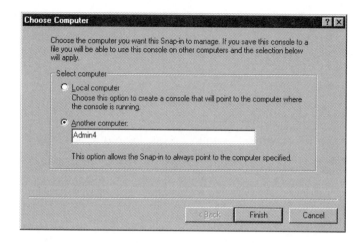

Figure 7.7   Creating an MMC to manage disks on a remote computer

Practice: Working with Dynamic Storage

After completing this practice, you will be able to

- Upgrade a basic disk to a dynamic disk.
- Create a new volume.
- Mount a simple volume.

Before working on this practice, you should have completed this chapter so that you are familiar with disk management and the Disk Management snap-in.

Exercise 1: Upgrading a Disk

In this exercise, you use Disk Management to upgrade a basic disk to a dynamic disk.

▶ **To upgrade a basic disk**

1. Ensure that you are logged on as Administrator.
2. Right-click My Computer, and then click Manage.

   The Computer Management (Local) window appears.
3. In the console tree, double-click Storage, and then click Disk Management.

   Note   If the Upgrade Disk wizard starts automatically, click Cancel. This can occur if your computer contains a disk configured for basic storage that does not contain the Windows 2000 boot partition.

4. Using the information supplied by Disk Management, complete the following questions.

What is the storage type of Disk 0?

Is drive C a primary partition or a logical drive in an extended partition?

5. In the lower-right pane of the Computer Management (Local) window, right-click Disk 0, and then click Upgrade To Dynamic Disk.

   The Upgrade To Dynamic Disk dialog box appears.

6. Ensure that Disk 0 is the only disk selected for upgrade, and then click OK.

   The Confirm Upgrade To Dynamic Disk dialog box appears.

7. Click Upgrade.

   The Disk Management dialog box appears, warning that this change will require a reboot, and that you will not be able to boot previous versions of Windows from any volumes on this disk.

   > **Caution**   If you are dual-booting with another operating system, for example Windows 95 or Windows 98 loaded on drive C, these operating systems will no longer run. Only Windows 2000 can access a dynamic drive.

8. Click Yes.

   After completing the upgrade, the Found New Hardware Wizard will appear, notifying you that the volume will not work until you restart the machine.

9. Select the Restart The Computer When I Click Finish check box, and then click Finish.

   Your computer restarts.

▶   **To confirm the upgrade**

1. Log on as Administrator.

2. Wait for the Found New Hardware wizard to appear, and then click Finish.

   > **Note**   The Found New Hardware wizard will appear twice. Click Finish to close it the second time it appears.

3. Right-click My Computer, and then click Manage.

   The Computer Management (Local) window appears.

4. In the console tree, double-click Storage, and then click Disk Management.

   > **Note**   If your computer has more than one disk, the Upgrade Disk wizard might appear. If it does, click Cancel to close it.

5. Using the information provided by Disk Management, complete the following questions.

What is the storage type of Disk 0?

Is drive C a primary partition or a logical drive in an extended partition?

What has changed?

6. Minimize the Computer Management (Local) window.

Exercise 2: Extending a Volume

In this exercise, you use Disk Management to create a new simple volume. You then mount the new volume onto an existing folder on another volume. If drive C is formatted NTFS, you create a folder named Mount under the root directory of drive C. If drive C is not formatted NTFS, you create the folder named Mount on the volume that is formatted NTFS and contains the Windows 2000 files.

▶   **To create a folder for mounting the new volume**

1. Right-click My Computer.
2. Click Explore.
3. Click Local Disk C if it is formatted NTFS; otherwise click the disk that is formatted NTFS and contains your Windows 2000 files.
4. On the File menu, click New, and then click Folder.
5. Type **Mount** and then press Enter.

▶   **To create a new simple volume**

1. Restore the Computer Management (Local) window.
2. Right-click the remaining unallocated space on Disk 0 in the lower-right pane, and then click Create Volume.

The Create Volume wizard appears.

3. Click Next.

The Select Volume Type page appears.

Notice that Simple Volume is the only available option.

4. Click Next.

The Select Disks page appears.

The value in the For All Selected Disks box represents the remaining free space on Drive 0.

5. Click Next.

The Assign Drive Letter or Path page appears.

6. Click Mount This Volume At An Empty Folder Which Supports Drive Paths, and then type *x:***mount** where *x* is the letter of the drive containing the Mount folder.

7. Click Next.

The Format Volume page appears.

8. In the Volume Label box, type **Mounted Volume**

9. Click Perform A Quick Format, and then click Next.

10. Click Finish.

The new volume is created, formatted, and mounted on the C:\Mount folder; or if C is not formatted NTFS, it is mounted where you created the Mount folder.

11. Leave the Computer Management (Local) window open.

▶   **To examine the new volume**

1. Open Microsoft Windows Explorer.

2. Click Local Disk (C:) (if necessary) to display the Local Disk (C:) window.

Important   If you mounted your volume on a drive other than drive C, click that drive instead.

---

3. Right-click Mount, and then click Properties.

The Mount Properties dialog box appears.

What type of folder is C:\Mount or *x:*\Mount (where *x* is the drive on which you mounted the volume)?

4. Click OK.

5. Create a new text document in the C:\Mount folder.

6. Close Windows Explorer.

7. Open a command prompt.

8. Change the working directory to the root directory of drive C (if necessary) or to the root directory of the drive where you mounted your volume, type **dir** and then press Enter.

How much free space does the Dir command report?

Why is there a difference between the free space reported for drive C and the free space reported for C:\Mount? (If you mounted your volume on a drive other than drive C, replace C with the appropriate drive letter.)

9. Close the command prompt.

Lesson Summary

The Disk Management snap-in provides a central location for disk information and management tasks, such as creating and deleting partitions and volumes. With the proper permissions, you can manage disks locally and on remote computers. In addition to monitoring disk information, some of the other disk management tasks that you might need to perform include adding and removing hard disks and changing the disk storage type.

This lesson introduced you to the following disk management tasks: working with simple volumes, spanned volumes, and striped volumes. It also introduced adding disks, changing storage type, viewing and updating information, and managing disks on a remote computer.

Review

Here are some questions to help you determine if you have learned enough to move on to the next chapter. If you have difficulty answering these questions, please go back and review the material in this chapter before beginning the next chapter. The answers for these questions are located in Appendix A, "Questions and Answers."

1. You install a new 10-GB disk drive that you want to divide into five equal 2-GB sections. What are your options?

2. You are trying to create a striped volume on your Windows NT Server in order to improve performance. You confirm that you have enough unallocated disk space on two disks in your computer, but when you right-click an area of unallocated space on a disk, your only option is to create a partition. What is the problem and how would you resolve it?

3. You add a new disk to your computer and attempt to extend an existing volume to include the unallocated space on the new disk, but the option to extend the volume is not available. What is the problem and how would you resolve it?

4. You dual boot your computer with Windows 98 and Windows 2000. You upgrade a second drive, which you are using to archive files, from basic storage to dynamic storage. The next time you try to access your archived files from Windows 98, you are unable to read the files. Why?

CHAPTER 8

Installing and Configuring Network Protocols

About This Chapter

A *protocol* is a set of rules and conventions for sending information over a network. Microsoft Windows 2000 relies on the Transmission Control Protocol/Internet Protocol (TCP/IP) for logon, file and print services, replication of information between one domain controller and another, and other common functions.

This chapter presents the skills and knowledge necessary to configure TCP/IP and to install other network protocols, including NWLink, NetBIOS Extended User Interface (NetBEUI), and Data Link Control (DLC). The chapter also discusses the process for configuring network bindings, which are links that enable communication between network adapter cards, protocols, and services.

Before You Begin

To complete this chapter, you must have

- A computer that meets the minimum hardware requirements listed in "Hardware Requirements," on page xxxiii.
- Installed the Windows 2000 Server software on the computer.
- Configured the computer as a stand-alone server in a workgroup.

Lesson 1: TCP/IP

TCP/IP provides communication across networks of computers with various hardware architectures and operating systems. Microsoft's implementation of TCP/IP enables enterprise networking and connectivity on computers running Windows 2000.

After this lesson, you will be able to

- Describe the TCP/IP protocol suite and the TCP/IP utilities that ship with Windows 2000.
- Configure TCP/IP.

Estimated lesson time: 65 minutes

Understanding the TCP/IP Protocol Suite

TCP/IP is an industry-standard suite of protocols that enables enterprise networking and connectivity on Windows 2000–based computers. Adding TCP/IP to a Windows 2000 configuration offers the following advantages:

- A routable networking protocol supported by most operating systems. Most large networks rely on TCP/IP.
- A technology for connecting dissimilar systems. You can use many standard connectivity utilities to access and transfer data between dissimilar systems. Windows 2000 includes several of these standard utilities.
- A robust, scaleable, cross-platform client/server framework. TCP/IP supports the Microsoft Windows Sockets (WinSock) interface, which is ideal for developing client/server applications for WinSock-compliant stacks.
- A method of gaining access to Internet resources.

The TCP/IP suite of protocols provides a set of standards for how computers communicate and how networks are interconnected. The TCP/IP suite of protocols map to a four-layer conceptual model: network interface, Internet, transport, and application. These layers can be seen in Figure 8.1.

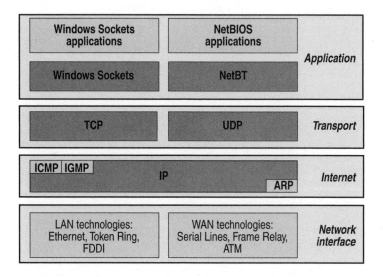

Figure 8.1   The TCP/IP suite of protocols within four layers

Network Interface Layer

At the base of the model is the network interface layer. This layer puts frames on the wire and pulls frames off the wire.

Internet Layer

Internet layer protocols encapsulate packets into Internet datagrams and run all the necessary routing algorithms. The four Internet layer protocols are Internet Protocol (IP), Address Resolution Protocol (ARP), Internet Control Message Protocol (ICMP), and Internet Group Management Protocol (IGMP). Table 8.1 describes these four Internet layer protocols.

Table 8.1   Protocols Included in the Internet Layer

Protocol	Description
IP	Provides connectionless packet delivery for all other protocols in the suite. Does not guarantee packet arrival or correct packet sequence.
ARP	Provides IP address mapping to the media access control (MAC) sublayer address to acquire the physical MAC control address of the destination. IP broadcasts a special ARP inquiry packet containing the IP address of the destination system. The system that owns the IP address replies by sending its physical address to the requester. The MAC sublayer communicates directly with the network adapter card and is responsible for delivering error-free data between two computers on a network.

(continued)

Protocol	Description
ICMP	Provides special communication between hosts, allowing them to share status and error information. Higher level protocols use this information to recover from transmission problems. Network administrators use this information to detect network trouble. The ping utility uses ICMP packets to determine whether a particular IP device on a network is functional.
IGMP	Provides multicasting, which is a limited form of broadcasting, to communicate and manage information between all member devices in a multicast group. IGMP informs neighboring multicast routers of the host group memberships present on a particular network. Windows 2000 supports multicast capabilities that allow developers to create multicast programs, such as Windows 2000 Server NetShow Services.

Transport Layer

Transport layer protocols provide communication sessions between computers. The desired method of data delivery determines the transport protocol. The two transport layer protocols are Transmission Control Protocol (TCP) and User Datagram Protocol (UDP). Table 8.2 describes the two protocols included in the transport layer.

Table 8.2   Protocols Included in the Transport Layer

Protocol	Description
TCP	Provides connection-oriented, reliable communications for applications that typically transfer large amounts of data at one time or that require an acknowledgment for data received. TCP guarantees the delivery of packets, ensures proper sequencing of the data, and provides a checksum feature that validates both the packet header and its data for accuracy.
UDP	Provides connectionless communications and does not guarantee that packets will be delivered. Applications that use UDP typically transfer small amounts of data at one time. Reliable delivery is the responsibility of the application.

Application Layer

At the top of the model is the application layer, in which applications gain access to the network. There are many standard TCP/IP utilities and services in the application layer, such as FTP, Telnet, Simple Network Management Protocol (SNMP), Domain Name System (DNS), and so on.

TCP/IP provides two interfaces for network applications to use the services of the TCP/IP protocol stack: WinSock and the NetBIOS over TCP/IP (NetBT) interface. Table 8.3 describes the two interfaces, which network applications use for TCP/IP services.

Table 8.3   Interfaces Through Which Applications Use TCP/IP Services

Interface	Description
WinSock	Serves as the standard interface between socket-based applications and TCP/IP protocols.
NetBT	Serves as the standard interface for NetBIOS services, including name, datagram, and session services. It also provides a standard interface between NetBIOS-based applications and TCP/IP protocols.

Configuring TCP/IP to Use a Static IP Address

By default, client computers running Windows 2000, Windows 95, or Windows 98 obtain TCP/IP configuration information automatically from the Dynamic Host Configuration Protocol (DHCP) Service. However, even in a DHCP-enabled environment, you should assign a static IP address to selected network computers. For example, the computer running the DHCP Service cannot be a DHCP client, so it must have a static IP address. If the DHCP Service is not available, you must also configure TCP/IP to use a static IP address. For each network adapter card that uses TCP/IP in a computer, you can configure an IP address, subnet mask, and default gateway, as shown in Figure 8.2.

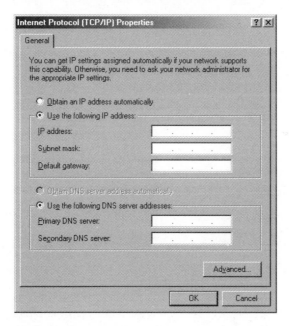

Figure 8.2   Configuring a static TCP/IP address

Table 8.4 describes the options used in configuring a static TCP/IP address.

Table 8.4   Options for Configuring a Static TCP/IP Address

Option	Description
IP address	A logical 32-bit address that identifies a TCP/IP host. Each network adapter card in a computer running TCP/IP requires a unique IP address, such as 192.168.0.108. Each address has two parts: a network ID, which identifies all hosts on the same physical network, and a host ID, which identifies a host on the network. In this example, the network ID is 192.168.0, and the host ID is 108.
Subnet mask	A network in a multiple-network environment that uses IP addresses derived from a single network ID. Subnets divide a large network into multiple physical networks connected with routers. A subnet mask blocks out part of the IP address, so that TCP/IP can distinguish the network ID from the host ID. When TCP/IP hosts try to communicate, the subnet mask determines whether the destination host is on a local or remote network. To communicate on a network, computers must have the same subnet mask.
Default gateway	The intermediate device on a local network that stores network IDs of other networks in the enterprise or Internet. To communicate with a host on another network, configure an IP address for the default gateway. TCP/IP sends packets for remote networks to the default gateway (if no other route is configured), which forwards the packets to other gateways until the packet is delivered to a gateway connected to the specified destination.

▶ **To configure TCP/IP to use a static IP address**

1. Right-click My Network Places, and then click Properties.

2. In the Network And Dial-Up Connections window, right-click Local Area Connection, and then click Properties.

3. In the Local Area Connection Properties dialog box, click Internet Protocol (TCP/IP), verify that the check box to its left is selected, and then click Properties.

4. In the Internet Protocol (TCP/IP) Properties dialog box, on the General tab, click Use The Following IP Address, type the TCP/IP configuration parameters, and then click OK.

5. Click OK to close the Local Area Connection Properties dialog box and then close the Network And Dial-Up Connections window.

Caution   IP communications can fail if duplicate IP addresses exist on a network. Therefore, you should always check with the network administrator to obtain a valid static IP address.

Configuring TCP/IP to Obtain an IP Address Automatically

If a server running the DHCP Service is available on the network, it can automatically assign TCP/IP configuration information to the DHCP client, as shown in Figure 8.3. Then you can configure any clients running Windows 2000, Windows 95, and Windows 98 to obtain TCP/IP configuration information automatically from the DHCP Service. Using DHCP to configure TCP/IP automatically on client computers can simplify administration and ensure correct configuration information.

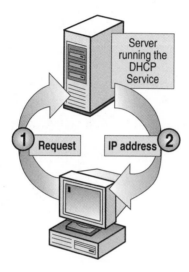

Figure 8.3   A server running the DHCP Service assigns TCP/IP addresses

Note   Windows 2000 also includes an Automatic Private IP Addressing feature that provides DHCP clients with limited network functionality if a DHCP server is unavailable during startup.

You can use the DHCP Service to provide clients with TCP/IP configuration information automatically. However, you must configure a computer as a DHCP client before it can interact with the DHCP Service.

▶ **To configure a DHCP client**

1. Right-click My Network Places, and then click Properties.
2. In the Network And Dial-Up Connections window, right-click Local Area Connection, and then click Properties.
3. In the Local Area Connection Properties dialog box, click Internet Protocol (TCP/IP), verify that the check box to its left is selected, and then click Properties.

4. In the Internet Protocol (TCP/IP) Properties dialog box, on the General tab, click Obtain An IP Address Automatically.

5. Click OK to close the Local Area Connection Properties dialog box and then close the Network And Dial-Up Connections window.

Note   For more information about the DHCP Service, see Chapter 9, "Configuring the DHCP Service."

Using Automatic Private IP Addressing

The Windows 2000 implementation of TCP/IP supports a new mechanism for automatic address assignment of IP addresses for simple LAN-based network configurations. This addressing mechanism is an extension of dynamic IP address assignment for local area network (LAN) adapters, enabling configuration of IP addresses without using static IP address assignment or installing the DHCP Service.

For the Automatic Private IP Addressing feature to function properly on a computer running Windows 2000, you must configure a network LAN adapter for TCP/IP and click Obtain An IP Address Automatically in the Internet Protocol (TCP/IP) Properties dialog box.

The process for the Automatic Private IP Addressing feature, as shown in Figure 8.4, is explained in the following steps:

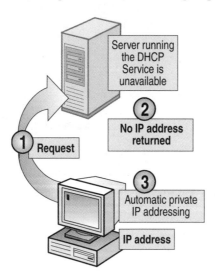

Figure 8.4   Automatic Private IP Addressing feature

1. Windows 2000 TCP/IP attempts to find a DHCP server on the attached network to obtain a dynamically assigned IP address.

2. In the absence of a DHCP server during startup, for example the server is down for maintenance or repairs, the client cannot obtain an IP address.

3. Automatic Private IP Addressing generates an IP address in the form of 169.254.x.y (where x.y is the client's unique identifier) and a subnet mask of 255.255.0.0.

Note The Internet Assigned Numbers Authority (IANA) has reserved 169.254.0.0–169.254.255.255 for Automatic Private IP Addressing. As a result, Automatic Private IP Addressing provides an address that is guaranteed not to conflict with routable addresses.

After the computer generates the address, it broadcasts to this address and then assigns the address to itself, if no other computer responds. The computer continues to use this address until it detects and receives configuration information from a DHCP server. This allows two computers to be plugged into a LAN hub to restart without any IP address configuration and to be able to use TCP/IP for local network access.

Note Windows 98 also supports Automatic Private IP Addressing.

Automatic Private IP Addressing can assign a TCP/IP address to DHCP clients automatically. However, Automatic Private IP Addressing does not generate all the information that typically is provided by DHCP, such as the address of a default gateway.

Consequently, computers enabled with Automatic Private IP Addressing can communicate only with computers on the same subnet that also have addresses of the form 169.254.x.y.

Disabling Automatic Private IP Addressing

By default, the Automatic Private IP Addressing feature is enabled. However, you can disable this feature by adding the IPAutoconfigurationEnabled *value* to the HKEY_LOCAL_MACHINE\SYSTEM\CurrentControlSet\Services\Tcpip\ Parameters\Interfaces*Adapter* subkey of the registry and setting its value to zero.

Note This subkey includes the globally unique identifier (GUID) for the computer's LAN adapter. For more information about GUIDs, see Chapter 12, "Implementing Active Directory." For more information about the registry, see Chapter 6, "Using the Registry."

The IPAutoconfigurationEnabled entry takes a REG_DWORD data type. To disable Automatic Private IP Addressing, specify a value of 0 for the entry. Specify a value of 1 to enable Automatic Private IP Addressing, the default state when this value is omitted from the registry.

Using TCP/IP Utilities

Windows 2000 includes the utilities diagrammed in Figure 8.5 that you can use to troubleshoot TCP/IP and test connectivity.

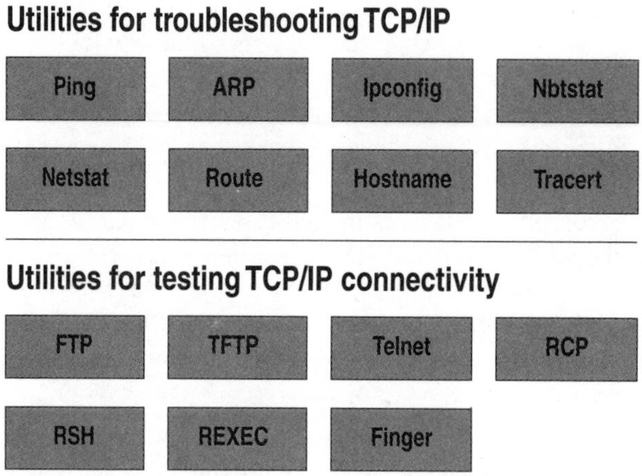

Utilities for troubleshooting TCP/IP

Ping	ARP	Ipconfig	Nbtstat

Netstat	Route	Hostname	Tracert

Utilities for testing TCP/IP connectivity

FTP	TFTP	Telnet	RCP

RSH	REXEC	Finger

Figure 8.5   TCP/IP utilities included with Windows 2000

Troubleshooting TCP/IP

Windows 2000 offers several utilities to assist you in troubleshooting TCP/IP. Table 8.5 describes the Windows 2000 utilities that you can use to troubleshoot TCP/IP.

Table 8.5   **Utilities Used to Troubleshoot TCP/IP**

Option	Description
Ping	Verifies configurations and tests connections
ARP	Displays locally resolved IP addresses as physical addresses
Ipconfig	Displays the current TCP/IP configuration
Nbtstat	Displays statistics and connections using NetBIOS over TCP/IP
Netstat	Displays TCP/IP protocol statistics and connections
Route	Displays or modifies the local routing table
Hostname	Returns the local computer's host name for authentication by the Remote Copy Protocol (RCP), remote shell (RSH), and remote execution (REXEC) utilities.
Tracert	Checks the route to a remote system

Testing TCP/IP Connectivity

Windows 2000 also provides utilities for testing TCP/IP connectivity. Table 8.6 describes these Windows 2000 utilities.

Table 8.6   Utilities Used to Test TCP/IP Connectivity

Option	Description
FTP	Provides bidirectional file transfer between a computer running Windows 2000 and any TCP/IP host running FTP. Windows 2000 Server ships with the ability to serve as an FTP client or server.
Trivial File Transfer Protocol (TFTP)	Provides bidirectional file transfer between a computer running Windows 2000 and a TCP/IP host running TFTP.
Telnet	Provides terminal emulation to a TCP/IP host running Telnet. Windows 2000 Server ships with the ability to serve as a Telnet client.
Remote Copy Protocol (RCP)	Copies files between a client and a host that support RCP; for example, a computer running Windows 2000 and a UNIX host.
Remote shell (RSH)	Runs commands on a UNIX host.
Remote execution (REXEC)	Runs a process on a remote computer.
Finger	Retrieves system information from a remote computer that supports TCP/IP and the finger utility.

Testing a TCP/IP Configuration

After configuring TCP/IP and restarting the computer, you should use the ipconfig and ping command-prompt utilities to test the configuration and connections to other TCP/IP hosts and networks. Such testing helps to ensure that TCP/IP is functioning properly.

Using Ipconfig

You use the ipconfig utility to verify the TCP/IP configuration parameters on a host. This helps to determine whether the configuration is initialized, or if a duplicate IP address exists. Use the ipconfig command with the /all switch to verify configuration information.

Tip   Type **ipconfig /all | more** to prevent the ipconfig output from scrolling off the screen; to scroll down and view additional output, press Spacebar.

The result of the ipconfig /all command is as follows:

- If a configuration has initialized, the ipconfig utility displays the IP address and subnet mask, and, if it is assigned, the default gateway.

- If a duplicate IP address exists, the ipconfig utility indicates that the IP address is configured; however, the subnet mask is 0.0.0.0.

- If the computer is unable to obtain an IP address from a server running the DHCP Service on the network, the ipconfig utility displays the IP address as the address provided by Automatic Private IP Addressing.

Using Ping

After you have verified the TCP/IP configuration, use the ping utility to test connectivity. The *ping* utility is a diagnostic tool that you can use to test TCP/IP configurations and diagnose connection failures. Use the ping utility to determine whether a particular TCP/IP host is available and functional. To test connectivity, use the Ping command with the following syntax:

ping *IP_address*

Using Ipconfig and Ping

Figure 8.6 outlines the steps for verifying a computer's configuration and for testing router connections.

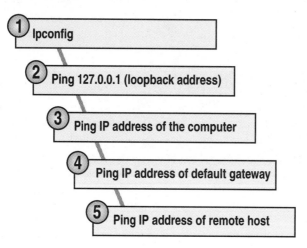

Figure 8.6   Using ipconfig and ping

The following list explains the steps outlined in Figure 8.6:

1. Use the ipconfig command to verify that the TCP/IP configuration has been initialized.

2. Use the ping command with the loopback address (ping 127.0.0.1) to verify that TCP/IP is correctly installed and bound to your network adapter card.

3. Use the ping command with the IP address of the computer to verify that your computer is not a duplicate of another IP address on the network.

4. Use the ping command with the IP address of the default gateway to verify that the default gateway is operational and that your computer can communicate with the local network.

5. Use the ping command with the IP address of a remote host to verify that the computer can communicate through a router.

Note Typically, if you ping the remote host (step 5) and the ping command is successful, steps 1 through 4 are successful by default. If the ping command is not successful, ping the IP address of another remote host before completing the entire diagnostic process because the current host might be turned off.

By default, the following message appears four times in response to a successful ping command:

Reply from *IP_address*

Practice: Installing and Configuring TCP/IP

In this practice you use two TCP/IP utilities to verify your computer's configuration. Then you configure your computer to use a static IP address and verify your computer's new configuration. Next you configure your computer to use a DHCP server to automatically assign an IP address to your computer, whether or not there is a DHCP server available on your network. Finally, you test the Automatic Private IP Addressing feature in Windows 2000 by disabling the DHCP server, if there is one on your network.

After completing this practice, you will be able to

- Verify a computer's TCP/IP configuration.

- Configure TCP/IP to use a static IP address using Automatic IP Addressing.

- Configure TCP/IP to obtain an IP address automatically using DHCP.

- Determine what happens when there is no server running the DHCP Service to provide an IP address.

To complete this practice, you need

- TCP/IP as the only installed protocol.

- Optional: A server running the DHCP Service to provide IP addresses. If you are working on a computer that is not part of a network and there is not a server running the DHCP service, there are certain procedures in this practice that you will not be able to do.

In the following table, record the IP address, subnet mask, and default gateway that your network administrator provides for you to use during this practice. Also ask your network administrator if there is another computer that you can use to test your computer's connectivity, and record the IP address of that computer as well. If you are not on a network, you can use the suggested values.

Variable value	Suggested value	Your value
Static IP address	192.168.1.201	
Subnet mask	255.255.255.0	
Default gateway (if required)	None	
Computer to test connectivity	NA	

Exercise 1: Verifying a Computer's TCP/IP Configuration

In this exercise, you use two TCP/IP utilities, ipconfig and ping, to verify your computer's configuration.

Note   As you complete the exercises in this practice, you will use the command prompt and Network Connections windows frequently. For the sake of efficiency, you will open the windows one time, and then minimize and restore them as necessary.

▶   **To verify a computer's configuration**

1. Open a command prompt.
2. At the command prompt, type **ipconfig /all | more** and then press Enter.

    The Windows 2000 IP Configuration utility displays the TCP/IP configuration of the physical and logical adapters configured on your computer.
3. Press Spacebar as necessary to display the heading Local Area Connection. Use the information displayed in this section to complete as much of the following table as possible. Press Spacebar to display additional information, as necessary, and to return to the command prompt.

Local Area Connection setting	Value
Host name	
DNS servers	
Description	
Physical address	
DHCP enabled	
Autoconfiguration enabled	
IP address	
Subnet mask	
Default gateway	

4. Press Spacebar as necessary to scroll through the configuration information and return to the command prompt.

5. To verify that the IP address is working and configured for your adapter, type **ping 127.0.0.1** and then press Enter.

A response similar to the following indicates a successful ping:

```
Pinging 127.0.0.1 with 32 bytes of data:

Reply from 127.0.0.1: bytes=32 time<10ms TTL=128

Reply from 127.0.0.1: bytes=32 time<10ms TTL=128

Reply from 127.0.0.1: bytes=32 time<10ms TTL=128

Reply from 127.0.0.1: bytes=32 time<10ms TTL=128

Ping statistics for 127.0.0.1:

    Packets: Sent = 4, Received = 4, Lost = 0 <0% loss>,

    Approximate round trip times in milliseconds:

    Minimum = 0ms, Maximum = 0ms, Average = 0ms
```

6. Minimize the command prompt.

Exercise 2: Configuring TCP/IP to Use a Static IP Address

In this exercise, you configure TCP/IP to use a static IP address.

▶   **To configure TCP/IP to use a static IP address**

1. Right-click My Network Places, and then click Properties.

   The Network And Dial-Up Connections window appears.

2. Right-click Local Area Connection, and then click Properties.

   The Local Area Connection Properties dialog box appears, displaying the network adapter in use and the network components used in this connection.

3. Click Internet Protocol (TCP/IP), and then verify that the check box to the left of the entry is selected.

4. Click Properties.

   The Internet Protocol (TCP/IP) Properties dialog box appears.

5. Click Use The Following IP Address.

6. In the IP Address box, the Subnet Mask box, and the Default Gateway box (if required), type the values that you entered in the table on page 166, or the suggested values listed in the table.

Important   Be careful when manually entering IP configuration settings, especially numeric addresses. The most frequent cause of TCP/IP connection problems is incorrectly entered IP address information.

---

7. Click OK.

   You are returned to the Local Area Connection Properties dialog box.

8. Click OK to close the Local Area Connection Properties dialog box.

9. Minimize the Network And Dial-Up Connections window.

▶ **To test the static TCP/IP configuration**

1. Restore the command prompt.

2. At the command prompt, type **ipconfig /all | more** and then press Enter.

   The Windows 2000 IP Configuration utility displays the physical and logical adapters configured on your computer.

3. Press Spacebar as needed to scroll through the configuration information and locate the Local Area Connection information.

4. Record the current TCP/IP configuration settings for your Local Area Connection in the following table.

Setting	Value
IP address	
Subnet mask	
Default gateway	

5. Press Spacebar as necessary to scroll through the configuration information and return to the command prompt.

6. To verify that the IP address is working and configured for your adapter, type **ping 127.0.0.1** and then press Enter.

   What happens?

7. If you have a computer that you are using to test connectivity, type **ping *ip_address*** (where *ip_address* is the IP address of the computer you are using to test connectivity), and then press Enter. If you do not have a computer to test connectivity, skip to step 8.

   What happens?

8. Minimize the command prompt.

Exercise 3: Configuring TCP/IP to Automatically Obtain an IP Address

In this exercise, you configure TCP/IP to automatically obtain an IP address. You then test the configuration to verify that the DHCP Service has provided the appropriate IP addressing information. Be sure to perform the first part of this exercise even if you have no DHCP Service server because these settings will also be used in Exercise 4.

▶ **To configure TCP/IP to automatically obtain an IP address**

1. Restore the Network And Dial-Up Connections window, right-click Local Area Connection, and then click Properties.

    The Local Area Connection dialog box appears.

2. Click Internet Protocol (TCP/IP), and then verify that the check box to the left of the entry is selected.

3. Click Properties.

    The Internet Protocol (TCP/IP) Properties dialog box appears.

4. Click Obtain An IP Address Automatically.

    What IP address settings will the DHCP Service configure for your computer?

5. Click OK to close the Internet Protocol (TCP/IP) Properties dialog box.

6. Click OK to close the Local Area Connection Properties dialog box.

7. Minimize the Network Connections window.

▶ **To test the TCP/IP configuration**

Note   If there is not an available server running the DHCP Service to provide an IP address, skip this procedure and continue with Exercise 4.

1. Restore the command prompt, type **ipconfig /release** and then press Enter.

2. At the command prompt, type **ipconfig /renew** and then press Enter.

3. At the command prompt, type **ipconfig | more** and then press Enter.

4. Pressing Spacebar as necessary, record the current TCP/IP configuration settings for your Local Area Connection in the following table.

Setting	Value
IP address	
Subnet mask	
Default gateway	

5. To test that TCP/IP is working and bound to your adapter, type **ping 127.0.0.1** and then press Enter.

    The internal loop-back test displays four replies if TCP/IP is bound to the adapter.

Exercise 4: Obtaining an IP Address
By Using Automatic Private IP Addressing

In this exercise, if you have a server running the DHCP Service, you need to disable it on that server, so that a DHCP server will not be available to provide an IP address for your computer. Without a DHCP server available to provide an IP address, the Windows 2000 Automatic Private IP Addressing feature will provide unique IP addresses for your computer. If the DHCP Service cannot be disabled, you can simply disconnect your network adapter cable.

▶ **To obtain an IP address by using Automatic Private IP Addressing**

1. At the command prompt, type **ipconfig /release** and then press Enter.

2. At the command prompt, type **ipconfig /renew** and then press Enter.

   There will be a pause while Windows 2000 attempts to locate a DHCP server on the network.

   What message appears, and what does it indicate?

3. Click OK to close the dialog box.

▶ **To test the TCP/IP configuration**

1. At the command prompt, type **ipconfig | more** and then press Enter.

   Pressing Spacebar as necessary, record the current TCP/IP settings for your Local Area Connection in the following table.

Setting	Value
IP address	
Subnet mask	
Default gateway	

   Is this the same IP address assigned to your computer in Exercise 3? Why or why not?

2. Press Spacebar to finish scrolling through the configuration information, as necessary.

3. To verify that TCP/IP is working and bound to your adapter, type **ping 127.0.0.1** and then press Enter.

   The internal loop-back test displays four replies if TCP/IP is bound to the adapter.

4. If you have a computer to test TCP/IP connectivity with your computer, type **ping** *ip_address* (where *ip_address* is the IP address of the computer that you are using to test connectivity), and then press Enter. If you do not have a computer to test connectivity, skip this step and proceed to Exercise 5.

Were you successful? Why or why not?

Exercise 5: Obtaining an IP Address by Using DHCP

In this exercise, enable the DHCP Service running on the computer that is acting as a DHCP server (or reconnect your network cable if you disconnected it in Exercise 4). Your computer will obtain IP addressing information from the DHCP server.

Note If there is not an available server running the DHCP Service to provide an IP address, skip this exercise.

▶   **To obtain an IP address by using DHCP**

1. At the command prompt, type **ipconfig /release** and then press Enter.

2. At the command prompt, type **ipconfig /renew** and then press Enter.

   After a short wait, a message box indicates that a new IP address was assigned.

3. Click OK to close the message box.

4. At the command prompt, type **ipconfig /all | more** and then press Enter.

5. Verify that the DHCP server has assigned an IP address to your computer.

6. Close the command prompt.

Lesson Summary

In this lesson you learned that Microsoft's implementation of TCP/IP enables enterprise networking and connectivity on computers running Windows 2000. It provides a robust, scaleable, cross-platform client/server framework that is supported by most large networks, including the Internet. You learned that the TCP/IP suite of protocols map to a four-layer conceptual model: network interface, Internet, transport, and application.

By default, client computers running Windows 2000 obtain TCP/IP configuration information automatically from the Dynamic Host Configuration Protocol (DHCP) Service. However, even in a DHCP-enabled environment, some computers, such as the computer running the DHCP Service, require a static IP address. For each network adapter card that uses TCP/IP in a computer, you can configure an IP address, subnet mask, and default gateway.

You also learned that Windows 2000 includes utilities that you can use to troubleshoot TCP/IP and test connectivity. Ping and ipconfig are two of the common troubleshooting utilities, and FTP and telnet are two of the connectivity utilities.

Finally, in this lesson you learned that the Windows 2000 implementation of TCP/IP supports automatic private IP addressing. Automatic private IP addressing is a new mechanism for automatic address assignment of IP addresses for simple LAN-based network configurations. It is an extension of dynamic IP address assignment for LAN adapters, and enables configuration of IP addresses without using static IP address assignments or installing the DHCP Service. By default, the Automatic Private IP Addressing feature is enabled. However, you can disable this feature by adding IPAutoconfigurationEnabled to the registry.

Lesson 2: NWLink

The NWLink IPX/SPX/NetBIOS compatible transport protocol (usually referred to as NWLink) is Microsoft's implementation of Novell's NetWare Internetwork Packet Exchange/Sequenced Packet Exchange (IPX/SPX) protocol. NWLink is most commonly used in environments where clients running Microsoft operating systems are used to access resources on NetWare servers, or where clients running NetWare are used to access resources on computers running Microsoft operating systems.

After this lesson, you will be able to

- Install and configure NWLink.

Estimated lesson time: 30 minutes

Understanding NWLink Features

NWLink allows computers running Windows 2000 to communicate with other network devices that are using IPX/SPX. NWLink also can be used in small network environments that use only clients running Windows 2000 and other Microsoft operating systems.

NWLink supports the networking application programming interfaces (APIs) that provide the interprocess communications (IPC) services described in Table 8.7.

Table 8.7   Networking APIs Supported by NWLink

Networking API	Description
WinSock	Supports existing NetWare applications written to comply with the NetWare IPX/SPX Sockets interface
NetBIOS over IPX	Implemented as NWLink NetBIOS; supports communication between a NetWare client running NetBIOS and a computer running Windows 2000 and NWLink NetBIOS

NWLink also provides NetWare clients with access to applications designed for Windows 2000 Server, such as Microsoft SQL Server and Microsoft SNA Server. To provide NetWare client access to file and print resources on a computer running Windows 2000 Server, you should install File and Print Services for NetWare (FPNW).

In summary, the 32-bit Windows 2000 implementation of NWLink provides the following features:

- Supports communications with NetWare networks
- Supports sockets and NetBIOS over IPX
- Provides NetWare clients with access to Windows 2000 servers

Installing NWLink

The procedure for installing NWLink is the same process that you use to install any network protocol in Windows 2000.

▶ **To install NWLink**

1. Right-click My Network Places, and then click Properties.
2. In the Network And Dial-Up Connections window, right-click Local Area Connection, and then click Properties.

   The Local Area Connection Properties dialog box appears, displaying the network adapter in use and the network components configured for this adapter.
3. Click Install.
4. In the Select Network Component Type dialog box, click Protocol, and then click Add.
5. In the Select Network Protocol dialog box, in the Network Protocol list, click NWLink IPX/SPX/NetBIOS Compatible Transport Protocol (see Figure 8.7), and then click OK.

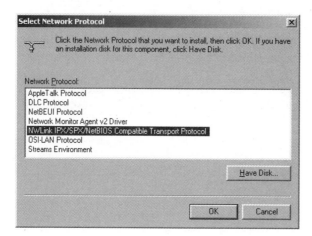

Figure 8.7   The Select Network Protocol dialog box

Configuring NWLink

NWLink configuration involves three components: frame type, network number, and internal network number. By default, Windows 2000 detects a frame type and a network number automatically when you install NWLink. Windows 2000 also provides a generic internal network number. However, you must manually specify an internal network number if you plan to run FPNW or IPX routing, as shown in Figure 8.8.

Note   Each network adapter card bound to NWLink in a computer requires a frame type and network number.

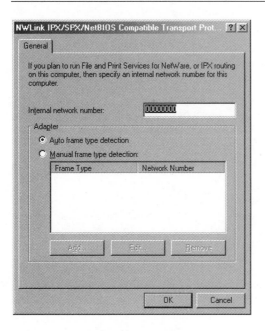

Figure 8.8   Configuring NWLink

Frame Type

A *frame type* defines the way that the network adapter card formats data. To ensure proper communication between a computer running Windows 2000 and a NetWare server, you must configure the NWLink frame type to match the frame type on the NetWare server.

Note   A connection between two computers that use different frame types is possible if the NetWare server is acting as a router. However, this is inefficient and could result in a slow connection.

Table 8.8 lists the topologies and frame types supported by NWLink.

Table 8.8   Topologies and Frame Types Supported by NWLink

Topology	Frame type
Ethernet	Ethernet II, 802.3, 802.2, and Sub Network Access Protocol (SNAP), which defaults to 802.2
Token Ring	802.5 and SNAP
Fiber Distributed Data Interface (FDDI)	802.2 and SNAP

Note   On Ethernet networks, the standard frame type for NetWare 2.2 and NetWare 3.11 is 802.3. For NetWare 3.12 and later, the default is 802.2.

When you install NWLink, Windows 2000 automatically determines which IPX frame type is in use on the network and sets the NWLink frame type accordingly. If Windows 2000 detects frame types in addition to 802.2 during NWLink installation, the frame type for NWLink defaults to 802.2.

Network Number

Each frame type configured on a network adapter card requires a *network number,* which must be unique for each network segment. All computers on a segment using the same frame type *must* use the same network number to communicate with one another.

Note   On a computer running Windows 2000, type **ipxroute config** at a command prompt to display the network number, frame type, and device in use.

Although Windows 2000 automatically detects a network number during NWLink installation by default, you can also manually specify a network number by using the Registry Editor.

Setting a network number in the registry for a given frame type requires entering two corresponding entries, NetworkNumber and PktType, in the HKEY_LOCAL_MACHINE\SYSTEM\CurrentControlSet\Services\Nwlnkipx\Parameters\Adapters*Adapter* subkey of the registry.

- NetworkNumber specifies the network number (in hexadecimal) for the adapter. If the value for this entry is 0, NWLink gets the network number from the network while it is running. Network numbers are four bytes (eight hexadecimal characters). The NetworkNumber entry takes a REG_MULTI_SZ data type.

- PktType specifies the packet form to use. The PktType entry takes a REG_MULTI_SZ data type. Table 8.9 lists the values for the PktType entry and the packet forms supported by NWLink.

Table 8.9   Packet Types or Forms Supported by NWLink

Value	Packet form
0	Ethernet_II
1	Ethernet_802.3
2	802.2
3	SNAP
4	ArcNet
FF (default)	Auto-detect

Note   If an adapter uses multiple packet types, you can specify the network number for each packet type by adding corresponding values in the NetworkNumber entry.

Internal Network Number

An *internal network number* uniquely identifies a computer on the network for internal routing. This eight-digit hexadecimal number, or virtual network number, is by default set to 00000000.

The internal network number identifies a virtual network segment inside the computer. That is, the internal network number identifies another (virtual) segment on the network. So, if an internal network number is configured for a computer running Windows 2000, a NetWare server or a router adds an extra hop in its route to the computer.

You must manually assign a unique, nonzero internal network number in the following situations:

- FPNW is installed, and there are multiple frame types on a single adapter.
- FPNW is installed, and NWLink is bound to multiple adapters in the computer.
- An application is using the NetWare Service Advertising Protocol (SAP). SQL Server and SNA Server are examples of applications that can use SAP.

Note   If a computer has multiple network adapter cards bound to NWLink, and if you want each one to use a different frame type, configure each network adapter card to use the Manual Frame Type Detection option. You also must specify a frame type, network number, and internal network number for each network adapter card.

Practice: Installing and Configuring NWLink

In this practice, you install and configure the NWLink IPX/SPX/NetBIOS Compatible Transport Protocol. Then you install and configure NWLink. With multiple protocols installed, you change the binding order of a protocol, unbind a protocol from a network adapter card, and remove NWLink from a computer.

Note   You can install any of the available protocols in Windows 2000 by using this procedure.

▶ **To install and configure NWLink**

1. Restore the Network Connections window.

2. Right-click Local Area Connection, and then click Properties.

   The Local Area Connection Properties dialog box appears, displaying the network adapter card in use and the network components used in this connection.

3. Click Add.

   The Select Network Component Type dialog box appears.

4. Click Protocol, and then click Add.

   The Select Network Protocol dialog box appears.

   What protocols can you install?

5. Select NWLink IPX/SPX/NetBIOS Compatible Transport Protocol, and then click OK.

   The Local Area Connection Properties dialog box appears.

6. Select NWLink IPX/SPX/NetBIOS Compatible Transport Protocol, and then click Properties.

   What type of frame detection is selected by default?

7. Click Manual Frame Type Detection, and then click Add.

   What is the default frame type?

8. Click Add, and then Click OK.

   The Local Area Connection Properties dialog box appears.

9. Click OK.

Lesson Summary

NWLink is Microsoft's implementation of Novell's NetWare Internetwork Packet Exchange/Sequenced Packet Exchange (IPX/SPX) protocol. NWLink is most commonly used in environments where clients running Microsoft operating systems are used to access resources on NetWare servers, or where clients running NetWare are used to access resources on computers running Microsoft operating systems. NWLink supports WinSock and NetBIOS over IPX networking APIs. Winsock supports existing NetWare applications written to comply with the NetWare IPX/SPX Sockets. NetBIOS over IPX is implemented as NWLink NetBIOS and supports communication between a NetWare client running NetBIOS and a computer running Windows 2000 and NWLink NetBIOS.

Lesson 3: Other Protocols Supported by Windows 2000

Windows 2000 also supports other protocols, including NetBEUI, DLC, AppleTalk Protocol, and the Network Monitor Agent v2 Driver.

After this lesson, you will be able to

- Explain the capabilities and limitations of NetBEUI.
- Explain the capabilities and limitations of DLC.
- Describe other protocols supported by Windows NT.

Estimated lesson time: 20 minutes

NetBEUI

NetBEUI is a protocol developed for LANs with 20–200 computers. However, while NetBEUI is a small, fast, and efficient protocol, it is not routable and therefore is unsuitable for use in a wide area network (WAN) environment.

NetBEUI Capabilities

NetBEUI provides compatibility with existing LANs that use the NetBEUI protocol. NetBEUI provides computers running Windows 2000 with the following capabilities:

- Connection-oriented and connectionless communication between computers
- Self-configuration and self-tuning
- Error protection
- Small memory overhead

NetBEUI Limitations

NetBEUI also has a number of limitations. NetBEUI is

- Designed for department-sized LANs.
- Nonroutable. Because of this limitation, you must connect computers running Windows 2000 and NetBEUI by using bridges instead of routers.
- Broadcast-based. NetBEUI protocol relies on broadcasts for many of its functions, such as name registration and discovery, which creates more broadcast traffic than other protocols.

DLC

As shown in Figure 8.9, Data Link Control (DLC) is a special purpose, non-routable protocol that enables computers running Windows 2000 to communicate with the following:

- Other computers running the DLC protocol stack, such as IBM mainframes.
- Network peripherals that use a network adapter card to connect directly to the network, such as a Hewlett-Packard LaserJet 4Si print device, which can connect directly to the network by using an HP JetDirect network adapter.

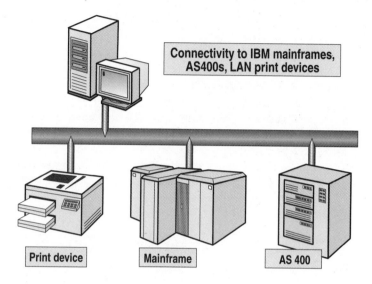

Figure 8.9   DLC connectivity

Note   You must install the DLC protocol on the print server for the print device. Computers sending print jobs to the print server do not require DLC.

DLC is not designed to be a primary protocol for use between personal computers and should be installed only on computers performing the previously mentioned tasks.

AppleTalk Protocol

The AppleTalk protocol allows computers running Windows 2000 Server and Apple Macintosh clients to share files and printers.

Note   For the AppleTalk protocol to function properly, a computer running Windows 2000 Server configured with Windows 2000 Services for Macintosh must be available on the network.

Network Monitor Agent v2 Driver

The Network Monitor Agent on a Windows 2000–based computer collects and displays statistics about activity detected by the network card in the computer. You can view these statistics on a computer that is running Network Monitor Agent. You can also use Microsoft Systems Management Server (SMS) and Network Monitor to collect statistics from computers that are running Network Monitor Agent.

Lesson Summary

In this lesson you learned that Windows 2000 supports protocols besides TCP/IP and NWLink. These other protocols include NetBEUI, DLC, AppleTalk protocol, and the Network Monitor Agent v2 Driver. NetBEUI is a protocol developed for LANs with 20–200 computers. It is a small, fast, and efficient protocol, but it is not routable and therefore is unsuitable for use in a WAN environment. NetBEUI provides compatibility with existing LANs that use the NetBEUI protocol. DLC is a special purpose, nonroutable protocol that enables computers running Windows 2000 to communicate with other computers running the DLC protocol stack, such as IBM mainframes. DLC is also used to communicate with network peripherals that use a network adapter card to connect directly to the network, such as a Hewlett-Packard LaserJet 4Si print device.

Lesson 4: Network Bindings

Network bindings enable communication between network adapter card drivers, protocols, and services. Figure 8.10 shows an example of network bindings. In Figure 8.10, the workstation service is bound to each of three protocols, and each protocol is bound to at least one network adapter card. This lesson describes the function of bindings in a network and the process for configuring them.

The Windows 2000 network architecture uses a series of interdependent layers. The bottom layer of the network architecture ends at the network adapter card, which places information on the cable, allowing information to flow between computers.

After this lesson, you will be able to

- Explain how to configure network bindings.

Estimated lesson time: 20 minutes

Binding Between Architectural Levels

Binding is the process of linking network components on different levels to enable communication between those components. A network component can be bound to one or more network components above or below it. The services that each component provides can be shared by all other components that are bound to it. For example, in Figure 8.10, TCP/IP is bound to both the Workstation service and the Server service.

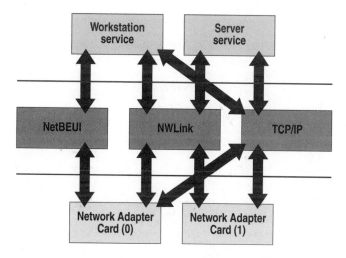

Figure 8.10   Network bindings

Combining Network Bindings

Many combinations of network bindings are possible. In the example shown in Figure 8.10, all three protocols are bound to the Workstation service, but only the routable protocols, NWLink and TCP/IP, are bound to the Server service. It is possible to select which protocols are bound to the network adapter cards. Network adapter card (0) is bound to all three protocols, while network adapter card (1) is bound only to the routable protocols. To control which components are bound together, you must be a member of the Administrators group.

When adding network software, Windows 2000 automatically binds all dependent network components accordingly. Network Driver Interface Specification (NDIS) 5.0 provides the capability to bind multiple protocols to multiple network adapter card drivers.

Configuring Network Bindings

You can configure your network bindings by using My Network Places.

▶ **To configure network bindings**

1. Right-click My Network Places, and then click Properties.
2. In the Network And Dial-Up Connections window, click Advanced, and then click Advanced Settings.
3. In the Advanced Settings dialog box, under Client For Microsoft Networks do one of the following:

   - To bind the protocol to the selected adapter, click to select the adapter.
   - To unbind the protocol from the selected adapter, click to clear the adapter.

Note   Only an experienced network administrator who is familiar with the requirements of the network software should attempt to change binding settings.

Specifying Binding Order

You also can specify binding order to optimize network performance. For example, a computer running Windows 2000 Workstation has NetBEUI, NWLink IPX/SPX, and TCP/IP installed. However, most of the servers to which this computer connects are running only TCP/IP. Verify that the Workstation binding to TCP/IP is listed *before* the Workstation bindings for the other protocols. In this way, when a user attempts to make a connection to a server, the Workstation service first attempts to use TCP/IP to establish the connection.

▶ **To specify binding order**

1. Right-click My Network Places, and then click Properties.

2. In the Network And Dial-Up Connections window, click Advanced, and then click Advanced Settings.

3. In the Advanced Settings dialog box, under Client For Microsoft Networks, click the protocol for which you want to change the binding order.

4. Use the Up Arrow and Down Arrow buttons to change the binding order for protocols that are bound to a specific adapter:

    -   To move the protocol higher in the binding order, click the Up Arrow button.

    -   To move the protocol lower in the binding order, click the Down Arrow button.

Practice: Working with Network Bindings

In this practice you change the binding order of the protocols bound to your network adapter card. Next you unbind a protocol from your network adapter card, and then bind a protocol to your network adapter card. Finally you uninstall a network protocol.

After completing this practice you will be able to

-   Change the binding order of protocols.

-   Bind and unbind a protocol.

-   Remove a protocol.

Exercise 1: Changing the Binding Order for a Protocol

In this exercise, you change the binding order of the protocols bound to your network adapter card.

▶   **To change the protocol binding order**

1. Right-click My Network Places and click Properties.

2. Maximize the Network And Dial-Up Connections window, and on the Advanced menu, click Advanced Settings.

    The Advanced Settings dialog box appears.

    What is the order of the protocols listed under Client For Microsoft Networks?

3. Under Client For Microsoft Networks, click NWLink IPX/SPX/NetBIOS Compatible Transport Protocol.

4. Click the Up Arrow button.

    Notice that the order of the protocols listed under Client For Microsoft Networks has changed. NWLink IPX/SPX/NetBIOS Compatible Transport Protocol is listed above Internet Protocol (TCP/IP).

5. Leave the Advanced Settings window open.

Exercise 2: Unbinding a Protocol

In this exercise, you unbind TCP/IP from your network adapter card, which will leave NWLink as the only protocol available to access other computers.

▶ **To unbind TCP/IP**

1. In the Advanced Settings dialog box, under Client For Microsoft Networks, unbind Internet Protocol (TCP/IP) by clearing the check box to the left of the entry.

2. Click OK.

   TCP/IP is now unbound from your network adapter card.

Exercise 3: Binding a Protocol

In this exercise, you bind TCP/IP to your network adapter card.

▶ **To bind TCP/IP**

1. On the Advanced menu of the Network And Dial-Up Connections window, click Advanced Settings.

   The Advanced Settings dialog box appears.

2. Under Client For Microsoft Networks, select Internet Protocol (TCP/IP) by clicking the check box to the left of the option.

3. Click OK.

   TCP/IP is now bound to your network adapter card.

Exercise 4: Uninstalling NWLink

In this exercise, you uninstall the NWLink IPX/SPX/NetBIOS Compatible Transport Protocol.

▶ **To remove NWLink**

1. In the Network And Dial-Up Connections window, right-click Local Area Connection, and then click Properties.

   The Local Area Connection Properties dialog box appears, displaying the adapter in use and the network components configured for this connection.

2. Click NWLink IPX/SPX/NetBIOS Compatible Transport Protocol, and then click Uninstall.

   The Uninstall NWLink IPX/SPX/NetBIOS Compatible Transport Protocol dialog box appears.

3. Click Yes to continue.

4. Click OK.

5. In the Network And Dial-Up Connections window, right-click Local Area Connection, and then click Properties.

   Notice that NWLink IPX/SPX/NetBIOS Compatible Transport Protocol is no longer listed as an installed protocol.

6. Click Cancel.

7. Close the Network Connections window.

Lesson Summary

In this lesson you learned that binding is the process of linking network components on different levels to enable communication between them. A network component can be bound to one or more network components above or below it, which allows the services that each component provides to be shared by all other components that are bound to it. When you install network software, Windows 2000 automatically binds all dependent network components accordingly. It is NDIS 5.0 that provides the capability to bind multiple protocols to multiple network adapter card drivers, and you can optimize network performance by specifying the binding order.

Review

Here are some questions to help you determine if you have learned enough to move on to the next chapter. If you have difficulty answering these questions, please go back and review the material in this chapter before beginning the next chapter. The answers for these questions are located in Appendix A, "Questions and Answers."

1. Your computer running Windows 2000 Workstation was configured manually for TCP/IP. You can connect to any host on your own subnet, but you cannot connect to or even ping any host on a remote subnet. What is the likely cause of the problem and how would you fix it?

2. Your computer running Windows 2000 Professional can communicate with some, but not all, of the NetWare servers on your network. Some of the NetWare servers are running frame type 802.2 and some are running 802.3. What is the likely cause of the problem?

3. What are the limitations of the NetBEUI protocol?

4. What is the primary function of the DLC protocol?

5. What is the significance of the binding order of network protocols?

C H A P T E R   9

Configuring the DHCP Service

About This Chapter

The Dynamic Host Configuration Protocol (DHCP) Service in Microsoft Windows 2000 centralizes and manages the allocation of Microsoft Transmission Control Protocol/Internet Protocol (TCP/IP) configuration information by assigning Internet Protocol (IP) addresses automatically to computers that are configured as DHCP clients. Implementing the DHCP Service can eliminate many of the configuration problems associated with configuring TCP/IP manually. This chapter presents the skills and knowledge necessary to install and configure the DHCP Service. The chapter also discusses the DHCP lease process.

Before You Begin

To complete this chapter, you must have

- A computer that meets the minimum hardware requirements listed in "Hardware Requirements," on page xxxiii.

- Installed the Windows 2000 Server software on the computer.

- Configured the computer as a stand-alone server in a workgroup with TCP/IP the only installed protocol.

Important A second computer running Windows 2000 Server to test connectivity is ideal. If you are working on a computer that is not part of a network and there is not a second computer to test connectivity, you will not be able to do all the exercises in this chapter.

Lesson 1: Understanding DHCP

DHCP is a TCP/IP standard for simplifying management of IP configuration. In this lesson you will learn about the differences between manually configuring the TCP/IP addresses on your network and using a DHCP server to automatically configure the TCP/IP addresses. You will learn the requirements for a server to run the DHCP Service and the requirements for a DHCP client. Finally, this lesson introduces the DHCP lease process, and you learn how to renew a lease or release a TCP/IP address.

After this lesson, you will be able to

- Explain the function of DHCP.
- Explain the DHCP lease process and how DHCP clients obtain IP addresses from a server running the DHCP Service.
- Explain IP lease renewal and release.

Estimated lesson time: 20 minutes

Bootstrap Protocol

The Bootstrap Protocol (BOOTP), based on the User Datagram Protocol/Internet Protocol (UDP/IP), enables a booting host to configure itself dynamically. DHCP is an extension of BOOTP, which enables diskless clients to start up and automatically configure TCP/IP. Each time that a DHCP client starts, it requests IP addressing information from a DHCP server, including the following:

- An IP address
- A subnet mask
- Optional values, such as the following:
  - A default gateway address
  - A Domain Name System (DNS) server address
  - A Windows Internet Name Service (WINS) server address

When a DHCP server receives a request for an IP address, it selects IP addressing information from a pool of addresses that are defined in its database and offers the IP addressing information to the DHCP client, as can be seen in Figure 9.1. If the client accepts the offer, the DHCP server leases the IP addressing information to the client for a specified period of time.

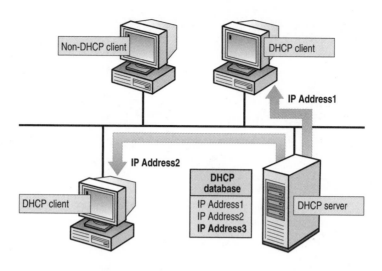

Figure 9.1   A DHCP Server provides IP addresses to DHCP clients

Manual vs. Automatic TCP/IP Configuration

To understand why the DHCP Service is beneficial for configuring TCP/IP on clients, it is useful to contrast the manual method of configuring TCP/IP with the automatic method using DHCP, as shown in Table 9.1.

Table 9.1   Configuring TCP/IP Manually vs. Using the DHCP Service

Configuring TCP/IP manually	Configuring TCP/IP using DHCP
Users can pick an IP address at random rather than obtaining a valid IP address from the network administrator. Using incorrect addresses can lead to network problems that can be very difficult to trace to the source.	Users no longer need to acquire IP addressing information from an administrator to configure TCP/IP. The DHCP Service supplies all the necessary configuration information to all the DHCP clients.
Typing in the IP address, subnet mask, or default gateway can lead to problems ranging from difficulty communicating, if the default gateway or subnet mask is incorrect, to problems associated with a duplicate IP address.	Correct configuration information ensures correct configuration, which eliminates most difficult-to-trace network problems.
There is administrative overhead for networks if you frequently move computers from one subnet to another. For example, you must change the IP address and default gateway address for a client to communicate from a new location.	Having servers running the DHCP Service on each subnet eliminates the overhead of having to manually reconfigure IP addresses, subnet masks, and default gateways when you move computers from one subnet to another.

To implement DHCP, you must install and configure the DHCP Service on at least one computer running Windows 2000 Server within the TCP/IP network. The computer can be configured as a domain controller or as a stand-alone server. In addition, for DHCP to function properly, you must configure the server and all of the clients.

Requirements for a Server Running the DHCP Service

A DHCP server requires a computer running Windows 2000 Server that is configured with the following:

- The DHCP Service.
- A static IP address (it cannot be a DHCP client itself), subnet mask, default gateway (if necessary), and other TCP/IP parameters.
- A DHCP scope. A *scope* is a range of IP addresses that are available for lease or assignment to clients.

Requirements for DHCP Clients

A DHCP client requires a computer that is DHCP enabled and running any of the following supported operating systems:

- Windows 2000, Windows NT Server version 3.51 or later, or Windows NT Workstation version 3.51 or later.
- Microsoft Windows 95 or later.
- Windows for Workgroups version 3.11 running Microsoft TCP/IP-32, which is included on the Windows 2000 Server CD-ROM.
- Microsoft Network Client version 3.0 for Microsoft MS-DOS with the real-mode TCP/IP driver, which is included on the Windows 2000 Server CD-ROM.
- LAN Manager version 2.2c, which is included on the Windows 2000 Server CD-ROM. LAN Manager 2.2c for OS/2 is not supported.

The DHCP Lease Process

To understand the DHCP lease process, you must first understand when the lease process occurs. The DHCP lease process occurs when one of the following events happens.

- TCP/IP is initialized for the first time on a DHCP client.
- A client requests a specific IP address and is denied, possibly because the DHCP server dropped the lease.
- A client previously leased an IP address but released the IP address and requires a new one.

DHCP uses a four-phase process to lease IP addressing information to a DHCP client for a specific period of time: DHCPDISCOVER, DHCPOFFER, DHCPREQUEST, and DHCPACK (see Figure 9.2).

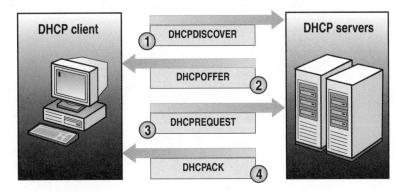

Figure 9.2   The DHCP lease process

DHCPDISCOVER

The first step in the DHCP lease process is DHCPDISCOVER. To begin the DHCP lease process, a client initializes a limited version of TCP/IP and broadcasts a DHCPDISCOVER message requesting the location of a DHCP server and IP addressing information. Because the client does not know the IP address of a DHCP server, the client uses 0.0.0.0 as the source address and 255.255.255.255 as the destination address.

The DHCPDISCOVER message contains the client's hardware address and computer name, so that the DHCP servers can determine which client sent the request.

DHCPOFFER

The second step in the DHCP lease process is DHCPOFFER. All DHCP servers that receive the IP lease request and have a valid client configuration broadcast a DHCPOFFER message that includes the following information:

- The client's hardware address
- An offered IP address
- A subnet mask
- The length of the lease
- A server identifier (the IP address of the offering DHCP server)

The DHCP server sends a broadcast because the client does not yet have an IP address. The DHCP client selects the IP address from the first offer that it receives. The DHCP server that is issuing the IP address reserves the address so that it cannot be offered to another DHCP client.

DHCPREQUEST

The third step in the DHCP lease process occurs after the client receives a DHCPOFFER from at least one DHCP server and selects an IP address. The client broadcasts a DHCPREQUEST message to all DHCP servers, indicating that it has accepted an offer. The DHCPREQUEST message includes the server identifier (IP address) of the server whose offer it accepted. All other DHCP servers then retract their offers and retain their IP addresses for the next IP lease request.

DHCPACK

The final step in a successful DHCP lease process occurs when the DHCP server issuing the accepted offer broadcasts a successful acknowledgment to the client in the form of a DHCPACK message. This message contains a valid lease for an IP address and possibly other configuration information.

When the DHCP client receives the acknowledgment, TCP/IP is completely initialized and the client is considered a bound DHCP client. Once bound, the client can use TCP/IP to communicate on the network.

DHCPNACK

If the DHCPREQUEST is not successful, the DHCP server broadcasts a negative acknowledgement (DHCPNACK). A DHCP server broadcasts a DHCPNACK if

- The client is trying to lease its previous IP address, and the IP address is no longer available.
- The IP address is invalid because the client physically has been moved to a different subnet.

When the client receives an unsuccessful acknowledgment, it resumes the DHCP lease process.

Note   If a computer has multiple network adapters that are bound to TCP/IP, the DHCP process occurs separately over each adapter. The DHCP Service assigns a unique IP address to each adapter in the computer that is bound to TCP/IP.

IP Lease Renewal and Release

All DHCP clients attempt to renew their lease when 50 percent of the lease time has expired. To renew its lease, a DHCP client sends a DHCPREQUEST message directly to the DHCP server from which it obtained the lease. If the DHCP server is available, it renews the lease and sends the client a DHCPACK message with the new lease time and any updated configuration parameters, as shown in Figure 9.3. The client updates its configuration when it receives the acknowledgment.

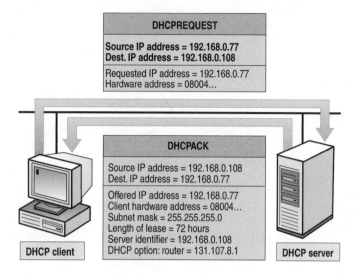

Figure 9.3   Renewing an IP lease

Note   Each time a DHCP client restarts, it attempts to lease the same IP address from the original DHCP server. If the lease request is unsuccessful and lease time is still available, the DHCP client continues to use the same IP address until the next attempt to renew the lease.

If a DHCP client cannot renew its lease with the original DHCP server at the 50 percent interval, the client broadcasts a DHCPREQUEST to contact any available DHCP server when 87.5 percent of the lease time has expired. Any DHCP server can respond with a DHCPACK message (renewing the lease) or a DHCPNACK message (forcing the DHCP client to reinitialize and obtain a lease for a different IP address).

If the lease expires, or if a DHCPNACK message is received, the DHCP client must immediately discontinue using that IP address. The DHCP client then begins the DHCP lease process to lease a new IP address.

Using Ipconfig to Renew a Lease

Use the ipconfig command with the /renew switch to send a DHCPREQUEST message to the DHCP server to receive updated options and lease time. If the DHCP server is unavailable, the client continues using the current DHCP-supplied configuration options.

Using Ipconfig to Release a Lease

Use the ipconfig command with the /release switch to cause a DHCP client to send a DHCPRELEASE message to the DHCP server and to release its lease. This is useful when you are moving a client to a different network and the client will not need its previous lease. TCP/IP communications with the client will stop after you issue this command.

Microsoft DHCP clients do not initiate DHCPRELEASE messages when shutting down. If a client remains shut down for the length of its lease (and the lease is not renewed), the DHCP server might assign that client's IP address to a different client after the lease expires. A client has a better chance of receiving the same IP address during initialization if it does not send a DHCPRELEASE message.

Lesson Summary

In this lesson you learned that when you manually configure IP addresses, you can pick an IP address at random rather than obtaining a valid IP address from the network administrator. When you pick your own IP address and type it in, you run the risk of making a typing mistake, of selecting an invalid address or subnet mask, or of choosing an address that is already in use. Using incorrect addresses can lead to network problems that can be very difficult to trace to the source. Using a DHCP server eliminates these problems.

Each time that a DHCP client starts, it requests IP addressing information from a DHCP server, including an IP address, a subnet mask, and any optional values, such as a default gateway address. When a DHCP server receives a request for an IP address, it selects IP addressing information from a pool of addresses that are defined in its database and offers the IP addressing information to the DHCP client. If the client accepts the offer, the DHCP server leases the IP addressing information to the client for a specified period of time.

Finally in this lesson, you learned that DHCP uses a four-phase process to lease IP addressing information to a DHCP client. All DHCP clients automatically attempt to renew their leases when 50 percent of the lease is expired. If the renewal fails, the client continues to use the same lease and continues to try to renew the lease. You also learned how to use the ipconfig command to manually renew or release a lease.

Lesson 2: Installing and Configuring the DHCP Service

In this lesson you learn how to install and configure the DHCP Service on a computer running Windows 2000 Server. You learn what a DHCP scope is and how to create and configure scopes. You also learn how to configure a client reservation to make sure that a DHCP client always is assigned the same IP address.

After this lesson, you will be able to

- Install the DHCP Service.
- Create a scope for the DHCP Service and configure a range of addresses for the scope to distribute.
- Exclude addresses from a scope's range of addresses and configure a reservation for a DHCP scope.
- Activate a DHCP scope.

Estimated lesson time: 55 minutes

The first step in implementing DHCP is to install the DHCP Service. Before you install the DHCP Service, you should specify a static IP address, subnet mask, and default gateway address for the network adapter bound to TCP/IP in the computer designated as the DHCP server.

▶ **To install the DHCP Service**

1. In Control Panel, double-click Add/Remove Programs.
2. In the Add/Remove Programs window, click Configure Windows, and then click Components.
3. Minimize the Add/Remove Programs window.
4. When the Windows Components wizard appears, click Next.
5. Select Optional Networking Components, and then click Details.
6. In the Optional Networking Components dialog box, in the Subcomponents Of Networking Options list, click to place a check mark in the box to the left of Microsoft DHCP Server, and then click OK (see Figure 9.4).
7. Click Next to install the required components.

To complete the installation of the DHCP Service, you must specify the location of the Windows 2000 setup files, such as the CD-ROM drive, when prompted.

Note The DHCP Service starts automatically during installation and must be running to communicate with DHCP clients.

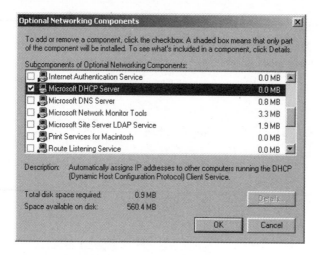

Figure 9.4   Installing Microsoft DHCP server

Creating a DHCP Scope

Before a DHCP server can lease an address to DHCP clients, you must create a scope. A scope is a pool of valid IP addresses available for lease to DHCP clients. After you have installed the DHCP Service and it is running, the next step is to create a scope.

When creating a DHCP scope, consider the following points:

- You must create at least one scope for every DHCP server.

- You must exclude static IP addresses from the scope.

- You can create multiple scopes on a DHCP server to centralize administration and to assign IP addresses specific to a subnet. You can assign only one scope to a specific subnet.

- DHCP servers do *not* share scope information. As a result, when you create scopes on multiple DHCP servers, ensure that the same IP addresses do not exist in more than one scope to prevent duplicate IP addressing.

Table 9.2 describes some of the parameters that you can specify when creating a new scope.

Table 9.2   Parameters for Creating a New Scope

Parameter	Description
Name	The name of the scope.
Comment	An optional comment for the scope.
IP Address Range From Address	The starting IP address that can be assigned to a DHCP client from this scope.
IP Address Range To Address	The ending IP address that can be assigned to a DHCP client from this scope.
Mask	The subnet mask to assign to DHCP clients.
Exclusion Range Start Address	The starting IP address of the range to exclude from the pool of addresses. The addresses in this exclusion will not be assigned to DHCP clients. This is important if you have static IP addresses configured on non-DCHP clients. (This is optional.)
Exclusion Range End Address	The ending IP address of the range to exclude from the pool of addresses. The addresses in this exclusion will not be assigned to DHCP clients. This is important if you have static IP addresses configured on non-DCHP clients. (This is optional.)
Lease Duration Unlimited	A parameter that indicates that DHCP leases assigned to clients never expire.
Lease Duration Limited To	The number of days, hours, and minutes that a DHCP client lease is available before it must be renewed. The default lease duration is three days.

▶ **To create a DHCP scope**

1. Start the DHCP Server Management snap-in.

2. In the DHCP window, right-click the entry for the DHCP server, point to New, and then click Scope.

3. In the Create Scope wizard, click Next, and then specify a name for the scope. You can also specify an optional comment for the scope.

4. Click Next, and then specify the range of IP addresses included in the scope. You can also specify the subnet mask by length or as an IP address.

5. Click Next, and then specify any exclusions.

Note An *exclusion* is an address or range of addresses that the server should not distribute. You *can* exclude multiple ranges of addresses.

---

6. Click Next, and then specify a duration for the leases issued by the DHCP server.

7. Click Next, and then click Finish.

> **Note**   Once you have created the scope, you must activate it to make it available for lease assignments.

8. In the DHCP window, right-click the entry for the scope that you just defined, point to Task, and then click Activate.

> **Important**   You must delete and recreate a scope to specify a new subnet mask or range of IP addresses.

Configuring a DHCP Scope

Once you have created the DHCP scope, you can configure options for DHCP clients. There are three levels of scope options—global, scope, and client.

Global Options

Global options are available to all DHCP clients. Use global options when all clients on all subnets require the same configuration information. For example, you might want all clients configured to use the same WINS server. Global options are always used, unless scope or client options are configured. To configure global options, right-click Server Options, and then click Configure Options.

Scope Options

Scope options are available only to clients who lease an address from the scope. For example, if you have a different scope for each subnet, you can define a unique default gateway address for each subnet. Scope options override global options. To configure scope options, right-click Scope Options, and then click Configure Options.

Client Options

Client options are available to specific clients. Create client options for a specific client using a reserved DHCP address lease. Client options are always used before scope or global options. To configure client options, right-click Client Options, and then click Configure Options.

Configuring Options for a DHCP Scope

▶   **To configure options for a DHCP scope**

1. In the DHCP window, expand the scope entry, if necessary.
2. Right-click the Scope Options icon, and then click Configure Options.

The following table describes some of the available options in the Configure DHCP Options: Scope Properties dialog box and includes all of the options supported by Microsoft DHCP clients.

Option	Description
003 Router	The IP address of a router, such as the default gateway address. A locally defined default gateway on a client takes precedence over the DHCP option.
006 DNS Servers	The IP address of a DNS server.
015 DNS Domain Name	The DNS domain name for client resolutions.
044 WINS/NBNS servers	The IP address of a WINS server available to clients. If a WINS server address is configured manually on a client, that configuration overrides the values configured for this option.
046 WINS/NBT node type	The type of network basic input/output system (NetBIOS) over TCP/IP name resolution to be used by the client. Options are 1 = B-node (broadcast) 2 = P-node (peer) 4 = M-node (mixed) 8 = H-node (hybrid)
047 NetBIOS Scope ID	The local NetBIOS scope ID. NetBIOS over TCP/IP will communicate only with other NetBIOS hosts that are using the same scope ID.

3. In the Available Options list, select the DHCP option to configure, and then enter the appropriate value in the Data Entry section of the dialog box.

The following table describes the available value types.

Value type	Description
IP Address	The IP address of a server that you added in the Configure DHCP Options: Scope Properties dialog box. For example, 003 Routers.
Long	A 32-bit numeric value. For example, 035 ARP Cache Time-out.
String	A string of characters. For example, 015 Domain Name.
Word	A 16-bit numeric value of specific block sizes. For example, 022 Max DG Reassembly Size.
Byte	A numeric value consisting of a single byte. For example, 046 WINS/NBT Node Type.
Binary	A binary value. For example, 043 Vendor-Specific Information.

4. Configure the appropriate value, and then click OK.

Configuring a Client Reservation

For some DHCP clients, it is important that the same IP address be reassigned when their lease expires. For these clients, you can configure the DHCP service so that it always assigns the same IP address to them. This is called a *client reservation* and is created using the Add Reservation dialog box shown in Figure 9.5. For example, if the server known as SRV187 is on a network that contains clients that are not WINS-enabled, SRV187 should be set up with a client reservation. Setting up the reservation ensures that SRV187 always leases the same IP address from the DHCP server. The clients that are on that network and are not WINS-enabled must use LMHOSTS to resolve NetBIOS computer names. Since the LMHOSTS file is a static file containing NetBIOS name to IP address mappings, name resolution using LMHOSTS will fail if the IP address of SRV187 changes.

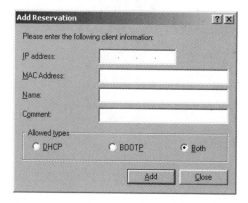

Figure 9.5 Adding client reservations

▶ **To configure a client reservation**

1. In the DHCP window, under the scope entry, right-click Reservations, point to New, and then click Reservation.

2. In the Add Reservation dialog box, in the IP Address box, type the IP address that you want to reserve for a specific client.

3. In the MAC Address box, type the hardware address (media access control address) of the host's network adapter card. Do not use dashes in the hardware address.

Important If you type the value for MAC Address incorrectly, it will not match the value sent by the DHCP client, and the DHCP Service will assign the client any available IP address instead of the IP address reserved for that client.

---

4. In the Name box, type a name to identify the client.

The DHCP Server Management snap-in uses a name associated with the hardware address of the network adapter card to identify a client.

5. In the Comment box, type an optional comment for the client.

6. Under Allowed Client Types, click to specify which method the client uses.

7. To add the reservation to the database, click Add.

Practice: Installing and Configuring the DHCP Service

In this practice, you install and configure the DHCP Service. You create a scope and configure a small range of addresses for the scope. For this practice you need an IP address and a subnet mask. In the following table, record the IP address, subnet mask, and default gateway that your network administrator provides for you to use during this practice. Also ask your network administrator if there is another computer that you can use to test your computer's connectivity, and record the IP address of that computer as well. If you are not on a network, use the suggested values in the following table.

Variable	Suggested value	Your value
Static IP address	192.168.1.201	
Subnet mask	255.255.255.0	
Default gateway (if required)	None	
IP address of second computer used to test connectivity	NA	

Exercise 1: Configuring TCP/IP to Use a Static IP Address

In this exercise, you configure TCP/IP to use a static IP address.

▶ **To configure TCP/IP to use a static IP address**

1. Right-click My Network Places, and then click Properties.

   The Network And Dial-Up Connections window appears.

2. Right-click Local Area Connection, and then click Properties.

   The Local Area Connection Properties dialog box appears, displaying the network adapter in use and the network components used in this connection.

3. Click Internet Protocol (TCP/IP), and then verify that the check box to the left of the entry is selected.

4. Click Properties.

   The Internet Protocol (TCP/IP) Properties dialog box appears.

5. Make sure that Use The Following IP Address is selected.

6. In the IP Address box, the Subnet Mask box, and the Default Gateway (if required) box, verify that the values that you entered in the table above or the suggested values listed in the table are being used. If not, enter the correct values.

Important   Be careful when entering IP configuration settings manually, especially numeric addresses. The most frequent cause of TCP/IP connection problems is incorrectly entered IP address information.

---

7. Click OK.

   You are returned to the Local Area Connection Properties dialog box.

8. Click OK to close the Local Area Connection Properties dialog box.

9. Minimize the Network And Dial-Up Connections window.

Optional Exercise 2: Determining the Physical Address of a Computer

In this exercise, if you have a second computer for testing connectivity, you determine the physical address of this second computer. You use this physical address (media access control address) in a later exercise to configure a DHCP reservation.

Note   If you do not have a second computer to use to determine the physical address, just read through Exercise 2 to see how it can be done.

▶   **To determine the physical address of a computer**

1. Open a command prompt, and ping the IP Address of the computer for which you want to determine the physical address.

2. Type **arp -a** and then press Enter.

3. Record the physical address of the computer that you used in step 1.

   The physical address is the hardware address or the Media Access Control (MAC) address. It is the address permanently burned into your network adapter and should look something like 00-aa-00-4a-de-14.

4. Minimize the command prompt.

Exercise 3: Installing the DHCP Service

In this exercise you install the DHCP Service on your computer.

▶   **To install the DHCP Service**

1. Click Start, point to Programs, and then point to Administrative Tools.

   Are there any entries for DHCP?

2. Open Control Panel.

3. Double-click Add/Remove Programs.

   The Add/Remove Programs window appears.

4. Click Configure Windows.

   The Add Or Remove Windows Components page appears.

5. Click Components.

   The Windows Components wizard appears.

6. Click Next to continue.

7. Click Optional Networking Components, but do not click or change the status of the check box to the left of the component.

   Note If the Optional Network Components check box is already checked, it means that some optional networking components have already been installed on this computer.

8. Click Details.

   The Optional Networking Components dialog box appears.

9. In the Subcomponents Of Optional Networking Components list, click to place a check mark in the box to the left of Microsoft DHCP Server.

10. Click OK.

    You are returned to the Windows NT Components page.

11. Click Next.

    Windows 2000 Server begins installing the required components.

    The Insert Disk dialog box appears.

12. Insert the Microsoft Windows 2000 Server Beta CD-ROM, and then click OK.

13. If the Windows 2000 CD-ROM window appears, close it.

    Note If the Files Needed dialog box appears, ensure that the path to the source files is correct and then click OK.

    Windows 2000 Server Setup copies the required files.

14. Remove the CD-ROM.

15. Click Finish to close the Windows Components wizard.

16. Close the Add/Remove Programs window.

17. Minimize Control Panel.

18. Click Start, point to Programs, and then point to Administrative Tools.

    Are there any entries for DHCP?

Exercise 4: Creating and Configuring a DHCP Scope

In this exercise, you create and configure a DHCP scope.

▶   **To create and configure a DHCP scope**

1. On the Administrative Tools menu, click DHCP Server Management.

   If the DHCP window appears along with a dialog box indicating that the DHCP server service is not running on the target machine, this means the DHCP server service is not starting automatically.

2. Click OK to close the dialog box, if necessary.

3. Maximize the DHCP window.

4. Double-click Server1. (If you named your computer a different name, double-click the name of your computer.)

5. Right-click Server1 (or the name of your computer), point to New, and then click Scope.

   The Create Scope wizard appears.

6. Click Next.

   The Scope Name page appears.

7. In the Name box, type **Server1 Scope** (or the name of your computer scope), and then click Next.

   The Set Address Range page appears.

8. Type **192.168.1.70** in the From box and type **192.168.1.90** in the To box.

   Caution   If you are on a network, do not assume that you can use this range of addresses. You must check with your network administrator to determine a range of addresses that you can use.

9. Ensure that the subnet mask is 255.255.255.0.

10. Click Next.

    The Add Exclusions page appears.

11. In the Start Address box, type **192.168.1.76**

12. In the End Address box, type **192.168.1.80**

13. Click Add.

14. Notice that 192.168.1.76 to 192.168.1.80 appears in the Excluded Addresses box.

15. Click Next.

    The Lease Duration page appears.

    What is the default lease duration?

16. Click Next to accept the default lease duration.

    The Configure DHCP Options page appears, asking if you would like to configure the most common DHCP options now.

17. Click No and then click Next.

    The Completing The Create Scope Wizard page appears.

18. Click Finish.

    An icon representing the new scope appears in DHCP Manager.

    The red arrow pointing down indicates that the scope is not activated. You will activate the scope in the next exercise.

Optional Exercise 5: Adding a Reservation to a DHCP Scope

In this exercise, you use the physical address of the computer you determined in Optional Exercise 2 to add a reservation to a DHCP scope.

▶ **To add a reservation to a DHCP scope**

1. In DHCP Manager, in the console tree, expand Scope.

   What options appear?

2. In the console tree, click Reservations.

3. In the console tree, right-click Reservations, point to New, and then click Reservation.

   The Add Reservation dialog box appears.

4. In the IP Address box, type **192.168.1.76**

5. In the MAC Address box, type the physical address you determined in Exercise 2, without dashes.

   For example, for the physical address 00-aa-00-4a-de-14, you would type 00aa004ade14 in the MAC Address box.

6. In the Name box, type **Server1** (or the name of your computer).

7. Click Add.

8. Click Close.

9. Double-click Reservation.

   Notice that the reservation has been added.

10. Right click the Scope listing, point to All Tasks, and click Activate.

    Does the icon for the scope change?

11. Close the DHCP Server Management snap-in.

Lesson Summary

The first step in implementing the DHCP Service is to specify a static IP address, subnet mask, and default gateway address for all network adapters bound to TCP/IP in the computer designated as the DHCP server. You then use Add/Remove Programs in Control Panel to install the DHCP Service. After, you have installed the DHCP Service, you must create a scope. A scope is a pool of valid IP addresses available for lease to DHCP clients. You must create at least one scope for every DHCP server, and you must exclude static IP addresses from the scope.

For some DHCP clients, it is important that they always lease the same IP address. For these clients, you can configure the DHCP Service so that it always assigns them same IP address. This is called a client reservation.

Lesson 3: Backing Up and Restoring the DHCP Database

You can edit the registry to specify the interval at which Windows 2000 backs up the DHCP database. In addition, you can manually restore the DHCP database by editing the registry.

After this lesson, you will be able to

- Explain how to back up and restore the DHCP database.

Estimated lesson time: 5 minutes

Backing Up the DHCP Database

By default, Windows 2000 backs up the DHCP database every 60 minutes. Windows 2000 stores the backup copies of the file in the *systemroot*\System32\ DHCP\Backup\Jet directory, where *systemroot* indicates the Windows 2000 installation folder, typically C:\Winnt.

You can change the default backup interval by changing the value, representing the number of minutes between backups, of the BackupInterval entry located in the registry under the following key:

HKEY_LOCAL_MACHINE\SYSTEM\CurrentControlSet\Services \DHCPServer\Parameters

Windows 2000 stores a copy of this registry subkey in the *systemroot*\System32\ DHCP\Backup directory as DHCPCFG.

Restoring the DHCP Database

By default, the DHCP Service restores a corrupt DHCP database automatically when you restart the DHCP Service. However, you can also manually restore the DHCP database file.

To manually restore the DHCP database, edit the registry and set the value for the RestoreFlag entry to 1 and then restart the DHCP Service. The RestoreFlag entry is located in the registry under the following subkey:

HKEY_LOCAL_MACHINE\SYSTEM\CurrentControlSet\Services \DHCPServer\Parameters

Note   After the DHCP Service successfully restores the database, the server automatically changes the RestoreFlag parameter to the default value of 0.

You can also restore the DHCP database file manually by copying the contents of the *systemroot*\System32\DHCP\Backup\Jet directory to the *systemroot*\ System32\DHCP directory and then restarting the DHCP Service.

Table 9.3 describes some of the files that are stored in the *\systemroot* System32\ DHCP directory.

Table 9.3   Files stored in \systemroot\System32\DHCP

File	Description
Dhcp.mdb	The DHCP database file.
Tmp.edb	A temporary file that the DHCP Service creates for temporary database information while the DHCP Service is running.
J50.log and J50*.LOG	Log files, including all transactions done with the database. The DHCP Service uses these files to recover data, if necessary.

Important   Do not tamper with or remove these files.

Lesson Summary

In this lesson you learned about backing up and restoring the DHCP database. By default, Windows 2000 backs up the DHCP database every 60 minutes. However, you can edit the registry and change the default backup interval. To change the backup interval, change the value of the BackupInterval entry, which represents the number of minutes between backups.

By default, the DHCP Service restores a corrupt DHCP database automatically when you restart the DHCP Service. However, you can also manually restore the DHCP database file. To manually restore the DHCP database, edit the registry and set the value for the RestoreFlag entry to 1 and then restart the DHCP Service.

Review

Here are some questions to help you determine if you have learned enough to move on to the next chapter. If you have difficulty answering these questions, please go back and review the material in this chapter before beginning the next chapter. The answers for these questions are located in Appendix A, "Questions and Answers."

1. What are the benefits of using the DHCP Service to automatically configure IP addressing information?

2. What are the steps in the DHCP lease process?

3. When do DHCP clients attempt to renew their leases?

4. Why might you create multiple scopes on a DHCP server?

5. How can you manually restore the DHCP database?

6. What three things should you consider when planning DHCP implementation?

C H A P T E R   1 0

Configuring the
Windows Internet Name Service

About This Chapter

This chapter explains the purpose and function of the Windows Internet Name Service (WINS), as well as name registration. It also explains the WINS server and client configuration, support for non-WINS clients, and DHCP server for WINS configuration.

Before You Begin

To complete this chapter, you must have

- A computer that meets the minimum hardware requirements listed in "Hardware Requirements," on page xxxiii.
- Installed the Windows 2000 Server software on the computer.
- Configured the computer as a stand-alone server in a workgroup.
- Installed TCP/IP as the only protocol.

Lesson 1: Understanding the Windows Internet Name Service

In a mixed network environment, down-level clients, such as computers running Microsoft Windows 98 or Microsoft Windows NT version 4.0, use Network Basic Input/Output System (NetBIOS) names to communicate. As a result, a Microsoft Windows 2000 network with down-level clients requires a means of resolving NetBIOS names to Internet Protocol (IP) addresses. The *Windows Internet Name Service (WINS)* is an enhanced NetBIOS name server that registers NetBIOS computer names and resolves them to IP addresses. WINS also provides a dynamic database that maintains mapping of computer names to IP addresses.

After this lesson, you will be able to

- Explain the purpose and function of the WINS process.
- Explain WINS name registration.
- Explain WINS name renewal and name release.
- Explain WINS name query.

Estimated lesson time: 15 minutes

The WINS Name Resolution Process

The WINS name resolution process allows WINS clients to register their name and IP address with WINS servers. The WINS clients can query the WINS servers to locate and communicate with other resources on the network. Figure 10.1 shows the WINS name resolution process and the steps by which WINS resolves NetBIOS names to IP addresses.

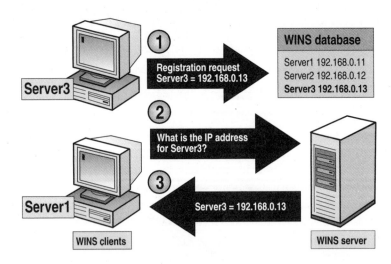

Figure 10.1   WINS name resolution process

The steps in the WINS name resolution process are explained below.

1. Every time that a WINS client starts, it registers its NetBIOS name/IP address mapping with a designated WINS server. It then queries the WINS server for computer name resolution.

Note A WINS client automatically updates the WINS database whenever its IP addressing information changes, for example, when dynamic addressing through the Dynamic Host Configuration Protocol (DHCP) results in a new IP address for a computer that moved between subnets.

---

2. When a WINS client initiates a NetBIOS command to communicate with another network resource, it sends the name query request directly to the WINS server instead of broadcasting the request on the local network.

3. The WINS server finds a NetBIOS name/IP address mapping for the destination resource in this database, and it returns the IP address to the WINS client.

Name Registration

Each WINS client is configured with the IP address of a primary WINS server and optionally, a secondary WINS server. When a client starts, it registers its NetBIOS name and IP address by sending a name registration request directly to the configured WINS server.

If the WINS server is available and another WINS client has not registered the name already, the WINS server returns a successful registration message to the client. This message contains the amount of time that the NetBIOS name is registered to the client, specified as the *Time to Live (TTL)*. In addition, the WINS server stores the client's NetBIOS name/IP address mapping in its database. In Figure 10.1, Server3 sends a name registration request to the WINS server. The name registration is successful, so when Server1 requests the IP address of Server3 from the WINS server, the WINS server can respond with the IP address for Server3.

When a Name Is Already Registered

When a name is already registered in the WINS database, the WINS server sends a name query request to the currently registered owner of the name. The WINS server sends the request three times at 500-millisecond intervals. If the registered computer is a multihomed computer, which means it has more than one network adapter card bound to TCP/IP and has an IP address for each network adapter card, the WINS server tries each IP address it has for the computer until it receives a response or until it has tried all the IP addresses.

If the current registered owner responds successfully to the WINS server, the WINS server sends a negative name registration response to the WINS client that is attempting to register the name. However, if the current registered owner does not respond to the WINS server, the WINS server sends a successful name registration response to the WINS client that is attempting to register the name.

When the WINS Server Is Unavailable

A WINS client makes three attempts to find the primary WINS server. If the client fails after the third attempt, it sends the name registration request to the secondary WINS server (if one is configured for the client). If neither server is available, the WINS client might initiate a broadcast to register its name.

Name Renewal

A WINS server registers all NetBIOS names on a temporary basis so that other computers can use the same name later if the original owner stops using it. Since client name registrations with a WINS server are temporary, a WINS client must renew its name or the lease will expire.

To continue using the same NetBIOS name, a client must renew its lease before the lease expires. If a client does not renew its lease, the WINS server makes the lease available for another WINS client.

A WINS client first attempts to refresh its lease after one-eighth of the TTL interval has expired. If the WINS client does not receive a name refresh response, it continues attempting to refresh its lease every two minutes, until half of the TTL interval has expired.

When half of the TTL interval has expired, the WINS client attempts to refresh its lease with a secondary WINS server, if configured. When switching to a secondary WINS server, the WINS client attempts to refresh its lease as if it were the first refresh attempt—every one-eighth of the TTL interval until successful or until half the TTL interval has expired (four tries). The WINS client then reverts to the primary WINS server.

When a WINS server receives the name refresh request, it sends the client a name refresh response with a new TTL. After a client successfully refreshes its lease one time, it will attempt to refresh its lease when half the TTL interval has expired.

Name Release

In addition, when a WINS client's name is no longer in use, the client sends a message to the WINS server to release the name.

When you shut down a WINS client properly, the client sends a name release request directly to the WINS server for each registered name. The request includes the client's IP address and the NetBIOS name to remove from the WINS database.

When the WINS server receives the name release request, it checks its database for the specified name. If the WINS server encounters a database error, or if a different IP address maps the registered name, it sends a negative name release to the WINS client. Otherwise, the WINS server sends a positive name release, and then the server designates the specified name as released in its database. The name release response contains the released NetBIOS name and a TTL value of zero.

Name Query

After a WINS client has registered its NetBIOS name and IP address with a WINS server, it can communicate with other hosts by obtaining the IP address of other NetBIOS-based computers from the WINS server.

By default, a WINS client attempts to resolve another host's NetBIOS name to an IP address in the following manner:

1. The client checks its NetBIOS name cache for the NetBIOS name/IP address mapping of the destination computer.

2. If the client cannot resolve the name from its cache, it sends a name query request directly to its primary WINS server.

3. If the primary WINS server is unavailable, the client resends the request two more times before switching to the secondary WINS server.

4. If either WINS server, primary or secondary, resolves the name, it sends a response to the client with the IP address for the requested NetBIOS name.

5. If no WINS server can resolve the name, the client receives a `Requested name does not exist` message, and then the client initiates a network broadcast.

Note   All WINS communications use directed datagrams over User Datagram Protocol (UDP) port 137 (NetBIOS Name Service).

Lesson Summary

In this lesson you learned about the WINS name resolution process. Name registration is an important part of the name resolution process. Each WINS client is configured with the IP address of a primary WINS server and, optionally, a secondary WINS server. Each time a WINS client starts, it registers its NetBIOS name and IP address by sending a name registration request directly to the configured WINS server.

Another important part of the name resolution process is the name query. By default, a WINS client attempts to resolve another host's NetBIOS name to an IP address by checking its NetBIOS name cache. If the client cannot resolve the name from its cache, it sends a name query request directly to its primary WINS server. If the WINS server finds the NetBIOS name/IP address mapping for the destination resource in this database, it returns the IP address to the WINS client. If the primary WINS server is unavailable, the client resends the request two more times before switching to the secondary WINS server. If neither WINS server can resolve the name, the client receives a message indicating that the requested name does not exist, and then the client initiates a network broadcast.

Two other important parts of the name resolution process are name renewal and name release. A WINS server registers all NetBIOS names on a temporary basis, so a WINS client must renew its name or the lease will expire. When a WINS server receives the name refresh request, it sends the client a name refresh response with a new TTL. In addition, when a WINS client's name is no longer in use, the client sends a message to the WINS server to release the name. When the WINS server receives the name release request, it checks its database for the specified name. If the WINS server finds the correct NetBIOS name/IP address mapping in its database, it sends a positive name release, and then the server designates the specified name as released in its database.

Lesson 2: Implementing WINS

To implement WINS, you must install and configure WINS on a computer running Windows 2000 Server. In addition, you must configure selected options on computers that participate as WINS clients. This lesson describes the process for implementing WINS, with information on using the Windows Internet Name Service snap-in. This lesson also includes information on support for non-WINS clients and configuration for a server running the DHCP Service for WINS.

After this lesson, you will be able to
- Explain how to implement WINS.

Estimated lesson time: 20 minutes

WINS Server Configuration

A WINS server requires a computer running Windows 2000 Server; however, the server does not need to be a domain controller. In addition, you must configure the following:

- The Windows Internet Name Service
- A static IP address, subnet mask, and default gateway

In addition, you also can configure the following, as necessary:

- A static mapping for all non-WINS clients to allow communication with WINS clients on remote networks
- A WINS proxy agent to extend the name resolution capabilities of WINS to non-WINS clients
- WINS support on a DHCP server

WINS Client Configuration

A WINS client must be running one of the following operating systems:

- Windows 2000.
- Windows NT Server version 3.5 or later or Windows NT Workstation version 3.5 or later.
- Windows 95 or later.
- Windows for Workgroups version 3.11 running Microsoft TCP/IP-32, which is included on the Windows 2000 Server CD-ROM.

- Microsoft Network Client version 3.0 for Microsoft MS-DOS with the real-mode TCP/IP driver, which is included on the Windows 2000 Server CD-ROM.

- LAN Manager version 2.2c for MS-DOS, which is included on the Windows 2000 Server CD-ROM. LAN Manager version 2.2c for OS/2 is not supported.

A WINS client also requires the IP address of a primary WINS server, and, optionally, the IP address of a secondary WINS server.

WINS Installation

WINS is not installed as part of the default Windows 2000 installation. You must add the service, as outlined below.

▶ **To install WINS**

1. In Control Panel, double-click Add/Remove Programs.
2. In the Add/Remove Programs window, click Configure Windows, and then click Components.

   The Windows Components wizard appears.
3. Click Next.

   Note In the following step, do not change the status of the check box to the left of Optional Networking Components. If the check box is already selected, it indicates some other networking components, such as DHCP, have already been installed.

   ---

4. In the Components list box, click Optional Networking Components, and then click Details.
5. On the Optional Networking Components page, shown in Figure 10.2, in the Subcomponents Of Optional Networking Components list, select the check box to the left of Windows Internet Name Service, and then click OK.
6. Click Next on the Windows NT Components page to install WINS.
7. When installation is complete, close Add/Remove Programs.

After you install WINS on a computer, you should configure its TCP/IP properties so that the computer points to itself. You do this on the WINS tab of the Advanced TCP/IP Settings dialog box.

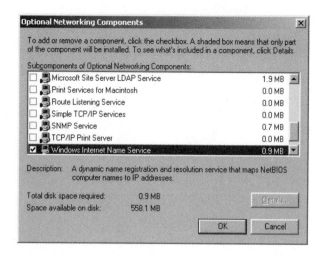

Figure 10.2 The Optional Networking Components dialog box

▶ **To configure TCP/IP properties so that the computer points to itself**

1. Right-click My Network Places, and choose Properties to open the Network and Dial-Up Connections dialog box.

2. Right-click Local Area Connection, and choose Properties.

3. Select Internet Protocol (TCP/IP), and click Properties.

4. Click the Advanced button on the Internet Protocol (TCP/IP) Properties dialog box.

5. Click the WINS tab of the Advanced TCP/IP Properties dialog box, and then click the Add button.

6. Add the IP address of the computer running the WINS service as one of the WINS addresses. If the computer you are operating is the one running the WINS service, the IP address is the one shown on the IP Settings tab.

7. Click Add to add the IP address, and repeat steps 5 and 6 to add a secondary WINS IP address.

8. Click OK to close each dialog box, and then close the Network Connections dialog box.

The Windows Internet Name Service Snap-In

Use the Windows Internet Name Service (WINS) snap-in, shown in Figure 10.3, for all WINS management and configuration tasks. The Windows Internet Name Service snap-in provides access to detailed information about the WINS servers on a network. The snap-in also provides the ability to view the contents of the WINS database and search for specific entries.

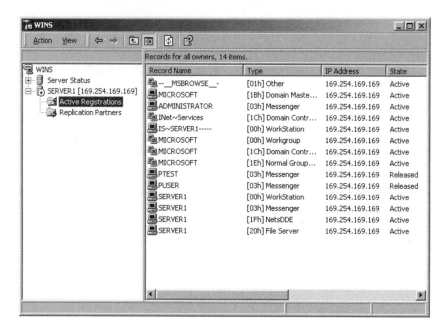

Figure 10.3   The WINS snap-in

Launch the WINS snap-in from the Administrative Tools menu on computers running Windows 2000.

Note   You must install WINS before you can use the Windows Internet Name Service snap-in.

Support for Non-WINS Clients

In a WINS environment, you can provide support for non-WINS clients by using static mappings and configuring a WINS proxy agent.

Static Mappings

On a network that includes non-WINS clients, you can configure a static NetBIOS name/IP address mapping for each non-WINS client. This ensures that WINS clients can resolve the NetBIOS names of the non-WINS clients.

Note   If you have DHCP clients that require a static mapping, you must reserve an IP address for the DHCP client so that its IP address is always the same.

▶   **To configure a static entry for non-WINS clients**

1. Start the Windows Internet Name Service snap-in.

2. In the WINS window, expand the entry for the WINS servers.

3. Right-click Active Registrations, point to New, and then click Static Mapping.

4. In the Create Static Mapping dialog box, in the Computer Name box, type the computer name of the non-WINS client.

5. In the Scope box, type an optional scope.

   A NetBIOS *scope* is an optional extension to a computer name that you can use to group computers in a network.

6. Under Type, select an option to specify the type of entry that you are creating, as described in the following table.

Option	Description
Unique	A unique name that maps to a single IP address.
Group	A name that maps to a group. When adding an entry to a group by using the Windows Internet Name Service snap-in, enter the computer name and IP address. The IP addresses of group members are not stored in the WINS database, so there is no limit to the number of members that you can add.
Domain Name	A NetBIOS name/IP address mapping with 0x1C as the 16th byte. A domain group stores up to 25 addresses for members. For registrations after the 25th address, WINS overwrites a replica address or, if none is present, it overwrites the oldest registration.
Internet Group	User-defined groups that you use to group resources, such as printers, for reference and browsing. An Internet group can store up to 25 addresses for members. A dynamic member, however, does not replace a static member that you add by using WINS Manager or by importing the LMHOSTS file.
Multihomed	A unique name that can have more than one address. Use this option for computers with multiple network adapters. You can register up to 25 multihomed addresses. For registrations after the 25th address, WINS overwrites a replica address or, if none is present, it overwrites the oldest registration.

7. In the IP Address box, type the IP address of the non-WINS client.

8. In the Create Static Mapping dialog box, click OK.

Note The Windows Internet Name Service snap-in adds a static mapping to the WINS database when you click OK. If you enter incorrect information for a static mapping, you must delete the entries for the mapping from the list of active registrations for the specific WINS server and then create a new static mapping.

Configuring a WINS Proxy Agent

A WINS proxy agent extends the name resolution capabilities of the WINS server to non-WINS clients by listening for broadcast name registrations and broadcast resolution requests and then forwarding them to a WINS server.

- **NetBIOS name registration.**   When a non-WINS client broadcasts a name registration request, the WINS proxy agent forwards the request to the WINS server to verify that no other WINS client has registered that name. The NetBIOS name does not get registered, only verified.

- **NetBIOS name resolution.**   When a WINS proxy agent detects a name resolution broadcast, it checks its NetBIOS name cache and attempts to resolve the name. If the name is not in cache, the request is sent to a WINS server. The WINS server sends the WINS proxy agent the IP address for the requested NetBIOS name. The WINS proxy agent returns this information to the non-WINS client.

To configure a WINS proxy agent, edit the registry and set the value for the EnableProxy entry to 1, and then restart the computer. The EnableProxy entry is located in the registry under the following subkey:

HKEY_LOCAL_MACHINE\SYSTEM\CurrentControlSet\Services \NetBT\Parameters.

DHCP Server Configuration

If a computer is a DHCP client, you can configure WINS support by using the DHCP Server Management snap-in (see Figure 10.4).

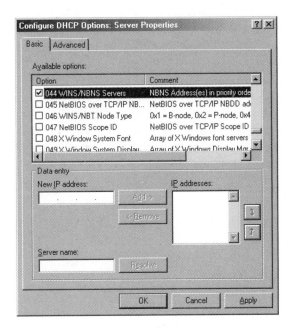

Figure 10.4   The DHCP Server Management snap-in

You use the DHCP Server Management snap-in to add and configure the DHCP scope option **044 WINS/NBNS Servers** and configure the address of primary and secondary servers.

When the DHCP client leases or renews an address lease, it receives this DHCP scope option, and the client is configured for WINS support.

Note   If you configure a client computer with IP addresses for a primary and secondary WINS server, those values take precedence over the same parameters provided by a DHCP server.

You also can configure the following DHCP scope option **046 WINS/NBT Node Type** and configure to 0x8 (H-node).

Note   For more information about node types, see RFC 1001 and RFC 1002. An *RFC (Request for Comment)* is a document in which a standard, a protocol, or other information pertaining to the operation of the Internet is published. The RFC is actually issued *after* discussion and serves as the standard. You can find the text of each RFC that is cited in this book (as well as much associated discussion material) on the Internet. Use your Web browser and search, using any of the popular search engines on the Internet, to find the RFC of interest. In this case, search for "RFC 1001" and then search again for "RFC 1002."

Lesson Summary

In this lesson you learned that to implement WINS, you must install and configure WINS on a computer running Window 2000 Server. To install WINS, you use the Windows Components wizard. You access the Windows Components wizard through Add/Remove Programs in Control Panel. In addition to installing WINS, you must configure selected options on computers that participate as WINS clients. This lesson also described using the Windows Internet Name Service snap-in, which provides access to detailed information about the WINS servers on a network and provides the ability to view the contents of the WINS database and search for specific entries.

Review

Here are some questions to help you determine if you have learned enough to move on to the next chapter. If you have difficulty answering these questions, please go back and review the material in this chapter before beginning the next chapter. The answers for these questions are located in Appendix A, "Questions and Answers."

1. Why would a WINS client broadcast a name query request?

2. What happens when a WINS server receives a name registration request with a NetBIOS name/IP address mapping that is already registered in the WINS database?

3. When does a WINS client first attempt to refresh its name registrations?

4. By default, where does a WINS client first check in an attempt to resolve another host's NetBIOS name to an IP address?

5. What are the configuration requirements for a WINS server?

CHAPTER 11

Configuring the DNS Service

About This Chapter

Domain Name System (DNS) is a distributed database that is used in Transmission Control Protocol/Internet Protocol (TCP/IP) networks to translate computer names to Internet Protocol (IP) addresses.

This chapter begins with an introduction to DNS and name resolution. It also presents the skills and knowledge necessary to install and configure the DNS service.

Before You Begin

To complete this chapter, you must have

- A computer that meets the minimum hardware requirements listed in "Hardware Requirements," on page xxxiii.
- Installed the Windows 2000 Server software on the computer.
- Configured the computer as a stand-alone server in a workgroup.
- Installed TCP/IP as the only protocol.

Lesson 1: Understanding DNS

DNS is most commonly associated with the Internet. However, private networks use DNS extensively to resolve computer names and to locate computers within their local networks and the Internet. DNS provides the following benefits:

- DNS names are user-friendly, which means that they are easier to remember than IP addresses.

- DNS names remain more constant than IP addresses. An IP address for a server can change, but the server name remains the same.

- DNS allows users to connect to local servers by using the same naming convention as the Internet.

Note   For more information on DNS, see RFC 1034 and RFC 1035. To read the text of these RFCs (Requests for Comment), use your Web browser to search for "RFC 1034" and "RFC 1035."

After this lesson, you will be able to
- Explain the function of DNS and its components.

Estimated lesson time: 15 minutes

Domain Name Space

The *domain name space* is the naming scheme that provides the hierarchical structure for the DNS database. Each node represents a partition of the DNS database. These nodes are referred to as *domains*.

The DNS database is indexed by name; therefore, each domain must have a name. As you add domains to the hierarchy, the name of the parent domain is appended to its child domain (called a subdomain). Consequently, a domain's name identifies its position in the hierarchy. For example, in Figure 11.1, the domain name

sales.microsoft.com

identifies the sales domain as a subdomain of the microsoft.com domain and microsoft as a subdomain of the com domain.

The hierarchical structure of the domain name space consists of a root domain, top-level domains, second-level domains, and host names.

Note   The term domain, in the context of DNS, is not related to domain as used in the Microsoft Windows 2000 directory services. A Windows 2000 domain is a grouping of computers and devices that are administered as a unit.

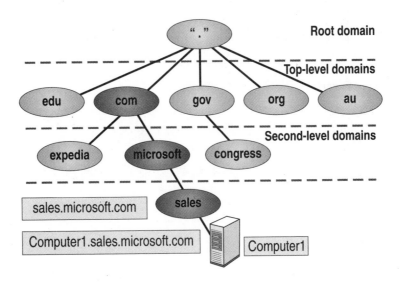

Figure 11.1 Hierarchical structure of a domain name space

Root Domain

The root domain is at the top of the hierarchy and is represented as a period (.). The Internet root domain is managed by several organizations, including Network Solutions, Inc.

Top-Level Domains

Top-level domains are two- or three-character name codes. Top-level domains are organized by organization type or geographic location. Table 11.1 provides some examples of top-level domain names.

Table 11.1   Top-Level Domains

Top-level domain	Description
gov	Government organizations
com	Commercial organizations
edu	Educational institutions
org	Noncommercial organizations
au	Country code of Australia

Top-level domains can contain second-level domains and host names.

Second-Level Domains

Organizations, such as Network Solutions, Inc., assign and register second-level domains to individuals and organizations for the Internet. A second-level name has two name parts: a top-level name and a unique second-level name. Table 11.2 provides some examples of second-level domains.

Table 11.2   Second-Level Domains

Second-level domain	Description
Ed.gov	United States Department of Education
Microsoft.com	Microsoft Corporation
Stanford.edu	Stanford University
W3.org	World Wide Web Consortium
Pm.gov.au	Prime Minister of Australia

Host Names

Host names refer to specific computers on the Internet or a private network. For example, in Figure 11.1, Computer1 is a host name. A host name is the leftmost portion of a *fully qualified domain name (FQDN),* which describes the exact position of a host within the domain hierarchy. In Figure 11.1, Computer1.sales.microsoft.com. (including the end period, which represents the root domain) is an FQDN.

DNS uses a host's FQDN to resolve a name to an IP address.

Note   The host name does not have to be the same as the computer name. By default, TCP/IP setup uses the computer name for the host name, replacing illegal characters, such as the underscore (_), with a hyphen (-). For the accepted domain naming conventions, see RFC 1035.

Domain Naming Guidelines

When you create a domain name space, consider the following domain guidelines and standard naming conventions:

- Limit the number of domain levels. Typically, DNS host entries should be three or four levels down the DNS hierarchy and no more than five levels down the hierarchy. The numbers of levels increase the administrative tasks.

- Use unique names. Each subdomain must have a unique name within its parent domain to ensure that the name is unique throughout the DNS name space.

- Use simple names. Simple and precise domain names are easier for users to remember and enable users to search intuitively and locate Web sites or other computers on the Internet or an intranet.

- Avoid lengthy domain names. Domain names can be up to 63 characters, including the periods. The total length of an FQDN cannot exceed 255 characters. Case-sensitive naming is not supported.

- Use standard DNS characters and Unicode characters.

- Windows 2000 supports the following standard DNS characters: A–Z, a–z, 0–9, and the hyphen (-), as defined in RFC 1035.

- The DNS Service also supports the Unicode character set. The Unicode character set includes additional characters not found in the American Standard Code for Information Exchange (ASCII) character set, which are required for languages such as French, German, and Spanish.

Note   Use Unicode characters only if all servers running the DNS Service in your environment support Unicode. For more information on the Unicode character set, read RFC 2044 by searching for "RFC 2044" with your Web browser.

Zones

A zone represents a discrete portion of the domain name space. Zones provide a way to partition the domain name space into manageable sections.

- Multiple zones in a domain name space are used to distribute administrative tasks to different groups. For example, Figure 11.2 depicts the microsoft.com domain name space divided into two zones. The two zones allow one administrator to manage the microsoft and sales domains and another administrator to manage the development domain.

- A zone must encompass a contiguous domain name space. For example in Figure 11.2, you could not create a zone that consists of only the sales.microsoft.com and development.microsoft.com domains, because these two domains are not contiguous.

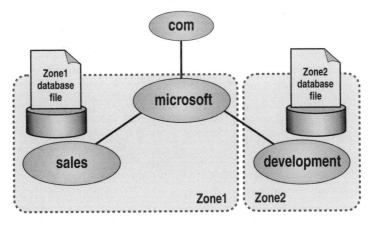

Figure 11.2   Domain name space divided into zones

The name-to-IP-address mappings for a zone are stored in the zone database file. Each zone is anchored to a specific domain, referred to as the zone's root domain. The zone database file does not necessarily contain information for all subdomains of the zone's root domain, only those subdomains within the zone.

In Figure 11.2, the root domain for Zone1 is microsoft.com, and its zone file contains the name to IP address mappings for the microsoft and sales domains. The root domain for Zone2 is development, and its zone file contains the name to IP address mappings for the development domain only. The zone file for Zone1 does not contain the name to IP address mappings for the development domain, although development is a subdomain of the microsoft domain.

Name Servers

A DNS name server stores the zone database file. Name servers can store data for one zone or multiple zones. A name server is said to have authority for the domain name space that the zone encompasses.

One name server contains the master zone database file, referred to as the *primary zone database file,* for the specified zone. As a result, there must be at least one name server for a zone. Changes to a zone, such as adding domains or hosts, are performed on the server that contains the primary zone database file.

Multiple name servers act as a backup to the name server containing the primary zone database file. Multiple name servers provide the following advantages. They

- Perform zone transfers. The additional name servers obtain a copy of the zone database file from the name server that contains the primary database zone file. This is called a *zone transfer*. These name servers periodically query the name server containing the primary zone database file for updated zone data.

> **Note**   To configure the zone transfer interval rate, use the DNS Manager snap-in.

- Provide redundancy. If the name server containing the primary zone database file fails, the additional name servers can provide service.

- Improve access speed for remote locations. If there are a number of clients in remote locations, use additional name servers to reduce query traffic across slow wide area network (WAN) links.

- Reduce the load on the name server containing the primary zone database file.

Lesson Summary

In this lesson you learned that DNS is most commonly associated with the Internet. However, many private networks also use DNS to resolve computer names and to locate computers within their local networks and the Internet. You also learned some of the benefits DNS provides. These benefits include providing user-friendly DNS names that are less likely to change than IP addresses and allowing users to connect to local servers by using the same naming convention as the Internet.

In this lesson you learned that the domain name space is the naming scheme that provides the hierarchical structure for the DNS database. The DNS database is indexed by name, so each domain (node) must have a name. The hierarchical structure of the domain name space consists of a root domain, top-level domains, second-level domains, and host names. Host names refer to specific computers on the Internet or a private network. A host name is the leftmost portion of a fully qualified domain name (FQDN), which describes the exact position of a host within the domain hierarchy.

In this lesson you also learned some domain naming guidelines, such as limiting the number of domain levels, using unique names, and using simple names. You learned that zones provide a way to partition the domain name space into smaller sections and that a zone represents a discrete portion of the domain name space. Finally, in this lesson you learned that a DNS name server stores the zone database file and that name servers can store data for one zone or multiple zones.

Lesson 2: Understanding Name Resolution

Name resolution is the process of resolving names to IP addresses. Name resolution is similar to looking up a name in a telephone book, where the name is associated with a telephone number. For example, when you connect to the Microsoft Web site, you use the name www.microsoft.com. DNS resolves www.microsoft.com to its associated IP address. The mapping of names to IP addresses is stored in the DNS distributed database.

DNS name servers resolve forward and reverse lookup queries. A forward lookup query resolves a name to an IP address. A reverse lookup query resolves an IP address to a name. A name server can only resolve a query for a zone for which it has authority. If a name server cannot resolve the query, it passes the query to other name servers that can resolve the query. The name server caches the query results to reduce the DNS traffic on the network.

After this lesson, you will be able to
- Explain the name resolution process.

Estimated lesson time: 5 minutes

Forward Lookup Query

The DNS Service uses a client/server model for name resolution. To resolve a forward lookup query, a client passes a query to a local name server. The local name server either resolves the query or queries another name server for resolution.

Figure 11.3 represents a client querying the name server for an IP address of www.microsoft.com. The numbers in the figure depict the following activities:

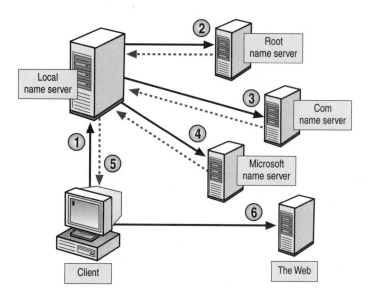

Figure 11.3   Resolving a forward lookup query

1. The client passes a forward lookup query for www.microsoft.com to its local name server.

2. The local name server checks its zone database file to determine whether it contains the name to IP address mapping for the client query. The local name server does not have authority for the microsoft.com domain. So it passes the query to one of the DNS root servers, requesting resolution of the host name. The root name server sends back a referral to the com name servers.

3. The local name server sends a request to a com name server, which responds with a referral to the Microsoft name servers.

4. The local name server sends a request to the Microsoft name server. The Microsoft name server receives the request. Because the Microsoft name server has authority for that portion of the domain name space, it returns the IP address for www.microsoft.com to the local name server.

5. The name server sends the IP address for www.microsoft.com to the client.

6. The name resolution is complete, and the client can access www.microsoft.com.

Name Server Caching

When a name server is processing a query, it might be required to send out several queries to find the answer. With each query, the name server discovers other name servers that have authority for a portion of the domain name space. The name server caches these query results to reduce network traffic.

When a name server receives a query result the following actions take place (see Figure 11.4):

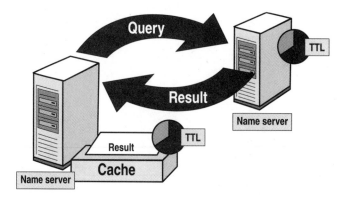

Figure 11.4 Caching query results

1. The name server caches the query result for a specified amount of time, referred to as Time to Live (TTL).

Note The zone that provided the query results specifies the TTL. TTL is configured by using the DNS Manager snap-in. The default value is 60 minutes.

---

2. Once the name server caches the query result, TTL starts counting down from its original value.
3. When TTL expires, the name server deletes the query result from its cache.

Caching query results enable the name server to resolve other queries to the same portion of the domain name space quickly.

Note Use shorter TTL values to help ensure that data about the domain name space is more current across the network. Shorter TTL values *do* increase the load on name servers, however. A longer TTL value decreases the time required to resolve information. However, if a change does occur, the client will not receive the updated information until the TTL expires and a new query to that portion of the domain name space is resolved.

Reverse Lookup Query

A reverse lookup query maps an IP address to a name. Troubleshooting tools, such as the nslookup command-line utility, use reverse lookup queries to report back host names. Additionally, certain applications implement security based on the ability to connect to names, not IP addresses.

Because the DNS distributed database is indexed by name and not by IP address, a reverse lookup query would require an exhaustive search of every domain name. To solve this problem, a special second-level domain called *in-addr.arpa* was created.

The in-addr.arpa domain follows the same hierarchical naming scheme as the rest of the domain name space; however, it is based on IP addresses, not domain names:

- Subdomains are named after the numbers in the dotted-decimal representation of IP addresses.

- The order of the IP address octets is reversed.

- Companies administer subdomains of the in-addr.arpa domain based on their assigned IP addresses and subnet mask.

For example, Figure 11.5 shows a dotted-decimal representation of the IP address 169.254.16.200. A company that has an assigned IP address range of 169.254.16.0 to 169.254.16.255 with a subnet mask of 255.255.255.0 will have authority over the 16.254.169.in-addr.arpa domain.

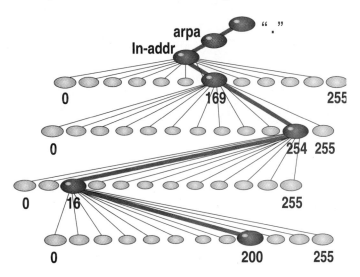

Figure 11.5   The in-addr.arpa domain

Lesson Summary

In this lesson you learned that name resolution is the process of resolving names to IP addresses and that the mapping of names to IP addresses is stored in the DNS distributed database. You learned that DNS name servers resolve forward lookup queries and what happens when a client queries the name server for an IP address. You also learned about name server caching and that the name server caches the query results to reduce the DNS traffic on the network.

In addition to forward lookup queries, DNS name servers resolve reverse lookup queries. A reverse lookup query resolves an IP address to a name. Because the DNS distributed database is indexed by name and not by IP address, a special second-level domain called in-addr.arpa was created. The in-addr.arpa domain follows the same hierarchical naming scheme as the rest of the domain name space; however, it is based on IP addresses instead of domain names.

Lesson 3: Installing the DNS Service

Now that you have been introduced to DNS, the Windows 2000 DNS Service, and name resolution, you are ready to learn how to install the Microsoft DNS Server Service on a computer running Windows 2000 Server. To implement DNS, you must configure the server and then install the DNS Service.

After this lesson, you will be able to

- Install the DNS Service.

Estimated lesson time: 25 minutes

Preinstallation Configuration

Configure the following options on the server on which you are going to install the DNS Service:

- Assign a static IP address in the Internet Protocol (TCP/IP) Properties dialog box.

- Configure the appropriate IP address of the DNS server and DNS domain name. Using My Network Places, click Advanced in the Internet Protocol (TCP/IP) Properties dialog box to configure the advanced TCP/IP settings. On the DNS tab, type the DNS address and domain name.

Installation Process

Install the DNS Service anytime after the Windows 2000 initial setup, or you can choose to install the DNS Service during setup. In addition to installing the DNS Service, the DNS installation process does the following:

- Installs DNS Manager and adds a shortcut to Administrative Tools on the Start menu. DNS Manager is the Microsoft Management Console (MMC) snap-in that you use to manage local and remote DNS name servers.

- Adds the following key for the DNS Service to the registry:

  HKEY_LOCAL_MACHINE\System\CurrentControlSet\Services\Dns

- Creates the C:\Winnt\System32\Dns directory, which contains the DNS database files that are described in Table 11.3.

Note Generally, you will not need to edit the DNS database files. However, you might use them to troubleshoot DNS. For additional information and sample files, see the C:\Winnt\System32\Dns\Samples directory after you have installed the DNS Service.

Table 11.3   DNS Database

Filename	Description
Domain.dns	The zone database file that maps host names to IP addresses for a zone.
z.y.w.x.in-addr.arpa	The reverse lookup file that maps IP addresses to host names.
Cache.dns	The cache file that contains the required host information for resolving names outside of authoritative domains. The default file contains records for all the root servers on the Internet.
Boot	The boot file that controls how the DNS Service starts up. In Windows 2000, the boot file is optional, because the boot settings are also stored in the registry.

Note   The boot file is not defined in an RFC and is not needed for RFC compliance. The boot file is a part of the Berkeley Internet Name Daemon (BIND)–specific implementation of DNS. If you are migrating from a BIND DNS server, copying the boot file allows easy migration of your existing configuration.

Practice: Installing the DNS Service

In this practice you install the DNS Server Service. In Exercise 1 you configure TCP/IP in preparation for Exercise 2, in which the actual DNS Service is installed.

Exercise 1: Configuring TCP/IP for DNS

In this exercise, you configure TCP/IP for DNS. This is part of the configuration you do to prepare to install Microsoft DNS Server.

▶   **To configure TCP/IP for DNS**

1. Log on as Administrator.

2. Right-click My Network Places, and then click Properties.

   The Network And Dial-up Connections window appears.

3. Right-click Local Area Connection, and then click Properties.

   The Local Area Connection Properties dialog box appears, displaying the network adapter in use and the network components used in this connection.

4. Click Internet Protocol (TCP/IP), and then verify that the check box to the left of the entry is selected.

5. Click Properties.

   The Internet Protocol (TCP/IP) Properties dialog box appears.

6. Verify that Use The Following IP Address is selected.

7. In the IP Address box, type **192.168.1.201**

In the Subnet Mask box, ensure that 255.255.255.0 is the value and leave the Default Gateway box empty.

If you are not using these suggested values, enter the IP address, subnet mask, and default gateway that you are using.

Important   Be careful when manually entering IP configuration settings, especially numeric addresses. The most frequent cause of TCP/IP connection problems is incorrectly entered IP address information.

---

8. Ensure that Use The Following DNS Server Addresses is selected.

9. In the Preferred DNS Server box, type your computer's assigned IP address.

10. Click Advanced.

    The Advanced TCP/IP Settings dialog box appears.

11. Click the DNS tab.

12. In the DNS Domain Name box, type **microsoft.com** and then click OK. (If you are on a network, check with your network administrator to make sure it is OK to use this as your DNS domain name.).

13. Click OK to close the Internet Protocol (TCP/IP) Properties dialog box.

14. Click OK to close the Local Area Connection Properties dialog box.

15. Close the Network And Dial-up Connections window.

▶   **To configure the DNS domain name of your computer**

1. Right-click My Computer, and then click Properties.

   The System Properties dialog box appears.

2. On the Network Identification tab, click Advanced.

   The Identification Changes dialog box appears.

3. Click More.

   The NetBIOS And DNS Domain Names dialog box appears.

4. In the DNS Domain Name Of This Computer box, type **microsoft.com** and then click OK.

5. Click OK to close the Identification Changes dialog box.

   A Network Identification warning box appears, stating that you must reboot this computer for the changes to take effect.

6. Click OK.

7. Click OK to close the System Properties dialog box.

   A System Settings Change box appears, asking if you want to restart your computer.

8. Click Yes to restart your computer.

Exercise 2: Installing the DNS Service

In this exercise, you install Microsoft DNS Server.

▶ **To install the DNS Service**

1. Log on as Administrator.
2. Open Control Panel.
3. Double-click Add/Remove Programs.

   The Add/Remove Programs window appears.
4. Click Configure Windows.

   The Add Or Remove Windows Components page appears.
5. Click Components.

   The Windows Components wizard appears.
6. Click Next to continue.
7. Click Optional Networking Options, but do not click or change the status of the check box to the left of the component. If the DHCP Service or any other Optional Networking Component is installed on your computer, a check mark will appear in the box to the left of Networking Options.
8. Click Details.
9. In the Subcomponents Of Optional Networking Components list box, select the check box to the left of Microsoft DNS Server.
10. Click OK.

    You are returned to the Windows NT Components page.
11. Click Next.

    The Insert Disk dialog box appears.
12. Insert the CD-ROM you used to install Windows 2000 on your computer, wait about 10 seconds, and then click OK.

    Note   If the Files Needed dialog box appears, ensure that the path to the source files is correct, and then click OK.

    ---
13. If the Windows 2000 CD-ROM window appears, close it.

    Windows 2000 Server Setup copies the required files.
14. Click Finish to close the Windows Components wizard.
15. Close the Add/Remove Programs window.
16. Close Control Panel.
17. Remove the CD-ROM.

Lesson Summary

In this lesson you learned that there are some configuration changes you need to make before you install the Microsoft DNS Server Service. As a part of this pre-installation configuration, you should assign a static IP address to the computer on which you are going to install the DNS Service, and you should configure the appropriate IP address of the DNS server and DNS domain name.

You can install the DNS Service anytime after the Windows 2000 initial setup, or you can choose to install the DNS Service during setup. In addition to installing the DNS Service, the DNS installation process installs DNS Manager and adds a shortcut to Administrative Tools on the Start menu. Finally, in the practice portion of this lesson, you did the preinstallation configuration and then you installed the DNS Service.

Lesson 4: Configuring the DNS Service

Once the DNS Service is installed, you can configure it by using the DNS snap-in in the Computer Management snap-in. You'll find the DNS snap-in by expanding Server Applications And Services in the console tree. When you double-click the DNS snap-in for the first time, you will be able to configure these options:

- A root name server
- A forward lookup zone
- A reverse lookup zone

You can also use the DNS snap-in to add additional entries, called *resource records,* to the zone database file and to configure the DNS Service for *Dynamic DNS (DDNS)*, which enables automatic updates to your zone files by other servers or services.

After this lesson, you will be able to

- Configure the DNS Service.
- Configure Dynamic DNS.
- Configure the Dynamic Host Configuration Protocol (DHCP) Service for DNS.

Estimated lesson time: 45 minutes

Configuring a DNS Name Server

When you start the DNS snap-in for the first time, you have the option of configuring the server as a root name server. Root name servers store the location of name servers with authority for all the top-level domains in the domain name space (for example, the com domain). These top-level name servers can then provide a list of name servers with authority for the second-level domains (for example, the microsoft.com domain).

Configure a root name server for your intranet only when the following conditions apply:

- You are not connecting to the Internet. Therefore, the root level domain is for your intranet only.
- You are using a proxy service to gain access to the Internet. You are creating the root of your local DNS domain name space, and the proxy service will do the translation and connection necessary to access the Internet.

Creating Forward Lookup Zones

A forward lookup zone enables forward lookup queries. On name servers, you must configure at least one forward lookup zone in order for the DNS Service to work.

To create a new forward lookup zone, right-click the Forward Lookup Zone folder, and click Create A New Zone. The Create New Zone wizard guides you through the process. The wizard presents the following configuration options: Zone Type, Zone Name, and Zone Database File Name.

Zone Type

There are three types of zones that you can configure:

- **Standard Primary.**   A standard primary zone is the master copy of a new zone and is stored in a standard text file. You administer and maintain a primary zone on the computer at which you create the zone.

- **Standard Secondary.**   A standard secondary zone is a replica of an existing zone. Secondary zones are read-only and are stored in standard text files. A primary zone must be configured in order to create a secondary zone. When creating a secondary zone, you must specify the DNS server, called the master server, which will transfer zone information to the name server containing the standard secondary zone. You create a secondary zone to provide redundancy and to reduce the load on the name server containing the primary zone database file.

- **Active Directory Integrated.**   An Active Directory Integrated zone is the master copy of a new zone. The zone uses Active Directory to store and replicate zone files.

Note   For more information on Active Directory, see Chapter 12, "Implementing Active Directory."

Zone Name

Typically, a zone is named after the highest domain in the hierarchy that the zone encompasses—that is, the root domain for the zone. For example, for a zone that encompasses both microsoft.com and sales.microsoft.com, the zone name would be microsoft.com.

Zone Database File Name

The zone database file name defaults to the zone name with a .DNS extension; for example, if your zone name is microsoft.com, the default zone database file name is microsoft.com.dns.

When migrating a zone from another server, you can import the existing zone file. You must place the existing file in the *systemroot*\System32\DNS directory on the target computer before creating the new zone, where *systemroot* indicates the Windows 2000 installation folder, typically C:\Winnt.

Creating Reverse Lookup Zones

A reverse lookup zone enables reverse lookup queries. Reverse lookup zones are not required. However, a reverse lookup zone is required to run troubleshooting tools, such as nslookup, and to record a name instead of an IP address in Internet Information Services (IIS) log files.

To create a new reverse lookup zone, right-click Reverse Lookup Zone under DNS in Computer Management, click Create A New Zone, and a wizard guides you through the process. The wizard presents the configuration options described in the following sections.

Zone Type

For the zone type, select Standard Primary, Standard Secondary, or Active Directory Integrated, as defined previously.

Network ID and Subnet Mask

Enter your network ID and subnet mask; for example, an IP address of 169.254.16.200 and a subnet mask of 255.255.0.0 would result in a network ID of 169.254. All reverse lookup queries within the 169.254 network are resolved in this new zone.

Zone File Name

The network ID and subnet mask determine the default zone file name. DNS reverses the IP octets and adds the in-addr.arpa suffix. For example, the reverse lookup zone for the 169.254 network becomes 254.169.in-addr.arpa.dns.

When migrating a zone from another server, you can import the existing zone file. You must place the existing file in the *systemroot*\System32\DNS directory on the target computer before creating the new zone.

Adding Resource Records

Once you create your zones, you can continue with the DNS snap-in to add resource records. Resource records are entries in the zone database file. To add a resource record, right-click the zone to which you want to add the record, click New, and then select the type of record that you want to add.

There are many different types of resource records. When a zone is created, DNS automatically adds two resource records: the Start of Authority (SOA) and the Name Server (NS) records. Table 11.4 describes these records, along with the most commonly used resource records.

Table 11.4   Types of Resource Records

Resource record	DNS snap-in name	Description
SOA	Start of Authority	Identifies which name server is the authoritative source of information for data within this domain. The first record in the zone database file must be the Start of Authority record.
NS	Name Server	Lists the name servers that are assigned to a particular domain.
A	Host	Lists the host name to IP address mappings for a forward lookup zone.
PTR	Pointer	Points to another part of the domain name space. For example, in a reverse lookup zone, it lists the IP address to name mapping.
SRV	Service	Identifies which servers are hosting a particular service. For example, if a client needs to find a server to validate logon requests, the client can send a query to the DNS server to obtain a list of domain controllers and their associated IP addresses.
CNAME	Alias	Creates an alias, or alternate name, for the specified host name. You can use a Canonical Name (CNAME) record to use more than one name to point to a single IP address. For example, you can host a File Transfer Protocol (FTP) server, such as ftp.microsoft.com, and a Web server, such as www.microsoft.com, on the same computer.
MX	Mail Exchanger	Identifies which mail exchanger to contact for a specified domain and in what order to use each mail host.
HINFO	Host Information	Identifies the CPU and operating system used by the host. Use this record as a low-cost resource-tracking tool.

Note   For more information on resource records, use your Web browser to search for "RFC 1034," "RFC 2052," and "RFC 2065" to retrieve the contents of these RFCs.

Configuring Dynamic DNS

The DNS Service includes a dynamic update capability called Dynamic DNS (DDNS). With DNS, when there are changes to the domain for which a name server has authority, you must manually update the zone database file on the primary name server. With DDNS, name servers and clients within a network automatically update the zone database files, as shown in Figure 11.6.

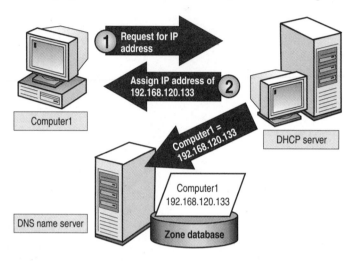

Figure 11.6   Dynamic DNS updates the zone database when IP addresses change

Dynamic Updates

You can configure a list of authorized servers to initiate dynamic updates. This list can include secondary name servers, domain controllers, and other servers that perform network registration for clients, such as servers running the Dynamic Host Configuration Protocol (DHCP) Service or the Microsoft Windows Internet Name Service (WINS).

DDNS and DHCP

DDNS interacts with the DHCP Service to maintain synchronized name to IP mappings for network hosts. By default, the DHCP Service allows clients to add their own A (Host) records to the zone, and the DHCP Service adds the PTR (Pointer) record to the zone. The DHCP Service cleans up both the A (Host) and PTR records in the zone when the lease expires.

Note   To send dynamic updates, use the DHCP Manager snap-in to configure the DHCP server to point to the appropriate DNS servers.

▶   **To configure a zone for DDNS**

1. From the DNS snap-in, right-click the forward or reverse lookup zone that you want to configure, and then click Properties. If you don't see Properties on the menu, click Advanced on the View menu and try again.

2. On the General tab, under Dynamic Update Field, click one of the following options:

    ▪ **None.**   Do not allow dynamic updates for this zone.

    ▪ **Allow Updates.**   Allow all dynamic DNS update requests for this zone.

    ▪ **Allow Secure Updates.**   Allow only dynamic DNS updates that use secure DNS for this zone.

    Allow Secure Updates only appears if the zone type is Active Directory Integrated. If you click Allow Secure Updates, the requester's permission to update the records in the zone database is tested by using mechanisms specified in a subsequent secure DNS update protocol.

    Note   For more information on Dynamic DNS, read RFC 2136 and RFC 2137 by using your Web browser to search for "RFC 2136" and "RFC 2137."

Practice: Configuring the DNS Service

In this practice, you configure the elements of the DNS Service. In Exercise 1 you create a forward and a reverse lookup zone for the DNS Service. In Exercise 2 you configure Dynamic DNS. The DHCP Service for DNS is configured in Exercise 3, and finally you test your DNS Server in Exercise 4.

Exercise 1: Configuring the DNS Service

In this exercise, you configure the DNS Service by creating a forward lookup zone and a reverse lookup zone.

▶   **To create a forward lookup zone**

1. Click Start, point to Programs, point to Administrative Tools, and then click Computer Management.

    The Computer Management window appears.

2. Double-click Server Applications And Services, and then double-click DNS.

3. Double-click Server1 (or the name of your computer).

4. Right-click Server1, and then click Create a New Zone.

    The Create New Zone wizard appears.

5. Click Next to continue.

    The Select A Zone Type page appears.

6. Ensure that Standard Primary is selected, and then click Next.

The Select The Zone Lookup Type page appears.

7. Ensure that Forward Lookup is selected, and then click Next.

The Zone Name page appears.

8. Type **microsoft.com** and then click Next. (If you are on a network, check with your network administrator to make sure it is OK to use this as your DNS domain name. This should be the same domain name that you used in step 12 of Exercise 1 in Lesson 3 of this chapter.)

The File Name page appears.

9. Ensure that New File is selected and that the name of the file to be created is microsoft.com.dns. (If you did not use microsoft.com as the domain name in step 8, this will be the domain name you typed in step 8 with a .DNS extension on the end.)

10. Click Next.

The Completing The Create New Zone Wizard page appears.

11. Click Finish.

A DNS dialog box appears indicating that the zone microsoft.com has been successfully created.

12. Click OK to close the dialog box.

▶   **To create a reverse lookup zone**

1. Right-click Server1, and then click Create a New Zone.

The Create New Zone wizard appears.

2. Click Next to continue.

The Select A Zone Type page appears.

3. Ensure that Standard Primary is selected, and then click Next.

The Select The Zone Lookup Type page appears.

4. Ensure that Reverse Lookup is selected, and then click Next.

The Network ID page appears.

5. Ensure that Specify The Network ID And The Subnet Mask For The Reverse Lookup Zone is selected, and type **192.168.1** in the Network ID box. (If you are on a network and did not use 192.168.1.201 as your IP address, type in the first three octets of your static IP address. This should be the same IP address that you used in step 7 of Exercise 1 in Lesson 3.)

Note   In the Name box at the bottom of the screen, notice that the in-addr arpa name is typed in and is 1.168.192.in-addr.arpa. If you did not use 192.168.1.201, your name will match the IP address and subnet mask that you are using.

---

6. Click Next.

   The File Name page appears.

7. Ensure that New File is selected and that the name of the file to be created is 1.168.192.in-addr.arpa.dns. (If you did not use 192.168.1.201 as your IP address in step 5, the file name will match the IP address and subnet mask that you used.)

8. Click Next.

   The Completing The Create New Zone Wizard page appears.

9. Review the information on the Completing The Create New Zone Wizard page, and then click Finish.

   A DNS dialog box appears indicating that the zone 1.168.192.in-add.arpa has been successfully created.

10. Click OK.

Exercise 2: Configuring Dynamic DNS Service

In this exercise, you configure the DNS Service to allow Dynamic updates.

▶ **To configure Dynamic DNS**

1. In the Computer Management console tree, double-click Server1 (or the name of your server).

2. Double-click Forward Lookup Zones, and then double-click microsoft.com. (If you did not use microsoft.com as your DNS domain name, double-click your DNS domain name.)

3. Right-click microsoft.com (or your DNS domain name), and then click Properties.

   The Microsoft.com Properties dialog box appears. (If you did not use microsoft.com as your DNS domain name, the name of the dialog box will reflect your DNS domain name.)

4. In the Dynamic Update box on the General tab, click Allow Updates, and then click OK.

   This configures Dynamic DNS for the forward lookup zone.

5. Double-click Reverse Lookup Zones, and then click 192.168.1.*x* Subnet.

6. Right-click 192.168.1.*x* Subnet, and then click Properties.

   The 192.168.1.*x* Subnet Properties dialog box appears.

7. In the Dynamic Update box on the General tab, click Allow Updates, and then click OK.

   This configures Dynamic DNS for the reverse lookup zone.

8. Minimize the Computer Management window.

Exercise 3: Configuring the DHCP Service for DNS

In this exercise, you configure the DHCP Service for DNS.

Important   Perform this exercise only if you have the DHCP Service installed on your computer.

▶   **To configure the DHCP Service for DNS**

1. Click Start, point to Programs, point to Administrative Tools, and then click DHCP Server Management.

    The DHCP window appears.

2. Double-click server1.microsoft.com[192.168.1.201], if necessary, to expand the console tree. (If you used a different name for your server or domain, or a different IP address, the name listed will vary. Click the appropriate name.)

3. Click Server Options.

4. Right-click Server Options, and then click Configure Options.

    The Configure DHCP Options: Server Properties dialog box appears.

5. In the Available Options list box, select the check box to the left of 006 DNS Servers.

6. In the Data Entry section, in the Server Name box, type **Server1** (or the name of your server).

7. Click Resolve.

    Notice that the New IP Address box contains the static IP address assigned to your computer.

8. Click Add.

9. In the Available Options list, select the check box to the left of 015 DNS Domain Name.

10. In the Data Entry section, type **microsoft.com** in the String Value box. (If you did not use microsoft.com as your DNS domain name, type the appropriate DNS domain name.)

11. Click OK.

12. Close the DHCP window.

Exercise 4: Testing Your DNS Server

In this exercise, you confirm that your DNS Service is working.

▶   **To test your DNS Service using the DNS snap-in**

1. Restore the Computer Management window.

2. In the console tree, right-click Server1 (or the name of your server name), and then click Properties.

The Server1 Properties dialog box appears. (If you did not use Server1 as your server name, the dialog box will reflect your server name.)

3. Click the Monitoring tab.

4. Under Tests Performed, select Simple Query and Recursive Query.

5. Click Test Now.

   Under Test Results, you should see PASS in the Simple Query column. If you are on a stand-alone server, you will see Fail in the Recursive Query column.

6. Click OK.

▶ **To create a pointer record for your DNS server**

1. In the console tree, click Reverse Lookup Zones.

2. Click 192.168.1.*x* Subnet. (If you did not use 192.168.1.201 as the static IP address for your server name, click the appropriate subnet.)

   What types of records exist in the reverse lookup zone?

3. In the console tree, right-click 192.168.0.*x* Subnet. (If you did not use 192.168.0.201 as the static IP address for your server name, click the appropriate subnet.) Point to New, and then click Pointer.

4. In the Host IP Number box, type **201** in the highlighted octet of your IP address.

5. In the Host Name box, type the fully qualified domain name of your computer, followed by a period.

   For example, if your computer name is Server1, type **server1.microsoft.com.** *Remember to include the trailing period.*

6. Click OK.

   A Pointer record appears in the details pane.

7. Close the Computer Management window.

▶ **To test your DNS Server using nslookup**

1. Open a command prompt.

2. At the command prompt, type **nslookup** and then press Enter.

   Record your results in the following table.

Parameter	Value
Default server	
Address	

3. Type **exit** and then press Enter.

Close the command prompt.

Lesson Summary

In this lesson you learned that you can configure the DNS Service by using the DNS snap-in. When you first start the DNS snap-in, you can configure a root name server, a forward lookup zone, and a reverse lookup zone. Root name servers store the location of name servers with authority for all the top-level domains in the domain name space, and the top-level name servers can provide a list of name servers with authority for the second-level domains. In the practice portion of this lesson, you configured your DNS Service by creating a forward lookup zone and a reverse lookup zone.

In this lesson you learned that you can also use the DNS snap-in to add additional entries, called resource records, to the zone database file and to configure the DNS Service for Dynamic DNS (DDNS), which enables automatic updates to your zone files by other servers or services.

Lesson 5: Configuring a DNS Client

Now that you know how to install and configure the DNS Service on computers running Windows 2000 Server, you need to know how to configure your DNS clients. In this lesson you will learn how to configure DNS clients.

After this lesson, you will be able to

- Configure a DNS client.

Estimated lesson time: 5 minutes

You must install TCP/IP on a client running Windows 2000 before configuring the client to use the DNS Service.

▶ **To configure a client to use the DNS Service**

1. Right-click My Network Places, and then click Properties.

2. Right-click Local Area Connection, and then click Properties.

3. Select Internet Protocol (TCP/IP), and then click Properties.

4. In the Internet Protocol (TCP/IP) Properties dialog box, select Use The Following DNS Server Addresses.

5. Type the IP address of the primary and secondary name servers for this client, and then click Advanced.

6. In the TCP/IP Advanced Settings dialog box (see Figure 11.7), click the DNS tab.

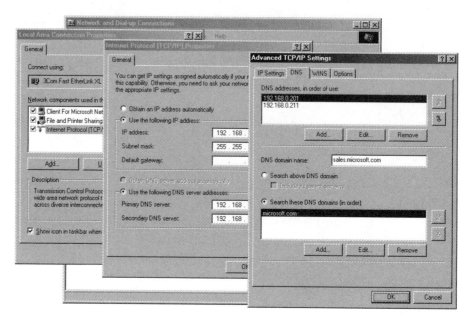

Figure 11.7   TCP/IP Advanced Settings dialog box

7. In the box labeled DNS Addresses, In Order Of Use, use the Up Arrow and Down Arrow buttons to set the client search order when sending queries to a name server.

    A client will attempt to send its query requests to the name server at the top of the search order list. If that name server is not responding, the client will send the query request to subsequent name servers on the search order list.

    Configure some of the clients to use the secondary server as the initial name server. This reduces the load on the primary server.

8. In the DNS Domain Name box, type the name of the DNS domain name.

9. In the Search These DNS Domains (In Order) box, click Add to add the names of the domains to search in order.

    When searching for a host name in the zone database file, a DNS server first searches for the name only and then for the name combined with each specified domain suffix.

10. Click OK in each of the three dialog boxes.

Lesson Summary

In this lesson, you learned that you must first install TCP/IP on a client running Windows 2000 before you can configure the client to use the DNS Service. Once you have TCP/IP installed, you can click the Advanced button to access the DNS tab and configure the IP addresses of the DNS servers and the DNS domain names your client will be using.

Lesson 6: Troubleshooting the DNS Service

Troubleshoot name servers by using the DNS snap-in monitoring and logging options and the nslookup command-line utility.

After this lesson, you will be able to

- Troubleshoot the DNS Service.

Estimated lesson time: 5 minutes

Monitoring the DNS Server

The DNS snap-in has an option that allows you to monitor the DNS Service. Double-click DNS in the Computer Management console tree, right-click the name server to monitor, click Properties, and then click the Monitoring tab. Test the name server by performing two types of queries:

- **Simple query.**   Select this option to perform a simple query test of the DNS server. This will be a local test using the DNS client on this computer to query the name server.

- **Recursive query.**   Select this option to perform a more complex, recursive query test of the name server. This query tests the name server by forwarding a recursive query to another name server.

Setting Logging Options

The DNS snap-in allows you to set additional logging options for debugging purposes. In the DNS snap-in, right-click the name server, click Properties, and then click the Logging tab. You can select from 11 options: Query, Notify, Update, Questions, Answers, Send, Receive, UDP, TCP, Full Packets, and Write Through.

Using Nslookup

Nslookup is the primary diagnostic tool for the DNS Service, and it is installed when the TCP/IP protocol is installed. Use nslookup to view any resource record and direct queries to any name server, including UNIX DNS implementations.

Nslookup has two modes: interactive and noninteractive.

- When you require more than one piece of data, use interactive mode. To run interactive mode, at the command prompt, type **nslookup**

   To exit interactive mode, type **exit**

- When you require a single piece of data, use noninteractive mode. Type the nslookup syntax at the command line, and the data is returned.

The syntax for nslookup is as follows:

```
nslookup [-option ...] [computer-to-find | - [server]]
```

Table 11.5   describes the optional parameters for nslookup.

Table 11.5   Nslookup Optional Parameters

Syntax	Description
-option...	Specifies one or more nslookup commands. For a list of commands, type a question mark (**?**) in interactive mode to open Help.
computer-to-find	If the computer to find is an IP address, nslookup returns the host name. If the computer to find is a name, nslookup returns an IP address. If the computer to find is a name and does not have a trailing period, the default DNS domain name is appended to the name. To look up a computer outside the current DNS domain, append a period to the name.
-server	Use this server as the DNS name server. If the server is omitted, the currently-configured default name server is used.

Lesson Summary

In this lesson you learned how to troubleshoot name servers by using the DNS snap-in monitoring and logging options and the nslookup command-line utility. You can test the name server by performing a simple query or by performing a recursive query. A simple query performs a local test using the DNS client on the computer to query the name server. A recursive query performs a more complex test. This query tests the name server by forwarding a recursive query to another name server.

You also learned that nslookup is the primary diagnostic tool for the DNS Service. It is installed along with the TCP/IP protocol. You can use nslookup to view any resource record and direct queries to any name server, including UNIX DNS implementations.

Review

Here are some questions to help you determine if you have learned enough to move on to the next chapter. If you have difficulty answering these questions, go back and review the material in this chapter before beginning the next chapter. The answers for these questions are located in Appendix A, "Questions and Answers."

1. What is the function of the following DNS components?

   Domain name space

   Zones

   Name servers

2. Why would you want to have multiple name servers?

3. What is the difference between a forward lookup query and a reverse lookup query?

4. When would you configure a server as a root server?

5. Why do you create forward and reverse lookup zones?

6. What is the difference between Dynamic DNS and DNS?

CHAPTER 12

Implementing Active Directory

About This Chapter

You use a directory service to uniquely identify users and resources on a network. Active Directory in Microsoft Windows 2000 is a significant enhancement over the directory services provided in previous versions of Windows 2000. Active Directory provides a single point of network management, allowing you to add, remove, and relocate users and resources easily.

This chapter introduces you to Active Directory and to how to plan your Active Directory implementation. It also presents the skills and knowledge necessary to install and explore Active Directory.

Before You Begin

To complete this chapter, you must have

- A computer that meets the minimum hardware requirements listed in "Hardware Requirements," on page xxxiii.
- Installed the Windows 2000 Server software on the computer.
- Configured the computer as a stand-alone server in a workgroup.

- Installed TCP/IP as the only protocol with the computer using a static IP address.

- Completed the exercises in Chapter 11, so that your Windows 2000 server is running the Domain Name System (DNS) Service and so that the DNS Service has been configured with Dynamic DNS enabled on the forward lookup zone and the reverse lookup zone.

Lesson 1: Understanding Active Directory

Before you implement Active Directory, it is important to understand the overall purpose of a directory service and the role that Active Directory plays in a Windows 2000 network. In addition, you should know about the key features of Active Directory, which have been designed to provide flexibility and ease of administration.

After this lesson, you will be able to

- Explain the purpose and function of Active Directory.

Estimated lesson time: 15 minutes

What Is Active Directory?

Active Directory is the directory service included in Windows 2000 Server. A *directory service* is a network service that identifies all resources on a network and makes them accessible to users and applications.

Active Directory includes the *Directory,* which stores information about network resources, as well as all the services that make the information available and useful. The resources stored in the Directory, such as user data, printers, servers, databases, groups, computers, and security policies, are known as objects.

Simplified Administration

Active Directory organizes resources hierarchically in domains. A *domain* is a logical grouping of servers and other network resources under a single domain name. The domain is the basic unit of replication and security in a Windows 2000 network.

Each domain includes one or more domain controllers. A *domain controller* is a computer running Windows 2000 Server that stores a complete replica of the domain directory. To simplify administration, all domain controllers in the domain are peers. You can make changes to any domain controller, and the updates are replicated to all other domain controllers in the domain.

Active Directory further simplifies administration by providing a single point of administration for all objects on the network. Since Active Directory provides a single point of logon for all network resources, an administrator can log on to one computer and administer objects on any computer in the network.

Scalability

In Active Directory, the Directory stores information by organizing the Directory into sections that permit storage for a very large number of objects. As a result, the Directory can expand as an organization grows, allowing you to scale from a small installation with a few hundred objects to a very large installation with millions of objects.

Note   You can distribute directory information across several computers in a network.

Open Standards Support

Active Directory integrates the Internet concept of a namespace with the Windows 2000 directory services. This allows you to unify and manage the multiple namespaces that now exist in the heterogeneous software and hardware environments of corporate networks. Active Directory uses Domain Name System (DNS) for its name system and can exchange information with any application or directory that uses Lightweight Directory Access Protocol (LDAP) or Hypertext Transfer Protocol (HTTP).

Important   Active Directory also shares information with other directory services that support LDAP version 2 and version 3, such as Novell Directory Services (NDS).

Domain Name System

Because Active Directory uses DNS as its domain naming and location service, Windows 2000 domain names are also DNS names. Windows 2000 Server uses Dynamic DNS (DDNS), which enables clients with dynamically assigned addresses to register directly with a server running the DNS Service and update the DNS table dynamically. DDNS eliminates the need for other Internet naming services, such as Windows Internet Name Service (WINS), in a homogeneous environment.

Important   For Active Directory and associated client software to function correctly, you must have installed and configured the DNS Service.

Support for LDAP and HTTP

Active Directory further embraces Internet standards by directly supporting LDAP and HTTP. LDAP is an Internet standard for accessing directory services, which was developed as a simpler alternative to the Directory Access Protocol (DAP). For more information about LDAP, use your Web browser to search for "RC 1777" and retrieve the text of this Request for Comment. Active Directory supports both LDAP version 2 and version 3. HTTP is the standard protocol for displaying pages on the World Wide Web. You can display every object in Active Directory as an HTML page in a Web browser. Thus, users receive the benefit of the familiar Web browsing model when querying and viewing objects in Active Directory.

Note   Active Directory uses LDAP to exchange information between directories and applications.

Support for Standard Name Formats

Active Directory supports several common name formats. Consequently, users and applications can access Active Directory by using the format with which they are most familiar. Table 12.1 describes some standard name formats supported by Active Directory.

Table 12.1   Standard Name Formats Supported by Active Directory

Format	Description
RFC 822	RFC 822 names are in the form *somename@domain* and are familiar to most users as Internet e-mail addresses.
HTTP URL	HTTP Uniform Resource Locators (URLs) are familiar to users with Web browsers and take the form http://*domain/path-to-page*.
UNC	Active Directory supports the Universal Naming Convention (UNC) used in Windows 2000 Server–based networks to refer to shared volumes, printers, and files. An example is \\microsoft.com\xl\budget.xls.
LDAP URL	An LDAP URL specifies the server on which the Active Directory services reside and the attributed name of the object. Active Directory supports a draft to RFC 1779 and uses the attributes in the following example: LDAP://someserver.microsoft.com/CN=FirstnameLastname,OU=sys, OU=product,OU=division,DC=devel CN represents CommonName OU represents OrganizationalUnitName DC represents DomainComponentName

Lesson Summary

In this lesson you learned that Active Directory is the directory service included in Windows 2000 Server. A directory service is a network service that identifies all resources on a network and makes them accessible to users and applications. Active Directory includes the Directory, which stores information about network resources, such as user data, printers, servers, databases, groups, computers, and security policies. The Directory can scale from a small installation with a few hundred objects to a very large installation with millions of objects.

In this lesson you also learned that Active Directory uses DNS as its domain naming and location service. Since Active Directory uses DNS as its domain naming and location service, Windows 2000 domain names are also DNS names. Windows 2000 Server uses Dynamic DNS (DDNS), so clients with dynamically assigned addresses can register directly with a server running the DNS Service and dynamically update the DNS table. Finally, you learned that in a homogeneous environment DDNS eliminates the need for other Internet naming services, such as WINS.

Lesson 2: Active Directory Structure and Replication

Active Directory provides a method for designing a directory structure that meets the needs of your organization. As a result, before installing Active Directory, you should examine your organization's business structure and operations.

Many companies have a centralized structure. Typically, these companies have strong information technology (IT) departments that define and implement the network structure down to the smallest detail. Other organizations, especially large enterprises, are very decentralized. These companies have multiple businesses, each of which is very focused. They need decentralized approaches to managing their business relationships and networks.

With the flexibility of Active Directory, you can create the network structure that best fits your company's needs. Active Directory completely separates the logical structure of the domain hierarchy from the physical structure.

After this lesson, you will be able to

- Explain Active Directory structure and replication.

Estimated lesson time: 15 minutes

Logical Structure

In Active Directory, you organize resources in a logical structure. Grouping resources logically enables you to find a resource by its name rather than by its physical location. Since you group resources logically, Active Directory makes the network's physical structure transparent to users.

Object

An *object* is a distinct, named set of attributes that represents a network resource. Object *attributes* are characteristics of objects in the Directory. For example, the attributes of a user account might include the user's first and last names, department, and e-mail address (see Figure 12.1).

In Active Directory, you can organize objects in *classes*, which are logical groupings of objects. For example, an object class might be user accounts, groups, computers, domains, or organizational units.

Note Some objects, known as *containers,* can contain other objects. For example, a domain is a container object.

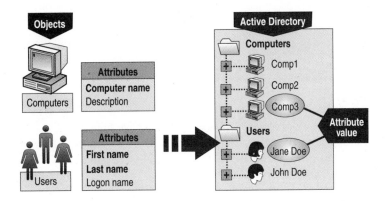

Figure 12.1   Active Directory objects and attributes

Organizational Units

An *organizational unit (OU)* is a container that you use to organize objects within a domain into logical administrative groups. An OU can contain objects such as user accounts, groups, computers, printers, applications, file shares, and other OUs (see Figure 12.2).

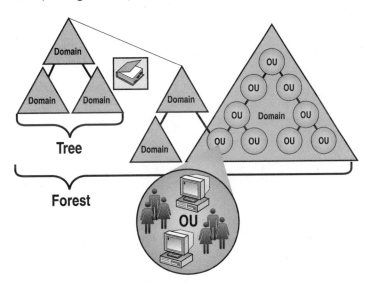

Figure 12.2   Resources organized in a logical hierarchical structure

The OU hierarchy within a domain is independent of the OU hierarchy structure of other domains—each domain can implement its own OU hierarchy. There are no restrictions on the depth of the OU hierarchy. However, a shallow hierarchy performs better than a deep one, so you should not create an OU hierarchy any deeper than necessary.

Note   You can delegate administrative tasks by assigning permissions to OUs.

Domain

The core unit of logical structure in Active Directory is the domain. Grouping objects into one or more domains allows your network to reflect your company's organization. Domains share these characteristics:

- All network objects exist within a domain, and each domain stores information only about the objects that it contains. Theoretically, a domain directory can contain up to 10 million objects, but 1 million objects per domain is more practical.

- A domain is a security boundary. Access to domain objects is controlled by *access control lists (ACLs)*. ACLs contain the permissions associated with objects that control which users can gain access to an object and what type of access users can gain to the objects. In Windows 2000 objects include files, folders, shares, printers, and Active Directory objects. All security policies and settings—such as administrative rights, security policies, and ACLs—do not cross from one domain to another. The domain administrator has absolute rights to set policies only within that domain.

Tree

A *tree* is a grouping or hierarchical arrangement of one or more Windows 2000 domains that share a contiguous namespace:

- Following DNS standards, the domain name of a child domain is the relative name of that child domain appended with the name of the parent domain.

- All domains within a single tree share a common *schema,* which is a formal definition of all object types that you can store in an Active Directory deployment.

- All domains within a single tree share a common *global catalog,* which is the central repository of information about objects in a tree.

Forest

A *forest* is a grouping or hierarchical arrangement of one or more domain trees that form a disjointed namespace. As such, forests have the following characteristics:

- All trees in a forest share a common schema.

- Trees in a forest have different naming structures, according to their domains.

- All domains in a forest share a common global catalog.

- Domains in a forest operate independently, but the forest enables communication across the entire organization.

Sites

The physical structure of Active Directory is based on sites. A *site* is a combination of one or more Internet Protocol (IP) subnets, which should be connected by a high-speed link. Typically, a site has the same boundaries as a local area network (LAN). When you group subnets on your network, you should combine only those subnets that have fast, cheap, and reliable network connections with one another. "Fast" network connections are at least 512 kilobits per second (Kbps). An available bandwidth of 128 Kbps and higher is sufficient.

With Active Directory, sites are not part of the namespace. When you browse the logical namespace, you see computers and users grouped into domains and OUs, not sites. Sites contain only computer objects and connection objects used to configure replication between sites.

Note   A single domain can span multiple geographical sites, and a single site can include user accounts and computers belonging to multiple domains.

Replication Within a Site

Active Directory also includes a replication feature. Replication ensures that changes to a domain controller are reflected in all domain controllers within a domain. To understand replication, you must understand domain controllers. A domain controller is a computer running Windows 2000 Server that stores a replica of the domain directory. A domain can contain one or more domain controllers.

The following list describes the functions of domain controllers:

- Each domain controller stores a complete copy of all Active Directory information for that domain, manages changes to that information, and replicates those changes to other domain controllers in the same domain.

- Domain controllers in a domain automatically replicate all objects in the domain to each other. When you perform an action that causes an update to Active Directory, you are actually making the change at one of the domain controllers. The domain controller then replicates the change to all other domain controllers within the domain. You can control replication of traffic between domain controllers in the network by specifying how often replication occurs and the amount of data that Windows 2000 replicates at one time.

- Domain controllers immediately replicate certain important updates, such as a user account being disabled.

- Active Directory uses multimaster replication, in which no one domain controller is the master domain controller. Instead, all domain controllers within a domain are peers, and each domain controller contains a copy of the directory database that can be written to. Domain controllers may hold different information for short periods of time until all domain controllers have synchronized changes to Active Directory.

- Having more than one domain controller in a domain provides fault tolerance. If one domain controller is offline, another domain controller can provide all required functions, such as recording changes to Active Directory.

- Domain controllers manage all aspects of user domain interaction, such as locating Active Directory objects and validating user logon attempts.

Within a site, Active Directory automatically generates a ring topology for replication among domain controllers in the same domain. The topology defines the path for directory updates to flow from one domain controller to another until all domain controllers receive the directory updates (see Figure 12.3).

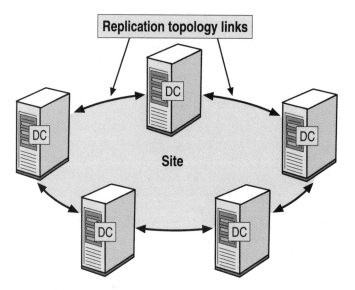

Figure 12.3   Replication topology

The ring structure ensures that there are at least two replication paths from one domain controller to another; if one domain controller is down temporarily, replication still continues to all other domain controllers.

Active Directory periodically analyzes the replication topology within a site to ensure that it is still efficient. If you add or remove a domain controller from the network or a site, Active Directory reconfigures the topology to reflect the change.

Lesson Summary

In this lesson you learned that Active Directory offers you a method for designing a directory structure to meet the needs of your organization's business structure and operations. Active Directory completely separates the logical structure of the domain hierarchy from the physical structure. In Active Directory, grouping resources logically enables you to find a resource by its name rather than by its physical location. Since you group resources logically, Active Directory makes the network's physical structure transparent to users.

You also learned that the core unit of logical structure in Active Directory is the domain. All network objects exist within a domain, and each domain stores information only about the objects that it contains. An organizational unit (OU) is a container that you use to organize objects within a domain into logical administrative groups, and an OU can contain objects such as user accounts, groups, computers, printers, applications, file shares, and other OUs. A tree is a grouping or hierarchical arrangement of one or more Windows 2000 domains that share a contiguous namespace. A forest is a grouping or hierarchical arrangement of one or more trees that form a disjointed namespace.

You also learned that the physical structure of Active Directory is based on sites. A site is a combination of one or more Internet Protocol (IP) subnets, connected by a high-speed link. Active Directory also includes replication to ensure that changes to a domain controller are reflected in all domain controllers within a domain. Within a site, Active Directory automatically generates a ring topology for replication among domain controllers in the same domain. The ring structure ensures that there are at least two replication paths from one domain controller to another; if one domain controller is down temporarily, replication still continues to all other domain controllers. If you add or remove a domain controller from the network or a site, Active Directory reconfigures the topology to reflect the change.

Lesson 3: Understanding Active Directory Concepts

There are several new concepts introduced with Active Directory. It is important that you understand their meaning as applied to Active Directory.

After this lesson, you will be able to
- Explain concepts associated with Active Directory.

Estimated lesson time: 15 minutes

Schema

The schema contains a formal definition of the contents and structure of Active Directory, including all attributes, classes, and class properties, as shown in Figure 12.4. For each object class, the schema defines what attributes an instance of the class must have, what additional attributes it can have, and what object class can be a parent of the current object class.

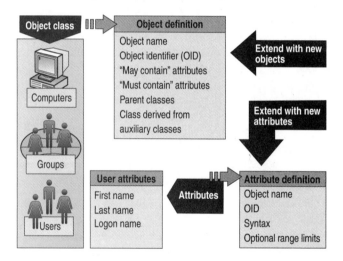

Figure 12.4   The schema contains a formal definition of the contents and structure of Active Directory

Installing Active Directory on the first domain controller in a network creates a default schema. The default schema contains definitions of commonly used objects and properties (such as user accounts, computers, printers, groups, and so on). The default schema also contains definitions of objects and properties that Active Directory uses internally to function.

The Active Directory schema is extensible, which means that you can define new directory object types and attributes and new attributes for existing objects. You can extend the schema by using the Schema Manager snap-in or the Active Directory Services Interface (ADSI).

The schema is implemented and stored within Active Directory itself (in the global catalog), and it can be updated dynamically. As a result, an application can extend the schema with new attributes and classes and then can use the extensions immediately.

Note Write access to the schema is limited to members of the Administrators group, by default.

Global Catalog

The global catalog is the central repository of information about objects in a tree or forest, as shown in Figure 12.5. Active Directory automatically generates the contents of the global catalog from the domains that make up the Directory through the normal replication process.

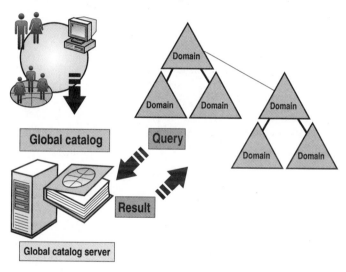

Figure 12.5   The global catalog is the central repository of information

The global catalog is a service and a physical storage location that contains a replica of selected attributes for every object in Active Directory. By default, the attributes stored in the global catalog are those most frequently used in search operations (such as a user's first and last names, logon name, and so forth), and those necessary to locate a full replica of the object. As a result, you can use the global catalog to locate objects anywhere in the network without replication of all domain information between domain controllers.

> **Note**   You use the Schema Manager snap-in to define which attributes are included in the global catalog replication process.

When you install Active Directory on the first domain controller in a new forest, that domain controller is, by default, a global catalog server. A *global catalog server* is a domain controller that stores a copy of the global catalog. The configuration of the initial global catalog server should have the capacity to support several hundred thousand to one million objects, with the potential for growth beyond those numbers.

You can designate additional domain controllers as global catalog servers by using the Sites And Servers Management snap-in. When considering which domain controllers to designate as global catalog servers, base your decision on the ability of your network structure to handle replication and query traffic. The more global catalog servers that you have, the greater the replication traffic. However, the availability of additional servers can provide quicker responses to user inquiries. It is recommended that every major site in your enterprise have a global catalog server.

Namespace

Active Directory, like all directory services, is primarily a namespace. A *namespace* is any bounded area in which a name can be resolved. Name resolution is the process of translating a name into some object or information that the name represents. The Active Directory namespace is based on the DNS naming scheme, which allows for interoperability with Internet technologies. An example namespace is shown in Figure 12.6.

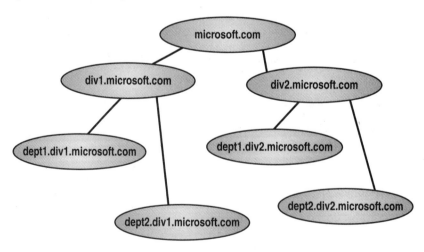

Figure 12.6   Namespace diagram

Using a common namespace allows you to unify and manage multiple hardware and software environments in your network. There are two types of namespaces:

- **Contiguous namespace.**   The name of the child object in an object hierarchy always contains the name of the parent domain. A tree is a contiguous namespace.

- **Disjointed namespace.**   The names of a parent object and of a child of the same parent object are not directly related to one another. A forest is a disjointed namespace.

Naming Conventions

Every object in Active Directory is identified by a name. Active Directory uses a variety of naming conventions: distinguished names, relative distinguished names, globally unique identifiers, and user principal names.

Distinguished Name

Every object in Active Directory has a *distinguished name (DN),* which uniquely identifies an object and contains sufficient information for a client to retrieve the object from the Directory. The DN includes the name of the domain that holds the object, as well as the complete path through the container hierarchy to the object.

For example, the following DN identifies the Firstname Lastname user object in the microsoft.com domain (where *Firstname* and *Lastname* represent the actual first and last names of a user account):

/DC=COM/DC=microsoft/OU=dev/CN=Users/CN=Firstname Lastname

Table 12.2 describes the attributes in the example.

Table 12.2   Distinguished Name Attributes

Attribute	Description
DC	DomainComponentName
OU	OrganizationalUnitName
CN	CommonName

DNs must be unique. Active Directory does not allow duplicate DNs.

Relative Distinguished Name

Active Directory supports querying by attributes, so you can locate an object even if the exact DN is unknown or has changed. The *relative distinguished name (RDN)* of an object is the part of the name that is an attribute of the object itself. In the preceding example, the RDN of the Firstname Lastname user object is *Firstname Lastname*. The RDN of the parent object is Users.

You can have duplicate RDNs for Active Directory objects, but you cannot have two objects with the same RDN in the same OU. For example, if a user account is named Jane Doe, you cannot have another user account called Jane Doe in the same OU. However, objects with duplicate RDN names can exist in separate OUs because they have different DNs (see Figure 12.7).

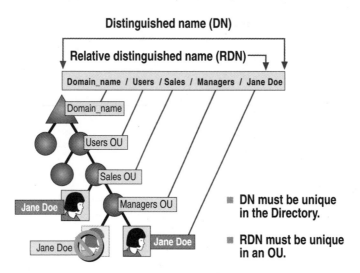

Figure 12.7   Distinguished names and relative distinguished names

Globally Unique Identifier

A *globally unique identifier (GUID)* is a 128-bit number that is guaranteed to be unique. GUIDs are assigned to objects when the objects are created. The GUID never changes, even if you move or rename the object. Applications can store the GUID of an object and use the GUID to retrieve that object regardless of its current DN.

User Principal Name

User accounts have a "friendly" name, the user principal name (UPN). The UPN is composed of a "shorthand" name for the user account and the DNS name of the tree where the user account object resides. For example, user *Firstname Lastname* (substitute the first and last names of an actual user) in the microsoft.com tree might have a UPN of FirstnameL@microsoft.com (using the full first name and the first letter of the last name).

Lesson Summary

In this lesson you learned that the schema contains a formal definition of the contents and structure of Active Directory, including all attributes, classes, and class properties. For each object class, the schema defines what attributes an instance of the class must have, what additional attributes it can have, and what object class can be a parent of the current object class. Installing Active Directory on the first domain controller in a network creates a default schema. The Active Directory schema is extensible.

You also learned that the global catalog is a service and a physical storage location that contains a replica of selected attributes for every object in Active Directory. Active Directory automatically generates the contents of the global catalog from the domains that make up the Directory through the normal replication process. By default, the attributes stored in the global catalog are those most frequently used in search operations (such as a user's first and last names, logon name, and so forth) and those necessary to locate a full replica of the object. As a result, you can use the global catalog to locate objects anywhere in the network without replication of all domain information between domain controllers.

Finally, you learned that there are contiguous namespaces and disjointed namespaces. In a contiguous namespace, the name of the child object in an object hierarchy always contains the name of the parent domain. A tree is an example of a contiguous namespace. In a disjointed namespace, the names of a parent object and of a child of the same parent object are not directly related to one another. A forest is an example of a disjointed namespace.

Lesson 4: Planning Active Directory Implementation

When you decide to establish a Windows 2000 network environment, you must consider how to implement a DNS namespace and Active Directory. First, examine the business structure and operation of your organization.

In many organizations, the IT department defines and implements the network structure down to the smallest detail. Other organizations, especially large enterprises, take a decentralized approach to managing business relationships and networks. These organizations may have multiple business units, each with different requirements for managing their network resources.

When planning the implementation of a namespace and Active Directory for your organization, consider the following issues: physical office locations, future growth and reorganization, and access to network resources. This lesson introduces some of the general considerations in planning for your Active Directory implementation.

Note Planning for implementing Active Directory can be an extremely complex undertaking, depending on the size and complexity of your organization. Individuals who are responsible for planning a Windows 2000 Active Directory structure should consider additional training that specifically covers Active Directory design issues.

After this lesson, you will be able to
- Explain considerations for planning an Active Directory implementation.

Estimated lesson time: 10 minutes

Planning a Namespace

If your network already has a presence on the Internet, you must decide whether to extend the external namespace for internal use or to create a new namespace.

Extending an Existing Namespace

You can extend an existing namespace to include it in Windows 2000 Server domains. You should consider using the same namespace for internal and external resources when you want

- To have consistent tree names for internal and external resources.
- To use the same logon and user names for internal and external resources.
- To reserve no more than one DNS namespace.

When you use the same namespace, you must create two separate DNS zones for your organization. One zone provides name resolution for internal resources, and the other provides name resolution for external resources, such as Web servers, File Transfer Protocol (FTP) servers, mail servers, and so on.

Creating a New Internal Namespace

You also can have different namespaces for internal and external resources. In this configuration, all internal corporate servers use one namespace, while external resources, such as Internet and FTP servers, use a different namespace. This configuration requires you to reserve two namespaces with an Internet DNS registration authority. Consider using different namespaces for internal and external resources when you want

- A clear distinction between internal and external resources.
- Separate internal and external resource management.
- Simple client browser and proxy client configuration.

Planning a Site

You maintain a domain structure and a site structure separately in Active Directory. A single domain can include multiple sites, and a single site can include multiple domains, or parts of multiple domains.

As you plan sites, consider the availability of bandwidth for the replication traffic that occurs within a domain. For example, assume that you have offices in Phoenix, Arizona, and Flagstaff, Arizona, and assume that both offices are in the same site. In this case, the domain controllers in each office would be replicating frequently. However, by establishing each office as a separate site, you can specify a replication schedule to take advantage of hours when there is less demand on network resources, when more connections are available, or even when dial-up connections are less expensive.

Use the following guidelines as you plan how to combine subnets into sites:

- Combine only those subnets that share fast, inexpensive, and reliable network connections of at least 512 Kbps.
- Configure sites so that replication within the site occurs at times or intervals that do not interfere with network performance.

Planning Organizational Units

In a single domain, you can organize user accounts and resources by using a hierarchy of OUs to reflect the structure of your company. Just as your organization can have multiple levels of management, you can establish multiple levels of management within a domain based on OUs.

Consider creating an OU if you want to

- Reflect your company's structure and organization within a domain. Without OUs, all user accounts are maintained and displayed in a single list, regardless of a user's department, location, or role. In Figure 12.8, by creating an OU for Sales and another for Repair, user accounts are divided into two groups.

- Delegate administrative control over network resources while maintaining the ability to manage them. You can grant administrative permissions to user accounts or groups at the OU level.

- Accommodate potential changes in your company's organizational structure. You can move user accounts between OUs easily, while moving user accounts between domains generally requires more time and effort.

- Group objects to allow administrators to locate similar network resources more easily to perform administrative tasks. For example, you could group all user accounts for temporary employees in an OU.

- Restrict visibility of network resources in Active Directory. Users can view only the objects to which they have access.

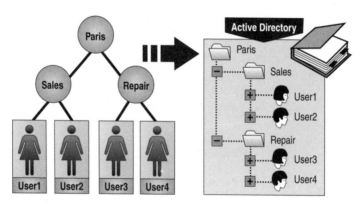

Figure 12.8 Designing OUs

Lesson Summary

In this lesson you learned that planning for implementing Active Directory can be extremely complex. For example, when you plan the implementation of a namespace and Active Directory for your organization, you must consider the following issues: physical office locations, future growth and reorganization, and access to network resources. If your network already has a presence on the Internet, you must decide whether to extend the external namespace for internal use or to create a new namespace.

You also learned that you should plan your sites. For example, when you plan your sites, you must consider the availability of bandwidth for the replication traffic within a domain. You might also want to determine how to take advantage of hours when there is less demand on network resources, when more connections are available, or even when dial-up connections are less expensive.

Finally, you learned that you also have to plan your OU structure. Your OU structure should have a purpose. For example, your OU structure could reflect your company's structure and organization within a domain, allow you to delegate administrative control over network resources while maintaining the ability to manage them, or restrict visibility of network resources in Active Directory.

Lesson 5: Installing Active Directory

This lesson presents information on installing Active Directory, including using the Active Directory Installation wizard. In addition, the lesson addresses the database and shared system volume that Active Directory creates during installation. Finally, the lesson discusses domain modes.

After this lesson, you will be able to

- Install Active Directory.

Estimated lesson time: 30 minutes

The Active Directory Installation Wizard

You use the Active Directory Installation wizard to perform the following tasks:

- Adding a domain controller to an existing domain
- Creating the first domain controller of a new domain
- Creating a new child domain
- Creating a new domain tree

To launch the Active Directory Installation wizard, run Windows 2000 Configure Server on the Administrative Tools menu of the Start menu, or run dcpromo.exe from the command prompt. These will run the Active Directory Installation wizard on a stand-alone server and step you through the process of installing Active Directory on the computer and creating a new domain controller.

As you install Active Directory, you can choose whether to add the new domain controller to an existing domain or create the first domain controller for a new domain.

Adding a Domain Controller to an Existing Domain

If you choose to add a domain controller to an existing domain, you create a peer domain controller. You create peer domain controllers for redundancy and to reduce the load on the existing domain controllers.

Creating the First Domain Controller for a New Domain

If you choose to create the first domain controller for a new domain, you create a new domain. You create domains on your network to partition your information, which enables you to scale Active Directory to meet the needs of very large organizations. When you create a new domain, you can create a new child domain or a new tree. Table 12.3 describes creating a new child domain and creating a new domain tree.

Table 12.3   Creating New Domains

Creating a new domain	Description
New child domain	When you create a child domain, the new domain is a child domain in an existing domain.
New domain tree	When you create a new tree, the new domain is not part of an existing domain. You can create a new tree in an existing forest, or you can create a new forest.

Caution   Running dcpromo.exe on a domain controller allows you to remove Active Directory from the domain controller and demotes it to a stand-alone server. If you remove Active Directory from all domain controllers in a domain, you also delete the directory database for the domain, and the domain no longer exists.

The Database and Shared System Volume

Installing Active Directory creates the database and database log files, as well as the shared system volume. Table 12.4 describes these files.

Table 12.4   Types of Files Created by Installing Active Directory

Type of file created	Description
Database and database log files	The database is the directory for the new domain. The default location for the database and database log files is *systemroot*\Ntds, where *systemroot* is the Windows 2000 directory.
	For best performance, place the database and the log file on separate hard disks.
Shared System Volume	The shared system volume is a folder structure that exists on all Windows 2000 domain controllers. It stores scripts and some of the group policy objects for both the current domain as well as the enterprise. The default location for the shared system volume is *systemroot*\Sysvol.
	The shared system volume must be located on a partition or volume formatted with Windows NT file system (NTFS) 5.0.

Replication of the shared system volume occurs on the same schedule as replication of Active Directory. As a result, you may not notice file replication to or from the newly created system volume until two replication periods have elapsed (typically, 10 minutes). This is because the first file replication period updates the configuration of other system volumes so that they are aware of the newly created system volume.

Domain Modes

There are two domain modes: mixed mode and native mode.

Mixed Mode

When you first install or upgrade a domain controller to Windows 2000 Server, the domain controller runs in mixed mode. Mixed mode allows the domain controller to interact with any domain controllers in the domain that are running previous versions of Windows 2000 Server (down-level domain controllers).

Native Mode

When all the domain controllers in the domain run Windows 2000 Server, and you do not plan to add any more down-level domain controllers to the domain, you can switch the domain from mixed mode to native mode.

Several things happen during the conversion from mixed mode to native mode:

- Support for down-level replication ceases. Since down-level replication is gone, you can no longer have any domain controllers in your domain that are not running Windows 2000 Server.
- You can no longer add new down-level domain controllers to the domain.
- The server that served as the primary domain controller during migration is no longer the domain master; all domain controllers begin acting as peers.

Note   The change from mixed mode to native mode is one way only; you cannot change from native mode to mixed mode.

▶   **To switch the domain mode**

1. Start the Domain Tree Management snap-in.
2. Right-click the domain name, and then click Properties.
3. On the General tab, click Change To Native Mode.
4. In the Warning dialog box, click Yes, and then click OK.

Practice: Installing Active Directory

In this practice you install Active Directory on your stand-alone server, which will make it a domain controller of a new domain. In Exercise 1 you use the dcpromo.exe program to install Active Directory. In Exercise 2 you view the domain you have created, and in Exercise 3 you are introduced to the Directory Management snap-in administrative tool.

Exercise 1: Promoting a Stand-Alone Server to a Domain Controller

In this exercise, you run dcpromo.exe to install the Active Directory service on your stand-alone server, making it a domain controller in a new domain.

▶ **To install the Active Directory service on a stand-alone server**

1. Restart your computer and log on as Administrator.

2. If the Windows 2000 Configure Server page opens, close it because the dcpromo.exe program will be used instead to accomplish the tasks in this practice.

3. Open a command prompt, and type **dcpromo.exe**

    The Active Directory Installation wizard appears.

4. Click Next.

    The Domain Controller Type page appears.

5. Select Domain Controller for a New Domain, and then click Next.

    The Create Tree Or Child Domain page appears.

6. Ensure that Create A New Domain Tree is selected, and then click Next.

    The Create Or Join Forest page appears.

7. Select Create A New Forest Of Domain Trees, and then click Next.

    The New Domain Name page appears.

8. In the Full DNS Name For The New Domain box, type **microsoft.com**

    (If you are not using microsoft.com as your DNS domain name, type the name you are using for your DNS domain name.)

9. Click Next.

    After a few moments, the NetBIOS Domain Name page appears.

10. Ensure that MICROSOFT (or a shortened form of the DNS name you have chosen) appears in the Domain NetBIOS Name box, and then click Next.

    The Database And Log Locations page appears.

11. Ensure that C:\Winnt\Ntds is the location of both the database and the log. (If you did not install Windows 2000 on the C drive or in the Winnt directory, both locations should default to the Ntds folder in the folder where you did install Windows 2000.)

12. Click Next.

    The Shared System Volume page appears.

13. Ensure that the Sysvol location is C:\Winnt\Sysvol. (If you did not install Windows 2000 on the C drive or in the Winnt directory, the Sysvol location should default to a Sysvol folder in the folder where you installed Windows 2000.)

    What is the one Sysvol location requirement?

What is the function of Sysvol?

14. Click Next to accept C:\Winnt\Sysvol (or the path where you installed Windows 2000) as the path for Sysvol.

    The Windows NT 4.0 RAS Servers page appears.

15. Unless your network administrator tells you to do otherwise, select No, Do Not Change The Permissions, and then click Next.

    The Summary page appears, listing the options that you selected.

16. Review the contents of the Summary page, and then click Next.

    The Configuring Active Directory progress indicator appears as the Active Directory service is installed on the server.

    This process will take several minutes.

17. When the Completing The Active Directory Installation Wizard page appears, click Finish, and then click Restart Now.

Exercise 2: Viewing Your Domain

In this exercise, you view your domain.

▶ **To explore My Network Places**

1. Log on as Administrator.

2. If the Windows 2000 Configure Server page appears, close it.

3. Double-click My Network Places.

    The My Network Places window appears.

    What selections do you see?

4. Double-click Entire Network, and then double-click Microsoft Windows Network.

    What do you see?

5. Close the Microsoft Windows Network window.

Exercise 3: Using Active Directory Manager

In this exercise, you use Active Directory Manager to view your domain.

▶ **To use Directory Management**

1. Click Start, point to Programs, point to Administrative Tools, and then click Directory Management.

    The Directory Management window appears.

2. In the console tree, double-click microsoft (or the name of your domain).

   What selections are listed under microsoft?

3. In the console tree, click Domain Controllers.

   Notice that Server1 appears in the details pane. (If you did not use Server1 as your server name, the name of your server appears in the details pane.)

4. Close Directory Management.

Lesson Summary

In this lesson you learned about installing Active Directory, including running Windows 2000 Configure Server to start the Active Directory wizard. You can also go to a command prompt and type **dcpromo** to launch the Active Directory wizard. You can use the Active Directory wizard to add a domain controller to an existing domain, to create the first domain controller of a new domain, to create a new child domain, and to create a new domain tree.

In addition, you learned about the database, which is the directory for the new domain, and the database log files. The default location for the database and database log files is *systemroot*\Ntds. You also learned about the shared system volume that Active Directory creates during installation. The shared system volume is a folder structure that exists on all Windows 2000 domain controllers. It stores scripts and some of the group policy objects for both the current domain and the enterprise. The default location for the shared system volume is *systemroot*\Sysvol.

You also learned about domain modes. When you first install or upgrade a domain controller to Windows 2000 Server, the domain controller runs in mixed mode. Mixed mode allows the domain controller to interact with any domain controllers in the domain that are running previous versions of Windows NT Server (down-level domain controllers). When all the domain controllers in the domain run Windows 2000 Server, and you do not plan to add any more down-level domain controllers to the domain, you can switch the domain from mixed mode to native mode. Native mode does not support down-level replication so you can no longer have any domain controllers in your domain that are not running Windows 2000 Server. One other difference between mixed mode and native mode is that the server that was the primary domain controller during migration is no longer the domain master, because all domain controllers in native mode act as peers.

Finally, in the practice exercises for this lesson, you used the Active Directory Installation wizard to install Active Directory on your computer, to promote your computer to a domain controller, and to create a domain. You then viewed your domain using My Network Places and the Directory Management snap-in to view your domain.

Lesson 6: Exploring a Multiple-Domain Environment

A domain tree is a hierarchical grouping of domains that you create by adding one or more child domains to an existing parent domain. All domains in a domain tree share the same Active Directory. However, domain controllers in each domain store the portion of Active Directory that contains only the objects from that domain. There is no one single master database that contains all objects from all domains in a domain tree. Instead, because the domains share a directory, users can locate and use network resources in any domain, provided they have the required permissions to gain access to the resource.

By creating a hierarchy of domains in a tree, you can retain security and allow for administration within an OU or within a single domain of a tree. Permissions can flow down the tree by granting permissions to users on an OU basis. This tree structure easily accommodates organizational changes.

Before you can support a multiple domain environment, you should understand trust relationships and interdomain security. You also should be aware of planning considerations for implementing a tree with multiple domains.

After this lesson, you will be able to

- Explain concepts related to multiple-domain environments.

Estimated lesson time: 10 minutes

Trust Relationships

A *trust relationship* is a link between two domains in which the trusting domain honors the logon authentications of the trusted domain. Active Directory supports two forms of trust relationships:

- **Two-way transitive trust.**   A relationship between parent and child domains within a tree and between the top-level domains in a forest. This is the default; trust relationships among domains in a tree are established and maintained *automatically*. Transitive trust is a feature of the Kerberos authentication protocol, which provides the distributed authentication and authorization in Windows 2000.

  For example, in Figure 12.9 a Kerberos transitive trust simply means that if Domain A trusts Domain B, and Domain B trusts Domain C, then Domain A trusts Domain C. As a result, a domain joining a tree immediately has trust relationships established with every domain in the tree. These trust relationships make all objects in all the domains of the tree available to all other domains in the tree.

  Transitive trust between domains eliminates the management of interdomain trust accounts. Domains that are members of the same tree automatically participate in a transitive, bidirectional trust relationship with their parent domain.

As a result, users in one domain can access resources to which they have been granted permission in all other domains in a tree.

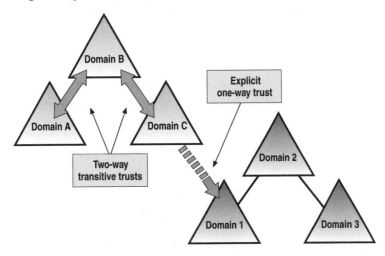

Figure 12.9   Active Directory supports two types of trust relationships

- **Explicit one-way trust.**   A relationship between domains that are not part of the same tree. This capability is provided to support connections to existing Windows NT 4.*x* and earlier domains and to allow the configuration of trust relationships with domains in other trees.

  For example, in Figure 12.9, Domain C trusts Domain 1, so that users in Domain 1 can access resources in Domain C.

Security

Because all domains in a tree trust one another, a tree allows users networkwide access, just as in a single domain. Users can log on in one domain and use resources in another domain, if they have the permissions to use those resources.

At the same time, the domain is a basic security boundary. As result, when you create a tree with multiple domains, you limit the scope of a domain administrator. By default, Windows 2000 sets the following security limitation on trees:

- Members of the built-in group Domain Admins only have control over the objects that reside in their domain.

- Administrative privileges do not flow down a tree. For example, a member of the Administrators group in the root domain does not by default have administrative privileges in any other domain.

A member of the Administrators group in one domain can grant administrative privileges to a member of the Administrators group from another domain by doing the following:

- Granting individual rights or permissions for specific objects and OUs. For example, you can designate a person to administer all user accounts by granting that person's user account the appropriate permissions in all OUs that contain user accounts in each domain.

- Adding a user account from another domain to the domain's Administrators group, thereby giving administrative privileges within the domain to that user. For example, if your company wants one person to have control over all domains, you can add that person's user account to the Domain Admins group in each domain.

Multiple Domains in a Tree

A tree is a grouping or hierarchical arrangement consisting of one or more Windows 2000 domains that share a contiguous namespace. Microsoft recommends that you use a single domain model if possible.

There are situations in which joining multiple domains into a tree can be useful. Consider structuring your network into a tree if the following conditions are met:

- Your organization is decentralized, and different administrators manage different groups of user accounts and resources. In a tree, each domain has its own administrators.

- Your organization is international, and you want the user account and resources for each country to be administered in the local language. By using a tree of domains that correspond to countries, you can ensure that a domain's administrator will understand the names and other attributes of network resources.

- Parts of your network are connected by a very slow link, and you do not want all the replication traffic to cross it. All domain controllers in a domain replicate Active Directory content changes to one another, even across slow links. In a tree, replication occurs only for key attributes of objects.

Lesson Summary

In this lesson you learned that a trust relationship is a link between two domains in which the trusting domain honors the logon authentications of the trusted domain. Active Directory supports two forms of trust relationships: two way transitive trusts and explicit one-way trusts.

A two-way transitive trust is a relationship between parent and child domains within a tree and between the top-level domains in a forest. These trust relationships make all objects in all the domains of the tree available to all other domains in the tree. This is the default and is a feature of the Kerberos authentication protocol. These trust relationships among domains in a tree are established and maintained automatically.

An explicit one-way trust is a relationship between domains that are not part of the same tree. This capability is provided to support connections to existing Windows NT 4.x and earlier domains and to allow the configuration of trust relationships with domains in other trees.

Finally, this lesson discussed multiple domains in a tree. When you create a tree with multiple domains, you limit the scope of a domain administrator.

Review

Here are some questions to help you determine if you have learned enough to move on to the next chapter. If you have difficulty answering these questions, please go back and review the material in this chapter before beginning the next chapter. The answers for these questions are located in Appendix A, "Questions and Answers."

1. What are four major features of Active Directory?

2. What are sites and domains, and how are they different?

3. What is the schema, and how can you extend it?

4. Your company has an Internet namespace reserved with a DNS registration authority. As you plan the Active Directory implementation for your company, you decide to recommend extending the existing namespace for the internal network. What benefits does this option provide?

5. What is the shared system volume, and what purpose does it serve?

6. What is the difference between two-way transitive trusts and explicit one-way trusts?

CHAPTER 13

Setting Up User Accounts

About This Chapter

This chapter introduces you to user accounts and to how to plan your user accounts. It also presents the skills and knowledge necessary to create domain and local user accounts and to set properties for them.

Before You Begin

To complete this chapter, you must have

- A computer that meets the minimum hardware requirements listed in "Hardware Requirements," on page xxxiii.

- Installed the Windows 2000 Server software on the computer.

- Configured the computer as a domain controller in a domain.

Lesson 1: Understanding User Accounts

A user account provides a user with the ability to log on to the domain to gain access to network resources or to log on to a computer to gain access to resources on that computer. Each person who regularly uses the network should have a user account.

Microsoft Windows 2000 provides different types of user accounts: domain user accounts and local user accounts. With a *domain user account,* a user can log on to the domain to gain access to network resources. With a *local user account,* a user logs on to a specific computer to gain access to resources on that computer.

Windows 2000 also provides built-in user accounts, which you use to perform administrative tasks or to gain access to network resources.

After this lesson, you will be able to

- Describe the role and purpose of user accounts.

Estimated lesson time: 10 minutes

Domain User Accounts

Domain user accounts allow users to log on to the domain and gain access to resources anywhere on the network. The user provides his or her password and user name during the logon process. By using this information, Windows 2000 authenticates the user and then builds an access token that contains information about the user and security settings. The access token identifies the user to computers running Windows 2000 on which the user tries to gain access to resources. Windows 2000 provides the access token for the duration of the logon session.

You create a domain user account in an organizational unit (OU) in the copy of the Active Directory database (called the Directory) on a domain controller, as shown in Figure 13.1. The domain controller replicates the new user account information to all domain controllers in the domain.

After Windows 2000 replicates the new user account information, all of the domain controllers in the domain tree can authenticate the user during the logon process.

Note   It can take a few minutes to replicate the domain user account information to all of the domain controllers. This delay might prevent a user from immediately logging on by using the newly created domain user account. By default, replication of Directory information occurs automatically every five minutes.

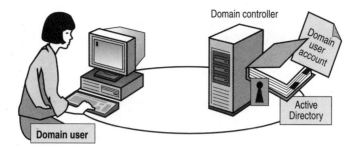

Domain user accounts

- ■ **Provide access to network resources**
- ■ **Provide the access token for authentication**
- ■ **Are created in Active Directory on a domain controller**

Figure 13.1   Domain user accounts

Local User Accounts

Local user accounts allow users to log on at and gain access to resources on only the computer where you create the local user account.

When you create a local user account, Windows 2000 creates the account *only* in that computer's security database, which is called the *local security database,* as shown in Figure 13.2. Windows 2000 does not replicate local user account information to domain controllers. After the local user account exists, the computer uses its local security database to authenticate the local user account, which allows the user to log on to that computer.

Do not create local user accounts on computers running Windows 2000 that are part of a domain, because the domain does not recognize local user accounts. Therefore, the user is unable to gain access to resources in the domain and the domain administrator is unable to administer the local user account properties or assign access permissions for domain resources.

Local user accounts

- Provide access to resources on the local computer
- Are created only on computers that are not in a domain
- Are created in the local security database

Figure 13.2   Local user accounts

Built-In User Accounts

Windows 2000 automatically creates accounts called *built-in accounts*. Two commonly used built-in accounts are Administrator and Guest.

Administrator

Use the built-in Administrator account to manage the overall computer and domain configuration, such as creating and modifying user accounts and groups, managing security policies, creating printers, and assigning permissions and rights to user accounts to gain access to resources.

If you are the administrator, you should create a user account that you use to perform nonadministrative tasks. Log on by using the Administrator account only when you perform administrative tasks.

Note   You can rename the Administrator account, but you cannot delete it. As a best practice, you should always rename the built-in Administrator account to provide a greater degree of security. Use a name that does not identify it as the Administrator account. This makes it difficult for unauthorized users to break into the Administrator account because they do not know which user account it is.

Guest

Use the built-in Guest account to give occasional users the ability to log on and gain access to resources. For example, an employee who needs access to resources for a short time can use the Guest account.

Note   The Guest account is disabled by default. Enable the Guest account only in low-security networks and always assign it a password. You can rename the Guest account, but you cannot delete it.

Lesson Summary

In this lesson you learned that Microsoft Windows 2000 provides different types of user accounts: domain user accounts and local user accounts. With a domain user account, a user can log on to the domain to gain access to network resources. With a local user account, a user logs on to a specific computer to gain access to resources on that computer. There are also built-in user accounts, which can be either domain user accounts or local user accounts. With built-in user accounts, you can perform administrative tasks or gain access to network resources.

When you create a domain user account, Windows 2000 creates the account in the copy of the Active Directory database (called the Directory) on a domain controller. The domain controller then replicates the new user account information to all domain controllers in the domain. When you create a local user account, Windows 2000 creates the account only in that computer's security database, which is called the local security database. Windows 2000 does not replicate local user account information to domain controllers. You do not create built-in user accounts; Windows 2000 automatically creates them.

Lesson 2: Planning New User Accounts

You can streamline the process of creating user accounts by planning and organizing the information for the user accounts. You should plan the following three areas:

- Naming conventions for user accounts
- Requirements for passwords
- Account options, such as logon hours, the computers from which users can log on, and account expiration

After this lesson, you will be able to

- Plan a strategy for creating new user accounts.

Estimated lesson time: 10 minutes

Naming Conventions

The naming convention establishes how users are identified in the domain. A consistent naming convention will help you and your users remember user logon names and locate them in lists.

Table 13.1 summarizes some points you might want to consider in determining a naming convention for your organization.

Table 13.1   Naming Convention Considerations

Consideration	Explanation
User logon names must be unique	User logon names for domain user accounts must be unique to the Directory. Domain user account names must be unique within the OU where you create the domain user account. Local user account names must be unique on the computer where you create the local user account.
20 characters maximum	User logon names can contain up to 20 uppercase or lowercase characters; the field accepts more than 20 characters, but Windows 2000 recognizes only the first 20.
Invalid characters	The following characters are invalid: " / \ [ ] : ;	= , + * ? < >

Consideration	Explanation
User logon names are not case sensitive	You can use a combination of special and alphanumeric characters to help uniquely identify user accounts. User logon names are *not* case sensitive, but Windows 2000 preserves the case.
Accommodate employees with duplicate names	If two users were named John Doe, you could use the first name and the last initial, and then add additional letters from the last name to differentiate the duplicate names. In this example, one user account logon name could be Johnd and the other Johndo. Another possibility would be to number each user logon name—for example, Johnd1 and Johnd2.
Identify the type of employee	In some organizations, it is useful to identify temporary employees by their user account. To identify temporary employees, you can use a *T* and a dash in front of the user's logon name—for example, T-Johnd. Alternatively, use parentheses in the name—for example, John Doe (Temp).

Password Requirements

To protect access to the domain or a computer, every user account should have a password. Consider the following guidelines for passwords:

- Always assign a password for the Administrator account to prevent unauthorized access to the account.

- Determine whether the Administrator or the users will control passwords. You can assign unique passwords for the user accounts and prevent users from changing them, or you can allow users to enter their own passwords the first time that they log on. In most cases, users should control their passwords.

- Use passwords that are hard to guess. For example, avoid using passwords with an obvious association, such as a family member's name.

- Passwords can be up to 128 characters; a minimum length of eight characters is recommended.

- Use both uppercase and lowercase letters, numerals, and valid nonalphanumeric characters. Table 13.1 lists the invalid nonalphanumeric characters .

Account Options

You should assess the hours when a user can log on to the network and the computers from which a user can log on, and you should determine if temporary user accounts need to expire. To determine account options, consider the following information.

Logon Hours

Set logon hours for users who only require access at specific times. For example, allow night shift workers to log on only during their working hours.

Computers from Which Users Can Log On

Determine the computers from which users can log on. By default, users can log on to the domain by using any computer in the domain. For security reasons, require users to log on to the domain only from their computer. This prevents users from gaining access to sensitive information that is stored on other computers.

Note   If you have disabled NetBIOS over Transmission Control Protocol/Internet Protocol (TCP/IP), Windows 2000 is unable to determine which computer you are logging on from, and therefore you cannot restrict users to specific computers.

Account Expiration

Determine whether a user account should expire. If so, set an expiration date on the user account to ensure that the account is disabled when the user should no longer have access to the network. As a good security practice, you should set user accounts for temporary employees to expire when their contract ends.

Practice: Planning New User Accounts

In this practice, you plan how to implement user accounts for employees who are listed on the New Hire List.

Scenario

As the Windows 2000 administrator for your corporate network, you need to set up the user accounts for new employees. Ten employees have recently been hired. You need to determine the following:

- A naming convention that will easily accommodate employees with duplicate or similar names and temporary contract personnel
- The hours during which users can log on
- The computers at which a user can log on

Criteria

Use the following criteria to make your decisions:

- All employees require a user account.
- Permanent employees should control their passwords.
- For security reasons, an administrator should control passwords for contract employees.

- Day shift hours are from 8 AM through 5 PM and night shift hours are from 6 PM through 6 AM.

- Permanent employees require access to the network 24 hours a day, seven days a week.

- Temporary employees log on at *only* their assigned computers and only during their shifts. The computer names for computers that temporary employees use are Temp1 and Temp2.

New Hire List

The following table provides fictitious names and hiring information for the new employees.

User name	Title	Department	Status	Shift
Don Hall	Representative	Sales	Temporary	Day
Donna Hall	Manager	Product Support	Permanent	Night
James Smith	Vice President	Training	Permanent	Day
James Smith	Representative	Sales	Permanent	Day
Jon Morris	Developer	Product Development	Temporary	Night
Judy Lew	Developer	Product Development	Temporary	Day
Kim Yoshida	President	Training	Permanent	Day
Laurent Vernhes	Engineer	Product Support	Temporary	Night
Sandra Martinez	Engineer	Product Support	Permanent	Day

Planning Questions

Complete the following table to determine a naming convention for the users in the new hire list by considering the information that is provided in the sections "Scenario," "Criteria," and "New Hire List" in this practice.

User name	Full name	User logon name
Don Hall		
Donna Hall		
James Smith		
James Smith		
Jon Morris		
Judy Lew		
Kim Yoshida		
Laurent Vernhes		
Sandra Martinez		

Complete the following table to determine logon hours and computer use for the users in the new hire list by considering the information that is provided in the sections "Scenario," "Criteria," and "New Hire List" in this practice.

User name	When can the user log on?	Where can the user log on?
Don Hall		
Donna Hall		
James Smith		
James Smith		
Jon Morris		
Judy Lew		
Kim Yoshida		
Laurent Vernhes		
Sandra Martinez		

Select the appropriate password setting for each user in the following table to determine who controls the user's password.

User name	User must change password the next time he or she logs on	User cannot change password
Don Hall	☐	☐
Donna Hall	☐	☐
James Smith	☐	☐
James Smith	☐	☐
Jon Morris	☐	☐
Judy Lew	☐	☐
Kim Yoshida	☐	☐
Laurent Vernhes	☐	☐
Sandra Martinez	☐	☐

Lesson Summary

In this lesson you learned that in planning user accounts, you should determine naming conventions for user accounts, requirements for passwords, and account options such as logon hours, the computers from which users can log on, and account expiration. You learned that domain user accounts can be up to 20 characters in length and must be unique within the OU where you create the domain user account. Local user account names can also be up to 20 characters in length and must be unique on the computer where you create the local user account. Making these decisions before you start creating user accounts will reduce the amount of time it takes to create the needed user accounts and will simplify managing these accounts.

In the practice portion of this lesson, you were presented a fictitious scenario and planned a naming convention that easily accommodated employees with duplicate or similar names and temporary contract personnel. You also had to plan the hours during which users can log on and the computers at which a user can log on, based on the scenario and criteria you were supplied.

Lesson 3: Creating Domain User Accounts

Use the Directory Management snap-in to create a new domain user account. When you create a domain user account, it is always created on the first available domain controller that is contacted by Microsoft Management Console (MMC), and then the account is replicated to all domain controllers.

After this lesson, you will be able to

▪ Create a domain user account.

Estimated lesson time: 10 minutes

Directory Management Snap-In

The Directory Management snap-in (illustrated in Figure 13.3) is the tool you use to create domain user accounts.

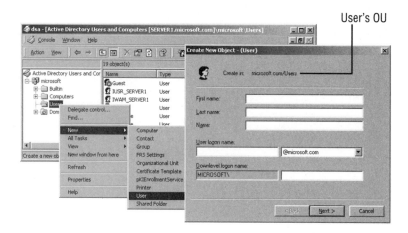

Figure 13.3   Directory Management snap-in

When you create the domain user account, User Logon Name defaults to the domain in which you are creating the domain user account. However, you can select any domain in which you have permissions to create domain user accounts. You must select the OU in which to create the new account. You can create the domain user account in the default Users OU or in an OU that you create to hold domain user accounts.

▶ **To create domain user accounts**

1. Click the Start button, point to Programs, point to Administrative Tools, and then click Directory Management.

2. Click the domain, right-click the Users OU, point to New, and click User.

Table 13.2 describes the domain user account options that you can configure.

Table 13.2   Domain User Account Options

Option	Description
First Name	The user's first name. This or Last Name is required.
Last Name	The user's last name. This or First Name is required.
Name	The user's complete name. The name must be unique within the OU where you create the user account. Windows 2000 completes this option if you enter information in First Name or Last Name. Windows 2000 displays this name in the OU where the user account is located in the Directory.
User Logon Name	The user's unique logon name, based on your naming conventions. This is required and must be unique within the Directory.
Down-Level Logon Name	The user's unique logon name that is used to log on from down-level clients, such as Windows NT 4.0 or Windows NT 3.51. This is required and must be unique within the domain.

Setting Password Requirements

In the Create New Object - (User) dialog box, shown in Figure 13.3, click Next to open a second Create New Object - (User) dialog box, shown in Figure 13.4, which contains password settings. In this dialog box, you set the password requirements for the domain user account.

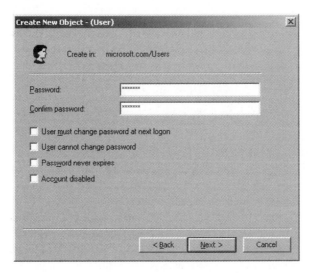

Figure 13.4   Create New Object - (User)

Table 13.3 describes the password options that you can configure.

Table 13.3   Password Options

Option	Description
Password	The password that is used to authenticate the user. For greater security, you should *always* assign a password. Notice that you do not see the password. It is represented as asterisks when you type the password, regardless of the length of the password.
Confirm Password	Confirm the password by typing it a second time to make sure that you typed the password correctly. This is required if you assign a password.
User Must Change Password At Next Logon	Select this check box if you want the user to change his or her password the first time that he or she logs on. This ensures that the user is the only person who knows the password.
User Cannot Change Password	Select this check box if you have more than one person using the same domain user account (such as Guest) or to maintain control over user account passwords. This allows only administrators to control passwords.
Password Never Expires	Select this check box if you never want the password to change—for example, for a domain user account that will be used by a program or a Windows 2000 service. User Must Change Password At Next Logon overrides Password Never Expires.
Account Disabled	Select this check box to prevent use of this user account—for example, for a new employee who has not yet started.

Note   Always require new users to change their passwords the first time that they log on. This will force users to use passwords that only they know.

Tip   For added security on networks, create random initial passwords for all new user accounts by using a combination of letters and numbers. Creating a random initial password will help keep the user account secure.

Note   Use the Local User Manager snap-in to create local user accounts. A local user account gives a user access to resources only on the computer where you create the account. You create local user accounts only on computers running Windows 2000 Professional and on stand-alone servers or member servers running Windows 2000 Server. Do not create local user accounts on computers that are part of a domain, because the domain does not recognize them. Local user accounts are not stored in the Directory for the domain; they are stored in the security database of the computer where you create them.

Practice: Creating Domain User Accounts

In this practice, you create the user accounts shown in the following table:

First name	Last name	User logon name	Password	Change password
User	One	User1	(blank)	Must
User	Three	User3	(blank)	Must
User	Five	User5	User5	Must
User	Seven	User7	User7	Must
User	Nine	User9	User9	Cannot

Note The following procedure outlines the steps that are required to create the first user account by using the Directory Management snap-in. After you have created the first user account, follow the same steps to create the remaining user accounts.

▶ **To create a domain user account**

1. Log on as Administrator.
2. Click the Start button, point to Programs, point to Administrative Tools, and then click Directory Management.

   Windows 2000 displays the Directory Management snap-in.
3. Expand Microsoft (if you did not use Microsoft as your domain name, expand your domain), and then double-click Users.

   In the details pane, notice the default user accounts.

   Which user accounts does the Active Directory Installation wizard create by default?

   _____

4. Right-click Users, point to New, and then click User.

   Windows 2000 displays the Create New Object - (User) dialog box.

   Where in Active Directory will the new user account be created?

   _____

5. Type **User** in the First Name box.
6. Type **One** in the Last Name box.

   Notice that Windows 2000 completes the Full Name box for you.

   Note To add a middle initial to a user's full name, complete the First Name and Last Name text boxes and then click the Name box to edit the full name.

7. Type **User1** in the User Logon Name box.

8. In the box to the right of the User Logon Name box, select @microsoft.com. (The domain name will vary, if you did not use microsoft.com as your DNS domain name.)

   The user logon name, combined with the domain name in the box that appears to the right of the User Logon Name box, is the user's full Internet logon name. This name uniquely identifies the user throughout the entire network (for example, user1@microsoft.com).

   Notice that Windows 2000 completes the Downlevel Logon Name box for you.

   When is the down-level logon name used?

9. Click Next to continue.

   Windows 2000 displays the Create New Object - (User) dialog box, prompting you to supply password options and restrictions.

10. In the Password box and the Confirm Password box, type the password or leave these boxes blank if you are not assigning a password.

    If you enter a password, notice that the password is displayed as asterisks as you type. This prevents onlookers from viewing the password as it is entered.

    In high-security environments, you should assign initial passwords to user accounts and then require users to change their password the next time that they log on. This prevents a user account from existing without a password, and once the user logs on and changes his or her password, only the user knows the password.

11. Specify whether or not the user can change his or her password.

    What are the results of selecting both the User Must Change Password At Next Logon check box and the User Cannot Change Password check box? Explain.

    Under what circumstances would you select the Account Disabled check box while you create a new user account?

12. After you have selected the appropriate password options, click Next.

    Windows 2000 displays the Create New Object - (User) dialog box, displaying the options and restrictions that you have configured for this user account.

13. Verify that the user account options are correct, and then click Finish.

    Note   If the user account options are incorrect, click Back to modify the user account options.

    In the details pane of Directory Management, notice that the user account that you just created now appears.

14. Complete steps 4–13 for the remaining user accounts.

Lesson Summary

In this lesson you learned that you use the Directory Management snap-in to create a new domain user account. When you create a domain user account, it is always created on the first available domain controller that is contacted by Microsoft Management Console (MMC), and then the account is replicated to all domain controllers. You also learned that you can configure options for the accounts you create, including a user name, a user last name, and a user logon name. Finally in this lesson you learned that you can also configure password options such as whether users must change their passwords at next logon, whether users can ever change their passwords, and whether the passwords expire. In the practice portion of this lesson you created five domain user accounts.

Lesson 4: Setting Properties for User Accounts

A set of default properties is associated with each domain user account that you create. These account properties equate to object attributes.

You can use the properties that you define for a domain user account to search for users in the Directory. For this reason, you should provide detailed property definitions for each domain user account that you create. For example, you can search for a person's telephone number, office location, and manager's name by using the person's last name.

After you create a domain user account, you can configure personal and account properties, logon options, and dial-in settings.

After this lesson, you will be able to

- Set properties for user accounts.

Estimated lesson time: 15 minutes

Setting Personal Properties

The tabs in the Properties dialog box contain information about each user account. The tabs are General, Address, Telephone/Notes, and Organization. Completing the properties on each of these tabs enables you to locate user accounts in the Directory. For example, if all of the properties on the Address tab are complete, as shown in Figure 13.5, you can locate that person by using the street address or another field.

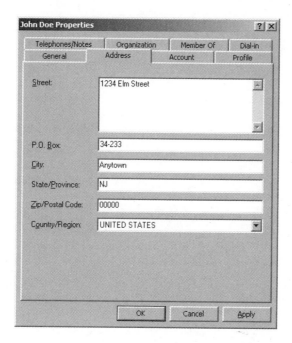

Figure 13.5   Address tab of the Properties dialog box

Table 13.4 describes the tabs in the Properties dialog box.

Table 13.4   Tabs in the Properties Dialog Box

Tab	Description
General	Use this tab to document the user's first name, last name, display name, description, office location, telephone number(s), e-mail address, home page, and additional Web pages.
Address	Use this tab to document the user's street address, post office box, city, state or province, zip or postal code, and country or region.
Account	Use this tab to document the user's account options. The account options include the following: user logon name, if and when a user can change passwords, and if and when the user account expires.
Profile	Use this path to set a profile path, logon script path, home directory, and shared document folder.
Telephone/Notes	Use this tab to document the user's home, pager, mobile, fax, and Internet Protocol (IP) telephone numbers, and to add comments.
Organization	Use this tab to document the user's title, department, company, manager, and direct reports.

(continued)

Tab	Description
Member Of	Use this tab to document the groups to which the user belongs.
Dial-In	Use this tab to document the dial-in properties for the user.

▶ **To set Personal Properties**

1. On the Administrative Tools menu, click Directory Management, and then click the domain.
2. Click the appropriate OU to view available domain user accounts.
3. Right-click the appropriate domain user account, and then click Properties.
4. Click the appropriate tab for the personal properties that you want to enter or change, and then enter values for each property.

Setting Account Properties

Use the Account tab in the Properties dialog box, shown in Figure 13.6, to set options for a domain user account.

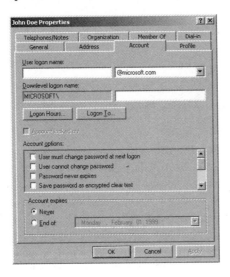

Figure 13.6   Account properties

Some of the domain user account options are the same for both the Account tab and the Create New Object - (User) dialog box. Table 13.5 describes the additional account options that are not available when you create a domain user account.

Table 13.5   Additional Account Options

Option	Description
Save Password As Encrypted Clear Text	Select this check box to enable Macintosh users to log on. Macintosh computers only send this type of password.
User Must Logon Using A Smart Card	Select this check box to allow a user to log on with a smart card. Additional hardware is required.
Account Expires	Select Never if you do not want the account to expire. Select End Of and then enter a date in the adjoining text box if you want Windows 2000 to automatically disable the user account on the date you specify. Use the End Of option for user accounts for temporary or part-time employees.

Setting Logon Hours

Set logon hours to control when a user can log on to the domain. Restricting logon hours limits the hours that users can explore the network. By default, Windows 2000 permits access for all hours on all days. You might want to allow users to log on only during working hours. Setting logon hours reduces the amount of time that the account is open to unauthorized access.

▶ **To set logon hours**

1. In the Properties dialog box, on the Account tab, click Logon Hours.

   A blue box indicates that the user can log on during the hour. A white box indicates that the user cannot log on (see Figure 13.7).

2. To allow or deny access, do one of the following:

   ■ Select the rectangles on the days and hours for which you want to *deny* access, click the start time, drag to the end time, and then click Logon Denied.

   ■ Select the rectangles on the days and hours for which you want to *allow* access, click the start time, drag to the end time, and then click Logon Permitted.

   Note   The days and hours for which you have allowed access are now shown in blue.

3. Click OK.

It is important that you remember that any connections to network resources on the domain are not disconnected when the user's logon hours run out. However, the user will not be able to make any new connections.

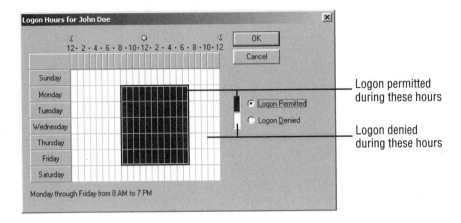

Logon permitted during these hours

Logon denied during these hours

Figure 13.7   Logon hours

Setting the Computers from Which Users Can Log On

Setting logon options for a domain user account allows you to control the computers from which a user can log on to the domain. By default, each user can log on from all computers in the domain. Setting the computers from which a user can log on prevents users from accessing another user's data that is stored on that user's computer.

▶   **To set logon workstations**

1. In the Properties dialog box, on the Account tab, click Logon To (see Figure 13.8).

2. Select the option that specifies from which computers a user can log on.

3. Add the computers from which a user can log on.

   Use the computer name that you specified when you installed Windows 2000, which is the name of the computer account in the Directory.

4. If necessary, delete or edit the name of a computer from which the user can log on.

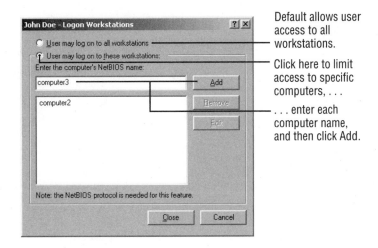

Default allows user access to all workstations.

Click here to limit access to specific computers, . . .

. . . enter each computer name, and then click Add.

Figure 13.8   Logon workstations

Configuring Dial-In Settings

Configuring dial-in settings for a user account permits you to control how a user can make a dial-in connection to the network from a remote location. To gain access to the network, the user dials in to a computer running the Windows 2000 Remote Access Service (RAS).

Note   In addition to configuring dial-in settings and having RAS on the server to which the user is dialing in, you must also set up a dial-up connection for the server on the client computer. Set up a dial-up connection by using the Network Connection wizard, which you can access from Network Connections in My Computer.

Configure dial-in settings on the Dial-In tab of the Properties dialog box. Table 13.6 describes the required options for setting up security for a dial-up connection.

Table 13.6   Additional Account Options

Option	Description
Allow Access or Deny Access	Specify whether to turn on dial-in settings (Allow Access) or to turn them off (Deny Access).
Verify Caller-ID	In the box, type the telephone number that the user must use to dial in.

(continued)

Option	Description
Callback Options	Select the callback method. Options include
	■ **No Callback.** The RAS server will not call the user back and the user pays the telephone charges. This is the default.
	■ **Set By Caller (RAS Only).** The user provides the telephone number for the RAS server to call back. The company pays the telephone charges for the session.
	■ **Always Callback To.** The RAS server uses the specified telephone number to call back the user. The user must be at the specified telephone number to make a connection to the server. This reduces the risk of an unauthorized person dialing in because the number is preconfigured. Use this option in a high-security environment.

Practice: Modifying User Account Properties

In this practice, you modify user account properties. You configure the Logon Hours and Account Expiration settings for several of the user accounts that you created in the previous practice. You add these user accounts to the Print Operators group so that the accounts can log on to the domain controller. Then you then test the Logon Hours restrictions, the password restrictions that you set up when you created the accounts, and the Account Expiration Settings.

Exercise 1: Configuring Logon Hours and Account Expiration

In this exercise you configure the hours during which User3 and User5 can log on to the computer, and for User5 you also set a date for the account to expire.

Scenario

Modify the following user accounts with the properties specified in the following table.

User account	Logon hours	Account expires . . .
User3	6 PM–6 AM, Monday–Friday	
User5		Today

Important   Complete the following procedure while you are logged on as Administrator with Directory Management running and your domain expanded in the console tree.

▶   **To specify logon hours**

1. In the console tree of Directory Management, expand Users.

2. In the details pane, right-click User Three, and then click Properties.

   Windows 2000 displays the User3 Properties dialog box with the General tab active.

   On the General tab, what information can you specify for the user account in addition to first and last name? How would this information be useful?

3. Click the Account tab, and then click Logon Hours.

   Windows 2000 displays the Logon Hours For User3 dialog box.

   Currently, when can User3 log on?

4. To restrict the user's logon hours, click the start time of the first period during which you want to prevent the user from logging on and then drag the pointer to the end time for the period.

   A frame outlines the blocks for all of the selected hours.

   Note   To select the same block of time for all days in the week, above the Sunday row, click the gray block that represents the start time, and then drag the pointer to the end time. To select an entire day, click the gray block that is labeled with the name of the day.

5. Click Logon Denied.

   The outlined area is now a white block, indicating that the user will not be permitted to log on during those hours.

6. Repeat steps 4 and 5 as necessary until only the correct logon hours are allowed.

7. Click OK to close the Logon Hours For User3 dialog box.

8. In the User3 Properties dialog box, click OK to apply your settings and return to Directory Management.

▶   **To set account expiration for a user account**

1. In the console tree of Directory Management, click Users.

2. In the details pane, right-click User Five, and then click Properties.

Windows 2000 displays the User5 Properties dialog box with the General tab active.

3. Click the Account tab.

   When will the account expire?

4. Click End Of, and then set the date to today's date.

5. Click OK to apply your changes and return to Directory Management.

6. Close Directory Management, and then log off Windows 2000.

Exercise 2: Testing User Accounts

In this exercise, you log on each of the user accounts that you created in the previous exercises and then test the effects of the account settings.

▶ **To test log on capabilities of user accounts**

1. Attempt to log on as User1 with no password.

   Windows 2000 displays the Logon Message message box, indicating that you must change your password.

2. In the Change Password dialog box, in the New Password box and the Confirm New Password box, type **student** and then click OK.

   Windows 2000 displays the Change Password message box indicating that your password was changed.

3. Click OK to close the Change Password message box.

   Were you able to successfully log on? Why or why not?

There are several ways to allow regular users to log on at a domain controller. In the next procedure you add the users to the Print Operators group, because this group has the right to log on to a domain controller. A *group* is a collection of user accounts. Groups simplify administration by allowing you to assign permissions to a group of users rather than having to assign permissions to each individual user account. For more information on groups, see Chapter 14, "Setting Up Groups."

▶ **To add users to the Print Operators group**

1. Log on as administrator.

2. In the console tree of Directory Management, expand Users.

3. In the details pane, right-click User One, and then click Properties.

   Windows 2000 displays the User1 Properties dialog box with the General tab active.

4. Click Member Of.

5. Click Add, and then click Print Operators.

6. Click Add, and then click OK to close the Select Groups window.

7. Click OK to close the User1 Properties window.

8. Repeat steps 3 through 7 for User3, User 5, User7, and User9.

9. Close Directory Management.

10. Log off Windows 2000.

▶ **To test restrictions on logon hours**

1. Attempt to log on as User1 with a password of student.

   Were you able to successfully log on? Why or why not?

2. Attempt to log on as User3 with no password.

3. When prompted, change the password to student.

   Were you able to successfully log on? Why or why not?

▶ **To test password restrictions**

1. Attempt to log on as User7 with no password.

   Were you able to successfully log on? Why or why not?

2. Attempt to log on as User7 with a password of User7.

3. When prompted, change the password to student.

   Were you able to log on? Why or why not?

4. Log off Windows 2000.

5. Attempt to log on as User9 with a password of user9.

   Were you able to successfully log on? Why or why not?

▶ **To test password restrictions by attempting to change a password**

1. Press Ctrl+Alt+Delete.

   Windows 2000 displays the Windows 2000 Security dialog box.

2. Click Change Password.

   Windows 2000 displays the Change Password dialog box.

3. In the Old Password box, type the password for the user account, in the New Password and Confirm New Password boxes, type **student** and then click OK.

   Were you able to change the password? Why or why not?

4. Click OK to close the Change Password message box, and then click Cancel to return to the Windows 2000 Security dialog box.

5. Click Log Off.

   Windows 2000 displays the Log Off Windows dialog box, prompting you to verify that you want to log off.

6. Click Yes to log off.

▶ **To test account expiration**

1. Attempt to log on as User5.

2. When prompted, change your password to student.

   Were you successful? Why or why not?

3. Log off Windows 2000.

▶ **To change the system time**

1. Log on to your domain as Administrator, click the Start button, point to Settings, and then click Control Panel.

2. In Control Panel, double-click Date/Time.

   Windows 2000 displays the Date/Time Properties dialog box.

3. Under Date, enter tomorrow's date, and then click OK to apply your changes and return to Control Panel.

4. Close Control Panel and log off Windows 2000.

▶ **To test account expiration**

1. Attempt to log on as User5 with a password of student.

   Were you successful? Why or why not?

▶ **To change the system time**

1. Log on to your domain as Administrator, click the Start button, point to Settings, and then click Control Panel.

2. In Control Panel, double-click Date/Time.

Windows 2000 displays the Date/Time Properties dialog box.

3. Under Date, enter today's date, and then click OK to apply your changes and return to Control Panel.

4. Close Control Panel and log off Windows 2000.

Lesson Summary

In this lesson you learned that there is a set of default properties associated with each domain user account that you create. You learned that these account properties equate to object attributes, so you can use these properties to search for users in the Directory. For example, you can search for a person's telephone number, office location, and manager's name by using the person's last name.

You also learned that after you create a domain user account, you can use the Directory Management snap-in to easily configure or modify personal and account properties. Personal properties allow you to change properties such as a person's name, address, and phone number in case he or she gets married, moves, or gets a different phone number. Account options allow you to control the time of day a user can log on, which workstations a user can log on to, whether a password expires, and whether a user can change his or her password.

In the practice portion of this lesson, you were able to create five domain user accounts. You then configured account properties including modifying the logon hours, setting account expiration, and determining when and if a user can change his or her password. Finally, you tested these properties to verify that they worked as expected.

Review

Here are some questions to help you determine if you have learned enough to move on to the next chapter. If you have difficulty answering these questions, please go back and review the material in this chapter before beginning the next chapter. The answers for these questions are located in Appendix A, "Questions and Answers."

1. Where does Windows 2000 create domain user accounts and local user accounts?

2. What different capabilities do domain user accounts and local user accounts provide to users?

3. What should you consider when you plan new user accounts?

4. What information is required to create a domain user account?

5. A user wants to gain access to network resources remotely from home. The user does not want to pay the long distance charges for the telephone call. How would you set up the user account to accomplish this?

C H A P T E R   1 4

Setting Up Groups

About This Chapter

This chapter introduces you to groups and to how to group user accounts to allow for easier assignment of permissions. It also presents the skills and knowledge necessary to implement groups, local groups, and built-in groups.

Before You Begin

To complete this chapter, you must have

- A computer that meets the minimum hardware requirements listed in "Hardware Requirements," on page xxxiii.
- Installed the Windows 2000 Server software on the computer.
- Configured the computer as a domain controller in a domain.
- Created the User1 and User5 accounts as directed in Chapter 13.

Lesson 1: Understanding Groups

In this lesson you will learn what groups are and how groups are used to simplify user account administration. You will also learn the group scopes and the group types you can create in Microsoft Windows 2000 and how these group scopes and types are used. Finally, you will learn the rules for group membership.

After this lesson, you will be able to

- Describe the key features of groups.

Estimated lesson time: 15 minutes

Group Administration

A *group* is a collection of user accounts. Groups simplify administration by allowing you to assign permissions and rights to a group of users rather than having to assign permissions to each individual user account (see Figure 14.1).

Permissions control what users can do with a resource, such as a folder, file, or printer. When you assign permissions, you give users the capability to gain access to a resource, and you define the type of access that they have. For example, if several users need to read the same file, you would add their user accounts to a group. Then, you would give the group permission to read the file. Rights allow users to perform system tasks, such as changing the time on a computer, backing up or restoring files, or logging on locally.

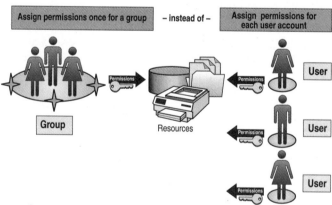

- Groups are a collection of user accounts.
- Members receive permissions given to groups.
- Users can be members of multiple groups.
- Groups can be members of other groups.

Figure 14.1   Groups simplify administration

In addition to user accounts, you can add groups and computers to groups. You add computers to groups to simplify giving a system task on one computer access to a resource on another computer.

When you add members to groups, consider the following:

- Users can be members of multiple groups.

  A group contains a list of members, with references to the actual user account. Therefore, users can be members of more than one group.

- Groups can be members of other groups.

  Adding groups to other groups (*nesting*) creates a consolidated group and can reduce the number of times that you need to assign permissions. For example, you could add the managers in each region to a group that is specific to that region. Administrators in each region control the membership of the group that represents managers in their region. Then, you could add all of the regional groups to a Worldwide Managers group. When all managers need access to resources, you assign permissions only to the Worldwide Managers group.

- Minimize levels of nesting.

  Tracking permissions becomes more complex with multiple levels of nesting. One level of nesting is the most effective to use. Troubleshooting becomes difficult if you have to trace permission assignments due to multiple levels of nesting. Therefore, you must document group membership to keep track of permissions assignments.

Group Types

Sometimes you create groups for security-related purposes, such as assigning permissions. Other times you use them for nonsecurity purposes, such as sending e-mail messages. To facilitate this, Windows 2000 includes two group types: *security* and *distribution*. The group type determines how you use the group. Both types of groups are stored in the database component of Active Directory, which allows you to use them anywhere in your network.

Security Groups

Windows 2000 uses only security groups, which you use to assign permissions to gain access to resources. Programs that are designed to search Active Directory can also use security groups for nonsecurity-related purposes, such as sending e-mail messages to a number of users at the same time. A security group also has all the capabilities of a distribution group. Since Windows 2000 uses only security groups, this chapter will focus on security groups.

Distribution Groups

Applications use distribution groups as lists for nonsecurity-related functions. Use distribution groups when the only function of the group is nonsecurity related, such as sending e-mail messages to a group of users at the same time. You cannot use distribution groups to assign permissions.

Note Only programs that are designed to work with Active Directory can use distribution groups. For example, future versions of Microsoft Exchange Server will be able to use distribution groups as distribution lists for sending e-mail messages.

Group Scopes

When you create a group you must select a group type and a group scope. Group *scopes* allow you to use groups in different ways to assign permissions. The scope of a group determines where in the network you are able to use the group to assign permissions to the group. The three group scopes are global, domain local, and universal, as shown in Figure 14.2.

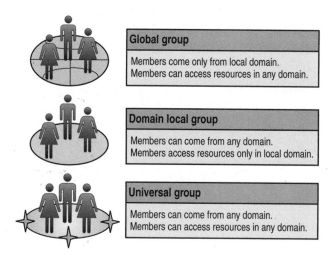

Global group
Members come only from local domain.
Members can access resources in any domain.

Domain local group
Members can come from any domain.
Members access resources only in local domain.

Universal group
Members can come from any domain.
Members can access resources in any domain.

Figure 14.2 Group scopes

Global Group

Global security groups are most often used to organize users who share similar network access requirements. A global group has the following characteristics:

- **Limited membership.** You can add members only from the domain in which you create the global group.

- **Access to resources in any domain.** You can use a global group to assign permissions to gain access to resources that are located in any domain.

Domain Local Groups

Domain local security groups are most often used to assign permissions to resources. A domain local group has the following characteristics:

- **Open membership.** You can add members from any domain.

- **Access to resources in one domain.** You can use a domain local group to assign permissions to gain access to resources that are located only in the same domain where you create the domain local group.

Universal Groups

Universal security groups are most often used to assign permissions to related resources in multiple domains. A universal security group has the following characteristics:

- **Open membership.** You can add members from any domain.

- **Access to resources in any domain.** You can use a universal group to assign permissions to gain access to resources that are located in any domain.

- **Only available in native mode.** Universal security groups are not available in mixed mode. The full feature set of Windows 2000 is only available in native mode.

Rules for Group Membership

The group scope determines the membership of the group. *Membership rules* consist of the members that a group can contain and the groups of which a group can be a member. Group members consist of user accounts and other groups. To assign the correct members to groups and to use nesting, it is important to understand group membership rules.

Table 14.1 describes group membership rules, including what each group scope can contain, as well as the groups of which each group scope can be a member.

Table 14.1   Group Scope Membership Rules

Group scope	Scope can contain	Scope can be a member of
Global	User accounts and global groups from the same domain.	Universal and domain local groups in any domain.
		Global groups in the same domain.
Domain local	User accounts, universal groups, and global groups from any domain.	Domain local groups in the same domain.
	Domain local groups from the same domain.	

Group scope	Scope can contain	Scope can be a member of
Universal	User accounts, universal groups, and global groups from any domain.	Domain local or universal groups in any domain.

Lesson Summary

In this lesson you learned that a group is a collection of user accounts. Groups can also contain other groups. Groups simplify administration by allowing you to assign permissions and rights to a group of users rather than having to assign permissions to each individual user account.

You also learned that when you create a group, you must choose a group type and a group scope. Windows 2000 includes two group types, security groups and distribution groups, but only uses security groups. Applications designed to work with Active Directory can use distribution groups as lists for nonsecurity-related functions, such as e-mail. Windows 2000 includes three group scopes: domain local, global, and universal.

Finally you learned that there are rules for group membership. These rules determine the members that a domain local security group, a global security group, and a universal security group can contain. These rules also determine the groups of which each of these three group scopes can be a member.

Lesson 2: Planning Group Strategies

To use groups effectively, you need a strategy for using the different group scopes. The following are two common group strategies, depending on your Windows 2000 network environment:

- In a single domain, the best strategy is to use global and domain local groups to assign permissions to network resources.

- In a domain tree, you can use global and universal groups.

After this lesson, you will be able to

- Plan a group strategy.

Estimated lesson time: 30 minutes

Using Global and Domain Local Groups

It is important to have a group strategy in place before you create groups. The recommended method is to use global and domain local groups. When you plan to use global and domain local groups, use the following strategy:

1. Identify users with common job responsibilities and add the user accounts to a global group. For example, in an accounting department, add user accounts for all accountants to a global group called Accounting.

2. Identify what resources or group of resources, such as related files, to which users need access, and then create a domain local group for that resource. For example, if you have a number of color printers in your company, create a domain local group called Color Printers.

3. Identify all global groups that share the same access needs for resources and make them members of the appropriate domain local group. For example, add the global groups Accounting, Sales, and Management to the domain local group Color Printers.

4. Assign the required permissions to the domain local group. For example, assign the necessary permissions to use color printers to the Color Printers group.

Figure 14.3 illustrates the strategy for using groups: place user accounts into global groups, create a domain local group for a group of resources to be shared in common, place the global groups into the domain local group, and then assign permissions to the domain local group. This strategy gives you the most flexibility for growth and reduces permissions assignments.

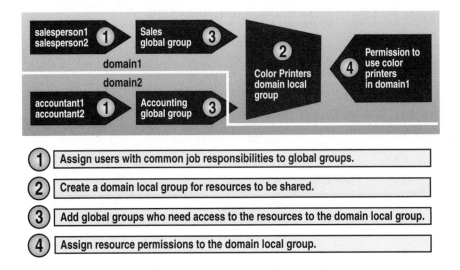

1. Assign users with common job responsibilities to global groups.

2. Create a domain local group for resources to be shared.

3. Add global groups who need access to the resources to the domain local group.

4. Assign resource permissions to the domain local group.

Figure 14.3   Planning a group strategy

Some of the possible limitations of other strategies include the following:

- Placing user accounts in domain local groups and assigning permissions to the domain local groups does not allow you to assign permissions for resources outside of the domain. This strategy reduces the flexibility when your network grows.

- Placing user accounts in global groups and assigning permissions to the global groups can complicate administration when you are using multiple domains. If global groups from multiple domains require the same permissions, you have to assign permissions for each global group.

Using Universal Groups

When you plan to use universal groups, follow these guidelines:

- Use universal groups to give users access to resources that are located in more than one domain. Unlike domain local groups, you can assign permissions to universal groups for resources in any domain in your network. For example, if executives need access to printers throughout your network, you can create a universal group for this purpose and assign it permissions for using printers on print servers in all domains.

- Use universal groups only when their membership is static. In a domain tree, universal groups can cause excessive network traffic between domain controllers whenever you change membership for the universal group because changes to the membership of universal groups may be replicated to a larger number of domain controllers.

- Add global groups from several domains to a universal group, and then assign permissions for access to a resource to the universal group. This allows you to use a universal group in the same way as domain local groups to assign permissions for resources. However, unlike a domain local group, you can assign permissions to a universal group to give users access to a resource that is located in any domain.

Practice: Planning New User Accounts

In this practice, you plan the groups that are required for a business scenario.

You determine the following:

- Which groups are needed.
- The membership of each group. This can be user accounts or other groups.
- The type and scope for each group.

Scenario

You are an administrator for the Customer Service division of a manufacturing company. You administer a domain that is part of your company's domain tree. You do not have to administer other domains, but you may have to give selected user accounts from other domains access to resources in your domain. Users at the company use several shared network resources. The company is also planning to implement an e-mail program that uses Active Directory.

The following table provides the job function and number of employees in each job function in the Customer Service division:

Job function	Number of employees
Product tester	20
Customer service representative	250
Maintenance worker	5
Manager	5
Sales representative	5
Network administrator	2

The following table lists the information access requirements for the classes of employees:

Information access	Required by
Full access to the customer database	Customer service representatives and managers

(continued)

Information access	Required by
Access to the customer database to read records only	Sales representatives
Read access to company policies	All employees
Receive company announcements through e-mail	All employees
Use a shared installation of Microsoft Office	All employees, except maintenance workers
Full access to all resources in the company	Network administrators
Receive periodic announcements through e-mail about manufacturing design topics	Any employees in the domain who are interested in these topics
Access sales reports	Sales representatives from your domain and all other domains

For each group, enter the group name, type and scope, and members in the following table:

Group name	Type and scope	Members
Testers	Security Global	All product testers

Does your network require local groups?

Does your network require universal groups?

Sales representatives at the company frequently visit the company headquarters and other divisions. Therefore, you need to give sales representatives with user accounts in other domains the same permissions for resources that sales representatives in your domain have. You also want to make it easy for administrators in other domains to assign permissions to sales representatives in your domain. How can you accomplish this?

Lesson Summary

In this lesson you learned a couple of common group strategies. The group strategy you choose depends on your Windows 2000 network environment. In a single domain, the best strategy is to use global and domain local groups to assign permissions to network resources, and this is Microsoft's recommendation for most Windows 2000 installations.

You also learned that the strategy for using global and domain local groups is to place user accounts into global groups. You then create a domain local group for a group of resources to be shared in common, and place the global groups into the domain local group. Finally, you assign permissions to the domain local group. This strategy gives you the most flexibility for growth and reduces permissions assignments.

Lesson 3: Implementing Groups

After you assess user needs and have a group plan in place, you are ready to implement your groups. To implement your group strategy, you should be familiar with the guidelines for creating groups. You should also be able to add members to existing groups, delete groups, and change the scope of a group.

After this lesson, you will be able to

- Create and delete groups.
- Add members to groups.
- Change the group scope.

Estimated lesson time: 25 minutes

Preparing to Create Groups

Important guidelines for creating groups include the following:

- Determine the required group scope based on how you want to use the group. For example, use global groups to group user accounts. Alternatively, use domain local groups to assign permissions to a resource.
- Determine if you have the necessary permissions to create a group in the appropriate domain:
  - Members of the Administrators group or the Account Operators group in a domain, by default, have the necessary permissions to create groups. The Administrators built-in group and the Account Operators built-in group are discussed in Lesson 6, "Implementing Built-In Groups," of this chapter.
  - An administrator can give a user the permission to create groups in the domain or in a single organizational unit (OU).
- Determine the name of the group. Consider the following:
  - Make the name intuitive, especially if administrators from other domains search for it in Active Directory.
  - If there are parallel groups in multiple domains, make sure that the names are also parallel. For example, if there is a group for managers in each domain, these groups should use a similar naming scheme, such as Managers USA and Managers Australia.

Creating and Deleting Groups

Use the Directory Management snap-in to create and delete groups. When you create groups, create them in the Users OU or in an OU that you have created specifically for groups. As your organization grows and changes, you may discover that there are groups that you no longer need. Be sure that you delete groups when you no longer need them. This will help you maintain security so that you do not accidentally assign permissions for accessing resources to groups that you no longer need.

To create a group, start Directory Management, click the Users OU, click the Action menu, point to New, and then click Group to open the dialog box shown in Figure 14.4. Table 14.2 describes the information that you need to provide in the Create New Object - (Group) dialog box.

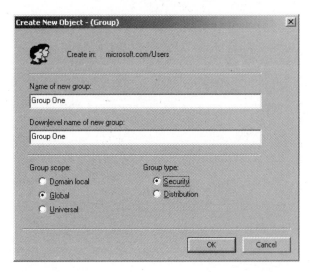

Figure 14.4 Create New Object - (Group) dialog box

Table 14.2 Create New Object - (Group) Options

Option	Description
Name Of New Group	The name of the new group. The name must be unique in the domain where you create the group.
Downlevel Name Of New Group	The down-level name of the group. This is filled in automatically for you based on the name you type in.
Group Scope	The group scope. Click Domain Local, Global, or Universal.
Group Type	The type of group. Click Distribution or Security.

Deleting a Group

Each group that you create has a unique, nonreusable identifier, called the security identifier (SID). Windows 2000 uses the SID to identify the group and the permissions that are assigned to it. When you delete a group, Windows 2000 does not use the SID for that group again, even if you create a new group with the same name as the group that you deleted. Therefore, you cannot restore access to resources by recreating the group.

When you delete a group, you delete only the group and remove the permissions and rights that are associated with it. Deleting a group does not delete the user accounts that are members of the group. To delete a group, right-click the group, and then click Delete.

Adding Members to a Group

After you create a group, you add members. Members of groups can include user accounts, other groups, and computers. You can add a computer to a group to give one computer access to a shared resource on another computer, for example, for remote backup. To add members, use the Directory Management snap-in.

To add members to a group, start the Directory Management snap-in and expand Users. Right-click the appropriate group, and then click Properties. In the Properties dialog box, click the Members tab, and then click Add. The Select Users, Contacts, Or Computers dialog box appears, as shown in Figure 14.5.

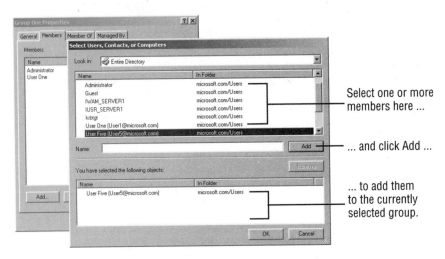

Figure 14.5   The Select Users, Contacts, Or Computers dialog box

In the Look In list, you can select a domain from which to display user accounts and groups, or you can select Entire Directory to view user accounts and groups from anywhere in Active Directory. Now select the user account or group that you want to add, and then click Add.

Note If there are multiple user accounts or groups that you want to add, you can repeat the process of selecting them one at a time and then click Add, or you can hold down the Shift or Ctrl key to select multiple user accounts or groups at a time. The Shift key allows you to select a consecutive range of accounts, while the Ctrl key allows you to pick some accounts and skip others. Click Add once you have selected all the accounts that you wish to add.

Clicking Add lists the accounts you have selected in the Name box. Once you review the accounts to make sure that they are the accounts you wish to add to the group, click OK to add the members.

Note You can also add a user account or group to a group by using the Member Of tab in the Properties dialog box for that user account or group. Use this method to quickly add the same user or group to multiple groups.

Changing the Group Scope

As your network changes, you may need to change a group scope. For example, you may want to change an existing domain local group to a universal group when you need to assign permissions to allow users to gain access to resources in other domains. You change the scope of a group on the General tab of the Properties dialog box for the group.

Note If you are running in mixed mode and you select the group type of security, the group scope universal will be inactive.

You can make the following changes:

- Change a global group to a universal group. You can do this only if the global group is not a member of another global group.
- Change a domain local group to a universal group. You can do this only if the domain local group that you are converting does not contain another domain local group.

Tip Windows 2000 does not permit changing the scope of a universal group because all other groups have more restrictive membership and scope than universal groups.

Practice: Creating Groups

In this practice, you create a security global group. You then add members to the group. To add members to the group, you add two user accounts, User1 and User5, that you created previously. Next you create a domain local group which you use to assign permissions to gain access to the sales reports. Finally, you provide access to the sales reports for the members of the security global group, by adding the security global group to the domain local group.

Exercise 1: Creating a Global Group and Adding Members

In this exercise, you create a security global group, and then add members to the group.

▶ **To create a global group in a domain**

1. Log on to your domain as Administrator.
2. Click the Start button, point to Programs, point to Administrative Tools, and then click Directory Management.
3. Expand your domain, and then double-click Users.

   In the details pane, Directory Management displays a list of current user accounts and built-in global groups.
4. To create a new group, on the Action menu, point to New, and then click Group.

   Directory Management displays the Create New Object - (Group) dialog box.

   Notice the different group types and scopes that are available.

   You use global security groups to group user accounts.
5. Type **Sales** in the Name Of New Group box.
6. For Group Type, confirm that Security is selected, and for Group Scope, click Global.
7. Click OK.

   Windows 2000 creates the group and adds it to the list of users and groups.

▶ **To add members to a global group**

1. In the details pane of Directory Management, double-click Sales.

   The Sales Properties dialog box displays the properties of the group.
2. To view the members of the group, click the Members tab.

   The Sales Properties dialog box displays a list of group members. This list is currently empty.
3. To add a member to the group, click Add.
4. In the Select Users, Contacts, Or Computers dialog box, in the Look In box, ensure your domain is selected.
5. In the list, select User One, and then click Add.
6. In the list, select User Five, and then click Add.

7. Click OK.

  User One and User Five are now members of the Sales security global group.

8. Click OK to close the Sales Properties dialog box.

Exercise 2: Creating a Domain Local Group and Adding Members

In this exercise, you create a domain local group which you use to assign permissions to gain access to sales reports. Because you use the group to assign permissions, you make it a domain local group. You then add members to the group by adding the security global group you created in Exercise 1.

▶ **To create a domain local group in a domain**

1. Make sure that Directory Management is open with the Users OU selected in the console tree.

2. To create a new group, on the Action menu, point to New, and then click Group.

  Directory Management displays the Create New Object - (Group) dialog box.

3. In the Name Of New Group box, enter Reports.

4. For Group Type, confirm that Security is selected, and for Group Scope, click Domain Local.

5. Click OK.

  Windows 2000 creates the domain local group and adds it to the list of user accounts and groups.

▶ **To add members to a domain local group**

1. In the details pane of Directory Management, double-click Reports.

  The Reports Properties dialog box displays the properties of the group.

2. To view the members of the group, click the Members tab.

  The Reports Properties dialog box displays a list of group members. This list is currently empty.

3. To add a member to the group, click Add.

4. In the Select Users, Contacts, Or Computers dialog box, in the Look In box, select Entire Directory.

  The Select Users, Contacts, Or Computers dialog box displays user accounts and groups from all domains and shows the location of each user account or group as *domain*/Users.

5. Above the list of user accounts, groups, and computers, click Name.

  Directory Management sorts all entries in the list alphabetically by name.

6. Click Sales, click Add, and then click OK.

7. The Sales group is now a member of the Reports domain local group.

8. Click OK to close the Reports Properties dialog box.

Lesson Summary

In this lesson you learned some important guidelines for creating groups. First you should determine the required group scope based on how you want to use the group. Then you should determine if you have the necessary permissions to create a group in the appropriate domain. By default, in a domain, members of the Administrators group or the Account Operators group have the necessary permissions to create groups. An administrator can give a user the permission to create groups in the domain or in a single organizational unit (OU).

You also learned that when naming a group, you should make the name intuitive. If there are parallel groups in multiple domains, make sure that the names are also parallel. You also learned that you use the Directory Management snap-in to create groups, to add members to a group, and to delete groups. In the practice portion of this lesson, you created a security global group and added members to it. You then created a security domain local group and added members by adding the security global group you created.

Lesson 4: Changing the Domain Mode

Windows 2000 has two domain modes. The initial mode is mixed mode to allow compatibility with previous versions of Windows NT. The second mode is native mode and is only used when all domain controllers in the domain are running Windows 2000 Server. In this lesson you will learn how to change from mixed mode to native mode.

After this lesson, you will be able to

- Change the domain mode.

Estimated lesson time: 5 minutes

Mixed Mode vs. Native Mode

When you create a domain, Windows 2000 sets the domain mode to mixed to enable compatibility with previous versions of Windows NT. You can change the domain mode to native, which makes available all of the group features of Windows 2000. Table 14.3 compares the two types of domain mode: mixed and native.

To change from mixed mode to native mode, on the Directory Management snap-in, right-click the domain and then click Properties. On the General tab of the Properties dialog box for the domain, click Change Mode.

Note After you change to native mode, you cannot return to a mixed mode domain. Change to native mode only when all domain controllers in the domain are running Windows 2000. Native mode prevents you from using domain controllers that run previous versions of Windows NT.

Table 14.3   Comparison of Mixed and Native Mode Operation in Windows 2000

Mixed mode	Native mode
Domain controllers can run any version of Windows NT, including Windows NT version 3.*x*, Windows NT version 4.0, or Windows 2000.	All domain controllers must run Windows 2000. However, client computers and member servers can run any version of Windows NT.
Global and domain local groups are available. Universal groups are not available.	Global, domain local, and universal groups are available.
Adding global groups to domain local groups is the only type of nesting that is available. You can use only one level of nesting.	You have more nesting options and can use multiple levels of nesting.

(continued)

Mixed mode	Native mode
By default, Windows 2000 is installed as mixed mode. You can convert mixed mode to native mode.	After you change to native mode, you cannot return to a mixed mode domain. Change to native mode only when all domain controllers in the domain are running Windows 2000.

Practice: Changing the Domain Mode

In this practice, you use Directory Management to change your domain mode. The default is mixed mode. However, to take advantage of all features relating to groups in Windows 2000, your domain should be in native mode.

▶ **To change the domain mode to native mode**

1. In the console tree, right-click your domain, and then click Properties.

   Directory Management displays the Microsoft Properties dialog box. (If your domain name is not microsoft, the Properties dialog box will display the name of your domain.)

   Notice that your domain is currently in mixed mode. Also notice the warning about changing the domain mode.

   What are the implications of changing the domain mode to native mode?

2. Click Change Mode.

   Directory Management displays a warning, informing you that this change is irreversible.

3. To acknowledge the warning, click Yes.

   The Microsoft Properties dialog box shows that you changed the domain to native mode. (If your domain name is not microsoft, the Properties dialog box will display the name of your domain.)

4. To complete the mode change, click Yes.

5. Click OK to close the Microsoft Properties dialog box.

   An Active Directory Service message box appears indicating that the operation was successful and telling you that you must reboot all domain controllers in the domain.

6. Click OK to close the dialog box.

7. Close Directory Management.

8. Restart your computer.

Lesson Summary

In this lesson you learned that Windows 2000 has two domain modes. When you first install Windows 2000 the initial mode is mixed mode. Mixed mode allows you to have domain controllers running previous versions of Windows NT. When all domain controllers in your domain are running Windows 2000 Server, you may switch to native mode. You learned how to change from mixed mode to native mode.

Lesson 5: Implementing Local Groups

A local group is a collection of user accounts on a computer. Use local groups to assign permissions to resources residing on the computer on which the local group is created. Windows 2000 creates local groups in the local security database.

After this lesson, you will be able to

- Describe local groups.

Estimated lesson time: 5 minutes

Preparing to Use Local Groups

Guidelines for using local groups include the following:

- You cannot create local groups on domain controllers because domain controllers cannot have a security database that is independent of the database in Active Directory.

- Use local groups on computers that do not belong to a domain.

  You can use local groups only on the computer where you create the local groups. Although local groups are available on member servers and domain computers running Windows 2000 Professional, do not use local groups on computers that are part of a domain. Using local groups on domain computers prevents you from centralizing group administration. Local groups do not appear in Active Directory, and you have to administer local groups separately for each computer.

- You can assign permissions to local groups for access to only the resources on the computer where you create the local groups.

Membership rules for local groups include the following:

- Local groups can contain local user accounts from the computer where you create the local groups.

- Local groups cannot be a member of any other group.

Creating Local Groups

Use the Local Users And Groups snap-in to create local groups, as shown in Figure 14.6. You create local groups in the Groups folder.

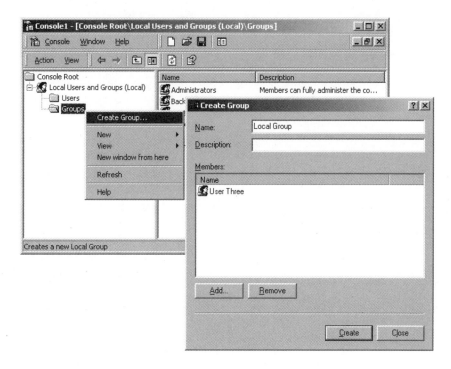

Figure 14.6   Local Users And Groups snap-in

▶   **To create a local group**

1. In Local User Manager, click Groups.
2. On the Action menu, click Create Group.

Table 14.4 describes the options presented in the Create Group dialog box.

Table 14.4   New Local User Account Options

Option	Description
Name	A unique name for the local group. This is the only required entry. Use any character except for the backslash (\). The name can contain up to 256 characters; however, very long names may not display in some windows.
Description	A description of the group.
Add	Adds a user to the list of members.
Remove	Removes a user from the list of members.
Create	Creates the group.

You can add members to a local group while you create the group or after you create the local group.

Lesson 6: Implementing Built-In Groups

Windows 2000 has four categories of built-in groups: global, domain local, local, and system. Built-in groups have a predetermined set of user rights or group membership. Windows 2000 creates these groups for you so you don't have to create groups and assign rights and permissions for commonly used functions.

After this lesson, you will be able to

- Describe the Microsoft Windows 2000 built-in groups.

Estimated lesson time: 15 minutes

Built-In Global Groups

Windows 2000 creates built-in global groups to group common types of user accounts. By default, Windows 2000 automatically adds members to some built-in global groups. You can add user accounts to these built-in groups to provide additional users with the privileges and permissions that you assign to the built-in group.

When you create a domain, Windows 2000 creates built-in global groups in Active Directory. By default, these built-in global groups do not have any inherent rights. You assign rights by either adding the global groups to domain local groups or explicitly assigning user rights or permissions to the built-in global groups.

The Users OU contains the built-in global groups in a domain. Table 14.5 describes the default membership of the most commonly used built-in global groups.

Table 14.5   Default Membership of Commonly Used Built-In Global Groups

Global group	Description
Domain Users	Windows 2000 automatically adds Domain Users to the Users domain local group. By default, the Administrator account is initially a member, and Windows 2000 automatically makes each new domain user account a member.
Domain Admins	Windows 2000 automatically adds Domain Admins to the Administrators domain local group so that members of Domain Admins can perform administrative tasks on any computer anywhere in the domain. By default, the Administrator account is a member.
Domain Guests	Windows 2000 automatically adds Domain Guests to the Guests domain local group. By default, the Guest account is a member.
Enterprise Admins	You can add user accounts to Enterprise Admins for users who should have administrative control for the entire network. Then, add Enterprise Admins to the Administrators domain local group in each domain. By default, the Administrator account is a member.

Built-In Domain Local Groups

Windows 2000 creates built-in domain local groups to provide users with user rights and permissions to perform tasks on domain controllers and in Active Directory. Domain local groups give predefined rights and permissions to user accounts when you add user accounts or global groups as members. Table 14.6 describes the most commonly used domain local groups and the capabilities that the members have.

Table 14.6   Commonly Used Built-In Domain Local Global Groups

Global group	Description
Account Operators	Members can create, delete, and modify user accounts and groups; members cannot modify the Administrators group or any of the operators groups.
Server Operators	Members can share disk resources and back up and restore files on a domain controller.
Print Operators	Members can set up and manage network printers on domain controllers.
Administrators	Members can perform all administrative tasks on all domain controllers and the domain itself. By default, the Administrator user account and the Domain Admins global group are members.
Guests	Members can perform only tasks for which you have granted rights; members can gain access only to resources for which you have assigned permissions; members cannot make permanent changes to their desktop environment. By default, the Guest user account and the Domain Guests global group are members.
Backup Operators	Members can back up and restore all domain controllers by using Windows Backup.
Users	Members can perform only tasks for which you have granted rights and gain access only to resources for which you have assigned permissions. By default, the Domain Users group is a member. Use this group to assign permissions and rights that every user with a user account in your domain should have.

Built-In Local Groups

All stand-alone servers, member servers, and computers running Windows 2000 Professional have built-in local groups. Built-in local groups give rights to perform system tasks on a single computer, such as backing up and restoring files, changing the system time, and administering system resources. Windows 2000 places the built-in local groups into the Groups folder in Local User Manager.

Table 14.7 describes the capabilities that members of the most commonly used built-in local groups have. Except where noted, there are no initial members in these groups.

Table 14.7   Commonly Used Built-In Local Groups

Local group	Description
Users	Members can perform only tasks for which you have specifically granted rights and can gain access only to resources for which you have assigned permissions.
	By default, Windows 2000 adds local user accounts that you create on the computer to the Users group. When a member server or a computer running Windows 2000 Professional joins a domain, Windows 2000 adds the Domain Users group to the local Users group.
Administrators	Members can perform all administrative tasks on the computer.
	By default, the built-in Administrator user account for the computer is a member. When a member server or a computer running Windows 2000 Workstation joins a domain, Windows 2000 adds the Domain Admins group to the local Administrators group.
Guests	Members can perform only tasks for which you have specifically granted rights and can gain access only to resources for which you have assigned permissions; members cannot make permanent changes to their desktop environment.
	By default, the built-in Guest account for the computer is a member. When a member server or a computer running Windows 2000 Workstation joins a domain, Windows 2000 adds the Domain Guests group to the local Guests group.
Backup Operators	Members can use Windows Backup to back up and restore the computer.
Power Users	Members can create and modify local user accounts on the computer and share resources.

Built-In System Groups

Built-in system groups exist on all computers running Windows 2000. System groups do not have specific memberships that you can modify, but they can represent different users at different times, depending on how a user gains access to a computer or resource. You do not see system groups when you administer groups, but they are available for use when you assign rights and permissions to resources. Windows 2000 bases system group membership on how the computer is accessed, not on who uses the computer. Table 14.8 describes the most commonly used built-in system groups.

Table 14.8   Commonly Used Built-In System Groups

System group	Description
Everyone	Includes all users who access the computer. Be careful if you assign permissions to the Everyone group and enable the Guest account. Windows NT will authenticate a user who does not have a valid user account as Guest. The user automatically gets all rights and permissions that you have assigned to the Everyone group.
Authenticated Users	Includes all users with a valid user account on the computer or in Active Directory. Use the Authenticated Users group instead of the Everyone group to prevent anonymous access to a resource.
Creator Owner	Includes the user account for the user who created or took ownership of a resource. If a member of the Administrators group creates a resource, the Administrators group is owner of the resource.
Network	Includes any user with a current connection from another computer on the network to a shared resource on the computer.
Interactive	Includes the user account for the user who is logged on at the computer. Members of the Interactive group gain access to resources on the computer at which they are physically located. They log on and gain access to resources by "interacting" with the computer.
Anonymous Logon	Includes any user account that Windows 2000 did not authenticate.
Dialup	Includes any user who currently has a dial-up connection.

Lesson Summary

In this lesson you learned that Windows 2000 has four categories of built-in groups: global, domain local, local, and system. You also learned that built-in groups have a predetermined set of user rights or group membership. Windows 2000 creates these groups for you so you don't have to create groups and assign rights and permissions for commonly used functions.

Review

Here are some questions to help you determine if you have learned enough to move on to the next chapter. If you have difficulty answering these questions, please go back and review the material in this chapter before beginning the next chapter. The answers for these questions are located in Appendix A, "Questions and Answers."

1. Why should you use groups?

2. What is the purpose of adding a group to another group?

3. When should you use security groups instead of distribution groups?

4. What strategy should you apply when you use domain local and global groups?

5. Why should you not use local groups on a computer after it becomes a member of a domain?

6. What is the easiest way to give a user complete control over all computers in a domain?

7. Suppose the headquarters for this chapter's imaginary manufacturing company has a single domain that is located in Paris. The company has managers who need access to the inventory database to perform their jobs. What would you do to ensure that the managers have the required access to the inventory database?

8. Now suppose the company has a three-domain environment with the root domain in Paris and the other two domains in Australia and North America. Managers from all three domains need access to the inventory database in Paris to perform their jobs. What would you do to ensure that the managers have the required access and that there is a minimum of administration?

CHAPTER 1 5

Setting Up and Configuring Network Printers

About This Chapter

This chapter introduces you to setting up and configuring network printers so that users can print over the network. You will also learn how to troubleshoot common printing problems that are associated with setting up network printers.

Before You Begin

To complete this chapter, you must have

- A computer that meets the minimum hardware requirements listed in "Hardware Requirements," on page xxxiii.
- Installed the Windows 2000 Server software on the computer.
- Configured the computer as a domain controller in a domain.

Note You do *not* need a printer to complete the exercises in this chapter.

Lesson 1: Introduction to Windows 2000 Printing

With Windows 2000 printing, you can share printing resources across an entire network and administer printing from a central location. You can easily set up printing on client computers running Windows 2000, Windows NT 4.0, Microsoft Windows 98, and Windows 95.

After this lesson, you will be able to

- Define Microsoft Windows 2000 printing terms.

Estimated lesson time: 15 minutes

Terminology

Before you set up printing, you should be familiar with Windows 2000 printing terminology to understand how the different components fit together, as shown in Figure 15.1.

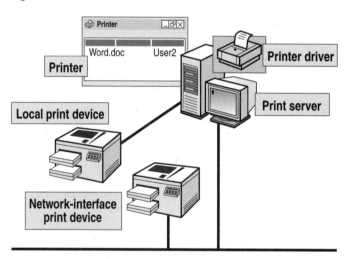

Figure 15.1   Printing terminology

If you are new to Windows 2000, you might find some of the printing terminology to be different from what you expected. The following list defines a few Windows 2000 printing terms:

- **Printer.**   A *printer* is the software interface between the operating system and the print device. The printer defines where a document will go to reach the print device (that is, to a local port, a port for a network connection, or a file), when it will go, and how various other aspects of the printing process will be handled.

When users make connections to printers, they use printer names, which point to one or more print devices.

- **Print device.**   A *print device* is the hardware device that produces printed documents.

  Windows 2000 supports the following print devices:

  - *Local print devices,* which are connected to a physical port on the print server.

  - *Network-interface print devices,* which are connected to a print server through the network instead of a physical port. Network-interface print devices require their own network interface cards and have their own network address or they are attached to an external network adapter.

- **Print server.**   A *print server* is the computer on which the printers that are associated with local and network-interface print devices reside. The print server receives and processes documents from client computers. You set up and share network printers on print servers.

- **Printer driver.**   A *printer driver* is one or more files containing information that Windows 2000 requires to convert print commands into a specific printer language, such as PostScript. This conversion makes it possible for a print device to print a document. A printer driver is specific to each print device model.

Requirements for Network Printing

The requirements for setting up printing on a Windows 2000 network include the following:

- At least one computer to operate as the print server. If the print server will manage many heavily used printers, Microsoft recommends a dedicated print server. The computer can run either of the following:

  - Windows 2000 Server, which can handle a large number of connections and supports Macintosh and UNIX computers and NetWare clients.

  - Windows 2000 Professional, which is limited to 10 concurrent connections from other computers for file and print services. It does not support Macintosh computers or NetWare clients but does support UNIX computers.

- Sufficient random access memory (RAM) to process documents.

  If a print server manages a large number of printers or many large documents, the server might require additional RAM beyond what Windows 2000 requires for other tasks. If a print server does not have sufficient RAM for its workload, printing performance deteriorates.

- Sufficient disk space on the print server to ensure that Windows 2000 can store documents that are sent to the print server until the print server sends the documents to the print device. This is critical when documents are large or likely to accumulate. For example, if 10 users send large documents to print at the same time, the print server must have enough disk space to hold all of the documents until the print server sends them to the print device. If there is not enough space to hold all of the documents, users will get error messages and be unable to print.

The requirements for network printing are as follows:

- A computer to operate as the print server running either Windows 2000 Server or, for networks with 10 or fewer concurrent client computers, Windows 2000 Professional
- Sufficient RAM to process documents
- Sufficient disk space on the print server to store documents until they print

Guidelines for a Network Printing Environment

Before you set up network printing, develop a network-wide printing strategy to meet users' printing needs without unnecessary duplication of resources or delays in printing. Table 15.1 provides some guidelines for developing a network printing strategy.

Table 15.1   Network Printing Environment Guidelines

Guideline	Explanation
Determine user's print requirements	Determine the number of users who print and the printing workload. For example, 15 people in a billing department who print invoices continually will have a larger printing workload and might require more printers, print devices, and possibly, more print servers than 15 software developers who do all their work online.
Determine company's printing requirements	Determine the printing needs of your company. This includes the number and types of print devices that are required. In addition, consider the type of workload that each print device will handle. Do not use a personal print device for network printing.
Determine the number of Print Servers required	Determine the number of print servers that your network requires to handle the number and types of printers that your network will have.
Determine where to be locate print devices	Determine where you will locate the print devices. It should easy for users to pick up their printed documents.

Lesson Summary

In this lesson you learned the Windows 2000 printing terminology. In Windows 2000 terminology, a printer is the software interface between the operating system and the print device. The print device is the hardware device that produces printed documents. You also learned that Windows 2000 supports local print devices, which are connected to a physical port on the print server, and network-interface print devices, which are connected to a print server through the network instead of through a physical port.

You also learned that a print server is the computer on which the printers reside. The print server receives and processes documents from client computers. You set up and share network printers on print servers. You learned that a printer driver is one or more files containing information that Windows 2000 requires to convert print commands into a specific printer language, such as PostScript. This conversion makes it possible for a print device to print a document. A printer driver is specific to each print device model.

You also learned that the requirements for setting up printing on a Windows 2000 network include at least one computer to operate as the print server. If the print server will manage many heavily used printers, Microsoft recommends that you use a dedicated print server and that the print server can run Windows 2000 Server or Windows 2000 Professional. Windows 2000 Professional is limited to 10 concurrent connections from other computers for file and print services, and it does not support Macintosh computers or NetWare clients but does support UNIX computers.

Lesson 2: Setting Up Network Printers

Setting up and sharing a network printer makes it possible for multiple users to print to it. You can set up a printer for a local print device that is connected directly to the print server, or you can set up a printer for a network-interface print device that is connected to the print server over the network. In larger organizations, most printers point to network-interface print devices.

After this lesson, you will be able to

- Identify the requirements for setting up a network printer and network printing resources.
- Add and share a new printer for a local print device or a network-interface print device.
- Set up client computers.

Estimated lesson time: 30 minutes

Adding and Sharing a Printer for a Local Print Device

The steps for adding a printer for a local print device or for a network-interface print device are similar. First, you add the printer for a local print device.

▶ **To add a printer for a local print device**

1. Log on as Administrator on the print server.
2. Click Start, point to Settings, and then click Printers.

   You add and share a printer by using the Add Printer wizard in the Printers folder.
3. Double-click Add Printer to launch the Add Printer wizard.

   The Add Printer wizard starts with the Welcome To The Add Printer Wizard Page displayed.

The Add Printer wizard guides you through the steps to add a printer for a print device that is connected to the print server. The number of local print devices that you can connect to a print server through physical ports depends on your hardware configuration.

Table 15.2 describes the Add Printer wizard options for adding a printer for a local print device.

Table 15.2   The Add Printer Wizard Options for a Local Print Device

Option	Description
Local Printer	The designation that you are adding a printer to the computer at which you are sitting, which is the print server.
Existing (ports)	The port on the print server to which you attached the print device.
	You can also add a port. Adding a port allows you to print to nonstandard hardware ports, such as a network-interface connection.
Manufacturer and Printers	The correct printer driver for the local print device. Enter the manufacturer and the printer model for your print device.
	If your print device is not in the list, you must provide a printer driver from the manufacturer or select a model that is similar enough that the print device can use it.
Printer Name	A name that will identify the printer to the users. Use a name that is intuitive and descriptive of the print device. Some applications might not support more than 31 characters in the server and printer name combinations.
	This name also appears in the result of an Active Directory search.
Default Printer	The default printer for all Windows-based applications. Select this option so that users do not have to set a printer for each application. The first time that you add a printer to the print server, this option does not appear because the printer is automatically selected as the default printer.
Shared As	A share name that users (with the appropriate permission) can use to make a connection to the printer over the network. This name appears when users browse for a printer or supply a path to a printer.
	Ensure that the share name is compatible with the naming conventions for all client computers on the network. By default, the share name is the printer name truncated to an 8.3 character filename. If you use a share name that is longer than an 8.3 character filename, some client computers might not be able to connect.
Location and Comment	Information about the print device. Provide information that helps users determine if the print device fits their needs.
	Users can search Active Directory for the information that you enter here. Because of this search capability, standardize the type of information that you enter so that users can compare printers in search results.

(continued)

Option	Description
Do You Want To Print A Testpage?	Verification that you have installed the printer correctly. Select this check box to print a test page.
Do You Want To Install Additional Drivers At This Time?	Additional printer drivers that you want to download for client computers running Windows 2000 (Intel only), Windows NT 4.0 (Intel only), Windows 95, and Windows 98. For other client computers, you have to add printer drivers later.
	Windows 2000 installs the printer drivers on the print server, from which most Windows client computers can download the drivers.

Adding and Sharing a Printer for a Network-Interface Print Device

In larger companies, most print devices are network-interface print devices. These print devices offer several advantages. You do not need to locate print devices with the print server. In addition, network connections transfer data more quickly than printer cable connections.

You add a printer for a network-interface print device by using the Add Printer wizard. The main differences between adding a printer for a local print device and adding a printer for a network-interface print device is that for a typical network-interface print device, you provide additional port and network protocol information.

The default network protocol for Windows 2000 is Transmission Control Protocol/Internet Protocol (TCP/IP), which many network-interface print devices use. For TCP/IP, you provide additional port information in the Add Standard TCP/IP Printer Port wizard.

Table 15.3 describes the options on the Select The Printer Port page of the Add Printer wizard that pertain to adding a network-interface print device.

Table 15.3   Options on the Select The Printer Port Page That Affect Adding a Network-Interface Print Device

Option	Description
Other (port)	This selection starts the process of creating a new port for the print server to which the network-interface print device is connected. In this case, the new port points to the network connection of the print device.
Additional Port Type	This selection determines the network protocol to use for the connection. The default protocol for Windows 2000 is TCP/IP.

Table 15.4 describes the options on the Add Port page of the Add Standard TCP/IP Printer Port wizard, which Windows 2000 displays when you select TCP/IP as the port type, as shown in Figure 15.2.

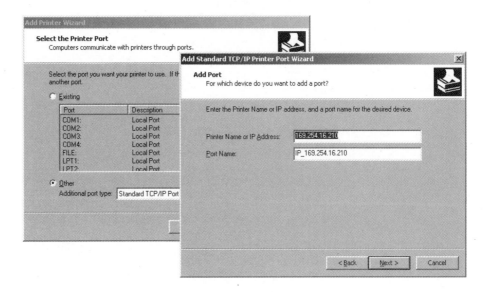

Figure 15.2   Add Standard TCP/IP Printer Port wizard

Table 15.4   Options on the Select The Printer Port Page That Affect Adding a Network-Interface Print Device

Option	Description
Printer Name Or IP Address	The network location of the print device. You must enter either the TCP/IP address or a Domain Name System (DNS) name of the network-interface print device.
	If you provide a TCP/IP address, Windows 2000 automatically supplies a suggested port name for the print device in the form IP_*Ipaddress*.
	If Windows 2000 cannot connect to and identify the network-interface print device, you must supply additional information about the type of print device. To enable automatic identification, make sure that the print device is powered on and connected to the network.
Port Name	The name that Windows 2000 assigns to the port that you created and defined. You can enter a different name.
	After you create the port, Windows 2000 displays it on the Select The Printer Port page of the Add Printer wizard. You do not have to redefine the port if you point additional printers to the same print device.

Note   If your print device uses a network protocol other than TCP/IP, you must install the network protocol before you can add a printer for this device. After you install the protocol, you can add additional ports that use the protocol. The tasks and setup information that are required to configure a printer port depend on the network protocol.

Setting Up Client Computers

After you add and share a printer, you need to set up client computers so that users can print. Although the tasks to set up client computers vary depending on which operating systems are running on the client computers, all client computers require that a printer driver be installed. The following summarizes the installation of printer drivers according to the computer's operating system:

- Windows 2000 automatically downloads the printer drivers for client computers running Windows 2000, Windows NT version 4 and earlier, Windows 95, or Windows 98.

- Client computers running other Microsoft operating systems require installation of printer drivers.

- Client computers running non-Microsoft operating systems require installation of both printer drivers and the print service on the print server.

Client Computers Running Windows 2000, Windows NT, Windows 95, or Windows 98

Users of client computers running Windows 2000, Windows NT, Windows 95, and Windows 98 only need to make a connection to the shared printer. The client computer automatically downloads the appropriate printer driver, as long as there is a copy of it on the print server.

You need to make sure that the appropriate printer drivers are on the print server. Printer drivers for different hardware platforms are *not* interchangeable. If you have an Alpha-based print server and Intel-based client computers, you must add the printer drivers for both platforms on the print server.

Client Computers Running Other Microsoft Operating Systems

For client computers running other Microsoft operating systems (such as Windows 3.*x* or MS-DOS) to print to a shared Windows 2000–based printer, you must manually install a printer driver on the client computer. You can get the appropriate printer driver for a Windows-based client computer from the installation disks for that client computer or from the printer manufacturer.

Note   For more information about setting up additional Windows 2000 print services, see the "Printing" topic in the "Managing Files and Printers" book in the Windows 2000 Server online documentation. (To access the documentation, click Start on the Windows 2000 desktop, and then click Help.)

Client Computers Running Non-Microsoft Operating Systems

To enable users of client computers running non-Microsoft operating systems to print, the print server must have additional services installed on it. Table 15.5 lists services that are required for Macintosh and UNIX client computers or computers running a NetWare client.

Table 15.5   Services Required for Client Computers Running Non-Microsoft Operating Systems

Client computer	Required services
Macintosh	Services for Macintosh are included with Windows 2000 Server but are not installed by default.
UNIX	TCP/IP Printing, which is also called Line Printer Daemon (LPD) Service, is included with Windows 2000 Server but is not installed by default.
NetWare	File and Print Services for NetWare (FPNW), an optional add-on service for Windows 2000 Server, is not included with Windows 2000 Server.

Practice: Installing A Network Printer

In this practice, you use the Add Printer wizard to install and share a local printer. By sharing the printer, it becomes available to other users on the network. You also take the printer offline and then print a document. Printing a document with the printer offline loads the document into the print queue.

Exercise 1: Adding and Sharing a Printer

In this exercise, you use the Add Printer wizard to add a local printer to your computer and share it.

▶ **To add a local printer**

1. Log on to your domain as Administrator.
2. Click the Start button, point to Settings, and then click Printers.

   Windows 2000 displays the Printers system folder. If you added a fax modem, a Fax icon appears in the Printers system folder.
3. Double-click Add Printer.
4. In the Add Printer wizard, click Next.

   The Add Printer wizard prompts you for the location of the printer. Because you are creating the printer on the computer at which you are sitting and not on a different computer, this printer is referred to as a local printer.
5. Click Local printer, and then click Next.

   The wizard prompts you to specify how the computer is connected to the print device: either directly or over the network.

Which port types are available depends on the installed network protocols. For this exercise, assume that the print device that you are adding is directly attached to your computer and using the LPT1 port.

Note   If the print device is connected to a port that is not listed, click Other, and then enter the port type.

---

6. Verify that Existing is selected, and then under Existing, click LPT1.

7. Click Next.

The wizard prompts you for the printer manufacturer and model. You will add an HP LaserJet 5Si printer.

Tip   The list of printers is sorted in alphabetical order. If you cannot find a printer name, make sure that you are looking in the correct location.

---

8. Under Manufacturers, click HP; under Printers, click HP LaserJet 5Si; and then click Next.

The wizard displays the Name Your Printer page. In the Printer Name box, Windows 2000 automatically defaults to the printer name HP LaserJet 5Si. For this exercise, do not change this name.

9. If other printers are already installed, the wizard will also ask whether you want to make this the default printer. If the wizard displays the message, Do You Want Your Windows-Based Programs To Use This Printer As The Default Printer?, click Yes.

10. To accept the default printer name, click Next.

The Printer Sharing page appears, prompting you for printer sharing information.

▶   **To share a printer**

1. In the Add Printer wizard, on the Printer Sharing page, verify that Share As is selected.

Notice that you can assign a shared printer name, even though you already supplied a printer name. The shared printer name is used to identify a printer on the network and must conform to a naming convention. This shared name is different from the printer name that you entered previously. The printer name is a description that will appear with the printer's icon in the Printers system folder and in Active Directory.

2. In the Shared As box, type **Printer1** and then click Next.

The Location And Comment page appears.

Note   Windows 2000 displays the values that you enter for Location and Comment when a user searches Active Directory for a printer. Entering this information is optional, but it can help users locate the printer more easily.

---

3. In the Location box and the Comment box, enter some applicable information, and then click Next.

    The wizard displays the Print Test Page page.

    Notice that you can print a test page to confirm that your printer is set up properly. You can also install additional drivers for other versions of Microsoft Windows.

4. Under Do You Want To Print A Test Page?, click No, clear the Install Additional Drivers At This check box, and then click Next.

    The wizard displays the Completing The Add Printer Wizard page and provides a summary of your installation choices.

Note As you review the summary, you might notice an error in the information you entered. To modify these settings, click Back.

---

5. Confirm the summary of your installation choices, and then click Finish.

    If necessary, Windows 2000 displays the Files Needed dialog box, prompting you for the location of the Windows 2000 Server distribution files.

6. Insert the Windows 2000 Server CD-ROM, and wait for about 10 seconds.

7. If Windows displays the Windows 2000 CD-ROM window, close it.

8. Click OK to close the Insert Disk dialog box.

    Windows 2000 copies the printer files.

    Windows 2000 creates the shared printer. An icon for the HP LaserJet 5Si printer appears in the Printers system folder.

    Notice that Windows 2000 displays an open hand under the printer icon. This indicates that the printer is shared.

    Notice the check mark next to the printer, which indicates that the printer is the default printer.

Exercise 2: Taking a Printer Offline and Printing a Test Document

In this exercise, you take the printer that you created offline. Taking a printer offline causes documents that you send to this printer to be held on the computer while the print device is not available. Doing this will eliminate error messages about unavailable print devices in later exercises. Windows 2000 will display such error messages when it attempts to send documents to a print device that is not connected to the computer.

▶ **To take a printer offline**

1. In the Printers system folder, click the HP LaserJet 5Si icon.

2. On the File menu, click Use Printer Offline.

Notice that Windows 2000 changes the icon to reflect that the printer is not available.

▶ **To print a test document**

1. In the Printers system folder, double-click the HP LaserJet 5Si icon.

   Notice that the list of documents to be sent to the print device is empty.

2. Click the Start button, point to Programs, point to Accessories, and then click Notepad.

3. In Notepad, type any text that you want.

4. Arrange Notepad and the HP LaserJet 5Si window so that you can see the contents of each.

5. In Notepad, on the File menu, click Print.

   Windows 2000 displays the Print dialog box, allowing you to select the printer and print options.

   Note Many programs running under Windows 2000 use the same Print dialog box.

   The Print dialog box displays the location and comment information that you entered when you created the printer, and it shows that the printer is currently offline. You can also use this dialog box to search Active Directory for a printer.

   Notice that HP LaserJet 5Si is selected as the printer.

   Why did Windows 2000 make that selection for you?

6. Click Print.

   Notepad briefly displays a message, stating that the document is printing on your computer. On a fast computer, you might not be able to see this message.

   In the HP LaserJet 5Si window, you will see the document waiting to be sent to the print device. Windows 2000 holds the document because you took the printer offline. Otherwise, Windows 2000 would have sent the document to the print device.

7. Close Notepad and click No when prompted to save changes to your document.

8. Because we don't want to print the document sitting in the print queue, select the document in the HP LaserJet 5Si window, click the Printer menu item, and then click Cancel All Documents.

   The document will be removed.

9. Close the HP LaserJet 5Si window.

10. Close the Printers window.

Lesson Summary

In this lesson you learned how to install network printers. You learned that to set up and share a printer for a local print device or for a network-interface print device you use the Add Printer wizard in the Printers folder. You also learned that sharing a local printer makes it possible for multiple users on the network to print to it.

You also learned that users of client computers running Windows 2000, Windows NT, Windows 95, or Windows 98 only need to make a connection to the shared printer to be able to print. The client computer automatically downloads the appropriate printer driver, as long as there is a copy of it on the print server. For client computers running other Microsoft operating systems (such as Windows 3.x or MS-DOS) to print to a shared Windows 2000-based printer, you must manually install a printer driver on the client computer. You can get the appropriate printer driver for a Windows-based client computer from the installation disks for that client computer or from the printer manufacturer. Finally, you learned that to enable users of client computers running non-Microsoft operating systems to print, the print server must have additional services installed on it.

Lesson 3: Connecting to Network Printers

After you have set up the print server with all required printer drivers for the shared printers, users on client computers running Windows 2000, Windows NT, Windows 95, and Windows 98 can easily make a connection and start printing. For most Windows-based client computers, if the appropriate printer drivers are on the print server, the client computer automatically downloads the printer when the user makes a connection to the printer.

When you add and share a printer, by default, all users can make a connection to that printer and print documents. The method that is used to make a connection to a printer depends on the client computer. Client computers running Windows 2000, Windows NT, Windows 98, or Windows 95 can use the Add Printer wizard, although the Add Printer wizard in Windows 2000 provides more features than in the earlier versions. Client computers running Windows 2000 can also use a Web browser to make a connection to the printer.

After this lesson, you will be able to

- Make a connection to a network printer by using the Add Printer wizard or a Web browser.

Estimated lesson time: 10 minutes

Using the Add Printer Wizard

The Add Printer wizard is one method that client computers running Windows 2000, Windows NT, Windows 98, or Windows 95 can use to connect to a printer. This is the same wizard that you use to add and share a printer. The options that are available in the Add Printer wizard that allow you to locate and connect to a printer vary depending on the operating system that the client computer is running (see Figure 15.3).

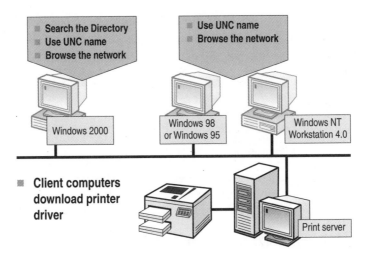

Figure 15.3   Using the Add Printer wizard to locate and connect to a network printer

Client Computers Running Windows 2000

By using the Add Printer wizard on client computers running Windows 2000, you can make a connection to a printer by using the following methods:

- Search Active Directory.

   You can find the printer by using Active Directory search capabilities. You can search either the entire Active Directory or just a portion of it. You can also narrow the search by providing features of the printer, such as color printing.

- Use the universal naming convention (UNC) name.

   You can use the UNC name (*print_server**printer_name*) to make connections by selecting Connect To The Printer Using A Network Name on the Locate Your Printers page of the Add Printer wizard. If you know the UNC name, this can be a quick method to use.

- You can also browse the network for the printer by selecting the Connect To The Printer Using A Network Name option, and clicking Browse.

Client Computers Running Windows NT 4.0, Windows 95, or Windows 98

On client computers running Window NT 4.0, Windows 95, or Windows 98, the Add Printer wizard only allows you to enter a UNC name or to browse Network Neighborhood to locate the printer.

Note   You can also make a connection to a printer by using the Run command on the Start menu. Type the UNC name of the printer in the Open box, and click OK.

Client Computers Running Other Microsoft Operating Systems

Users at client computers running Windows 3.x and Windows for Workgroups use Print Manager instead of the Add Printer wizard to make a connection to a printer.

Users at any Windows-based client computer can make a connection to a network printer by using the following command:

```
net use lptx: \\server_name\share_name
```

where x is the number of the printer port.

The Net Use command is also the only method that is available for making a connection to a network printer from client computers running MS-DOS or OS/2 with Microsoft LAN Manager client software installed.

Using a Web Browser

If you are using a client computer running Windows 2000, you can make a connection to a printer through your corporate intranet. You can type a Uniform Resource Locator (URL) in your Web browser, and you do not have to use the Add Printer wizard. After you make a connection, Windows 2000 automatically copies the correct printer drivers to the client computer.

A Web designer can customize this Web page, such as displaying a floor plan that shows the location of print devices to which users can connect. There are two ways to make a connection to a printer by using a Web browser:

- http://*server_name*/printers

  The Web page lists all of the shared printers on the print server that you have permission to use. The page includes information about the printers, including the printer name, status of print jobs, location, model, and any comments that were entered when the printer was installed. This information helps you select the correct printer for their needs. You must have permission to use the printer.

- http://*server_name*/*printer_share_name*

  You provide the intranet path for a specific printer. You must have permission to use the printer.

Downloading Printer Drivers

When users at client computers running Windows 2000, Windows NT, Windows 95, or Windows 98 make the first connection to a printer on the print server, the client computer automatically downloads the printer driver. The print server must have a copy of the printer driver.

Thereafter, client computers running Windows 2000 and Windows NT verify that they have the current printer driver each time that they print. If not, they download the new printer driver. For these client computers, you only need to update printer drivers on the print server. Client computers running Windows 95 or Windows 98 do not check for updated printer drivers. You must manually install updated printer drivers.

Lesson Summary

In this lesson you learned that client computers running Windows 2000, Windows NT, Windows 98, or Windows 95 can use the Add Printer wizard to connect to a printer. On client computers running Windows 2000, you can make a connection to a printer by using Active Directory search capabilities, or you can select Connect To The Printer Using A Network Name on the Locate Your Printers page of the Add Printer wizard. If you know the UNC name, you can use it, or you can browse the network for the printer.

On client computers running Windows NT 4.0, Windows 95, or Windows 98, the Add Printer wizard only allows you to enter a UNC name or to browse Network Neighborhood to locate the printer. Users at client computers running Windows 3.*x* and Windows for Workgroups use Print Manager to make a connection to a printer.

You also learned that users at any Windows-based client computer can make a connection to a network printer by using the Net Use command. The Net Use command is also the only method that is available for making a connection to a network printer from client computers running MS-DOS or OS/2 with Microsoft LAN Manager client software installed.

Lesson 4: Configuring Network Printers

After you have set up and shared network printers, user and company printing needs might require you to configure printer settings so that your printing resources better fit these needs.

Three common configuration changes you can make are as follows:

- You can share an existing nonshared printer if your printing load increases.
- You can create a printer pool so that the printer automatically distributes print jobs to the first available print device so that users do not have to search for an available printer.
- You can set priorities between printers so that critical documents always print before noncritical documents.

After this lesson, you will be able to

- Share an existing printer.
- Create a printer pool.
- Set priorities between printers.

Estimated lesson time: 15 minutes

Sharing an Existing Printer

If the printing demands on your network increase and your network has an existing, nonshared printer for a print device, you can share it so that users can print to the print device.

When you share a printer

- You need to assign the printer a share name, which appears in My Network Places. Use an intuitive name to help users when they are browsing for a printer.
- You can add printer drivers for all versions of Windows NT, for Windows 95 and Windows 98, and for Windows 2000 and Windows NT running on different hardware platforms.
- You can choose to publish the printer in Active Directory so that users can search for the printer.

Use the Sharing tab, in the Properties dialog box for the printer, to share an existing printer (see Figure 15.4).

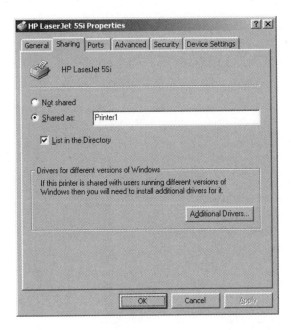

Figure 15.4   Sharing Tab in the Properties dialog box for a printer

▶   **To access the Sharing tab**

1. In the Printers folder, click the icon for the printer that you want to share.

2. On the File menu, click Properties.

3. In the Properties dialog box for the printer, click the Sharing tab.

After you have shared the printer, Windows 2000 puts an open hand under the printer icon, indicating that the printer is shared.

Setting Up a Printer Pool

A *printer pool* is one printer that is connected to multiple print devices through multiple ports on a print server. The print devices can be local or network-interface print devices. Print devices should be identical; however, you can use print devices that are not identical but use the same printer driver. See Figure 15.5.

When you create a printer pool, users can print documents without having to find out which print device is available—the printer checks for an available port.

Note   When you set up a printer pool, place the print devices in the same physical area so that users can easily locate their documents.

A printer pool has the following advantages:

- In a network with a high volume of printing, it decreases the time that documents wait on the print server.
- It simplifies administration because you can administer multiple print devices from a single printer.

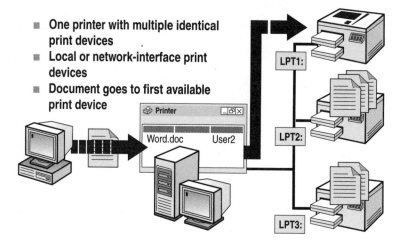

- **One printer with multiple identical print devices**
- **Local or network-interface print devices**
- **Document goes to first available print device**

Figure 15.5   Printer pool

Before you create a printer pool, make sure that you connect the print devices to the print server.

▶   **To create a printer pool**

1. In the Properties dialog box for the printer, click the Ports tab.
2. Select the Enable Printer Pooling check box.
3. Select the check box for each port to which a print device that you want to add to the pool is connected, and then click OK.

Setting Priorities Between Printers

Setting priorities between printers makes it possible to set priorities between groups of documents that all print on the same print device. Multiple printers point to the same print device, which allows users to send critical documents to a high priority printer and noncritical documents to a lower priority printer. The critical documents always print first.

▶ **To set priorities between printers**

- Point two or more printers to the same print device—that is, the same port. The port can be either a physical port on the print server or a port that points to a network-interface print device.

- Set a different priority for each printer that is connected to the print device, and then have different groups of users print to different printers, or have users send different types of documents to different printers.

  For an example, see Figure 15.6. User1 sends documents to a printer with the lowest priority of 1, while User2 sends documents to a printer with the highest priority of 99. In this example, User2's documents always print before User1's.

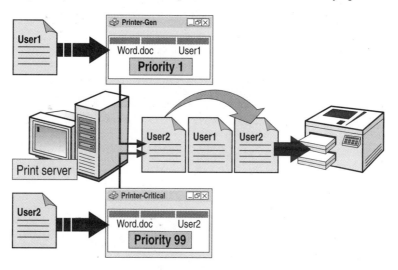

Figure 15.6   Printer pool with different priorities set

▶ **To set the priority for a printer**

1. In the Properties dialog box for the printer, click the Advanced tab.
2. In the Priority box, select the appropriate priority, and then click OK.

   Windows 2000 sets the priority for the printer.

Lesson Summary

In this lesson you learned that you can share an existing, nonshared printer. To share an existing printer, use the Sharing tab in the Properties dialog box for the printer and select Shared As. After you have shared the printer, Windows 2000 puts an open hand under the printer icon, indicating that the printer is shared.

You also learned that a printer pool is one printer that is connected to multiple print devices through multiple ports on a print server. The print devices in a printer pool should be identical; however, you can use print devices that are not identical if all the print devices use the same printer driver. A printer pool has several advantages. A printer pool can decrease the time that documents wait on the print server. It also simplifies administration because you can administer multiple print devices from a single printer. To create a printer pool, in the Properties dialog box for the printer, use the Ports tab to select the Enable Printer Pooling check box.

You also learned that setting priorities between printers makes it possible to set priorities between groups of documents that all print on the same print device. Multiple printers point to the same print device, which allows users to send critical documents to a high priority printer and noncritical documents to a lower priority printer. The critical documents always print first.

Lesson 5: Troubleshooting Network Printers

During setup and configuration of a printer, problems can sometimes occur. This lesson introduces you to a few common problems that you might encounter and provides some suggested solutions.

After this lesson, you will be able to

■ Troubleshoot network printing problems.

Estimated lesson time: 5 minutes

Common Troubleshooting Scenarios

Table 15.6 lists some of the common setup and configuration problems that you might encounter. It also lists some probable causes of the problems, and some possible solutions.

Table 15.6   Common Printer Problems and Possible Solutions

Problem	Probable cause	Possible solution
Test page does not print. You have confirmed that the print device is connected and turned on.	The selected port is not correct.	Configure the printer for the correct port. For a printer that uses a network-interface print device, make sure that the network address is correct.
Test page or documents print incorrectly, as garbled text.	The installed printer driver is not correct.	Reinstall the printer with the correct printer driver.
Users report an error message that asks them to install a printer driver when they print to a print server running Windows 2000.	Printer drivers for the client computers are not installed on the print server.	On the print server, add the appropriate printer drivers for the client computers. Use the client computer operating system CD-ROM or a printer driver from the vendor.
Documents from one client computer do not print, but documents from other client computers do.	The client computer is connected to the wrong printer.	On the client computer, remove the printer, and then add the correct printer.

(continued)

Problem	Probable cause	Possible solution
Documents print correctly on some print devices in a printer pool but not all of them.	The print devices in the printer pool are not identical.	Verify that all print devices in the printer pool are identical or that they use the same printer driver. Remove inappropriate devices.
Documents do not print in the right priority.	The printing priorities between printers are set incorrectly.	Adjust the printing priorities for the printers associated with the print device.

Lesson Summary

Troubleshooting is something you learn through experience. Certain problems can be solved based on the troubleshooting scenarios in this lesson or because you have encountered the problem before. However, in many cases you simply have to eliminate the possible causes one at a time until the problem is resolved.

Review

Here are some questions to help you determine if you have learned enough to move on to the next chapter. If you have difficulty answering these questions, please go back and review the material in this chapter before beginning the next chapter. The answers for these questions are located in Appendix A, "Questions and Answers."

1. What is the difference between a printer and a print device?

2. A print server can connect to two different types of print devices. What are these two types of print devices, and what are the differences?

3. You have added and shared a printer. What must you do to set up client computers running Windows 2000 so that users can print, and why?

4. What advantages does connecting to a printer by using http://*server_name*/ printers provide for users?

5. Why would you connect multiple printers to one print device?

6. Why would you create a printer pool?

CHAPTER 16

Securing Resources with NTFS Permissions

About This Chapter

This chapter introduces you to Microsoft Windows 2000 file system (NTFS) folder and file permissions. You will learn how to assign NTFS folder and file permissions to user accounts and groups and how moving or copying files and folders affects NTFS file and folder permissions. You will also learn how to troubleshoot common resource access problems.

Before You Begin

To complete this chapter, you must have

- A computer that meets the minimum hardware requirements listed in "Hardware Requirements," on page xxxiii.
- Installed the Windows 2000 Server software on the computer.
- Configured the computer as a domain controller in a domain.

Lesson 1: Understanding NTFS Permissions

Use NTFS permissions to specify which users and groups can gain access to files and folders and what they can do with the contents of the file or folder. NTFS permissions are only available on NTFS volumes. NTFS permissions are *not* available on volumes that are formatted with the file allocation table (FAT) or FAT32 file systems. NTFS security is effective whether a user gains access to the file or folder at the computer or over the network. The permissions you assign for folders are different from the permissions you assign for files.

After this lesson, you will be able to

- Define the standard NTFS folder and file permissions.

Estimated lesson time: 5 minutes

NTFS Folder Permissions

You assign folder permissions to control the access that users have to folders and to the files and subfolders that are contained within the folder.

Table 16.1 lists the standard NTFS folder permissions that you can assign and the type of access that each permission provides.

Table 16.1   NTFS Folder Permissions

NTFS folder permission	Allows the user to
Read	See files and subfolders in the folder and view folder ownership, permissions, and attributes (such as Read-only, Hidden, Archive, and System).
Write	Create new files and subfolders within the folder, change folder attributes, and view folder ownership and permissions.
List Folder Contents	See the names of files and subfolders in the folder.
Read & Execute	Move through folders to reach other files and folders, even if the users do not have permission for those folders, and perform actions permitted by the Read permission and the List Folder Contents permission.
Modify	Delete the folder *plus* perform actions permitted by the Write permission and the Read & Execute permission.
Full Control	Change permissions, take ownership, and delete subfolders and files, *plus* perform actions permitted by all other NTFS folder permissions.

You can deny permission to a user account or group. To deny all access to a user account or group for a folder, deny the Full Control permission.

NTFS File Permissions

You assign file permissions to control the access that users have to files. Table 16.2 lists the standard NTFS file permissions that you can assign and the type of access that each permission provides.

Table 16.2   NTFS File Permissions

NTFS file permission	Allows the user to
Read	Read the file, and view file attributes, ownership, and permissions.
Write	Overwrite the file, change file attributes, and view file ownership and permissions.
Read & Execute	Run applications *plus* perform the actions permitted by the Read permission.
Modify	Modify and delete the file *plus* perform the actions permitted by the Write permission and the Read & Execute permission.
Full Control	Change permissions and take ownership, *plus* perform the actions permitted by all other NTFS file permissions.

Lesson Summary

In this lesson you learned that you use NTFS permissions to specify which users and groups can gain access to files and folders, and what these permissions allow users to do with the contents of the files or folders. NTFS permissions are only available on NTFS volumes. NTFS security is effective whether a user gains access to the file or folder at the computer or over the network. You also learned that the folder permissions are Read, Write, List folder contents, Read & Execute, Modify, and Full Control. The file permissions are similar to the folder permissions. The file permissions are Read, Write, Read & Execute, Modify, and Full Control.

Lesson 2: Applying NTFS Permissions

Administrators, the owners of files or folders, and users with Full Control permission can assign NTFS permissions to users and groups to control access to files and folders.

After this lesson, you will be able to

- Describe the result when you combine user account and group permissions.
- Describe the result when folder permissions are different from those of the files in the folder.

Estimated lesson time: 5 minutes

Access Control List

NTFS stores an *access control list* (ACL) with every file and folder on an NTFS volume. The ACL contains a list of all user accounts and groups that have been granted access for the file or folder, as well as the type of access that they have been granted. When a user attempts to gain access to a resource, the ACL must contain an entry, called an *access control entry* (ACE), for the user account or a group to which the user belongs. The entry must allow the type of access that is requested (for example, Read access) in order for the user to gain access. If no ACE exists in the ACL, the user cannot gain access to the resource.

Multiple NTFS Permissions

You can assign multiple permissions to a user account by assigning permissions to his or her individual user account and to each group of which the user is a member. You need to understand the rules and priorities that are associated with how NTFS assigns and combines multiple permissions. You also need to understand NTFS permission inheritance.

Permissions Are Cumulative

A user's *effective permissions* for a resource are the sum of the NTFS permissions that you assign to the individual user account and to all of the groups to which the user belongs. If a user has Read permission for a folder and is a member of a group with Write permission for the same folder, the user has both Read and Write permission for that folder.

File Permissions Override Folder Permissions

NTFS file permissions take priority over NTFS folder permissions. A user with access to a file will be able to gain access to the file even if he or she does not have access to the folder containing the file. A user can gain access to the files for which he or she has permissions by using the full universal naming convention (UNC) or local path to open the file from its respective application, even

though the folder in which it resides will be invisible if the user has no corresponding folder permission. In other words, if you do not have permission to
access the folder containing the file you want to access, you would have to know
the full path to the file to access it. Without permission to access the folder, you
cannot see the folder, so you cannot browse for the file you want to access.

Deny Overrides Other Permissions

You can deny permission to a user account or group for a specific file, although
this is not the recommended way to control access to resources. Denying a permission overrides all instances where that permission is allowed. Even if a user
has permission to gain access to the file or folder as a member of a group, denying permission to the user blocks any other permission that the user might have
(see Figure 16.1).

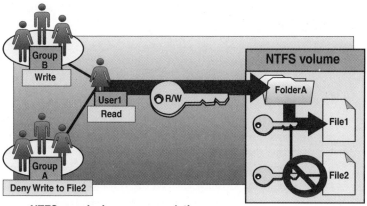

- NTFS permissions are cumulative.
- File permissions override folder permissions.
- Deny overrides other permissions.

Figure 16.1   Multiple NTFS permissions

In Figure 16.1, User1 has Read permission for FolderA and is a member of Group
A and Group B. Group B has Write permission for FolderA. Group A has been
denied Write permission for File2.

The user can read and write to File1. The user can also read File2, but she cannot
write to File2 because she is a member of Group A, which has been denied Write
permission for File 2.

NTFS Permissions Inheritance

By default, permissions that you assign to the parent folder are inherited by and
propagated to the subfolders and files that are contained in the parent folder.
However, you can prevent permissions inheritance, as shown in Figure 16.2.

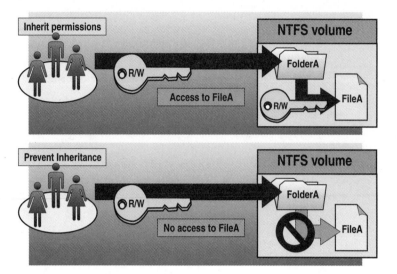

Figure 16.2   Inheritance

Understanding Permissions Inheritance

Files and subfolders inherit permissions from their parent folder. Whatever permissions you assign to the parent folder also apply to subfolders and files that are contained within the parent folder. When you assign NTFS permissions to give access to a folder, you assign permissions for the folder and for any existing files and subfolders, as well as for any new files and subfolders that are created in the folder.

Preventing Permissions Inheritance

You can prevent permissions that are assigned to a parent folder from being inherited by subfolders and files that are contained within the folder. That is, the subfolders and files will not inherit permissions that have been assigned to the parent folder containing them.

The folder at which you prevent permissions inheritance becomes the new parent folder, and permissions that are assigned to this folder will be inherited by the subfolders and files that are contained within it.

Lesson Summary

In this lesson you learned about applying NTFS permissions. You learned that Administrators, the owners of files or folders, and users with Full Control permission can assign NTFS permissions to users and groups to control access to files and folders. NTFS stores an ACL with every file and folder on an NTFS volume. The ACL contains a list of all user accounts and groups that have been granted access for the file or folder, as well as the type of access that they have been granted. A user attempting to gain access to a resource must have permission for the type of access that is requested in order for the user to gain access.

You also learned that you can assign multiple permissions to a user account by assigning permissions to his or her individual user account and to each group of which the user is a member. There are rules and priorities that control how NTFS assigns and combines multiple permissions. You also learned that a user's effective permissions for a resource are based on the NTFS permissions that you assign to the individual user account and to all of the groups to which the user belongs. Finally, you learned that NTFS file permissions take priority over NTFS folder permissions.

Lesson 3: Assigning NTFS Permissions

There are certain guidelines you should follow for assigning NTFS permissions. Assign permissions according to group and user needs, which includes allowing or preventing permissions inheritance from parent folders to subfolders and files that are contained in the parent folder.

After this lesson, you will be able to

- Assign NTFS folder and file permissions to user accounts and groups.

Estimated lesson time: 60 minutes

Planning NTFS Permissions

If you take the time to plan your NTFS permissions and follow a few guidelines, you will find that NTFS permissions are easy to manage. Use the following guidelines when you assign NTFS permissions:

1. To simplify administration, group files into application, data, and home folders. Centralize home and public folders on a volume that is separate from applications and the operating system. Doing so provides the following benefits:

    - You assign permissions only to folders, not to individual files.

    - Backup is less complex because there is no need to back up application files, and all home and public folders are in one location.

2. Allow users only the level of access that they require. If a user only needs to read a file, assign the Read permission to his or her user account for the file. This reduces the possibility of users accidentally modifying or deleting important documents and application files.

3. Create groups according to the access that the group members require for resources, and then assign the appropriate permissions to the group. Assign permissions to individual user accounts only when necessary.

4. When you assign permissions for working with data or application folders, assign the Read & Execute permission to the Users group and the Administrators group. This prevents application files from being accidentally deleted or damaged by users or viruses.

5. When you assign permissions for public data folders, assign the Read & Execute permission and the Write permission to the Users group and the Full Control permission to Creator Owner. The user who creates a file is by default the creator and owner of the file. After you create a file, you may grant another user permission to take ownership of the file. The person who takes ownership would then become the owner of the file. If you assign the Read & Execute permission and the Write permission to the Users group and the Full Control permission to Creator Owner, users have the ability to read and mod-

ify documents that other users create and the ability to read, modify, and delete the files and folders that they create.

6. Deny permissions only when it is essential to deny specific access to a specific user account or group.

7. Encourage users to assign permissions to the files and folders that they create and educate users about how to do so.

Setting NTFS Permissions

By default, when you format a volume with NTFS, the Full Control permission is assigned to the Everyone group. You should change this default permission and assign other appropriate NTFS permissions to control the access that users have to resources.

Assigning or Modifying Permissions

Administrators, users with the Full Control permission, and the owners of files and folders (Creator Owner) can assign permissions to user accounts and groups.

To assign or modify NTFS permissions for a file or a folder, on the Security tab of the Properties dialog box for the file or folder, configure the options that are described in Table 16.3 and shown in Figure 16.3.

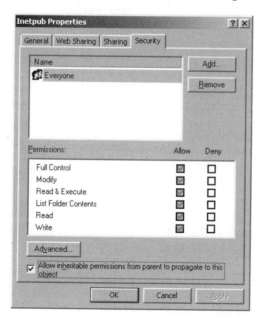

Figure 16.3   The Security tab of the Properties dialog box for a folder

Table 16.3   Security Tab Options

Option	Description
Name	Select the user account or group for which you want to change permissions or which you want to remove from the list.
Permission	To allow a permission, select the Allow check box.
	To deny a permission, select the Deny check box.
Add	Opens the Select User, Groups, or Computers dialog box, which you use to select user accounts and groups to add to the Name list.
Remove	Remove the selected user account or group and the associated permissions for the file or folder.

Preventing Permissions Inheritance

By default, subfolders and files inherit permissions that you assign to their parent folder. This is indicated on the Security tab in the Properties dialog box by a check in the Allow Inheritable Permissions From Parent To Propagate To This Object check box. To prevent a subfolder or file from inheriting permissions from a parent folder, clear the Allow Inheritable Permissions From Parent To Propagate To This Object check box. If you clear this check box, you are prompted to select one of the options that are described in Table 16.4.

Table 16.4   Preventing Permissions Inheritance Options

Option	Description
Copy	Copy the permissions from the parent folder to the current folder and then deny subsequent permissions inheritance from the parent folder.
Remove	Remove the permissions that are assigned to the parent folder and retain only the permissions that you explicitly assign to the file or folder.
Cancel	Cancel the dialog box and restore the checkmark in the Allow Inheritable Permissions From Parent To Propagate To This Object check box.

Practice: Planning and Assigning NTFS Permissions

In this practice you plan NTFS permissions for folders based and files based on a business scenario. Then you apply NTFS permissions for folders and files on your computer, based on a second scenario. Finally, you test the NTFS permissions that you set up to make sure that they are working properly.

Before beginning the exercises below, create the users and groups listed in the following table:

Group	User account
Managers	User81 (member of Print Operators)
Sales	User82 (member of Sales and Print Operators)
Sales	User83 (member of Managers and Print Operators)

Create the following folders:

- C:\Data
- C:\Data\Managers
- C:\Data\Managers\Report
- C:\Data\Sales

Exercise 1: Planning NTFS Permissions

In this exercise, you plan how to assign NTFS permissions to folders and files on a computer running Windows 2000 Server, based on the scenario that is described in the next section.

Scenario

The default NTFS folder and file permissions are Full Control for the Everyone group. Figure 16.4 shows the folder and file structure used for this practice. You need to review the following security criteria and record the changes that you should make to the NTFS folder and file permissions to meet the security criteria.

Figure 16.4   Folder and file structure for practice

To plan NTFS permissions, you must determine the following:

- What groups to create and what built-in groups to use.
- What permissions users will require to gain access to folders and files.
- Whether or not to clear the Allow Inheritable Permissions From Parent To Propagate To This Object check box for the folder or file for which you are assigning permissions.

Keep the following general guidelines in mind:

- NTFS permissions that are assigned to a folder are inherited by all of the folders and files that it contains. To assign permissions for all of the folders and files in the Apps folder, you need only assign NTFS permissions to the Apps folder.
- To assign more restrictive permissions to a folder or file that is inheriting permissions, you must either *deny* the unwanted permissions or block inheritance

by clearing the Allow Inheritable Permissions From Parent To Propagate To This Object check box.

The decisions that you make are based on the following criteria:

- In addition to the default built-in groups, the following groups have been created in the domain:
  - Accounting
  - Managers
  - Executives
- Administrators require the Full Control permission for all folders and files.
- All users will run programs in the WordProc folder, but they should not be able to modify the files in the WordProc folder.
- Only members of the Accounting, Managers, and Executives groups should be able to read documents in the Spreadsh and Database application folders by running the associated spreadsheet and database applications, but they should not be able to modify the files in those folders.
- All users should be able to read and create files in the Public folder.
- All users should be prevented from modifying files in the Public\Library folder.
- Only User81 should be able to modify and delete files in the Public\Manuals folder.

  When you apply custom permissions to a folder or file, which default permission entry should you remove?

Complete the following table to plan and record your permissions:

Path	User account or group	NTFS permissions	Block inheritance (yes/no)
Apps			
Apps\WordProc			
Apps\Spreadsh			
Apps\Database			

Public

Public\Library

Public\Manuals

Exercise 2: Assigning NTFS Permissions for the Data Folder

In this exercise, you assign NTFS permissions for the C:\Data folder based on the scenario that is described next.

Scenario

The permissions that you assign are based on the following criteria:

- All users in the domain should be able to read documents and files in the Data folder.
- All users in the domain should be able to create documents in the Data folder.
- All users in the domain should be able to modify the contents, properties, and permissions of the documents that they create in the Data folder.

▶ **To remove permissions from the Everyone group**

1. Log on to your domain as Administrator.
2. Right-click My Computer, and then click Explore.
3. Expand Local Disk (C:), right-click the C:\Data folder, and then click Properties.

    Windows 2000 displays the Data Properties dialog box with the General tab active.
4. Click the Security tab to display the permissions for the Data folder.

    Windows 2000 displays the Data Properties dialog box with the Security tab active.

    What are the existing folder permissions?

    Notice that the current allowed permissions cannot be modified.
5. Under Name, select the Everyone group, and then click Remove.

    What do you see?
6. Click OK to close the message box.

7. Clear the Allow Inheritable Permissions From Parent To Propagate To This Object check box to block permissions from being inherited.

Windows 2000 displays the Security dialog box, prompting you to copy the currently inherited permissions to the folder or remove all permissions for the folder except those that you explicitly specify.

8. Click Remove.

What are the existing folder permissions?

▶ **To assign permissions to the Users group for the Data folder**

1. In the Data Properties dialog box, click Add.

Windows 2000 displays the Select User Computer, Or Group dialog box.

2. In the Look In box at the top of the dialog box, select your domain.

The Look In box allows you to select the computer or domain from which to select user accounts, groups, or computers when you assign permissions. You should specify your domain to select from the user accounts and groups that you created.

3. In the Name box, type **Users** and then click Add.

The dialog box displays Users under Name at the bottom of the dialog box.

Note   On a domain controller, you can select a domain local group by typing its name in the Name box. On a member server, typing the name of a domain local group selects an identically named local group on the member server instead.

---

4. Click OK to return to the Data Properties dialog box.

What are the existing allowed folder permissions?

5. Make sure that Users is selected, and then next to Write, select the Allow check box.

6. Click Apply to save your changes.

▶ **To assign permissions to the Creator Owner group for the Data folder**

1. In the Data Properties dialog box, click Add.

Windows 2000 displays the Select User Computer, Or Group dialog box.

2. In the Look In box at the top of the dialog box, select your domain.

3. In the Name list, select Creator Owner, and then click Add.

Creator Owner appears under Name at the bottom of the dialog box.

4. Click OK to return to the Data Properties dialog box.

   What are the existing allowed folder permissions?

5. Make sure that Creator Owner is selected, and next to Full Control, select the Allow check box, and then click Apply to save your changes.

   What do you see?

6. Click Advanced to display the additional permissions.

   Windows 2000 displays the Access Control Settings for Data dialog box.

7. Under Name, select Creator Owner.

   What permissions are assigned to Creator Owner and where do these permissions apply? Why?

   The user who creates the new file or folder receives the permissions that are assigned to Creator Owner for the parent folder.

▶ **To test the folder permissions that you assigned for the Data folder**

1. Log on to your domain as User81, and then start Windows Explorer.
2. Expand the C:\Data directory.
3. In the Data folder, attempt to create a text file named User81.txt.

   Were you successful? Why or why not?

4. Attempt to perform the following tasks for the file that you just created, and then record those tasks that you are able to complete.

   Open the file

   Modify the file

   Delete the file

   The tasks that you can complete are opening, modifying, and deleting the file because Creator Owner has been assigned the NTFS Full Control permission for the Data folder.

5. Close all applications, and then log off Windows 2000.

Exercise 3: Assigning NTFS Permissions

In this exercise, you assign NTFS permissions to the Data, Managers, Reports, and Sales folders based on the scenario that is described in the following section.

Scenario

Assign the appropriate permissions to folders as listed in the following table:

Folder name	User account or group	Permissions
C:\Data	Users group Administrators group	Read & Execute Full Control
C:\Data\Managers	Users group Administrators group Managers group	Read & Execute Full Control Modify
C:\Data\Managers\Reports	Users group Administrators group User82	Read & Execute Full Control Modify
C:\Data\Sales	Users group Administrators group Sales group	Read & Execute Full Control Modify

▶ **To assign NTFS permissions for a folder**

1. Log on to your domain as Administrator, and then start Windows Explorer.

2. Expand the C:\ directory.

3. Right-click the folder for which you are modifying permissions, and then click Properties.

    Windows 2000 displays the Properties dialog box for the folder with the General tab active.

4. In the Properties dialog box for the folder, click the Security tab.

5. On the Security tab, if you need to modify the inherited permissions for a user account or group, clear the Allow Inheritable Permissions From Parent To Propagate To This Object check box, and then when prompted to copy or remove inherited permissions, click Copy.

6. To add permissions to user accounts or groups for the folder, click Add.

    Windows 2000 displays the Select User Computer, Or Group dialog box.

7. Make sure that your domain appears in the Look In box at the top of the dialog box.

8. In the Name box, type the name of the appropriate user account or group, based on the preceding scenario, and then click Add.

    Windows 2000 displays the user account or group under Name at the bottom of the dialog box.

9. Repeat step 8 for each user account or group that is listed for the folder in the preceding scenario.

10. Click OK to return to the Properties dialog box for the folder.

11. If the Properties dialog box for the folder contains user accounts and groups that are not listed in the preceding scenario, select the user account or group, and then click Remove.

12. For all user accounts and groups that are listed for the folder in the preceding scenario, under Name, select the user account or group, and then under Permissions, select the Allow check box or the Deny check box next to the appropriate permissions that are listed for the folder in the preceding scenario.

13. Click OK to apply your changes and close the Properties dialog box for the folder.

14. Repeat this procedure for each folder for which you are assigning permissions as specified in the preceding scenario.

15. Log off Windows.

Exercise 4: Testing NTFS Permissions

In this exercise, you log on using various user accounts and test NTFS permissions.

▶ **To test permissions for the Reports folder while logged on as User81**

1. Log on as User81, and then start Windows Explorer.

2. In Windows Explorer, expand the C:\\Data\s directory.

3. Attempt to create a file in the Reports folder.

Were you successful? Why or why not?

4. Log off Windows 2000.

▶ **To test permissions for the Reports folder while logged on as User82**

1. Log on as User82, and then start Windows Explorer.

2. Expand the C:\\Data\Manager\Reports directory.

3. Attempt to create a file in the Reports folder.

Were you successful? Why or why not?

4. Log off Windows 2000.

▶ **To test permissions for the Sales folder while logged on as Administrator**

1. Log on to your domain as Administrator, and then start Windows Explorer.

2. Expand the C:\\Data\Sales directory.

3. Attempt to create a file in the Sales folder.

Were you successful? Why or why not?

4. Close Windows Explorer, and then log off Windows 2000.

▶ **To test permissions for the Sales folder while logged on as User81**

1. Log on as User81, and then start Windows Explorer.
2. Expand the C:\Data\Sales directory.
3. Attempt to create a file in the Sales folder.

Were you successful? Why or why not?

▶ **To test permissions for the Sales folder while logged on as User82**

1. Log on as User82, and then start Windows Explorer.
2. Expand the C:\Data\Sales directory.
3. Attempt to create a file in the Sales folder.

Were you successful? Why or why not?

4. Close all applications, and then log off Windows 2000.

Lesson Summary

In this lesson you learned that by default, when you format a volume with NTFS, the Full Control permission is assigned to the Everyone group. You learned that you should change this default permission and assign other appropriate NTFS permissions to control the access that users have to resources. You learned how to assign or modify NTFS permissions for a file or a folder by using the Security tab of the Properties dialog box for the file or folder.

You also learned that by default, subfolders and files inherit permissions that you assign to their parent folder, and you learned how to disable this feature, so that subfolders and files do not inherit the permissions assigned to their parents. In the practice exercises, you created some folders, assigned NTFS permissions, and then tested the permissions you had set up to determine if you set them up correctly.

Lesson 4: Assigning Special Access Permissions

The standard NTFS permissions generally provide all of the access control that you need to secure your resources. However, there are instances where the standard NTFS permissions do not provide the specific level of access that you may want to assign to users. To create a specific level of access, you can assign NTFS special access permissions.

After this lesson, you will be able to

- Give users the ability to change permissions on files or folders.
- Give users the ability to take ownership of files and folders.

Estimated lesson time: 5 minutes

Special Access Permissions

There are 14 special access permissions. Two of them, shown in Figure 16.5, are particularly useful for controlling access to resources: Change Permissions and Take Ownership.

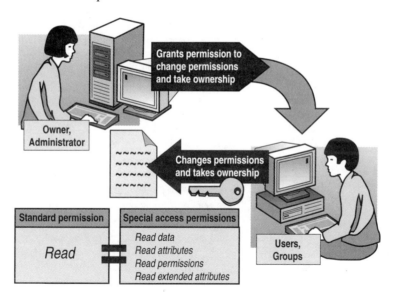

Figure 16.5   Change Permissions and Take Ownership special access permissions

When you assign special access permissions to folders, you can choose where to apply the permissions down the tree to subfolders and files.

Change Permissions

You can give other administrators and users the ability to change permissions for a file or folder without giving them the Full Control permission over the file or folder. In this way, the administrator or user cannot delete or write to the file or folder but can assign permissions to the file or folder.

To give administrators the ability to change permissions, assign Change Permissions to the Administrators group for the file or folder.

Take Ownership

You can transfer ownership of files and folders from one user account or group to another user account or group. You can give someone the ability to take ownership and, as an administrator, you can take ownership of a file or folder.

The following rules apply for taking ownership of a file or folder:

- The current owner or any user with Full Control permission can assign the Full Control standard permission or the Take Ownership special access permission to another user account or group, allowing the user account or a member of the group to take ownership.
- An administrator can take ownership of a folder or file, regardless of assigned permissions. If an administrator takes ownership, the Administrators group becomes the owner and any member of the Administrators group can change the permissions for the file or folder and assign the Take Ownership permission to another user account or group.

  For example, if an employee leaves the company, an administrator can take ownership of the employee's files, assign the Take Ownership permission to another employee, and then that employee can take ownership of the former employee's files.

Note You cannot *assign* anyone ownership of a file or folder. The owner of a file, an administrator, or anyone with Full Control permission can assign Take Ownership permission to a user account or group, allowing them to take ownership. To become the owner of a file or folder, a user or group member with Take Ownership permission must explicitly take ownership of the file or folder, as explained later in this chapter.

Setting Special Access Permissions

You assign special access permissions to enable users to change permissions and take ownership of files and folders.

▶ **To set Change Permissions or Take Ownership permissions**

1. In the Access Control Settings dialog box for a file or folder, on the Permissions tab, select the user account or group for which you want to apply NTFS special access permissions.

2. Click View/Edit to open the Permissions Entry dialog box (see Figure 16.6).

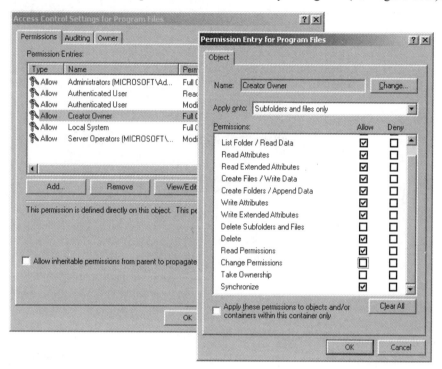

Figure 16.6 Permissions Entry dialog box

The options in the Permissions Entry dialog box are described in Table 16.5.

Table 16.5 Options in the Permissions Entry Dialog Box

Option	Description
Name	The user account or group name. To select a different user account or group, click Change Account.
Apply Onto	The level of the folder hierarchy at which the special NTFS permissions are inherited. The default is This Folder, Subfolders, And Files.
Permissions	The special access permissions. To allow the Change Permissions permission or Take Ownership permission, select the Allow check box.

(continued)

Option	Description
Apply These Permissions To Objects And/Or Containers Within This Container Only	Specify whether subfolders and files within a folder inherit the special access permissions from the folder. Select this check box to propagate the special access permissions to files and subfolders. Clear this check box to prevent permissions inheritance.
Clear All	Click this button to clear all selected permissions.

Note In the Access Control Settings dialog box, on the Permissions tab, you can view the permissions that are applied to the file or folder, the owner, and where the permissions apply. When special access permissions have been assigned, Windows 2000 displays Special under Permissions.

Taking Ownership of a File or Folder

To take ownership of a file or folder, the user or a group member with Take Ownership permission must explicitly take ownership of the file or folder.

▶ **To take ownership of a file or folder**

1. In the Access Control Settings dialog box, on the Owner tab, in the Change Owner To list, select your name.

2. Select the Replace Owner On Subdirectories And Objects check box to take ownership of all subfolders and files that are contained within the folder.

Lesson Summary

In this lesson you learned that there are 14 special access permissions. You learned specifically about two of them: Change Permissions and Take Ownership. You can give administrators and other users the ability to change permissions for a file or folder without giving them the Full Control permission over the file or folder. This prevents the administrator or user from deleting or writing to the file or folder, but it allows them to assign permissions to the file or folder.

You also learned how to transfer ownership of files and folders from one user account or group to another user account or group. The current owner or any user with Full Control permission can assign the Full Control standard permission or the Take Ownership special access permission to another user account or group, allowing the user account or a member of the group to take ownership. An administrator can take ownership of a folder or file, regardless of assigned permissions. When an administrator takes ownership of a file or folder, the Administrators group becomes the owner and any member of the Administrators group can change the permissions for the file or folder and assign the Take Ownership permission to another user account or group.

Lesson 5: Copying and Moving Files and Folders

When you copy or move files and folders, the permissions you set on the files or folders might change. There are rules that control how and when permissions change. It is important that you understand how and when permissions change during a copy or move.

After this lesson, you will be able to

- Describe the effect on NTFS file and folder permissions when files and folders are copied.
- Describe the effect on NTFS file and folder permissions when files and folders are moved.

Estimated lesson time: 5 minutes

Copying Files and Folders

When you copy files or folders from one folder to another folder, or from one volume to another volume, permissions change, as shown in Figure 16.7.

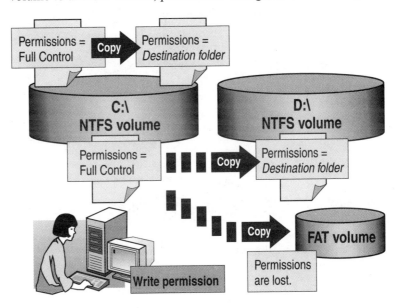

Figure 16.7   Copying files or folders between folders or volumes

When you copy a file within a single NTFS volume or between NTFS volumes:

- Windows 2000 treats it as a new file. As a new file, it takes on the permissions of the destination folder.
- You must have Write permission for the destination folder to copy files and folders.
- You become the Creator Owner.

Note When you copy files or folders to FAT volumes, the folders and files lose their NTFS permissions because FAT volumes do not support NTFS permissions.

Moving Files and Folders

When you move a file or folder, permissions might or might not change, depending on where you move the file or folder. (See Figure 16.8.)

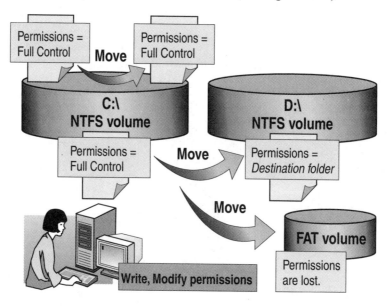

Figure 16.8   Moving files or folders between folders or volumes

Moving Within a Single NTFS Volume

When you move a file or folder within a single NTFS volume

- The folder or file retains the original permissions.
- You must have the Write permission for the destination folder to move files and folders into it.

- You must have the Modify permission for the source folder or file. The Modify permission is required to move a folder or file because Windows 2000 deletes the folder or file from the source folder after it is copied to the destination folder.

- You become the Creator Owner.

Moving Between NTFS Volumes

When you move a file or folder between NTFS volumes

- The folder or file inherits the permissions of the destination folder.

- You must have the Write permission for the destination folder to move files and folders into it.

- You must have the Modify permission for the source folder or file. The Modify permission is required to move a folder or file because Windows 2000 deletes the folder or file from the source folder *after* it is copied to the destination folder.

- You become the Creator Owner.

Note   When you move files or folders to FAT volumes, the folders and files lose their NTFS permissions because FAT volumes do not support NTFS permissions.

Lesson Summary

In this lesson you learned that when you copy or move files and folders, the permissions you set on the files or folders might change. You also learned that there are rules that control how and when permissions change. For example, when you copy files or folders from one folder to another folder, or from one volume to another volume, permissions change. Windows 2000 treats the file or folder as a new file or folder, and therefore it takes on the permissions of the destination folder. You must have Write permission for the destination folder to copy files and folders. When you copy a file, you become the Creator Owner of the file. When you move a file or folder within a single NTFS volume, the file or folder retains the original permissions. However, when you move a file or folder between NTFS volumes, the file or folder inherits the permissions of the destination folder.

Lesson 6: Solving Permissions Problems

When you assign or modify NTFS permissions to files and folders, problems might arise. Troubleshooting these problems is important in order to keep resources available to users.

After this lesson, you will be able to

- Troubleshoot resource access problems.

Estimated lesson time: 20 minutes

Troubleshooting Permissions Problems

Table 16.6 describes some common permissions problems that you might encounter and provides solutions that you can try to resolve these problems.

Table 16.6   Permissions Problems and Troubleshooting Solutions

Problem	Solution
A user cannot gain access to a file or folder.	If the file or folder was copied, or if it was moved to another NTFS volume, the permissions might have changed.
	Check the permissions that are assigned to the user account and to groups of which the user is a member. The user might not have permission or might be denied access either individually or as a member of a group.
You add a user account to a group to give that user access to a file or folder, but the user still cannot gain access.	For access permissions to be updated to include the new group to which you have added the user account, the user must either log off and then log on again or close all network connections to the computer on which the file or folder resides and then make new connections.
A user with Full Control permission to a folder deletes a file in the folder although that user does not have permission to delete the file itself. You want to stop the user from being able to delete more files.	You would have to clear the special access permission Delete Subfolders And Files check box on the folder to prevent users with Full Control of the folder from being able to delete files in the folder.

Note   Windows 2000 supports POSIX applications that are designed to run on UNIX. On UNIX systems, Full Control permission allows you to delete files in a folder. In Windows 2000, the Full Control permission includes the Delete Subfolders and Files special access permission, allowing you the same ability to delete files in that folder regardless of the permissions that you have for the files in the folder.

Avoiding Permissions Problems

The following list provides best practices for implementing NTFS permissions. These guidelines will help you avoid permission problems.

- Assign the most restrictive NTFS permissions that still enable users and groups to accomplish necessary tasks.

- Assign all permissions at the folder level, not at the file level. Group files in a separate folder for which you want to restrict user access, and then assign that folder restricted access.

- For all application executable files, assign Read & Execute and Change Permissions to the Administrators group and assign Read & Execute to the Users group. Damage to application files is usually a result of accidents and viruses. By assigning Read & Execute to Users and Read & Execute and Change Permissions to Administrators, you can prevent users or viruses from modifying or deleting executable files. To update files, members of the Administrators group can assign Full Control to their user account to make changes and then reassign Read & Execute and Change Permissions to their user account.

- Assign Full Control to Creator Owner for public data folders so that users can delete and modify files and folders that they create. Doing so gives the user who creates the file or folder (Creator Owner) full access to only the files or folders that he or she creates in the public data folder.

- For public folders, assign Full Control to Creator Owner and Read and Write to the Everyone group. This gives users full access to the files that they create, but members of the Everyone group can only read files in the folder and add files to the folder.

- Use long, descriptive names if the resource will be accessed only at the computer. If a folder will eventually be shared, use folder and file names that are accessible by all client computers.

- Allow permissions rather than denying permissions. If you do not want a user or group to gain access to a particular folder or file, do not assign permissions. Denying permissions should be an exception, not a common practice.

Practice: Managing NTFS Permissions

In this practice you observe the effects of taking ownership of a file. Then you determine the effects of permission and ownership when you copy or move files. Finally you determine what happens when a user has full Control permission to a folder, but has been denied all access to a file in that folder, and the user attempts to delete the file.

To successfully complete this practice, you must have completed "Practice: Planning and Assigning NTFS Permissions," in Lesson 3 of this chapter.

Exercise 1: Taking Ownership of a File

In this exercise, you observe the effects of taking ownership of a file. To do this, you determine permissions for a file, assign the Take Ownership permission to a user account, and then take ownership as that user.

▶ **To determine the permissions for a file**

1. Log on to your domain as Administrator, and then start Windows Explorer.

2. In the C:\Data directory, create a text file named Owner.txt.

3. Right-click Owner.txt, and then click Properties.

   Microsoft Windows 2000 displays the Owner Properties dialog box with the General tab active.

4. Click the Security tab to display the permissions for the Owner.txt file.

   What are the current allowed permissions for Owner.txt?

   The Users group has the Read & Execute permission.

5. Click Advanced.

   Windows 2000 displays the Access Control Settings For Owner dialog box with the Permissions tab active.

6. Click the Owner tab.

   Who is the current owner of the Owner.txt file?

▶ **To assign permission to a user to take ownership**

1. In the Access Control Settings For Owner dialog box, click the Permissions tab.

2. Click Add.

   Windows 2000 displays the Select User, Computer, Or Group dialog box.

3. In the Look In box at the top of the dialog box, select your domain.

4. Under Name, click User84, and then click OK.

   Windows 2000 displays the Permission Entry For Owner dialog box.

   Notice that all of the permission entries for User84 are blank.

5. Under Permissions, select the Allow check box next to Take Ownership.

6. Click OK.

   Windows 2000 displays the Access Control Settings For Owner dialog box with the Permissions tab active.

7. Click OK to return to the Owner Properties dialog box.

8. Click OK to apply your changes and close the Owner Properties dialog box.

9. Close all applications, and then log off Windows 2000.

▶   **To take ownership of a file**

1. Log on to your domain as User84, and then start Windows Explorer.

2. Expand the C:\Data directory.

3. Right-click Owner.txt, and then click Properties.

    Windows 2000 displays the Owner Properties dialog box with the General tab active.

4. Click the Security tab to display the permissions for Owner.txt.

    Windows 2000 displays the Security message box, indicating that you can only view the current permission information on Owner.txt.

5. Click OK.

    Windows 2000 displays the Owner Properties dialog box with the Security tab active.

6. Click Advanced to display the Access Control Settings For Owner dialog box, and then click the Owner tab.

    Who is the current owner of Owner.txt?

7. Under Name, select User84, and then click Apply.

    Who is the current owner of Owner.txt?

8. Click OK to close the Security dialog box.

9. Click Cancel to close the Access Control Settings For Owner dialog box.

    Windows 2000 displays the Owner Properties dialog box with the Security tab active.

10. Click OK to close the Owner Properties dialog box.

▶   **To test permissions for a file as the owner**

1. While you are logged on as User84, assign User84 the Full Control permission for the Owner.txt file, and click Apply.

2. Clear the Allow Inheritable Permissions From Parent To Propagate To This Object check box.

3. In the Security dialog box, click Remove.

4. Remove permissions from the Users group and the Administrators group for the Owner.txt file.

Were you successful? Why or why not?

5. Delete the Owner.txt file.

Exercise 2: Copying and Moving Folders

In this exercise, you see the effects of permissions and ownership when you copy and move folders.

▶ **To create a folder while logged on as a user**

1. While you are logged on as User84, in Windows Explorer, in C:\, create a folder named Temp1.

   What are the permissions that are assigned to the folder?

   Who is the owner? Why?

2. Close all applications, and then log off Windows 2000.

▶ **To create a folder while logged on as Administrator**

1. Log on to your domain as Administrator, and then start Windows Explorer.
2. In C:\, create the following two folders: Temp2 and Temp3.

   What are the permissions for the folders that you just created?

   Who is the owner of the Temp2 and Temp3 folders? Why?

3. Remove the Everyone group, and then assign the following permissions to the Temp2 and Temp3 folders. You will have to clear the Allow Inheritable Permissions From Parent To Propagate To This Object check box. To select a group, type the group name in the Name box and then click Add.

Folder	Assign these permissions
C:\Temp2	Administrators: Full Control Users: Read & Execute
C:\Temp3	Backup Operators: Read & Execute Users: Full Control

▶ **To copy a folder to another folder within a Windows 2000 NTFS volume**

1. Copy C:\Temp2 to C:\Temp1.

2. Select C:\Temp1\Temp2, and then compare the permissions and ownership with C:\Temp2.

    Who is the owner of C:\Temp1\Temp2 and what are the permissions? Why?

    The Everyone group has the Full Control permission because when a folder or file is copied within an NTFS volume, the folder or file inherits the permissions of the folder into which it is copied.

▶ **To move a folder within the same NTFS volume**

1. Log on to your domain as User84.
2. Select C:\Temp3, and then move it to C:\Temp1.

    What happens to the permissions and ownership for C:\Temp1\Temp3? Why?

Exercise 3: Deleting a File with All Permissions Denied

In this exercise, you grant a user Full Control permission to a folder, but deny all permissions to a file in the folder. You then observe what happens when the user attempts to delete that file.

▶ **To assign the Full Control permission for a folder**

1. Log on to your domain as Administrator, and then start Windows Explorer.
2. Expand C:\, and then create a folder named Fullaccess.
3. Verify that the Everyone group has the Full Control permission for the C:\Fullaccess folder.

▶ **To create a file and deny access to it**

1. In C:\Fullaccess, create a text file named Noaccess.txt.
2. Deny the Everyone group the Full Control permission for the Noaccess.txt file.

    Windows 2000 displays the Security dialog box with the following message:

    ```
    Caution! Deny entries take priority over Allow entries, and you have
    denied everyone access to Noaccess. No one will be able to access
    Noaccess. Not even the owner will be able to change permissions.

    Do you wish to continue?
    ```

3. Click Yes to apply your changes and close the Security dialog box.

▶ **To view the result of the Full Control permission for a folder**

1. In Windows Explorer, double-click Noaccess.txt in C:\Fullaccess to open the file. Were you successful? Why or why not?

2. Click the Start button, point to Programs, and then click Command Prompt.

3. Change to C:\Fullaccess.

4. Delete Noaccess.txt.

   Were you successful? Why or why not?

   How would you prevent users with Full Control permission for a folder from deleting a file in that folder for which they have been denied the Full Control permission?

Lesson Summary

When you assign or modify NTFS permissions for files and folders, problems might arise. Troubleshooting these problems is important in order to keep resources available to users. In this lesson, you learned some common permissions problems and some possible solutions to resolve these problems. In the practice exercises for this lesson you determined the permissions for a file, assigned the Take Ownership permission to a user account, and then took ownership as that user. You also observed the effects of permissions and ownership when you copy and move folders. Finally, in these exercises you practiced assigning permissions to a folder and a file, and then observed the results when a user has Full Control permission to a folder and has been denied all permissions to a file in that folder.

Review

Here are some questions to help you determine if you have learned enough to move on to the next chapter. If you have difficulty answering these questions, please go back and review the material in this chapter before beginning the next chapter. The answers for these questions are located in Appendix A, "Questions and Answers."

1. What is the default permission when a volume is formatted with NTFS? Who has access to the volume?

2. If a user has Write permission for a folder and is also a member of a group with Read permission for the folder, what are the user's effective permissions for the folder?

3. If you assign the Modify permission to a user account for a folder and the Read permission for a file, and then copy the file to that folder, what permission does the user have for the file?

4. What happens to permissions that are assigned to a file when the file is moved from one folder to another folder on the same NTFS volume? What happens when the file is moved to a folder on another NTFS volume?

5. If an employee leaves the company, what must you do to transfer ownership of his or her files and folders to another employee?

6. What three things should you check when a user cannot gain access to a resource?

C H A P T E R   1 7

Administering Shared Folders

About This Chapter

In Chapter 16, "Securing Resources with NTFS Permissions," you learned about NTFS permissions. You use NTFS permissions to specify which users and groups can gain access to files and folders and what these permissions allow users to do with the contents of the file or folder. NTFS permissions are only available on NTFS volumes. NTFS security is effective whether a user gains access to the file or folder at the computer or over the network. In this chapter you will learn how to make folders accessible over the network. You can only access a computer's folders and their contents by physically sitting at the computer and logging on to it or by accessing a shared folder on a remote computer. Sharing folders is the only way to make folders and their contents available over the network. Shared folders also provide another way to secure file resources, one that can be used on FAT or FAT32 partitions. In this chapter, you will learn how to share file resources, secure them with permissions, and provide access to them.

Before You Begin

To complete this chapter, you must have

- A computer that meets the minimum hardware requirements listed in "Hardware Requirements," on page xxxiii.
- Installed the Windows 2000 Server software on the computer.
- Configured the computer as a domain controller in a domain.

Lesson 1: Understanding Shared Folders

You use shared folders to provide network users with access to file resources. When a folder is shared, users can connect to the folder over the network and gain access to the files that it contains. However, to gain access to the files, users must have permissions to access the shared folders.

After this lesson, you will be able to

- Use shared folders to provide access to network resources.

- Describe how permissions affect access to shared folders.

Estimated lesson time: 15 minutes

Shared Folder Permissions

A shared folder can contain applications, data, or a user's personal data, called a home folder. Each type of data requires different shared folder permissions.

The following are characteristics of shared folder permissions:

- Shared folder permissions apply to folders, not individual files. Since you can only apply shared folder permissions to the entire shared folder, and not to individual files or subfolders in the shared folder, shared folder permissions provide less detailed security than Microsoft Windows NT file system (NTFS) permissions.

- Shared folder permissions do not restrict access to users who gain access to the folder at the computer where the folder is stored. They only apply to users who connect to the folder over the network.

- Shared folder permissions are the only way to secure network resources on a file allocation table (FAT) volume. NTFS permissions are not available on FAT volumes.

- The default shared folder permission is Full Control, and it is assigned to the Everyone group when you share the folder.

Note A shared folder appears in Microsoft Windows Explorer as an icon of a hand holding the shared folder (Figure 17.1 shows the sharing icon).

To control how users gain access to a shared folder, you assign shared folder permissions.

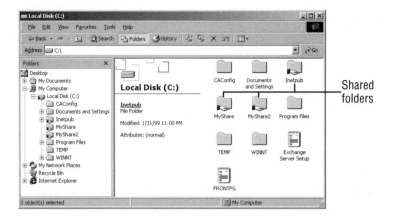

Figure 17.1   Shared folders in Windows Explorer

Table 17.1 explains what each of the shared folder permissions allows a user to do. The permissions are presented from most restrictive to least restrictive.

Table 17.1   Shared Folder Permissions

Shared folder permission	Allows the user to
Read	Display folder names, file names, file data and attributes; run program files; and change folders within the shared folder.
Change	Create folders, add files to folders, change data in files, append data to files, change file attributes, delete folders and files, *plus* it allows the user to perform actions permitted by the Read permission.
Full Control	Change file permissions, take ownership of files, *and* perform all tasks permitted by the Change permission.

You can allow or deny shared folder permissions. Generally, it is best to allow permissions and to assign permissions to a group rather than to individual users. You deny permissions only when it is necessary to override permissions that are otherwise applied. In most cases, you should deny permissions only when it is necessary to deny permission to a specific user who belongs to a group to which you have given the permission. If you deny a shared folder permission to a user, the user will not have that permission. For example, to deny *all* access to a shared folder, deny Full Control permission.

How Shared Folder Permissions Are Applied

Applying shared permissions to user accounts and groups affects access to a shared folder. Denying permission takes precedence over the permissions that you allow.

Multiple Permissions Combine

A user can be a member of multiple groups, each with different permissions that provide different levels of access to a shared folder. When you assign permission to a user for a shared folder, and that user is a member of a group to which you assigned a different permission, the user's *effective permissions* are the combination of the user and group permissions. For example, if a user has Read permission and is a member of a group with Change permission, the user's effective permission is Change, which includes Read.

Deny Overrides Other Permissions

Denied permissions take precedence over any permissions that you otherwise allow for user accounts and groups. If you deny a shared folder permission to a user, the user will not have that permission, even if you allow the permission for a group of which the user is a member.

NTFS Permissions Are Required on NTFS Volumes

Shared folder permissions are sufficient to gain access to files and folders on a FAT volume, but not on an NTFS volume. On a FAT volume, users can gain access to a shared folder for which they have permissions, as well as all of the folder's contents. When users gain access to a shared folder on an NTFS volume, they need the shared folder permission and also the appropriate NTFS permissions for each file and folder to which they gain access.

Copied or Moved Shared Folders Are No Longer Shared

When you copy a shared folder, the original shared folder is still shared, but the copy is not shared. When you move a shared folder, it is no longer shared.

Guidelines for Shared Folder Permissions

The following list provides some general guidelines for managing your shared folders and assigning shared folder permissions:

- Determine which groups need access to each resource and the level of access that they require. Document the groups and their permissions for each resource.

- Assign permissions to groups instead of user accounts to simplify access administration.

- Assign to a resource the most restrictive permissions that still allow users to perform required tasks. For example, if users need only to read information in a folder, and they will never delete or create files, assign the Read permission.

- Organize resources so that folders with the same security requirements are located within a folder. For example, if users require Read permission for several application folders, store the application folders within the same folder. Then share this folder instead of sharing each individual application folder.

- Use intuitive share names so that users can easily recognize and locate resources. For example, for the Application folder, use Apps for the share name. You should also use share names that all client operating systems can use.

Table 17.2 describes share and folder naming conventions for different client computer operating systems.

Table 17.2   Client Computer Operating Systems and Share Name Length

Client computer operating system	Share name length
Windows 2000, Windows NT, Windows 98, and Windows 95	12 characters
MS-DOS, Windows 3.x, and Windows for Workgroups	8.3 characters

Microsoft Windows 2000 provides 8.3-character equivalent names, but the resulting names might not be intuitive to users. For example, a Windows 2000 folder named Accountants Database would appear as Account~1 on client computers running MS-DOS, Windows 3.x, and Windows for Workgroups.

Practice: Applied Permissions

In the following practice, User1 has been assigned permissions to gain access to resources as an individual and as a member of a group, as shown in Figure 17.2. Determine what effective permissions User1 has in each situation:

1. User1 is a member of Group1, Group2, and Group3. Group1 has Read permission and Group3 has Full Control permission for Folder A. Group2 has no permissions for FolderA. What are User1's effective permissions for FolderA?

2. User1 is also a member of the Sales group, which has Read permission for FolderB. User1 has been denied the shared folder permission Full Control for FolderB as an individual user. What are User1's effective permissions for FolderB?

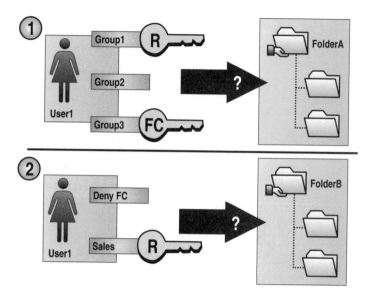

Figure 17.2   Applied permissions

Lesson Summary

In this lesson you learned that you can make a folder and its contents available to other users over the network by sharing the folder. Shared folder permissions are the only way to secure file resources on FAT volumes. Shared folder permissions apply to folders, not individual files. You also learned that shared folder permissions do not restrict access to users who gain access to the folder at the computer where the folder is stored. They only apply to users who connect to the folder over the network.

Three shared folder permissions are Read, Change, and Full Control. Read permission allows users to display folder names, file names, file data, and attributes. Read permission also allows users to run program files and to change folders within the shared folder. Change permission allows users to create folders, add files to folders, change data in files, append data to files, change file attributes, and delete folders and files, *plus* it allows the user to perform actions permitted by the Read permission. Full control permission allows users to change file permissions, take ownership of files, *and* perform all tasks permitted by the Change permission. The default shared folder permission is Full Control, and it is assigned to the Everyone group when you share the folder.

Lesson 2: Planning Shared Folders

When you plan shared folders, you can reduce administrative overhead and ease user access. Organize resources that will be shared and put them into folders according to common access requirements. Determine which resources you want shared, and then organize resources according to function and use, as well as how you will administer the resources.

Shared folders can contain applications and data. Use shared application folders to centralize administration. Use shared data folders to provide a central location for users to store and gain access to common files. If all data files are centralized in one shared folder, users will find them easily. It will be easier for you to back up data folders if data folders are centralized, and it will be easier to upgrade application software if applications are centralized.

After this lesson, you will be able to

- Plan which shared folder permissions to assign to user accounts and groups for application and data folders.

Estimated lesson time: 5 minutes

Application Folders

Shared application folders are used for applications that are installed on a network server and can be used from client computers. The main advantage of shared applications is that you do not need to install and maintain most components of the applications on each computer. While program files for applications can be stored on a server, configuration information for most network applications is often stored on each workstation. The exact way in which you share application folders will vary depending on the application and your particular network environment and company organization.

When you share application folders, consider the points in Figure 17.3. These points are explained in more detail as follows:

- Create one shared folder for applications and organize all of your applications under this folder. When you combine all applications under one shared folder, you designate one location for installing and upgrading software.

- Assign the Administrators group the Full Control permission for the applications folder so that they can manage the application software and control user permissions.

- Remove the Full Control permission from the Everyone group and assign Read permission to the Users group. This provides more security because the Users group includes only user accounts that you created, whereas the Everyone group includes anyone who has access to network resources, including the Guest account.

- Assign the Change permission to groups that are responsible for upgrading and troubleshooting applications.

- Create a separate shared folder outside your application folder hierarchy for any application for which you need to assign different permissions. Then assign the appropriate permissions to that folder.

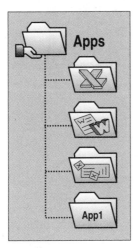

- Create a shared folder for applications.

- Assign Full Control to Administrators.

- Remove Full Control from Everyone and assign Read to Users.

- Assign Change to groups that upgrade and troubleshoot.

- Create a separate shared folder for each set of permissions.

Figure 17.3   Creating and sharing application folders

Data Folders

Users on a network use data folders to exchange public and working data. Working data folders are used by members of a team who need access to shared files. Public data folders are used by larger groups of users who all need access to common data.

When you use data folders, create and share common data folders on a volume that is separate from the operating system and applications. Data files should be backed up frequently, and with data folders on a separate volume, you can conveniently back them up. If the operating system requires reinstallation, the volume containing the data folder remains intact.

Public Data

When you share a common public data folder, do the following:

- Use centralized data folders so that data can be easily backed up.

- Assign the Change permission to the Users group for the common data folder (see Figure 17.4). This will provide users with a central, publicly accessible location for storing data files that they want to share with other users. Users will be able to gain access to the folder and read, create, or change files in it.

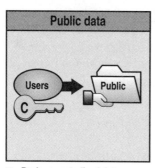 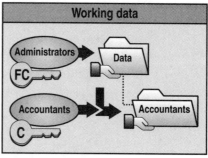

■ Back up centralized data   ■ Share lower-level folders.
    folders consistently.

Figure 17.4   Public data and working data shared folders

Working Data

When you share a data folder for working files, do the following:

- Assign the Full Control permission to the Administrators group for a central data folder so that administrators can perform maintenance.
- Share lower-level data folders below the central folder with the Change permission for the appropriate groups when you need to restrict access to those folders.

  For an example, see Figure 17.4. To protect data in the Accountants folder, which is a subfolder of the Data folder, share the Accountants folder and assign the Change permission only to the Accountants group so that only members of the Accountants group can gain access to the Accountants folder.

Lesson Summary

In this lesson you learned that you use shared application folders to centralize administration and make it easier to upgrade application software. When you use shared application folders, you should assign the Administrators group the Full Control permission for the applications folder so that members of this group can manage the application software and control user permissions. You should also remove the Full Control permission from the Everyone group and assign Read permission to the Users group. This provides more security because the Users group includes only user accounts that you created, whereas the Everyone group includes anyone who has access to network resources, including the Guest account.

You also learned that you use shared data folders to provide a central location for users to store and gain access to common files. When you use data folders, you should create and share common data folders on a volume that is separate from the operating system and applications. Data files should be backed up frequently, and with data folders on a separate volume, you can conveniently back them up.

Lesson 3: Sharing Folders

You can share resources with others by sharing folders containing those resources. To share a folder, you must be a member of one of several groups, depending on the role of the computer where the shared folder resides. When you share a folder you can control access to the folder by limiting the number of users who can simultaneously gain access to it, and you can also control access to the folder and its contents by assigning permissions to selected users and groups. Once you have shared a folder, users must connect to the shared folder and must have the appropriate permissions to gain access to it. After you have shared a folder, you may want to modify it. You can stop sharing it, change its share name, and change user and group permissions to gain access to it.

After this lesson, you will be able to

- Create and modify shared folders.
- Make a connection to a shared folder.

Estimated lesson time: 20 minutes

Requirements for Sharing Folders

In Windows 2000, members of the built-in Administrators, Server Operators, and Power Users groups are able to share folders. Which of the groups can share folders and on which machines they can share them depends on whether it is a workgroup or a domain and the type of computer on which the shared folders reside:

- In a Windows 2000 domain, the Administrators and Server Operators groups can share folders residing on any machines in the domain. The Power Users group is a local group and can only share folders residing on the stand-alone server or computer running Windows 2000 Professional where the group is located.
- In a Windows 2000 workgroup, the Administrators and Power Users groups can share folders on the Windows 2000 Server stand-alone server or the computer running Windows 2000 Professional on which the group exists.

Note If the folder to be shared resides on an NTFS volume, users must also have at least the Read permission for that folder to be able to share it.

Administrative Shared Folders

Windows 2000 automatically shares folders for administrative purposes. These shares are appended with a dollar sign ($). The $ hides the shared folder from users who browse the computer. The root of each volume, the system root folder, and the location of the printer drivers are all hidden shared folders that you can gain access to across the network.

Table 17.3 describes the purpose of the administrative shared folders that Windows 2000 automatically provides.

Table 17.3   Windows 2000 Administrative Shared Folders

Share	Purpose
C$, D$, E$, and so on	The root of each volume on a hard disk is automatically shared, and the share name is the drive letter appended with a dollar sign ($). When you connect to this folder, you have access to the entire volume. You use the administrative shares to remotely connect to the computer to perform administrative tasks. Windows 2000 assigns the Full Control permission to the Administrators group.
	Windows 2000 also automatically shares CD-ROM drives and creates the share name by appending the $ to the CD-ROM drive letter.
Admin$	The system root folder, which is C:\Winnt by default, is shared as Admin$. Administrators can gain access to this shared folder to administer Windows 2000 without knowing in which folder it is installed. Only members of Administrators have access to this share. Windows 2000 assigns the Full Control permission to the Administrators group.
Print$	When you install the first shared printer, the *systemroot*\System32\Spool\Drivers folder is shared as Print$. This folder provides access to printer driver files for clients. Only members of Administrators, Server Operators, and Print Operators have the Full Control permission. The Everyone group has the Read permission.

Hidden shared folders are not limited to those that the system automatically creates. You can share additional folders and append a $ to the end of the share name. Then, only users who know the folder name can gain access to it, if they also possess the proper permissions to it.

Sharing a Folder

When you share a folder, you can give it a share name, provide comments to describe the folder and its content, limit the number of users who have access to the folder, assign permissions, and share the same folder multiple times.

▶   **To share a folder**

1. Right-click the folder that you want to share, and then click Properties.
2. On the Sharing tab of the Properties dialog box, configure the options shown in Figure 17.5 and described in Table 17.4.

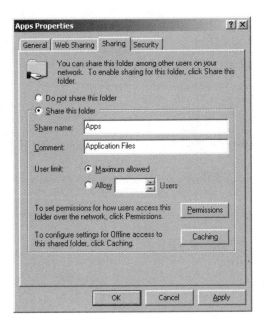

Figure 17.5 Sharing tab of a folder's Properties dialog box

Table 17.4 Sharing Tab Options

Option	Description
Share Name	The name that users from remote locations use to make a connection to the shared folder. You must enter a share name.
Comment	An optional description for the share name. The comment appears in addition to the share name when users at client computers browse the server for shared folders. This comment can be used to identify contents of the shared folder.
User Limit	The number of users who can concurrently connect to the shared folder. If you click Maximum Allowed as the user limit, Windows 2000 Professional supports up to 10 connections. Windows 2000 Server can support an unlimited number of connections, but the number of Client Access Licenses (CALs) that you purchased limits the connections.
Permissions	The shared folder permissions that apply *only* when the folder is accessed over the network. By default, the Everyone group is assigned Full Control for all new shared folders.
Caching	The settings to configure offline access to this shared folder.

Assigning Shared Folder Permissions

After you share a folder, the next step is to specify which users have access to the shared folder by assigning shared folder permissions to selected user accounts and groups.

▶ **To assign permissions to user accounts and groups for a shared folder**

1. On the Sharing tab of the Properties dialog box of the shared folder, click Permissions.

2. In the Permissions dialog box, ensure that the Everyone group is selected and then click Remove.

3. In the Permissions dialog box, click Add (see Figure 17.6).

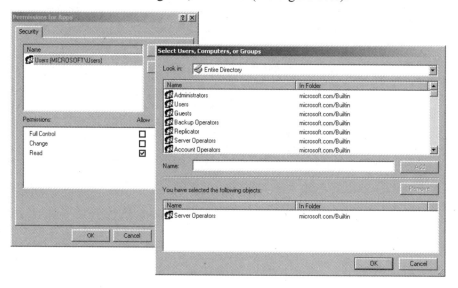

Figure 17.6 Setting permissions for a shared folder

4. In the Select Users, Computers, Or Groups dialog box, click the user accounts and groups to which you want to assign permissions.

5. Click Add to add the user account or group to the shared folder. Repeat this step for all user accounts and groups to which you want to assign permissions.

6. Click OK.

7. In the Permissions dialog box for the shared folder, click the user account or group, and then, under Permissions, select the Allow check box or the Deny check box of the appropriate permissions for the user account or group.

Note   In the Select User, Computers, Or Groups dialog box, click the Look In arrow to see a list of other domains or the local computer from which you can select user account and group names for assigning permissions. You can also search Active Directory for user accounts and groups by selecting Entire Directory from the Look In list.

Modifying Shared Folders

You can modify shared folders. You can stop sharing a folder, modify the share name, and modify shared folder permissions.

▶ **To modify a shared folder**

1. Click the Sharing tab in the Properties dialog box of the shared folder.

2. To complete the appropriate task, use the steps in Table 17.5.

Table 17.5   Steps to Modify a Shared Folder

To	Do this
Stop sharing a folder	Click Do Not Share This Folder.
Modify the share name	Click Do Not Share This Folder to stop sharing the folder; click Apply to apply the change; click Share This Folder, and then enter the new share name in the Share Name box.
Modify shared folder permissions	Click Permissions. In the Permissions dialog box, click Add or Remove. In the Select Users, Computers, Or Groups dialog box, click the user account or group whose permissions you want to modify.
Share folder multiple times	Click New Share to share a folder with an additional shared folder name. Do so to consolidate multiple shared folders into one while allowing users to continue to use the same shared folder name that they used before you consolidated the folders.
Remove a share name	Click Remove Share. This option only appears after the folder has been shared more than once.

Note   If you stop sharing a folder while a user has a file open, the user might lose data. If you click Do Not Share This Folder and a user has a connection to the shared folder, Windows 2000 displays a dialog box, notifying you that a user has a connection to the shared folder.

Connecting to a Shared Folder

You can gain access to a shared folder on another computer by using the Map Network Drive wizard, the Run command, or My Network Places.

▶ **To connect to a shared folder by using the Map Network Drive wizard**

1. Right-click the My Network Places icon on your desktop, and then click Map Network Drive.

2. In the Map Network Drive wizard, shown in Figure 17.7, click Folder, and then type a Universal Naming Convention (UNC) path to the folder (*computer_name**sharedfolder_name*).

Figure 17.7   Map Network Drive wizard

3. Enter a drive letter for the shared folder in the Drive list box.

4. Select the Reconnect At Logon check box if you want to reconnect to the shared folder each time that you log on.

5. Click the link labeled Click Here To Connect Using A Different User Name to connect to a shared folder with a different user account, and then enter the user name and password in the Connect As dialog box.

▶ **To connect to a shared folder by using the Run command**

1. Click the Start button, click Run, and then type *computer_name* in the Open box. Windows 2000 displays shared folders for the computer.

2. Double-click the shared folder to which you want to connect.

▶   **To connect to a shared folder by using My Network Places**

1. Double-click the My Network Places icon.

2. Locate the computer on which the shared folder is located.

3. Double-click the shared folder to which you want to connect.

Lesson Summary

In this lesson you learned that you can share resources with others by sharing folders containing those resources. To share a folder, you must be a member of one of several groups, depending on the role of the computer where the shared folder resides. You can control access to a shared folder by limiting the number of users who can simultaneously gain access to it, and you can also control access to the folder and its contents by assigning permissions to selected users and groups. To access a shared folder, users must connect to it and must have the appropriate permissions. You also learned that you may modify a shared folder. You can stop sharing it, change its share name, and change user and group permissions to gain access to it.

Lesson 4: Combining Shared Folder Permissions and NTFS Permissions

You share folders to provide network users with access to resources. If you are using a FAT volume, the shared folder permissions are all that is available to provide security for the folders you have shared and the folders and files they contain. If you are using an NTFS volume, you can assign NTFS permissions to individual users and groups to better control access to the files and subfolders in the shared folders. When you combine shared folder permissions and NTFS permissions, the more restrictive permission is always the overriding permission.

After this lesson, you will be able to

- Combine shared folder permissions and NTFS permissions.

Estimated lesson time: 45 minutes

Strategies for Combining Shared Folder Permissions and NTFS Permissions

One strategy for providing access to resources on an NTFS volume is to share folders with the default shared folder permissions and then control access by assigning NTFS permissions. When you share a folder on an NTFS volume, both shared folder permissions and NTFS permissions combine to secure file resources.

Shared folder permissions provide limited security for resources. You gain the greatest flexibility by using NTFS permissions to control access to shared folders. Also, NTFS permissions apply whether the resource is accessed locally or over the network.

When you use shared folder permissions on an NTFS volume, the following rules apply:

- You can apply NTFS permissions to files and subfolders in the shared folder. You can apply different NTFS permissions to each file and subfolder that a shared folder contains.

- In addition to shared folder permissions, users must have NTFS permissions for the files and subfolders that shared folders contain in order to gain access to those files and subfolders. This is in contrast to FAT volumes where permissions for a shared folder are the only permissions protecting files and subfolders in the shared folder.

- When you combine shared folder permissions and NTFS permissions, the more restrictive permission is always the overriding permission.

In Figure 17.8, the Everyone group has the shared folder Full Control permission for the Public folder and the NTFS Read permission for FileA. The Everyone group's effective permission for FileA is Read because Read is the more restrictive permission. The effective permission for FileB is Full Control because both the shared folder permission and the NTFS permission allow this level of access.

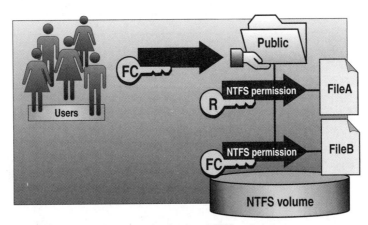

■ **NTFS permissions are required on NTFS volumes.**
■ **Apply NTFS permissions to files and subfolders.**
■ **Most restrictive permission is the effective permission.**

Figure 17.8   Combining shared folder permissions and NTFS permissions

Practice: Managing Shared Folders

In this practice, you determine users' effective permissions, plan shared folders, plan permissions, share a folder, assign shared folder permissions, connect to a shared folder, stop sharing a folder, and test the combined effects of shared folder permissions and NTFS permissions.

Important   To complete Optional Exercises 5 and 8, you must have two computers running Windows 2000 Server. This practice also assumes that one of the two computers is configured as a domain controller and the other computer is configured as a member server in the domain.

Exercise 1: Combining Permissions

Figure 17.9 shows examples of shared folders on NTFS volumes. These shared folders contain subfolders that also have been assigned NTFS permissions. Determine a user's effective permissions for each example.

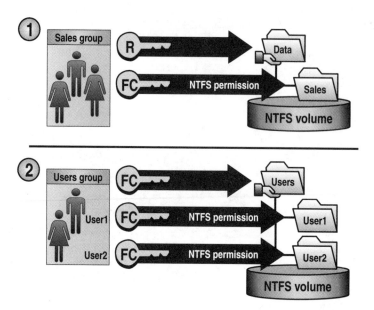

Figure 17.9   Combined permissions

1. In the first example, the Data folder is shared. The Sales group has the shared folder Read permission for the Data folder and the NTFS Full Control permission for the Sales subfolder.

   What are the Sales group's effective permissions for the Sales subfolder when they gain access to the Sales subfolder by making a connection to the Data shared folder?

2. In the second example, the Users folder contains user home folders. Each user home folder contains data that is only accessible to the user for whom the folder is named. The Users folder has been shared, and the Users group has the shared folder Full Control permission for the Users folder. User1 and User2 have the NTFS Full Control permission for *only* their home folder and no NTFS permissions for other folders. These users are all members of the Users group.

   What permissions does User1 have when he or she accesses the User1 subfolder by making a connection to the Users shared folder? What are User1's permissions for the User2 subfolder?

Exercise 2: Planning Shared Folders

In this exercise, you plan how to share resources on servers in the main office of a manufacturing company. Record your decisions in the table at the end of this exercise.

Figure 17.10 illustrates a partial folder structure for the servers at the manufacturing company.

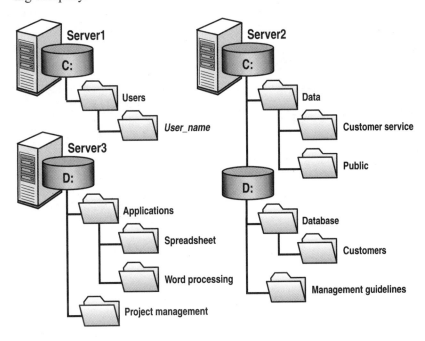

Figure 17.10   Partial folder structure for the servers at a manufacturing company

You need to make resources on these servers available to network users. To do this, determine which folders to share and what permissions to assign to groups, including the appropriate built-in groups.

Base your planning decisions on the following criteria:

- Members of the Managers group need to read and revise documents in the Management Guidelines folder. Nobody else should have access to this folder.

- Administrators need complete access to all shared folders, except for Management Guidelines.

- The Customer Service department requires its own network location to store working files. All customer service representatives are members of the Customer Service group.

- All employees need a network location to share information with each other.

- All employees need to use the spreadsheet, database, and word processing software.
- Only members of the Managers group should have access to the project management software.
- Members of the CustomerDBFull group need to read and update the customer database.
- Members of the CustomerDBRead group need to read the customer database only.
- Each user needs a private network location to store files. This location must be accessible by that user only.
- Share names must be accessible from Windows 2000, Windows NT, Windows 95, and non-Windows-NT-based platforms.

Record your answers in the following table.

Folder name and location	Shared name	Groups and permissions
Example: Management Guidelines	MgmtGd	Managers: Full Control

Exercise 3: Sharing Folders

In this exercise, you share a folder.

▶ **To share a folder**

1. Log on to your domain as Administrator.
2. Start Windows Explorer, create a folder C:\Apps, right-click Apps, and then click Properties.
3. In the Apps Properties dialog box, click the Sharing tab.

    Notice that the folder is currently not shared.
4. Click Share This Folder.

    Notice that Share Name defaults to the name of the folder. If you want the share name to be different from the folder's name, change it here.

5. In the Comment box, type **Shared Productivity Applications** and then click OK.

   How does Windows Explorer change the appearance of the Apps folder to indicate that it is a shared folder?

Exercise 4: Assigning Shared Folder Permissions

In this exercise, you determine the current permissions for a shared folder and assign shared folder permissions to groups in your domain.

▶ **To determine the current permissions for the Apps shared folder**

1. In Windows Explorer, right-click C:\Apps, and then click Properties.

2. In the Apps Properties dialog box, click the Sharing tab, and then click Permissions.

   Windows 2000 displays the Permissions For Apps dialog box.

   What are the default permissions for the Apps shared folder?

▶ **To remove permissions for a group**

1. Verify that Everyone is selected.

2. Click Remove.

▶ **To assign Full Control to the Administrators group**

1. Click Add.

   Windows 2000 displays the Select Users, Computers, Or Groups dialog box.

2. In the Look In box, select your domain, in the Name box, click Administrators, and then click Add.

3. Click OK.

   Windows 2000 adds Administrators to the list of names with permissions.

   What type of access does Windows 2000 assign to Administrators by default?

4. In the Permissions box, under Allow, click Full Control.

   Why did Windows Explorer also select the Change permission for you?

5. Click OK.

6. Click OK to close the Apps Properties dialog box.

7. Close Windows Explorer.

Optional Exercise 5: Connecting to a Shared Folder

In this exercise, you use two methods to connect to a shared folder.

Important   To complete Exercise 5, you must have two computers running Windows 2000 Server. This exercise also assumes that one of the two computers is configured as a domain controller and the other computer is configured as a member server in the domain.

▶ **To connect to a network drive by using the Run command**

1. Log on to your second computer as Administrator.

2. Click the Start button, and then click Run.

3. In the Open box, type **\\server1** (if you did not use server1 as the name of your domain controller, use the appropriate name here and in the following steps), and then click OK.

   Windows 2000 displays the Server1 window.

   Notice that only the folders that are shared appear to network users.

   Which shared folders are currently available?

Note   The DEBUG shared folder exists for debugging and testing purposes and will be removed prior to product release.

---

4. Double-click Apps to confirm that you can gain access to its contents.

5. Close the Apps On Server1 window.

▶ **To connect a network drive to a shared folder by using the Map Network Drive command**

1. Right-click My Network Places, and then click Map Network Drive.

2. In the Map Network Drive wizard, in the Folder box, type **\\server1\apps** (if you did not use server1 as the name of your domain controller, use the appropriate name here and in the following steps).

3. In the Drive box, select P.

4. Clear the Reconnect At Logon check box.

   You will gain access to this shared folder only in this exercise. Disabling the option to reconnect will ensure that Windows 2000 will not automatically attempt to reconnect to this shared folder later.

5. To complete the connection, click Finish.

6. To confirm that Windows Explorer has successfully completed the drive mapping, on your desktop, double-click My Computer.

   Notice that Windows 2000 has added drive P as Apps On Server1 (P:).

   How does Windows Explorer indicate that this drive points to a remote shared folder?

   _____

▶ **To disconnect from a network drive by using Windows Explorer**

1. In Windows Explorer, right-click Apps On Server1 (P:), and then click Disconnect.

   Windows 2000 removes Apps On Server1 (P:) from the My Computer window.

2. Close the My Computer window.

▶ **To attempt to connect to a shared folder on your domain controller**

1. Log off Windows 2000, and then log on to your domain as User91.

2. Click the Start button, and then click Run.

3. In the Open box, type \\server1\apps (if you did not use server1 as the name of your domain controller, use the appropriate name), and then click OK.

   Windows 2000 displays a message, stating that access is denied.

   Why were you denied access to the Apps shared folder?

   _____

4. Close all open windows and dialog boxes.

▶ **To connect to a shared folder by using another user account**

1. Right-click My Network Places, and then click Map Network Drive.

2. In the Map Network Drive wizard, in the Folder box, type \\server1\apps (if you did not use server1 as the name of your domain controller, use the appropriate name).

3. In the Drive box, select J.

4. Click the link labeled Click Here To Connect Using A Different User Name.

The Connect As dialog box appears. This dialog box lets you specify a different user account to use to make a connection to the shared folder. When would you use this option?

5. In the Connect As dialog box, in the User Name box, type *domain1*\administrator (where domain1 is your domain).

6. In the Password box, type **password** and then click OK.

7. Confirm that the Reconnect At Logon check box is cleared, and then click Finish.

In Windows Explorer, can you gain access to drive J? Why or why not?

8. Close all windows and log off Windows 2000.

Exercise 6: Stopping Folder Sharing

In this exercise, you stop sharing a shared folder.

▶ **To stop sharing a folder**

1. Log on to your domain as Administrator at your domain controller, and then start Windows Explorer.

2. Right-click C:\Apps, and then click Properties.

3. In the Apps Properties dialog box, click the Sharing tab.

4. Click Do Not Share This Folder, and then click OK.

Notice that Windows 2000 no longer displays the hand that identifies a shared folder under the Apps folder. You might need to refresh the screen; press F5 to refresh the screen.

5. Close Windows Explorer.

Exercise 7: Assigning NTFS Permissions and Sharing Folders

In this exercise, you assign NTFS permissions to the Apps, Wordprocessing, Database, Public, and Manuals folders. Then, you share the Apps and the Public folders.

▶ **To assign NTFS permissions**

Use Windows Explorer to create the necessary folders and to assign the NTFS permissions that are listed in the table below. For each folder, do not allow inherited permissions to propagate to the object and remove any previously existing NTFS permissions.

Path	User account or group in the domain	NTFS permissions
C:\Apps	Administrators Users	Full Control Read & Execute
C:\Apps\Wordprocessing	Administrators Users	Full Control Read & Execute
C:\Apps\Database	Administrators	Read & Execute
C:\Public	Administrators Users	Full Control Modify
C:\Public\Manuals	Administrators Users User93	Full Control Read & Execute Full Control

▶ **To share folders and assign shared folder permissions**

Share the appropriate application folders and assign permissions to network user accounts based on the information in the table below. Remove all other shared folder permissions.

Path and shared folder name	User account or group	Shared folder permissions
C:\Apps shared as Apps	Administrators Users	Read Read
C:\Public shared as Public	Administrators Users	Full Control Full Control

Optional Exercise 8: Testing NTFS and Shared Folder Permissions

In this exercise, you use different user accounts to test the permissions that you assigned in Exercise 1. To answer the questions in this exercise, refer to the tables in Exercise 7.

Note To complete Exercise 8, you must have two computers running Windows 2000 Server. This exercise also assumes that one of the two computers is configured as a domain controller and the other computer is configured as a member server in the domain.

▶ **To test permissions for the Manuals folder when a user logs on locally**

1. Log on to your domain as User92 at your domain controller.

2. In Windows Explorer, expand C:\Public\Manuals.

3. In the Manuals folder, attempt to create a file.

   Were you successful? Why or why not?

4. Close Windows Explorer.

▶ **To test permissions for the Manuals folder when a user makes a connection over the network**

1. Log on to your domain as User92 at your second computer, not at your domain controller.

2. Click the Start button, and then click Run.

3. In the Open box, type **\\server1\public** (where server1 is your domain controller), and then click OK.

4. In the Public On Server1 window, double-click Manuals.

5. In the Manuals folder on your domain controller, attempt to create a file.

   Were you successful? Why or why not?

6. Close all windows and log off Windows 2000.

▶ **To test permissions for the Manuals folder when a user logs on locally as User93**

1. Log on to your domain as User93 at your domain controller.

2. In Windows Explorer, expand C:\Public\Manuals.

3. In the Manuals folder, attempt to create a file.

   Were you successful? Why or why not?

4. Close all windows and log off Windows 2000.

▶ **To test permissions for the Manuals folder when a user logs on as User93 and connects over the network**

1. Log on to your domain as User93 at your second computer, not at your domain controller.

2. Make a connection to the Public shared folder on your second computer.

3. In the Public On Server1 window, double-click Manuals.

4. In the Manuals folder on your domain controller, attempt to create a file.

Were you successful? Why or why not?

5. Close all windows and log off Windows 2000.

Lesson Summary

In this lesson you learned that you share folders to provide network users with access to resources. On a FAT volume, the shared folder permissions are all that is available to provide security for the folders you have shared and for the folders and files they contain. On an NTFS volume, you can assign NTFS permissions to individual users and groups to better control access to the files and subfolders in the shared folders. You also learned that when you combine shared folder permissions and NTFS permissions, the more restrictive permission is always the overriding permission.

In the practice portion of this lesson, you created and shared folders, stopped sharing a folder, created folders, applied NTFS permissions, and then shared the folders. If you have a second computer, you were able to test how the shared folder permissions and NTFS permissions combined to provide access to resources.

Lesson 5: Configuring Dfs to Gain Access to Network Resources

The Microsoft distributed file system (Dfs) for Windows 2000 Server provides users with convenient access to shared folders that are distributed throughout a network. A single Dfs shared folder serves as an access point to other shared folders in the network.

After this lesson, you will be able to

- Configure Dfs for Windows 2000 Server to provide user access to shared folders.

Estimated lesson time: 40 minutes

Understanding Dfs

Dfs is a single hierarchical file system whose contents are distributed across the enterprise network. Dfs provides a logical tree structure for file system resources that might be anywhere on the network. Since the Dfs tree is a single point of reference, regardless of the actual location of the underlying resources, users can easily gain access to network resources.

Dfs organizes shared folders that can reside on different computers, as shown in Figure 17.11. Dfs provides users with easy navigation to these shared folders. Users do not need to know where a resource is on a network to gain access to it. Dfs facilitates administering multiple shared folders.

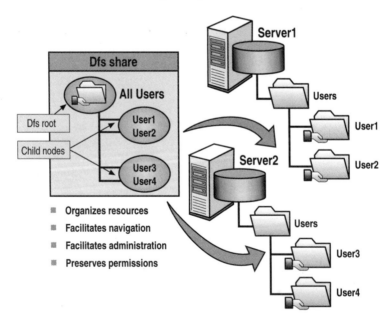

Figure 17.11   Overview of Dfs

To share file resources across the network, Dfs does the following:

- **Organizes resources in a tree structure.**   A Dfs share uses a tree structure containing a root and child nodes. To create a Dfs share, you must first create a Dfs root. Each Dfs root can have multiple child nodes beneath it, each of which points to a shared folder. The child nodes of the Dfs root represent shared folders that can be physically located on different file servers. Table 17.6 describes the two types of Dfs.

Table 17.6   Types of Dfs

Type of Dfs	Description
Stand-alone Dfs	Stores the Dfs topology on a single computer. This type of Dfs provides no fault tolerance if the computer that stores the Dfs topology or any of the shared folders that Dfs uses fails.
Fault-tolerant Dfs	Stores the Dfs topology in Active Directory. This type of Dfs allows child nodes to point to multiple identical shared folders for fault tolerance. In addition, it supports Domain Name System (DNS), multiple levels of child volumes, and file replication.

- **Facilitates network navigation.**   A user who navigates a Dfs-managed shared folder does not need to know the name of the server on which the folder is shared. This simplifies network access because users no longer need to locate the network server on which a specific resource is located. After connecting to a Dfs root, users can browse and gain access to all resources below the root, regardless of the location of the server on which the resource is located.

- **Facilitates network administration.**   Dfs also simplifies network administration. If a server fails, you can move a child node from one server to another without users being aware of the change. All that is required to move a child node is to modify the Dfs folder to refer to the new server location of the shared folders. Users continue to use the same Dfs path for the child node.

- **Preserves network permissions.**   A user can gain access to a shared folder through Dfs as long as the user has the required permission to gain access to the shared folder.

Note   Only client computers with Dfs client software can gain access to Dfs resources. Computers running Windows NT 4.0 and later or Windows 98 include a Dfs client. You must download and install a Dfs client for Windows 95.

Setting Up a Stand-Alone Dfs Root

A stand-alone Dfs root is physically located on the server to which users initially connect. The first step in setting up stand-alone Dfs is to create the Dfs root.

To create a Dfs root, you use the Distributed File System Manager snap-in to start the New Dfs Root Volume wizard. Table 17.7 describes the wizard options that you can configure.

Table 17.7   Dfs Root Volume Wizard Options

Option	Description
Select Dfs Root Type	Click the Create A Standalone Dfs Root option.
Specify Server To Host Dfs	The initial connection point for all resources in the Dfs tree, or the host server. You can create a Dfs root on any computer running Windows 2000 Server.
Path To Share Dfs	A shared folder to host the Dfs root. You can choose an existing shared folder or create a new share.
Dfs Share Name	A descriptive name for the Dfs root.

Setting Up Dfs Child Nodes

In a network environment, it might be difficult for users to keep track of the physical locations of shared resources. When you use Dfs, the network and file system structures become transparent to users. This enables you to centralize and optimize access to resources based on a single tree structure. Users can browse the child nodes under a Dfs root without knowing where the referenced resources are physically located.

After you create a Dfs root, you can create Dfs child nodes. You use the Distributed File System Manager snap-in to create child nodes.

In the Distributed File System Manager snap-in, click the Dfs root to which you will attach a child node. Then on the Action menu, click New Dfs Child Node. The Add To Dfs dialog box appears (see Figure 17.12).

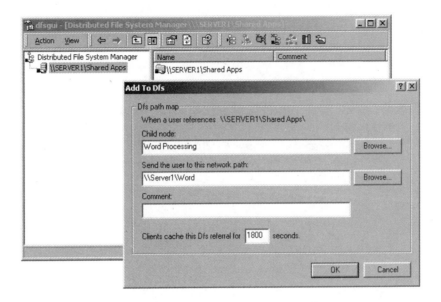

Figure 17.12   Add To Dfs dialog box

In the Add To Dfs dialog box, you configure the options described in Table 17.8.

Table 17.8   Add to Dfs Dialog Box Options

Option	Description
Child Node	The name that users will see when they connect to Dfs.
Send The User To This Network Path	The UNC name for the actual location of the shared folder to which the child node refers.
Comment	Additional information (optional) to help keep track of the shared folder (for example, the actual name of the shared folder).
Clients Cache This Dfs Referral For X Seconds	Length of time for which clients cache a referral to a Dfs child node. After the referral time expires, a client queries the Dfs server about the location of the child node, even if the client has previously established a connection with the child node.

The child node will appear below the Dfs root volume in the Distributed File System Manager snap-in.

Practice: Using Dfs

In this practice, you share some existing folders, create and share some folders, create a new Dfs root, and then create some DNS child nodes.

Important   To complete all procedures in this practice, you must have two computers running Windows 2000 Server. This practice also assumes that one of the two computers is configured as a domain controller and the other computer is configured as a member server in the domain. If you have only one computer, read through the steps in the procedures marked optional to learn how to perform them in the future.

▶ **To share existing folders**

1. Log on to your domain at your domain controller as Administrator.
2. Start Windows Explorer and share the folders listed in the following table, using all default permissions. These folders were created in Exercise 7 of Lesson 4, earlier in this chapter.

Folder	Share name
C:\Apps\Database	DB
C:\Apps\Wordprocessing	Word

▶ **To create new shared folders**

In Windows Explorer, create the folders listed in the following table and share them, using all default permissions.

Folder	Share name
C:\MoreApps\Maintenance	Maint
C:\MoreApps\CustomerService	Custom

▶ **To create a new Dfs root**

1. Click the Start button, point to Programs, point to Administrative Tools, and then click Dfs Manager.

    A Microsoft Management Console (MMC) opens and displays the Distributed File System Manager snap-in.

2. On the Action menu, click New Dfs Root Volume.

    Windows starts the Create New Dfs Root wizard.

3. Click Next.

    The wizard displays the Select Dfs Root Type page.

    Notice that there are two types of Dfs you can create:

A fault tolerant Dfs root that uses Active Directory to store the Dfs tree topology and supports DNS, multiple levels of child volumes, and file replication.

A stand-alone Dfs root that does not use Active Directory and that permits a single level of child volumes.

In this exercise, you will create a stand-alone Dfs root.

4. Click Create A Standalone Dfs Root, and then click Next.

   The wizard displays the Specify Server To Host Dfs page. You will create a Dfs root on your own server.

5. In the Server Name box, confirm that the name of your server is displayed, and then click Next.

   The wizard displays the Select Share For Dfs Root Volume page. Notice that you can use an existing share for the Dfs root or the wizard can create a new shared folder for you.

   In this exercise, you will let the wizard create a new shared folder for you. You have to provide both the location of the folder on your computer and a share name.

6. Select the Create New Share option. Type **C:\App-Dfs** in the Path To Share box, and then type **Shared Apps** in the Share Name box.

7. Click Next.

   The wizard displays the Provide The Dfs Root Name page.

   The wizard fills in the Dfs name for you. You can choose whether you want to add this Dfs root to the current MMC console (Distributed File System Manager) for easy administrative access.

8. Clear the Add The Dfs Root To My Current Console check box, and then click Next.

   The wizard displays the Completing The Create New Dfs Root Wizard page, which contains a summary of the choices that you made. Notice that several choices are listed as not applicable because you chose to create a stand-alone Dfs root and not a fault-tolerant Dfs root.

9. Confirm that the options that the wizard displays are correct, and then click Finish.

10. Close Distributed File System Manager.

In the following two procedures, you will create Dfs child nodes according to the following table.

Child node	Shared folder	Folder name
Word Processing	\\Server1\Word	C:\Apps \Wordprocessing
Customer Service	\\Server1\Custom	C:\MoreApps \CustomerService
Maintenance	\\second computer\Maint	C:\MoreApps \Maintenance
Database	\\second computer\DB	C:\Apps\Database

▶   **To add a Dfs child node on your domain controller**

1. Open the Distributed File System Manager and in the console tree, click \\SERVER1\SharedApps (where Server1 is the name of your domain controller).

2. On the Action menu, click New Dfs Child Node.

   Distributed File System Manager displays the Add To Dfs dialog box.

3. Type **Word Processing** in the Child Node box.

4. In the Send The User To This Network Path box, type **Server1\Word** (where Server1 is the name of your domain controller).

5. Click OK.

6. Repeat steps 1–5 to add a child node called Customer Service, which points to the shared folder \\Server1\Custom (where Server1 is the name of your domain controller).

▶   **To add a Dfs child node on a remote computer (Optional)**

1. In the console tree, click \\SERVER1\SharedApps (where Server1 is the name of your domain controller).

2. On the Action menu, click New Dfs Child Node.

   Distributed File System Manager displays the Add To Dfs dialog box.

3. Type **Maintenance** in the Child Node box.

4. In the Send The User To This Network Path box, type *Second_computer***Maint** (where Second_computer is the name of your non-domain controller computer), and then click OK.

5. Repeat steps 1–4 to add a child node called Database, which points to the shared folder *Second_computer*\DB (where Second_computer is the name of your non-domain controller computer).

6. Close the Distributed File System Manager snap-in.

▶   **To gain access to a Dfs root (Optional)**

1. Double-click My Network Places, and then double-click Computers Near Me.

2. Double-click *Second_computer* (where Second_computer is the name of your non-domain controller computer).

   Windows Explorer displays a list of all shared folders on your second computer. Notice that one of the shared folders is SharedApps, your second Dfs root.

   Does Windows 2000 provide an indication that SharedApps is a Dfs root and not an ordinary shared folder?

3. To view the Dfs child nodes on your second computer, double-click SharedApps located with your Server 1 folders.

   Windows Explorer displays the Shared Apps On Server 1 window, which shows all the child nodes of SharedApps.

   Does Windows 2000 indicate that the folders inside SharedApps are Dfs child nodes and not ordinary folders?

4. Create a text file in SharedApps\Word Processing and give it your first name.

5. Close all open windows.

Lesson Summary

In this lesson you learned the Microsoft Distributed file system (Dfs) for Windows 2000 Server provides users with convenient access to shared folders that are distributed throughout a network. A Dfs share uses a tree structure containing a root and child nodes. The child nodes of the Dfs root represent shared folders that can be physically located on different file servers.

It might be difficult for users to keep track of the physical locations of shared resources in a network environment. When you use Dfs, the network and file system structures become transparent to users. A user who navigates a Dfs-managed shared folder does not need to know the name of the server on which the folder is shared.

After connecting to a Dfs root, users can browse and gain access to all resources below the root, regardless of the location of the server on which the resource is located. If a server fails, you can move a child node from one server to another without users being aware of the change. All that is required to move a child node is to modify the Dfs folder to refer to the new server location of the shared folders. Users continue to use the same Dfs path for the child node.

Review

Here are some questions to help you determine if you have learned enough to move on to the next chapter. If you have difficulty answering review questions, please go back and review the material in this chapter before beginning the next chapter. The answers for these questions are located in Appendix A, "Questions and Answers."

1. When a folder is shared on a FAT volume, what does a user with the Full Control shared folder permissions for the folder have access to?

2. What are the shared folder permissions?

3. By default, what are the permissions that are assigned to a shared folder?

4. When a folder is shared on an NTFS volume, what does a user with the Full Control shared folder permission for the folder have access to?

5. When you share a public folder, why should you use centralized data folders?

6. What is the best way to secure files and folders that you share on NTFS partitions?

7. How does Dfs facilitate network navigation for users?

CHAPTER 18

Administering Active Directory

About This Chapter

This chapter builds upon Chapter 12, "Implementing Active Directory." Active Directory is the Microsoft Windows 2000 directory service. A directory service stores information about resources on the network and provides the services that make these resources easy to locate, use, and manage. The information about network resources is stored in the database component of Active Directory. Active Directory allows users, applications, and Windows 2000 to search the database in Active Directory for network resources. Active Directory also provides administrators with a way to centrally organize, manage, and control access to network resources.

Before You Begin

To complete the lessons in this chapter, you must have

- A computer that meets the minimum hardware requirements listed in "Hardware Requirements," on page xxxiii.
- Installed the Windows 2000 Server software on the computer.
- Configured the computer as a domain controller in a domain.

Lesson 1: Creating Active Directory Objects

Active Directory is the directory service included in Windows 2000 Server. It identifies all resources on a network and makes them accessible to users and applications. Active Directory objects represent network resources. Each object is a distinct, named set of attributes that represents a specific network resource. In this lesson you will learn how to create Active Directory objects.

After this lesson, you will be able to

- Describe the general procedure for creating Active Directory objects.

- Identify the types of Active Directory objects.

Estimated lesson time: 10 minutes

Adding Resources

When you add new resources to your network, such as user accounts, groups, or printers, you create new Active Directory objects that represent these resources. To create a new object, you must have the required permissions. For example, to add a new user, you must have the permission to add new objects to the organizational unit (OU) where you want to add the user. By default, members of the Administrators group have the permissions to add objects anywhere in the domain.

When you create objects

- The rules of the schema, wizard, or snap-in that you use define the objects that are available for you to create.

- Not all attributes are always available for definition. Often, to completely define all of the object attributes, you must modify the object after you create it.

Note   *Object attributes* (also referred to as properties) are categories of information that define the characteristics for all objects of a defined object type. All objects of the same type have the same attributes. The *values* of the attributes make the objects unique. For example, all user account objects have a First Name attribute; however, the value for the First Name attribute can be any name, such as John or Jane.

Understanding Common Active Directory Objects

Adding new resources to your network creates new Active Directory objects that represent these resources. You should be familiar with some of the common Active Directory objects. Table 18.1 describes the most common object types that you can add to Active Directory.

Table 18.1   Common Objects and Their Contents

Object	Contents
User account	The information that allows a user to log on to Windows 2000, such as user logon name. This information also has many optional fields including first name, last name, display name, telephone number, e-mail, and home page.
Group	A collection of user accounts, groups, or computers that you can create and use to simplify administration.
Shared folder	A pointer to the shared folder on a computer. A *pointer* contains the address of certain data, rather than the data itself. Shared folders and printers exist in the registry of a computer. When you publish a shared folder or printer in Active Directory, you are creating an object that contains a pointer to the shared folder or printer.
Printer	A pointer to a printer on a computer. You must manually publish a printer on a computer that is not in Active Directory. Windows 2000 automatically adds printers that you create on domain computers to Active Directory.
Computer	The information about a computer that is a member of the domain.
Domain controllers	The information about a domain controller including an optional description, its DNS name, its downlevel name, the version of the operating system loaded on the domain controller, the location, and who is responsible for managing the domain controller.
Organizational unit (OU)	An OU can contain other objects, including other OUs. Used to organize Active Directory objects.

Practice: Creating an Organizational Unit

In this practice, you create part of the organizational structure of a domain by creating an OU. You then create three user accounts that you use in a later practice.

▶ **To create an OU**

1. Log on to your domain as Administrator.

2. Open Directory Management.

   What are the default OUs in your domain?

   To ensure that you are creating a new OU in the correct location, you must first select the location where you want to create this OU.

3. In the console tree, click your domain.

4. On the Action menu, point to New, and then click Organizational Unit.

   Directory Management displays the Create New Object - (Organizational Unit) dialog box.

   Notice that the only required information is the name. The dialog box indicates the location where the object will be created. This should be your domain.

5. In the Name box, type **Sales1** and then click OK.

   Directory Management displays the newly created OU in addition to the default OUs in your domain.

6. Under the domain, create another OU, called Servers1.

▶   **To create user accounts**

1. In the console tree, click Users.

2. On the Action menu, point to New, and then click User.

   Notice that the Create New Object - (User) dialog box shows that the new user account is being created in the User folder of your domain.

   Note   User objects can be created in any OU. In this practice, you will create most user objects in the Users OU; however, this is not a requirement for creating these objects.

   ---

3. Create a new user account, using your choice of name. Record the user logon name and user name below. You will need to refer to this user account name and user logon name later in this procedure. Leave the password blank and select all default settings for this user account. Make the user a member of the Print Operators group or another group with the right to log on locally to a domain controller.

   User logon name:
   User name:

4. Edit the properties of the user account that you created, and on the General tab of the Properties dialog box, in the Telephone box, enter **555-1234**

5. Repeat steps 1 through 3 to create two more user accounts in the Users OU, using your choice of names.

Record the user account names below. You will need to refer to these user account names later in this chapter.

User logon name:
User name:

Lesson Summary

In this lesson you learned that when you add new resources to your network, you create new Active Directory objects that represent these resources. To create a new object, you must have the required permissions, and that by default members of the Administrators group have the permissions to add objects anywhere in the domain.

You also learned that object attributes (properties) are categories of information that define the characteristics for all objects of a defined object type. All objects of the same type have the same attributes; it is the values of the attributes that make an object unique. Finally, you learned that common Active Directory objects include user accounts, groups, shared folders, printers, computers, and OUs.

Lesson 2: Locating Active Directory Objects

In this lesson you will learn how to use the Find command of the Directory Management snap-in to locate Active Directory objects. You will also learn what fields are available in the Find dialog box and how to use them to search for objects in Active Directory.

After this lesson, you will be able to
- Use the Find command to locate any type of Active Directory object.

Estimated lesson time: 10 minutes

Using the Find Command

To locate Active Directory objects, open the Directory Management snap-in located in the Administrative Tools folder. Then right-click a domain or OU in the console tree and click Find. The Find dialog box provides options that allow you to search the global catalog to locate user accounts, groups, and printers (see Figure 18.1). The global catalog contains a partial replica of the Entire Directory, so it stores information about every object in a domain tree or forest. Since global catalog contains information about every object, a user can find information regardless of which domain in the tree or forest contains the data. The contents of the global catalog are automatically generated by Active Directory from the domains that make up the directory.

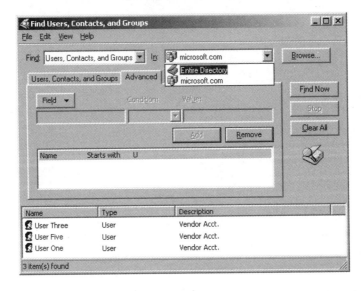

Figure 18.1   Using Directory Management to locate objects

Table 18.2 describes the options in the Find dialog box.

Table 18.2   Find Dialog Box Elements

Element	Description
Find	The objects for which you can search are users, contacts, and groups; computers; printers; shared folders; directory folders (each OU is placed in its own folder); custom search; and routers.
In	The location that you want to search, which can be the entire Active Directory, a specific domain, or an OU.
Advanced	The tab on which you define the search criteria to locate the object that you need.
Field	A list of the attributes for which you can search on the object type that you select; located on the Advanced tab.
Condition	The methods that are available to further define the search for an attribute. The options are Starts With, Ends With, Is (Exactly), Is Not, Present, or Not Present; located on the Advanced tab.
Value	The value for the condition of the field (attribute) that you are using to search the Directory; located on the Advanced tab. You can search for an object by using an attribute of the object only if you enter a value for the attribute. For example, if the Field you select is First Name and the Condition is Starts With, the Value would be R if you were looking for the users whose first name starts with the letter R.
Search Criteria	The box that lists each search criteria that you have defined; located on the Advanced tab. To define a search criteria you use Field, Condition, and Value fields, and then click Add. You can add or remove search criteria to narrow or widen your search.
Results	A text box that opens at the bottom of the Find window and displays the results of your search after you click Find Now; located on the Advanced tab.

Practice: Searching Active Directory

In this practice, you search Active Directory for objects based on search criteria that you provide. You first find a user account based on his or her primary phone number, and then find a printer that is able to staple the pages it prints.

Important   You need to have a local printer installed on your computer. (You do *not* need a printing device connected to the computer.) If you do not have a local printer, create one now. Remember that *printing device* refers to the physical machine that prints and that *local printer* refers to the software that Windows 2000 needs in order to send data to the printing device.

► **To find user accounts in the domain**

1. Log on to your domain as Administrator, and then open Directory Management.

2. In the console tree, right-click your domain, and then click Find.

   Windows 2000 displays the Find dialog box.

   In the Find dialog box, what object type can you select for a search?

3. Ensure that Users, Contacts, And Groups is selected in the Find box, and then click Find Now. What do you see?

   Notice how Windows 2000 can find objects, such as user accounts, regardless of their location.

4. In the Find Users, Contacts, And Groups dialog box, click Clear All, and then click OK to acknowledge that you want to clear the search results.

5. In the In box, select your domain.

6. Click the Advanced tab.

7. Click Field, point to User, and then click Primary Phone.

   Notice that Windows 2000 fills in Starts With in the Condition box.

8. In the Value box, type **555** and then click Add.

9. Click Find Now.

   In the Find Users, Contacts, And Groups dialog box, Windows 2000 displays the user account for which you entered a telephone number of 555-1234.

10. Close the Find Users, Contacts, And Groups dialog box.

► **To view printers in Directory Management**

1. On the View menu, click Users, Groups, And Computers As Containers.

   By default, Directory Management does not show printers. You have to change the view options.

2. In the console tree, expand Domain Controllers to view your computer.

   Directory Management displays your computer in the console tree. Notice that you can expand the computer because it is now shown as a container.

3. In the console tree, click your computer.

   Directory Management displays all printers on your computer as objects that are associated with your computer.

4. To view the properties of a printer, double-click the printer.

5. To mark the printer as one that can staple, click Staple, and then click OK.

6. Minimize Directory Management.

7. Click the Start button, point to Search, and then click For Printers.

8. In the Find Printers dialog box, click the Features tab.

9. Click Can Staple.

10. In the In box, select your domain, and then click Find Now.

    Windows 2000 displays the printer that you modified in the list of printers that are capable of stapling.

11. Close the Find Printers dialog box.

Lesson Summary

In this lesson you learned how to locate Active Directory objects by using the Directory Management snap-in. You learned to use the Find command by starting the Directory Management snap-in, right-clicking a domain or OU in the console tree, and clicking Find. The Find dialog box provides fields that allow you to search for objects including user accounts, groups, and printers. The Find dialog box includes the Find field, which allows you to specify the object you want to locate; the In field, which allows you to specify the location that you want to search, such as a specific domain; and the Advanced tab, which provides several additional fields so that you can be more precise in specifying the object for which you are searching.

Lesson 3: Controlling Access to Active Directory Objects

Windows 2000 uses an object-based security model to implement access control for all Active Directory objects. This security model is similar to the one that Windows 2000 uses to implement Windows NT file system (NTFS) security. Every Active Directory object has a security descriptor that defines who has the permissions to gain access to the object and what type of access is allowed. Windows 2000 uses these security descriptors to control access to objects.

To reduce administrative overhead, you can group objects with identical security requirements into an OU. You can then assign access permissions to the entire OU and all objects in it.

After this lesson, you will be able to

- Set permissions on Active Directory objects to control user access.
- Move Active Directory objects.

Estimated lesson time: 30 minutes

Understanding Active Directory Permissions

Active Directory permissions provide security for resources by allowing you to control who can gain access to individual objects or object attributes and the type of access that you will allow.

Active Directory Security

Use Active Directory permissions to determine who has the permissions to gain access to the object and what type of access is allowed. An administrator or the object owner must assign permissions to the object before users can gain access to the object. Windows 2000 stores a list of user access permissions, called the access control list (ACL), for every Active Directory object. The ACL for an object lists who can access the object and the specific actions that each user can perform on the object.

You can use permissions to assign administrative privileges to a specific user or group for an OU, a hierarchy of OUs, or a single object, without assigning administrative permissions for controlling other Active Directory objects.

Object Permissions

The object type determines which permissions you can select. Permissions vary for different object types. For example, you can assign the Reset Password permission for a user object but not for a printer object.

A user can be a member of multiple groups, each with different permissions that provide different levels of access to objects. When you assign a permission to a user for access to an object and that user is a member of a group to which you assigned a different permission, the user's effective permissions are the combination of the user and group permissions. For example, if a user has Read permission and is a member of a group with Write permission, the user's effective permission is Read and Write.

You can allow or deny permissions. Denied permissions take precedence over any permissions that you otherwise allow for user accounts and groups. If you deny permission to a user to gain access to an object, the user will not have that permission, even if you allow the permission for a group of which the user is a member. You should deny permissions only when it is necessary to deny permission to a specific user who is a member of a group with allowed permissions.

Note Always ensure that all objects have at least one user with the Full Control permission. Failure to do so might result in some objects being inaccessible to the person using the Directory Management snap-in, even an administrator.

Standard Permissions and Special Permissions

You can set standard permissions and special permissions on objects. Standard permissions are the most frequently assigned permissions and are composed of special permissions. Special permissions provide you with a finer degree of control for assigning access to objects.

For example, the standard Write permission is composed of the Write All Properties, Add/Remove Self As Member, and Read permissions.

Table 18.3 lists standard object permissions that are available for most objects (some object types have additional permissions that are available) and the type of access that each permission allows.

Table 18.3   Standard Object Permissions and Type of Access Allowed

Object permission	Allows the user to
Read	View objects and object attributes, the object owner, and Active Directory permissions.
Write	Change object attributes.
Delete All Child Objects	Remove any type of object from an OU.
Create All Child Objects	Add any type of child object to an OU.
Full Control	Change permissions and take ownership, *plus* perform the tasks that are allowed by all other standard permissions.

Assigning Active Directory Permissions

You can use the Directory Management snap-in to set standard permissions for objects and attributes of objects. You use the Security tab of the Properties dialog box for the object to assign permissions (see Figure 18.2).

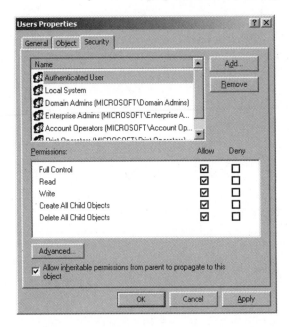

Figure 18.2   Setting Active Directory permissions

► **To assign standard permission for an object**

1. In Directory Management, on the View menu, ensure that Advanced Features is selected.

2. Select the object, click Properties on the Action menu, and then click the Security tab in the Properties dialog box.

3. To assign standard permissions

   ▪ To add a new permission, click Add, click the user account or group to which you want to assign permissions, click Add, and then click OK.

   ▪ To change an existing permission, click the user account or group.

4. Under Permissions, select the Allow check box or the Deny check box for each permission that you want to add or remove.

Standard permissions are sufficient for most administrative tasks. However, you might need to view the special permissions that constitute a standard permission.

▶ **To view special permissions**

1. On the Security tab in the Properties dialog box for the object, click Advanced.

2. In the Access Control Settings dialog box shown in Figure 18.3, on the Permissions tab, click the entry that you want to view, and then click View/Edit.

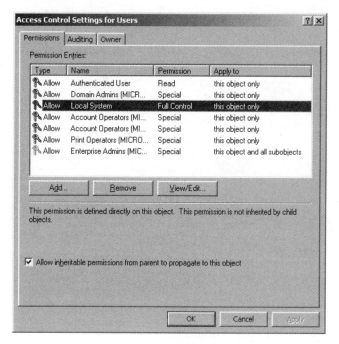

Figure 18.3   Access Control Settings dialog box

3. To view the permissions for specific attributes, click the Properties tab of the Permission Entry dialog box, as shown in Figure 18.4.

Note   Avoid assigning permissions for specific attributes of objects because this can complicate system administration. Errors can result, such as Active Directory objects not being visible, which prevents users from completing tasks.

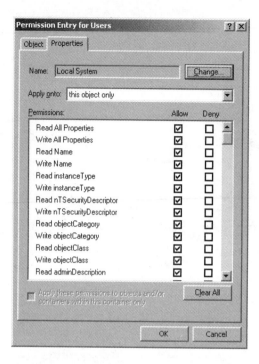

Figure 18.4   Permission Entry dialog box

Using Permissions Inheritance

Similar to other permissions inheritance in Windows 2000, permissions inheritance in Active Directory minimizes the number of times that you need to assign permissions for objects. When you assign permissions, you can apply the permissions to subobjects (child objects), which propagates the permissions to all of the subobjects for a given object, as shown in Figure 18.5. To indicate that permissions are inherited, the check boxes for inherited permissions are unavailable in the user interface.

For example, you can assign Full Control for an OU that contains printers to a group and then apply this permission for all subobjects. The result is that all group members can administer all printers in the OU.

You can specify that permissions for a given object are propagated to all subobjects. You can also prevent permissions inheritance. When you copy previously inherited permissions, you are starting with exactly the same permissions that the object currently inherits from its parent object. However, any permissions for the parent object that you modify after blocking inheritance no longer apply. When you remove previously inherited permissions, Windows 2000 assigns no permissions to the object. You have to assign any permissions you want for the object.

■ Permissions flow down to child objects.

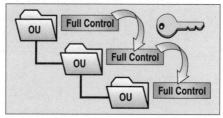

■ Preventing inheritance stops the flow of permissions.

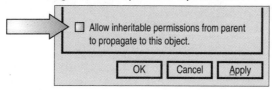

Figure 18.5   Inheriting Permissions and Blocking Inheritance

Preventing Permissions Inheritance

You can prevent permissions inheritance so that a child object does not inherit permissions from its parent object by deselecting the Allow Inheritable Permissions From Parent To Propagate To This Object check box. When you prevent inheritance, only the permissions that you explicitly assign to the object apply. You use the Security tab in the Properties dialog box to prevent permissions inheritance.

When you prevent permissions inheritance, Windows 2000 allows you to

- Copy previously inherited permissions to the object. The new explicit permissions for the object are a copy of the permissions that it previously inherited from its parent object. Then, according to your needs, you can make any necessary changes to the permissions.

- Remove previously inherited permissions from the object. Windows 2000 removes any previously inherited permissions. No permissions exist for the object. Then, according to your needs, you can assign any permissions for the object.

Moving Objects

You can move objects between OUs in Active Directory. You move objects from one location to another when organizational or administrative functions change— for example, when an employee moves from one department to another. To move an object, in Directory Management select the object to move, and then on the Action menu, click Move. In the Move dialog box, you select the OU to which you want the object to move (see Figure 18.6).

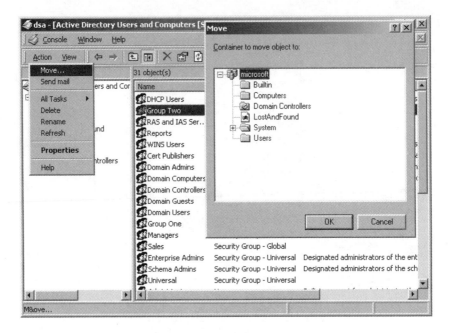

Figure 18.6   Moving objects in Active Directory

The following conditions apply when you move objects between OUs:

- Permissions that are assigned directly to objects remain the same.
- The objects inherit permissions from the new OU. Any permissions that were previously inherited from the old OU no longer affect the objects.
- You can move multiple objects at the same time.

Note   To simplify assigning permissions for printers, move printers on different print servers that require identical permissions to the same OU. Printers are located in the Computer object for the print server. To view a printer, click View, and then click Users, Groups, And Computers As Containers.

Practice: Controlling Access to Active Directory Objects

In this practice you move objects in a domain, log on from another user account, create an OU with two users, and review permissions in Active Directory.

Exercise 1: Moving Objects in a Domain

In this exercise you move three user accounts from one organizational unit to another. You also attempt to log on using a different account.

▶ **To move objects in the domain**

1. In the console tree, click Users.

2. To select all three user accounts that you created in lesson 1, click one of the user accounts, press Ctrl, and then click the remaining two user accounts.

3. On the Action menu, click Move.

4. In the Move dialog box, to select the new location for the user accounts, expand your domain, click Sales1, and then click OK.

   Notice that the user accounts that you moved no longer appear in the Users OU.

5. To verify that the user accounts were moved to the correct location, in the console tree, click **Sales1**

   Notice that the user accounts that you moved are now located in the Sales1 OU.

6. Close the Directory Management snap-in.

▶ **To log on as a user in a nonstandard OU**

1. Log off and then log on to your domain by using one of the user accounts that you created in the preceding procedure.

   Did Windows 2000 require you to specify the OU in which your user account is located as part of the logon process? Why or why not?

2. Log off Windows 2000.

Exercise 2: Reviewing Active Directory Permissions

In this exercise, you review the default security settings on Active Directory components.

Caution   In this exercise, do not change any security settings in Active Directory. Making changes could result in losing access to portions of Active Directory.

▶ **To create an OU containing two user accounts**

1. Start Directory Management.

2. In the console tree, click your domain.

3. On the Action menu, point to New, and then click Organizational Unit.

4. In the Name box, type **Security1** and then click OK.

5. In the Security1 OU, create a user account which has the First Name field and the User Logon Name field set to Assistant1. Type **password** as the password and accept the defaults for all other options.

6. In the same OU, create another user account that has the First Name field and the User Logon Name set to Secretary1. Type **password** as the password and accept the defaults for all other options.

7. Grant both users membership in the Print Operators group or another group with the right to log on locally to the domain controller.

▶ **To view default Active Directory permissions for an OU**

1. On the View menu, click Advanced Features.

   Enabling the viewing of advanced features allows you to review and configure Active Directory permissions.

2. In the console tree, right-click Security1, and then click Properties.

3. Click the Security tab.

4. In the following table, list the groups that have permissions for the Security1 OU. You will need to refer to these permissions in the next exercise.

User account or group	Assigned permissions

How can you tell if any of the default permissions are inherited from the domain, which is the parent object?

▶ **To view advanced permissions for an OU**

1. In the Security1 Properties dialog box, on the Security tab, click Advanced.

   Directory Management displays the Access Control Settings For Security1 dialog box.

2. To view the permissions for Account Operators, in the Permission Entries box, click each entry for Account Operators, and then click View/Edit.

   Directory Management displays the Permission Entry For Security1 dialog box.

   What object permissions are assigned to Account Operators? What can Account Operators do in this OU? (Hint: check both permission entries for Account Operators.)

Do any objects within this OU inherit the permissions assigned to the Account Operators group? Why or why not?

3. Close all open dialog boxes, but do not close Directory Management.

▶ **To view the default Active Directory permissions for a user object**

1. In the Directory Management console tree, click Security1.
2. In the details pane, right-click Secretary1, and then click Properties.
3. Click the Security tab.
4. In the following table, list the groups that have permissions for the Secretary1 user account. You will need to refer to these permissions in the next practice. If the dialog box indicates that additional permissions are present for a group, do not list the additional permissions to which you can gain access through the Advanced button.

Group	Assigned permissions

Are the default permissions for a user object the same as those for an OU object? Why or why not?

Are any of the default permissions inherited from Security1, the parent object? How can you tell?

What do the permissions of the Account Operators group allow its members to do with the user object?

5. Close all programs and log off Windows 2000.

Lesson Summary

In this lesson you learned that every Active Directory object has a security descriptor that defines who has permission to gain access to the object and what type of access is allowed. An administrator or the object owner must assign permissions to an object before users can gain access to it. Windows 2000 stores a list of user access permissions, called the access control list (ACL), for every Active Directory object.

You also learned how to set standard permissions and special permissions on objects. The standard permissions are Read, Write, Delete All Child Objects, Create All Child Objects, and Full Control. Special permissions provide you with a finer degree of control over assigning access to objects. Permissions inheritance in Active Directory minimizes the number of times that you need to assign permissions for objects. When you assign permissions, you can apply the permissions to subobjects (child objects), which propagates the permissions to all of the subobjects for a given object. You also learned to how to block permissions inheritance.

Finally, you learned how to move objects between OUs in Active Directory. You learned that to move an object, in Directory Management you select the object to move, and then on the Action menu, click Move. In the Move dialog box, you select the OU to which you want the object to move.

Lesson 4: Delegating Administrative Control of Active Directory Objects

In this lesson you will learn that you can delegate administrative control of objects to individuals so that they can perform administrative tasks on the objects. You will learn that there are different ways to delegate control of objects and that there are guidelines for delegating control.

After this lesson, you will be able to

- Delegate administrative control of OUs and objects.

Estimated lesson time: 20 minutes

Guidelines for Delegating Control

You delegate administrative control of objects to individuals so that they can perform administrative tasks on the objects. There are different ways to delegate control of objects, and there are also guidelines for delegating control. After you determine who to assign control to, use the Delegation Of Control wizard to delegate control of objects.

You delegate administrative control of objects by assigning permissions to the object to allow users or groups of users to administer the objects. An administrator can delegate the following types of control:

- Assigning to a user permissions to create or modify objects in a specific OU
- Assigning to a user the permissions to modify specific permissions for the attributes of an object, such as assigning the permission to reset passwords on a user account object

Because tracking permissions at the OU level is easier than tracking permissions on objects or object attributes, the most common method of delegating administrative control is to assign permissions at the OU level. Assigning permissions at the OU level allows you to delegate administrative control for the objects that are contained in the OU. Use the Delegation Of Control wizard to assign permissions at the OU level.

For example, you can delegate administrative control by assigning Full Control for an OU to the appropriate manager, only within his or her area of responsibility. By delegating control of the OU to the manager, you can decentralize administrative operations and issues. This reduces your administration time and costs by distributing administrative control closer to its point of service.

To help you delegate administrative control, you may want to follow these suggestions:

- Assign control at the OU level whenever possible. Assigning control at the OU level allows for easier tracking of permission assignments. Tracking permission assignments becomes more complex for objects and object attributes.
- Use the Delegation Of Control wizard. The wizard assigns permissions only at the OU level. The wizard simplifies the process of assigning object permissions by stepping you through the process.
- Track the delegation of permission assignments. Tracking assignments allows you to maintain records to easily review security settings.
- Follow business requirements. Follow any guidelines that your organization has in place for delegating control.

Delegation Of Control Wizard

The Delegation Of Control wizard steps you through the process of assigning permissions at the OU level. For more specialized permissions, you must manually assign permissions.

In Directory Management, click the OU for which you want to delegate control, and then on the Action menu, click Delegate Control to start the wizard.

Table 18.4 describes the Delegation Of Control wizard options.

Table 18.4   Delegation Of Control Wizard Options

Option	Description
Users And Groups	The user accounts or groups to which you want to delegate control
Object Type(s) To Delegate Control On	Either all objects or only specific types of objects within the specified OU
Access Rights Selection	The permissions to assign to the object or objects. Select one of the following:
	Show General Rights: The most commonly assigned permissions that are available for the object
	Show Property Rights: The permissions that you can assign to the attributes of the object
	Show Creation/Deletion Of Subobject Rights: The permissions to create and delete child objects

Guidelines for Administrating Active Directory

The following list provides best practices for administering Active Directory:

- In larger organizations, coordinate your Active Directory structure with other administrators. You can move objects later, but this might create extra work.

- When you create Active Directory objects, such as user accounts, complete all attributes that are important to your organization. Completing the attributes gives you more flexibility when you search for objects.

- Use deny permissions sparingly. If you assign permissions correctly, you should not need to deny permissions. In most cases, denied permissions indicate mistakes that were made in assigning group membership.

- Always ensure that at least one user has Full Control for each Active Directory object. Failure to do so might result in objects being inaccessible.

- Ensure that delegated users take responsibility and can be held accountable. You gain nothing if you delegate administrative control without ensuring future accountability. As an administrator, you are ultimately responsible for all of the administrative changes that are made. If the users to whom you delegate responsibility are not performing the administrative tasks, you will need to assume responsibility for their failure.

- Provide training for users who have control of objects. Ensure that the users to whom you delegate responsibility understand their responsibilities and know how to perform the administrative tasks.

Practice: Delegating Administrative Control in Active Directory

In this practice, you delegate to a user control over objects in an OU. Refer to the tables that you completed in Exercise 2 of the previous lesson to answer the questions below.

▶ **To test current permissions**

1. Log on to your domain as Assistant1, and type **password** as the password.
2. Start Directory Management.
3. In the console tree, expand your domain, and then click Security1.

   What user objects are visible in the Security1 OU?

   Which permissions allow you to see these objects?

For the user account with the logon name Secretary1, change the logon hours. Were you successful? Why or why not?

For the Assistant1 user account, under which you are currently logged on, change the logon hours. Were you successful? Why or why not?

4. Close Directory Management and log off Windows 2000.

▶   **To use the Delegation Of Control wizard to assign Active Directory permissions**

1. Log on to your domain as Administrator and open Directory Management.

2. On the View menu, select Advanced Features.

3. In the console tree, expand your domain.

4. Click Security1, and then on the Action menu, click Delegate Control.

5. In the Delegation Of Control wizard, click Next.

   The Delegation Of Control wizard displays the Active Directory Folder page.

   Notice that the wizard filled in microsoft.com/Security1, which is the name for the OU that you selected when you started the wizard.

6. Click Next.

   The Delegation Of Control wizard displays the Group or User Selection page.

   Notice that the wizard does not display any user accounts or groups. You will add a user account to which to delegate control.

7. Click Add.

   The Select Users, Groups, Or Computers dialog box appears.

8. Select Assistant1, click Add, and then click OK.

9. Click Next.

   The Delegation Of Control wizard displays the Active Directory Object Type page. If you only want to delegate control for certain types of objects, such as printers, you can select one or more object types.

10. For this exercise, confirm that Delegate Control Of This Container is selected, and then click Next.

    The Delegation Of Control wizard displays the Permissions page.

11. To show the most common permissions that you can delegate, make sure that only Show General Rights is selected.

    The Delegation Of Control wizard displays standard permissions in the Permissions To Delegate box.

12. Click Full Control.

   Notice that the Delegation Of Control wizard automatically selects all other permissions.

13. Click Next.

14. Review the Summary page.

   - If all choices reflect the delegation of control on all objects for Assistant1, click Finish.

   - To make changes, click Back.

15. Close Directory Management and log off Windows 2000.

▶ **To test delegated permissions**

1. Log on to your domain as Assistant1, and type **password** as your password.

2. Open Directory Management.

3. In the console tree, expand your domain, and then click Security1.

4. Attempt to change the logon hours for both user accounts in the Security1 OU.

   Were you successful? Why or why not?

5. Attempt to change the logon hours for a user account in the Users OU.

   Were you successful? Why or why not?

6. Close Directory Management and log off Windows 2000.

Lesson Summary

In this lesson you learned that you can delegate administrative control of objects to individuals so that they can perform administrative tasks on the objects. You learned that there are different ways to delegate control of objects and that there are guidelines for delegating control. You use the Delegation Of Control wizard to delegate control of objects. In the practice portion of this lesson, you used the Delegation Of Control wizard to assign Active Directory permissions.

Review

Here are some questions to help you determine if you have learned enough to move on to the next chapter. If you have difficulty answering these questions, please go back and review the material in this chapter before beginning the next chapter. The answers for these questions are located in Appendix A, "Questions and Answers."

1. What is the advantage of having all objects located in Active Directory?

2. What is the difference between an object attribute and an object attribute value? Give examples.

3. You want to allow the manager of the Sales department to create, modify, and delete only user accounts for sales personnel. How can you accomplish this?

4. What determines if a user can locate an object when using global catalog?

5. What happens to the permissions of an object when you move it from one OU to another OU?

C H A P T E R   1 9

Administering User Accounts

About This Chapter

Administering user accounts goes beyond creating user accounts for new users. It includes modifying user accounts, as well as setting up user profiles and home directories. This chapter explains how to administer user accounts and how group policies affect user accounts in your network.

Before You Begin

To complete this chapter, you must have

- A computer that meets the minimum hardware requirements listed in the "Hardware Requirements," on page xxxiii.
- Installed the Windows 2000 Server software on the computer.
- Configured the computer as a domain controller in a domain.

Lesson 1: Managing User Profiles

A *user profile* is a collection of folders and data that stores the user's current desktop environment and application settings, as well as personal data. A user profile also contains all of the network connections that are established when a user logs on to a computer, such as Start menu items and mapped drives to network servers. User profiles maintain consistency for users in their desktop environments by providing each user the same desktop environment that he or she had the last time that he or she logged on to the computer.

After this lesson, you will be able to

- Manage user profiles.

Estimated lesson time: 45 minutes

Local User Profiles

Windows 2000 creates a user profile the first time that a user logs on at a computer. After the user logs on for the first time, Windows 2000 stores the user profile on that computer. This user profile is also known as *a local user profile*.

User profiles operate in the following manner:

- When a user logs on to a client computer running Windows 2000, the user always receives his or her individual desktop settings and connections, regardless of how many users share the same client computer.

- The first time that a user logs on to a client computer running Windows 2000, Windows 2000 creates a default user profile for the user and stores it in the system partition root\Documents and Settings*user_logon_name* folder (typically C:\Documents and Settings*user_logon_name*), where *user_logon_name* is the name the user enters when logging on to the system.

- A user profile contains the My Documents folder, which provides a place for users to store personal files. My Documents is the default location for the File Open and Save As commands. By default, Windows 2000 creates a My Documents icon on the user's desktop. This makes it easier for users to locate their personal documents.

- A user can change his or her user profile by changing desktop settings. For example, a user makes a new network connection or adds a file to My Documents. Then, when the user logs off, Windows 2000 incorporates the changes into the user profile. The next time that the user logs on, the new network connection and the file are present.

Note You should have users store their documents in My Documents rather than in home directories. Home directories are covered later in this chapter. Windows 2000 automatically sets up My Documents and it is the default location for storing data for Microsoft applications.

To support users who work at multiple computers, you can set up roaming user profiles. Roaming user profiles are user profiles that are stored on a network server. Windows 2000 downloads and applies the roaming user profile to any domain computer at which the user logs on. You can also customize and assign a preconfigured roaming user profile that you assign to all user accounts, as well as make roaming user profiles read-only.

Roaming User Profiles

A *roaming user profile* is a user profile that you set up on a network server so that the profile is available to the user no matter where the user logs on in the domain. When a user logs on, Windows 2000 copies the roaming user profile from the network server to the client computer running Windows 2000 at which the user logs on. Consequently, the user always receives his or her individual desktop settings and connections. This is in contrast to a local user profile, which only resides on one client computer.

When a user logs on, Windows 2000 copies the roaming user profile from the network server to the client computer and applies the roaming user profile settings to that computer. The first time that a user logs on at a computer, Windows 2000 copies all documents to the local computer. Thereafter, when the user logs on to the computer, Windows 2000 compares the locally stored user profile files and the roaming user profile files. It copies only the files that have changed since the last time that the user logged on at the computer. Since Windows 2000 only copies the files that have changed, the logon process is shorter.

When a user logs off, Windows 2000 copies changes that were made to the local copy of the roaming user profile back to the server where it is stored.

Creating Customized Roaming User Profiles

You can create a customized roaming user profile by configuring the desktop environment for the user and then copying the customized profile to the user's roaming user profile location.

You use customized roaming user profiles for the following reasons:

- To provide users with the work environment that they need to perform their jobs and to remove connections and applications that the user does not require.

- To provide a standard desktop environment for multiple users with similar job responsibilities. These users require the same network resources.

- To simplify troubleshooting. Technical support would know the exact baseline setup of the desktops and could easily find a deviation or a problem.

Note You can customize local user profiles but this is not recommended. Customizing local user profiles is inefficient because they only reside on the client computer at which the user logs on. Therefore, you would have to customize the user profile at each client computer to which a user logs on.

Using Mandatory Profiles

A *mandatory profile* is a read-only roaming user profile. When the user logs off, Windows 2000 does not save any changes that the user made during the session. The next time that the user logs on, the profile is the same as the last time that he or she logged on.

You can assign one mandatory profile to multiple users who require the same desktop settings, such as bank tellers. This means that by changing one profile, you change the desktop environment for several users.

Note A hidden file in the profile (for example in C:\Documents and Settings\ *user_logon_name*) called Ntuser.dat contains that section of the Windows 2000 system settings that applies to the individual user account and contains the user environment settings, such as desktop appearance. This is the file that you make read-only by changing its name to Ntuser.man.

Setting Up a Roaming User Profile

When you set up a roaming user profile on a server, the next time that the user logs on to a computer in the domain, Windows 2000 copies the local user profile to the roaming user profile path on the server. When the user logs on thereafter, the roaming user profile copies from the server to the computer.

You should set up roaming user profiles on a file server that you frequently back up, so that you have copies of the latest roaming user profiles. To improve logon performance for a busy network, place the roaming user profile folder on a member server instead of a domain controller. The copying of roaming user profiles between the server and client computers can use a lot of system resources, such as bandwidth and computer processing. If the profiles are on the domain controller, this can delay the authentication of users by the domain controller.

If you want to set up a roaming user profile, do the following:

1. On a server, create a shared folder and use a path with the following format:
   *server_name**shared_folder_name*

   Note Use an intuitive name for the shared folder, such as Profiles.

2. On the Profile tab in the Properties dialog box for the user account, provide the path to the shared folder in the Profile Path box (such as *server_name*\ *shared_folder_name**logon_name*).

You can type the variable %username% instead of the user's logon name. When you use this variable, Windows 2000 automatically replaces the variable with the user account name for the roaming user profile.

Assigning a Customized Roaming User Profile

You can customize a roaming user profile and assign it to multiple users, who will then have the same settings and connections when they log on. Before you can customize and assign a roaming user profile, you must first create a user profile template, which contains the customized desktop settings that you want the users to have.

▶ **To create a customized roaming user profile**

1. Create the template account, such as a user account named Sales Profile.

2. Log on by using the template account and configure the desktop environment, such as the desktop appearance, network connections, applications, shortcuts, and Start menu items.

3. Log off. Windows 2000 creates a user profile on the computer in the system partition root\Documents and Settings*user_logon_name* folder (typically C:\Documents and Settings*user_logon_name*) folder. Use this user profile for your template.

After you have created your user profile template, log on as administrator and copy the user profile template to the user's roaming user profile folder on the server. Assign the profile to the appropriate users and groups by using System in Control Panel.

▶ **To copy and assign a template user profile**

1. In the System Properties dialog box, on the User Profiles tab, select the template profile under Name, and then click Copy To.

2. In the Copy To dialog box, in the Copy Profile To box, type the path to the server (*server_name**shared_folder_name**user_logon_name*), or browse the path, and then click Change.

3. In the Choose User dialog box, click Show Users, select the appropriate users, click Add, and then click OK.

Since changes to the template profile affect all users who are assigned the profile, you should make the profile mandatory. To make the profile a mandatory (read-only) user profile, change the extension on the Ntuser file in the user's profile template profile from .DAT to .MAN.

Practice: Managing User Profiles

In this practice you create two user accounts, Puser and Ptester. You add both accounts to the Print Operators group so that they can log on at a domain controller. You then log on as Puser to create a profile for Puser. Then you log on as Administrator and use the System icon in Control Panel to verify that the profile for Puser was created. In optional Exercise 2, you can create and test a roaming user profile from a second computer.

Exercise 1: Creating a User Account

In this exercise, you create a user account that is used for a profile template and then define and test a local user profile.

▶ **To create a user account for a profile template**

1. Log on to your domain as Administrator.
2. Use Active Directory Manager to create the user accounts listed in the following table. For each account that you create, in the box to the right of the User Logon Name box, select @microsoft.com. Each user is added to the Print Operators group so that he or she can log on to the domain controller.

First name	Last name	Logon name	Password	Member of
Profile	User	Puser	None	Print Operators
Profile	Tester	Ptester	None	Print Operators

3. Log off Windows 2000.

▶ **To create a user profile by logging on**

1. Log on to your domain as Profile User (Puser).

   The first time that you log on to Windows 2000, a local user profile is created for you with default settings. Logging on as Profile User will create the local profile that you will customize, and then assign, to other users.

2. Log off Windows 2000.

▶ **To use Control Panel to determine existing profiles**

1. Log on to your domain as Administrator.
2. Click Start, point to Settings, click Control Panel, and then double-click System.
3. Click the User Profiles tab.

   Which users' profiles are stored on your computer?

4. Click OK to close the Systems Properties dialog box, and then close Control Panel.

5. Log off Windows 2000.

▶ **To define and test a local profile**

1. Log on to your domain as Profile Tester (Ptester).

2. Right-click anywhere on the desktop, and then click Properties.

   The Display Properties dialog box appears.

3. Click the Appearance tab.

   Notice the current color scheme.

4. In the Scheme box, select a different color scheme, and then click OK.

   This change takes effect immediately.

5. Log off and log on as the same user, Profile Tester (Ptester).

   Were screen colors saved? Why or why not?

6. Close all applications and log off Windows 2000.

Optional Exercise 2: Defining a Roaming User Profile

In this exercise, you define a roaming user profile by assigning a centralized path to it, and then you test it.

Note   To complete all the procedures in Exercise 2, you must have two computers running Windows 2000 Server. This exercise also assumes that one of the two computers is configured as a domain controller and the other computer is configured as a member server in the domain.

▶ **To create a shared folder in which to store roaming user profiles**

1. Log on to your domain as Administrator, at your domain controller.

2. In the C:\ folder, create a folder named Profiles.

3. Share the C:\Profiles folder as Profiles and assign the Everyone group the shared folder permission Full Control.

▶ **To assign a roaming user profile path**

Note   If you have only one computer, perform this procedure on your domain controller. If you have two computers, perform this procedure on your member server and not on your domain controller.

1. Logged on to the domain as Administrator, start Active Directory Manager.
2. Expand Domain1, and then click Users.
3. Right-click the account that you created for Profile Tester, and then click Properties.

   The Profile Tester Properties dialog box appears with the General tab active.
4. Click the Profile tab.
5. In the Profile path box, type **\\server1\profiles\ptester**
6. Click OK to apply your changes and return to Active Directory Manager.
7. Exit all applications.

▶ **To copy a profile template to the shared profile path**

Note Complete this procedure at the computer that is configured as the domain controller.

1. While logged on to your domain as Administrator, in Control Panel, double-click System.
2. Click the User Profiles tab.
3. Under Profiles Stored On This Computer, select Puser.
4. Click Copy To.

   The Copy To dialog box appears.
5. In the Copy Profile To box, type **\\server1\profiles\ptester**
6. Under Permitted To Use, click Change.

   The Choose User dialog box appears.
7. Click Show Users and under Names, click Ptester, and then click Add.

   DOMAIN1\ptester appears in the Add Name box.
8. Click OK to return to the Copy To dialog box.

   Notice that DOMAIN1\ptester is now permitted to use this profile.
9. Click OK to return to the System Properties dialog box.
10. Click OK to return to Control Panel.
11. Close all applications and log off Windows 2000.

▶ **To test the roaming user profile**

Note Complete this procedure at the computer that is configured as the member server.

1. Log on to your domain by using the account that you created for Profile Tester.

   Notice that the screen colors are different from when you logged on as the same user either on the member server or on the domain controller. Profile Tester's profile has been overwritten with Profile User's settings.

2. Right-click anywhere on the desktop, and then on the shortcut menu, click Properties.

3. Click the Appearance tab.

   Notice the current color scheme.

4. In the Scheme list, select a different color scheme from what was used on the member server.

5. Click the Background tab, change your wallpaper, and then click OK.

   The changes will take effect immediately.

6. Close all applications and log off Windows 2000.

▶ **To verify that the roaming user profile is assigned to Profile Tester**

Note   Complete this procedure at the computer that is configured as the domain controller.

1. Log on to your domain as Administrator, and then start Control Panel.

2. Double-click System, and then click the User Profiles tab.

   What type of profile is listed for the Profile Tester account?

3. Close all applications and log off Windows 2000.

▶ **To test the roaming user profile from another computer**

Note   Complete this procedure at the computer that is configured as the member server.

1. Log on by using the account that you created for Profile Tester.

2. If a dialog box appears which provides profile options, click Download.

   Are the screen colors and desktop the same or different from those set at the domain controller? Why or why not?

3. Close all applications and log off Windows 2000.

Lesson Summary

In this lesson you learned that a user profile is a collection of folders and data that stores the user's current desktop environment and application settings, as well as personal data. A user profile also contains all of the network connections that are established when a user logs on to a computer, such as Start menu items and mapped drives to network servers.

You learned that there are two main types of user profiles: local user profiles and roaming user profiles. Windows 2000 creates a local user profile the first time that a user logs on at a computer. Windows 2000 stores the user profile on that computer and the profile is referred to as the local user profile. Every time the user logs on to that computer, the user always receives his or her individual desktop settings and connections, regardless of how many users share the same client computer.

In contrast to a local user profile, which only resides on one computer, a roaming user profile is a user profile that you set up on a network server. When a user logs on, Windows 2000 copies the roaming user profile from the network server to the client computer running Windows 2000 at which the user logs on. The profile is available to the user no matter where the user logs on in the domain, and the user always receives his or her individual desktop settings and connections.

Lesson 2: Modifying User Accounts

Company needs and changes might require you to modify user accounts. For example, you might need to rename an existing user account for a new employee so that this employee can have the same permissions and network access as his or her predecessor. Other modifications are based on personnel changes or personal information. These include disabling, enabling, and deleting a user account. You might also need to reset a user's password or unlock a user account.

Note   To modify a user account, you make changes to the user account object in Active Directory. To successfully complete the tasks for modifying user accounts, creating roaming user profiles, and assigning home directories, you must have permission to administer the organizational unit (OU) in which the user accounts reside.

After this lesson, you will be able to

- Identify day-to-day user account administration tasks.
- Disable, enable, rename, and delete user accounts.
- Reset user passwords.
- Unlock user accounts.

Estimated lesson time: 30 minutes

Disabling, Enabling, Renaming, and Deleting User Accounts

Modifications that you make to user accounts that affect the functionality of the user accounts include the following:

- **Disabling and enabling a user account.**   You disable a user account when a user does not need a user account for an extended period, but will need it again. For example, if John takes a two-month leave of absence, you would disable his user account when he leaves. When he returns, you would enable his user account so that he could log on to the network again.

- **Renaming a user account.**   You rename a user account when you want to retain all rights, permissions, and group memberships for the user account and reassign it to a different user. For example, if there is a new company accountant, rename the account by changing the first, last, and user logon names to those of the new accountant.

- **Deleting a user account.**   Delete a user account when an employee leaves the company and you are not going to rename the user account. By deleting these user accounts, you do not have unused accounts in Active Directory.

The procedures for disabling, enabling, renaming, and deleting user accounts are very similar.

▶ **To disable, enable, rename, and delete user accounts**

1. In Active Directory Manager, expand the console tree until the appropriate user account is visible, and then select the user account.

2. On the Action menu, click the command for the type of modification that you want to make (see Figure 19.1).

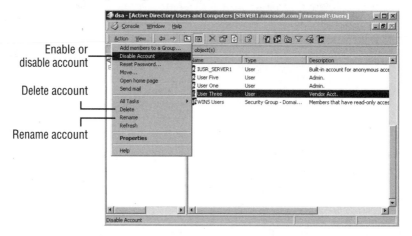

Figure 19.1   Disabling, enabling, deleting, or renaming user accounts

Note   If a user account is enabled, the Action menu displays the Disable Account command. If a user account is disabled, the Action menu displays the Enable Account command.

Resetting Passwords and Unlocking User Accounts

If a user cannot log on to the domain or to a local computer, you might need to reset the user's password or unlock the user's account. To perform these tasks, you must have administrative privileges for the OU in which the user account resides.

Resetting Passwords

If a user's password expires before he or she can change it, or if a user forgets his or her password, you need to reset the password.

Note   You do not need to know the old password to reset a password.

▶ **To reset user passwords**

1. In Active Directory Manager, expand the console tree until the appropriate user account is visible, and then select the user account.

2. On the Action menu, click Reset Password.

   The Reset Password dialog box appears.

In the Reset Password dialog box, you should always select User Must Change Password At Next Logon to force the user to change his or her password the next time he or she logs on.

Unlocking User Accounts

A Windows 2000 group policy locks out a user account when the user violates the policy. For example, the user exceeds the limit that a group policy allows for bad logon attempts. When a user account is locked out, Windows 2000 displays an error message.

▶ **To unlock a user's account**

1. In Active Directory Manager, expand the console tree until the appropriate user account is visible, and then select the user account.

2. On the Action menu, click Properties, and then in the Properties dialog box, click the Account tab.

   Notice that the Account Lock Out check box is selected.

3. Clear the check box.

Practice: Administering User Accounts

In this practice you work with disabling and enabling a user account, and you learn how to reset the password for a user account.

Exercise 1: Enabling a User Account

In this exercise, you disable a user account so that it can no longer be used to log on to the domain. You then enable the same account.

▶ **To disable a user account**

Note   If you have more than one computer, complete this procedure at the computer that is configured as the domain controller.

---

1. Log on to your domain as Administrator.

2. Start Active Directory Manager.

3. Expand Domain1, and click Users.

4. In the details pane, right-click the account you created for Profile User, and then click Disable Account.

   The Active Directory Service dialog box appears, stating that the account has been disabled.

5. Click OK to return to Active Directory Manager.

6. In the details pane of Active Directory Manager, right-click the user account that you just disabled to display the shortcut menu.

   How can you tell that the user account is disabled?

7. Log off Windows 2000.

8. Attempt to log on as Puser.

   Were you successful? Why or why not?

▶   **To enable a user account**

1. Log on as Administrator.

2. Start Active Directory Manager.

3. Expand Domain1, and then click Users.

4. In the details pane, right-click the account you created for Profile User, and then click Enable Account.

   Windows 2000 displays the Active Directory Service message box confirming that the account was enabled.

5. In the details pane of Active Directory Manager, right-click the user account that you just enabled to display the shortcut menu.

   How can you tell that the user account is enabled?

6. Log off Windows 2000.

▶   **To test account enabling and to change the password for a user account**

1. Log on as Puser.

   Were you successful? Why?

2. Change your password to student.

3. Log off Windows 2000.

Exercise 2: Resetting the Password for a User Account

In this exercise, you reset the password for a user account.

► **To reset the password for a user account**

1. Log on as Administrator.
2. Start Directory Management (in the Administrative Tools folder).
3. Expand Domain1, and then click Users.
4. Right-click the account you created for Profile User, and then click Reset Password.

   The Reset Password dialog box appears, prompting you for the new password for this account.

   Notice that the Administrator account is not able to view the current password. After the password has been set for a user account, either by the administrator or by the user, the password is not visible to any user, including the administrator. This improves security by preventing users, including the administrator, from learning another user's password. If passwords were readable, an administrator could look up a user's password, reset the password, and then log on as that user. After the administrator was through impersonating the user, the administrator could log back on and change the user's password back to what it was.

5. In the New Password box and the Confirm Password box, type **password** and check the box labeled User Must Change Password At Next Logon. Then click OK.

   Windows 2000 displays the Active Directory Service message box, confirming that the password has been changed.

6. Click OK to return to Active Directory Manager.
7. Log off Windows 2000.

► **To test password resetting**

1. Log on as Puser and type **password** as the password.

   Were you successful? Why?

2. Log off Windows 2000.

Lesson Summary

In this lesson you learned about disabling and enabling user accounts. You disable a user account when a user does not need a user account for an extended period, but will need it again. You enable the account when it is needed again.

You also learned about renaming user accounts and deleting user accounts. You rename a user account when you want to retain all rights, permissions, and group memberships for the user account and reassign it to a different user. You delete a user account when it is no longer needed.

Finally, in this lesson you learned about resetting the password for a user account and enabling a user account that is locked. If a user's password expires before he or she can change it, or if a user forgets his or her password, you need to reset the password so that the user can log on to the domain. You also learned that if a user forgets his or her password and gets locked out the system, you can log on as administrator and unlock the account.

Lesson 3: Creating Home Directories

In addition to the My Documents folder, Windows 2000 provides you with the means to create another location for users to store their personal documents. This additional location is the user's home directory.

After this lesson, you will be able to

- Manage home directories.

Estimated lesson time: 5 minutes

Introducing Home Directories

A home directory is an additional folder that you can provide for users to store personal documents, and, for older applications, it is sometimes the default folder for saving documents. You can store a home directory on a client computer or in a shared folder on a file server. Because a home directory is not part of a roaming user profile, its size does not affect network traffic during the logon process. You can locate all users' home directories in a central location on a network server.

Storing all home directories on a file server provides the following advantages:

- Users can gain access to their home directories from any client computer on the network.
- The backing up and administration of user documents is centralized.
- The home directories are accessible from a client computer running any Microsoft operating system (including MS-DOS, Windows 95, Windows 98, and Windows 2000).

Note You should store home directories on a Windows NT file system (NTFS) volume so that you can use NTFS permissions to secure user documents. If you store home directories on a file allocation table (FAT) volume, you can only restrict home directory access by using shared folder permissions.

Creating Home Directories on a Server

To create a home directory on a network file server, you must perform the following three tasks:

1. Create and share a folder in which to store all home directories on a network server. The home directory for each user will reside in this shared folder.
2. For the shared folder, remove the default permission Full Control from the Everyone group and assign Full Control to the Users group. This ensures that only users with domain user accounts can gain access to the shared folder.

3. Provide the path to the user's home directory folder in the shared home directory folder on the Profile tab of the Properties dialog box for the user account. Since the home directory is on a network server, click Connect and specify a drive letter to use to connect. In the To box you would specify a UNC name, for example *server_name**shared_folder_name**user_logon_name*. Type the %username% variable as the user's logon name to automatically name each user's home directory to the user logon name. For example, type **\\server_name\Users\ %username%**

If you use %username% to name a folder on an NTFS volume, the user is assigned the NTFS Full Control permission and all other permissions are removed for the folder, including those for the Administrator account.

Lesson Summary

In addition to the My Documents folder, Windows 2000 provides you with the means to create a home directory for users to store their personal documents. You can create a home directory on a client computer or in a shared folder on a file server. Because a home directory is not part of a roaming user profile, its size does not affect network traffic during the logon process.

Storing all home directories on a file server provides several advantages. The first advantage is that users can gain access to their home directories from any client computer on the network. The second advantage is that backup and administration of user documents is centralized. Another advantage is that the home directories are accessible from client computers running any Microsoft operating system (including MS-DOS, Windows 95, Windows 98, and Windows 2000).

Review

Here are some questions to help you determine if you have learned enough to move on to the next chapter. If you have difficulty answering these questions, please go back and review the material in this chapter before beginning the next chapter. The answers for these questions are located in Appendix A, "Questions and Answers."

1. Why would you rename a user account and what are the advantages of doing so?

2. What must you do to ensure that a user on a client computer running Windows 2000 has a user profile?

3. What is the difference between a user profile and a roaming user profile?

4. What do you do to ensure that a user on a client computer running Windows 2000 has a roaming user profile?

5. How can you ensure that a user has a centrally located home directory?

6. What can you do if a user whom you administer cannot gain access to a special printer that is needed to do the job because of a group policy restriction?

C H A P T E R   2 0

Auditing Resources and Events

About This Chapter

In this chapter, you will learn about Windows 2000 auditing, which is a tool for maintaining network security. Auditing allows you to track user activities and system-wide events. In addition, you will learn about audit policies and what you need to consider before you set one up. You also will learn how to set up auditing on resources and how to maintain security logs.

Before You Begin

To complete this chapter, you must have

- A computer that meets the minimum hardware requirements listed in "Hardware Requirements," on page xxxiii.
- Installed the Windows 2000 Server software on the computer.
- Configured the computer as a domain controller in a domain.
- Optionally configured a second computer as a member server in the domain.

Lesson 1: Understanding Auditing

Auditing in Microsoft Windows 2000 is the process of tracking both user activities and Windows 2000 activities, which are called *events*, on a computer. Through auditing, you can specify that Windows 2000 writes a record of an event to the security log. The *security log* maintains a record of valid and invalid logon attempts and events relating to creating, opening, or deleting files or other objects. An audit entry in the security log contains the following information:

- The action that was performed
- The user who performed the action
- The success or failure of the event and when the event occurred

After this lesson, you will be able to

- Describe the purpose of auditing.

Estimated lesson time: 5 minutes

Using an Audit Policy

An *audit policy* defines the types of security events that Windows 2000 records in the security log on each computer. The security log allows you to track the events that you specify.

Windows 2000 writes events to the security log on the computer where the event occurs. For example, any time someone tries to log on to the domain using a domain user account and the logon attempt fails, Windows 2000 writes an event to the security log on the domain controller. The event is recorded on the domain controller rather than on the computer at which the logon attempt was made because it is the domain controller that attempted to and could not authenticate the logon attempt.

You can set up an audit policy for a computer to do the following:

- Track the success and failure of events, such as logon attempts by users, an attempt by a particular user to read a specific file, changes to a user account or to group memberships, and changes to your security settings
- Eliminate or minimize the risk of unauthorized use of resources

You use Event Viewer to view events that Windows 2000 has recorded in the security log. You can also archive log files to track trends over time—for example, to determine the use of printers or files or to verify attempts at unauthorized use of resources.

Lesson Summary

In this lesson you learned that Windows 2000 auditing helps you ensure your network is secure by tracking user activities and system-wide events. Auditing allows you to have Windows 2000 write a record of these events to the security log. To specify which events to record, you set up an audit policy. You use Event Viewer to view the security log. Each audit entry in the security log contains the action that was performed, the user who performed the action, and the success or failure of the action. You can also archive log files to track trends over time.

Lesson 2: Planning an Audit Policy

When you plan an audit policy, you need to determine what you want to audit and the computers on which to configure auditing.

After this lesson, you will be able to

- Plan an audit strategy and determine which events to audit.

Estimated lesson time: 5 minutes

Audit Policy Guidelines

When you plan an audit policy you must determine the computers on which to set up auditing. Auditing is turned off by default. As you are determining which computers to audit, you must also plan what to audit on each computer. Windows 2000 records audited events on each computer separately.

The types of events that you can audit include the following:

- Access to files and folders
- Users logging on and off
- Shutting down and restarting a computer running Windows 2000 Server
- Changes to user accounts and groups
- Attempts to make changes to Active Directory objects

After you have determined the types of events to audit, you must also determine whether to audit the success and/or failure of events. Tracking successful events can tell you how often Windows 2000 or users gain access to specific files, printers, or other objects. You can use this information for resource planning. Tracking failed events can alert you to possible security breaches. For example, if you notice a lot of failed logon attempts by a certain user account, especially if these attempts are occurring outside normal business hours, you can assume that an unauthorized person is attempting to break into your system.

Other guidelines in determining your audit policy include the following:

- Determine if you need to track trends of system usage. If so, plan to archive event logs. Archiving these logs will allow you to view how usage changes over time and will allow you to plan to increase system resources before they become a problem.
- Review security logs frequently. You should set a schedule and regularly review security logs because configuring auditing alone does not alert you to security breaches.
- Define an audit policy that is useful and manageable. Always audit sensitive and confidential data. Audit only those events that will provide you with

meaningful information about your network environment. This will minimize usage of server resources and make essential information easier to locate. Auditing too many types of events can create excess overhead for Windows 2000.

- Audit resource access by the Everyone group instead of the Users group. This will ensure that you audit anyone who can connect to the network, not just the users for whom you create user accounts in the domain.

Lesson Summary

In this lesson you learned that in planning an audit policy you must determine the computers on which to set up auditing and what to audit on each computer. The types of events that you can audit include the following: access to files and folders, users logging on and off, shutting down and restarting a computer running Windows 2000 Server, changes to user accounts and groups, and attempts to make changes to Active Directory objects.

You also learned that you can audit the success and/or failure of events. You track successful events to determine how often Windows 2000 or users gain access to specific files or printers. You can use this information for resource planning. You track failed events to look for possible security breaches. Finally, you learned that you can archive the logs to track trends of system usage.

Lesson 3: Implementing an Audit Policy

Auditing is a powerful tool for tracking events that occur on computers in your organization. To implement auditing, you need to consider auditing requirements and set the audit policy. After you set an audit policy on a computer, you can implement auditing on files, folders, Active Directory objects, and printers.

After this lesson, you will be able to

- Set up auditing on files and folders.
- Set up auditing on Active Directory objects.
- Set up auditing on printers.

Estimated lesson time: 25 minutes

Configuring Auditing

You implement an audit policy based on the role of the computer in the Windows 2000 network. Auditing is configured differently for the following types of computers running Windows 2000:

- For member or stand-alone servers, or computers running Windows 2000 Professional, an audit policy is set for each individual computer. For example, to audit user access to a file on a member server, you set the audit policy on that computer.
- For domain controllers, an audit policy is set for all domain controllers in the domain. To audit events that occur on domain controllers, such as changes to Active Directory objects, you configure a group policy for the domain, which applies to all domain controllers.

Note The types of events that you can audit on a domain controller are identical to those on a computer that is not a domain controller. The procedure is similar as well, but you use a group policy for the domain to control auditing for domain controllers. For more information on how to configure a group policy, see Chapter 21, "Implementing Group Policy."

Auditing Requirements

The requirements to set up and administer auditing are as follows:

- You must have the Manage Auditing And Security Log user right for the computer where you want to configure an audit policy or review an audit log. By default, Windows 2000 grants these rights to the Administrators group.
- The files and folders to be audited must be on Windows NT file system (NTFS) volumes.

Setting Up Auditing

Setting up auditing is a two-part process:

1. Set the audit policy. The audit policy enables auditing of objects but does not activate auditing of specific objects.

2. Enable auditing of specific resources. You specify the specific events to audit for files, folders, printers, and Active Directory objects. Windows 2000 then tracks and logs the specified events.

Setting an Audit Policy

The first step in implementing an audit policy is selecting the types of events that Windows 2000 audits. For each event that you can audit, the configuration settings indicate whether to track successful or failed attempts. You set audit policies in the Group Policy snap-in. In the stored configuration settings that are found in the Group Policy Editor snap-in, On indicates that Windows 2000 tracks the event.

Table 20.1 describes the types of events that Windows 2000 can audit.

Table 20.1   Types of Events Audited by Windows 2000

Event	Description
Account logon	A domain controller received a request to validate a user account.
Account management	An administrator created, changed, or deleted a user account or group. A user account was renamed, disabled, or enabled, or a password was set or changed.
Directory service access	A user gained access to an Active Directory object. You must configure specific Active Directory objects for auditing to log this type of event.
Logon	A user logged on or logged off, or a user made or canceled a network connection to the computer.
Object access	A user gained access to a file, folder, or printer. You must configure specific files, folders, or printers for auditing. Directory service access is auditing a user's access to specific Active Directory objects. Object access is auditing a user's access to files, folders, and printers.
Policy change	A change was made to the user security options, user rights, or audit policies.
Privilege use	A user exercised a right, such as changing the system time (this does not include rights that are related to logging on and logging off).

(continued)

Event	Description
Process tracking	A program performed an action. This information is generally useful only for programmers who want to track details of program execution.
System	A user restarted or shut down the computer, or an event occurred that affects Windows 2000 security or the security log (for example, the audit log is full and Windows 2000 discards entries).

To set an audit policy on a computer that is not a domain controller, create a custom MMC console and add the Group Policy snap-in to it. When prompted, select Local Computer. If you don't know how to create custom MMC consoles, refer to Chapter 4, "Using Microsoft Management Console and Task Scheduler."

▶ **To set an audit policy on a computer that is not a domain controller**

1. Open your custom MMC console that contains the Group Policy snap-in.

2. In the Local Policy Editor MMC console tree, double-click Computer Configuration, double-click Windows Settings, double-click Security Settings, double-click Local Policies, and then click Audit Policy.

   The console displays the current audit policy settings in the details pane, as shown in Figure 20.1.

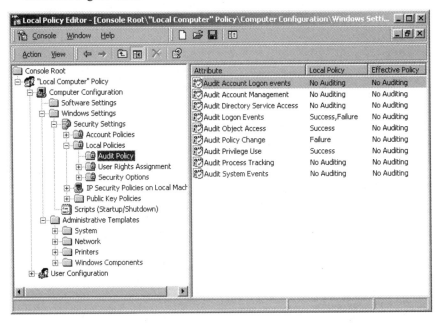

Figure 20.1   Custom console showing events that Windows 2000 can audit

3. Select the type of event to audit, and then, on the Action menu, click Security.

4. Select the Audit Successful Attempts check box and/or the Audit Failed Attempts check box.

   The Local Policy column will indicate one of the following for each auditable policy setting.

Local policy entry	Description
No Auditing	No auditing is occurring for this event in the policy.
Success	Auditing is in effect for successful attempts only.
Failure	Auditing is in effect for failed attempts only.
Success, Failure	Auditing is in effect for both successful and failed attempts.

5. Click OK.

Now you know how to set your audit policy for computers that are not domain controllers. Once you have set the audit policy, you must remember that the changes that you make to your computer's audit policy take effect when one of the following events occurs:

- You initiate policy propagation by typing **secedit /RefreshPolicy /MACHINE_POLICY** at the command prompt and then pressing Enter.

- You restart your computer. Windows 2000 applies changes that you made to your audit policy the next time that you restart your computer.

- Policy propagation occurs. Policy propagation is a process that applies policy settings, including audit policy settings, to your computer. Automatic policy propagation occurs at regular, configurable intervals. By default, policy propagation occurs every eight hours.

Auditing Access to Files and Folders

If security breaches are an issue for your organization, you can set up auditing for files and folders on NTFS partitions. To audit user access to files and folders, you must first set your audit policy to audit object access, which includes files and folders.

Once you have set your audit policy to audit object access, you enable auditing for specific files and folders and specify which types of access, by which users or groups, to audit.

▶ **To enable auditing for specific files and folders**

1. On the Security tab in the Properties dialog box for a file or folder, click Advanced.

2. On the Auditing tab, click Add, select the users for whom you want to audit file and folder access, and then click OK.

3. In the Audit Entry dialog box, select the Successful check box or the Failed check box for the events that you want to audit. For a list of the events, see Figure 20.2.

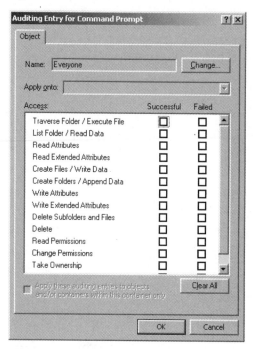

Figure 20.2   Events that can be audited for files and folders

Table 20.2 describes when to audit these events.

Table 20.2   User Events and What Triggers Them

Event	User activity that triggers the event
Traverse Folder/ Execute File	Running a program or gaining access to a folder to change directories
List Folder/Read Data	Displaying the contents of a file or a folder
Read Attributes And Read Extended Attributes	Displaying the attributes of a file or folder
Create Files/Write Data	Changing the contents of a file or creating new files in a folder
Write Attributes And Write Extended Attributes	Changing attributes of a file or folder
Delete Subfolders And Files	Deleting a file or subfolder in a folder
Delete	Deleting a file or folder
Read Permissions	Viewing permissions or the file owner for a file or folder

Change Permissions	Changing permissions for a file or folder
Take Ownership	Taking ownership of a file or folder
Synchronize	Synchronizing a file or folder with an offline copy of the file or folder

4. Click OK to return to the Access Control Settings dialog box.

   By default, any auditing changes that you make to a parent folder also apply to all child folders and all files in the parent and child folders.

5. To prevent changes that are made to a parent folder from applying to the currently selected file or folder, clear the Allow Inheritable Permissions From Parent To Propagate To This Object check box.

6. Click OK.

Auditing Access to Active Directory Objects

Similar to auditing file and folder access, to audit Active Directory object access, you have to configure an audit policy and then set auditing for specific objects, such as users, computers, organizational units (OUs), or groups by specifying which types of access and access by which users to audit. You audit Active Directory objects to track access to Active Directory objects, such as changing the properties on a user account. To enable auditing of user access to Active Directory objects, set the audit policy to track directory service access.

▶ **To enable auditing for specific Active Directory objects**

1. In Active Directory Manager, click View, and then click Advanced Features.

2. Select the object that you want to audit, click Properties on the Action menu, click the Security tab, and then click the Advanced button.

3. On the Auditing tab, click Add, select the users or groups for whom you want to audit file and folder access, and then click OK.

4. In the Apply Onto box, select where the auditing setting applies. For example, in Figure 20.3, Successful and Failed are both selected for Full Control access.

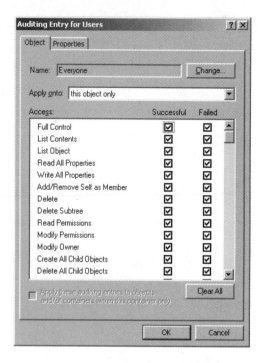

Figure 20.3   Events that can be audited for Active Directory objects

Table 20.3 describes the audit events for Active Directory objects and explains what action triggers the event to occur.

Table 20.3   Some Active Directory Object Events and What Triggers Them

Event	User activity that triggers the event
Full Control	Performing any type of access to the audited object
List Contents	Viewing the objects within the audited object
List Object	Viewing the audited object
Read All Properties	Viewing any attribute of the audited object
Write All Properties	Changing any attribute of the audited object
Create All Child Objects	Creating any object within the audited object
Delete All Child Objects	Deleting any object within the audited object
Read Permissions	Viewing the permissions for the audited object
Modify Permissions	Changing the permissions for the audited object
Modify Owner	Taking ownership of the audited object

Auditing Access to Printers

Audit access to printers to track access to sensitive printers. To audit access to printers, set your audit policy to audit object access, which includes printers. Then, enable auditing for specific printers and specify which types of access and access by which users to audit. After you select the printer, you use the same steps that you use to set up auditing on files and folders.

▶ **To set up auditing on a printer**

1. In the Properties dialog box for the printer, click the Security tab, and then click Advanced.

2. On the Auditing tab, click Add, select the appropriate users or groups for whom you want to audit printer access, click Add, and then click OK.

3. In the Apply Onto box, select where the auditing setting applies.

4. Under Events To Audit, select the Successful check box or the Failed check box for the events that you want to audit. (See Figure 20.4.)

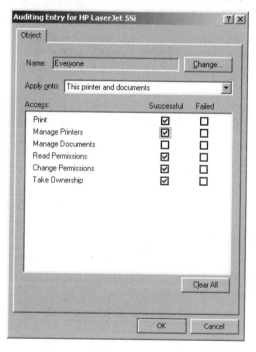

Figure 20.4   Printer events that can be audited

Table 20.4 describes audit events for printers and explains what action triggers the event to occur.

Table 20.4   Printer Events and What Triggers Them

Event	User activity that triggers the event
Print	Printing a file
Manage Printers	Changing printer settings, pausing a printer, sharing a printer, or removing a printer
Manage Documents	Changing job settings; pausing, restarting, moving, or deleting documents; sharing a printer; or changing printer properties
Read Permissions	Viewing printer permissions
Change Permissions	Changing printer permissions
Take Ownership	Taking printer ownership

5. Click OK in the appropriate dialog boxes to exit.

Lesson Summary

In this lesson you learned how to set up an audit policy. The first step in implementing an audit policy is selecting the types of events that Windows 2000 audits. For each event that you can audit, the configuration settings indicate whether to track successful or failed attempts. You set audit policies in the Group Policy snap-in.

Lesson 4: Using Event Viewer

You use Event Viewer to perform a variety of tasks, including viewing the audit logs that are generated as a result of setting the audit policy and auditing events. You can also use Event Viewer to view the contents of security log files and find specific events within log files.

After this lesson, you will be able to

- View a log.
- Locate events in a log.
- Archive security logs.
- Configure the size of audit logs.

Estimated lesson time: 45 minutes

Understanding Windows 2000 Logs

You use Event Viewer to view information contained in Windows 2000 logs. By default there are three logs available to view in Event Viewer. These logs are described in Table 20.5.

Table 20.5   Logs Maintained by Windows 2000

Log	Description
Application log	Contains errors, warnings, or information that programs, such as a database program or an e-mail program, generate. The program developer presets which events to record.
Security log	Contains information about the success or failure of audited events. The events that Windows 2000 records are a result of your audit policy.
System log	Contains errors, warnings, and information that Windows 2000 generates. Windows 2000 presets which events to record.

Note   If additional services are installed, they might add their own event log. For example, the Domain Name System (DNS) Service logs events that this service generates in the DNS server log.

Viewing Security Logs

The security log contains information about events that are monitored by an audit policy, such as failed and successful logon attempts.

▶   **To view the security log**

1. Click the Start button, point to Programs, point to Administrative Tools, and then click Event Viewer.

2. In the console tree, select Security Log.

    In the details pane, Event Viewer displays a list of log entries and summary information for each item, as shown in Figure 20.5.

    Successful Events appear with a key icon, and unsuccessful events appear with a lock icon. Other important information includes the date and time that the event occurred, the category of the event, and the user who generated the event.

    The category indicates the type of event, such as object access, account management, directory service access, or logon events.

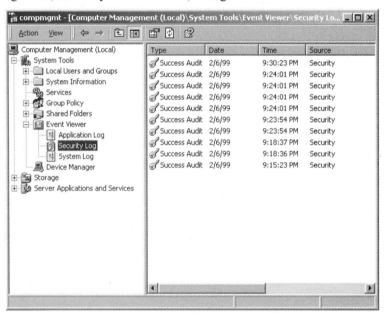

Figure 20.5   Event Viewer displaying a sample security log

3. To view additional information for any event, select the event, and then click Properties on the Action menu.

Windows 2000 records events in the security log on the computer at which the event occurred. You can view these events from any computer as long as you have administrative privileges for the computer where the events occurred. To view the security log on a remote computer, point Event Viewer to a remote computer when you add this snap-in to a console.

Locating Events

When you first start Event Viewer, it automatically displays all events that are recorded in the selected log. To change what appears in the log, you can locate selected events by using the Filter command. You can also search for specific events by using the Find command.

To filter or find events, start Event Viewer, and then click Filter or click Find on the View menu. (See Figure 20.6.)

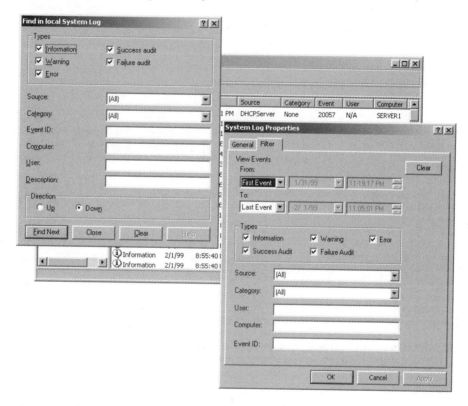

Figure 20.6 Using Event Viewer to filter or find events in a log

Table 20.6 describes the options for filtering and finding events.

Table 20.6   Options for Filtering and Finding Events

Option	Description
View Events	The dates for which to view events. (Only on the Filter tab.)
Types	The types of events to view.
Source	The software or component driver that logged the event.

(continued)

Option	Description
Category	The type of event, such as a logon or logoff attempt or a system event.
User	A user logon name.
Computer	A computer name.
Event ID	An event number to identify the event. This number helps product support representatives track events.
Description	Text that is in the description of the event. (Only in the Find dialog box.)
Direction	The direction in which to search the log (up or down). (Only in the Find dialog box.)

Managing Audit Logs

You can track trends in Windows 2000 by archiving event logs and comparing logs from different periods. Viewing trends helps you determine resource use and plan for growth. You can also use logs to determine a pattern if unauthorized use of resources is a concern. Windows 2000 allows you to control the size of the logs and to specify the action that Windows 2000 takes when a log becomes full.

You can configure the properties of each individual audit log. To configure the settings for logs, select the log in Event Viewer, and then display the Properties dialog box for the log.

Use the Properties dialog box for each type of audit log to control the following:

- The size of each log, which can be from 64 KB to 4,194,240 KB (4 GB). The default size is 512 KB.

- The action that Windows 2000 takes when the log fills up, by clicking one of the options described in Table 20.7.

Table 20.7   Options for Handling Full Audit Log Files

Option	Description
Overwrite Events As Needed	You might lose information if the log becomes full before you archive it. However, this setting requires no maintenance.
Overwrite Events Older Than X Days	Enter the number of days. You might lose information if the log becomes full before you archive it, but Windows 2000 will only lose information that is at least x days old.
Do Not Overwrite Events	This option requires you to clear the log manually. When the log becomes full, Windows 2000 will stop. However, no security log entries are overwritten.

Archiving Logs

Archiving security logs allows you to maintain a history of security-related events. Many companies have policies on keeping archive logs for a specified period to track security-related information over time.

If you want to archive, clear, or view an archived log, select the log you want to configure in Event Viewer, click the Action menu, and then click one of the options described in Table 20.8.

Table 20.8   Options to Archive, Clear, or View a Log File

To	Do this
Archive the log	Click Save Log File As, and then type a file name.
Clear the log	Click Clear All Events to clear the log. Windows 2000 creates a security log entry, stating that the log was cleared.
View an archived log	Point to New, and then click Log View; in the Add Another Log View dialog box, select Saved, and then provide the path to the log.

Practice: Auditing Resources and Events

In this practice you plan a domain audit policy. Then you set up an audit policy by enabling auditing on certain events. You set up auditing of a file, a printer, and an Active Directory object. Then you view the security log file and configure Event Viewer to overwrite events when the log file is filled.

Exercise 1: Planning a Domain Audit Policy

In this exercise, you plan an audit policy for your server. You need to determine the following:

- Which types of events to audit
- Whether to audit the success or failure of an event, or both

Use the following criteria to make your decisions:

- Record unsuccessful attempts to gain access to the network.
- Record unauthorized access to the files that make up the Customer database.
- For billing purposes, track color printer usage.
- Track whenever someone tries to tamper with the server hardware.
- Keep a record of actions that an administrator performs to track unauthorized changes.
- Track backup procedures to prevent data theft.
- Track unauthorized access to sensitive Active Directory objects.

Record your decisions to audit successful and/or failed events for the actions listed in the following table.

Action to audit	Successful	Failed
Account logon events	❑	❑
Account management	❑	❑
Directory service access	❑	❑
Logon events	❑	❑
Object access	❑	❑
Policy change	❑	❑
Privilege use	❑	❑
Process tracking	❑	❑
System events	❑	❑

Exercise 2: Setting Up an Audit Policy

In this exercise, you enable auditing for selected events.

Note   Complete this exercise on the computer that is a member server only. If you only have one computer that is a domain controller, you can also choose to complete this exercise at the domain controller, but the settings that you change will not take effect.

To set an audit policy on a computer that is not a domain controller, you first need to create a custom Microsoft Management Console and add the Group Policy snap-in to it.

▶ **To create and prepare a custom console**

1. Log on to your computer as Administrator.
2. Click Start, click Run, and then type **mmc** in the Open box. Click OK.

   Microsoft Management Console opens a new, blank console window labeled Console1.
3. Click the Console menu item and then click Add/Remove Snap-In.

   The Add/Remove Snap-In dialog box opens.
4. Click the Add button.

   The Add Standalone Snap-In dialog box opens.
5. Select Group Policy from the list and click Add.
6. Click Finish in the dialog box that appears.
7. Click Close and then click OK to close the remaining dialog boxes.

   The Console Root window now displays the Local Computer Policy snap-in.

8. Select Console, select Save As, and type **Local Policy Editor** in the file name box.

9. Click the Save button, and then leave the console open for the next procedure.

The custom console is now saved in the My Administrative Tools folder.

▶ **To set up an audit policy**

1. In the console tree of the Local Policy Editor console you just created, expand Computer Configuration, Windows Settings, and Local Policies, and then click Audit Policy.

2. To set the audit policy, in the details pane, double-click each type of event, and then select either the Audit successful attempts check box or the Audit failed attempts check box as listed in the following table.

Event	Audit successful attempts	Audit failed attempts
Account Logon	☐	☐
Account Management	☑	☐
Directory Service Access	☐	☑
Logon	☐	☑
Object Access	☑	☑
Policy Change	☑	☐
Privilege Use	☑	☐
Process Tracking	☐	☐
System	☑	☑

3. Close Local Policy Editor.

4. Start a command prompt.

5. At the command prompt, type **secedit /RefreshPolicy MACHINE_POLICY** and then press Enter.

Windows 2000 informs you that policy propagation was triggered and that you need to wait for a few minutes until the policy changes take effect.

6. Close the command prompt window.

Exercise 3: Setting Up Auditing of Files

In this exercise, you set up auditing for a file.

Note   Complete this exercise on the computer that is a member server only. If you only have one computer that is a domain controller, you can also choose to complete this exercise at the domain controller, but the settings that you change will not take effect.

▶   **To set up auditing of files**

1. In Windows Explorer, locate a file such as a simple text file.

2. Right-click the file name, and then click Properties.

3. In the Properties dialog box, click the Security tab, and then click Advanced.

4. In the Access Control Settings dialog box, click the Auditing tab.

5. Click Add.

6. In the Select User, Computer, Or Group dialog box, double-click Everyone in the list of user accounts and groups.

7. In the Audit Entry For dialog box, select the Successful check box and the Failed check box for each of the following events:

   ▪ Create Files / Write Data

   ▪ Delete

   ▪ Change Permissions

   ▪ Take Ownership

8. Click OK.

   Windows 2000 displays the Everyone group in the Access Control Settings For dialog box.

9. Click OK to apply your changes.

▶   **To change file permissions**

1. In the Properties dialog box, change the NTFS permissions for the file to only the Read permission for Everyone. Remove any other permissions and prevent inheritable permissions to propagate from the parent.

2. Click OK to close the Properties dialog box, and then close Windows Explorer.

Exercise 4: Setting Up Auditing of a Printer

In this exercise, you set up auditing of a printer.

Note   Complete this exercise on the computer that is a member server only. If you only have one computer that is a domain controller, you can also choose to complete this exercise at the domain controller, but the settings that you change will not take effect.

▶   **To set up auditing of a printer**

1. Click the Start button, point to Settings, and then click Printers.

2. In the Printers system folder, right-click HP LaserJet 5Si (installed in Chapter 15), and then click Properties.

3. Click the Security tab, and then click Advanced.

4. In the Access Control Settings for HP LaserJet 5Si dialog box, click the Auditing tab, and then click Add.

5. In the Select User, Computer, Or Group dialog box, double-click Everyone in the list box.

6. In the Audit Entry For HP LaserJet 5Si dialog box, select the Successful check box for all types of access.

7. Click OK.

   Windows 2000 displays the Everyone group in the Access Control Settings For HP LaserJet 5Si dialog box.

8. Click OK to apply your changes.

9. Click OK to close the HP LaserJet 5Si Properties dialog box.

10. Close the Printers system folder.

Exercise 5: Setting Up Auditing of an Active Directory Object

In this exercise, you set up auditing of an Active Directory object.

Note   Complete this exercise on the computer that is a member server only. If you only have one computer that is a domain controller, you can also choose to complete this exercise at the domain controller, but the settings that you change will not take effect.

▶   **To review auditing of an Active Directory object**

1. Start Active Directory Manager.

2. On the View menu, click Advanced Features.

3. In the console tree, click your domain.

4. In the details pane, click Users, and then on the Action menu, click Properties.

5. In the Users Properties dialog box, click the Security tab, and then click Advanced.

6. In the Access Control Settings For Users dialog box, click the Auditing tab, and then double-click Everyone.

   Active Directory Manager displays the Audit Entry For Users dialog box.

   Review the default audit settings for object access by members of the Everyone group. How do the audited types of access differ from the types of access that are not audited?

7. Click OK three times to close the Users Properties dialog box.

   At which computer or computers does Windows 2000 record log entries for Active Directory access? Will you be able to review them?

8. Close Active Directory Manager.

Exercise 6: Viewing the Security Log

In this exercise, you view the security log for your computer. Then, you use Event Viewer to filter events and to search for potential security breaches.

Note   Complete this exercise on the computer that is a member server only. If you only have one computer that is a domain controller, you can also choose to complete this exercise at the domain controller, but the settings that you change will not take effect.

▶   **To view the security log for your computer**

1. Click the Start menu, click Programs, click Administrative Tools, and then click Event Viewer.

2. In the console tree, click each of the three logs and view the contents. As you scroll through the logs, double-click a couple of events to view a description.

Note   If you only have one computer and are working on your domain controller, your security log will be empty.

Exercise 7: Managing the Security Log

In this exercise, you configure Event Viewer to overwrite events when the log file gets full. Then, you clear the security log and view an archived security log.

Note   Complete this exercise on the computer that is a member server only. If you only have one computer that is a domain controller, you can also choose to complete this exercise at the domain controller, but the settings that you change will not take effect.

▶   **To control the size and contents of a log file**

1. Verify that in the console tree, System Log is selected.

2. On the Action menu, click Properties.

3. In the System Log Properties dialog box, click Overwrite events as needed.

4. In the Maximum Log Size box, change the maximum log size to 2048 kilobytes (KB), and click OK.

Windows 2000 will now allow the log to grow to 2048 KB and will then over-write older events with new events as necessary.

5. Close Event Viewer.

Lesson Summary

In this lesson you learned about the Windows 2000 logs. You learned about Event Viewer and how to use Event Viewer to view the contents of the Windows 2000 logs. You learned how to use the Filter and Find commands in Event Viewer to locate specific events or types of events. You also learned to manage logs by archiving them and by controlling their size. The practice portion of this exercise gave you hands-on experience with these tasks.

Review

Here are some questions to help you determine if you have learned enough to move on to the next chapter. If you have difficulty answering these questions, please go back and review the material in this chapter before beginning the next chapter. The answers for these questions are located in Appendix A, "Questions and Answers."

1. On which computer do you set an audit policy to audit a folder that is located on a member server that belongs to a domain?

2. What is the difference between what the audit policy settings track for directory service access and object access?

3. What two tasks must you perform to audit access to a file?

4. Who can set up auditing for a computer?

5. When you view a security log, how do you determine if an event failed or was successful?

6. If you click the Do Not Overwrite Events option in the Properties dialog box for an audit log, what happens when the log file becomes full?

C H A P T E R   2 1

Implementing Group Policy

About This Chapter

Group policies are another method for defining a user's desktop environment.
Group policies can be used to control the programs that are available to users, the
programs that appear on a user's desktop, the Start menu options, and so on.

Before You Begin

To complete this chapter, you must have

- A computer that meets the minimum hardware requirements listed in
  "Hardware Requirements," on page xxxiii.
- Installed the Windows 2000 Server software on the computer.
- Configured the computer as a domain controller in a domain.

Lesson 1: Understanding Group Policy

Typically, you will not set group policies; rather group policy administrators set up and administer them. Group policies are typically set for the entire domain or network and are used to enforce corporate policies. However, even if you do not administer group policies, they affect the user accounts, groups, computers, and OUs that you administer. You should be aware of what group policies are and be familiar with the different types of group policies.

After this lesson, you will be able to

- Explain the structure of group policies, including group policy objects, group policy containers, and group policy templates.

Estimated lesson time: 30 minutes

Introduction to Group Policies

Group policies are a set of configuration settings that a group policy administrator applies to one or more Active Directory objects. A group policy administrator uses group policies to control the work environments for users in a domain. Group policies can also control the work environment of users with accounts that are located in a specific organizational unit (OU). You must consider the effect that group policies have on the user accounts and groups that you administer.

How Group Policies Work

A group policy consists of settings that govern how an object and its child objects behave. Group policies allow a group policy administrator to provide users with a fully populated desktop environment. This environment can include a customized Start menu, files that are copied automatically to the My Documents folder, applications that are set up, and restricted access to files, folders, and Microsoft Windows 2000 system settings. Group policies can also affect rights that are granted to user accounts and groups.

Group policies are typically set at the site and domain level in Active Directory. A site is a combination of one or more Internet Protocol (IP) subnets connected by a high-speed connection.

Effects of Group Policies

Conflicts can exist between group policies and local needs, such as when a policy restricts a user's ability to gain access to a resource that the user needs to perform his or her job. When this occurs, you must work with the group policy administrator to resolve the conflict. For example, if a group policy that is applied at the domain level prevents users in your network from gaining access to an application that they need to perform their jobs, contact the group policy administrator to correct the situation.

There is an exception to always having to contact the group policy administrator; you can unlock a user account that a group policy locked out, as explained in Lesson 2 of Chapter 19.

Be aware that you should not bother to perform tasks that a group policy overrides, such as implementing mandatory user profiles if a group policy overrides profile settings.

Types of Group Policies

Group policies influence a variety of network components and Active Directory objects. Table 21.1 describes the types of group policies.

Table 21.1 Types of Group Policies

Type of group policy	Description
Application deployment	Affects the applications to which users can gain access. These policies make application installations automatic in two ways: **Application assignment.** The group policy installs or upgrades applications automatically on the client computers or provides the user with a connection to an application, which users cannot delete. **Application publication.** The group policy administrator publishes applications in Active Directory. The applications then appear in the list of components that a user can install by using Add/Remove Programs in Control Panel. Users can uninstall these applications.
File deployment	Allows group policy administrators to place files in special folders on the user's client computer, such as Desktop and My Documents. For example, an Employee Handbook file stored on a server appears in each user's My Documents folder when he or she logs on.
Scripts	Allows group policy administrators to specify scripts and batch files to run at specified times, such as during system startup or system shutdown, or when a user logs on or logs off. Scripts automate repetitive tasks, such as mapping network drives.
Software	Allows group policy administrators to globally configure most of the settings in user profiles, such as desktop settings, the Start menu, and applications.
Security	Allows group policy administrators to restrict user access to files and folders. The group policy administrator can also use security group policies to set how many incorrect passwords a user can enter before Windows 2000 locks out the user account. These group policies also control user rights, such as which users are able to log on at a domain server.

Benefits of Group Policy

Total cost of ownership (TCO) is the cost involved in administering distributed personal computer networks. Recent studies on TCO cite lost user productivity as one of the major costs to corporations. Lost productivity is often due to user error, such as modifying system configuration files and thereby rendering the computer unusable, or to the confusing array of nonessential applications and features available to the user.

You can lower your network's TCO by using group policies to create a managed desktop environment tailored to the user's job responsibilities and experience level.

Securing a User's Environment

As an administrator in a high-security network, you might want to create a "locked down" environment on a computer. By implementing appropriate group policy settings for specific users, combined with Windows NT file system (NTFS) permissions and other Windows 2000 security features, you can prevent users from accessing unauthorized programs or data. You can also prevent users from deleting files that are important to the proper functioning of their applications or operating system.

Enhancing a User's Environment

You can use group policy to enhance a user's environment by doing the following:

- Automatically delivering applications to a user's Start menu
- Enabling applications so that users can easily find them on the network and install them
- Delivering files or shortcuts to useful places on the network or to a specific folder on a user's computer
- Automating the execution of tasks or programs when a user logs on or off and when a computer starts or shuts down

Group Policy Objects

Group Policy configuration settings are contained within a group policy object (GPO). You establish group policy settings in a GPO that you apply to a site, domain, or organizational unit (SDOU). One or more GPOs can apply to a SDOU, and multiple SDOUs can be associated with the same GPO.

GPOs store group policy information in two locations: a group policy container and a group policy template. GPOs contain properties that Windows 2000 stores in Active Directory in an object called a group policy container (GPC). GPOs also store group policy information in a folder structure called a group policy template (GPT).

Group Policy Containers

A group policy container (GPC) is an Active Directory object that contains GPO properties and includes subcontainers for computer and user group policy information. The GPC includes the following information:

- **Version information.**   Ensures that the information contained within the GPC synchronizes with the GPT information.
- **Status information.**   Indicates whether the GPO is enabled or disabled.

The GPC contains the class store information for application deployment. The Windows 2000 class store is a server-based repository for all applications, interfaces, and application programming interfaces (APIs) that provide application publishing and assigning functions.

Windows 2000 stores group policy data that is small in size and changes infrequently in GPCs. Windows 2000 stores group policy data that is large and might change frequently in GPTs.

Group Policy Templates

A group policy template (GPT) is a folder structure in the system volume folder (Sysvol) of domain controllers. The GPT is the container for all software policy, script, file and application deployment, and security settings information.

GPT Structure

When you create a GPO, Windows 2000 creates the corresponding GPT folder structure. The folder name of the GPT is the globally unique identifier (GUID) of the GPO that you created. For example, if you associate a GPO with a domain called MyDomain.microsoft.com, the resulting GPT folder name would be

```
systemroot\Sysvol\sysvol\MyDomain.microsoft.com\Policies\
{A3A2C853-F033-11D1-9BE4-00C0DFE00C63}
```

where *systemroot* refers to the Windows 2000 installation directory, such as C:\Winnt.

Gpt.ini File

The root folder of each GPT contains a file called Gpt.ini. The entries in this file include

- **Version=x.**   Where x represents the version number of the GPO. The version number begins at 0 when you first create the GPO and then is automatically incremented by 1 each time that you modify the GPO.
- **Disabled=y.**   Where y is either 0 or 1 and refers only to the local GPO. This switch indicates whether the local GPO is enabled or disabled.

The Gpt.ini file defines whether the local GPO is disabled or enabled; for all other GPOs, this information is stored in the GPC in Active Directory.

GPT Contents

Typically the default contents of GPT are \User and \Machine\Microsoft\Windows NT\SecEdit. As you can create and modify policies, additional folders will be created. The specific folder structure depends on the group policies that you set. Table 21.2 describes the subfolders that might be contained in the GPT folder.

Table 21.2   Group Policy Template (GPT) Subfolders

Subfolder	Contents
\ADM	The .ADM files that are associated with a specific GPT
\User	A Registry.pol file with the registry settings to apply to users
\User\Applications	The .AAS advertisement files used by the Microsoft Windows Installer
\User\Documents & Settings	Any files to deploy to the user's desktop as part of this GPT
\User\Scripts	The Logon and Logoff subfolders
\User\Scripts\Logon	The scripts and related files for logon scripting
\User\Scripts\Logoff	The scripts and related files for logoff scripting
\Machine	A Registry.pol file with the registry setting to apply to computers
\Machine\Applications	The advertisement files (.AAS files) used by the Windows installer
\Machine\Documents & Settings	Any files to deploy to all desktops for all users who log on to this computer as part of this GPT
\Machine\Microsoft\WindowsNT\SecEdit	The GptTmpl.ini Security Editor file
\Machine\Scripts	The Startup and Shutdown subfolders
\Machine\Scripts\Startup	The scripts and related files for startup scripting
\Machine\Scripts\Shutdown	The scripts and related files for shutdown scripting

Windows 2000 downloads and applies the Registry.pol file in the Machine subfolder to the registry during the boot process of the computer. When the user logs on, Windows 2000 downloads and applies the Registry.pol file in the User subfolder to the registry. In other words, computer settings apply when the computer is started, and user settings apply when the user logs on.

Note The format of the Registry.pol files for Windows 2000 differs from the format of the .POL files created with the System Policy Editors in Microsoft Windows 95 or later and Windows NT 4.0. You cannot apply files created using the earlier versions of the System Policy Editor to computers running Windows 2000. You cannot apply files created with the Windows 2000 Group Policy Editor to clients running Windows 95 or later or Windows NT version 4.0.

Lesson Summary

In this lesson you learned about group policies, group policy objects, group policy containers, and group policy templates. Group policies are a set of configuration settings that a group policy administrator applies to one or more Active Directory objects and are typically set for the entire domain or network to enforce corporate policies. Typically, a group policy administrator uses group policies to control the work environments for users in a domain. However, group policy can also control the work environment of users with accounts that are located in a specific organizational unit (OU).

The group policies configuration settings are contained within a group policy object (GPO). GPOs store group policy information in two locations: a group policy container (GPC) and a group policy template (GPT). You establish group policy settings in a GPO that you apply to a site, domain, or organizational unit (SDOU). One or more GPOs can apply to a SDOU, and multiple SDOUs can be associated with the same GPO.

Windows 2000 stores group policy data that is small in size and changes infrequently in GPCs. A GPC is an Active Directory object that contains GPO properties and includes subcontainers for computer and user group policy information. The GPC contains the class store information for application deployment.

Windows 2000 stores group policy data that is large and might change frequently in group policy templates (GPTs). A GPT is a folder structure in the system volume folder (Sysvol) of domain controllers. The GPT is the container for all software policy, script, file and application deployment, and security settings information.

Lesson 2: Applying Group Policy

Group policy is inherited and cumulative, and it affects all computers and user accounts in the Active Directory container with which the GPO is associated.

After this lesson, you will be able to

- Explain the hierarchy for applying group policies, including methods for modifying inheritance of policies.
- Describe the use of the Access Control List (ACL) Editor and security groups to filter the scope of a group policy.
- Create a group policy object (GPO) with the Group Policy Editor.
- Identify the settings nodes in Group Policy Editor.

Estimated lesson time: 50 minutes

Understanding Order of Inheritance

The order of group policy inheritance is site, domain, and then OU. Windows 2000 evaluates group policy starting with the Active Directory container furthest away from the computer object or user object. Sites contain domains, domains contain OUs, and OUs contain the computer objects and the user objects. Therefore, Windows 2000 first evaluates any group policy set up for the site and applies it to the computer object or user object. Next, Windows 2000 evaluates any group policy set up for the domain and applies it to the computer object or user object. Finally, Windows 2000 evaluates any group policy set up for the OU and applies it to the computer object or user object.

This default behavior allows a group policy setting in the Active Directory container closest to the computer or user to override a conflicting group policy setting in a container that is higher up in the Active Directory hierarchy. For example, if there is a conflict between the group policy set up for the domain and the group policy set up for the OU, because the OU is closer to the computer object or user object, the OU group policy is applied after the domain group policy and thereby overrides the domain group policy.

Note When there is a conflict between a computer policy and a user policy setting, the user policy setting applies.

Overriding Inheritance and Blocking Inheritance

Windows 2000 provides the following two options for changing the default group policy processing:

- **No Override**.   Use this option to prevent child containers from overriding policy that is set in a higher-level GPO. This option is useful for enforcing policies that represent company-wide business rules. The No Override option is set on a per-GPO basis. You can set this option on one or more GPOs as required.

- **Block Inheritance.**   Use this option to allow a child container to block policy inheritance from parent containers. This option is useful when an OU requires unique settings. The Block Inheritance setting applies to all GPOs from parent containers.

Note   In case of a conflict, the No Override option always takes precedence over the Block Inheritance option.

The No Override and Block Inheritance options are check boxes that you can select when you use Active Directory Manager.

Filtering the Scope of the GPO

The policies in a GPO apply only to users who have Read permission for that GPO. You can filter the scope of a GPO by creating Security groups and then assigning Read permission to selected groups. Thus, you can prevent a policy from applying to a specific group by denying that group Read permission to the GPO.

Use the ACL Editor to set access permissions on a selected GPO, allowing or denying access to the GPO for specific groups. Select the GPO you want to administer, open its Properties dialog box and click the Group Policy tab, select the policy and click Properties, click the Security tab, and finally click the Advanced button to open the Access Control Settings dialog box shown in Figure 21.1.

Network administrators (members of the Domain Administrators group) can use the ACL Editor to identify which groups of administrators can modify policies in GPOs. To do this, the network administrator defines groups of administrators (for example, Marketing Administrators), and then assigns the Read permission and the Write permission to selected GPOs for these groups. This allows the network administrator to delegate control of the GPO policies. Administrators with Read permission and Write permission to a GPO can control all aspects of the GPO.

Creating a GPO

The first step in creating a group policy is to create or open a GPO. Before you can access the Group Policy Editor, you need to create one or more GPOs. You then use the Group Policy Editor to specify settings for the GPO that you create.

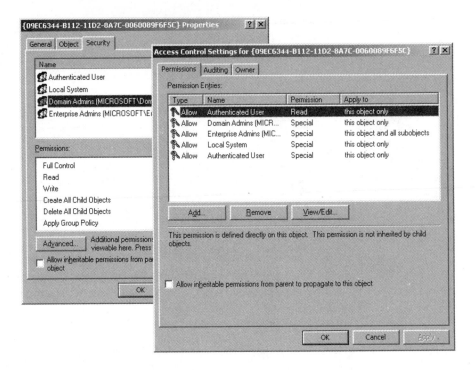

Figure 21.1 Access Control Settings dialog box

▶ **To create a GPO**

1. Start the Directory Management snap-in.

2. Right-click the Active Directory object (domain or OU) for which you want to create a GPO, click Properties, and select the Group Policy tab.

3. Click Add.

4. Under Group Policy Objects Linked To This Container, select the All tab, and then click the Create New Group Policy Object button (the middle button of three).

5. Type a name for the new GPO, and then click OK.

   Windows 2000 returns to the Group Policy tab of the Properties dialog box for the domain or OU.

   Use the Properties dialog box to manage GPOs.

6. On the Group Policy tab, select the GPO that you want to manage and choose from the following buttons:

   - Click the Up button or the Down button to change the priority for a GPO.

     You can associate more than one GPO with an Active Directory container. Windows 2000 processes GPOs from the top of the list to the bottom of the list.

   - Click Edit to open the GPO in Group Policy Editor.

   - Click Delete to remove or delete the GPO from the SDOU.

     When you click Delete, you are prompted with two choices. If you select Remove The Link From The List, you have selected remove. When you *remove* a GPO, it remains in Active Directory but does not apply to that SDOU. If you select Remove The Link And Delete The Group Policy Object Permanently, you have selected delete. When you *delete* a GPO, Windows 2000 removes it from Active Directory.

7. Select a GPO and then click the Options button to select from the following check boxes to control how Windows 2000 applies the GPO:

   - **No Override.**   Select this check box to prevent child containers from overriding the policy set in the selected GPO.

   - **Disabled.**   Select this check box to specify that the GPO does not apply to this SDOU.

     The following check box is located on the Group Policy tab and applies to all GPOs in the list:

   - **Block Policy Inheritance.**   Select this check box to prevent policy inheritance from parent containers.

8. Select a GPO, click Properties, and then click the Security tab to filter application of the GPO by setting ACL properties for security groups.

Using Group Policy Editor

You use the Group Policy Editor to specify group policy settings for computers and user accounts, application and file deployment, security, software, and scripts.

Group Policy Editor Interface

The Group Policy Editor user interface includes the Computer Configuration node and the User Configuration node. Each node displays the following extensions:

- Software Settings
- Windows Settings
- Application Templates

Computer Configuration

The Computer Configuration folders contain settings that you can use to customize the user's environment or enforce lockdown policies for *computers* on the network. Computer Configuration policies apply when the operating system initializes. If you assign user policies to computers, the user policies apply to every user who logs on to the computer, regardless of the OU to which the user belongs.

User Configuration

The User Configuration folders contain settings that you can use to customize the user's environment or enforce lockdown policies for *users* on the network. These settings include all user-specific policies, such as desktop appearance, application settings, logon and logoff scripts, and assigned and published applications. User Configuration policies apply when the user logs on to the computer.

Opening Group Policy Editor

Add the Group Policy snap-in to a Microsoft Management Console (MMC) as a stand-alone tool focused on a particular GPO. After saving it you can open it whenever necessary from the My Administrative Tools folder in the Start Menu's Programs folder.

Note   To edit a GPO for a site, use the Active Directory Sites and Services Manager.

Administrators with Read permission and Write permission to the GPO can make modifications to the group policy for the selected object.

Practice: Creating GPOs

In this exercise, you create a GPO named Domain Policy for your domain. Then you use the Group Policy Editor to modify security settings of the GPO to give Domain Users the right to log on locally at the domain controllers.

Exercise 1: Creating a GPO

In this exercise, you create a GPO at the domain level.

▶   **To create a GPO for your domain**

1. Log on to the domain as Administrator.
2. Click Start, point to Programs, point to Administrative Tools, and then click Directory Management.

   The Active Directory Manager window appears.

3. Right-click Microsoft (or the name of another domain you've created), and then click Properties.

4. Click the Group Policy tab, and then click Add.

   The Add A Group Policy Object Link dialog box appears.

5. Click the All tab, and then point to each of the three buttons on the toolbar and record below the function of the button.

   First button:

   Second button:

   Third button:

6. Click the middle button of the three buttons on the toolbar.

   A new GPO appears under Group Policy Objects list.

7. Name the new GPO Domain Policy, and then click OK.

   You are returned to the Group Policy tab of the Microsoft Properties dialog box. Notice that Domain Policy is now listed under Group Policy Object Links.

8. Click OK to close the Group Policy Properties dialog box.

9. Leave the Active Directory Manager window open.

Exercise 2: Modifying Security Settings

In this exercise, you use the Group Policy Editor to modify security settings in order to give the Domain Users group the right to log on locally.

▶ **To modify security settings**

1. In the Active Directory Manager window, in the console tree, double click Microsoft (or the name of the domain you are using).

2. In the console tree, right-click Domain Controllers, click Properties, and select the Group Policy tab.

3. In the Group Policy Object Links list, select Default Domain Controllers Policy (if necessary), and then click Edit.

   The gpedit - ["Default Domain Controllers Policy" Policy] window appears.

4. In the console tree, double-click Computer Configuration.

   The Computer Configuration policies appear.

5. In the console tree, double-click Windows Settings.

   The Windows Settings policies appear.

6. In the console tree, double-click Security Settings.

   The Security Settings policies appear.

7. In the console tree, double-click Local Policies.

   The Local Policies appear.

8. In the console tree, click User Rights Assignment.

   A list of User Rights Assignment attributes appears in the details pane.

9. Double-click Log On Locally in the details pane.

   The Log On Locally dialog box appears.

   What groups have the right to log on locally?

10. Click Add.

    The Select Users Or Groups dialog box appears.

11. In the Names list, select Domain Users, click Add, and then click OK.

    Domain Users appears in the list of users and groups with the right to log on locally.

12. Click OK, and then close the gpedit - ["Default Domain Controllers Policy" Policy] window.

13. Click OK to close the Domain Controllers Properties dialog box.

14. Close the Active Directory Manager window.

Lesson Summary

In this lesson you learned that you use the Group Policy snap-in to define software policy settings. This node contains all registry-based policy. You also learned that the order of group policy inheritance is site, domain, and then OU. This default behavior allows a group policy setting in the Active Directory container closest to the computer or user to override a conflicting group policy setting in a container that is higher up in the Active Directory hierarchy. When there is a conflict between a computer policy setting and a user policy setting, the user policy setting applies.

You also learned that group policy is inherited, cumulative, and affects all computers and user accounts in the Active Directory container with which the GPO is associated. However, Windows 2000 provides two options for changing the default group policy processing. The first option is No Override. You use No Override to prevent child containers from overriding policy that is set in a higher level GPO. No Override is useful for enforcing policies that represent company-wide business rules. The No Override option is set on a per-GPO basis. You can set this option on one or more GPOs as required. The second option is Block Inheritance. You use Block Inheritance to allow a child container to block policy inheritance from parent containers. Block Inheritance is useful when an OU requires unique settings. The Block Inheritance setting applies to all GPOs from parent containers.

Finally, you learned to use the ACL Editor to set access permissions on a selected GPO, allowing or denying access to the GPO by specified groups.

Lesson 3: Modifying Software Policies

Software policy settings include group policy for applications as well as for Windows 2000 and its components. You are able to modify these settings by using the Directory Management snap-in.

After this lesson, you will be able to

- Modify the software settings in a GPO.

Estimated lesson time: 25 minutes

How to Modify Software Policies

Windows 2000 saves computer settings under the **HKEY_LOCAL_MACHINE** key of the registry, and it saves user settings under the **HKEY_CURRENT_USER** key. There are times that you will want to modify these settings.

▶ **To modify a Software Policy**

1. Start Directory Management.
2. Right-click the Active Directory object (domain or OU) for which you want to modify a GPO, click Properties, and then click the Group Policy tab.
3. Select the GPO link you want to modify and click Edit.
4. Expand the item that represents the particular policy that you want to modify.

   For example, in Figure 21.2, User Configuration, Administrative Templates, and Control Panel were expanded, and then Display was selected.

5. In the details pane, right-click the policy that you want to modify, and then click Properties. In Figure 21.2, Wallpaper was selected in the details pane.

   - If the box on the Properties page contains a check mark, it is implemented. When Windows 2000 applies this policy, the user's computer conforms to the policy. If the box was checked the last time that the user logged on, no changes are made.

   - If the box on the Properties page does not contain a check mark, the policy is not implemented. If the settings were previously implemented, they are removed from the registry.

   - If the box on the Properties page is shaded and contains a check mark, Windows 2000 ignores the setting and makes no changes to the computer.

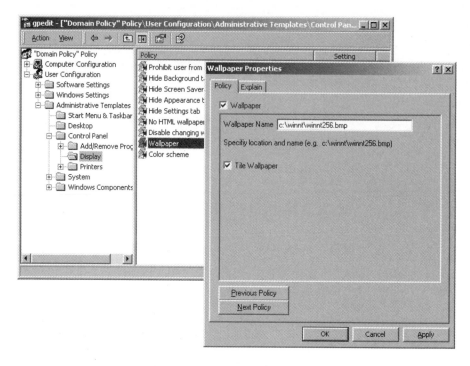

Figure 21.2   Group Policy Editor snap-in

Advanced Software Policies

Some software policies display Yes under More Properties in the details pane. These policies require you to provide more information in order for them to be implemented. For example, all properties listed under the Computer Configuration\ Windows NT Shell\Custom Shared Folders node require that you provide a Universal Naming Convention (UNC) path to the custom shared folder.

To access the Properties page, right-click the policy in the details pane, and then click Properties or double-click the policy.

Windows 2000 writes changes to software policies to Registry.pol immediately. You do not need to save changes.

Modifying the List of Software Policies

To modify the available software settings listed under the Software Settings nodes in Group Policy Editor, you create custom administrative templates (.ADM files).

If you plan to create custom entries for the Software Policies node, Microsoft recommends using the *CompanyName**Product**Version* (or *CompanyName**Product and Version*) naming convention that is also used in the registry. For example, the Windows 2000 settings are under \Microsoft\Windows NT.

Practice: Modifying Software Policies

In this practice, you modify software policies for an OU. You modify the Sales OU group policy by removing the Search menu from the Start menu and by removing the Run menu from the Start menu. You also disable the Lock Workstation policy. You then view the effects of these software policy modifications. In the last part of this practice, you prevent the Sales OU from overriding the group policy of its parent container, the domain.

Exercise 1: Modifying Software Policies

In this exercise, you modify software policies for the Sales OU.

Note   If you haven't set up a Sales OU in a previous chapter, open Directory Management, right-click Microsoft (or the name of your domain), point to New, and then click Organizational Unit. Type **Sales** in the Name box, and click OK.

▶   **To create a GPO for the Sales OU**

1. Log on to your domain as Administrator.

2. Click Start, point to Programs, point to Administrative Tools, and then click Directory Management.

   The Active Directory Manager window appears.

3. Double-click Microsoft.

4. In the console tree, right-click Sales, click Properties, and then click the Group Policy tab.

5. Click Add.

   The Add A Group Policy Object Link dialog box appears.

6. Select the All tab, and then click Create New Group Policy Object (the middle button of the three buttons on the toolbar).

   A new GPO appears under Group Policy Objects associated with this container.

7. Name the new GPO SalesSoftware, and then click OK.

   You are returned to the Group Policy tab of the Sales Properties dialog box.

▶   **To modify software policies for the Sales OU**

1. With SalesSoftware selected, click Edit.

   The gpedit - ["SalesSoftware" Policy] window appears.

2. In the console tree, double-click User Configuration, and then double-click Administrative Templates.

3. In the console tree, click Start Menu and Task Bar.

   The policies available for this category appear in the details pane.

4. In the details pane, double-click Remove Search Menu From Start Menu.

   The Remove Search Menu From Start Menu Properties dialog box appears.

5. On the Policy tab, click the Remove Search Menu From Start Menu box twice.

   The check box to the left of Remove Search Menu From Start Menu should now be selected.

6. Click OK.

7. Repeat steps 4 through 6 to enable the Remove Run Menu From Start Menu policy.

8. In the console pane, double-click System and then click Logon/Logoff.

   The policies available for this category appear in the details pane.

9. In the details pane, enable the Disable Lock Workstation policy.

10. Close the gpedit - ["SalesSoftware" Policy] window, and then click OK to close the Sales Properties dialog box.

11. Close the Active Directory Manager window.

Exercise 2: Testing Software Policies

In this exercise, you view the effects of the software policies implemented in the previous exercise.

Important   If you don't have a user account established in the Sales group, right-click Sales in Directory Management, point to New, and click User. Add a user account and then continue with this exercise.

▶   **To test the Sales OU software policies**

1. Log on as one of the users who is a member of the Sales group.

2. Press Ctrl+Alt+Delete.

   The Windows NT Security dialog box appears.

   Are you able to lock the workstation?

3. Click Cancel.

4. Click Start.

   Does the Search command appear on the Start menu?

   Does the Run command appear on the Start menu?

Exercise 3: Preventing Group Policy Override

In this exercise, you prevent the Sales OU from overriding the group policy of its parent container.

▶ **To prevent group policy override**

1. Log on as Administrator.
2. Click Start, point to Programs, point to Administrative Tools, and then click Directory Management.

   The Active Directory Manager window appears.
3. Double-click Microsoft, or the name of your domain.
4. Right-click Sales, click Properties, and then click the Group Policy tab.
5. Select SalesSoftware in the Group Policy Objects Link list, and then click Options.
6. Enable the check box labeled No Override: Prevents Other Group Policy Objects From Overriding Policy Set In This One, and then click OK.
7. Click OK again and then close the Active Directory Manager window.

Lesson Summary

In this lesson you learned that software policy settings include group policy for applications and for Windows 2000 and its components. You learned that Windows 2000 saves computer settings in the registry under the HKEY_LOCAL_MACHINE key, and it saves user settings under the HKEY_CURRENT_USER key. You also learned that to modify these settings you open the Active Directory Manager, right-click the Active Directory object (domain or OU) for which you want to modify a GPO, click Properties, and then click the Group Policy tab.

Lesson 4: Using Script Policies and Security Policy Settings

Windows 2000 group policy allows you to assign scripts. To help you create scripts Windows 2000 includes Windows Scripting host, a language-independent scripting host for 32-bit Windows platforms that includes both Visual Basic Scripting Edition (VBScript) and Jscript scripting engines. You can use Windows scripting host to run .VBS and .JS scripts directly on the Windows desktop or command console.

After this lesson, you will be able to
- Describe the use of scripts in Windows 2000.
- Describe the security settings in a GPO.

Estimated lesson time: 10 minutes

Types of Scripts

Windows 2000 group policy allows considerable flexibility when assigning scripts. You can assign startup and shutdown scripts to computers, which Windows 2000 processes when it starts up and shuts down. You can also assign logon and logoff scripts to users, which Windows 2000 processes when the user logs on and logs off, as shown in Figure 21.3.

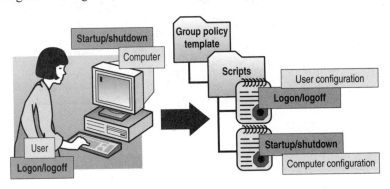

Figure 21.3   Types of scripts

Windows 2000 executes scripts as follows:

- When you assign multiple logon/logoff or startup/shutdown scripts to a user or computer, Windows 2000 executes the scripts from top to bottom. You can determine the order of execution for multiple scripts in the Properties dialog box.

- When a computer is shut down, Windows 2000 first processes logoff scripts and then shutdown scripts. By default, the timeout value for processing scripts is two minutes. If the logoff and shutdown scripts require more than two minutes to process, you must adjust the timeout value with a software policy.

Note   Windows 2000 stores scripts in the GPT, in the Scripts folder.

The Security Configuration Editor

You use the Security Configuration Editor extension to define security configurations for computers and groups. A security configuration consists of security settings applied to each security area supported for Windows 2000 Professional or Windows 2000 Server.

You can configure the following security areas for computers:

- **Account Policies.**   Use to configure password policies, account lockout policies, and Kerberos policies for the domain.

- **Local Policies.**   Use to configure auditing, user rights definition, and security options.

- **Restricted Group.**   Use to configure group memberships for specific groups that are security sensitive. By default, Restricted Group includes the built-in administrative groups, such as Administrators.

- **System Services.**   Use to configure security and startup settings for services running on a computer.

- **Registry.**   Use to configure security on registry keys.

- **File System.**   Use to configure security on specific file paths.

- **Active Directory.**   Use to configure security on specific directory objects in the domain.

- **Public Key Policies.**   Use to configure encrypted data recovery agents, domain roots, trusted certificate authorities, and so forth.

- **IP Security Policies.**   Use to configure network Internet Protocol (IP) security.

Lesson Summary

In this lesson you learned that Windows 2000 group policy allows you to assign scripts and that Windows 2000 includes Windows Scripting host. Windows Scripting host includes both Visual Basic Scripting Edition (VBScript) and Jscript scripting engines. You can use Windows scripting host to run .VBS and .JS scripts directly on the Windows desktop or command console. You learned that you can assign startup and shutdown scripts to computers, which Windows 2000 processes when it starts up and shuts down, or you can assign logon and logoff scripts to users, which Windows 2000 processes when the user logs on and logs off.

You also learned that you use the Security Configuration Editor extension to define security configurations for computers and groups. A security configuration consists of security settings applied to each security area supported for Windows 2000 Professional or Windows Server.

Review

Here are some questions to help you determine if you have learned enough to move on to the next chapter. If you have difficulty answering these questions, please go back and review the material in this chapter before beginning the next chapter. The answers for these questions are located in Appendix A, "Questions and Answers."

1. What is a GPO?

2. What is a GPC?

3. What is a GPT?

4. In what order is group policy implemented through the Active Directory structure?

CHAPTER 22

Administering Network Printers

About This Chapter

In this chapter, you will learn about setting up and administering network printers. You will learn how to manage printers and documents and how to troubleshoot common printing problems.

Before You Begin

To complete this chapter, you must have

- A computer that meets the minimum hardware requirements listed in "Hardware Requirements," on page xxxiii.
- Installed the Windows 2000 Server software on the computer.
- Configured the computer as a domain controller in a domain.

Lesson 1: Understanding Printer Administration

After your printing network is set up, you will be responsible for administering it. You can administer network printers at the print server or remotely over the network. In this lesson you will learn that there are four major types of tasks involved with administering network printers: managing printers, managing documents, troubleshooting printers, and performing tasks that require the Manage Printers permission. In this lesson you will also learn that before you can administer printers, you must know how to access them and control access to them.

After this lesson, you will be able to

- Identify the tasks and requirements for administering a printer.
- Gain access to printers for administration.
- Assign printer permissions to user accounts and groups.

Estimated lesson time: 25 minutes

Managing Printers

One of the most important aspects of printer administration is managing printers. Managing printers includes the following tasks:

- Assigning forms to paper trays
- Setting a separator page
- Pausing, resuming, and canceling documents on a printer
- Redirecting documents
- Taking ownership of a printer

Managing Documents

A second major aspect of printer administration is managing documents. Managing documents includes the following tasks:

- Pausing and resuming a document
- Setting notification, priority, and printing time
- Deleting a document

Troubleshooting Printers

A third major aspect of printer administration is troubleshooting printers. Troubleshooting printers means identifying and resolving all printer problems. The types of problems you need to troubleshoot include the following:

- Printers that are off or offline

- Printers that are out of paper or out of ink
- Users who cannot print or cannot print correctly
- Users who cannot access a printer

Performing Tasks That Require The Manage Printers Permission

The following tasks involved with administering printers require the Manage Printers permission:

- Adding and removing printers
- Sharing printers
- Taking ownership of a printer
- Changing printer properties or permissions

By default, members of the Administrators, Print Operators, Server Operators, and Power Users groups have the Manage Printers permission for all printers.

Note   The Power Users group is only available on computers running Windows 2000 Professional and on computers running Windows 2000 Server that are configured as stand-alone servers.

Accessing Printers

You can gain access to printers for administration by using either the Printers system folder on the Start menu, shown in Figure 22.1, or the Directory Management snap-in, shown in Figure 22.2. You can perform all administrative tasks by gaining access to the printer from the Printers system folder; however, you cannot perform some tasks from Directory Management, such as taking the printer offline.

▶   **To gain access to printers by using the Printers system folder**

1. Click the Start button, point to Settings, and then click Printers.
2. In the Printers system folder, select the appropriate printer icon.
3. On the File menu
   - Click Open to open the printer window to perform print document tasks.
   - Click Properties to open the Properties dialog box to change printer permissions or edit Active Directory information about the printer.

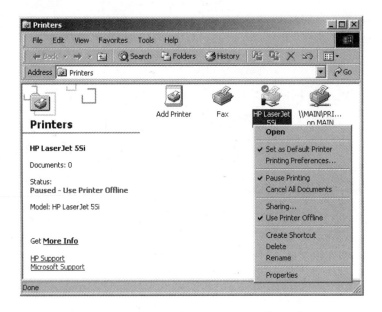

Figure 22.1   Accessing printers using the Printers folder

▶   **To gain access to printers by using Directory Management**

1. Click the Start button, point to Programs, point to Administrative Tools, and then click Directory Management.

2. In Directory Management, on the View menu, click Users, Groups, And Computers As Containers.

3. In the console tree, expand the organizational unit (OU) containing your print server, and then click the print server.

    Note   The printer you installed in Chapter 15 is installed on your domain controller, Server1, so your printer should be located in the Domain Controllers OU. Normally you install printers on a print server, not on a domain controller.

4. Right-click the printer icon in the details pane, and then click Open to open the printer window or click Properties to open the Properties dialog box.

    Important   In this chapter, unless stated otherwise, the procedures assume you are accessing and managing the printing devices from the Printers system folder.

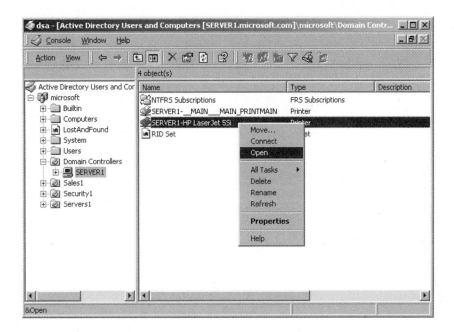

Figure 22.2   Accessing printers using the Directory Management snap-in

Setting Printer Permissions to Control Access

Microsoft Windows 2000 allows you to control printer usage and administration by assigning permissions. By using printer permissions, you can control who can use a printer. You can also assign printer permissions to control who can administer a printer and the level of administration, which can include managing printers and managing documents.

For security reasons, you might need to limit user access to certain printers. You can also use printer permissions to delegate responsibilities for specific printers to users who are not administrators. Windows 2000 provides three levels of printer permissions: Print, Manage Documents, and Manage Printers. Table 22.1 lists the capabilities of each level of permission.

Table 22.1   Printing Capabilities of Windows 2000 Printer Permissions

	Permissions		
Capabilities	Print	Manage documents	Manage printers
Print documents	✓	✓	✓
Pause, resume, restart, and cancel the user's own document	✓	✓	✓
Connect to a printer	✓	✓	✓

(continued)

Capabilities	Permissions		
	Print	Manage documents	Manage printers
Control job settings for all documents		✓	✓
Pause, resume, restart, and cancel all other users' documents		✓	✓
Cancel all documents			✓
Share a printer			✓
Change printer properties			✓
Delete a printer			✓
Change printer permissions			✓

You can allow or deny printer permissions. Denied permissions always override allowed permissions. For example, if you click the Deny check box next to Manage Documents for the Everyone group, no one can manage documents, even if you granted this permission to another user account or group. This is because all user accounts are members of the Everyone group.

Assigning Printer Permissions

By default, Windows 2000 assigns the Print permission for each printer to the built-in Everyone group, allowing all users to send documents to the printer. You can also assign printer permissions to users or groups.

▶   **To assign printer permissions**

1. Open the Properties dialog box for the printer, select the Security tab, and then click Add.
2. In the Select Users, Groups, Or Computers dialog box, select the appropriate user account or group, and then click Add. Repeat this step for all users or groups that you are adding.
3. Click OK.
4. On the Security tab, shown in Figure 22.3, select a user account or group, and then do one of the following:
   - Click the permissions in the bottom part of the dialog box that you want to assign.
   - Click Advanced and assign additional printer permissions that do not fit into the predefined permissions on the Security tab, and then click OK.

   The bottom part of the dialog box shows the permissions granted to the user or group selected in the upper part.
5. Click OK to close the Properties dialog box.

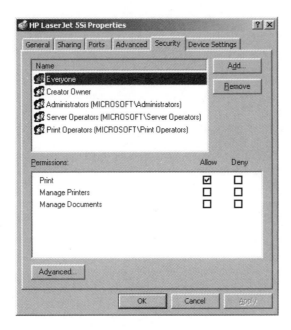

Figure 22.3 Assigning printer permissions

Modifying Printer Permissions

You can change the default printer permissions that Windows 2000 assigned, or that you previously assigned for any user or group.

▶ **To modify printer permissions**

1. Open the Printers folder by clicking Settings on the Windows 2000 Start menu.

2. Right-click the printer and choose Properties.

3. On the Security tab of the Properties dialog box for the printer, select the appropriate user account or group, and then do one of the following:

   ▪ Click the permissions that you want to change for the user or group.

   ▪ Click Advanced to modify additional printer permissions that do not fit into the predefined permissions on the Security tab.

4. Click OK.

Lesson Summary

In this lesson you learned that are four major types of tasks in administering printers: managing printers, managing documents, troubleshooting printers, and performing tasks that require the Manage Printers permission. You learned that you can gain access to printers for administration by using either the Printers system folder on the Start menu or Directory Management. You can perform all administrative tasks by gaining access to the printer from the Printers system folder; however, you cannot perform some tasks from Directory Management.

In this lesson you also learned that Windows 2000 allows you to control printer usage and administration by assigning permissions. You might need to limit access to certain printers, for example, the one used to print checks. You can also use printer permissions to delegate responsibilities for specific printers to users who are not administrators.

Lesson 2: Managing Printers

Managing printers includes assigning forms to paper trays and setting a separator page. In addition, you can pause, resume, and cancel a document if a problem occurs on a print device. If a print device is faulty or you add print devices to your network, you might need to redirect documents to a different printer. In addition, you might need to change who has administrative responsibility for printers, which involves changing ownership.

After this lesson, you will be able to

- Assign forms to paper trays.
- Set a separator page.
- Pause, resume, and cancel documents on a printer.
- Redirect documents to a different printer.
- Take ownership of a printer.

Estimated lesson time: 30 minutes

Assigning Forms to Paper Trays

If a print device has multiple trays that regularly hold different paper sizes, you can assign a form to a specific tray. A form defines a paper size. Users can then select the paper size from within their application. When the user prints, Windows 2000 automatically routes the print job to the paper tray that holds the correct form. Examples of forms include the following: Legal, A4, Envelopes #10, and Letter Small.

▶ **To assign a form to a paper tray**

1. Right-click the icon of the appropriate printing device, and then click Properties.
2. In the Properties dialog box for the printer, click the Device Settings tab.
3. In the box next to each paper tray, click the form for the paper type for the tray, as shown in Figure 22.4.
4. Click OK.

After you have set up a paper tray, users specify the paper size from within applications. Windows 2000 knows in which paper tray the form is located.

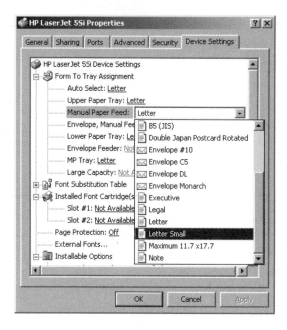

Figure 22.4 Setting forms for a printer

Setting a Separator Page

A separator page is a file that contains print device commands. Separator pages have two functions:

- To identify and separate printed documents.

- To switch print devices between print modes. Some print devices can switch between print modes that take advantage of different device features. You can use separator pages to specify the correct page description language. For example, you can specify PostScript or Printer Control Language (PCL) for a print device that can switch between different print modes but cannot automatically detect which language a print job uses.

Windows 2000 includes four separator page files. They are located in the *system-root*\System32 folder. Table 22.2 lists the file name and describes the function for each of the included separator page files.

Table 22.2 Separator Page Files

File name	Function
Sysprint.sep	Prints a page before each document. Compatible with PostScript print devices.
Pcl.sep	Switches the print mode to PCL for HP-series print devices and prints a page before each document.

| Pscript.sep | Switches the print mode to PostScript for HP-series print devices but does not print a page before each document. |
| Sysprtj.sep | A version of Sysprint.sep that uses Japanese characters. |

Once you have decided to use a separator page and have chosen an appropriate one, you use the Advanced tab in the printer's Properties dialog box to have the separator page printed at the beginning of each print job.

▶ **To set up a separator page**

1. On the Advanced tab in the Properties dialog box for the printer, click Separator Page.

2. In the Separator Page box, type the name of the separator page file. You can also browse for the file.

3. Click OK, and then click OK again.

Pausing, Resuming, and Canceling Documents

Pausing and resuming a printer or canceling all documents on a printer might be necessary if there is a printing problem.

To pause, resume, or cancel all documents, right-click a printing device, click Open, and then click the appropriate command. If you right-click a printer in the Printers folder, you can choose the commands directly from the shortcut menu.

Table 22.3 describes the tasks that you might perform when you manage printers, how to perform the tasks, and examples of situations in which you might perform these tasks.

Table 22.3   Managing Printers Tasks

Task	Action	Example
To pause printing	Click Pause Printing. A check mark appears next to the Pause Printing command, which indicates that the printer is paused.	Pause the printer if there is a problem with the printer or print device until you fix the problem.
To resume printing	Click Pause Printing. The check mark next to the Pause Printing command disappears, which indicates that the printer is active.	Resume printing after you fix a problem with a printer or print device.

(continued)

Task	Action	Example
To cancel all documents	Click Cancel All Documents. All documents are deleted from the printer.	Cancel all documents when you need to clear a print queue after old documents that no longer need to print have accumulated.

Note   You can also pause a printer by taking the printer offline. When you take a printer offline, documents stay in the print queue, even when the print server is shut down and then restarted. To take a printer offline, open the printer window, and on the Printer menu, click Use Printer Offline.

Redirecting Documents to a Different Printer

You can redirect documents to a different printer. For example, if a printer is connected to a faulty print device, redirect the documents so that users do not need to resubmit them. You can redirect all print jobs for a printer, but you cannot redirect specific documents. The new printer must use the same printer driver as the current printer.

▶   **To redirect documents to a different printer**

1. Open the printer window, and on the Printer menu, click Properties.
2. In the Properties dialog box, click the Ports tab.
3. Click Add Port.
4. In the Available Port Types list, click Local Port, and then click the New Port button.
5. In the Port Name dialog box, in the Enter A Port Name box, type the Universal Naming Convention (UNC) name for the printer to which you are redirecting documents (for example, \\prntsrv6\\HPLaser5), as shown in Figure 22.5.
6. Click OK.
7. Click Close.
8. Click OK.

If another print device is available for the current print server, you can continue to use the same printer and configure the printer to use the other print device. To configure a printer to use another local or network print device that uses the same printer driver, select the appropriate port on the print server, and cancel the selection of the current port.

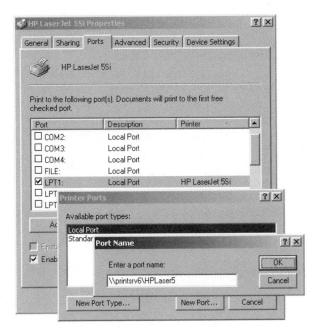

Figure 22.5   Redirecting documents to another printer

Taking Ownership of a Printer

There might be times when the owner of a printer can no longer manage that printer and you will need to take ownership. Taking ownership of a printer enables you to change administrative responsibility for a printer. By default, the user who installed the printer owns it. If that user can no longer administer the printer, you should take ownership of it—for example, if the current owner leaves the company.

The following users can take ownership of a printer:

- A user or a member of a group who has the Manage Printers permission for the printer.
- Members of the Administrators, Print Operators, Server Operators, and Power Users groups. By default these groups have the Manage Printers permission, which allows them to take ownership.

▶   **To take ownership of a printer**

1. In the Properties dialog box for the printer, click the Security tab, and then click Advanced.
2. In the Access Control Settings dialog box, click the Owner tab, and then click your user account under Change Owner To, as shown in Figure 22.6.

Note If you are a member of the Administrators group and you want the Administrators group to take ownership of the printer, click the Administrators group.

3. Click OK, and then click OK again.

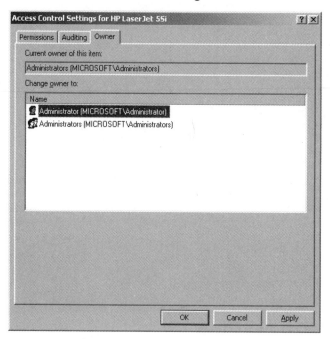

Figure 22.6 Taking ownership of a printer

Practice: Performing Printer Management

In this practice you perform three tasks that are part of managing printers. In the first exercise, you assign forms to paper trays. In the second exercise, you set up a separator page. In the third exercise you learn how to take ownership of a printer.

Exercise 1: Assigning Forms to Paper Trays

In this exercise, you assign a paper type (form) to a paper tray so that when users print to a specified form, the print job is automatically routed to and adjusted for the correct tray.

▶ **To assign forms to paper trays**

1. Select Printers from the Settings menu of the Windows 2000 Start menu.
2. Right-click the icon of your printer, and then click Properties.

3. In the Properties dialog box, click the Device Settings tab.

    Notice that there are multiple selections under Form To Tray Assignment. Some of the selections are labeled Not Available because they depend on options that are not installed.

4. Click Lower Paper Tray, and then select Legal.

    Whenever a user prints on legal size paper, Windows 2000 will instruct the printer to use paper from the Lower Paper Tray.

5. Click Apply and leave the Properties dialog box open for the next exercise.

Exercise 2: Setting Up Separator Pages

In this exercise, you set up a separator page to print between documents. This separator page includes the user's name and the date and time that the document was printed.

▶ **To set up a separator page**

1. Click the Separator Page tab of the Properties dialog box.

2. In the Separator Page dialog box, click Browse.

    Windows 2000 displays another Separator Page dialog box.

    What are the four separator page files from which you can select?

3. Select Sysprint.sep, and then click Open.

    Windows 2000 displays the first Separator Page dialog box again.

4. Click OK.

    Windows 2000 will now print a separator page between print jobs.

5. Leave the Properties dialog box open for the next exercise.

Exercise 3: Taking Ownership of a Printer

In this exercise, you practice taking ownership of a printer.

▶ **To take ownership of a printer**

1. Click the Security tab of the Properties dialog box.

2. On the Security tab, click Advanced, and then click the Owner tab.

    Who currently owns the printer?

3. To take ownership of the printer, select another user in the Name box.

4. If you actually wanted to take ownership you would click Apply now, but click Cancel instead to leave the ownership unchanged.

5. Close the Properties dialog box and the Printers folder, and then log off Windows 2000.

Lesson Summary

In this lesson you learned that managing printers includes assigning forms to paper trays, setting a separator page, pausing, resuming, and canceling documents on a printer, redirecting documents to a different printer, and taking ownership of a printer. In addition, you learned how to change who has administrative responsibility for printers, which involves changing ownership.

Lesson 3: Managing Documents

In addition to managing printers, Windows 2000 allows you to manage documents. Managing documents includes pausing, resuming, restarting, and canceling a document if there is a printing problem. In addition, you can set someone to notify when a print job is finished, the priority to allow a critical document to print before other documents, and a specific time for a document to print.

After this lesson, you will be able to

- Pause, resume, restart, and cancel the printing of a document.
- Set a notification, priority, and printing time.
- Delete a document from the print queue.

Estimated lesson time: 20 minutes

Pausing, Restarting, and Canceling a Document

If there is a printing problem with a specific document, you can pause and resume printing of the document. Additionally, you can restart or cancel a document. You must have the Manage Documents permission for the appropriate printer to perform these actions. Because the creator of a document has the default permissions to manage that document, users can perform any of these actions on their own documents.

To manage a document, right-click the printing device for the document and click Open. Select the appropriate document(s), click the Document menu, and then click the appropriate command to pause, resume, restart from the beginning, or cancel a document, as shown in Figure 22.7.

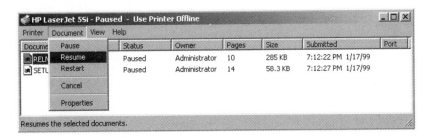

Figure 22.7   Managing documents

Table 22.4 describes the tasks that you might perform when you manage individual documents, how to perform the tasks, and examples of situations in which you might perform these tasks.

Table 22.4   Managing Document Tasks

Task	Action	Example
To pause printing a document	Select the documents for which you want to pause printing, and then click Pause. (The status changes to Paused.)	Pause printing when there is a problem with the document.
To resume printing a document	Select the documents for which you want to resume printing, and then click Resume. (The status changes to Printing.)	Resume printing after you fix a problem with a paused document.
To restart printing a document	Select the documents for which you want to restart printing, and then click Restart. Restart causes printing to start from the beginning of the document.	Restart printing of a partially printed document after you fix a problem with the document or the print device.
To cancel printing a document	Select the documents for which you want to cancel printing, and then click Cancel. You can also cancel a document by pressing the Delete key.	When a document has the wrong printer settings or is no longer needed, delete it before it prints.

Setting Notification, Priority, and Printing Time

You can control print jobs by setting the notification, priority, and printing time. To perform these document management tasks, you must have the Manage Documents permission for the appropriate printer.

You set the notification, priority, and printing time for a document on the General tab of the Properties dialog box for the document, as shown in Figure 22.8. To open the Properties dialog box for one or more documents, first select the documents in the Printer window, click Document on the Printer window menu bar, and then click Properties.

Table 22.5 describes the tasks that you might perform when you control print jobs, how to perform the tasks, and examples of situations in which you might perform these tasks.

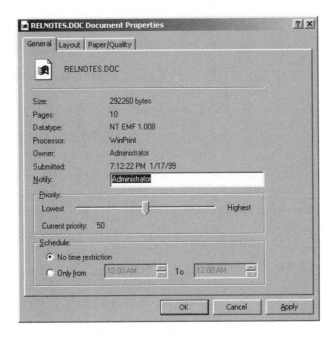

Figure 22.8   Setting notification, priority, and printing time for a document

Table 22.5   Setting a Notification, Changing Priority, and Scheduling Print Times

Task	Action	Example
Set a notification	In the Notify box, type the logon name of the user who should receive the notification. By default, Windows 2000 enters the name of the user who printed the document.	Change the print notification when someone other than the user who printed the document needs to retrieve it.
Change a document priority	Move the Priority slider to the priority that you want. The highest priority is 99 and the lowest is 1.	Change a priority so that a critical document prints before other documents.
Schedule print times	To restrict print times, click Only From in the Schedule section, and then set the hours between which you want the document to print.	Set the print time for a large document so that it will print during off hours, such as late at night.

Practice: Managing Documents

In this practice, you manage documents by printing a document, setting a notification for a document, changing the priority for a document, and then canceling a document.

▶   **To verify that a printer is offline**

1. Log on to your domain as Administrator.
2. Click the Start button, point to Settings, and then click Printers.
3. In the Printers system folder, click the printer icon.
4. Do one of the following to verify that the printer is offline:
   - On the File menu, verify that Use Printer Offline is selected.
   - Right-click the printer icon and verify that Use Printer Offline is selected.
   - If the Printers folder is displayed in Web view, verify that Use Printer Offline is displayed in the left portion of the folder window.
5. On the File menu (or by right-clicking the printer icon), verify that Set As Default Printer is selected.

   The printer icon will display a check mark to show it is the default. If necessary, press F5 to update the display.
6. Minimize the Printers system folder.

Note   Keep the printer offline to prevent it from trying to communicate with a nonexistent print device. This will eliminate error messages in later exercises when documents are spooled.

▶   **To print a document**

Print the file Relnotes. It is located in the root directory of the CD-ROM you used to install Windows 2000 Server.

▶   **To set a notification**

1. Restore the Printers system folder.
2. Double-click Printer1.
3. In the Printer window, select Relnotes, and then click Properties on the Document menu.

   Windows 2000 displays the Relnotes Document Properties dialog box with the General tab active.

   Which user is specified in the Notify box? Why?

Note   To change the person to be notified, you would type in the name of the user in the Notify box and click apply.

▶   **To increase the priority of a document**

1. In the Relnotes Document Properties dialog box, on the General tab, notice the default priority.

   What is the current priority? Is it the lowest or highest priority?

2. In the Priority box, move the slider to the right to increase the priority of the document, and then click OK.

   Nothing changes visibly in the Printer1 - Use Printer Offline window.

3. On the Printer menu, click Use Printer Offline to remove the check mark, and then immediately click Use Printer Offline again.

   Note If Windows 2000 displays a Printers Folder dialog box with an error message informing you that the printer port is unavailable, finish the following procedure, and then, in the dialog box, click Cancel.

4. Check the status of Relnotes to confirm that Windows 2000 has started to print this document.

▶   **To cancel a document**

1. Select Relnotes in the Printer window document list.

2. On the Document menu, click Cancel.

   Notice that the Status column changes to Deleting. After several minutes Relnotes will be removed from the document list.

   Tip You can also cancel a document by pressing the Delete key.

3. Close the Printer window, and then close the Printers folder.

Lesson Summary

In this lesson you learned that managing documents includes pausing, resuming, restarting, and canceling a document; setting who is notified when a print job is finished; setting the document priority to allow a critical document to print before other documents; and setting a specific time for a document to print. You must have the Manage Documents permission for the appropriate printer to perform these actions. The creator of a document has the default permissions to manage that document, so users can perform any of these actions on their own documents.

Lesson 4: Administering Printers Using a Web Browser

Windows 2000 enables you to manage printers from any computer running a Web browser, regardless of whether the computer is running Windows 2000 or has the correct printer driver installed. All management tasks that you perform with Windows 2000 management tools are the same when you use a Web browser. The difference in administering with a Web browser is the interface, which is a Web-based interface. To gain access to a printer by using a Web browser, the print server on which the printer resides must have Internet Information Services (IIS) installed.

After this lesson, you will be able to

- Describe the advantages of administering printers using a Web browser.
- Describe how to administer printers using a Web browser.

Estimated lesson time: 5 minutes

Using a Web Browser to Manage Printers

The following are the advantages of using a Web browser to manage printers:

- It allows you to administer printers from any computer running a Web browser, regardless of whether the computer is running Windows 2000 or has the correct printer driver installed.
- It allows you to customize the interface. For example, you can create your own Web page containing a floor plan with the locations of the printers and the links to the printers.
- It provides a summary page listing the status of all printers on a print server.
- It can report real-time print device data, such as whether the print device is in power saving mode, if the printer driver makes such information available. This information is not available from the Printers system folder.

Accessing Printers Using a Web Browser

If you want to gain access to all printers on a print server by using a Web browser, open the Web browser, and then in the Address box, type

http://*print_server_name*/printers

If you want to gain access to a specific printer by using a Web browser, open the Web browser, and then in the Address box, type

http://*server_name*/*printer_share_name*

Lesson Summary

In this lesson you learned about the advantages of using a Web browser to administer printers. One benefit of using a Web browser to administer printers is that it allows you to administer printers from any computer running a Web browser, regardless of whether the computer is running Windows 2000 or has the correct printer driver installed.

Lesson 5: Troubleshooting Common Printing Problems

In this lesson you will learn about some common printing problems and how to troubleshoot them.

After this lesson, you will be able to
- Describe how to troubleshoot some common printing problems.

Estimated lesson time: 5 minutes

Examining the Problem

When you detect a printing problem, always verify that the print device is plugged in, turned on, and that it is connected to the print server. For a network-interface print device, verify that there is a network connection between the print device and the print server.

To determine the cause of a problem, first try printing from a different program to verify that the problem is with the printer and not with the program. If the problem is with the printer, ask the following questions:

- Can other users print normally? If this is the case, the problem is most likely due to insufficient permissions, no network connection, or client computer problems.
- Does the print server use the correct printer driver for the print device?
- Is the print server operational and is there enough disk space for spooling?
- Does the client computer have the correct printer driver?

Reviewing Common Printing Problems

There are certain printing problems that are common to most network printing environments. Table 22.6 describes some of these common printing problems, as well as some possible causes and solutions.

Table 22.6   Common Printing Problems, Causes, and Solutions

Problem	Possible cause	Solution
A user receives an Access Denied message when trying to configure a printer from an application (for example, earlier versions of Microsoft Excel).	The user does not have the appropriate permission to change printer configurations.	Change the user's permission, or configure the printer for the user.

The document does not print completely or comes out garbled.	The printer driver is incorrect.	Install the correct printer driver.
The hard disk starts thrashing and the document does not reach the print server.	There is insufficient hard disk space for spooling.	Create more free space on the hard disk.

Lesson Summary

In this lesson you learned about a few basic things to check when you have a printing problem. You also were given a list of some common printing problems and some suggested causes and solutions. In many cases, you will find that in troubleshooting a problem you must investigate the problem as thoroughly as you can and then begin trying logical solutions until you discover one that works.

Review

Here are some questions to help you determine if you have learned enough to move on to the next chapter. If you have difficulty answering these questions, please go back and review the material in this chapter before beginning the next chapter. The answers for these questions are located in Appendix A, "Questions and Answers."

1. What printer permission does a user need to change the priority on another user's document?

2. In an environment where many users print to the same print device, how can you help reduce the likelihood of users picking up the wrong documents?

3. Can you redirect a single document?

4. A user needs to print a very large document. How can the user print the job after hours, without being present while the document prints?

5. What are the advantages of using a Web browser to administer printing?

CHAPTER 23

Managing Data Storage

About This Chapter

This chapter introduces data storage management on NTFS-formatted volumes. You will learn about compression, which allows you to store more data on a disk, and you will learn about disk quotas, which allow you to control how much space a user can use on a disk. You will also learn about defragmenting a disk. Defragmenting a disk allows your system to access files and save files and folders more efficiently.

Before You Begin

To complete this chapter, you must have

- A computer that meets the minimum hardware requirements listed in "Hardware Requirements," on page xxxiii.

- Installed the Windows 2000 Server software on the computer.

- Configured the computer as a domain controller in a domain.

Lesson 1: Managing NTFS Compression

NT file system (NTFS) compression enables you to compress files and folders. Compressed files and folders occupy less space on an NTFS-formatted volume, which enables you to store more data. Each file and folder on an NTFS volume has a *compression state*, which is either compressed or uncompressed.

After this lesson, you will be able to

- Manage disk compression.
- Compress and uncompress files and folders.

Estimated lesson time: 40 minutes

Using Compressed Files and Folders

Compressed files can be read, and written to, by any Microsoft Windows-based or MS-DOS-based application without first being uncompressed by another program. When an application, such as Microsoft Word for Windows, or an operating system command, such as Copy, requests access to a compressed file, NTFS automatically uncompresses the file before making it available. When you close or explicitly save a file, NTFS compresses it again.

NTFS allocates disk space based on the uncompressed file size. If you copy a compressed file to an NTFS volume with enough space for the compressed file, but not enough space for the uncompressed file, you may get an error message stating that there is not enough disk space for the file. The file will not be copied to the volume.

Compressing Files and Folders

You can set the compression state of folders and files and you can change the color that is used to display compressed files and folders in Microsoft Windows Explorer.

Note NTFS encryption and compression are mutually exclusive. For that reason, if you select the Encrypt Contents To Secure Data check box, you cannot compress the folder or file.

If you want to set the compression state of a folder or file, right-click the folder or file in Windows Explorer, click Properties, and then click the Advanced button. In the Advanced Attributes dialog box, select the Compress Contents To Save Disk Space check box, as shown in Figure 23.1. Click OK, and then click Apply in the Properties dialog box.

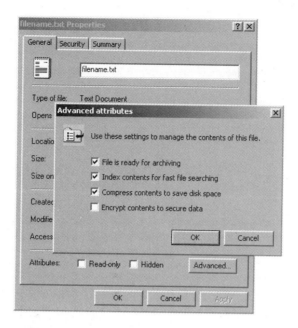

Figure 23.1   Advanced Attributes dialog box

Important   To change the compression state for a file or folder, you must have Write permission for the file or folder.

The compression state for a folder does not reflect the compression state of the files and subfolders in that folder. A folder can be compressed, yet all of the files in that folder can be uncompressed. Alternatively, an uncompressed folder can contain compressed files. When you compress a folder, Windows 2000 displays the Confirm Attribute Changes dialog box, which has the two additional options explained in Table 23.1.

Table 23.1   **Confirm Attribute Changes Dialog Box Options**

Option	Description
Apply Changes To This Folder Only	Compresses only the folder that you have selected.
Apply Changes To This Folder, Subfolder, And Files	Compresses the folder and all subfolders and files that are contained within it and added to it subsequently.

Note   Windows 2000 does not support NTFS compression for cluster sizes larger than 4 KB because compression on large clusters causes performance degradation. If you select a larger cluster size when you format an NTFS volume, compression is not available for that volume.

Selecting an Alternate Display Color for Compressed Files and Folders

Windows Explorer makes it easy for you to quickly determine if a file or folder is compressed, by allowing you to select a different display color for compressed files and folders to distinguish them from uncompressed files and folders.

▶ **To set an alternative display color for compressed files and folders**

1. In Windows Explorer, on the Tools menu, select Folder Options.
2. On the View tab, select the Display Compressed Files And Folders With Alternate Color check box.

Copying and Moving Compressed Files and Folders

There are rules that determine whether the compression state of files and folders is retained when you copy or move them within and between NTFS and FAT volumes. The following sections describe how Windows 2000 treats the compression state of a file or folder when you copy or move a compressed file or folder within or between NTFS volumes or between NTFS and file allocation table (FAT) volumes.

Copying a File Within an NTFS Volume

When you copy a file within an NTFS volume (shown as A in Figure 23.2), the file inherits the compression state of the target folder. For example, if you copy a compressed file to an uncompressed folder, the file is automatically uncompressed.

Moving a File or Folder Within an NTFS Volume

When you move a file or folder within an NTFS volume (shown as B in Figure 23.2), the file or folder retains its original compression state. For example, if you move a compressed file to an uncompressed folder, the file remains compressed.

Copying a File or Folder Between NTFS Volumes

When you copy a file or folder between NTFS volumes (shown as C in Figure 23.2), the file or folder inherits the compression state of the target folder.

Moving a File or Folder Between NTFS Volumes

When you move a file or folder between NTFS volumes (shown as C in Figure 23.2), the file or folder inherits the compression state of the target folder. Because Windows 2000 treats a move as a copy and then a delete, the files inherit the compression state of the target folder.

Moving or Copying a File or Folder to a FAT Volume

Windows 2000 supports compression only for NTFS files. Because of this, when you move or copy a compressed NTFS file or folder to a FAT volume, Windows 2000 automatically uncompresses the file or folder.

Moving or Copying a Compressed File or Folder to a Floppy Disk

When you move or copy a compressed NTFS file or folder to a floppy disk, Windows 2000 automatically uncompresses the file or folder.

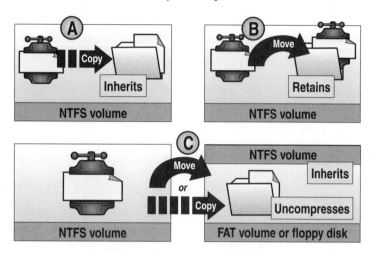

Figure 23.2   Effects of copying and moving compressed folders and files

---

Note   When you copy a compressed NTFS file, Windows 2000 uncompresses the file, copies the file, and then compresses the file again as a new file. This may cause performance degradation.

Using NTFS Compression

The following list provides best practices for using compression on NTFS volumes:

- Because some file types compress more than others, select file types to compress based on the anticipated resulting file size. For example, because Windows bitmap files contain more redundant data than application executable files, this file type compresses to a smaller size. Bitmaps will often compress to less than 50 percent of the original file size, whereas application files rarely compress to less than 75 percent of the original size.

- Do not store compressed files, such as PKZIP files, in a compressed folder. Windows 2000 will attempt to compress the file, wasting system time and yielding no additional disk space.

- To make it easier to locate compressed data, use a different display color for compressed folders and files.

- Compress static data rather than data that changes frequently. Compressing and uncompressing files incurs some system overhead. By choosing to compress files that are infrequently accessed, you minimize the amount of system time that is dedicated to compression and uncompression activities.

- NTFS compression can cause performance degradation when you copy and move files. When a compressed file is copied, it is uncompressed, copied, and then compressed again as a new file. Compress static data rather than data that changes frequently or is copied or moved frequently.

Practice: Managing NTFS Compression

In this practice you compress files and folders. You then display the compressed files and folders in a different color. Then you uncompress a file and test the effects that copying and moving files have on compression.

Note   In this practice it is assumed that you installed Windows 2000 on the C drive and that the C drive is formatted with NTFS. If you installed Windows 2000 on a different partition and that partition is formatted with NTFS, use that drive letter when the practice refers to drive C.

Exercise 1: Compressing Files in an NTFS Partition

In this exercise, you use Windows Explorer to compress files and folders to make more disk space available on your NTFS partition. You also configure Windows Explorer to display the compressed files and folders in a different color. Next you uncompress a file. Finally you view the effects that copying and moving files has on compressed files.

▶   **To view the capacity and free space for drive C**

1. Log on to your domain as Administrator, right-click the My Computer icon on your desktop, and then click Explore.

2. Right-click drive C, and then click Properties.

   Windows 2000 displays the Local Disk (C:) Properties dialog box with the General tab active.

   What is the capacity of drive C?

   What is the free space on drive C?

3. Click Cancel to close the Local Disk (C:) Properties dialog box and return to Windows Explorer.

▶ **To compress a folder tree**

1. In Windows Explorer, expand Local Disk (C:).

2. Create a folder in C:\ and name it CompTest.

Note   To create a folder in C:\, click Local Disk (C:), on the File menu click New, and then click Folder. Type **CompTest** and then press Enter.

---

3. Double-click CompTest to expand the folder.

4. Create a folder in C:\CompTest and name it CompTest2.

5. Right-click the CompTest folder, and then click Properties.

   Windows 2000 displays the CompTest Properties dialog box with the General tab active.

6. On the General tab, click the Advanced button.

   Windows 2000 displays the Advanced Attributes dialog box.

7. Select the Compress Contents To Save Disk Space check box.

   Why is the Encrypt Contents To Secure Data Option no longer available?

8. Click OK to return to the CompTest Properties dialog box.

9. Click Apply to apply your settings.

   Windows 2000 displays the Confirm Attribute Changes dialog box, prompting you to specify whether to compress only this folder or this folder and all sub-folders.

10. Select the Apply Changes To This Folder, Subfolders, And Files check box, and then click OK.

    Windows 2000 displays the Applying Attributes message box, indicating the progress of the operation and the paths and names of folders and files as they are compressed. Because there is little data on drive C, compression will complete too quickly for you to view this dialog box.

11. If Windows 2000 displays an Error Applying Attributes dialog box, click Ignore All to continue.

12. Click OK to close the Properties dialog box.

▶ **To display compressed files and folders with an alternate color**

1. In Windows Explorer, click Local Disk (C:) and, on the Tools menu, click Folder Options.

   The Folder Options window appears with the General tab selected.

2. Click the View tab.

3. In the Advanced Settings list, select the Display Compressed Files And Folders With Alternate Color check box.

4. Click OK to apply your changes.

The names of the compressed files and folders are displayed in blue.

► **To uncompress a folder**

1. In Windows Explorer, expand C:\CompTest.

2. In the CompTest folder, right-click CompTest2, and then click Properties.

Windows 2000 displays the CompTest2 Properties dialog box with the General tab active.

3. On the General tab, click the Advanced button.

Windows 2000 displays the Advanced Attributes dialog box.

4. Clear the Compress Contents To Save Disk Space check box, and then click OK to apply your settings and return to the CompTest2 Properties dialog box.

5. Click OK to apply your settings and close the CompTest2 Properties dialog box.

Since the CompTest2 folder is empty, Windows 2000 does not display the Confirm Attributes Changes dialog box asking you to specify whether to uncompress only this folder or this folder and all subfolders.

6. Press F5 to refresh the view in Windows Explorer.

What indication do you have that the CompTest2 folder is no longer compressed?

Exercise 2: Copying and Moving Files

In this exercise, you see the effects that copying and moving files has on compressed files.

► **To create a compressed file**

1. In Windows Explorer, click the CompTest folder.

2. On the File menu, click New, and then click Text Document.

3. Type **Text1** and then press Enter.

How can you verify that Text1 is compressed?

► **To copy a compressed file to an uncompressed folder**

1. Copy Text1 to the C:\CompTest\CompTest2 folder.

Make sure that you copy (hold down the Ctrl key while you drag the file) and do not move the file.

2. Examine the properties for Text1 in the CompTest2 folder.

   Is C:\CompTest\CompTest2\Text1.txt compressed or uncompressed? Why?

▶ **To move a compressed file to an uncompressed folder**

1. Examine the properties of C:\CompTest\Text1.txt.

   Is Text1.txt compressed or uncompressed?

2. Move Text1.txt to the C:\CompTest\CompTest2 folder. If the Confirm File Replace dialog box appears, click OK.

3. Examine the properties of Text1.txt in the CompTest2 folder.

   Is Text1.txt compressed or uncompressed? Why?

▶ **To uncompress the NTFS folder**

1. In Windows Explorer, right-click C:\CompTest, and then click Properties.

   Windows 2000 displays the CompTest Properties dialog box with the General tab active.

2. On the General tab, click the Advanced button.

   Windows 2000 displays the Advanced Attributes dialog box.

3. Clear the Compress Contents To Save Disk Space check box, and then click OK to return to the CompTest Properties dialog box.

4. Click Apply.

   Windows 2000 displays the Confirm Attributes Changes dialog box, prompting you to specify whether to uncompress only this folder or this folder and all subfolders.

5. Click Apply Changes To This Folder, Subfolders, And All Files, and then click OK.

   Windows 2000 briefly displays the Applying Attributes message box. This might happen so fast that you do not see it.

6. Click OK to close the Properties dialog box, and then close Windows Explorer.

Lesson Summary

In this lesson you learned how to compress and uncompress files and folders on an NTFS volume. You learned that compressed files can be read, and written to, by any Microsoft Windows-based or MS-DOS-based application without first being uncompressed by another program. The Windows NTFS file system automatically uncompresses the file before making it available, and when you close or explicitly save a file, NTFS compresses it again.

You learned how to change the color that is used to display compressed files and folders in Windows Explorer to distinguish them from uncompressed files and folders. You also learned that NTFS encryption and compression are mutually exclusive.

Finally, you learned about copying and moving compressed files. When you copy a file within an NTFS volume, the file inherits the compression state of the target folder. When you move a file or folder within an NTFS volume, the file or folder retains its original compression state. When you copy or move a file or folder between NTFS volumes, the file or folder inherits the compression state of the target folder. Finally, when you move or copy a compressed NTFS file or folder to a FAT volume or a floppy disk, Windows 2000 automatically uncompresses the file or folder.

Lesson 2: Managing Disk Quotas

You use disk quotas to manage storage growth in distributed environments. Disk quotas allow you to allocate disk space usage to users based on the files and folders that they own. You can set disk quotas, quota thresholds, and quota limits for all users and for individual users. You can also monitor the amount of hard disk space that users have used and the amount that they have left against their quota.

After this lesson, you will be able to

- Configure and manage disk quotas.

Estimated lesson time: 20 minutes

Understanding Windows 2000 Disk Quota Management

Windows 2000 disk quotas track and control disk usage on a per-user, per-volume basis. Windows 2000 tracks disk quotas for each volume, even if the volumes are on the same hard disk. Because quotas are tracked on a per-user basis, every user's disk space is tracked regardless of the folder in which the user stores files. Table 23.2 describes the characteristics of Windows 2000 disk quotas.

Table 23.2   Disk Quota Characteristics and Descriptions

Characteristic	Description
Disk usage is based on file and folder ownership.	Windows 2000 calculates disk space usage for users based on the files and folders that they own. When a user copies or saves a new file to an NTFS volume or takes ownership of a file on an NTFS volume, Windows 2000 charges the disk space for the file against the user's quota limit.
Disk quotas do not use compression.	Windows 2000 ignores compression when it calculates hard disk space usage. Users are charged for each uncompressed byte, regardless of how much hard disk space is actually used. This is done partially because file compression produces different degrees of compression for different types of files. Different uncompressed file types that are the same size may end up to be very different sizes when they are compressed.
Free space for applications is based on quota limit.	When you enable disk quotas, the free space that Windows 2000 reports to applications for the volume is the amount of space remaining within the user's disk quota limit.

Note   Disk quotas can only be applied to Windows 2000 NTFS volumes.

You use disk quotas to monitor and control hard disk space usage. System administrators can do the following:

- Set a disk quota limit to specify the amount of disk space for each user.
- Set a disk quota warning to specify when Windows 2000 should log an event, indicating that the user is nearing his or her limit.
- Enforce disk quota limits and deny users access if they exceed their limit, or allow them continued access.
- Log an event when a user exceeds a specified disk space threshold. The threshold could be when users exceed their quota limit, or when they exceed their warning level.

After you enable disk quotas for a volume, Windows 2000 collects disk usage data for all users who own files and folders on the volume. This allows you to monitor volume usage on a per-user basis. By default, only members of the Administrators group can view and change quota settings. However, you can allow users to view quota settings.

Setting Disk Quotas

You can enable disk quotas and enforce disk quota warnings and limits for all users or for individual users.

If you want to enable disk quotas, open the Properties dialog box for a disk, click the Quota tab, and configure the options that are described in Table 23.3 and displayed in Figure 23.3.

Table 23.3   Quota Tab Options

Option	Description
Enable Quota Management	Select this check box to enable disk quota management.
Deny Disk Space To Users Exceeding Quota Limit	Select this check box so that when users exceed their hard disk space allocation, they receive an "out of disk space" message and cannot write to the volume.
Do Not Limit Disk Usage	Click this option when you do not want to limit the amount of hard disk space for users.
Limit Disk Space To	Configure the amount of disk space that users can use.

Set Warning Level To	Configure the amount of disk space that users can fill before Windows 2000 logs an event, indicating that a user is nearing his or her limit.
Quota Entries	Click this button to open the Quota Entries For dialog box, where you can add a new entry, delete an entry, and view the per user quota information.

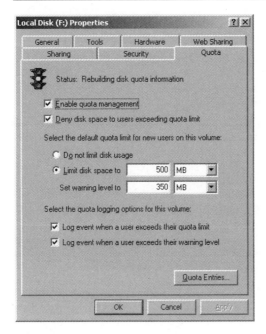

Figure 23.3 Quota tab of the Properties dialog box for a disk

▶ **To enforce identical quota limits for all users**

1. In the Limit Disk Space To box and the Set Warning Level To box, enter the values for the limit and warning level that you want to set.

2. Select the Deny Disk Space To Users Exceeding Quota Limit check box.

Windows 2000 will monitor usage and will not allow users to create files or folders on the volume when they exceed the limit.

Determining the Status of Disk Quotas

You can determine the status of disk quotas in the Properties dialog box for a disk by checking the traffic light icon, and reading the status message to its right (see Figure 23.3):

- A red traffic light indicates that disk quotas are disabled.
- A yellow traffic light indicates that Windows 2000 is rebuilding disk quota information.
- A green traffic light indicates that the disk quota system is active.

▶ **To enforce different quota limits for one or more specific users**

1. Open the Properties dialog box for a disk, click the Quota tab, and then click the Quota Entries button.
2. In the Quota Entries For dialog box, shown in Figure 23.4, double-click the user account for which you want to set a disk quota limit or create an entry by clicking New Quota Entry on the Quota menu.
3. Configure the disk space limit and the warning level for each individual user.

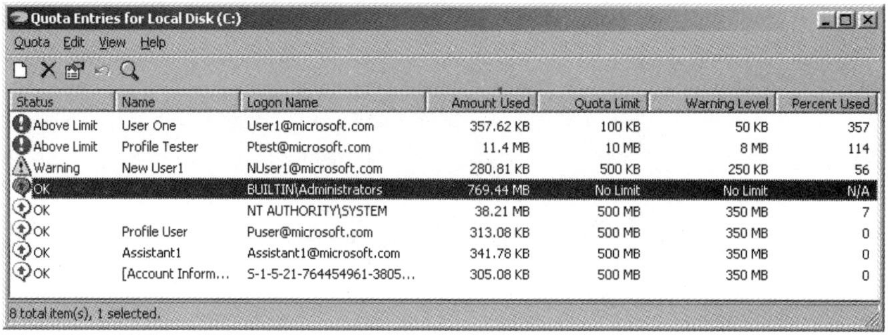

Figure 23.4   Quota Entries dialog box

Monitoring Disk Quotas

You use the Quota Entries For dialog box to monitor usage for all users who have copied, saved, or taken ownership of files and folders on the volume. Windows 2000 will scan the volume and monitor the amount of disk space in use by each user. Use the Quota Entries For dialog box to view the following:

- The amount of hard disk space that each user uses.
- Users who are over their quota-warning threshold, which is signified by a yellow triangle.
- Users who are over their quota limit, which is signified by a red circle.

- The warning threshold and the disk quota limit for each user.

Best Uses of Disk Quotas

The following list provides guidelines for using disk quotas:

- If you enable disk quota settings on the volume where Windows 2000 is installed and your user account has a disk quota limit, log on as Administrator to install additional Windows 2000 components and applications. By doing so, Window 2000 will not charge the disk space that you use to install applications against the disk quota allowance for your user account.

- You can monitor hard disk usage and generate hard disk usage information without preventing users from saving data. To do so, clear the Deny Disk Space To Users Exceeding Quota Limit check box when you enable disk quotas.

- Set more restrictive default limits for all user accounts, and then modify the limits to allow more disk space to users who work with large files.

- If client computers running Windows 2000 are shared by more than one user, set disk quota limits on client computer volumes so that disk space is shared by all users who share the computer.

- Generally, you should set disk quotas on shared volumes to limit storage for users. Set disk quotas on public folders and network servers to ensure that users share hard disk space appropriately. When storage resources are scarce, you may want to set disk quotas on all shared hard disk space.

- Delete disk quota entries for a user who no longer stores files on a volume. You can delete quota entries for a user account only after all files that the user owns have been removed from the volume or another user has taken ownership of the files.

- Before you can delete a quota entry for a user account, all files that the user owns must be removed from the volume or another user must take ownership of the files.

Practice: Enabling and Disabling Disk Quotas

In this practice you configure default quota management settings to limit the amount of data users may store on drive C (their hard disk drive). Next you configure a custom quota setting for a user account. You increase the amount of data the user may store on drive C to 20 MB with a warning level set to 16. Finally you turn off quota management for drive C.

Note   If you did not install Windows 2000 on drive C, substitute the NTFS partition on which you did install Windows 2000 whenever drive C is referred to in the practice.

Exercise 1: Configuring Quota Management Settings

In this exercise, you configure the quota management settings for drive C to limit the data that users may store on the volume. You then configure custom quota settings for a user account.

▶ **To configure default quota management settings**

1. In Windows Explorer, right-click the drive C icon, and then click Properties.

   Windows 2000 displays the Local Volume (C:) Properties dialog box with the General tab active.

2. Click the Quota tab.

   Notice that disk quotas are disabled by default.

3. On the Quota tab, click the Enable Quota Management check box.

   What is the default disk space limit for new users?

4. Click Limit Disk Space To.

5. Type **10** in the Limit Disk Space To box and then type **6** in the Set Warning Level To box.

   Notice the default unit size is KB.

6. Change the unit sizes to MB and then click Apply.

   Windows 2000 displays the Disk Quota dialog box, warning you that the volume will be rescanned to update disk usage statistics if you enable quotas.

7. Click OK to enable disk quotas.

▶ **To configure quota management settings for a user**

1. On the Quota tab of the Local Disk (C:) Properties dialog box, click the Quota Entries button.

   Windows 2000 displays the Quota Entries For Local Disk (C:) dialog box.

   Are any user accounts listed? Why or why not?

2. On the Quota menu, click New Quota Entry.

   Windows 2000 displays the Select Users dialog box.

3. In the Look In box, select your domain.

4. At the top of the dialog box, under Name, select a user for whom you want to set up a quota, and then click Add.

   The user name appears in the Name list at the bottom of the dialog box.

5. Click OK.

Windows 2000 displays the Add New Quota Entry dialog box.

What are the default settings for the user you just set a quota limit for?

6. Increase the amount of data that the user can store on drive C by changing the Limit disk space to 20 MB and the Set warning level to 16 MB.

7. Click OK to return to the Quota Entries dialog box.

Exercise 2: Disabling Quota Management

In this exercise, you disable quota management settings for drive C.

▶ **To disable quota management settings for drive C**

1. Log on to your domain as Administrator and start Windows Explorer.

2. Right-click the drive C icon, and then click Properties.

Windows 2000 displays the Local Disk (C:) Properties dialog box with the General tab active.

3. Click the Quota tab.

4. On the Quota tab, clear the Enable Quota Management check box.

Notice that all quota settings for drive C are no longer available.

5. Click Apply.

Windows 2000 displays the Disk Quota dialog box, warning you that if you disable quotas, the volume will be rescanned if you enable them later.

6. Click OK to close the Disk Quota dialog box.

7. Click OK to close the Local Disk (C:) Properties dialog box.

8. Close all applications and log off Windows 2000.

Lesson Summary

In this lesson you learned how to use disk quotas to allocate disk space usage to users. You can set disk quotas, quota thresholds, and quota limits for all users and for individual users. You can also monitor the amount of hard disk space that users have used and the amount that they have left against their quota. You also learned that Windows 2000 ignores compression when it calculates hard disk space usage and that you can apply disk quotas only to Windows 2000 NTFS volumes.

Windows 2000 disk quotas track and control disk usage on a per-user, per-volume basis. Windows 2000 tracks disk quotas for each volume, even if the volumes are on the same hard disk. Because quotas are tracked on a per-user basis, every user's disk space is tracked regardless of the folder in which the user stores files.

Lesson 3: Using Disk Defragmenter

Windows 2000 saves files and folders in the first available space on a hard disk and not necessarily in an area of contiguous space. This leads to file and folder fragmentation. When your hard disk contains a lot of fragmented files and folders, your computer takes longer to gain access to them because it requires several additional reads to collect the various pieces. Creating new files and folders also takes longer because the available free space on the hard disk is scattered. Your computer must save a new file or folder in various locations on the hard disk. This lesson introduces the Windows 2000 system tool, Disk Defragmenter, which helps organize your hard disks.

After this lesson, you will be able to

- Describe defragmentation.
- Use Disk Defragmenter to organize your hard disks.

Estimated lesson time: 15 minutes

Defragmenting Disks

The process of finding and consolidating fragmented files and folders is called *defragmenting*. Disk Defragmenter locates fragmented files and folders and defragments them. It does this by moving the pieces of each file or folder to one location so that each file or folder occupies a single, contiguous space on the hard disk. Consequently, your system can gain access to and save files and folders more efficiently. By consolidating files and folders, Disk Defragmenter also consolidates free space, making it less likely that new files will be fragmented. Disk Defragmenter can defragment FAT, FAT32, and NTFS volumes.

The Disk Defragmenter window is split into three areas, as shown in Figure 23.5.

The upper portion of the window lists the volumes that you can analyze and defragment. The middle portion provides a graphic representation of how fragmented the selected volume is. The lower portion provides a dynamic representation of the volume that continuously updates during defragmentation. The display colors indicate the condition of the volume as follows:

- Red indicates fragmented files.
- Dark blue indicates contiguous (nonfragmented) files.
- White indicates free space on the volume.
- Green indicates system files, which Disk Defragmenter cannot move.

By comparing the Analysis Display band to the Defragmentation Display band during and at the conclusion of defragmentation, you can quickly see the improvement in the volume.

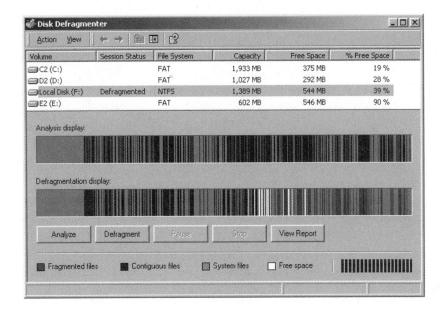

Figure 23.5   Disk Defragmenter window

If you want to analyze and defragment a volume, open Disk Defragmenter by selecting a drive you want to defragment in Windows Explorer or My Computer. Click the File menu, click Properties, select the Tools tab, and click the Defragment Now button. Then select one of the options that are described in Table 23.4.

Table 23.4   **Disk Defragmenter Options**

Option	Description
Analyze	Click this button to analyze the disk for fragmentation. After the analysis, the Analysis Display band provides a graphic representation of how fragmented the volume is.
Defragment	Click this button to defragment the disk. After defragmentation, the Defragmentation Display band provides a graphic representation of the defragmented volume.

Using Disk Defragmenter Effectively

The following list provides some guidelines for using Disk Defragmenter:

- Run Disk Defragmenter when the computer will receive the least usage. During defragmentation, data is moved around on the hard disk and the defragmentation process is microprocessor-intensive. The defragmentation process will adversely affect access time to other disk-based resources.

- Educate users to defragment their local hard disks at least once a month to prevent accumulation of fragmented files.

- Analyze the target volume before you install large applications, and then defragment the volume if necessary. Installations complete more quickly when the target media has adequate contiguous free space. Additionally, gaining access to the application, after it is installed, is faster.

- When you delete a large number of files or folders, your hard disk may become excessively fragmented, so be sure that you analyze it afterwards. Generally, you should defragment hard disks on busy file servers more often than those on single-user client computers.

Lesson Summary

In this lesson you learned that Windows 2000 saves files and folders in the first available space on a hard disk and not necessarily in an area of contiguous space. This leads to file and folder fragmentation. You learned that when your hard disk contains a lot of fragmented files and folders, your computer takes longer to gain access to these files and folders and to create new files and folders.

You also learned about the Windows 2000 system tool, Disk Defragmenter, which locates fragmented files and folders and defragments them. Consequently, your system can gain access to and save files and folders more efficiently. By consolidating files and folders, Disk Defragmenter also consolidates free space, making it less likely that new files will be fragmented. Disk Defragmenter can defragment FAT, FAT32, and NTFS volumes.

Review

Here are some questions to help you determine if you have learned enough to move on to the next chapter. If you have difficulty answering these questions, please go back and review the material in this chapter before beginning the next chapter. The answers for these questions are located in Appendix A, "Questions and Answers."

1. You are the administrator for a computer running Windows 2000 Server that is used to store a user's home folders and roaming user profiles. You want to restrict users to 25 MB of available storage for their home folder while monitoring, but not limiting, the disk space that is used for the roaming user profiles. How should you configure the volumes on the server?

2. The Sales department archives legacy sales data on a network computer running Windows 2000 Server. Several other departments share the server. You have begun to receive complaints from users in other departments that the server has very little remaining disk space. What can you do to alleviate the problem?

3. Your department has recently archived several gigabytes of data from a computer running Windows 2000 Server to CD-ROMs. As users have been adding files to the server, you have noticed that the server has been taking longer than usual to gain access to the hard disk. How can you increase disk access time for the server?

CHAPTER   2 4

Backing Up and Restoring Data

About This Chapter

Now that you have learned to install Microsoft Windows 2000 and set up a network, it is important that you are able to ensure that network data, such as Active Directory, is not lost. Windows 2000 provides the Windows Backup tool to allow you to back up your data. This chapter introduces you to backing up and restoring data.

Before You Begin

To complete this chapter, you must have

- A computer that meets the minimum hardware requirements listed in "Hardware Requirements," on page xxxiii.
- Installed the Windows 2000 Server software on the computer.
- Configured the computer as a domain controller in a domain.

Lesson 1: Understanding Backing Up and Restoring Data

The efficient recovery of lost data is the goal of all backup jobs. A *backup job* is a single process of backing up data. Regularly backing up the data on server hard disks and client computer hard disks prevents data loss due to disk drive failures, power outages, virus infections, and other such incidents. If data loss occurs, and you have carefully planned and performed regular backup jobs, you can restore the lost data, whether the lost data is a single file or an entire hard disk.

After this lesson, you will be able to

- Identify the purpose of backing up and restoring data.
- Identify the user rights and permissions that are necessary to back up and restore data.
- Identify planning issues for backing up data.
- Identify the different backup types.

Estimated lesson time: 20 minutes

Windows Backup

Windows 2000 provides Windows Backup, shown in Figure 24.1, which is a tool that allows you to easily back up and restore data. To launch Windows Backup, on the Start menu, point to Programs, point to Accessories, and then click Backup; or, on the Start menu, click Run, type **ntbackup** and then click OK. You can use it to back up data manually or to schedule unattended backup jobs on a regular basis. You can back up data to a file or to a tape. Files can be stored on hard disks, removable disks (such as Iomega Zip and Jaz drives), and recordable compact discs and optical drives.

To successfully back up and restore data on a computer running Windows 2000, you must have the appropriate permissions and user rights, as described in the following list:

- All users can back up their own files and folders. They can also back up files for which they have the Read, Read and Execute, Modify, or Full Control permission.
- All users can restore files and folders for which they have the Write, Modify, or Full Control permission.
- Members of the Administrators, Backup Operators, and Server Operators groups can back up and restore all files (regardless of the assigned permissions). By default, members of these groups have the Backup Files and Directories and Restore Files and Directories user rights.

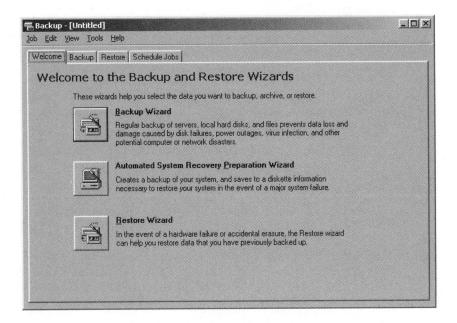

Figure 24.1   Windows 2000 Backup

Planning Issues for Windows Backup

You should plan your backup jobs to fit the needs of your company. The primary goal for backing up data is to be able to restore that data if necessary, so any backup plan that you develop should incorporate how you restore data. You should be able to quickly and successfully restore critical lost data. There is no single correct backup plan for all networks.

Consider the following issues in formulating your backup plan.

Determine Which Files and Folders to Back Up

Always back up critical files and folders that your company needs to operate, such as sales and financial records, the registry for each server, and Active Directory.

Determine How Often to Back Up

If data is critical for company operations, back it up daily. If users create or modify reports once a week, backing up the reports weekly is sufficient. You only need to back up data as often as it changes. For example, there is no need to do daily backups on files that rarely change, such as monthly reports.

Determine Which Target Media to Use for Storing Backup Data

With Windows Backup, you can back up to the following removable media:

- **Files.** You can store the files on a removable media device, such as an Iomega Zip drive, or on a network location, such as a file server. The file that is created contains the files and folders that you have selected to backup. The file has a .bkf extension. Users can back up their personal data to a network server. Use this only for temporary backup jobs.

- **Tape.** A less expensive medium than other removable media, a tape is more convenient for large backup jobs because of its high storage capacity. However, tapes have a limited life and can deteriorate. Be sure that you check the manufacturer's recommendations for usage.

    For information about tape rotation and archiving tapes, see Appendix D, "Managing Backup Tapes."

Note If you use a removable media device to back up and restore data, be sure that you verify that the device is supported on the Windows 2000 Hardware Compatibility List (HCL).

Determine Whether to Perform Network or Local Backup Jobs

A network backup can contain data from multiple network computers. This allows you to consolidate backup data from multiple computers to a single removable backup media. A network backup also allows one administrator to back up the entire network. Whether you perform a network or local backup job depends on the data that must be backed up. For example, you can only back up the registry and Active Directory at the computer where you are performing the backup.

If you decide to perform local backups, you must perform a local backup at each computer, including servers and client computers. There are several things to consider in performing local backups. First of all, you must move from computer to computer so that you can perform a backup at each computer, or you must rely on users to back up their own computers. Typically most users fail to back up their data on a regular basis. A second consideration with local backups is the number of removable storage media devices. If you use removable storage media devices, such as tape drives, you must have one for each computer, or you must move the tape drive from computer to computer so that you can perform a local backup on each computer.

You may also choose to use a combination of network and local backup jobs. Do this when critical data resides on client computers and servers and you do not have a removable storage media device for each computer. In this situation, users perform a local backup and store their backup files on a server. You then back up the server.

Backup Types

Windows Backup provides five backup types that define what data is backed up, such as only files that have changed since the last backup.

Some backup types use backup *markers,* also known as archive attributes, which mark a file as having changed. When a file changes, an attribute is set on the file that indicates that the file has changed since the last backup. When you back up the file, this clears or resets the attribute.

Normal

During a *normal* backup, all selected files and folders are backed up. A normal backup does not rely on markers to determine which files to back up. During a normal backup any existing marks are cleared and each file is marked as having been backed up. Normal backups speed up the restore process because the backup files are the most current and you do not need to restore multiple backup jobs.

Copy

During a *copy* backup, all selected files and folders are backed up. It neither looks for nor clears markers. If you do not want to clear markers and affect other backup types, use copy. For example, use a copy backup between a normal and an incremental backup to create an archival snapshot of network data.

Differential

During a *differential* backup, only selected files and folders that have a marker are backed up. It does not clear markers. Because a differential backup does not clear markers, if you did two differential backups in a row on a file and nothing changed in the file, the entire file would be backed up each time.

Incremental

During an *incremental* backup, only selected files and folders that have a marker are backed up. It clears markers. Because an incremental backup clears markers, if you did two incremental backups in a row on a file and nothing changed in the file, the file would not be backed up the second time.

Daily

During a *daily* backup, all selected files and folders that have changed during the day are backed up. It neither looks for nor clears markers. If you want to back up all files and folders that change during the day, use a daily backup.

Combining Backup Types

An effective backup strategy is likely to combine different backup types. Some backup types require more time to back up data but less time to restore data. Conversely, other backup types require less time to back up data but more time to restore data. If you combine backup types, markers are critical. Incremental and differential backup types check for and rely on the markers.

The following are some examples of combining different backup types:

- **Normal and differential backups.** On Monday a normal backup is performed, and on Tuesday through Friday differential backups are performed. Differential backups do not clear markers, which means that each backup includes all changes since Monday. If data becomes corrupt on Friday, you only need to restore the normal backup from Monday and the differential backup from Thursday. This strategy takes more time to back up but less time to restore.

- **Normal and incremental backups.** On Monday a normal backup is performed, and on Tuesday through Friday incremental backups are performed. Incremental backups clear markers, which means that each backup includes only the files that changed since the previous backup. If data becomes corrupt on Friday, you need to restore the normal backup from Monday and all incremental backups, from Tuesday through Friday. This strategy takes less time to back up but more time to restore.

- **Normal, differential, and copy backups.** This strategy is the same as the first example that used normal and incremental backups, except that on Wednesday, you perform a copy backup. Copy backups include all selected files and do not clear markers or interrupt the usual backup schedule. Therefore, each differential backup includes all changes since Monday. The copy backup type done on Wednesday is not part of the Friday restore. Copy backups are helpful when you need to create a snapshot of your data.

Lesson Summary

In this lesson you learned that the efficient recovery of lost data is the goal of all backup jobs. If data loss does occur, and you have carefully planned and performed regular backup jobs, you can restore the lost data. Windows 2000 provides the Windows Backup tool that allows you to easily back up and restore data. You can use it to back up data manually or to schedule unattended backup jobs on a regular basis. Windows Backup provides five backup types: normal, copy, differential, incremental, and daily. You can use one of these backup types or a combination of backup types to back up your data.

Lesson 2: Backing Up Data

In this lesson you will learn about backing up data. After you have planned your backup, including planning the backup type to use and when to perform backup jobs, the next step is to prepare to back up your data. There are certain preliminary tasks that must be completed before you can back up your data. After you have completed the preliminary tasks, you can perform the backup. You will also learn about scheduling and running an unattended backup.

After this lesson, you will be able to

- Back up data at a computer and over the network.
- Schedule a backup job.
- Set backup options for Windows Backup.

Estimated lesson time: 45 minutes

Performing Preliminary Tasks

An important part of each backup job is performing the preliminary tasks. One task that you must do is ensure that the files that you want to back up are closed. You should send a notification to users to close files before you begin backing up data. Windows Backup does not back up files that are locked open by applications. You can use e-mail or the Send Console Message dialog box, in the File Service Management snap-in, to send administrative messages to users.

Note For information on how to send a message using the Send Console Message dialog box, see Chapter 26, "Monitoring Access to Network Resources."

If you use a removable media device, make sure that the following preliminary tasks occur:

- The backup device is attached to a computer on the network and is turned on. If you are backing up to tape, you must attach the tape device to the computer on which you run Windows Backup.
- The media device is listed on the Windows 2000 HCL.
- The media is loaded in the media device. For example, if you are using a tape drive, ensure that a tape is loaded in the tape drive.

Selecting Files and Folders to Back Up

After you have completed the preliminary tasks, you can perform the backup. You can use the Backup wizard, shown in Figure 24.2. To start the Backup wizard, on the Backup window displayed by running Ntbackup, click Backup Wizard.

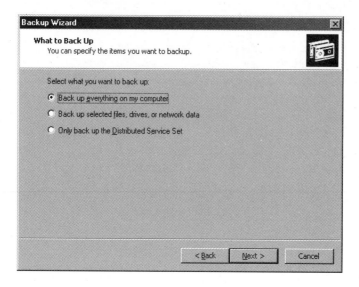

Figure 24.2   What To Back Up page of the Backup wizard

The first phase is to specify what to back up by choosing one of the following options:

- **Back Up Everything On My Computer.**   Backs up all files on the computer on which you are running Windows Backup, except those files that Windows Backup excludes by default, such as certain power management files.

- **Back Up Selected Files, Drives, Or Network Data.**   Backs up selected files and folders. This includes files and folders on the computer where you run Windows Backup and any shared file or folder on the network. When you click this option, the Backup wizard provides a hierarchical view of the computer and the network (through My Network Places).

- **Only Back Up The Distributed Services.**   Backs up Active Directory, File Replication Services, and Certificate Server for the computer on which you are running Windows Backup. This option is only available at a domain controller. Use this option to create a copy of Active Directory, which contains all domain objects and their attributes. Back up the Certificate Server and stop the Certificate Server service before running this option. Windows Backup will fail if the Certificate Server is running. You should keep the certificate store backup file created by backing up the Certificate Server with your backup.

Specifying Backup Destination and Media Settings

After you select what you want to back up, you need to provide information about the backup media. Table 24.1 describes the information that you must provide for the backup media options.

Table 24.1   Backup Media Options

Option	Description
Backup Media Type	The target medium to use, such as a tape or file. A file can be located on any disk-based media, including a hard disk, a shared network folder, or a removable disk, such as an Iomega Zip drive.
Backup Media Or File Name	The location where Windows Backup will store the data. For a tape, enter the tape name. For a file, enter the path for the backup file.

After you provide the media information, the Backup wizard displays the wizard settings and the opportunity to do either of the following:

- Start the backup. If you click Finish, during the backup process, the Backup wizard displays status information about the backup job in the Backup Progress dialog box.

- Specify advanced backup options. If you click Advanced, the Backup wizard allows you to select the advanced backup settings listed in Table 24.2.

Note   When the backup process is complete, you can choose to review the backup report, which is the backup log. A *backup log* is a text file that records backup operations and is stored on the hard disk of the computer on which you are running Windows Backup.

Specifying Advanced Backup Settings

When you specify advanced backup settings, you are changing the default backup settings for only the current backup job. The advanced settings cover the backup media and characteristics of the backup job, as shown in Figure 24.3.

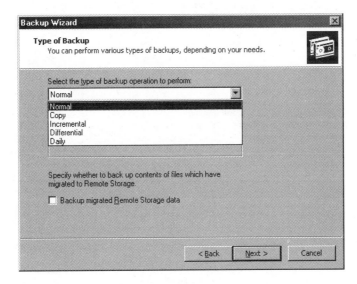

Figure 24.3   Type Of Backup page of the Backup wizard

Table 24.2   Advanced Backup Settings

Advanced option	Description
Select The Type Of Backup Operation To Perform	Allows you to choose the backup type that is used for this backup job. Select one of the following types: normal, copy, incremental, differential, and daily.
Backup Migrated Remote Storage Data	Backs up data that Hierarchical Storage Manager (HSM) has moved to remote storage.
Verify Data After Backup	Confirms that files are correctly backed up. Windows Backup compares the backup data and the source data to verify that they are the same. *Microsoft recommends that you select this option.*
Use Hardware Compression, If Available	Enables hardware compression for tape devices that support it. If your tape device does not support hardware compression, this option is unavailable.
If The Archive Media Already Contains Backups	Specifies whether to append or replace the existing backup on the backup media. Choose Append to store multiple backup jobs on a storage device, or choose Replace if you do not need to save previous backup jobs and you only want to save the most recent backup data.
Allow Only The Owner And The Administrator Access To The Backup Data, And Any Backups Appended To This Media	Allows you to restrict who can gain access to the completed backup file or tape. This option is only available if you choose to replace an existing backup on a backup media, rather than appending to the backup media.
	If you back up the registry or Active Directory, click this option to prevent others from getting copies of the backup job.
Backup Label	Allows you to specify a name and description for the backup job. The name and description appear in the backup log. The default is Set Created *Date* At *Time*. You can change the name and description to a more intuitive name (for example, Sales-normal backup September 14, 1998).

Media Label	Allows you to specify the name of the backup media (for example, the tape name). The default name is Media Created *Date* At *Time*. The first time that you back up to a new media or overwrite an existing backup job, you can specify the name, such as Active Directory backup.
When To Backup	Allows you to specify Now or Later. If you choose later, you specify the job name and the start date. You can also set the schedule.

Depending on whether you chose to back up now or later, the Backup wizard provides you with the opportunity to do either of the following:

- If you chose to finish the backup process, the Backup wizard displays the Completing The Backup Wizard settings and then presents the option to finish and immediately start the backup. During the backup, the wizard displays status information about the backup job.

- If you chose to backup later, you are shown additional dialog boxes to schedule the backup process to occur later, as described in the next section.

Scheduling Backup Jobs

Scheduling a backup job means that you can have an unattended backup job occur later when users are not at work and files are closed. You can also schedule backup jobs to occur at regular intervals. To enable this, Windows 2000 integrates Windows Backup with the Task Scheduler service.

▶   **To schedule a backup**

1. Click Later on the When To Back Up page of the Backup wizard.

   Task Scheduler presents the Set Account Information dialog box, prompting you for your password. The user account must have the appropriate user rights and permissions to perform backup jobs.

   Note   If the Task Scheduler service is not running or not set to start automatically, Windows 2000 displays a dialog box prompting you to start the service. Click OK, and the Set Account Information dialog box appears.

2. Enter your password in the Password box and Confirm password box, and then click OK.

   The When To Back Up page appears. You must provide a name for the backup job, and by default, the wizard displays the present date and time for the start date.

3. Type in the appropriate name in the Job Name box.

4. Click Set Schedule to set a different start date and time. This selection causes Task Scheduler to display the Schedule Job dialog box.

    In the Schedule Job dialog box, you can set the date, time, and number of occurrences for the backup job to repeat, such as every Friday at 10:00 PM. You can also display all of the scheduled tasks for the computer by selecting the Show Multiple Schedules check box. This helps to prevent you from scheduling multiple tasks on the same computer at the same time.

    By clicking the Advanced button, you can also schedule how long the backup can last and for how many days, weeks, months, or years you want this schedule to continue.

After you scheduled the backup job and completed the Backup wizard, Windows Backup places the backup job on the calendar on the Schedule Jobs tab in Windows Backup. The backup job automatically starts at the time that you specified.

Practice: Backing Up Files

In this practice you use the Backup wizard to back up some files to your hard disk. You then create a backup job to perform a backup operation at a later time by using Task Scheduler.

Exercise 1: Starting a Backup Job

In this exercise, you start Windows Backup and use the Backup wizard to back up files to your hard disk.

▶   **To back up files by using the Backup wizard**

1. Log on to your domain as Administrator.
2. Click Start, point to Programs, point to Accessories, and then click Backup.
3. On the Welcome tab, click Backup Wizard.

    The Backup wizard starts and displays the Welcome to the Backup Wizard page.
4. Click Next to continue creating the backup job.

    The Backup wizard displays the What To Back Up page, prompting you to choose the scope of the backup job.
5. Click Back Up Selected Files, Drives, Or Network Data, and then click Next to continue.

    The Backup wizard displays the Items To Back Up page, prompting you to select the local and network drives, folders, and files to be backed up.

6. Expand My Network Places.

Notice there is a selection called Directory that allows you to back up the Directory for your domain.

7. Expand My Computer and expand C: Local Disk.

8. In the details pane, select boot.ini.

Boot.ini is one of the boot files for Windows 2000. You will learn more about boot.ini in Chapter 27, "The Windows 2000 Boot Process."

9. Click Next to continue.

The Backup wizard displays the Where To Store The Backup page.

Note If there is no tape drive connected to your computer, File will be the only backup media type that is available.

10. In the Backup Media or File Name box, type **c:\backup1.bkf** and then click Next.

Note You would not normally back up files from a drive to a file on that same drive, as is done in this exercise. You would normally back up data to a tape or to a file stored on another hard disk, removable disks (such as Iomega Zip and Jaz drives), or recordable compact discs or optical drives.

The Backup wizard displays the Completing The Backup Wizard page, prompting you to finish the wizard and begin the backup job or to specify advanced options.

11. Click Advanced to specify additional backup options.

The Backup wizard displays the Type Of Backup page, prompting you to select a backup type for this backup job.

12. Make sure that Normal is selected in the Select The Type Of Backup Operation To Perform list.

13. Make sure that the Backup Migrated Remote Storage Data check box is cleared, and then click Next.

The Backup wizard displays the How To Backup page, prompting you to specify whether or not to verify the backed up data after the backup job.

Why is the Use Hardware Compression, If Available check box unavailable?

14. Select the Verify Data After Backup check box, and then click Next.

The Backup wizard displays the Media Options page, prompting you to specify whether to append this backup job to existing media or overwrite existing backup data on the destination media.

15. Click Replace The Data On The Media With This Backup.

   When is it appropriate to select the check box labeled Allow Only The Owner And The Administrator Access To The Backup Data And Any Backups Appended To This Media?

   _____

16. Make sure that the Allow Only The Owner And The Administrator Access To The Backup Data And To Any Backups Appended To This Media check box is cleared, and then click Next.

   The Backup wizard displays the Backup Label page, prompting you to supply a label for the backup job and a label for the backup media.

   Notice that Windows Backup generates a backup label and media label by using the current date and time.

17. In the Backup Label box, type **Documents backup on *date*** (where *date* is today's date).

18. In the Media label box, type **Backup file for Server1** and then click Next.

   The Backup wizard displays the When To Backup page, prompting you to choose whether to run the backup job now or schedule this backup job.

19. Make sure that Now is selected, and then click Next.

   The Backup wizard displays the Completing The Backup Wizard page, which lists the options and settings that you selected for this backup job.

20. Click Finish to start the backup job.

   Windows Backup briefly displays the Selection Information dialog box, indicating the estimated amount of data for, and the time to complete, the backup job.

   Then Windows Backup displays the Backup Progress dialog box, providing the status of the backup operation, statistics on estimated and actual amount of data being processed, the time that has elapsed, and the estimated time that remains for the backup operation.

▶ **To view the backup report**

1. When the Backup Progress dialog box indicates that the backup is complete, click Report.

   Notepad starts, displaying the backup report.

   The backup report contains key details about the backup operation, such as the time that it started and how many files were backed up.

2. Examine the report, and when you are finished, quit Notepad.

3. In the Backup Progress dialog box, click Close.

   Windows Backup appears with the Welcome tab active.

Exercise 2: Creating and Running an Unattended Backup Job

In this exercise, you create a backup job to perform a backup operation at a later time by using Task Scheduler.

▶ **To create a scheduled backup job**

1. On the Welcome tab, click Backup Wizard.

   The Backup wizard starts and displays the Welcome To The Backup Wizard page.

2. Click Next to continue creating the backup job.

   The Backup wizard displays the What To Backup page, prompting you to choose the scope of the backup job.

3. Click Back Up Selected Files, Drives, Or Network Data, and then click Next to continue.

   The Backup wizard displays the Items To Back Up page, prompting you to select the local and network drives, folders, and files to be backed up.

4. Expand My Computer, expand drive C, and then select the Inetpub check box.

5. Click Next to continue.

   The Backup wizard displays the Where To Store The Backup page, prompting you to select the destination for your backup data.

6. In the Backup media or file name box, type **C:\backup2.bkf** and then click Next.

   The Backup wizard displays the Completing The Backup Wizard page.

7. Click Advanced to specify additional backup options.

   The Backup wizard displays the Type Of Backup page, prompting you to select a backup type for this backup job.

8. Make sure that in the Select The Type Of Backup Operation To Perform box, Normal is selected.

9. Since your computer is a domain controller, make sure that the Backup The Active Directory check box is cleared, and then click Next.

   The Backup wizard displays the How To Backup page, prompting you to specify whether to verify the backed up data after the backup job.

10. Select the Verify Data After Backup check box, and then click Next.

    The Backup wizard displays the Media Options page, prompting you to specify whether to append this backup job to existing media or overwrite existing backup data on the destination media.

11. Click Replace The Data On The Media With This Backup.

12. Make sure you clear the check box labeled Allow Only The Owner And The Administrator Access To The Backup Data And To Any Backups Appended To This Media, and then click Next.

    The Backup wizard displays the Backup Label page, prompting you to supply a label for the backup job and a label for the backup media.

13. In the Backup Label box, type **Automated Inetpub backup on** *date* (where *date* is today's date).

14. In the Media Label box, type **Backup file 2 for Server1** and then click Next.

    The Backup wizard displays the When To Backup page, prompting you to choose whether to run the backup job now or schedule this backup job.

15. Click Later.

    The Set Account Information dialog box appears, prompting you for the password for the Administrator account. (If the Task Scheduler service isn't set to start automatically, you may first see a dialog box asking whether you want to start the Task Scheduler. Click OK, and then the Set Account Information dialog box appears.)

    Because the Task Scheduler service automatically runs applications within the security context of a valid user for the computer or domain, you are prompted for the name and password with which the scheduled backup job will run. For scheduled backup jobs, you should supply a user account that is a member of the Backup Operators group with permission to gain access to all of the folders and files to be backed up.

    For purposes of this lab, you will use the Administrator account to run the scheduled backup job.

16. Make sure that Microsoft\Administrator appears in the Run As box (or the name of your domain, if not Microsoft), and then in the Password box and the Confirm Password box, type **password**

17. Click OK.

18. In the Job Name box, type **Inetpub Backup** and then click Set Schedule.

    Windows Backup displays the Schedule Job dialog box, prompting you to select the start time and schedule options for the backup job.

19. In the Schedule Task box, select Once, and in the Start Time box, enter a time two minutes from the present time, and then click OK.

    The Backup wizard displays the When To Backup page along with the scheduled backup job information.

20. Click Next to continue.

    The Backup wizard displays the Completing The Backup Wizard page, displaying the options and settings that you selected for this backup job.

21. Click Finish to start the backup job.

22. If a warning dialog box appears, indicating that files have already been selected, click No.

Windows Backup appears with the Welcome tab active.

23. Close Windows Backup.

When the time for the backup job is reached, Windows Backup starts and performs the requested backup operation.

▶ **To verify that the backup job was performed**

1. Start Microsoft Windows Explorer and click drive C.

Does the Backup2.bkf file exist?

2. Log off Windows 2000.

Lesson Summary

In this lesson you learned that after you have planned your backup, the next step is to prepare to back up your data. An important part of each backup job is performing the preliminary tasks. One task that you must do is ensure that the files that you want to back up are closed because Windows Backup does not back up files that are locked open by applications. Next you perform the backup.

You also learned that in using the Backup wizard, the first phase is to specify what to back up. There are three options: back up everything on the computer; back up selected files, drives, or network data; or back up only the Registry and Active Directory. After you select what you want to back up, you need to provide the target destination, and the backup media or file name. Then you can finish the backup or you can specify any advanced backup options.

Finally, in the practice exercises, you were able to back up a portion of your files. Then you were able to create and run an unattended backup job.

Lesson 3: Restoring Data

In this lesson you will learn about restoring data. The ability to restore corrupt or lost data is critical to all corporations and is the goal of all backup jobs. To ensure that you can successfully restore data, you should follow certain guidelines, such as keeping thorough documentation on all of your backup jobs.

After this lesson, you will be able to

- Restore data, whether an entire volume or a single file.

Estimated lesson time: 30 minutes

Preparing to Restore Data

To restore data, you must select the backup sets, files, and folders to restore. You can also specify additional settings based on your restore requirements. Windows Backup provides a Restore wizard to help you restore data, or you can restore data without using the wizard.

When critical data is lost, you need to restore the data quickly. Use the following guidelines to help prepare for restoring data:

- Base your restore strategy on the backup type that you used for the backup. If time is critical when you are restoring data, your restore strategy must ensure that the backup types that you choose for backups expedite the restore process. For example, use normal and differential backups so that you only need to restore the last normal backup and the last differential backup.

- Perform a trial restore periodically to verify that Windows Backup is backing up your files correctly. A trial restore can uncover hardware problems that do not show up with software verifications. Restore the data to an alternate location, and then compare the restored data to the data on the original hard disk.

- Keep documentation for each backup job. Create and print a detailed backup log for each backup job. A detailed backup log contains a record of all files and folders that were backed up. By using the backup log, you can quickly locate which piece of media contains the files that you need to restore without having to load the catalogs. A *catalog* is an index of the files and folders from a backup job that Windows 2000 automatically creates and stores with the backup job and on the computer running Windows Backup.

- Keep a record of multiple backup jobs in a calendar format that shows the days on which you perform the backup jobs. For each job, note the backup type and identify the storage that is used, such as a tape number or the name of the Iomega Zip drive. Then, if you need to restore data, you can easily review several weeks' worth of backup jobs to select which tape to use.

Selecting Backup Sets, Files, and Folders to Restore

The first step in restoring data is to select the data to restore. You can select individual files and folders, an entire backup job, or a backup set. A *backup set* is a collection of files or folders from one volume that you back up during a backup job. If you back up two volumes on a hard disk during a backup job, the job has two backup sets. You select the data to restore in the catalog.

To restore data, use the Restore wizard, which you access through Windows Backup.

▶ **To restore data**

1. In the Restore wizard, expand the media type that contains the data that you want to restore. This can be either tape or file media.

2. Expand the appropriate media set until the data that you want to restore is visible. You can restore a backup set or specific files and folders.

3. Select the data that you want to restore, and then click Next.

   The Restore wizard displays the settings for the restore.

4. Do one of the following:

   - Finish the restore process. If you choose to finish the restore job, during the restore, the Restore wizard requests verification for the source of the restore media and then performs the restore. During the restore, the Restore wizard displays status information about the restore.

   - Specify advanced restore options.

Specifying Advanced Restore Settings

The advanced settings in the Restore wizard vary, depending on the type of backup media from which you are restoring, such as a tape device or an Iomega Zip drive. Table 24.3 describes the advanced restore options.

After you have finished the Restore wizard, Windows Backup does the following:

- Prompts you to verify your selection of the source media to use to restore data. After the verification, Windows Backup starts the restore process.

- Displays status information about the restore process. As with a backup process, you can choose to view the report (restore log) of the restore. It contains information about the restore, such as the number of files that have been restored and the duration of the restore process.

Table 24.3   Advanced Restore Settings

Option	Description
Restore Files To	The target location for the data that you are restoring. The choices are: **Original Location.** Replaces corrupted or lost data. **Alternate Location.** Restores an older version of a file or does a practice restore. **Single Folder.** Consolidates the files from a tree structure into a single folder. For example, use this option if you want copies of specific files but do not want to restore the hierarchical structure of the files. If you select either an alternate location or a single directory, you must provide the path.
When Restoring Files That Already Exist (Click Options on the Tool menu to access these options.)	Whether or not to overwrite existing files. The choices are: **Do Not Replace The File On My Disk (Recommended).** Prevents accidental overwriting of existing data. (This is the default.) **Replace The File On Disk Only If It Is Older Than The Backup Copy.** Verifies that the most recent copy exists on the computer. **Always Replace The File On Disk.** Windows Backup does not provide a confirmation message if it encounters a duplicate file name during the restore operation.
Select The Special Restore Options You Want To Use (Click the Start Restore button to access these options.)	Whether or not to restore security or special system files. The choices are: **Restore Security.** Applies the original permissions to files that you are restoring to a Windows NT file system (NTFS) volume. Security settings include access permissions, audit entries, and ownership. This option is only available if you have backed up data from an NTFS volume and are restoring to an NTFS volume. **Restore Removable Storage Management Database.** Restores the configuration database for Removable Storage Management (RSM) devices and the media pool settings. The database is located in *systemroot*\system32\remotestorage.

Restore Junction Points, Not The Folders And File Data They Reference.   Restores junction points on your hard disk as well as the data that the junction points refer to. If you have any mounted drives, and you want to restore the data that mounted drives point to, you should select this check box. If you do not select this check box, the junction point will be restored but the data your junction point refers to may not be accessible.

When Restoring Replicated Data Sets, Make The Restored Data As The Primary Data For All Replicas.   Restores the data for all replicated data sets.

Practice: Restoring Files

In this practice, you restore a few of the files that you backed up in Exercise 1 in Lesson 2 of this chapter.

Important   To complete this practice, you must have completed the practice in the previous lesson, or you must have some files you have backed up using Ntbackup that you can restore.

▶ **To restore files from a previous backup job**

1. In Windows Backup, on the Welcome tab, click Restore Wizard.

   The Restore wizard starts and displays the Welcome To The Restore Wizard page.

2. Click Next to continue creating the restore job.

   The Restore wizard displays the What To Restore page, prompting you to select the backup media from which you wish to restore files.

   Notice that the only media from which you can restore is a file and that the backup files are listed according to the media label that is specified.

3. Under What To Restore, expand the backup file that you created.

   Notice that drive C appears as the first folder in the backup file. Windows Backup creates a separate backup set for each volume that is backed up. All folders and files that are backed up from a single volume appear under the drive letter for the volume.

4. Expand drive C.

   The Backup File Name dialog box appears with C:\Backup1.bkf in the Catalog Backup File box.

5. Click OK, and then when you are returned to the What To Restore page, expand the subfolders, select My Document, and then click Next.

    The Restore wizard displays the Completing The Restore Wizard page, prompting you to start the restore operation and use the default restore settings.

6. Click Advanced to modify the default restore settings.

    The Restore wizard displays the Where To Restore page, prompting you for a target location to restore files.

7. In the Restore Files To list, select Alternate Location.

8. In the Alternate Location box, type **C:\Restored data** and then click Next.

    The Restore wizard displays the How to Restore page, prompting you to specify how to process duplicate files during the restore job.

9. Make sure that Do Not Replace The File On My Disk (Recommended) is selected, and then click Next.

    The Restore wizard displays the Advanced Restore Options page, prompting you to select security options for the restore job.

10. Make sure that all check boxes are cleared and then click Next.

    The Restore wizard displays the Completing The NT Restore Wizard page, displaying a summary of the restore options that you selected.

11. Click Finish to begin the restore process.

    Windows Backup displays the Enter Backup File Name dialog box, prompting you to supply or verify the name of the backup file that contains the folders and files to be restored.

12. Make sure that C:\Backup1.bkf is entered in the Restore From Backup File box, and then click OK.

    Windows Backup displays the Selection Information dialog box, indicating the estimated amount of data for, and the time to complete, the restore job.

    Then Windows Backup displays the Restore Progress dialog box, providing the status of the restore operation, statistics on estimated and actual amount of data that is being processed, the time that has elapsed, and the estimated time that remains for the restore operation.

▶   **To view the restore report**

1. When the Restore Progress dialog box indicates that the restore is complete, click Report.

    Notepad starts, displaying the report. Notice that the details about the restore operation are appended to the previous backup log. This provides a centralized location to view all status information for backup and restore operations.

2. Examine the report, and then exit Notepad.

3. In the Restore Progress dialog box, click Close.

   Windows Backup appears with the Welcome tab active.

▶ **To verify that the data was restored**

1. Start Windows Explorer and expand drive C.

   Does the Restored data folder exist?

2. Close Windows Explorer.

Lesson Summary

In this lesson you learned how to restore the data that you backed up. Windows Backup provides a Restore wizard to help you restore data, or you can restore data without using the wizard. The first step in restoring data is to select the data to restore. You can select individual files and folders, an entire backup job, or a backup set. The advanced settings in the Restore wizard vary, depending on the type of backup media from which you are restoring. Finally, in the practice section, you restored the data that you backed up in Exercise 1 of Lesson 2 in this chapter.

Lesson 4: Changing Windows Default Backup Options

Windows Backup allows you to change the default settings for all backup and restore jobs. These default settings are on the tabs in the Options dialog box. To access the Options dialog box, in Windows Backup, on the Tools menu, click Options.

After this lesson, you will be able to

- Explain how to change the Windows default backup options.

Estimated lesson time: 5 minutes

Understanding Windows Backup Settings

The following list provides an overview of the Windows default backup settings:

- General tab settings affect data verification, the status information for backup and restore jobs, alert messages, and what is backed up (see Figure 24.4). You should select the Verify Data After The Backup Completes check box because it is critical that your backup data is not corrupt.

- Restore tab settings affect what happens when the file to restore is identical to an existing file.

- Backup Type tab settings affect the default backup type when you perform a backup job. The options you select depend on how often you back up, how quickly you want to restore, and how much storage space you have.

- Backup Log tab settings affect the amount of information that is included in the backup log.

- Exclude Files tab settings affect which files are excluded from backup jobs.

You can modify some default settings in the Backup wizard for a specific backup job. For example, the default backup type is normal, but you can change it to another backup type in the Backup wizard. However, the next time that you run the Backup wizard, the default backup type (normal) is selected.

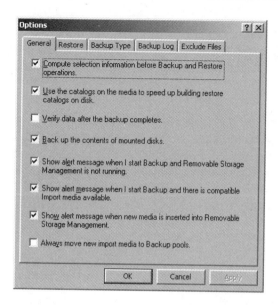

Figure 24.4   General tab of the Windows Backup Options dialog box

Lesson Summary

In this lesson you learned about the default Windows Backup options and how to change them using the tabs on the Windows Backup Options dialog box. You also learned that you can change the default settings for individual jobs.

Review

Here are some questions to help you determine if you have learned enough to move on to the next chapter. If you have difficulty answering these questions, please go back and review the material in this chapter before beginning the next chapter. The answers to these questions are located in Appendix A, "Questions and Answers."

1. If you want a user to perform network backups, what do you need to do?

2. You performed a normal backup on Monday. For the remaining days of the week, you only want to back up files and folders that have changed since the previous day. What backup type do you select?

3. What are the considerations for using tapes as your backup media?

4. You are responsible for backing up Active Directory. What must you consider?

5. Users are responsible for backing up their critical data, but there is only one tape device in your domain. In addition, you want to make sure that at least one copy of all backup data is stored offsite. What do you do?

6. You are restoring a file that has the same name as a file on the volume to which you are restoring. You are not sure which is the most current version. What do you do?

C H A P T E R   2 5

Implementing Disaster Protection

About This Chapter

In Chapter 24, "Backing Up and Restoring Data," you learned how to ensure that network data is not lost, by using the Windows Backup tool to back up and restore data. Now it is time to learn about techniques available in Microsoft Windows 2000 for preventing and recovering from computer disasters. A *computer disaster* is any event that renders a computer unable to start, such as any of the following:

- Destruction of the boot block stored on a computer's *system device* (the disk containing the files necessary to start the computer)
- Deletion of one or more operating system files
- Destruction of a computer's physical system device, leaving the rest of the computer intact
- Physical destruction of the computer itself

The causes of computer disasters are many, ranging from failure of a piece of hardware to a complete system loss, such as in the case of fire or other similar events. *Disaster protection* is a term that describes efforts by support professionals to prevent computer disasters and to minimize downtime in the event of system failure. You achieve disaster protection through a combination of fault (disaster) tolerance and disaster recovery techniques. This chapter will help you to prevent and recover from computer disasters by using the features available in Windows 2000.

Before You Begin

To complete this chapter, you must have

- A computer that meets the minimum hardware requirements listed in "Hardware Requirements," on page xxxiii.
- Installed the Windows 2000 Server software on the computer.
- Configured the computer as a domain controller in a domain.

Lesson 1: Configuring an Uninterruptible Power Supply

Disaster recovery is the restoration of a computer so that you can log on and access system resources after a computer disaster has occurred. One common type of computer disaster is the loss of local power, which can result in damaged or lost data on a server or client computer. While companies usually protect servers against this type of disaster, you might consider providing protection for client computers against power loss, as well, depending on the reliability of your local power supply.

An *uninterruptible power supply* (UPS) provides power if the local power fails and usually is rated to provide a specific amount of power for a specific period of time. In general, a UPS should provide power long enough for you to shut down a computer in an orderly way by quitting processes and closing sessions.

Note   Before purchasing a UPS for use with Windows 2000, determine whether the proposed device is on the Windows 2000 Hardware Compatibility List (HCL). The HCL is located in the support folder on the CD-ROM you used to install Windows 2000.

After this lesson, you will be able to

- Explain how to configure an uninterruptible power supply.

Estimated lesson time: 5 minutes

Configuring Options for the UPS Service

Use the UPS tab of Power Options in Control Panel to configure the UPS service by specifying the following:

- The serial port to which the UPS device is connected
- The conditions that trigger the UPS device to send a signal, such as a power failure, low battery power, and remote shutdown by the UPS device
- The time interval for maintaining battery power, recharging the battery, and sending warning messages after power failure.

Note   The configuration options for the UPS service can vary depending on the specific UPS device attached to your computer. For details about possible settings, see the documentation for your UPS device.

Testing a UPS Configuration

After you have configured the UPS service for your computer, you should test the configuration to ensure that your computer is protected from power failures. You can simulate a power failure by disconnecting the main power supply to the UPS device.

During the test, the computer and peripherals connected to the UPS device should remain operational, messages should display, and events should be logged.

Note   You should not use a production computer to test the UPS configuration. You should use a spare computer or test computer. If you use a production computer, you could lose some of the data on the computer and possibly have to reinstall Windows 2000. Remember when a computer suddenly stops, data can be lost or corrupted. The reason for having a UPS is to allow a graceful shutdown of the computers rather than an abrupt stop.

In addition, you should wait until the UPS battery reaches a low level to verify that an orderly shutdown occurs. Then, restore the main power to the UPS device and check the event log to ensure that all actions were logged and that there were no errors.

Note   Some UPS manufacturers provide their own UPS software to take advantage of the unique features of their UPS devices.

Lesson Summary

In this lesson you learned that a UPS provides power in case the local power fails. In general, a UPS should provide power long enough for you to shut down a computer in an orderly way by quitting processes and closing sessions. You learned that you use the UPS tab of Power Options in Control Panel to configure the UPS service. You can configure the serial port to which the UPS device is connected; the conditions that trigger the UPS device to send a signal, such as a power failure; and the time interval for maintaining battery power, recharging the battery, and sending warning messages after power failure.

Lesson 2: Implementing Fault Tolerance Using RAID

Fault tolerance is the ability of a computer or operating system to respond to a catastrophic event, such as a power outage or hardware failure, so that no data is lost and that work in progress is not corrupted. Fully fault tolerant systems use redundant disk controllers and power supplies as well as fault tolerant disk subsystems. In addition, fault tolerant systems often include a UPS to safeguard against local power failure.

Although the data is available and current in a fault tolerant system, you should still make backups to protect the information on hard disks from erroneous deletions, fire, theft, or other disasters. Disk fault tolerance is *not* an alternative to a backup strategy with offsite storage, which is the best insurance for recovering lost or damaged data.

If you experience the loss of a hard disk due to mechanical or electrical failure and have not implemented fault tolerance, your only option for recovering the data on the failed drive is to replace the hard disk and restore your data from a backup. However, the loss of access to the data while you replace the hard disk and restore your data can translate into lost time and money.

After this lesson, you will be able to

- Explain how to implement redundant array of independent disks (RAID) systems.

Estimated lesson time: 30 minutes

RAID Implementations

To maintain access to data during the loss of a single hard disk, Windows 2000 Server provides a software implementation of a fault tolerance technology known as redundant array of independent disks (RAID). RAID provides fault tolerance by implementing data redundancy. With *data redundancy*, a computer writes data to more than one disk, which protects the data in the event of a single hard disk failure.

Note Windows 2000 Professional does not support disk fault tolerance.

You can implement RAID fault tolerance as either a software or hardware solution.

Software Implementations of RAID

Windows 2000 Server supports two software implementations of RAID: mirrored volumes (RAID 1) and striped volumes with parity (RAID 5), otherwise known as RAID-5 volumes. However, you can create new RAID volumes only on Windows 2000 dynamic disks.

With software implementations of RAID, there is no fault tolerance following a failure until the fault is repaired. If a second fault occurs before the data lost from the first fault is regenerated, you can recover the data only by restoring it from a backup.

Hardware Implementations of RAID

In a hardware solution, the disk controller interface handles the creation and regeneration of redundant information. Some hardware vendors implement RAID data protection directly into their hardware, as with disk array controller cards. Because these methods are vendor-specific and bypass the fault tolerance software drivers of the operating system, they usually offer performance improvements over software implementations of RAID. In addition, hardware implementations of RAID usually include extra features, such as hot swapping of failed hard disks and dedicated cache memory for improved performance.

Note   The level of RAID supported in a hardware implementation is dependent on the hardware manufacturer.

Consider the following points when deciding whether to use a software or hardware implementation of RAID:

- Hardware fault tolerance is more expensive than software fault tolerance.
- Hardware fault tolerance generally provides faster computer performance than software fault tolerance.
- Hardware fault tolerance solutions might limit equipment options to a single vendor.
- Hardware fault tolerance solutions might implement hot swapping of hard disks to allow for replacement of a failed hard disk without shutting down the computer.

Note   When you upgrade Windows NT version 4.0 to Windows 2000, any existing mirror sets or stripe sets with parity are retained. Windows 2000 provides limited support for these fault tolerance sets, allowing you to manage and delete them.

Mirrored Volumes

A mirrored volume uses the Windows 2000 Server fault tolerance driver (Ftdisk.sys) to write the same data to a volume on each of two physical disks simultaneously, as diagrammed in Figure 25.1. Each volume is considered a *member* of the mirrored volume. Implementing a mirrored volume helps to ensure the survival of data in the event that one member of the mirrored volume fails.

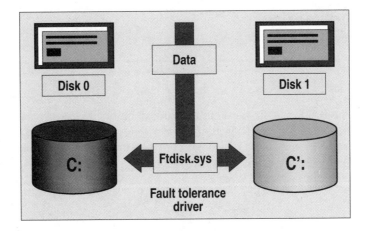

Figure 25.1   Mirrored volume

A mirrored volume can contain any partition, including the boot or system partition; however, both disks in a mirrored volume must be Windows 2000 dynamic disks.

Performance on Mirrored Volumes

Mirrored volumes can enhance read performance because the fault tolerance driver reads from both members of the volume at once. There can be a slight *decrease* in write performance, because the fault tolerance driver must write to both members. When one member of a mirrored volume fails, performance returns to normal because the fault tolerance driver works with only a single partition.

Because disk space usage is only 50 percent (two members for one set of data), mirrored volumes can be expensive.

Caution   Deleting a mirrored volume will delete all the information stored on that volume.

Disk Duplexing

If the same disk controller controls both physical disks in a mirrored volume, and the disk controller fails, neither member of the mirrored volume is accessible. You can install a second controller in the computer so that each disk in the mirrored volume has its own controller. This arrangement, called *disk duplexing,* can protect the mirrored volume against both controller failure and hard disk failure.

It also reduces bus traffic and potentially improves read performance. Disk duplexing is a hardware enhancement to a Windows 2000 mirrored volume and requires no additional software configuration.

RAID-5 Volumes

Windows 2000 Server also supports fault tolerance through striped volumes with parity (RAID 5). *Parity* is a mathematical method of determining the number of odd and even bits in a number or series of numbers, which can be used to reconstruct data if one number in a sequence of numbers is lost.

In a RAID-5 volume, Windows 2000 achieves fault tolerance by adding a parity-information stripe to each disk partition in the volume, as shown in Figure 25.2. If a single disk fails, Windows 2000 can use the data *and* parity information on the remaining disks to reconstruct the data that was on the failed disk.

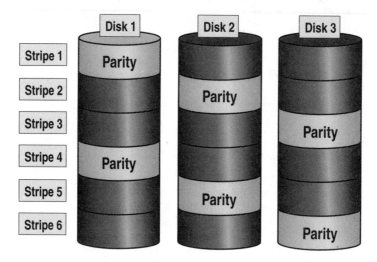

Figure 25.2   Raid-5 parity-information stripes

Because of the parity calculation, write operations on a RAID-5 volume are slower than on a mirrored volume. However, RAID-5 volumes provide better read performance than mirrored volumes, especially with multiple controllers, because data is distributed among multiple drives. If a disk fails, however, the read performance on a RAID-5 volume slows while Windows 2000 Server reconstructs the data for the failed disk by using parity information.

RAID-5 volumes have a cost advantage over mirrored volumes because disk usage is optimized. The more disks that you have in the RAID-5 volume, the less the cost of the redundant data stripe. Table 25.1 shows how the amount of space required for the data stripe decreases with the addition of 2-gigabyte (GB) disks to the RAID-5 volume.

Table 25.1   RAID-5 Disk Usage

Number of disks	Disk space used	Available disk space	Redundancy
3	6 GB	4 GB	33 percent
4	8 GB	6 GB	25 percent
5	10 GB	8 GB	20 percent

There are some restrictions on RAID-5 volumes. First of all, RAID-5 volumes involve a *minimum* of three drives and a *maximum* of 32 drives. Secondly, a RAID-5 volume *cannot* contain the boot or system partition.

Mirrored Volumes vs. RAID-5 Volumes

Mirrored volumes and RAID-5 volumes provide different levels of fault tolerance. Deciding which option to implement depends on the level of protection that you require and the cost of hardware. The major differences between mirrored volumes (RAID 1) and RAID-5 volumes are performance and cost. Table 25.2 describes some differences between RAID 1 and RAID 5.

Table 25.2   Comparison of Mirrored Volumes and RAID-5 Volumes

Mirrored volumes RAID 1	Striped volumes with parity RAID-5 volumes
Supports FAT and NTFS	Supports FAT and NTFS
Can protect system or boot partition	Cannot protect system or boot partition
Requires 2 hard disks	Requires a minimum of 3 hard disks, and allows a maximum of 32 hard disks
Has a higher cost per megabyte	Has a lower cost per megabyte
50 percent utilization	33 percent minimum utilization
Has good write performance	Has moderate write performance
Has good read performance	Has excellent read performance
Uses less system memory	Requires more system memory

Generally, mirrored volumes offer read and write performance comparable to that of single disks. RAID-5 volumes offer better read performance than mirrored volumes, especially with multiple controllers, because data is distributed among multiple drives. However, the need to calculate parity information requires more computer memory, which can slow write performance.

Mirroring only uses 50 percent of the available disk space, so it more expensive in cost per megabyte (MB) than disks without mirroring. RAID 5 uses 66 percent of the available disk space when you use the minimum number of hard disks (three). With RAID 5, disk utilization improves as you increase the number of hard disks (see Table 25.1 above).

Implementing RAID Systems

The fault tolerance features of Windows 2000 Server are only available on Windows 2000 dynamic disks.

Note   For more information about dynamic disks, see Chapter 7, "Managing Disks."

In Windows 2000 Server, you create mirrored and RAID-5 volumes by using the Create Volume wizard in the Computer Management snap-in.

▶   **To create a volume using the Create Volume wizard**

1. On the Taskbar, click the Start button, point to Programs, point to Administrative Tools, and then click Computer Management.

2. In the console tree, expand Storage, and then click Disk Management.

   The details pane of the Computer Management window displays a text view of the physical disks in your computer, while the lower-right pane displays a graphical view.

3. In the depiction of a dynamic disk, right click an area of unallocated space, and then select Create Volume.

4. In the Create Volume wizard, click Next.

   The Select Volume Type page appears.

   The wizard now requires you to make several choices. Table 25.3 describes the options that you can specify by using the Create Volume wizard.

5. After you specify the appropriate options, click Finish to close the wizard and create the volume.

Table 25.3   Create Volume Wizard Options

Option	Description
Select Disks	The dynamic disks that will participate in the volume. For mirrored volumes, you can select only two disks. For RAID-5 volumes, you must select at least three disks.
Volume Size	The amount of unallocated disk space to use on each selected dynamic disk.
Assign A Drive Letter Or Path	A drive letter or path for the volume that you are creating.
Format Volume	Formatting options for the volume.

Recovering from a Mirrored Volume Failure

In a mirrored volume, the computer saves data to each member simultaneously. If one member fails, the functional member continues to operate.

To replace the failed member, first you must "remove" the failed disk from the mirrored volume. Using the Computer Management snap-in, you can isolate the working member as a separate volume. Then, you can replace the failed disk with a functional disk.

To recreate the mirrored volume after replacing the failed disk, in the Computer Management window, click the working partition, and then click Add Mirror. The computer then presents the option to mirror this partition to the replacement disk.

In Figure 25.3, drive D on disk 1 is mirrored on disk 2. Drive D on disk 2 is the secondary member of the mirrored volume.

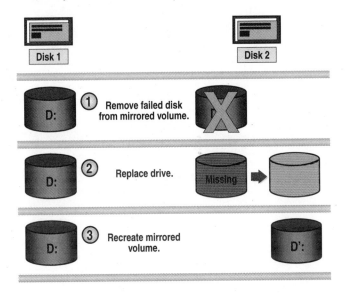

Figure 25.3   Replacing a failed disk in a mirrored volume

▶   **To replace a failed disk**

1. If disk 2 fails, physically remove the failed disk from the computer, and then remove the disk from the mirrored volume by using the Computer Management snap-in.

2. Physically replace disk 2 with another disk drive. The failed disk will show up as missing in the Computer Management snap-in to allow you to remove the drive from the mirrored volume.

3. Recreate the mirrored volume by adding the new disk 2 to the remaining volume on disk 1 to form a new mirrored volume.

▶ **To remove a mirrored volume from Windows 2000 when a member disk fails**

1. On the taskbar, click the Start button, point to Programs, point to Administrative Tools, and then click Computer Management.
2. Expand Storage, and then click Disk Management.
3. Under Failed Redundancy, right-click the depiction of the functioning member, and then click Remove Mirror.
4. In the Remove Mirror dialog box, click Missing, and then click Remove Mirror.

   The functioning member of the mirrored volume appears as a Simple Volume.

If the primary member of a mirrored volume, including the boot partition, fails, use a boot disk to start the computer and access the functioning member. The Boot.ini file on the boot disk must include the Advanced RISC Computing (ARC) path pointing to the mirrored partition. *It is recommended that you create and test a boot disk immediately after implementing a mirrored volume.*

Note   Replacing a failed member is not the only reason to remove a mirrored volume. You might also remove one member of a mirrored volume to reclaim the disk space for other purposes.

Repairing a RAID-5 Volume

If a member of a RAID-5 volume fails, the computer continues to operate with access to all data. However, as data is requested, the Windows 2000 Server fault tolerance driver uses the data and parity bits on the remaining members to regenerate the missing data in RAM. During this regeneration, computer performance decreases.

To restore the computer's level of performance, you can replace the failed drive and then repair the RAID-5 volume. The fault tolerance driver reads the parity information from the parity information stripes on the remaining members, and then recreates the data contained on the missing member. When complete, the fault tolerance driver writes the data to the new member.

▶ **To repair a failed RAID-5 volume**

1. In the Computer Management snap-in, expand Storage, and then click Disk Management.
2. Under Failed Redundancy, right-click the depiction of one of the volumes in the RAID-5 set, and then click Repair Volume.

3. In the Repair RAID-5 Volume dialog box, in the list of available hard drives, click a disk, and then click OK.

Windows 2000 regenerates the data and parity information on the new disk.

Lesson Summary

In this lesson you learned that Windows 2000 Server provides a software implementation of RAID, which provides fault tolerance by implementing data redundancy. With data redundancy, a computer writes data to more than one disk, which protects the data in the event of a single hard disk failure.

You learned that a mirrored volume (RAID 1) uses the Windows 2000 Server fault tolerance driver (Ftdisk.sys) to write the same data to a volume on each of two physical disks simultaneously. A mirrored volume can contain any partition, including the boot or system partition; however, both disks in a mirrored volume must be Windows 2000 dynamic disks.

You also learned that if the same disk controller controls both physical disks in a mirrored volume, and the disk controller fails, neither member of the mirrored volume is accessible. By installing a second controller in the computer, each disk in the mirrored volume has its own controller. This arrangement, called disk duplexing, can protect the mirrored volume against both controller failure and hard disk failure.

Finally, you learned that Windows 2000 Server also supports fault tolerance through striped volumes with parity (RAID 5). In a RAID-5 volume, Windows 2000 achieves fault tolerance by adding a parity-information stripe to each disk partition in the volume. If a single disk fails, Windows 2000 can use the data and parity information on the remaining disks to reconstruct the data that was on the failed disk.

Lesson 3: Implementing Automatic System Recovery

If you change the Windows 2000 configuration to load a driver and have problems rebooting, Windows 2000 has a feature that usually prevents you from having to reinstall. This feature allows you to try loading the Last Known Good configuration, which is stored in the registry, to boot Windows 2000. This Last Known Good Process is explained in Chapter 27, "The Windows 2000 Boot Process."

If Windows 2000 fails to start or function correctly, and using the Last Known Good configuration does not solve the problem, you can use Automatic System Recovery (ASR) to restore Windows 2000. The ASR process consists of two components: a login recovery component and a file restore component (Windows Backup).

After this lesson, you will be able to

- Explain how to implement Automatic System Recovery.

Estimated lesson time: 15 minutes

Understanding Login Recovery

The purpose of the login recovery component is to bring a nonbootable computer to a state in which you can log on and invoke the file restore component. The login recovery component is incorporated into both the text mode and the graphical mode of the Windows 2000 Setup program.

During login recovery, ASR restores the following:

- A computer's physical storage configuration, including the partition structure of each disk and the file format of each partition
- Windows 2000 operating system files, including all the files in the *systemroot* directory hierarchy
- Windows 2000 boot files (Ntldr and Ntdetect.com)

Understanding File Restore

The purpose of the file restore component is to recover additional computer and user files. When file restoration is complete, ASR has completely restored the computer to its predisaster state.

Creating an Automatic System Recovery Saveset

For ASR to function properly, the file restore component, or backup application, must preserve the computer's configuration information and operating system files. This information, together with the files necessary to recover a nonbootable computer, is called an ASR *saveset*.

▶ **To create an ASR saveset**

1. Click Start, point to Programs, point to Accessories, and then click Backup.

   The Welcome to the Backup and Restore Wizards screen appears.

2. Click Automated System Recovery and Preparation Wizard.

   The Welcome to the Automated System Recovery and Preparation Wizard screen appears.

3. Click Next.

   The Backup Destination screen appears.

4. Select the Backup Media Type and type in the Backup Media or File Name, and then click Next.

5. Click Finish to complete the Automated System Recovery Preparation wizard.

When you create an ASR saveset, the backup application does the following:

- Creates a setup information file (SIF) on the ASR floppy disk. The SIF contains the following configuration information:
  - The physical configuration of the disks that are attached to the computer
  - Partition attributes such as type, volume label, drive letter, size and starting sector, and so on
  - Computer configuration information (for example, computer name and Windows 2000 directory path)
  - The name and location of the required device driver files
  - One or more commands with which the backup and restore applications are invoked
- Copies the Setup.log, Autoexec.nt, and Config.nt files from *systemroot*\Repair to the ASR floppy disk.
- Copies device driver files to the ASR floppy disk. ASR requires these device driver files to support recovery commands for device drivers that are not part of the default device driver set installed by Winnt.
- Copies all the files from the system and boot partitions to removable media.

Performing Login Recovery

In ASR, login recovery occurs in two distinct phases: Phase I and Phase II.

Phase I

In Phase I of login recovery, ASR recovers and reformats the system and boot partitions and reinstalls the operating system, if necessary. Phase 1 does the following:

1. Repartitions all disks missing one or more partitions, as specified in the SIF.

2. Recreates the original information contained on each new partition.

3. Copies the Windows 2000 files from the CD-ROM into the boot partition under *systemroot*.

4. Copies the SIF into *systemroot*\System32 and modifies the registry so that one or more restore applications (specified in the SIF) launch when you restart the computer.

At the end of Phase I, the computer restarts, and then Phase II begins.

Phase II

Phase II of login recovery begins as graphical-mode Setup launches when the computer restarts. During Phase II, you run one or more applications to restore the original operating system files (including the registry, device drivers, and profiles) from removable media to the *systemroot* directory.

To complete Phase II of login recovery, graphical-mode Setup does the following:

1. Starts and reads the SIF in the *systemroot*\Repair directory.

2. Reestablishes the fault tolerance volumes.

3. Reestablishes other volumes on dynamic disks.

4. Restores all files to *systemroot* and other directories.

When Phase II is complete, the computer restarts, and then the logon prompt appears. At this point, the computer has a complete, though minimal, operating system, and you can start the file recovery component of ASR.

Repairing a Windows 2000 Installation

You can use ASR to attempt a repair of a Windows 2000 installation.

Table 25.4 describes the options that you can use during setup to determine the tasks that the ASR process performs.

Table 25.4   Options to Determine the Tasks That the ASR Process Performs

Option	Description
Inspect Startup Environment	Setup verifies that the Windows 2000 files on the system partition are the correct ones. Select this option if Windows 2000 is installed but does not appear in the list of bootable operating systems.

Verify Windows 2000 System Files	Setup verifies that each file in the installation matches the file installed from the distribution files. Setup also verifies the presence and functionality of the files needed to start, such as Ntldr and Ntoskrnl.exe. If Setup determines that a file on the disk does not match what was installed, it displays a message that identifies the file and asks whether to replace it.
Inspect Boot Sector	Setup copies a new boot sector to the hard disk. Select this option if you cannot boot from any system installed on the computer.

▶   **To use ASR to attempt to repair a Windows 2000 installation**

1. Start the computer by using the Windows 2000 CD-ROM or Setup disk 1.

2. When prompted, insert disk 2, and then disk 3.

3. When prompted, press R to select the Repair/Recovery option, and then press R again to enter the Repair A Damaged Installation screen.

4. Press F to select a Fast repair, which performs all repair tasks, or press M to select Manual Repair. If you press M, Setup displays the following options:

```
[X] Inspect startup environment

[X] Verify Windows 2000 system files

[X] Inspect boot sector

Continue (perform selected tasks)
```

5. Click to clear the options that you do not want to use, click Continue to perform selected tasks, and then press Enter.

6. When prompted, insert the ASR disk, and then follow the instructions.

   Setup displays the following messages after it has finished the repair process:

```
Setup has completed repairs.

If there is a floppy disk inserted in drive A:, remove it.

Press ENTER to restart your computer.
```

Lesson Summary

In this lesson you learned that if Windows 2000 fails to start or function correctly, and if using the Last Known Good configuration does not solve the problem, you can use ASR to restore Windows 2000. The ASR process consists of two components: a login recovery component and a file restore component (Windows Backup).

You learned that the purpose of the login recovery component is to bring a non-bootable computer to a state in which you can log on and invoke the file restore component. The purpose of the file restore component is to recover additional computer and user files. When file restoration is complete, ASR has completely restored the computer to its predisaster state.

Review

Here are some questions to help you determine if you have learned enough to move on to the next chapter. If you have difficulty answering these questions, please go back and review the material in this chapter before beginning the next chapter. The answers for these questions are located in Appendix A, "Questions and Answers."

1. What is the purpose of disaster protection, and what combination of techniques do you use to achieve it?

2. How can you test the configuration of the UPS service on a computer?

3. A computer running Windows 2000 Server has the following disk configuration:

    -   Disk 0: drive C (300 MB, system/boot partition), drive D (700 MB, data), and 500 MB of free space

    -   Disk 1: 750 MB of free space

    -   Disk 2: 1 GB of free space

    You want to install additional Microsoft BackOffice components on this computer. What is the best way both to protect your computer's data and to optimize its performance by using Windows 2000 fault tolerance?

4. What information is included in an ASR saveset?

CHAPTER 26

Monitoring Access to Network Resources

About This Chapter

This chapter prepares you to monitor network resources. You learn about the Shared Folders snap-in and how to use it to view and create shares. You also learn how to use the Shared Folders snap-in to view sessions and open files and how to use it to disconnect users from your shared folders.

Before You Begin

To complete this chapter, you must have

- A computer that meets or exceeds the minimum hardware requirements listed in "Hardware Requirements," on page xxxiii.
- Installed the Windows 2000 Server software on the computer.
- Configured the computer as a domain controller in a domain.

Lesson 1: Monitoring Network Resources

Microsoft Windows 2000 includes the Shared Folders snap-in so that you can easily monitor access to network resources and send administrative messages to users. You monitor access to network resources to assess and manage current usage on network servers.

After this lesson, you will be able to

- Identify three reasons for monitoring access to network resources.
- Identify the tool included with Windows 2000 to monitor access to network resources and to send administrative messages.
- Identify who can monitor access to network resources.

Estimated lesson time: 5 minutes

Understanding the Purposes For Monitoring Network Resources

Some of the reasons why it is important to assess and manage network resources are included in the following list:

- **Maintenance.**   You should determine which users are currently using a resource so that you can notify them before making the resource temporarily or permanently unavailable.
- **Security.**   You should monitor user access to resources that are confidential or need to be secure to verify that only authorized users are accessing them.
- **Planning.**   You should determine which resources are being used, and how much they are being used, so that you can plan for future system growth.

Microsoft Windows 2000 includes the Shared Folders snap-in so that you can easily monitor access to network resources and send administrative messages to users. When you add the Shared Folders snap-in to a Microsoft Management Console (MMC) console, you specify whether you want to monitor the resources on the local computer or a remote computer.

Understanding the Requirements To Monitor Network Resources

Not all users can monitor access to network resources. Table 26.1 lists the group membership requirements for monitoring access to network resources.

Table 26.1   Groups That Can Access Network Resources

A member of these groups	Can monitor
Administrators or Server Operators for the domain	All computers in the domain
Administrators or Power Users for a member server, stand-alone server, or computer running Microsoft Windows 2000 Workstation	That computer

Lesson Summary

In this lesson you learned some of the reasons why it is important to monitor network resources. Monitoring network resources helps you to determine if the network resource is still needed and if it is secure. Monitoring resources also helps you to plan for future growth.

You learned that Windows 2000 includes the Shared Folders snap-in so that you can monitor access to network resources. You can monitor resources on the local computer or on a remote computer. To monitor resources on a remote computer, you specify the computer on which you want to monitor resources when you add the Shared Folders snap-in to an MMC console.

Finally, you learned that not all users can monitor resources. Only members of the Administrators or Server Operators for the domain can monitor resources on all the computers in the domain. Administrators or Power Users for a member server, stand-alone server, or a computer running Microsoft Windows 2000 Workstation can monitor resources on that computer.

Lesson 2: Monitoring Access to Shared Folders

You monitor access to shared folders to determine how many users currently have a connection to each folder. You can also monitor open files to determine which users are gaining access to the files, and you can disconnect users from one open file or from all open files.

After this lesson, you will be able to

- Determine the shared folders on a computer.
- Monitor shared folders.
- View and modify the properties of a shared folder.
- Monitor open files.
- Disconnect users from one or all open files.

Estimated lesson time: 15 minutes

Monitoring Shared Folders

You use the Shares folder in the Shared Folders snap-in to view a list of all shared folders on the computer and to determine how many users have a connection to each folder. In Figure 26.1, the Shares folder has been selected in the Computer Management console tree and all the shared folders on that computer are shown in the details pane.

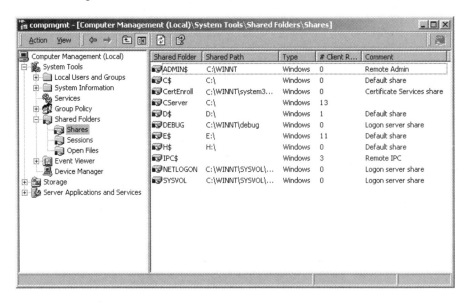

Figure 26.1 Shares folder of the Shared Folders snap-in

Table 26.2 explains the information provided in the details pane shown in Figure 26.1.

Table 26.2   Fields in the Details Pane for the Shares Folder

Column name	Description
Shared Folder	The shared folders on the computer. This is the name that was given to the folder when it was shared.
Shared Path	The path to the shared folder.
Type	The operating system that must be running on a computer so that it can be used to gain access to the shared folder.
# Client Redirections	The number of clients who have made a remote connection to the shared folder.
Comment	Descriptive text about the folder. This comment was provided when the folder was shared.

Note   Microsoft Windows 2000 does not update the list of shared folders, open files, and user sessions automatically. To update these lists, on the Action menu, click Refresh.

Determining How Many Users Can Access a Shared Folder Concurrently

You can use the Shared Folders snap-in to determine the maximum number of users that are permitted to gain access to a folder. In the Shared Folders details pane, click the shared folder for which you want to determine the maximum number of concurrent users that can access the folder. On the Action menu, click Properties, and the Properties dialog box for the shared folder appears. The General tab shows you the user limit.

You can also use the Shared Folders snap-in to determine if the maximum number of users that are permitted to gain access to a folder has been reached. This is one quick and easy way to troubleshoot connectivity problems. If a user cannot connect to a share, determine the number of connections to the share and the maximum connections allowed. If the maximum number of connections have already been made, the user cannot connect to the shared resource.

Modifying Shared Folder Properties

You can modify existing shared folders, including shared folder permissions, from the Shares folder. To change a shared folder's properties, click the shared folder, and then on the Action menu, click Properties. The General tab of the Properties dialog box shows you the Share name, the path to the shared folder, and any comment that has been entered. The General tab also allows you to view and set a user limit for accessing the shared folder. The Security tab allows you to view and change the shared folders permissions.

Monitoring Open Files

Use the Open Files folder in the Shared Folders snap-in to view a list of open files that are located in shared folders and the users who have a current connection to each file (see Figure 26.2). You can use this information when you need to contact users to notify them that you are shutting down the system. Additionally, you can determine which users have a current connection and should be contacted when another user is trying to gain access to a file that is in use.

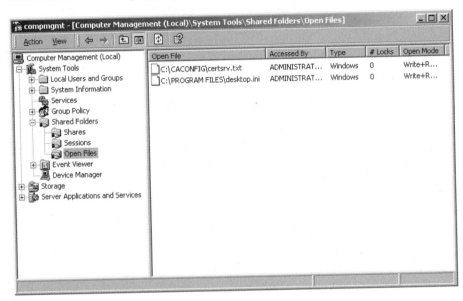

Figure 26.2   Open Files folder of the Shared Folders snap-in

Table 26.3 describes the information that is available in the Open Files folder.

Table 26.3   Information Available in the Open Files Folder

Column name	Description
Open File	The name of the open files on the computer.
Accessed By	The logon name of the user who has the file open.
Type	The operating system running on the computer where the user is logged on.
# Locks	The number of locks on the file. Programs can request the operating system to lock a file in order to gain exclusive access and prevent other programs from making changes to the file.
Open Mode	The type of access that the user's application requested when it opened the file, such as Read or Write.

Disconnecting Users from Open Files

You can disconnect users from one open file or from all open files. If you make changes to Windows NT file system (NTFS) permissions for a file that is currently opened by a user, the new permissions will not affect the user until he or she closes and then attempts to reopen the file.

You can force these changes to take place immediately by doing either of the following:

- Disconnecting all users from all open files. To disconnect all users from all open files, in the Shared Folders snap-in console tree, click Open Files, and then on the Action menu, click Disconnect All Open Files.

- Disconnecting all users from one open file. To disconnect users from one open file, in the Shared Folders snap-in console tree, click Open Files. In the details pane select the open file, and then on the Action menu, click Close Open File.

Caution   Disconnecting users from open files can result in data loss.

Practice: Managing Shared Folders

In this practice you use the Shared Folders snap-in to view the shared folders and open files on your server. You will disconnect all users from all open files.

▶ **To view the shared folders on your computer**

1. Click the Start button, point to Programs, point to Administrative Tools, and then click Computer Management.

2. In the console tree of Computer Management, expand System Tools, and then expand Shared Folders.

3. In the console tree, click Shares under Shared Folders.

   Notice that the details pane shows a list of the existing Shared Folders on your computer.

▶ **To view the open files on your computer**

1. In the console tree, click Open Files under Shared Folders.

   If you are working on a computer that is not connected to a network, there will not be any open files because the open files only show connections from a remote computer to a share on your computer.

▶   **To disconnect all users from open files on your computer**

1. In the console tree, select Open Files under Shared Folders, and then click Disconnect All Open Files on the Action menu.

    If you are not on a network, there will not be any open files to disconnect.

2. Leave Computer Management open. You will use it in the next practice.

Lesson Summary

In this lesson you learned that you use the Shares folder in the Shared Folders snap-in to view a list of all shared folders on the computer and to determine how many users have a connection to each folder. The General tab of the Properties page for a shared folder shows you the user limit, or maximum number of users that can concurrently connect to that share.

You also learned that you can modify existing shared folders, including shared folder permissions. To change a shared folder's properties, click the shared folder, and then on the Action menu, click Properties. The General tab of the Properties dialog box lets you view and change the user limit for accessing the shared folder. The Security tab allows you to view and change the shared folders permissions.

Lesson 3: Sharing a Folder Using the Shared Folders Snap-In

You can use the Shared Folders snap-in to share an existing folder or to create a new folder and share it on the local computer or on a remote computer. You can also modify the shared folder and NTFS permissions when you share the folder.

After this lesson, you will be able to

- Share a folder by using the Shared Folders snap-in.
- Stop sharing a folder by using the Shared Folders snap-in.

Estimated lesson time: 15 minutes

When you use the Shared Folders snap-in to share an existing folder or to create a new folder and share it, Windows 2000 assigns the Full Control shared folder permission to the Everyone group. You can also assign NTFS permissions when you share the folder.

Note Using the Shared Folders snap-in is the only way to create a shared folder on a remote computer. Otherwise, you need to be physically located at the computer where the folder resides to share it.

Practice: Creating a Shared Folder

In this practice, you use the Shared Folders snap-in to create a new Shared Folder on your server.

▶ **To create a new shared folder on your computer**

1. In the console tree, under Shared Folders, click Shares.
2. On the Action menu, click New File Share.

   The Create Shared Folder wizard starts.
3. In the Create Shared Folder wizard, in the Folder name box, type **C:\MyShare**
4. Click Next.

   A message box appears asking you if you want to create C:\MyShare.
5. Click Yes.

   A message box appears informing you that C:\MyShare has been created.
6. Click OK.

   The Set Permissions page appears. Whether the wizard creates a folder for you or you select an existing folder, you can keep the original NTFS permissions, or you can change the existing permissions for the folder. If you used the wizard to create the folder, the folder inherits permissions from its parent folder.

The NTFS permissions options are described in the following table. The first three permissions options are radio button selections indicating that you must select one and only one of the three options.

Option	Description
Keep The Current Permissions	The wizard maintains the current permissions, whether this is an existing folder or whether this is a new folder created using the wizard. This is the default.
Only I Have Full Control, But Others Can Read Files In This Folder	The wizard assigns the Full Control NTFS permission for the folder to the user who is sharing the folder. The wizard also assigns the Read NTFS permission for the folder to the Everyone group.
Everyone Has Access And Full Control	The wizard assigns the Full Control permission for the folder to the Everyone group. The wizard also assigns the Full Control NTFS permission for the folder to the user who is sharing the folder.
Apply These Permissions To All Folders And Files Within This Folder	Select this check box to allow permissions inheritance, or clear it to prevent permissions inheritance. This check box is not available if you select Keep The Current Permissions.

7. Click Next to accept the current permissions.

   The Name The Shared Folder And Control Computer Access page appears with the shared folder name selected. The shared folder name is limited to 12 characters.

8. Press the Tab key to accept the suggested shared folder name of MyShare and move to the Description box.

9. Type **Practice Share** in the Description box.

   Users will see the description for the shared folder when they browse for the shared folder.

10. Click Next.

   The Completing The Create Shared Folder Wizard page appears and summarizes for you the shared folder the wizard will create.

11. Click Finish to close the wizard and finish creating the shared folder.

   A message box appears asking if you want to set access for another folder.

12. Click No.

   The wizard finishes. Does the new shared folder appear in the details pane? Why or why not?

You also can use the Shared Folders snap-in to stop sharing a shared folder.

▶ **To stop sharing a folder**

1. In the console tree, under Shared Folders, click Shares.
2. Select the MyShare folder in the details pane.
3. On the Action menu, click Stop Sharing.

   A message box appears asking if you are sure you want to stop sharing the Share.

4. Click OK.

   The MyShare share disappears from the list of shared folders.

Caution   If you stop sharing a folder while a user has a file open, the user might lose data.

Lesson Summary

In this lesson you learned that you can use the Shared Folders snap-in to share an existing folder or to create a new folder and share it on the local computer or on a remote computer. The Shared Folders snap-in is the only tool available in Windows 2000 that allows you to create a shared folder on a remote computer. You can set the shared folder and NTFS permissions when you share the folder.

Lesson 4: Monitoring Network Users

You can also use the Shared Folders snap-in to monitor which users are currently gaining access to shared folder resources on a server from a remote computer, and you can view the resources to which the users have connections. You can disconnect users and send administrative messages to computers and users, including computers and users who are not currently gaining access to network resources.

After this lesson, you will be able to

- Disconnect a specific user from his or her network connection.
- Send administrative messages to users.

Estimated lesson time: 20 minutes

Monitoring User Sessions

You can use the Shared Folders snap-in to view users who have a connection to open files on a server and the files to which they have a connection. This information enables you to determine which users you should contact when you need to stop sharing a folder or shut down the server on which the shared folder resides. You can disconnect one or more users to free idle connections to the shared folder, to prepare for a backup or restore operation, to shut down a server, and to change group membership and permissions for the shared folder.

You use the Sessions folder in the Shared Folders snap-in to view a list of the users with a current network connection to the computer that you are monitoring (see Figure 26.3).

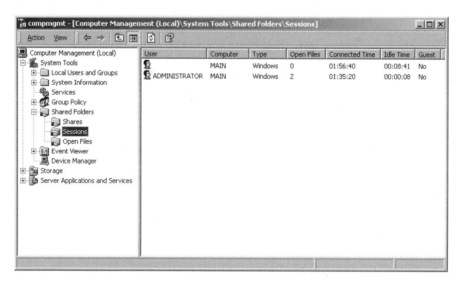

Figure 26.3   Sessions folder of the Shared Folders snap-in

Table 26.4 describes the information that is available in the Sessions folder.

Table 26.4   Information Available in the Sessions Folder

Column name	Description
User	The users with a current network connection to this computer
Computer	The name of the user's computer
Type	The operating system running on the user's computer
Open Files	The number of files that the user has open on this computer
Connected Time	The time that has elapsed since the user established the current session
Idle Time	The time that has elapsed since the user last gained access to a resource on this computer
Guest	Whether this computer authenticated the user as a member of the built-in Guest account

Disconnecting Users

You can disconnect one or all users with a network connection to a computer. You disconnect users so that you can do any of the following:

- Have changes to shared folder and NTFS permissions take effect immediately. A user retains all permissions for a shared resource that Windows 2000 assigned when the user connected to it. Windows 2000 evaluates the permissions again the next time that a connection is made.

- Free idle connections on a computer so that other users can make a connection when you reach the maximum number of connections. User connections to resources might remain active for several minutes after a user finishes gaining access to a resource.

- Shut down a server.

Note   After you disconnect a user, the user can immediately make a new connection. If the user gains access to a shared folder from a Windows-based client computer, the client computer will automatically reestablish the connection with the shared folder. This connection will be established without user intervention unless you change the permissions to prevent the user from gaining access to the shared folder or you stop sharing the folder to prevent all users from gaining access to the shared folder.

▶   **To disconnect a specific user**

1. In the console tree, under Shared Folders, click Sessions.

2. In the list of users in the details pane, select the user that you want to disconnect, and then click Close Session on the Action menu.

Note If you want to disconnect all users, click Sessions in the console tree, and then click Disconnect All Sessions on the Action menu.

To prevent data loss, you should always notify users who are accessing shared folders or files that you are ready to stop sharing a folder or shut down the computer.

Sending Administrative Messages to Users

You can send administrative messages to one or more users or computers. Send administrative messages to users who have a current connection to a computer on which network resources are shared when there will be a disruption to the computer or resource availability. Some common reasons for sending administrative messages are to notify users when you intend to do any of the following:

- Perform a backup or restore operation
- Disconnect users from a resource
- Upgrade software or hardware
- Shut down the computer

Use the Shared Folders snap-in to send administrative messages to users. By default, all currently connected computers to which you can send a message appear in the list of recipients. You can add other users or computers to this list even if they do not have a current connection to resources on the computer.

Practice: Sending Console Messages

In this practice, you use the Shared Folders snap-in to send a console message.

▶ **To send a console message**

1. In the console tree, under Shared Folders, select Shares.
2. On the Action menu, point to All Tasks, and then click Send Console Message.
3. In the Message box, type **Log Off Now — Server1 is shutting down in 5 minutes**

   If your computer is not connected to a network, you will notice that the Send button is unavailable and that the Recipients box is empty.
4. Click Add.

   The Add Recipients dialog box appears.
5. Type **Server1** in the Recipients box.

   Server1 should be the name of your computer. If you did not name your computer Server1, type the name of your server in the Recipients box.

6. Click OK.

Notice that the Send button is now available.

7. Click Send.

A message box briefly appears showing that the message is being sent, and then the Messenger Service dialog box appears, as shown in Figure 26.4. It confirms that a message was sent from Server1 to Server1, indicating the date and time the message was sent, and displaying the message that was sent.

8. Click OK to close the message box.

Figure 26.4   Messenger Service dialog box

Lesson Summary

In this lesson you learned how to use the Shared Folders snap-in to view users who have a connection to open files on a server and the files to which they have a connection. It is the Sessions folder that allows you to view connections to open files on a server and allows you to disconnect a specific user or all users with a network connection to a computer.

You also learned that the Shared Folders snap-in allows you to send administrative messages to one or more users or computers, and that by default all currently connected computers appear in the list of recipients to which you can send a message. Finally, you learned how to use the Add button to add other users or computers to the list of recipients for administrative messages, even if they do not have a current connection to any resources on the computer.

Review

Here are some questions to help you determine if you have learned enough to move on to the next chapter. If you have difficulty answering these questions, please go back and review the material in this chapter before beginning the next chapter. The answers for these questions are located in Appendix A, "Questions and Answers."

1. What are the reasons for monitoring access to network resources?

2. What can you monitor on a network with the Shared Folders snap-in?

3. Why would you send an administrative message to users with current connections?

4. What can you do to prevent a user from reconnecting to a shared folder after you have disconnected the user from the shared folder?

5. How does the Shared Folders snap-in use shared folder permissions and NTFS permissions when you share a folder?

C H A P T E R   2 7

The Windows 2000 Boot Process

About This Chapter

This chapter introduces you to the Microsoft Windows 2000 boot process. You will learn about the Intel-based boot process and the Alpha-based boot process. You will also learn about using the Boot.ini file and about creating a Windows 2000 boot disk.

Before You Begin

To complete this chapter, you must have

- A computer that meets the minimum hardware requirements listed in "Hardware Requirements," on page xxxiii.
- A blank, high-density floppy disk, which you will use to create a Windows 2000 boot disk.
- Installed the Windows 2000 Server software on the computer.
- Configured the computer as a domain controller in a domain.

Lesson 1: The Intel-Based Boot Process

In this lesson you will learn that the Windows 2000 boot process occurs in five stages: the preboot sequence, boot sequence, kernel load, kernel initialization, and logon. You will learn how to troubleshoot more effectively by learning about the phases in the Windows 2000 Intel-based boot process and the files used in each phase.

After this lesson, you will be able to

- Explain the boot process for Intel-based computers.

Estimated lesson time: 25 minutes

Files Used in the Intel-Based Boot Process

An Intel-based boot sequence requires certain files. Table 27.1 lists the files used in the Windows 2000 Intel-based boot process, the appropriate location of each file, and the stages of the boot process associated with each file. *Systemroot* represents the path to your Windows 2000 installation directory, which will be C:\Winnt if you've followed the installation instructions in Chapter 2, "Installing Windows 2000."

Table 27.1   Files Used in the Windows 2000 Intel-Based Boot Process

File	Location	Boot stage
Ntldr (hidden)	System partition root (C:\)	Preboot and boot
Boot.ini	System partition root	Boot
Bootsect.dos (optional)	System partition root	Boot
Ntdetect.com (hidden)	System partition root	Boot
Ntbootdd.sys (optional)	System partition root	Boot
Ntoskrnl.exe	*systemroot*\System32	Kernel load
Hal.dll	*systemroot*\System32	Kernel load
System	*systemroot*\System32\Config	Kernel initialization
Device drivers (*.sys)	*systemroot*\System32\Drivers	Kernel initialization

Preboot Sequence

During startup, a Windows 2000–based computer initializes and then locates the boot portion of the hard disk.

The following four steps occur during the preboot sequence:

1. The computer runs power-on self test (POST) routines to determine the amount of physical memory, whether the hardware components are present, and so on. If the computer has a Plug and Play basic input/output system (BIOS), enumeration and configuration of hardware devices occurs at this stage.

2. The computer BIOS locates the boot device and loads and runs the master boot record (MBR).

3. The MBR scans the partition table to locate the active partition, loads the boot sector on the active partition into memory, and then executes it.

4. The computer loads and initializes the Ntldr file, which is the operating system loader.

Note   Windows 2000 modifies the boot sector during installation so that Ntldr loads during system startup.

Boot Sequence

After the computer loads Ntldr into memory, the boot sequence gathers information about hardware and drivers in preparation for the Windows 2000 load phases. The boot sequence uses the following files: Ntldr, Boot.ini, Bootsect.dos (optional), Ntdetect.com, and Ntoskrnl.exe.

There are four phases in the boot sequence: initial boot loader phase, operating system selection, hardware detection, and configuration selection.

Initial Boot Loader Phase

During the initial boot loader phase, Ntldr switches the microprocessor from real mode to 32-bit flat memory mode, which Ntldr requires to carry out any additional functions. Next, Ntldr starts the appropriate minifile system drivers. The minifile system drivers are built into Ntldr so that Ntldr can find and load Windows 2000 from partitions formatted with either the file allocation table (FAT) or Windows NT file system (NTFS).

Operating System Selection

During the boot sequence, Ntldr reads the Boot.ini file, and then the Operating System Selection menu appears, listing the operating systems specified in the Boot.ini file. You use the Operating System Selection menu to specify which operating system to load. If you do not select an entry before the timer reaches zero, Ntldr loads the operating system specified by the default parameter in the Boot.ini file. Windows 2000 Setup sets the default parameter to the most recent Windows 2000 installation.

Note   If the Boot.ini file is not present, Ntldr attempts to load Windows 2000 from \Winnt on the first partition of the first disk, typically C:\Winnt.

Hardware Detection

On Intel-based computers, Ntdetect.com and Ntoskrnl.exe perform hardware detection. Ntdetect.com executes after you select Windows 2000 on the operating system selection menu (or after the timer times out).

Note   If you select an operating system other than Windows 2000, such as Microsoft Windows 98, Ntldr loads and executes Bootsect.dos. Bootsect.dos is a copy of the boot sector that was on the system partition at the time that Windows 2000 was installed. Passing execution to Bootsect.dos starts the boot process for the selected operating system.

Ntdetect.com collects a list of currently installed hardware components and returns this list to Ntldr for later inclusion in the registry under the HKEY_LOCAL_ MACHINE\HARDWARE key.

Ntdetect.com detects the following components:

- Bus/adapter type
- Communication ports
- Floating-point coprocessor
- Floppy disks
- Keyboard
- Mouse/pointing device
- Parallel ports
- Small Computer System Interface (SCSI) adapters
- Video adapters

Configuration Selection

After Ntldr starts loading Windows 2000 and collects hardware information, OS Loader presents you with the option of pressing the Spacebar to invoke the Hardware Profile/Configuration Recovery menu. The Hardware Profile/Configuration Recovery menu contains a list of the hardware profiles that are set up on the computer. The first hardware profile is highlighted. If you have created additional hardware profiles, you can press the Down arrow key to select another profile. You also can press L to invoke the Last Known Good configuration.

If you do not press the Spacebar, or if there is only a single hardware profile, Ntldr loads Windows 2000 using the default hardware profile configuration.

Kernel Load

After configuration selection, the Windows 2000 kernel (Ntoskrnl.exe) loads and initializes. Ntoskrnl.exe also loads and initializes device drivers and loads services. If you press Enter when the Hardware Profile/Configuration Recovery menu displays, or if Ntldr makes the selection automatically, the computer enters the kernel load phase. The screen clears and progress periods (…) appear across the top of the screen.

During the kernel load phase, Ntldr does the following:

- Loads Ntoskrnl.exe but does not initialize it.

- Loads the hardware abstraction layer file (Hal.dll).

- Loads the HKEY_LOCAL_MACHINE\SYSTEM registry key from *systemroot*\System32\Config\System.

- Selects the control set it will use to initialize the computer. A *control set* contains configuration data used to control the system, such as a list of the device drivers and services to load and start.

- Loads device drivers with a value of 0x0 for the Start entry. These typically are low-level hardware device drivers, such as those for a hard disk. The value for the List entry, which is specified in the HKEY_LOCAL_MACHINE\ SYSTEM\CurrentControlSet\Control\ServiceGroupOrder subkey of the registry, defines the order in which Ntldr loads these device drivers.

Kernel Initialization

When the kernel load phase is complete, the kernel initializes, and then Ntldr passes control to the kernel. At this point, the system displays a graphical screen with a status bar indicating load status. Four tasks are accomplished during the kernel initialization stage:

1. **The Hardware key is created.**   Upon successful initialization, the kernel uses the data collected during hardware detection to create the registry key HKEY_LOCAL_MACHINE\HARDWARE. This key contains information about hardware components on the system board and the interrupts used by specific hardware devices.

2. **The Clone control set is created.**   The kernel creates the Clone control set by copying the control set referenced by the value of the Current entry in the HKEY_LOCAL_MACHINE\SYSTEM\Select subkey of the registry. The Clone control set is never modified, as it is intended to be an identical copy of the data used to configure the computer and should not reflect changes made during the startup process.

3. **Device drivers are loaded and initialized.**   After creating the Clone control set, the kernel initializes the low-level device drivers that were loaded during the kernel load phase. The kernel then scans the HKEY_LOCAL_MACHINE\ SYSTEM\CurrentControlSet\Services subkey of the registry for device drivers with a value of 0x1 for the Start entry. As in the kernel load phase, a device driver's value for the Group entry specifies the order in which it loads. Device drivers initialize as soon as they load.

If an error occurs while loading and initializing a device driver, the boot process proceeds based on the value specified in the ErrorControl entry for the driver.

Table 27.2 describes the possible ErrorControl values and the resulting boot sequence actions.

Table 27.2   ErrorControl Values and Resulting Action

ErrorControl value	Action
0x0 (Ignore)	The boot sequence ignores the error and proceeds without displaying an error message.
0x1 (Normal)	The boot sequence displays an error message but ignores the error and proceeds.
0x2 (Severe)	The boot sequence fails and then restarts using the LastKnownGood control set. If the boot sequence is currently using the LastKnownGood control set, the boot sequence ignores the error and proceeds.
0x3 (Critical)	The boot sequence fails and then restarts using the LastKnownGood control set. However, if the Last-KnownGood control set is causing the critical error, the boot sequence stops and displays an error message.

ErrorControl values appear in the registry under the subkey HKEY_LOCAL_ MACHINE\SYSTEM\CurrentControlSet\Services*name_of_service_or_driver*\ ErrorControl.

4. **Services are started.**   After the kernel loads and initializes devices drivers, the Session Manager (Smss.exe) starts the higher-order subsystems and services for Windows 2000. Session Manager executes the instructions in the BootExecute data item, and in the Memory Management, DOS Devices, and Subsystems keys.

Table 27.3 describes the function of each instruction set and the resulting Session Manager action.

Table 27.3   Session Manager Reads and Executes the Following Instruction Sets

Data item or key	Action
BootExecute data item	Session Manager executes the commands specified in this data item before it loads any services.
Memory Management key	Session Manager creates the paging file information required by the Virtual Memory Manager.
DOS Devices key	Session Manager creates symbolic links that direct certain classes of commands to the correct component in the file system.
SubSystems key	Session Manager starts the Win32 subsystem, which controls all input/output (I/O) and access to the video screen and starts the WinLogon process.

Logon

The logon process begins at the conclusion of the kernel initialization phase. The Win32 subsystem automatically starts Winlogon.exe, which starts the Local Security Authority (Lsass.exe) and displays the logon dialog box. You can log on at this time, even though Windows 2000 might still be initializing network device drivers.

Next, the Service Controller executes and makes a final scan of the HKEY_LOCAL_MACHINE\SYSTEM\CurrentControlSet\Services subkey, looking for services with a value of 0x2 for the Start entry. Services with a value of 0x2 for the Start entry are marked to load automatically. These include the Workstation service and the Server service.

The services that load during this phase do so based on their values for the DependOnGroup or DependOnService entries in the registry subkey HKEY_LOCAL_MACHINE\SYSTEM\CurrentControlSet\Services.

Windows 2000 startup is not considered good until a user successfully logs on to the system. After a successful logon, the system copies the Clone control set to the LastKnownGood control set.

Lesson Summary

In this lesson you learned that the Windows 2000 Intel-based boot process occurs in five stages: the preboot sequence, boot sequence, kernel load, kernel initialization, and logon. You also learned the files that are used in the Intel-based boot process, where these files are stored, and which stage of the boot process uses them.

Lesson 2: The Alpha-Based Boot Process

In this lesson you will learn that the Windows 2000 Alpha-based boot process occurs in two stages: the preboot sequence and boot sequence. You will learn how to troubleshoot the Alpha-based boot process more effectively by learning about the phases in the Windows 2000 Alpha-based boot process and the files used in each phase.

After this lesson, you will be able to

- Explain the boot process for Alpha-based computers.

Estimated lesson time: 5 minutes

Files Used in the Alpha-Based Boot Process

On Alpha-based computers, Ntldr functionality is built into the firmware. Osloader.exe performs the initial stages of loading the Windows 2000 operating system on Alpha-based computers, a process that Ntldr controls on Intel-based computers. As a result, the Ntldr, Boot.ini, and Bootsect.dos files used to boot Intel-based computers are not necessary on Alpha-based computers.

Additionally, Ntdetect.com is not necessary to boot Alpha-based computers. The Alpha POST routine collects hardware information and passes it to Osloader.exe.

Table 27.4 lists the files that are required for the boot sequence on Alpha-based computers and the location of each file.

Table 27.4   Files Used in the Windows 2000 Alpha-Based Boot Process

Alpha-based file	Folder
Osloader.exe	os\<winnt>
Ntoskrnl.exe	*Systemroot*\System32
Hal.dll	os\<winnt>
*.pal	os\<winnt>
System	*Systemroot*\System32\Config
Device drivers (*.sys)	*Systemroot*\System32\Drivers

Preboot Sequence

On Alpha-based computers, the following steps occur prior to the boot sequence:

1. The read-only memory (ROM) firmware selects a boot device by reading a boot precedence table from nonvolatile random access memory (RAM). If the nonvolatile RAM is invalid or blank, the firmware either issues a query for the boot device or defaults to a floppy disk or hard disk sequence.

2. For a hard-disk boot, the firmware reads the MBR to determine whether a system partition is present.

3. If a system partition exists, the firmware reads the first sector of the partition into memory and examines the BIOS parameter block (BPB) to determine whether the volume's file system is supported by the firmware.

4. If the file system is supported by the firmware, the firmware searches the root directory of the volume for Osloader.exe, loads the program, and then passes control to it, along with a list of the hardware that is available on the system.

Boot Sequence

During the boot sequence on Alpha-based computers, Osloader.exe does the following:

1. Loads Ntoskrnl.exe, Hal.dll, the *.pal files, and the System hive.

2. Scans the System hive and loads the device drivers that are configured to start at boot time.

3. Passes control to Ntoskrnl.exe, at which point the boot process ends, and the load phases begin.

Lesson Summary

In this lesson you learned that the Windows 2000 Alpha-based boot process occurs in two stages: the preboot sequence and the boot sequence. You learned that on Alpha-based computers, the Ntldr functionality is built into the firmware, and that Osloader.exe performs the initial stages of loading the Windows 2000 operating system on Alpha-based computers. You also learned what files are used in the Alpha-based boot process, and where these files are stored.

Lesson 3: Control Sets in the Registry

This lesson discusses the Windows 2000 control sets. A *control set* contains configuration data used to control the system, such as a list of which device drivers and services to load and start.

After this lesson, you will be able to

- Explain Windows 2000 control sets.

Estimated lesson time: 15 minutes

Windows 2000 Control Sets

A typical Windows 2000 installation contains the following control set subkeys: Clone, ControlSet001, ControlSet002, and CurrentControlSet. Control sets are stored as subkeys of the registry key HKEY_LOCAL_MACHINE\SYSTEM. The registry might contain several control sets depending on how often you change or have problems with system settings.

The CurrentControlSet subkey is a pointer to one of the ControlSet00x keys. The Clone control set is a clone of the control set used to initialize the computer (either Default or LastKnownGood), and is created by the kernel initialization process each time that you start your computer. The Clone control set is not available after you log on.

To better understand control sets, you should know about the registry subkey HKEY_LOCAL_MACHINE\SYSTEM\Select. The entries contained in this subkey include Current, Default, Failed, and LastKnownGood.

- **Current.**   Identifies which control set is the CurrentControlSet. When you use Control Panel options or the Registry Editor to change the registry, you modify information in the CurrentControlSet.

- **Default.**   Identifies the control set to use the next time that Windows 2000 starts, unless you select the LastKnownGood configuration. Default and Current typically contain the same control set number.

- **Failed.**   Identifies the control set that was designated as failed the last time that the computer was started using the LastKnownGood control set.

- **LastKnownGood.**   Identifies a copy of the control set that was used the last time that the computer started Windows 2000 successfully. After a successful logon, the Clone control set is copied to the LastKnownGood control set.

Each of these entries in HKEY_LOCAL_MACHINE\SYSTEM\Select takes a REG_DWORD data type, and the value for each entry refers to a specific control set. For example, if the value for the Current entry is set to 0x1, the CurrentControlSet points to ControlSet001. Similarly, if the value for the

LastKnownGood entry is set to 0x2, the LastKnownGood control set points to ControlSet002.

The Last Known Good Process

If you change the Windows 2000 configuration to load a driver and have problems rebooting, you can use the last known good process to recover your working configuration. The last known good process uses the LastKnownGood configuration, stored in the registry, to boot Windows 2000.

Windows 2000 provides two configurations for starting a computer, Default and LastKnownGood. Figure 27.1 shows the events that occur when you make configuration changes to your system. Any configuration changes (for example, adding or removing drivers), are saved in the Current control set.

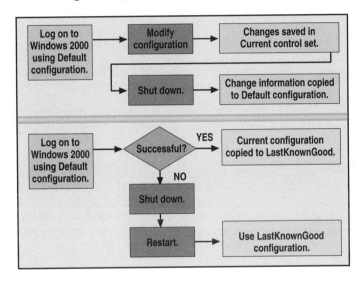

Figure 27.1   Using Default and LastKnownGood configurations

After you reboot the computer, the kernel copies the information in the Current control set to the Clone control set during the kernel initialization phase. When you successfully log on to Windows 2000, the information in the Clone control set is copied to the LastKnownGood control set.

If you experience startup problems that you think might relate to Windows 2000 configuration changes, shut down the computer *without* logging on, and then restart it. After the OS Loader V5.0 prompt appears on the screen, press F8 to open the Windows NT Advanced Options menu and select the Last Known Good Configuration option, or after you select Windows 2000 on the OS Loader V5.0 screen, you can press Spacebar to open the Hardware Profile/Configuration Recovery menu, and then press L to select Last Known Good Configuration.

The next time you log on, the Current configuration is copied to the Default configuration. If your configuration changes work correctly, the next time you log on, the Current configuration is copied to the Default configuration. If your configuration changes do not work, you can restart and use the Last Known Good Configuration option to log on.

Table 27.5 summarizes the purpose of the Default and LastKnownGood configurations.

Table 27.5 Default and LastKnownGood Configurations

Configuration	Description
Default	Contains information that the system saves when a computer shuts down. To start a computer using the default configuration, select Windows 2000 on the operating system selection menu.
LastKnownGood	Contains information that the system saves after a successful logon. The LastKnownGood configuration loads only if the system is recovering from a severe or critical device driver loading error or if it is selected during the boot process.

Table 27.6 lists situations in which you can use the Last Known Good configuration and the related solutions.

Table 27.6 Situations When You Use the LastKnownGood Configuration

Situation	Solution
After a new device driver is installed, Windows 2000 restarts, but the system stops responding.	Use the Last Known Good Configuration option to start Windows 2000 because the LastKnownGood configuration does not contain any reference to the new, and possibly faulty, driver.
You accidentally disable a critical device driver (such as the Scsiport driver).	Some critical drivers are written to keep users from making the mistake of disabling them. With these drivers, the system automatically reverts to the LastKnownGood control set if a user disables the driver. If the driver does not automatically cause the system to revert to the LastKnownGood control set, you must manually select LastKnownGood.

Using the LastKnownGood configuration does *not* help in the following situations:

- When the problem is not related to Windows 2000 configuration changes. Such a problem might arise from incorrectly configured user profiles or incorrect file permissions.

- After you log on. The system updates the LastKnownGood configuration with Windows 2000 configuration changes after a successful logon.

- When startup failures relate to hardware failures or missing or corrupted files.

Important   Starting Windows 2000 using the LastKnownGood configuration overwrites any changes made since the last successful boot of Windows 2000.

Lesson Summary

In this lesson you learned that a control set contains configuration data used to control the system, such as a list of which device drivers and services to load and which to start. Control sets are stored as subkeys of the registry key HKEY_LOCAL_MACHINE\SYSTEM, and a typical Windows 2000 installation contains the following control set: Clone, ControlSet001, ControlSet002, and CurrentControlSet. The registry might contain several other control sets, depending on how often you have changed or had problems with system settings.

You also learned about the last known good process. If you make incorrect changes to a computer's configuration, you might have problems restarting your computer. If you cannot restart your computer due to a configuration change, Windows 2000 provides the last known good process so that you do not have to reinstall your Windows 2000 software in order to restart your computer. You can boot your computer using the LastKnownGood control set. The LastKnownGood control set contains the configuration settings from the last successful restart and logon to your computer. After restarting your computer using the LastKnownGood control set, you can reconfigure the computer. The last known good process uses the LastKnownGood configuration, stored in the registry, to restart Windows 2000.

Lesson 4: Advanced Boot Options

In this lesson you will learn about the Windows 2000 advanced boot options. These options include Safe Mode, Enable Boot Logging, Enable VGA Mode, Last Known Good Configuration, Directory Services Restore Mode, and Debugging Mode.

After this lesson, you will be able to

- Explain advanced boot options.

Estimated lesson time: 5 minutes

Safe Mode

If your computer will not start, you might be able to start it by using the Safe Mode advanced boot option. Pressing F8 during the operating system selection phase displays a screen with advanced options for booting Windows 2000. You can select Safe Mode. In safe mode, Windows 2000 only loads and uses basic files and drivers, including the mouse, VGA monitor, keyboard, mass storage, default system services, and no network connections. If you choose to start your computer in safe mode, the background will be black and Safe Mode will appear in all four corners of the screen. If your computer does not start using safe mode, you can try Windows 2000 Automatic System Recovery.

Note   Safe Mode is not fully functional in some early-release beta versions of Windows 2000.

There are a couple of variations of safe mode. You can select Safe Mode With Networking, which is identical to safe mode except that it adds the drivers and services necessary to enable networking to function when you restart your computer. A second variation of safe mode is Safe Mode With Command Prompt, which is the same as safe mode, but when the computer restarts it displays a command prompt.

Enable Boot Logging

Selecting the Enable Boot Logging advanced boot option logs the loading and initialization of drivers and services for troubleshooting boot problems. All drivers and services that are loaded and initialized or that are not loaded in a file are logged. The log file, ntbtlog.txt, is located in the %windir% folder. All three versions of safe mode automatically create this boot log file.

Enable VGA Mode

Selecting the Enable VGA Mode advanced boot option starts Windows 2000 with a basic VGA driver.

Last Known Good Configuration

Selecting the Last Known Good Configuration advanced boot option starts Windows 2000 using the registry information that Windows 2000 saved at the last shutdown.

Directory Services Restore Mode

Selecting the Directory Services Restore Mode advanced boot option only applies to Windows 2000 Server and not to Windows 2000 Professional. This option allows the restoration of Active Directory on domain controllers.

Debugging Mode

Selecting the Debugging Mode advanced boot option only applies to Windows 2000 Server and not to Windows 2000 Professional. Selecting this advanced boot option turns on debugging.

Note   When using the advanced boot options in Windows 2000, logging is enabled with every option except Last Known Good Configuration. The system writes the log file (ntbtlog.txt) to the *systemroot* folder. In addition, each option except Last Known Good Configuration loads the default video graphics adapter (VGA) driver.

Using an advanced boot option to boot the system sets the environment variable %SAFEBOOT_OPTION% to indicate the mode used to boot the system.

Lesson Summary

In this lesson you learned about the advanced boot options available in Windows 2000. These advanced boot options include Safe Mode, Enable Boot Logging, Enable VGA Mode, Last Known Good Configuration, Directory Services Restore Mode, and Debugging Mode. These options allow you to attempt to restart your computer when there is a problem with a normal boot.

Lesson 5: The Boot.ini File

In this lesson you will learn about the Boot.ini file. When you install Windows 2000 on an Intel-based computer, Windows 2000 Setup saves the Boot.ini file in the active partition. Ntldr uses information in the Boot.ini file to display the boot loader screen, from which you select the operating system to start. In this lesson you will learn how to modify the Boot.ini file, including modifying ARC paths and using the optional Boot.ini switches.

After this lesson, you will be able to

- Explain the purpose and function of the Boot.ini file.

Estimated lesson time: 15 minutes

Components of the Boot.ini File

The Boot.ini file includes two sections, [boot loader] and [operating systems], which contain information which Ntldr uses to create the Boot Loader Operating System Selection menu. A typical Boot.ini might contain the following lines:

```
[boot loader]
timeout=30
default=multi(0)disk(0)rdisk(1)partition(2)\WINNT


[operating systems]
multi(0)disk(0)rdisk(1)partition(2)\WINNT="Windows 2000 Server" /fastde-
tect
multi(0)disk(0)rdisk(1)partition(1)\WINNT="Windows NT Server Version
4.00"
multi(0)disk(0)rdisk(1)partition(1)\WINNT="Windows NT Server Version
4.00 [VGA mode]" /basevideo /sos
C:\="Previous Operating System on C:"
```

The [operating systems] section of a Boot.ini file that is created during a default installation of Windows 2000 Professional contains a single entry for Windows 2000. If your computer is a Windows 95- or 98-based dual-boot system, the [operating systems] section also contains an entry for starting the system using the other operating system, for example, C:\="Previous Operating System on C". If you installed Windows 2000 on a computer and kept an installation of NT 4.0 on another partition of the same computer, the [operating systems] section also contains an entry for starting the system using this version of Windows NT, for example, C:\="Windows NT Server Version 4.00".

ARC Paths

During installation, Windows 2000 generates the Boot.ini file, which contains Advanced RISC Computing (ARC) paths pointing to the computer's boot partition. (*RISC* stands for Reduced Instruction Set Computing, a microprocessor design that uses a small set of simple instructions for fast execution.) The following is an example of an ARC path:

```
multi(0)disk(0)rdisk(1)partition(2)
```

Table 27.7 describes the naming conventions for ARC paths.

Table 27.7   ARC Path Naming Conventions

Convention	Description
Multi (x) | scsi (x)	The adapter/disk controller. Use scsi to indicate a SCSI controller on which SCSI BIOS is *not* enabled. For all other adapter/disk controllers, use multi, including SCSI disk controllers *with* the BIOS enabled.
	x represents a number that indicates the load order of the hardware adapter. For example, if you have two SCSI adapters in a computer, the first to load and initialize receives number 0, and the next SCSI adapter receives number 1.
Disk(y)	The SCSI ID. For multi, this value is always 0.
Rdisk(z)	A number that identifies the disk (ignored for SCSI controllers).
Partition(a)	A number that identifies the partition.

In both multi and scsi conventions, multi, scsi, disk, and rdisk numbers are assigned starting with (0). Partition numbers start with (1). All nonextended partitions are assigned numbers first, followed by logical drives in extended partitions.

See Figure 27.2 for some examples of how to determine the ARC path name.

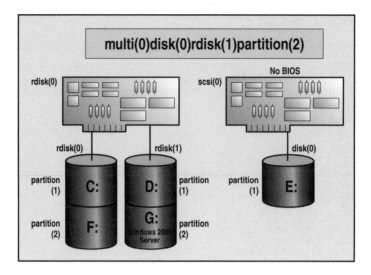

Figure 27.2   ARC paths

The scsi ARC naming convention varies the disk(y) parameter for successive disks on one controller, while the multi format varies the rdisk(z) parameter.

Boot.ini Switches

You can add a variety of switches to the entries in the [operating systems] section of the Boot.ini file to provide additional functionality. Table 27.8 describes optional switches that you can use for entries in the Boot.ini file.

Table 27.8   Boot.ini Optional Switches

Switch	Description
/basevideo	Boots the computer using the standard VGA video driver. If a new video driver is not working correctly, use this switch to start Windows 2000, and then change to a different driver.
/fastdetect= [com$x$ | comx,y,z.]	Disables serial mouse detection. Without a port specification, this switch disables peripheral detection on all COM ports. This switch is included in every entry in the Boot.ini file by default.
/maxmem:n	Specifies the amount of RAM that Windows 2000 uses. Use this switch if you suspect that a memory chip is bad.
/noguiboot	Boots the computer without displaying the graphical boot status screen.
/sos	Displays the device driver names as they are loading. Use this switch when startup fails while loading drivers to determine which driver is triggering the failure.

Modifications to Boot.ini

You can modify the timeout and default parameter values in the Boot.ini file by using System Properties in Control Panel. In addition, you can manually edit these and other parameter values in the Boot.ini file. For example, you might modify the Boot.ini file to add more descriptive entries for the Boot Loader Operating System Selection menu or to include various switches to aid in troubleshooting the boot process.

During Windows 2000 installation, Windows 2000 Setup sets the read-only and system attributes for the Boot.ini file. Before editing the Boot.ini file with a text editor, you must make the file visible and turn off the read-only attribute. You can change file attributes by using My Computer, Windows Explorer, or the command prompt.

▶ **To change file attributes by using My Computer or Windows Explorer**

1. Double-click the icon for the drive containing the Boot.ini file.
2. On the View menu, click Folder Options.
3. In the Folder Options dialog box, click the View tab.
4. Under Hidden Files, click Show All Files, and then click OK.
5. Right-click Boot.ini, and then click Properties.
6. On the General tab, under Attributes, click to clear the Read-Only check box, and then click OK.

To change file attributes by using the command prompt, change to the directory containing the Boot.ini file if necessary, and then type

```
attrib -s -r boot.ini
```

Once you have changed the attributes of the Boot.ini file, you can open and modify the file using a text editor.

Lesson Summary

In this lesson you learned about the Boot.ini file. When you install Windows 2000 on an Intel-based computer, Windows 2000 Setup saves the Boot.ini file in the active partition. Ntldr uses information in the Boot.ini file to display the boot loader screen, from which you select the operating system to start. You also learned how to modify the Boot.ini file, including modifying ARC paths and using the optional Boot.ini switches.

Lesson 6: The Windows 2000 Boot Disk

In this lesson you will learn about the Windows 2000 boot disk. If some of the Windows 2000 files on the system partition are missing or corrupt, you cannot start your computer. If this occurs, you can use a Windows 2000 boot disk to start your computer and restore the corrupt or missing file or files to the hard disk.

After this lesson, you will be able to

- Create a Microsoft Windows 2000 boot disk.

Estimated lesson time: 25 minutes

Creating a Windows 2000 Boot Disk

You should create a boot disk immediately after installing Windows 2000. If any of the Windows 2000 files on the system partition get deleted, you can easily restore them.

▶ **To create a boot disk**

1. On a computer running Windows 2000, format a floppy disk.

   This writes information to the boot track of the floppy disk so that the boot track looks for the appropriate loader file when the system starts.

2. Display hidden files if necessary, and then copy the files shown in the following table from the primary partition of the computer running Windows 2000 to the boot disk.

For Intel-based computers	For Alpha-based computers
Ntldr	Osloader.exe
Ntdetect.com	Hal.dll
Ntbootdd.sys (for SCSI controllers without a SCSI BIOS)	*.pal
Boot.ini	

   Certain boot files load directly from the hard disk of a computer running Windows 2000. If Ntoskrnl.exe or other files on the hard disk are corrupt or missing, you must use the Automatic System Recovery (ASR) process.

   Note For more information on ASR, see Chapter 25, "Implementing Disaster Protection."

3. Test the boot disk immediately by using it to boot Windows 2000.

Practice: Troubleshooting the Windows 2000 Boot Process

In this practice you create a Windows 2000 boot disk for Intel-based computers and identify the phases of the boot process for Intel-based computers. In addition, you repair a boot problem by using a Windows 2000 boot disk and by using the Last Known Good configuration.

Exercise 1: Creating a Windows 2000 Boot Disk

In this exercise, you use the attrib command to make some necessary files available. You then format a floppy disk and copy the required files to it to create a Windows 2000 boot disk.

▶ **To prepare files for copying**

1. Ensure that you are logged on as Administrator.
2. Start a command prompt.
3. Type **attrib -s -r -h boot.ini** and press Enter.

▶ **To create a Windows 2000 boot disk**

1. Place a floppy disk in drive A.
2. From a command prompt in Windows 2000, type **format a:** to format the floppy disk using Windows 2000.
3. Type each of the following commands and press Enter to copy the following files from the root directory of drive C to the root directory of drive A:

```
copy boot.ini a:
copy ntdetect.com a:
copy ntldr. a:
copy bootsect.dos a:
copy ntbootdd.sys a:
```

If the last two files listed above are not present on your system, they will not be needed on the Windows 2000 boot disk.

Note   Essentially, the boot disk is a copy of the system partition files from a computer running Windows 2000.

If you were to use this boot disk to restart another computer running Windows 2000 that included different hardware, what, if anything, would you need to change about the disk?

Exercise 2: Identifying the Phases of the Boot Process

In this exercise, you test the boot disk that you created for Intel-based computers by using it to restart Windows 2000. Next, you examine the various phases of the Windows 2000 boot process, noting in particular what is happening in each phase.

▶ **To restart your computer running Windows 2000**

Note Read the following procedure in its entirety *before* starting it. You are required to pause the boot process at various points, and you will be asked to answer questions during this exercise to help you recognize the phases of the boot process and to understand how to troubleshoot boot problems.

---

1. Ensure that the boot disk that you created in the previous exercise is in drive A.

2. Restart the computer.

3. At any stage during the POST, press the Pause key to pause the boot process.

    A common error that occurs at the conclusion of the POST is a black screen with the text Missing operating system. What might be the cause of this error?

    How could you restart your computer and boot to Windows 2000?

4. Press Spacebar to continue the boot process.

5. When the Boot Loader menu appears, press Pause to pause the boot process.

    Which file or files does the system use to produce this menu?

6. Press Spacebar to continue the boot process.

7. In the Boot Loader menu, ensure that Windows 2000 Server is selected, and then press Enter.

    The following text appears for a short period of time:

    NTDETECT V5.0 Checking Hardware . . .

    This indicates that Ntdetect.com is building a list of installed hardware. When Ntdetect.com completes hardware detection, the following text appears in the top-left corner of the screen:

    OS Loader V5.0

    Notice that the floppy disk drive activity light goes out. This indicates that the Windows 2000 boot process is finished reading files from the boot disk.

How could you display a list of the files loaded at this stage rather than the periods?

8. Log on as Administrator.

This completes the Windows 2000 boot process.

Exercise 3: Repairing a Boot Problem Using a Windows 2000 Boot Disk

In this exercise you run a batch file to cause a system boot failure. You verify and observe the failure by restarting your computer. Next, you repair your system by booting from the boot disk that you created in Exercise 1.

▶ **To create a system boot failure**

1. Rename Ntldr to Oldntldr.

2. Remove the boot disk from the floppy disk drive, and then restart the computer.

What error do you receive when attempting to restart the computer?

▶ **To fix the problem of the missing file**

1. Insert the Windows 2000 boot disk in the floppy disk drive, and then restart your computer.

Windows 2000 restarts.

2. Log on as Administrator.

3. At the root directory of drive C, rename Oldntldr as Ntldr.

Your computer is now repaired.

4. Remove the boot disk from the floppy disk drive.

Exercise 4: Using the Last Known Good Configuration

In this exercise you simulate a boot problem by restarting your computer and selecting the Last Known Good Configuration.

▶ **To use the Last Known Good Configuration**

1. Restart the computer.

2. When the initial Boot Loader menu appears, press F8.

3. On the Windows 2000 Advanced Options menu, select Last Known Good Configuration, and then press Enter.

The initial Boot Loader menu appears. What line appears in red at the bottom of the screen?

4. Ensure that Windows 2000 Server is selected, and then press Enter.

   The Hardware Profile/Configuration Recovery menu appears.

5. Press Enter.

   The computer restarts successfully by using the LastKnownGood configuration.

Lesson Summary

In this lesson you learned about the Windows 2000 boot disk. You learned about the files stored on the disk and you learned that you should create one as soon as you install Windows 2000. You also learned how to create a boot disk.

Review

Here are some questions to help you determine if you have learned enough to move on to the next chapter. If you have difficulty answering these questions, please go back and review the material in this chapter before beginning the next chapter. The answers for these questions are located in Appendix A, "Questions and Answers."

1. What are the five major phases of the boot process for Intel-based computers?

2. Which files used in the boot process for Intel-based computers are not necessary on Alpha-based computers?

3. What are the various safe mode options for booting Windows 2000, and how do they differ?

4. What are the two sections of the Boot.ini file, and what information does each section contain?

5. Suppose that you created a Windows 2000 boot disk that contains the following files:

   Ntldr
   Ntdetect.com
   Boot.ini
   Ntbootdd.sys

   When you try to boot Windows 2000 with the boot disk, you receive the following error message:

   ```
   Non-System disk or disk error
   Replace and press any key when ready
   ```

   What did you do wrong?

6. You install a new device driver for a SCSI adapter in your computer. When you restart the computer, however, Windows 2000 stops responding after the kernel load phase. How can you get Windows 2000 to restart successfully?

APPENDIX   A

Questions and Answers

Chapter 1

Review Questions

1. What is the major difference between a workgroup and a domain?

   The major difference between a workgroup and a domain is where the user account information resides for user logon authentication. For a workgroup, user account information resides in the local security database on each computer in the workgroup. For the domain, the user account information resides in the Active Directory database.

2. What is Active Directory and what does it provide?

   Active Directory is the Windows 2000 directory service. A directory service consists of a database that stores information about network resources, such as computer and printers, and the services that make this information available to users and applications. Active Directory also provides administrators with the capability to control access to resources.

3. What information must a user provide when he or she logs on to a computer in a domain?

   A user name, password, and, optionally, the name of the domain to log on to.

4. What happens when a user logs on to a domain?

   Windows 2000 sends the logon information to a domain controller, which compares it to the user's information in the Directory. If they match, the domain controller authenticates the user and issues an access token for the user.

5. How would you use the Windows 2000 Security dialog box?

   The Windows 2000 Security dialog box provides easy access to important security options, which include the ability to lock a computer, change a password, log off of a computer, stop programs that are not responding, and shut down the computer. You can also determine the domains to which you are logged on and the user account that you used to log on.

Chapter 2

Practice Questions

Lesson 2: Installing Windows 2000 from a CD-ROM

Practice: Installing Windows 2000 from a CD-ROM

▶ **To begin the installation phase of Windows 2000 Server Setup**

7. Select the partition and press Enter.

    You are prompted to select a file system partition for the partition.

    If you are installing another operating system, such as Microsoft Windows 98, in a dual-boot configuration on the same computer, which file system should you choose? Why?

    FAT. Windows 2000 and Windows NT are the only operating systems that can run on an NTFS-formatted partition.

▶ **To complete the gathering information phase of Windows 2000 Server Setup**

3. In the Name box, type your name, in the Organization box, type the name of your company or organization, and then click Next.

    Setup displays the Licensing Modes page, prompting you to select a licensing mode. By default, the Per Server licensing mode is selected. Setup prompts you to enter the number of licenses that you have purchased for this server.

    Which licensing mode should you select if users in your organization require frequent access to multiple servers? Why?

    Per Seat. The Per Seat licensing mode requires the fewest number of licenses when users make connections to multiple servers. Per Server licensing requires a license for each concurrent user with a connection to the server; this is the best option for organizations where users make connections to only one server.

Review Questions

1. Your company has decided to install Windows 2000 Professional on all new computers that are purchased for desktop users. What should you do before you purchase new computers to ensure that Windows 2000 can be installed and run without difficulty?

    Verify that the hardware components meet the minimum requirements for Windows 2000. Also, verify that all of the hardware components that are installed in the new computers are on the Windows 2000 HCL. If a component is not listed, contact the manufacturer to verify that a Windows 2000 driver is available.

2. You are attempting to install Windows 2000 Professional from a CD-ROM; however, you have discovered that your computer does not support booting from the CD-ROM drive. How can you install Windows 2000?

Start the computer by using the Setup boot disks. When prompted, insert the Windows 2000 Professional CD-ROM, and then continue Setup.

3. You are installing Windows 2000 Server on a computer that will be a member server in an existing Windows 2000 domain. You want to add the computer to the domain during installation. What information do you need, and what computers must be available on the network, before you run the Setup program?

You need the DNS domain name of the domain that you are joining. You must also make sure that a computer account for the member server exists in the domain or you must have the user name and password of a user account in the domain with the authority to create computer accounts in the domain. A server running the DNS service and a domain controller in the domain you are joining must be available on the network.

4. You are using a CD-ROM to install Windows 2000 Server on a computer that was previously running another operating system. How should you configure the hard disk to simplify the installation process?

Use a disk partitioning tool to remove any existing partitions, and then create and format a new partition for the Windows 2000 installation.

5. You are installing Windows 2000 over the network. Before you install to a client computer, what must you do?

Locate the path to the shared installation files on the distribution server. Create a 500-MB FAT partition on the target computer (1 GB recommended). Create a client disk with a network client so that you can connect from the computer, without an operating system, to the distribution server.

Chapter 3

Review Questions

1. What environment subsystems ship with Windows 2000? Which of these subsystems is responsible for controlling screen-oriented I/O?

Windows 2000 ships with the Win32 subsystem, the POSIX subsystem, and the OS/2 subsystem. The Win32 subsystem controls all screen-oriented I/O.

2. What component of the Windows 2000 architecture provides portability across multiple hardware platforms?

The hardware abstraction layer (HAL).

3. Why is a symmetric multiprocessing operating system more efficient than an asymmetric multiprocessing operating system?

   A symmetric multiprocessing operating system has the ability to run process threads on any available microprocessor. An asymmetric multiprocessing operating system will always run process threads on the same microprocessor, even if another microprocessor is available.

4. What is a page fault?

   The microprocessor issues a page fault when a thread requests access to an invalid page; an invalid page is one not available to the process or a page that is stored on disk rather than in physical memory.

5. What does the term *working set* mean?

   ***Working set* refers to pages for a process that currently reside in physical memory.**

Chapter 4

Practice Questions

Lesson 2: Using MMC Consoles

Practice: Using Microsoft Management Console

Exercise 1: Using a Preconfigured MMC Console

▶ **To use a preconfigured MMC Console**

2. Click the Start button, point to Programs, point to Administrative Tools, and then click Event Viewer.

   Windows 2000 displays the Event Viewer console, which gives you access to the contents of the event log files on your computer. You use Event Viewer to monitor various hardware and software activities.

   Looking at the console tree, what three logs are listed?

   Application log, Security log, System log.

   Can you add snap-ins to this console? Why or why not?

   No. This is a preconfigured console, and therefore it was saved in User mode. You cannot modify consoles that are saved in User mode.

Exercise 2: Creating a Customized MMC Console

▶ **To create a customized console**

5. To view the currently configured options, click Options on the Console menu.

   MMC displays the Options dialog box with the User tab active.

What are the default user options?

The default user options are to show Taskpad views by default and not to open console files in Author mode, regardless of the mode in which the consoles were saved.

6. Click the Console tab.

The Console tab allows you to configure the console mode.

How does a console that is saved in User mode differ from one that is saved in Author mode?

You can modify consoles that are saved in Author mode. You cannot modify consoles that are saved in User mode after they have been saved. Different levels of User mode restrict the degree of user access.

8. On the Console menu, click Save As.

MMC displays the Save As dialog box.

What is the default folder for customized consoles? What is the advantage of saving files in this folder?

The default folder for saving a customized console is My Administrative Tools, which MMC creates when you save the first customized console. You can gain access to consoles that are saved in this folder from the Start menu.

▶   **To remove extensions from a snap-in**

12. Click Computer Management (Local), and then click the Extensions tab.

MMC displays a list of available extensions for the Computer Management snap-in.

What determines which extensions MMC displays in this dialog box?

The available extensions depend on which snap-in you select.

15. Expand Computer Management and then expand System Tools to confirm that Device Manager and System Information have been removed.

When should you remove extensions from a console?

To customize the console for limited administrative tasks. This allows you to include only those extensions that are relevant to the computer that you are administering. You should also remove extensions when you create consoles for administrators who perform only limited tasks.

Review Questions

1. When and why would you use an extension?

When specific snap-ins need additional functionality—extensions are snap-ins that provide additional administrative functionality to another snap-in.

2. You need to create a custom MMC console for an administrator who only needs to use the Computer Management and Active Directory Manager snap-ins. The administrator

- Must not be able to add any additional snap-ins.

- Needs full access to all snap-ins.

- Must be able to navigate between snap-ins.

What console mode would you use to configure the custom MMC console?

User mode, Full Access.

3. Why do you create custom MMC consoles?

Create custom MMC consoles to meet your administrative requirements. Combine snap-ins that you use together to perform common administrative tasks.

Creating custom MMC consoles allows you to perform most administrative tasks with one MMC console file. You do not have to switch between different programs or MMC console files, because all of the snap-ins that you need to use are located in the same MMC console file.

4. What do you need to do to remotely administer a computer running Windows 2000 Server from a computer running Windows 2000 Professional?

Windows 2000 Professional does not include all snap-ins that are included with Windows 2000 Server. To enable remote administration of many Windows 2000 Server components from a computer running Windows 2000 Professional, you need to add the required snap-ins on the computer running Windows 2000 Professional.

5. You need to schedule a maintenance utility to run once a week on a computer running Windows 2000 Server. What do you use to accomplish this?

Use Task Scheduler to schedule the necessary maintenance utilities to run at specific times.

Chapter 5

Practice Questions

Lesson 3: Configuring Operating System Settings

Practice: Using Control Panel to Change Operating System Settings

Exercise 1: Decreasing the Boot Delay

▶   **To decrease the boot delay**

2. In Control Panel, double-click the System icon.

The System Properties dialog box appears.

What is an alternate method for accessing the System Properties dialog box?

Right-click My Computer, and then click Properties.

3. On the Advanced tab, click Startup And Recovery.

The Startup And Recovery dialog box appears.

What is the default operating system?

Windows 2000 Server.

How long will the countdown timer run before automatically starting the default operating system?

30 seconds.

6. Restart the computer.

Does the boot loader menu appear?

No.

Why might you not want the boot loader menu to appear?

To prevent a user from being able to select another operating system.

Exercise 2: Changing the Paging File Size

▶ **To change the paging file size**

4. In the Initial Size box, increase the value by 10, and then click Set.

Why would you want to increase the initial size of the paging file?

If the actual size of the paging file is consistently greater than the initial size setting, increasing the initial size will provide a performance increase because the Virtual Memory Manager will not have to increase the page file size as often.

Exercise 3: Adding a System Environment

▶ **To test the new variable**

2. At the command prompt, type **set | more** and then press Enter.

The list of current environment variables is displayed.

Is Ntdir listed as an environment variable?

Yes.

6. Type **cd %ntdir%** and then press Enter.

What happens?

The command processor resolves the variable Ntdir to its value and then carries out the cd command. The working directory is changed to C:\Winnt, in this example, or to another folder you specified above in step 4.

Review Questions

1. What should you do if you cannot see any output on the secondary display?

   If you cannot see any output on the secondary display, try the following:

   Activate the device in the Display Properties dialog box.

   Confirm you chose the correct video driver.

   Restart the computer and check its status in Device Manager.

   Switch the order of the display adapters on the motherboard.

2. You have configured recovery options on a computer running Windows 2000 Server to write debugging information to a file if a stop error occurs. You notice, however, that the file is not being created. What could be causing this problem?

   The problem could be one or more of the following:

   The paging file size could be set to less than the amount of physical RAM in your system.

   The paging file might not be located on your system partition.

   You might not have enough free space to create the Memory.dmp file.

3. How can you optimize virtual memory performance?

   To optimize virtual memory, do the following:

   If you have multiple hard disks, create a separate paging file on each hard disk.

   Move the paging file off of the disk that contains the Windows 2000 system files.

   Set the minimum size of the paging file to be equal to or greater than the amount of disk space that is allocated by VMM when your system is operating under a typical load.

4. You installed a new network card in your computer, but it does not seem to be working. Describe how you would troubleshoot this problem.

   You would do the following to troubleshoot the problem:

   Check Device Manager to determine whether Windows 2000 properly detected the network card.

   If the card is not listed in Device Manager, run the Add/Remove Hardware wizard to have Windows 2000 detect the new card. If the card is listed in Device Manager but the icon representing the new card contains either an exclamation mark or a stop sign, view the properties of the card for further details. You might need to reinstall the drivers for the card, or the card might be causing a resource conflict.

Chapter 6

Practice Questions

Lesson 2: Using Registry Editor

Practice: Using Registry Editor

Exercise 1: Exploring the Registry

▶ **To view information in the registry**

6. Double-click the HARDWARE\DESCRIPTION\System subkey to expand it, and then answer the following questions:

   What is the basic input/output system (BIOS) version of your computer and its date?

   Answer will vary based on contents of the SYSTEMBIOSVERSION and SYSTEMBIOSDATE entries.

   What is the computer type of your local machine according to the Identifier entry?

   Answer may vary; will likely be AT/AT compatible.

7. Expand the SOFTWARE\Microsoft\Windows NT\CurrentVersion subkey, and then fill in the following information.

Software configuration	Value and string
Current build number	**1950 (for RC0 of beta 3)**
Current version	**5.0.**
Registered organization	**Answer will vary.**
Registered owner	**Answer will vary.**

Exercise 3: Modifying the Registry

▶ **To verify the new registry value**

2. Click the Advanced tab, and then click Environment Variables.

   The Environment Variables dialog box appears.

   Does the test variable appear in the User Variables For Administrator list?

   Yes.

   What value has been assigned to the test variable? Why?

   C:\WINNT\System32 (unless you installed Windows 2000 in another directory) has been assigned. The data type assigned in the registry was REG_EXPAND_SZ, and the %windir% portion of the value data has been expanded to C:\WINNT.

Exercise 4: Saving a Subtree as a File

▶   **To save a subtree as a file**

12. Scroll down (if necessary) to see the data for CurrentBuildNumber.

What is this value's data?

1950.

Review Questions

1. What is the registry and what does it do?

    The registry is a hierarchical database that stores Windows 2000 hardware and software settings. The registry controls the Windows 2000 operating system by providing the appropriate initialization information to start applications and load components, such as device drivers and network protocols. The registry contains a variety of different types of data, including the hardware installed on the computer, the installed device drivers, applications, network protocols, and network adapter card settings.

2. What is a hive?

    A hive is a discrete body of keys, subkeys, and entries. Each hive has a corresponding registry file and .LOG file located in *systemroot*\System32\Config. Windows 2000 uses the .LOG file to record changes and to ensure the integrity of the registry.

3. What is the recommended editor for viewing and modifying the registry?

    Regedt32.exe is the recommended editor for viewing and modifying the registry.

4. What option should you turn on when you are viewing the contents of the registry? Why?

    Using Registry Editor incorrectly can cause serious, system-wide problems that could require reinstallation of Windows 2000. When using Registry Editor to view data, save a backup copy of the registry file before viewing and select Read Only Mode on the Options menu to prevent accidental updating or deleting of configuration data.

Chapter 7

Practice Questions

Lesson 2: Common Disk Management Tasks

Practice: Working with Dynamic Storage

Exercise 1: Upgrading a Disk

▶ **To upgrade a basic disk**

4. Using the information supplied by Disk Management, complete the following questions.

   What is the storage type of Disk 0?

   Basic.

   Is drive C a primary partition or a logical drive in an extended partition?

   Primary partition.

▶ **To confirm the upgrade**

5. Using the information provided by Disk Management, complete the following questions.

   What is the storage type of Disk 0?

   Dynamic.

   Is drive C a primary partition or a logical drive in an extended partition?

   Neither—it is a simple volume.

   What has changed?

   Drive 0 has been changed from a basic disk to a dynamic disk, and Drive C has been changed from a primary partition to a simple volume. If you had a logical drive in an extended partition on Drive 0, it is now a simple volume as well.

Exercise 2: Extending a Volume

▶ **To examine the new volume**

3. Right-click Mount, and then click Properties.

   The Mount Properties dialog box appears.

   What type of folder is C:\Mount or *x*:\Mount (where *x* is the drive on which you mounted the volume)?

   Mounted Volume

8. Change the working directory to the root directory of drive C (if necessary) or to the root directory of the drive where you mounted your volume, type **dir** and then press Enter.

How much free space does the dir command report?

Answer will vary.

Why is there a difference between the free space reported for drive C and the free space reported for C:\Mount? (If you mounted your volume on a drive other than drive C, replace C with the appropriate drive letter.)

The amount of free space reported for C:\Mount is the amount of free space available on the mounted volume.

Review Questions

1. You install a new 10-GB disk drive that you want to divide into five equal 2-GB sections. What are your options?

   You can leave the disk as a basic disk and then create a combination of primary partitions (up to three) and logical drives in an extended partition; or, you can upgrade the disk to a dynamic disk and create five 2-GB simple volumes.

2. You are trying to create a striped volume on your Windows NT Server in order to improve performance. You confirm that you have enough unallocated disk space on two disks in your computer, but when you right-click an area of unallocated space on a disk, your only option is to create a partition. What is the problem and how would you resolve it?

   You can create striped volumes on dynamic disks only. The option to create a partition rather than a volume indicates that the disk you are trying to use is a basic disk. You will need to upgrade all of the disks that you want to use in your striped volume to dynamic disks before you stripe them.

3. You add a new disk to your computer and attempt to extend an existing volume to include the unallocated space on the new disk, but the option to extend the volume is not available. What is the problem and how would you resolve it?

   The existing volume is not formatted with NTFS. You can extend NTFS volumes only. You should back up any data on the existing volume, convert it to NTFS, and then extend the volume.

4. You dual boot your computer with Windows 98 and Windows 2000. You upgrade Disk 1, which you are using to archive files, from basic storage to dynamic storage. The next time you try to access your files on Disk 1 from Windows 98, you are unable to read the files. Why?

   Only Windows 2000 can read dynamic storage.

Chapter 8

Practice Questions

Lesson 1: TCP/IP

Practice: Installing and Configuring TCP/IP

Exercise 2: Configuring TCP/IP to Use a Static IP Address

▶ **To test the static TCP/IP configuration**

6. To verify that the IP address is working and configured for your adapter, type **ping 127.0.0.1** and then press Enter.

   What happens?

   If TCP/IP is bound to the adapter, the internal loop-back test displays four replies similar to the following:

   Reply from 127.0.0.1: bytes=32 time<10ms TTL=128

7. If you have a computer that you are using to test connectivity, type **ping *ip_address*** (where *ip_address* is the IP address of the computer you are using to test connectivity), and then press Enter. If you do not have a computer to test connectivity, skip to step 8.

   What happens?

   Four Reply from *ip_address* **messages should appear.**

Exercise 3: Configuring TCP/IP to Automatically Obtain an IP Address

▶ **To configure TCP/IP to automatically obtain an IP address**

4. Click Obtain An IP Address Automatically.

   What IP address settings will the DHCP Service configure for your computer?

   IP Address and Subnet Mask.

Exercise 4: Obtaining an IP Address by Using Automatic Private IP Addressing

▶ **To obtain an IP address by using Automatic Private IP Addressing**

2. At the command prompt, type **ipconfig /renew** and then press Enter.

   There will be a pause while Windows 2000 attempts to locate a DHCP server on the network.

   What message appears, and what does it indicate?

   Your computer was not assigned an address from the network. It may require a network address for full access to the network. It will continue

to try and obtain an address on its own from the network address server (DHCP).

▶ **To test the TCP/IP configuration**

1. At the command prompt, type **ipconfig | more** and then press Enter.

   Pressing Spacebar as necessary, record the current TCP/IP settings for your Local Area Connection in the following table.

Setting	Value
IP address	
Subnet mask	
Default gateway	

   Is this the same IP address assigned to your computer in Exercise 3? Why or why not?

   No, the IP address is not the same as the one assigned in Exercise 3. In this exercise, the Automatic Private IP Addressing feature of Windows 2000 assigned the IP address because a DHCP server was not available. In Exercise 3, the DHCP Service assigned an IP address.

4. If you have a computer to test TCP/IP connectivity with your computer, type **ping *ip_address*** (where *ip_address* is the IP address of the computer that you are using to test connectivity), and then press Enter. If you do not have a computer to test connectivity, skip this step and proceed to step 5.

   Were you successful? Why or why not?

   Answers will vary. If you don't have a computer that you can use to test your computer's connectivity, you cannot do this exercise.

   No, if the computer you are using to test your computer's connectivity is configured with a static IP address in another network and there is no default gateway configured on your computer.

   Yes, if the computer you are using to test your computer's connectivity is also configured with an IP address assigned by Automatic Private IP Addressing and it is on the same subnet so that a default gateway is unnecessary.

Lesson 2: NWLink

Practice: Installing and Configuring NWLink

▶ **To install and configure NWLink**

4. Click Protocol, and then click Add.

   The Select Network Protocol dialog box appears.

   What protocols can you install?

AppleTalk protocol, DLC protocol, NetBEUI protocol, Network Monitor Agent v2 Driver, and NWLink IPX/SPX/NetBIOS Compatible Transport Protocol, OSI-LAN protocol, and Streams Environment.

6. Select NWLink IPX/SPX/NetBIOS Compatible Transport Protocol, and then click Properties.

   What type of frame detection is selected by default?

   Auto frame type detection.

7. Click Manual Frame Type Detection, and then click Add.

   What is the default frame type?

   Ethernet 802.2.

Lesson 4: Network Bindings

Practice: Working with Network Bindings

Exercise 1: Changing the Binding Order for a Protocol

▶ **To change the protocol binding order**

2. Maximize the Network And Dial-Up Connections window, and on the Advanced menu, click Advanced Settings.

   The Advanced Settings dialog box appears.

   What is the order of the protocols listed under Client For Microsoft Networks?

   The first protocol listed under Client For Microsoft Networks is Internet Protocol (TCP/IP), and the second one is NWLink IPX/SPX/NetBIOS Compatible Transport Protocol.

Review Questions

1. Your computer running Windows 2000 Workstation was configured manually for TCP/IP. You can connect to any host on your own subnet, but you cannot connect to or even ping any host on a remote subnet. What is the likely cause of the problem and how would you fix it?

   The default gateway might be missing or incorrect. You specify the default gateway in the Internet Protocol (TCP/IP) Properties dialog box (under Network And Dial-Up Connections in My Network Places). Other possibilities are that the default gateway is offline or that the subnet mask is incorrect.

2. Your computer running Windows 2000 Professional can communicate with some, but not all, of the NetWare servers on your network. Some of the NetWare servers are running frame type 802.2 and some are running 802.3. What is the likely cause of the problem?

Although the NWLink implementation in Windows 2000 can automatically detect a frame type for IPX/SPX compatible protocols, it can only automatically detect one frame type. This network uses two frame types; you must manually configure the additional frame type (802.3).

3. What are the limitations of the NetBEUI protocol?

NetBEUI cannot be routed and therefore is not suitable for WANs. Since NetBEUI is not routable, you must connect computers running Windows 2000 and NetBEUI by using bridges instead of routers.

The NetBEUI protocol relies on broadcasts for many of its functions, such as name registration and discovery, so it creates more broadcast traffic than other protocols.

4. What is the primary function of the DLC protocol?

DLC provides connectivity to IBM mainframes and to LAN print devices that are directly attached to the network.

5. What is the significance of the binding order of network protocols?

You specify the binding order to optimize network performance. For example, a computer running Windows 2000 Workstation has NetBEUI, NWLink IPX/SPX, and TCP/IP installed. However, most of the servers to which this computer connects are running only TCP/IP. You would adjust the binding order so that the Workstation binding to TCP/IP is listed before the Workstation bindings for the other protocols. In this way, when a user attempts to connect to a server, the Workstation service first attempts to use TCP/IP to establish the connection.

Chapter 9

Practice Questions

Lesson 2: Installing and Configuring the DHCP Service

Practice: Installing and Configuring the DHCP Service

Optional Exercise 2: Determining the Physical Address of a Computer

▶ To determine the physical address of a computer

3. Record the physical address of the computer that you used in step 1.

The physical address is the hardware address or the Media Access Control (MAC) address. It is the address permanently burned into your network adapter and should look something like 00-aa-00-4a-de-14.

Answer will vary.

Exercise 3: Installing the DHCP Service

▶　**To install the DHCP Service**

1. Click Start, point to Programs, and then point to Administrative Tools.

   Are there any entries for DHCP?

   No.

18. Click Start, point to Programs, and then point to Administrative Tools.

    Are there any entries for DHCP?

    Yes, DHCP Server Management was added to the Administrative Tools menu when the DHCP Service was installed.

Exercise 4: Creating and Configuring a DHCP Scope

▶　**To create and configure a DHCP scope**

15. Click Next.

    The Lease Duration page appears.

    What is the default lease duration?

    Three days.

Exercise 5: Adding a Reservation to a DHCP Scope

▶　**To add a reservation to a DHCP scope**

1. In DHCP Manager, in the console tree, expand Scope.

   What options appear?

   Address Pool, Address Leases, Reservations, and Scope Options

10. Right-click the Scope listing, point to New, and click Activate.

    Does the icon for the scope change?

    Yes, the red arrow is removed from the icon.

Review Questions

1. What are the benefits of using the DHCP Service to automatically configure IP addressing information?

   Users no longer need to acquire IP addressing information from an administrator to configure TCP/IP, because the DHCP Service supplies all of the necessary configuration information to all the DHCP clients. Most difficult-to-trace network problems will be eliminated.

2. What are the steps in the DHCP lease process?

First, a DHCP-enabled client broadcasts a DHCPDISCOVER message to lease an IP address. Second, All DHCP servers respond with a DHCPOFFER message. Third, the DHCP-enabled client selects an offer from the first DHCP server and sends a DHCPREQUEST message. Finally, the DHCP server responds with a DHCPACK or DHCPNACK message, depending on whether or not the lease request is successful.

3. When do DHCP clients attempt to renew their leases?

Initially, with the DHCP server that leased the address, when 50 percent of the lease life has expired. Subsequently, with any DHCP server, when 87.5 percent of its lease life has expired.

4. Why might you create multiple scopes on a DHCP server?

You might create multiple scopes on a DHCP server to centralize administration and to assign IP addresses specific to a subnet (for example, a default gateway). You can assign only one scope to a specific subnet.

5. How can you manually restore the DHCP database?

You can change an entry in the registry and restart the DHCP Service, or you can manually copy the files in the DHCP backup folder to the DHCP directory and then restart the service.

6. What three things should you consider when planning DHCP implementation?

(1) Whether all computers will become DHCP clients, (2) whether a DHCP server will supply IP addresses to multiple subnets, and (3) what IP addressing options clients will obtain from the DHCP server.

Chapter 10

Review Questions

1. Why would a WINS client broadcast a name query request?

When a WINS client initiates a NetBIOS command to communicate with another network resource, the name query request is sent directly to a WINS server. If a WINS server is unavailable, the WINS client uses a broadcast in an attempt to resolve the name.

2. What happens when a WINS server receives a name registration request with a NetBIOS name/IP address mapping that is already registered in the WINS database?

If a WINS server receives a name registration request with a NetBIOS name/IP address mapping that is already registered in the WINS database, it sends a name query request to the currently registered owner of the name.

If the current registered owner responds successfully to the WINS server, the WINS server sends a negative name registration response to the WINS client that is attempting to register the name. If the current registered owner does not respond to the WINS server, the WINS server sends a successful name registration response to the WINS client that is attempting to register the name.

3. When does a WINS client first attempt to refresh its name registrations?

A WINS client first attempts to refresh its name registrations after one-eighth of the TTL interval has expired.

4. By default, where does a WINS client first check in an attempt to resolve another host's NetBIOS name to an IP address?

The client checks its NetBIOS name cache for the NetBIOS name/IP address mapping of the destination computer.

5. What are the configuration requirements for a WINS server?

A computer running Windows 2000 Server configured with WINS, and a static IP address, subnet mask, and default gateway.

You also can configure a static mapping for all non-WINS clients, a WINS proxy agent, and WINS support on a DHCP server.

Chapter 11

Practice Questions

Lesson 4: Configuring the DNS Service
Practice: Configuring the DNS Service
Exercise 4: Testing Your DNS Server

▶ **To create a pointer record for your DNS server**

2. Click 192.168.0.*x* Subnet. (If you did not use 192.168.0.201 as the static IP address for your server name, click the appropriate subnet.)

What types of records exist in the reverse lookup zone?

Start of Authority (SOA) and Name Server (NS).

▶ **To test your DNS Server using nslookup**

2. At the command prompt, type **nslookup** and then press Enter.

Record your results in the following table.

Parameter	Value
Default server	Server1.microsoft.com. (Answer will vary if you did not use Server1 as your computer name or microsoft as your DNS domain name.)
Address	192.168.1.201. (Answer will vary if you did not use 192.168.1.201 as the static IP address for your server.)

Review Questions

1. What is the function of the following DNS components?

   Domain name space

   The domain name space provides the hierarchical structure for the DNS distributed database.

   Zones

   Zones are used to divide the domain name space into administrative units.

   Name servers

   Name servers store the zone information and perform name resolution for their authoritative domain name spaces.

2. Why would you want to have multiple name servers?

   Installing multiple name servers provides redundancy, reduces the load on the server that stores the primary zone database file, and allows for faster access speed for remote locations.

3. What is the difference between a forward lookup query and a reverse lookup query?

   A forward lookup query resolves a name to an IP address. A reverse lookup query resolves an IP address to a name.

4. When would you configure a server as a root server?

   Configure a name server as a root server only if you will not be connecting to the Internet or if you are using a proxy server to gain access to the Internet.

5. Why do you create forward and reverse lookup zones?

   A name server must have at least one forward lookup zone. A forward lookup zone enables name resolution.

   A reverse lookup zone is needed for troubleshooting utilities, such as nslookup, and to record names instead of IP addresses in IIS logs.

6. What is the difference between Dynamic DNS and DNS?

Dynamic DNS allows automatic updates to the primary server's zone file. In DNS, you must manually update the file when new hosts or domains are added.

Dynamic DNS also allows a list of authorized servers to initiate updates. This list can include secondary name servers, domain controllers, and other servers that perform network registration for clients, such as servers running WINS and the DHCP Service.

Chapter 12

Practice Questions

Lesson 5: Installing Active Directory

Practice: Installing Active Directory

Exercise 1: Promoting a Stand-Alone Server to a Domain Controller

► **To install the Active Directory service on a stand-alone server**

13. Ensure that the Sysvol location is C:\Winnt\Sysvol. (If you did not install Windows 2000 on the C drive or in the Winnt directory, the Sysvol location should default to a Sysvol folder in the folder where you installed Windows 2000.)

    What is the one Sysvol location requirement?

    Sysvol must be located on a Windows 2000 partition that is formatted as Windows NT file system (NTFS).

    What is the function of Sysvol?

    Sysvol is a system volume hosted on all Windows 2000 domain controllers. It stores scripts and part of the group policy objects for both the current domain and the enterprise.

Exercise 2: Viewing Your Domain

► **To explore My Network Places**

3. Double-click My Network Places.

    The My Network Places window appears.

    What selections do you see?

    Add Network Place, Entire Network, and Computers Near Me.

4. Double-click Entire Network, and then double-click Microsoft Windows Network.

    What do you see?

Your domain, Microsoft. Answer may vary.

Exercise 3: Using Active Directory Manager

▶ **To use Directory Management**

2. In the console tree, double-click microsoft (or the name of your domain). What selections are listed under domain1?

   Builtin, Computers, Users, and Domain Controllers.

Review Questions

1. What are four major features of Active Directory?

   Active Directory offers simplified administration, scalability, open standards support, and support for standard name formats.

2. What are sites and domains, and how are they different?

   A site is a combination of one or more IP subnets that should be connected by a high-speed link.
   A domain is a logical grouping of servers and other network resources organized under a single name.
   A site is a component of Active Directory's physical structure, while a domain is a component of the logical structure.

3. What is the schema, and how can you extend it?

   The schema contains a formal definition of the contents and structure of Active Directory, including all attributes, classes, and class properties. You can extend the schema by using the Schema Manager snap-in or the Active Directory Services Interface (ADSI).

4. Your company has an Internet namespace reserved with a DNS registration authority. As you plan the Active Directory implementation for your company, you decide to recommend extending the existing namespace for the internal network. What benefits does this option provide?

   Extending an existing namespace provides consistent tree names for internal and external resources. In addition, this plan allows your company to use the same logon and user account names for internal and external resources. Finally, you do not have to reserve an additional DNS namespace.

5. What is the shared system volume, and what purpose does it serve?

   The shared system volume is a folder structure that exists on all Windows 2000 domain controllers. It stores scripts and some of the group policy objects for both the current domain and the enterprise.

6. What is the difference between two-way transitive trusts and explicit one-way trusts?

A two-way transitive trust is a trust between domains that are part of the Windows 2000 scalable namespace, for example, between parent and child domains within a tree and between the top-level domains in a forest. These trust relationships make all objects in all the domains of the tree available to all other domains in the tree.

An explicit one-way trust is a relationship between domains that are not part of the same tree. One-way trusts support connections to existing Windows NT version 4.x and earlier domains to allow the configuration of trust relationships with domains in other trees.

Chapter 13

Practice Questions

Lesson 2: Planning New User Accounts

Practice: Planning New User Accounts

Complete the table to determine a naming convention for the users in the new hire list by considering the information that is provided under "Scenario," "Criteria," and "New Hire List" earlier in this practice.

Answers may vary. The sample answers use a full name with the department name for duplicate names and a user logon name with the first name and last initial and additional characters from the last name for duplicate names. All user logon names and full names must be unique.

Complete the table to determine logon hours and computer use for the users in the new hire list by considering the information that is provided under "Scenario," "Criteria," and "New Hire List" earlier in this practice.

Temporary employees share Temp1 and Temp2. Only two temporary workers are able to log on during a shift, so you must share two computers between four employees.

Select the appropriate password setting for each user in the following table to determine who controls the user's password.

User name	User must change password the next time he or she logs on	User cannot change password
Don Hall	☐	☑
Donna Hall	☑	☐
James Smith	☑	☐
James Smith	☑	☐
Jon Morris	☐	☑

(continued)

User name	User must change password the next time he or she logs on	User cannot change password
Judy Lew	☐	☑
Kim Yoshida	☑	☐
Laurent Vernhes	☐	☑
Sandra Martinez	☑	☐

Lesson 3: Creating Domain User Accounts

Practice: Creating Domain User Accounts

▶   **To create a domain user account**

3. Expand Domain1 (if you did not use Domain1 as your domain name, expand your domain), and then double-click Users.

    In the details pane, notice the default user accounts.

    Which user accounts does the Active Directory Installation wizard create by default?

    Administrator, Cet Publishers, DnsAdmins, Domain Admins, Domain Guests, Domain Users, Enterprise Admins, Guest, IUSR_SERVER1, IWAM_SERVER1, krbtgt, RAS and IAS Servers, and SchemaAdmins. (Answers may vary.)

4. Right-click Users, point to New, and then click User.

    Windows 2000 displays the Create New Object - (User) dialog box.

    Where in Active Directory will the new user account be created?

    microsoft/Users. (Answer may vary if your domain name is not microsoft.com.)

8. In the box to the right of the User Logon Name box, select @domain1.msft. (The domain name will vary, if you did not use domain1.msft as your DNS domain name.)

    The user logon name, combined with the domain name in the box that appears to the right of the User Logon Name box, is the user's full Internet logon name. This name uniquely identifies the user throughout the entire network (for example, user1@domain1.msft).

    Notice that Windows 2000 completes the Downlevel Logon Name box for you.

    When is the down-level logon name used?

    The user's down-level logon name is used to log on to the Windows 2000 domain from a computer running a previous version of Microsoft Windows.

11. Specify whether or not the user can change his or her password.

What are the results of selecting both the User Must Change Password At Next Logon check box and the User Cannot Change Password check box? Explain.

Windows 2000 displays a warning box with the following message:

```
You cannot check both 'User must change password at next logon'
and 'User cannot change password' for the same user.
```

The next time that the user attempts to log on, the user would be prompted to change his or her password and would not be able to log on until the password has been changed. However, Windows 2000 will not allow the user to change his or her password, so the user would not be able to log on successfully.

Under what circumstances would you select the Account Disabled check box while you create a new user account?

Answer may vary. Some possible answers include
This account is for a user who has not yet started at the company.
The user has taken a leave of absence.

Lesson 4: Setting Properties for User Accounts

Practice: Modifying User Account Properties

Exercise 1: Configuring Logon Hours and Account Expiration

▶ **To specify logon hours**

2. In the details pane, right-click User Three, and then click Properties.

Windows 2000 displays the User3 Properties dialog box with the General tab active.

On the General tab, what information can you specify for the user account in addition to first and last name? How would this information be useful?

Display Name, Description, Office, Telephone, E-Mail, and Home page. Active Directory can store user information that might otherwise require a separate application or book. Also, user information that is entered here can be used to locate the user when you search Active Directory.

3. Click the Account tab, and then click Logon Hours.

Windows 2000 displays the Logon Hours For User3 dialog box.

Currently, when can user3 log on?

All hours on all days are allowed by default.

▶ **To set account expiration for a user account**

3. Click the Account tab.

When will the account expire?

Never.

Exercise 2: Testing User Accounts

▶ **To test logon capabilities of user accounts**

3. Click OK to close the Change Password message box.

Were you able to successfully log on? Why or why not?

No, by default administrators have the right to log on to a domain controller, but regular users, like User1, do not.

▶ **To test restrictions on logon hours**

1. Attempt to log on as User1 with a password of student.

Were you able to successfully log on? Why or why not?

Yes, because User1 has access to the network 24 hours a day, seven days a week, and now has the user right to log on interactively.

3. When prompted, change the password to student.

Were you able to successfully log on? Why or why not?

No, because User3 is only allowed to log on between 6 PM and 6 AM. (Answer is Yes if reader is logging on between 6 PM and 6 AM.)

▶ **To test password restrictions**

1. Attempt to log on as User7 with no password.

Were you able to successfully log on? Why or why not?

No, because User7 was assigned a password when the user accounts were created.

3. When prompted, change the password to student.

Were you able to log on? Why or why not?

Yes, because you entered the correct password for the User7 user account.

5. Attempt to log on as User9 with a password of user9.

Were you able to successfully log on? Why or why not?

Yes, because you entered the correct password for the User9 user account.

▶ **To test password restrictions by attempting to change a password**

3. In the Old Password box, type the password for the user account, in the New Password and Confirm New Password boxes, type **student** and then click OK.

Were you able to change the password? Why or why not?

No, User9 has been restricted from changing passwords.

▶ **To test account expiration**

2. When prompted, change your password to student.

Were you successful? Why or why not?

Yes, because the account for User5 does not expire until the end of the day today.

▶ **To test account expiration**

1. Attempt to log on as User5 with a password of student.

Were you successful? Why or why not?

No, because the account for User5 has expired.

Review Questions

1. Where does Windows 2000 create domain user accounts and local user accounts?

Windows 2000 creates a domain user account in an OU in the copy of the Active Directory database (called the Directory) on a domain controller. When you create a local user account, Windows 2000 creates the account only in that computer's security database.

2. What different capabilities do domain user accounts and local user accounts provide to users?

A domain user account allows a user to log on to the domain from any computer in the network and to gain access to resources anywhere in the domain, provided the user has permission to access these resources. A local user account allows the user to log on at and gain access to resources on only the computer where you create the local user account.

3. What should you consider when you plan new user accounts?

- **A naming convention that ensures unique but consistent user account names**
- **Whether you or the user will determine the user account password**
- **The hours when users need to have access to the network or be restricted from using the network**
- **Whether the user account should be disabled**

4. What information is required to create a domain user account?

A first or last name, name, logon name, and down-level logon name.

5. A user wants to gain access to network resources remotely from home. The user does not want to pay the long distance charges for the telephone call. How would you set up the user account to accomplish this?

On the Dial-In tab of the Properties dialog box for the user account, click the Set By Caller (RAS Only) option to have the RAS server call the user back at a telephone number that he or she specifies. You can also click the Always Callback To option to have the RAS server use a specified telephone number to call back the user. However, the user must be at the specified telephone number to make a connection to the server.

Chapter 14

Practice Questions

Lesson 2: Planning Group Strategies

Practice: Planning New User Accounts

For each group, enter the name, type and scope, and members in the table.

Does your network require local groups?

No. The scenario presents no need to create local groups, which you can only use on a single computer.

Does your network require universal groups?

No. The scenario presents no need to create universal groups. Your domain has no groups that need to have access to resources in multiple domains and also need to have members from multiple domains.

Sales representatives at the company frequently visit the company headquarters and other divisions. Therefore, you need to give sales representatives with user accounts in other domains the same permissions for resources that sales representatives in your domain have. You also want to make it easy for administrators in other domains to assign permissions to sales representatives in your domain. How can you accomplish this?

Create global groups for sales representatives in all other domains. Add these global groups to the appropriate domain local groups in your domain. Tell administrators in other domains about the global group that represents sales representatives in your domain. Have the administrators add the sales representatives group from your domain to the appropriate domain local groups in their domains.

Lesson 4: Changing the Domain Mode
Practice: Changing the Domain Mode

▶ **To change the domain mode to native mode**

1. In the console tree, right-click your domain, and then click Properties.

   Directory Management displays the Microsoft Properties dialog box. (If your domain name is not microsoft, the Properties dialog box will display the name of your domain.)

   Notice that your domain is currently in mixed mode. Also notice the warning about changing the domain mode.

   What are the implications of changing the domain mode to native mode?

   Pre-Windows 2000 domain controllers cannot participate in a native mode domain.
   Pre-Windows 2000 stand-alone servers and computers running Windows NT Workstation can still participate in the domain.
   After you change to native mode, you cannot change back to mixed mode.

Review Questions

1. Why should you use groups?

   Use groups to simplify administration by granting rights and assigning permissions once to the group rather than multiple times to each individual member.

2. What is the purpose of adding a group to another group?

   Adding groups to other groups (nesting groups) creates a consolidated group and can reduce the number of times that you need to assign permissions.

3. When should you use security groups instead of distribution groups?

   Use security groups to assign permissions. Use distribution groups when the only function of the group is not security related, such as an e-mail distribution list. You cannot use distribution groups to assign permissions.

4. What strategy should you apply when you use domain local and global groups?

   Place user accounts into global groups, place global groups into domain local groups, and then assign permissions to the domain local group.

5. Why should you not use local groups on a computer after it becomes a member of a domain?

   Local groups do not appear in Active Directory, and you have to administer local groups separately for each computer.

6. What is the easiest way to give a user complete control over all computers in a domain?

    Add his or her user account to the Domain Admins group. Then, he or she can perform all administrative tasks on all domain computers and in Active Directory. The user receives administrative control because Windows 2000 makes Domain Admins a member of both the Administrators domain local group and the Administrators local group on each member server and computer running Windows 2000 Professional. The Administrators domain local group has complete control over all domain controllers and Active Directory. Each Administrators local group has complete control over the computer on which it exists.

7. Suppose the headquarters for this chapter's imaginary manufacturing company has a single domain that is located in Paris. The company has managers who need access to the inventory database to perform their jobs. What would you do to ensure that the managers have the required access to the inventory database?

    Place all of the managers into a global group. Create a domain local group for inventory database access. Make the global group a member of the domain local group and assign permissions to gain access to the inventory database to the domain local group.

8. Now suppose the company has a three-domain environment with the root domain in Paris and the other two domains in Australia and North America. Managers from all three domains need access to the inventory database in Paris to perform their jobs. What would you do to ensure that the managers have the required access and that there is a minimum of administration?

    In each domain, create a global group and add user accounts for the managers in that domain to the global group. Create a domain local group in the domain where the database is located and add the global groups from each of the domain's members to the domain local group. Then, assign permissions to gain access to the inventory database to the domain local group.

Chapter 15

Practice Questions

Lesson 2: Setting Up Network Printers

Practice: Installing a Network Printer

Exercise 2: Taking a Printer Offline and Printing a Test Document

▶ **To print a test document**

5. In Notepad, on the File menu, click Print.

Windows 2000 displays the Print dialog box, allowing you to select the printer and print options.

The Print dialog box displays the location and comment information that you entered when you created the printer, and it shows that the printer is currently offline. You can also use this dialog box to search Active Directory for a printer.

Notice that HP LaserJet 5Si is selected as the printer.

Why did Windows 2000 make that selection for you?

HP LaserJet 5Si is the default printer.

Review Questions

1. What is the difference between a printer and a print device?

   A printer is the software interface between the operating system and the print device. The print device is the hardware device that produces printed documents.

2. A print server can connect to two different types of print devices. What are these two types of print devices, and what are the differences?

   The two types are local and network-interface print devices. A local print device is connected directly to a physical port of the print server. A network-interface print device is connected to the print server through the network. Also, a network-interface print device requires a network interface card.

3. You have added and shared a printer. What must you do to set up client computers running Windows 2000 so that users can print, and why?

   You (or the user) must make a connection to the printer from the client computer. When you make a connection to the printer from the client computer, Windows 2000 automatically copies the printer driver to the client computer.

4. What advantages does connecting to a printer by using http://*server_name*/printers provide for users?

   It allows a user to make a connection to a printer without having to use the Add Printer wizard. It makes a connection to a Web site, which dis-

plays all of the printers for which the user has permission. The Web site also provides information on the printers to help the user make the correct selection. Also, a Web designer can customize this Web page, such as by displaying a floor plan that shows the location of print devices, which makes it easier for users to choose a print device.

5. Why would you connect multiple printers to one print device?

To set priorities between the printers so that users can send critical documents to the printer with the highest priority. These documents will always print before documents that are sent from printers with lower priorities.

6. Why would you create a printer pool?

To speed up printing. Users can print to one printer that has several print devices so that documents do not wait in the print queue. It also simplifies administration: it is easier to manage one printer for several print devices than it is to manage one printer for each print device.

Chapter 16

Practice Questions

Lesson 3: Assigning NTFS Permissions

Exercise 1: Planning NTFS Permissions

When you apply custom permissions to a folder or file, which default permission entry should you remove?

The Full Control permission for the Everyone group.

Complete the following table to plan and record your permissions:

Path	User account or group	NTFS permissions	Block inheritance (yes/no)
Apps	Administrative group	Full Control	No
Apps\WordProc	Users group	Read & Execute	No
Apps\Spreadsh	Accounting group Managers group Executives group	Read & Execute Read & Execute Read & Execute	No
Apps\Database	Accounting group Managers group Executives group	Read & Execute Read & Execute Read & Execute	No
Public	Administrators group Creator Owner Users group	Full Control Full Control Write	No

Public\Library	Administrators group	Full Control	Yes
	Users group	Read & Execute	
Public\Manuals	Administrators group	Full Control	Yes
	Users group	Read & Execute	
	User81	Full Control	

Exercise 2: Assigning NTFS Permissions for the Data Folder

▶ **To remove permissions from the Everyone group**

4. Click the Security tab to display the permissions for the Data folder.

   Windows 2000 displays the Data Properties dialog box with the Security tab active.

   What are the existing folder permissions?

   The Everyone group has Full Control.

   Notice that the current allowed permissions cannot be modified.

5. Under Name, select the Everyone group, and then click Remove.

   What do you see?

   Windows 2000 displays a message box, indicating that the folder is inheriting the permissions for Everyone from its parent folder. To change permissions for Everyone, you must first block inheritance.

8. Click Remove.

   What are the existing folder permissions?

   No permissions are currently assigned.

▶ **To assign permissions to the Users group for the Data folder**

4. Click OK to return to the Data Properties dialog box.

   What are the existing allowed folder permissions?

   The Users group has the following permissions: Read & Execute, List Folder Contents, and Read. These are the default permissions that Windows 2000 assigns when you add a user account or group to the list of permissions.

▶ **To assign permissions to the Creator Owner group for the Data folder**

4. Click OK to return to the Data Properties dialog box.

   What are the existing allowed folder permissions?

   Users has the following permissions: Read & Execute, List Folder Contents, Read, and Write. Creator Owner has the following permissions: Read & Execute, List Folder Contents, and Read.

5. Make sure that Creator Owner is selected, and next to Full Control, select the Allow check box, and then click Apply to save your changes.

What do you see?

Under Permissions, the Allow check boxes are checked and under Name, the Creator Owner group is listed along with Users.

7. Under Name, select Creator Owner.

What permissions are assigned to Creator Owner and where do these permissions apply? Why?

Full Control permission is applied to subfolders and files only. Permissions that are assigned to the Creator Owner group are not applied to the folder but only to new files and folders that are created within the folder.

▶ **To test the folder permissions that you assigned for the Data folder**

3. In the Data folder, attempt to create a text file named User81.txt.

Were you successful? Why or why not?

Yes, because the Users group is assigned the Write permission for the Data folder.

Exercise 4: Testing NTFS Permissions

▶ **To test permissions for the Reports folder while logged on as User81**

3. Attempt to create a file in the Reports folder.

Were you successful? Why or why not?

No, because only User82 has NTFS permissions to create and modify files in the Reports folder.

▶ **To test permissions for the Reports folder while logged on as User82**

3. Attempt to create a file in the Reports folder.

Were you successful? Why or why not?

Yes, because User82 has the Modify permission for the folder.

▶ **To test permissions for the Sales folder while logged on as Administrator**

3. Attempt to create a file in the Sales folder.

Were you successful? Why or why not?

Yes, because the Administrators group has the Full Control permission for the Sales folder.

▶ **To test permissions for the Sales folder while logged on as User81**

3. Attempt to create a file in the Sales folder.

   Were you successful? Why or why not?

   No, because Users only has the Read & Execute permission for the Sales folder.

▶ **To test permissions for the Sales folder while logged on as User82**

3. Attempt to create a file in the Sales folder.

   Were you successful? Why or why not?

   Yes, because User82 is a member of the Sales group, which has been assigned the Modify permission for the Sales folder.

Lesson 6: Solving Permissions Problems

Exercise 1: Taking Ownership of a File

▶ **To determine the permissions for a file**

4. Click the Security tab to display the permissions for the Owner.txt file.

   What are the current allowed permissions for Owner.txt?

   The Administrators group has the Full Control permission.

   The Users group has the Read & Execute permission.

6. Click the Owner tab.

   Who is the current owner of the Owner.txt file?

   The Administrators group.

▶ **To test permissions for a file as the owner**

4. Remove permissions from the Users group and the Administrators group for the Owner.txt file.

   Were you successful? Why or why not?

   Yes, because User84 is the owner of Owner.txt, and the owner of a folder or file can always change the permissions on folders and files that he or she owns.

Exercise 2: Copying and Moving Folders

▶ **To create a folder while logged on as a user**

1. While you are logged on as User84, in Windows Explorer, in C:\, create a folder named Temp1.

   What are the permissions that are assigned to the folder?

   The Everyone group has Full Control.

   Who is the owner? Why?

   User84 is the owner because the person who creates a folder or file is the owner.

▶ **To create a folder while logged on as Administrator**

2. In C:\, create the following two folders: Temp2 and Temp3.

   What are the permissions for the folders that you just created?

   The Everyone group has Full Control.

   Who is the owner of the Temp2 and Temp3 folders? Why?

   The Administrators group is the owner of Temp2 and Temp3 because a member of the Administrators group created these folders.

▶ **To copy a folder to another folder within a Windows 2000 NTFS volume**

2. Select C:\Temp1\Temp2, and then compare the permissions and ownership with C:\Temp2.

   Who is the owner of C:\Temp1\Temp2 and what are the permissions? Why?

   The owner is still the Administrators group because you are logged on as Administrator. When a folder or file is copied within an NTFS volume, the person who copies the folder or file becomes the owner.

   The Everyone group has the Full Control permission because when a folder or file is copied within an NTFS volume, the folder or file inherits the permissions of the folder into which it is copied.

▶ **To move a folder within the same NTFS volume**

2. Select C:\Temp3, and then move it to C:\Temp1.

   What happens to the permissions and ownership for C:\Temp1\Temp3? Why?

   The Everyone group has Full Control permission for C:\Temp1\Temp3, and the owner is the Administrators group.

   C:\Temp1\Temp3 retains the same permissions and owner as C:\Temp3. This is because when a folder or file is moved within the same NTFS volume, the folder or file retains its original permissions and owner.

Exercise 3: Deleting a File With All Permissions Denied

▶ **To view the result of the Full Control permission for a folder**

1. In Windows Explorer, double-click Noaccess.txt in C:\Fullaccess to open the file.

   Were you successful? Why or why not?

   No. The Everyone group has been denied the Full Control permission for C:\FullControl\Noaccess.txt. The Administrator user account is a member of the Everyone group.

4. Delete Noaccess.txt.

   Were you successful? Why or why not?

   Yes, because Full Control includes the Delete Subfolders and Files special permission for POSIX compliance. This special permission allows a user to delete files in the root of a folder to which the user has been assigned the Full Control permission. This permission overrides the file permissions.

   How would you prevent users with Full Control permission for a folder from deleting a file in that folder for which they have been denied the Full Control permission?

   Allow users all of the individual permissions, and then deny users the Delete Subfolders and Files special permission.

Review Questions

1. What is the default permission when a volume is formatted with NTFS? Who has access to the volume?

   The default permission is Full Control. The Everyone group has access to the volume.

2. If a user has Write permission for a folder and is also a member of a group with Read permission for the folder, what are the user's effective permissions for the folder?

   The user has both Read permission and Write permission for the folder because NTFS permissions are cumulative.

3. If you assign the Modify permission to a user account for a folder and the Read permission for a file, and then copy the file to that folder, what permission does the user have for the file?

   The user can modify the file because the file inherits the Modify permission from the folder.

4. What happens to permissions that are assigned to a file when the file is moved from one folder to another folder on the same NTFS volume? What happens when the file is moved to a folder on another NTFS volume?

   When the file is moved from one folder to another folder on the same NTFS volume, the file retains its permissions. When the file is moved to a

folder on a different NTFS volume, the file inherits the permissions of the destination folder.

5. If an employee leaves the company, what must you do to transfer ownership of his or her files and folders to another employee?

   You must be logged on as Administrator to take ownership of the employee's folders and files. Assign the Take Ownership special access permission to another employee to allow that employee to take ownership of the folders and files. Notify the employee to whom you assigned Take Ownership to take ownership of the folders and files.

6. What three things should you check when a user cannot gain access to a resource?

   Check the permissions that are assigned to the user account and to groups of which the user is a member.

   Check whether the user account, or a group of which the user is member, has been denied permission for the file or folder.

   Check whether the folder or file has been copied to any other file or folder or moved to another volume. If it has, the permissions will have changed.

Chapter 17

Practice Questions

Lesson 1: Understanding Shared Folders

Practice: Applied Permissions

1. User1 is a member of Group1, Group2, and Group3. Group1 has Read permission and Group3 has Full Control permission for Folder A. Group2 has no permissions for FolderA. What are User1's effective permissions for FolderA?

   Since User1 gets the permissions of all groups, User1's effective permission for FolderA is Full Control, which also includes all capabilities of the Read permission.

2. User1 is also a member of the Sales group, which has Read permission for FolderB. User1 has been denied the shared folder permission Full Control for FolderB as an individual user. What are User1's effective permissions for FolderB?

   User1 has no access to FolderB. Even though User1 is a member of the Sales group, which has Read permission for FolderB, User1 has been denied Full Control access to FolderB. Denied permissions override all other permissions.

Lesson 4: Combining Shared Folder Permissions and NTFS Permissions

Practice: Managing Shared Folders

Exercise 1: Combining Permissions

1. In the first example, the Data folder is shared. The Sales group has the shared folder Read permission for the Data folder and the NTFS Full Control permission for the Sales subfolder.

   What are the Sales group's effective permissions for the Sales subfolder when they gain access to the Sales subfolder by making a connection to the Data shared folder?

   The Sales group has Read permission for the Sales subfolder because when shared folder permissions are combined with NTFS permissions, the more restrictive permission applies.

2. In the second example, the Users folder contains user home folders. Each user home folder contains data that is only accessible to the user for whom the folder is named. The Users folder has been shared, and the Users group has the shared folder Full Control permission for the Users folder. User1 and User2 have the NTFS Full Control permission for *only* their home folder and no NTFS permissions for other folders. These users are all members of the Users group.

   What permissions does User1 have when he or she accesses the User1 subfolder by making a connection to the Users shared folder? What are User1's permissions for the User2 subfolder?

   User1 has the Full Control permission for the User1 subfolder because both the shared folder permission and the NTFS permission allow full control. User1 cannot access the User2 subfolder because she or he has no NTFS permissions to gain access to it.

Exercise 2: Planning Shared Folders

Record your answers in the table.

You have two choices for permissions. You can rely entirely on NTFS permissions and assign Full Control for all shared folders to Everyone, or you can use shared folder permissions according to resource needs. The following suggested shared folders include required permissions if you decide to assign shared folder permissions.

Share Management Guidelines as MgmtGd. Assign the Full Control permission to the Managers group.

Share Data as Data. Assign the Full Control permission to the Administrators built-in group.

Share Data\Customer Service as CustServ. Assign the Change permission to the Customer Service group.

Share Data\Public as Public. Assign the Change permission to the Users built-in group.

Share Applications as Apps. Assign the Read permission to the Users built-in group and the Full Control permission to the Administrators built-in group.

Share Project Management as ProjMan. Assign the Change permission to the Managers group and the Full Control permission to the Administrators built-in group.

Share Database\Customers as CustDB. Assign the Change permission to the CustomerDBFull group, the Read permission to the CustomerDBRead group, and the Full Control permission to the Administrators built-in group.

Share Users as Users. Create a folder for every employee below this folder. Assign the Full Control permission to each employee for his or her own folder. Preferably, have Windows 2000 create the folder and assign permissions automatically when you create each user account.

Exercise 3: Sharing Folders

▶ **To share a folder**

5. In the Comment box, type **Shared Productivity Applications** and then click OK.

   How does Windows Explorer change the appearance of the Apps folder to indicate that it is a shared folder?

   Windows Explorer shows a hand holding the Apps folder. The hand indicates that the folder is shared.

Exercise 4: Assigning Shared Folder Permissions

▶ **To determine the current permissions for the Apps shared folder**

2. In the Apps Properties dialog box, click the Sharing tab, and then click Permissions.

   Windows 2000 displays the Permissions For Apps dialog box.

   What are the default permissions for the Apps shared folder?

   Everyone has Full Control.

▶ **To assign Full Control to the Administrators group**

3. Click OK.

   Windows 2000 adds Administrators to the list of names with permissions.

   What type of access does Windows 2000 assign to Administrators by default?

   Read permission.

4. In the Permissions box, under Allow, click Full Control.

Why did Windows Explorer also select the Change permission for you?

Full Control includes both the Change permission and the Read permission.

Optional Exercise 5: Connecting to a Shared Folder

▶ **To connect to a network drive by using the Run command**

3. In the Open box, type **\\server1** (if you did not use server1 as the name of your domain controller, use the appropriate name here and in the following steps), and then click OK.

Windows 2000 displays the Server1 window.

Notice that only the folders that are shared appear to network users.

Which shared folders are currently available?

In addition to the folders that you shared on your domain controller, the following folders are also shared: Printers, Scheduled Tasks, DEBUG, NETLOGON, and SYSVOL. Any printers that you have shared also appear.

▶ **To connect a network drive to a shared folder by using the Map Network Drive command**

6. To confirm that Windows Explorer has successfully completed the drive mapping, on your desktop, double-click My Computer.

Notice that Windows 2000 has added drive P as Apps On Server1 (P:).

How does Windows Explorer indicate that this drive points to a remote shared folder?

Windows Explorer uses an icon that shows a network cable attached to the drive. The network cable icon indicates a mapped network drive.

▶ **To attempt to connect to a shared folder on your domain controller**

3. In the Open box, type **\\server1\apps** (if you did not use server1 as the name of your domain controller, use the appropriate name), and then click OK.

Windows 2000 displays a message, stating that access is denied.

Why were you denied access to the Apps shared folder?

Because the user account that you used to log on does not have the required permissions to gain access to the shared folder. Only the Administrators group can gain access to the Apps shared folder.

▶ **To connect to a shared folder by using another user account**

4. Click the link labeled Click Here To Connect Using A Different User Name.

The Connect As dialog box appears. This dialog box lets you specify a different user account to use to make a connection to the shared folder. When would you use this option?

Choose to connect as a different user when the user account that you are currently using does not have the necessary permissions for a shared folder and you have another user account that does. In this situation, you do not have to log off and log on again to gain access to the shared folder.

7. Confirm that the Reconnect At Logon check box is cleared, and then click Finish.

In Windows Explorer, can you gain access to drive J? Why or why not?

Yes. The Administrator account has appropriate permissions to gain access to the shared folder.

Optional Exercise 8: Testing NTFS and Shared Folder Permissions

▶ **To test permissions for the Manuals folder when a user logs on locally**

3. In the Manuals folder, attempt to create a file.

Were you successful? Why or why not?

No. Only Administrators and User93 have the NTFS permission to create and modify files in the Manuals folder.

▶ **To test permissions for the Manuals folder when a user makes a connection over the network**

5. In the Manuals folder on your domain controller, attempt to create a file.

Were you successful? Why or why not?

No. Although the Users group has the Full Control shared folder permission for \\Server1\Public, only Administrators and User93 have the NTFS permission to create and modify files in the Manuals folder.

▶ **To test permissions for the Manuals folder when a user logs on locally as User93**

3. In the Manuals folder, attempt to create a file.

Were you successful? Why or why not?

Yes. User93 has the Full Control NTFS permission for the folder.

▶ **To test permissions for the Manuals folder when a user logs on as User93 and connects over the network**

4. In the Manuals folder on your domain controller, attempt to create a file.

Were you successful? Why or why not?

Yes. The Users group has Full Control for the Public shared folder. User93 also has the Full Control NTFS permission for the Manuals folder.

Lesson 5: Configuring Dfs to Gain Access to Network Resources

▶ **To gain access to a Dfs root**

2. Double-click *Second_computer* (where Second_computer is the name of your non-domain controller computer).

Windows Explorer displays a list of all shared folders on your second computer. Notice that one of the shared folders is SharedApps, your second Dfs root.

Does Windows 2000 provide an indication that SharedApps is a Dfs root and not an ordinary shared folder?

Windows 2000 does not indicate that the share is a Dfs root share.

3. To view the Dfs child nodes on your second computer, double-click SharedApps located with your Server 1 folders.

Windows Explorer displays the Shared Apps On Server 1 window, which shows all the child nodes of SharedApps.

Does Windows 2000 indicate that the folders inside SharedApps are Dfs child nodes and not ordinary folders?

Windows 2000 does not indicate that the folders are Dfs child nodes.

Review Questions

1. When a folder is shared on a FAT volume, a user with the Full Control shared folder permissions for the folder has access to what?

All folders and files in the shared folder.

2. What are the shared folder permissions?

Full Control, Change, and Read.

3. By default, what are the permissions that are assigned to a shared folder?

The Everyone group is assigned the Full Control permission.

4. When a folder is shared on an NTFS volume, a user with the Full Control shared folder permission for the folder has access to what?

Only the folder, not necessarily any of the folder's contents. The user would also need NTFS permissions for each file and subfolder in the shared folder to gain access to those files and subfolders.

5. When you share a public folder, why should you use centralized data folders?

Centralized data folders enable data to be backed up easily.

6. What is the best way to secure files and folders that you share on NTFS partitions?

Put the files that you want to share in a shared folder and keep the default shared folder permission (the Everyone group with the Full Control permission for the shared folder). Assign NTFS permissions to users and groups to control access to all contents in the shared folder or to individual files.

7. How does Dfs facilitate network navigation for users?

A user who navigates a Dfs-managed shared folder does not need to know the name of the server where the folder is actually shared. After connecting to the Dfs root, users can browse for and gain access to all of the resources that are contained within each child node, regardless of the location of the server on which the resource is located.

Chapter 18

Practice Questions

Lesson 1: Creating Active Directory Objects

Practice: Creating an Organizational Unit

▶ **To create an OU**

2. Open Directory Management.

What are the default OUs in your domain?

Builtin, Computers, Users, and Domain Controllers. If you enabled Advanced Features, the Foreign Security Principals, LostAndFound, System, and Infrastructure OUs also appear.

Lesson 2: Locating Active Directory Objects

Practice: Searching Active Directory

▶ **To find user accounts in the domain**

2. In the console tree, right-click your domain, and then click Find.

Windows 2000 displays the Find dialog box.

In the Find dialog box, what object type can you select for a search?

Users, Contacts, And Groups; Computers; Printers; Shared Folders; Directory Folders (OUs are directory folders); Custom Search; and Routers.

3. Ensure that Users, Contacts, And Groups is selected in the Find box, and then click Find Now. What do you see?

The list of users and groups in the domain.

Lesson 3: Controlling Access to Active Directory Objects
Practice: Controlling Access to Active Directory Objects
Exercise 1: Moving Objects in a Domain

▶ **To log on as a user in a nonstandard OU**

1. Log off and then log on to your domain by using one of the user accounts that you created in the preceding procedure.

   Did Windows 2000 require you to specify the OU in which your user account is located as part of the logon process? Why or why not?

   No. Windows 2000 automatically locates the user object in Active Directory, independent of its exact location.

Exercise 2: Reviewing Active Directory Permissions

▶ **To view default Active Directory permissions for an OU**

4. In the following table, list the groups that have permissions for the Security1 OU. You will need to refer to these permissions in the next exercise.

User account or group	Assigned permissions
Authenticated User	Read
Local System	Full Control
Domain Admins	Full Control
Enterprise Administrators	Inherits the Read, Write, and Create All Child Objects permissions and also has advanced permissions
Account Operators	Advanced permissions
Print Operators	Advanced permissions

How can you tell if any of the default permissions are inherited from the domain, which is the parent object?

The permissions that are assigned to Administrators are inherited from the parent object. The check boxes for inherited permissions are shown as shaded.

▶ **To view advanced permissions for an OU**

2. To view the permissions for Account Operators, in the Permission Entries box, click each entry for Account Operators, and then click View/Edit.

   Directory Management displays the Permission Entry For Security1 dialog box.

What object permissions are assigned to Account Operators? What can Account Operators do in this OU? (Hint: check both permission entries for Account Operators.)

The permissions that are assigned to Account Operators are Create User Objects, Delete User Objects, Create Group Objects, and Delete Group Objects. Account Operators can only create and delete user accounts and groups.

Do any objects within this OU inherit the permissions assigned to the Account Operators group? Why or why not?

No. Objects within this OU do not inherit these permissions. The dialog box shows that permissions are applied on this object only.

▶ **To view the default Active Directory permissions for a user object**

4. In the following table, list the groups that have permissions for the Secretary1 user account. You will need to refer to these permissions in the next exercise. If the dialog box indicates that additional permissions are present for a group, do not list the additional permissions to which you can gain access through the Advanced button.

Group	Assigned permissions
Everyone	Change Password
Principal Self	Read, Phone and Mail Options, Personal Information, Receive As, Send As, Change Password, and Web Information
Authenticated User	Advanced
Local System	Full Control
Domain Admins	Full Control
Cert Publishers	Advanced
Enterprise Administrators	Inherits all permissions, except the Full Control and Delete All Child Objects permissions, and also has advanced permissions
RAS and IAS Servers	Advanced
Account Operators	Full Control

Are the default permissions for a user object the same as those for an OU object? Why or why not?

No. Default permissions for each type of object are different. The reason for the differences is that different object types are used for different tasks, and therefore the security needs for each object type differ.

Are any of the default permissions inherited from Security1, the parent object? How can you tell?

Only the default permissions that are assigned to Administrators are inherited from the parent object. The check boxes for inherited permissions are shown as shaded.

What do the permissions of the Account Operators group allow its members to do with the user object?

Account Operators have Full Control. A member of the group can make any changes to a user object, including deleting it.

Lesson 4: Delegating Administrative Control of Active Directory Objects

Practice: Delegating Administrative Control in Active Directory

▶   **To test current permissions**

3.   In the console tree, expand your domain, and then click Security1.

What user objects are visible in the Security1 OU?

The Secretary1 and Assistant1 user accounts.

Which permissions allow you to see these objects? (Hint: refer to your answers in the preceding exercise.)

The Assistant1 user account automatically belongs to the Authenticated Users built-in group, which has the Read permission for the OU.

For the user account with the logon name Secretary1, change the logon hours. Were you successful? Why or why not?

No. The Assistant1 user account does not have the Write permission for this object.

For the Assistant1 user account, under which you are currently logged on, change the logon hours. Were you successful? Why or why not?

No. The Assistant1 user account does not have the Write permission for this object.

▶   **To test delegated permissions**

4.   Attempt to change the logon hours for both user accounts in the Security1 OU. Were you successful? Why or why not?

Yes. The Assistant1 user account has been assigned the Full Control permission for all objects in the OU. This includes the permission to change the logon hours.

5.   Attempt to change the logon hours for a user account in the Users OU. Were you successful? Why or why not?

No. The Assistant1 user account has been assigned no permissions for the Users OU.

Review Questions

1. What is the advantage of having all objects located in Active Directory?

   Because the Directory contains all objects, it provides a centralized way to create, view, manage, and locate objects.

2. What is the difference between an object attribute and an object attribute value? Give examples.

   Attributes (also referred to as properties) are categories of information and define the characteristics for all objects of a defined object type. All objects of the same type have the same attributes. Values of the attributes make the objects unique. For example, all user account objects have a First Name attribute; however, the value for the First Name attribute can be any name, such as John or Jane.

3. You want to allow the manager of the Sales department to create, modify, and delete only user accounts for sales personnel. How can you accomplish this?

   Place all of the sales personnel user accounts in an OU, and then delegate control of the OU to the manager of the Sales department.

4. What determines if a user can locate an object when using global catalog?

   The global catalog contains a partial replica of the Entire Directory. It stores information about every object in a domain tree or forest. This enables a user to find information regardless of which domain in the tree or forest contains the data.

5. What happens to the permissions of an object when you move it from one OU to another OU?

   Permissions assigned directly to the object remain the same. The object also inherits permissions from the new OU. Any permissions previously inherited from the old OU no longer affect the object.

Chapter 19

Practice Questions

Lesson 1: Managing User Profiles

Practice: Managing User Profiles

Exercise 1: Creating a User Account

▶ **To use Control Panel to determine existing profiles**

3. Click the User Profiles tab.

   Which users' profiles are stored on your computer?

Domain1\Administrator, Domain1\Puser, and users who have logged on to the computer.

▶ **To define and test a local profile**

5. Log off and log on as the same user, Profile Tester (Ptester).

   Were screen colors saved? Why or why not?

   Yes, because the screen colors are saved in the user's profile.

Optional Exercise 2: Defining a Roaming User Profile

▶ **To verify that the roaming user profile is assigned to Profile Tester**

2. Double-click System, and then click the User Profiles tab.

   What type of profile is listed for the Profile Tester account?

   A roaming user profile.

▶ **To test the roaming user profile from another computer**

2. If a dialog box appears which provides profile options, click Download.

   Are the screen colors and desktop the same or different from those set at the domain controller? Why or why not?

   The screen colors are the same because the roaming profile for the Profile Tester account was downloaded from a network location and applied to whatever computer Profile Tester logs on to.

Lesson 2: Modifying User Accounts

Practice: Administering User Accounts

Exercise 1: Enabling a User Account

▶ **To disable a user account**

6. In the details pane of Active Directory Manager, right-click the user account that you just disabled to display the shortcut menu.

   How can you tell that the user account is disabled?

   The Enable Account option appears on the shortcut menu, and a red X appears on the user icon in the details pane.

8. Attempt to log on as puser.

   Were you successful? Why or why not?

   No, because the account is disabled.

▶   **To enable a user account**

5. In the details pane of Active Directory Manager, right-click the user account that you just enabled to display the shortcut menu.

How can you tell that the user account is enabled?

The Disable Account option appears on the shortcut menu, and the red X is removed from the user icon in the details pane.

▶   **To test account enabling and to change the password for a user account**

1. Log on as puser.

Were you successful? Why?

Yes, because the account is enabled.

Exercise 2: Resetting the Password for a User Account

▶   **To test password resetting**

1. Log on as puser with the password password.

Were you successful? Why?

Yes, because the password has been reset to password.

Review Questions

1. Why would you rename a user account and what are the advantages of doing so?

You rename a user account if you want a new user to have all of the properties of a former user, including permissions, desktop settings, and group membership. The advantages of renaming an account are that you do not have to rebuild all of the properties as you do for a new user account.

2. What must you do to ensure that a user on a client computer running Windows 2000 has a user profile?

Nothing. When a user logs on for the first time at a computer running Windows 2000, Windows 2000 creates a default user profile for that user. Windows 2000 automatically saves the user profile within the system root folder (*systemroot*\Profiles).

3. What is the difference between a user profile and a roaming user profile?

A user profile is stored on the computer where the user logs on. A roaming user profile is stored on a domain server and is copied to the client computer where the user logs on.

4. What do you do to ensure that a user on a client computer running Windows 2000 has a roaming user profile?

First, create a shared folder on a network server. Second, for each user account, in the Properties dialog box for each user, provide a path to the folder on the server. The next time that the user logs on, the roaming user profile is created.

5. How can you ensure that a user has a centrally located home directory?

First, create and share a parent folder on a server. Second, change the permission for the folder to Full Control for the Users group. Third, provide a path to the folder, including the name of the individual user's home directory (*server_name**shared_folder_name**user_logon_name*).

6. What can you do if a user whom you administer cannot gain access to a special printer that they need to do their job because of a group policy restriction?

You must contact the group policy administrator and resolve the conflict with this administrator.

Chapter 20

Practice Questions

Lesson 4: Using Event Viewer

Practice: Auditing Resources and Events

Exercise 2: Setting Up an Audit Policy

▶ To set up an audit policy

2. To set the audit policy, in the details pane, double-click each type of event, and then select either the Audit Successful Attempts check box or the Audit Failed Attempts check box as listed in the table.

Answers may vary. Possible answers include the following:

Account logon events: Failed (for network access attempts)

Account management: Successful (for administrator actions)

Directory service access: Failed (for unauthorized access)

Logon events: Failed (for network access attempts)

Object access: Successful (for printer use) and Failed (for unauthorized access)

Policy change: Successful (for administrator actions)

Privilege use: Successful (for administrator actions and backup procedures)

Process tracking: Nothing (useful primarily for programmers)

System events: Successful and Failed (for attempts to breach the server).

Exercise 5: Setting Up Auditing of an Active Directory Object

▶   **To review auditing of an Active Directory object**

6. In the Access Control Settings For Users dialog box, click the Auditing tab, and then double-click Everyone.

    Active Directory Manager displays the Audit Entry For Users dialog box.

    Review the default audit settings for object access by members of the Everyone group. How do the audited types of access differ from the types of access that are not audited?

    All types of access that result in a change of the object are audited; types of access that do not result in a change of the object are not audited.

7. Click OK three times to close the Users Properties dialog box.

    At which computer or computers does Windows 2000 record log entries for Active Directory access? Will you be able to review them?

    Windows 2000 records auditing events for Active Directory access at domain controllers. Because you did not configure auditing for the computer in your domain that is acting as a domain controller, you will not be able to view auditing events for Active Directory access.

Review Questions

1. On which computer do you set an audit policy to audit a folder that is located on a member server that belongs to a domain?

    You set the audit policy on the member server; the audit policy must be set on the computer where the file is located.

2. What is the difference between what the audit policy settings track for directory service access and object access?

    Directory service access tracks if a user gained access to an Active Directory object. Object access tracks if a user gained access to a file, folder, or printer.

3. What two tasks must you perform to audit access to a file?

    Set the audit policy for object access and configure the file for the type of access to audit.

4. Who can set up auditing for a computer?

    By default, only members of the Administrators group can set up and administer auditing. You can also give other users the Manage Auditing and Security log user right, which is required to configure an audit policy and review audit logs.

5. When you view a security log, how do you determine if an event failed or was successful?

Successful events appear with a key icon; unsuccessful events appear with a lock icon.

6. If you click the Do Not Overwrite Events option in the Properties dialog box for an audit log, what happens when the log file becomes full?

When the log becomes full, Windows 2000 will stop. You must clear the log manually.

Chapter 21

Practice Questions

Lesson 2: Applying Group Policy

Practice: Creating GPOs

Exercise 1: Creating a GPO

▶ **To create a GPO for your domain**

5. Click the All tab, and then point to each of the three buttons on the toolbar and record below the function of the button.

First button: **Up One Level**

Second button: **Create New Group Policy Object**

Third button: **View Menu**

Exercise 2: Modifying Security Settings

▶ **To modify security settings**

9. Double-click Log On Locally in the details pane.

The Log On Locally dialog box appears.

What groups have the right to log on locally?

Account Operators, Administrators, Backup Operators, IUSR_SERVER1, IWAM_SERVER1, Print Operators, and Server Operators.

Lesson 3: Modifying Software Policies

Practice: Modifying Software Policies

Exercise 2: Testing Software Policies

▶ **To test the Sales OU software policies**

2. Press Ctrl+Alt+Delete.

The Windows 2000 Security dialog box appears.

Are you able to lock the workstation?

No.

4. Click Start.

Does the Search command appear on the Start menu?

No.

Does the Run command appear on the Start menu?

No.

Review Questions

1. What is a GPO?

    A GPO is a group policy object. Group Policy configuration settings are contained within a GPO. You establish group policy settings in a GPO that you apply to a site, domain, or organizational unit (SDOU). GPOs store group policy information in two locations: a GPC and a GPT.

2. What is a GPC?

    A GPC, group policy container, is an Active Directory object that contains GPO properties and includes subcontainers for computer and user group policy information. The GPC contains the class store information for application deployment. The Windows 2000 class store is a server-based repository for all applications, interfaces, and application programming interfaces (APIs) that provide application publishing and assigning functions.

3. What is a GPT?

    A GPT, group policy template, is a folder structure in the system volume folder (Sysvol) of domain controllers. The GPT is the container for all software policy, script, file and application deployment, and security settings information. The folder name of the GPT is the globally unique identifier (GUID) of the GPO that you created.

4. In what order is group policy implemented through the Active Directory structure?

    Group policy is implemented in the following order: site, domain, and then organizational unit (OU).

Chapter 22

Practice Questions

Lesson 2: Managing Printers
Practice: Performing Printer Management
Exercise 2: Setting Up Separator Pages

▶ **To set up a separator page**

2. In the Separator Page dialog box, click Browse.

   Windows 2000 displays another Separator Page dialog box.

   What are the four separator page files from which you can select?

   Pcl.sep, Pscript.sep, Sysprint.sep, and Sysprtj.sep.

Exercise 3: Taking Ownership of a Printer

▶ **To take ownership of a printer**

2. On the Security tab, click Advanced, and then click the Owner tab.

   Who currently owns the printer?

   The Administrators group.

Lesson 3: Managing Documents
Practice: Managing Documents

▶ **To set a notification**

3. In the Printer window, select Relnotes, and then click Properties on the Document menu.

   Windows 2000 displays the Relnotes Document Properties dialog box with the General tab active.

   Which user is specified in the Notify box? Why?

   The Notify box currently displays the user Administrator because Administrator printed the document.

▶ **To increase the priority of a document**

1. In the Relnotes Document Properties dialog box, on the General tab, notice the default priority.

What is the current priority? Is it the lowest or highest priority?

The current priority is the default of 1, which is the lowest priority.

Review Questions

1. What printer permission does a user need to change the priority on another user's document?

   The Manage Documents permission.

2. In an environment where many users print to the same print device, how can you help reduce the likelihood of users picking up the wrong documents?

   Create a separator page that identifies and separates printed documents.

3. Can you redirect a single document?

   No. You can only change the configuration of the print server to send documents to another printer or print device, which redirects all documents on that printer.

4. A user needs to print a very large document. How can the user print the job after hours, without being present while the document prints?

   You can control print jobs by setting the printing time. You set the printing time for a document on the General tab of the Properties dialog box for the document. To open the Properties dialog box for a document, select the document in the Printer window, click Document on the Printer window menu bar, and then click Properties. Click Only From in the Schedule section of the Properties dialog box, and then set the Only From hour to the earliest time you want the document to begin printing after regular business hours. Set the To time to a couple of hours before normal business hours start. To set the printing time for a document, you must be the owner of the document or have the Manage Documents permission for the appropriate printer.

5. What are the advantages of using a Web browser to administer printing?

   You can administer any printer on a Windows 2000 print server on the intranet by using any computer running a Web browser, regardless of whether the computer is running Windows 2000 or has the correct printer driver installed. Additionally, a Web browser provides a summary page and reports real-time print device status, and you can customize the interface.

Chapter 23

Practice Questions

Lesson 1: Managing NTFS Compression

Practice: Managing NTFS Compression

Exercise 1: Compressing Files in an NTFS Partition

▶ **To view the capacity and free space for drive C**

2. Right-click drive C, and then click Properties.

   Windows 2000 displays the Local Disk (C:) Properties dialog box with the General tab active.

   What is the capacity of drive C?

   Answer will vary.

   What is the free space on drive C?

   Answer will vary.

▶ **To compress a folder tree**

7. Select the Compress Contents To Save Disk Space check box.

   Why is the Encrypt Contents To Secure Data Option no longer available?

   Encryption and compression are mutually exclusive options.

▶ **To uncompress a folder**

6. Press F5 to refresh the view in Windows Explorer.

   What indication do you have that the CompTest2 folder is no longer compressed?

   The Library folder name is displayed in black.

Exercise 2: Copying and Moving Files

▶ **To create a compressed file**

3. Type **Text1** and then press Enter.

   How can you verify that Text1 is compressed?

   The name of the file is displayed in blue. You could also check the properties for the file.

▶ **To copy a compressed file to an uncompressed folder**

2. Examine the properties for Text1 in the CompTest2 folder.

   Is C:\CompTest\CompTest2\Text1.txt compressed or uncompressed? Why?

   Uncompressed. A new file inherits the compression attribute of the folder in which it is created.

▶ **To move a compressed file to an uncompressed folder**

1. Examine the properties of C:\CompTest\Text1.txt.

   Is Text1.txt compressed or uncompressed?

   Compressed.

3. Examine the properties of Text1.txt in the Compress2 folder.

   Is Text1.txt compressed or uncompressed? Why?

   Compressed. When a file is moved to a new folder on the same partition, its compression attribute does not change.

Lesson 2: Managing Disk Quotas

Practice: Enabling and Disabling Disk Quotas

Exercise 1: Configuring Quota Management Settings

▶ **To configure default quota management settings**

3. On the Quota tab, click the Enable Quota Management check box.

   What is the default disk space limit for new users?

   Do Not Limit Disk Usage is the default setting.

▶ **To configure quota management settings for a user**

1. On the Quota tab of the Local Disk (C:) Properties dialog box, click the Quota Entries button.

   Windows 2000 displays the Quota Entries For Local Disk (C:) dialog box.

   Are any user accounts listed? Why or why not?

   Yes. The accounts listed are those that have logged on and gained access to drive C.

5. Click OK.

   Windows 2000 displays the Add New Quota Entry dialog box.

   What are the default settings for the user you just set a quota limit for?

Limit disk space to 10 MB and Set warning level to 6 MB. These are the default settings that are selected for drive C.

Review Questions

1. You are the administrator for a computer running Windows 2000 Server that is used to store user's home folders and roaming user profiles. You want to restrict users to 25 MB of available storage for their home folder while monitoring, but not limiting, the disk space that is used for the roaming user profiles. How should you configure the volumes on the server?

   Create two volumes: one to store home folders and one to store roaming user profiles. Format both volumes with NTFS and enable disk quotas for both volumes. For the home folder volume, specify a limit of 25 MB and select the Deny Disk Space To Users Exceeding Quota Limit check box. For the roaming user profile volume, do not specify a limit and clear the Deny Disk Space To Users Exceeding Quota Limit check box.

2. The Sales department archives legacy sales data on a network computer running Windows 2000 Server. Several other departments share the server. You have begun to receive complaints from users in other departments that the server has very little remaining disk space. What can you do to alleviate the problem?

   Compress the folders that the Sales department uses to store archive data.

3. Your department has recently archived several gigabytes of data from a computer running Windows 2000 Server to CD-ROMs. As users have been adding files to the server, you have noticed that the server has been taking longer than usual to gain access to the hard disk. How can you increase disk access time for the server?

   Use Disk Defragmenter to defragment files on the server's hard disk.

Chapter 24

Practice Questions

Lesson 2: Backing Up Data

Practice: Backing Up Files

Exercise 1: Starting a Backup Job

▶   **To back up files by using the Backup wizard**

13. Make sure that the Backup Migrated Remote Storage Data check box is cleared, and then click Next.

    The Backup wizard displays the How To Backup page, prompting you to specify whether or not to verify the backed up data after the backup job.

Why is the Use Hardware Compression, If Available check box unavailable?

This option is only available for tape drives. (If you have a tape drive installed, the box is available.)

15. Click Replace The Data On The Media With This Backup.

When is it appropriate to select the check box labeled Allow Only The Owner And The Administrator Access To The Backup Data And Any Backups Appended To This Media?

Unless the data that is being backed up will be restored by anyone other than the person backing up or an administrator, you should consider selecting this check box if you want to minimize the risk of unauthorized access to your data.

Exercise 2: Creating and Running an Unattended Backup Job

▶   **To verify that the backup job was performed**

1. Start Microsoft Windows Explorer and click drive C.

   Does the Backup2.bkf file exist?

   Yes.

Lesson 3: Restoring Data

Practice: Restoring Files

▶   **To verify that the data was restored**

1. Start Windows Explorer and expand drive **C**.

   Does the Restored data folder exist?

   Yes.

Review Questions

1. If you want a user to perform network backups, what do you need to do?

   Make sure that the user is a member of the Administrators, Backup Operators, or Server Operators groups.

2. You performed a normal backup on Monday. For the remaining days of the week, you only want to back up files and folders that have changed since the previous day. What backup type do you select?

   Incremental. The incremental backup type backs up changes since the last markers were set and then clears the markers. Thus, for Tuesday through Friday, you only back up changes since the previous day.

3. What are the considerations for using tapes as your backup media?

Tapes are a less expensive medium and are more convenient for large backups because of their higher storage capacity. However, the medium deteriorates with time and thus has a limited lifespan.

4. You are responsible for backing up Active Directory. What must you consider?

You must run Windows Backup at a domain controller. If you use a removable media device, such as a tape device, attach it to the domain controller. After the backup is complete, store the backup media in a physically secure location.

5. Users are responsible for backing up their critical data, but there is only one tape device in your domain. In addition, you want to make sure that at least one copy of all backup data is stored offsite. What do you do?

Have users back up critical data to files on a network file server. You can then back up the file server to tapes, which you can store offsite.

6. You are restoring a file that has the same name as a file on the volume to which you are restoring. You are not sure which is the most current version. What do you do?

Do not replace the file. Restore the file to another location, and then compare the two files.

Chapter 25

Review Questions

1. What is the purpose of disaster protection, and what combination of techniques do you use to achieve it?

The purpose of disaster protection is to prevent computer disasters and to minimize downtime in the event of computer failure. You achieve disaster protection through a combination of fault (disaster) tolerance and disaster recovery techniques.

2. How can you test the configuration of the UPS service on a computer?

You can simulate a power failure by disconnecting the main power supply to the UPS device. During the test, the computer and peripherals connected to the UPS device should remain operational, messages should display, and events should be logged.

In addition, you should wait until the UPS battery reaches a low level to verify that a graceful shutdown occurs. Then restore the main power to the UPS device and check the event log to ensure that all actions were logged and there were no errors.

3. A computer running Windows 2000 Server has the following disk configuration:

   - Disk 0: drive C (300 MB, system/boot partition), drive D (700 MB, data),
     and 500 MB of free space
   - Disk 1: 750 MB of free space
   - Disk 2: 1 GB of free space

   You want to install additional Microsoft BackOffice components on this computer. What is the best way both to protect your computer's data and to optimize its performance by using Windows 2000 fault tolerance?

   **Mirror drive C on disk 2, and create a 1.5-GB RAID-5 volume that spans
   all three disks.**

4. What information is included in an ASR saveset?

   **An ASR saveset contains a computer's configuration information and
   operating system files, including the following:**

   **The *systemroot* directory and all of its subdirectories and files on offline
   storage.**

   **The configuration of the physical storage (for example, partition struc-
   ture, file format, and other attributes) on which the system and boot partitions reside.**

Chapter 26

Practice Questions

Lesson 3: Sharing a Folder Using the Shared Folders Snap-In
Practice: Creating a Shared Folder

▶ **To create a new shared folder on your computer**

12. Click No.

   The wizard finishes. Does the new shared folder appear in the details pane?
   Why or why not?

   **Yes. Microsoft Windows 2000 automatically updates the list of shared
   folders.**

Review Questions

1. What are the reasons for monitoring access to network resources?

   Maintenance (to notify users before making the resource unavailable), security (to monitor which users are gaining access to which resources), and planning (to determine which resources are being used).

2. What can you monitor on a network with the Shared Folders snap-in?

   You can monitor the number of users who have a current connection to the computer that you are monitoring, the files to which users are currently gaining access and which users are currently gaining access to each file, the shared folders to which users are currently gaining access on the network, and how many users have a connection to each folder. You can monitor all this information on the computer where you are physically located or on a remote computer.

3. Why would you send an administrative message to users with current connections?

   To inform the users that you are about to disconnect them from the resource so that you can perform a backup or restore operation, upgrade software or hardware, or shut down the computer.

4. What can you do to prevent a user from reconnecting to a shared folder after you have disconnected the user from the shared folder?

   To prevent all users from reconnecting, stop sharing the folder. To prevent only one user from reconnecting, change the permissions for the folder so that the user no longer has access, and then disconnect the user from the shared folder.

5. How does the Shared Folders snap-in use shared folder permissions and NTFS permissions when you share a folder?

   The Shared Folders snap-in assigns the shared folder Full Control permission to the Everyone group. For an existing shared folder, it allows you to keep the original NTFS permissions. For a new shared folder, it allows you to keep the NTFS permissions that the folder inherited when the folder was created. For an existing or new shared folder, you can assign any one of three sets of NTFS permissions and you can choose to allow or prevent inheritance to all subfolders and files within the shared folder.

Chapter 27

Practice Questions

Lesson 6: The Windows 2000 Boot Disk

Practice: Troubleshooting the Windows 2000 Boot Process

Exercise 1: Creating a Windows 2000 Boot Disk

▶ **To create a Windows 2000 boot disk**

3. Type each of the following commands and press Enter to copy the following files from the root directory of drive C to the root directory of drive A:

   copy boot.ini a:
   copy ntdetect.com a:
   copy ntldr. a:
   copy bootsect.dos a:
   copy ntbootdd.sys a:

   If the last two files listed above are not present on your system, they will not be needed on the Windows 2000 boot disk.

   If you were to use this boot disk to restart another computer running Windows 2000 that included different hardware, what, if anything, would you need to change about the disk?

   You might need to edit the Boot.ini file to change the Advanced RISC Computing (ARC) path to the Windows 2000 boot partition on a new system if Windows 2000 was installed in a different location.

Exercise 2: Identifying the Phases of the Boot Process

▶ **To restart your computer running Windows 2000**

3. At any stage during the POST, press the Pause key to pause the boot process.

   A common error that occurs at the conclusion of the POST is a black screen with the text `Missing operating system`. What might be the cause of this error?

   This error occurs before any Windows 2000 files are loaded from the hard disk, which indicates that there is something wrong with the hard disk configuration. This error can be caused by failure to set an active partition, or by the boot sector being invalid as a result of incorrect disk configuration or damaged sectors.

   How could you restart your computer and boot to Windows 2000?

   To restart Windows 2000, boot from a Windows 2000 boot disk. To fix the error, check the hard disk configuration in the basic input/output system

(BIOS), and if this is correct, use the Automatic System Recovery (ASR) repair process to repair the boot sector.

5. When the Boot Loader menu appears, press Pause to pause the boot process.

   Which file or files does the system use to produce this menu?

   Ntldr and Boot.ini.

7. In the Boot Loader menu, ensure that Windows 2000 Server is selected, and then press Enter.

   The following text appears for a short period of time:

   ```
   NTDETECT V5.0 Checking Hardware . . .
   ```

   This indicates that Ntdetect.com is building a list of installed hardware. When Ntdetect.com completes hardware detection, the following text appears in the top-left corner of the screen:

   ```
   OS Loader V5.0
   ```

   Notice that the floppy disk drive activity light goes out. This indicates that the Windows 2000 boot process is finished reading files from the boot disk.

   How could you display a list of the files loaded at this stage rather than the periods?

   Edit the Boot.ini file and add the /SOS switch to the end of the line that is loading Windows 2000.

Exercise 3: Repairing a Boot Problem Using a Windows 2000 Boot Disk

▶ **To create a system boot failure**

2. Remove the boot disk from the floppy disk drive, and then restart the computer.

   What error do you receive when attempting to restart the computer?

   ```
   Ntldr is missing
   Press any key to restart
   ```

Exercise 4: Using the Last Known Good Configuration

▶ **To use the Last Known Good Configuration**

3. On the Windows 2000 Advanced Options menu, select Last Known Good Configuration, and then press Enter.

   The initial Boot Loader menu appears. What line appears in red at the bottom of the screen?

   Last Known Good Configuration.

Review Questions

1. What are the five major phases of the boot process for Intel-based computers?

   The boot process for Intel-based computers includes the preboot sequence, boot sequence, kernel load, kernel initialization, and logon phases.

2. Which files used in the boot process for Intel-based computers are not necessary on Alpha-based computers?

   The Ntldr, Boot.ini, Bootsect.dos, and Ntdetect.com files are not necessary. On Alpha-based computers, Ntldr functionality is built into the firmware. Osloader.exe performs the initial stages of loading the Windows 2000 operating system on Alpha-based computers. In addition, the Alpha POST routine collects hardware information and passes it to Osloader.exe.

3. What are the various safe mode options for booting Windows 2000, and how do they differ?

   The Safe Mode option loads only the basic devices and drivers required to start the system, including the mouse, keyboard, mass storage devices, base video, and the standard/default set of system services.

   The Safe Mode With Networking option loads the devices and drivers loaded with the Safe Mode option, but it also loads the services and drivers required for networking.

   The Safe Mode With Command Prompt option is identical to the Safe Mode option, but it launches a command prompt instead of Windows Explorer.

4. What are the two sections of the Boot.ini file, and what information does each section contain?

   The two sections of the Boot.ini file are [boot loader] and [operating systems]. The [boot loader] section of Boot.ini specifies the default operating system and provides a timeout value.

   The [operating systems] section of Boot.ini contains the list of operating systems that appear in the Boot Loader Operating System Selection menu. Each entry includes the path to the operating system and the name that appears in the Boot Loader Operating System Selection menu (the text between the quotation marks). Each entry can also contain optional parameters.

5. Suppose that you created a Windows 2000 boot disk that contains the following files:

   Ntldr
   Ntdetect.com
   Boot.ini
   Ntbootdd.sys

When you try to boot Windows 2000 with the boot disk, you receive the following error message:

```
Non-System disk or disk error
Replace and press any key when ready
```

What did you do wrong?

The disk that you used was not formatted by Windows 2000.

6. You install a new device driver for a SCSI adapter in your computer. When you restart the computer, however, Windows 2000 stops responding after the kernel load phase. How can you get Windows 2000 to restart successfully?

Use the LastKnownGood configuration to start Windows 2000 because it does not contain any reference to the new, and possibly faulty, driver.

APPENDIX B

Computing the Number
Of Client Access Licenses

Use the following table to calculate the number of Client Access Licenses you need to buy and whether you should use Per Seat or Per Server licensing.

Per Server	Number of computers running Microsoft Windows 2000 Server (also replace E in the bottom box of this table with this number)	**A** ☐
	Maximum number of simultaneous workstation connections to each server	**B** ☐
	Number of Client Access Licenses required equals (A × B)	**C** ☐
Per Seat	Number of seats that will access any server	**D** ☐
Choosing a licensing mode	Check one: The number next to D is greater than the number next to C. Use the number that is next to C to replace F in the box below. Use Per Server licensing.	☐
	The number next to C is greater than the number next to D. Use the number that is next to D to replace F in the box below. Use Per Seat licensing.	☐
What to buy	The number of copies of Windows 2000 Server you need to buy is	**E** ☐
	The number of Client Access Licenses you need to purchase is	**F** ☐

A P P E N D I X   C

Creating Setup Disks

Unless your computer supports booting from a CD-ROM drive, you must have the four Windows 2000 Server Setup disks to complete the installation of Microsoft Windows 2000 Server. To create these three Setup disks, complete the following procedure.

Important   You must complete this procedure on a computer running Windows 2000 or Windows NT with access to a CD-ROM drive. This procedure requires four blank, formatted 1.44-MB disks. If you use disks that contain data already, the data will be overwritten without warning.

▶ **To create Windows 2000 Server Setup disks**

1. Label the four blank, formatted 1.44-MB disks as follows:
   - Windows 2000 Server Setup Disk 1
   - Windows 2000 Server Setup Disk 2
   - Windows 2000 Server Setup Disk 3
   - Windows 2000 Server Setup Disk 4

2. Insert the Microsoft Windows 2000 Server CD-ROM into the CD-ROM drive.

3. If the Windows 2000 CD-ROM dialog box appears prompting you to upgrade to Windows NT, click No.

4. Open a command prompt.

5. At the command prompt, change to your CD-ROM drive. For example, if your CD-ROM drive name is E, type **e:** and press Enter.

6. At the command prompt, change to the Bootdisk folder by typing **cd bootdisk** and pressing Enter.

7. With Bootdisk as the active folder, type **makeboot a:** (where a: is the name of your floppy disk drive) and then press Enter.

Windows 2000 displays a message indicating that this script creates the four Windows 2000 Setup disks for installing from a CD-ROM. It also indicates that four blank formatted floppy disks are required.

8. Press any key to continue.

Windows 2000 displays a message prompting you to insert the disk labeled Disk 1.

9. Insert the blank formatted disk labeled Windows 2000 Server Setup Disk 1 into your floppy disk drive, and then press any key to continue.

After Windows 2000 creates the disk image, it displays a message prompting you to insert the disk labeled Disk 2.

10. Remove Disk 1, insert the blank formatted disk labeled Windows 2000 Server Setup Disk 2 into drive A, and then press any key to continue.

After Windows 2000 creates the disk image, it displays a message prompting you to insert the disk labeled Disk 3.

11. Remove Disk 2, insert the blank formatted disk labeled Windows 2000 Server Setup Disk 3 into your floppy disk drive, and then press any key to continue.

After Windows 2000 creates the disk image, it displays a message prompting you to insert the disk labeled Disk 4.

12. Remove Disk 3, insert the blank formatted disk labeled Windows 2000 Server Setup Disk 4 into drive A, and then press any key to continue.

After Windows 2000 creates the disk image, it displays a message indicating that the imaging process is done.

13. At the command prompt, type **exit** and then press Enter.

14. Remove the disk from the floppy disk drive and the CD-ROM from the CD-ROM drive.

A P P E N D I X   D

Managing Backup Tapes

If you use tapes as your backup medium, consider the distinction between rotating tapes and archiving tapes. *Rotating tapes* means reusing them when the data stored on them is no longer viable for restoring. This common practice helps to lower the cost of backing up data. *Archiving tapes* means storing the tape to keep a record of the data rather than as prevention against data loss. When you archive a tape, you remove that tape from the tape rotation. Archived tapes are useful for maintaining a record of data for a specific date and time, such as employee records at the end of a fiscal year.

Rotating and Archiving Tapes

The following two examples provide strategies for rotating and archiving tapes.

Example 1

The following table illustrates one strategy for rotating and archiving tapes and is explained below.

	Monday	**Tuesday**	**Wednesday**	**Thursday**	**Friday**
Week 1	Tape 1	Tape 2	Tape 3	Tape 4	Tape 5 (Archive)
Week 2	Tape 1 (Replace or Append)	Tape 2 (Replace or Append)	Tape 3 (Replace or Append)	Tape 4 (Replace or Append)	Tape 6 (Archive)

Week 1

The backup job for each day of the week is on a different tape. The backup tape for Friday is archived and removed from rotation.

Week 2

For this week, you reuse the tapes for the same day of the week (the Monday backup job is on the previous Monday tape 1). You can either replace or append to the existing backup job. However, on Friday, use a new tape that you archive and remove from rotation.

Example 2

This table illustrates another strategy for rotating and archiving tapes and is explained below.

	Monday	Tuesday	Wednesday	Thursday	Friday
Week 1	Tape 1	Tape 1 (Append)	Tape 1 (Append)	Tape 1 (Append)	Tape 2 (Archive)
Week 2	Tape 1	Tape 1 (Append)	Tape 1 (Append)	Tape 1 (Append)	Tape 3 (Archive)

Week 1

The backup job for each day of the week, except Friday, is on the same tape. The backup tape for Friday is archived and removed from rotation.

Use the same tape for the Monday through Thursday backup jobs and append each new backup job to the previous one. The Friday backup job is on a different tape (tape 2) that you archive and remove from rotation.

Week 2

For this week, reuse the tape from the previous week (tape 1) for all backup jobs. The Friday backup job is on a tape (tape 3) that is different from the one that you used the previous Friday. You archive and remove this tape from rotation.

Determining the Number of Tapes Required

When determining the number of tapes you need, consider the tape rotation and archival schedule, the amount of the data that you back up, and the tape life cycle.

The life cycle of a tape depends on the tape itself and storage conditions. Follow the tape manufacturer's usage guidelines. If your company does not have a suitable storage facility, consider using a third-party company that specializes in off-site storage for backup media.

INDEX

The *intelligent* way to practice for the *MCP exam.*

If you took the Microsoft, Certified Professional (MCP) exam today, would you pass? With the READINESS REVIEW MCP exam simulation on CD-ROM, you get a low-risk, low-cost way to find out! Use this electronic assessment tool to take randomly generated, 60-question practice tests covering actual MCP objectives. Test and retest with different question sets each time, then consult the companion study guide to review all featured exam items and identify areas for further study. READINESS REVIEW—it's the smart way to prep!

Register Today!

Return this
Microsoft® Windows® 2000 Beta Training Kit
registration card today

Microsoft® Press

mspress.microsoft.com

0-7356-0644-7

Microsoft® Windows® 2000 Beta Training Kit

FIRST NAME   MIDDLE INITIAL   LAST NAME

INSTITUTION OR COMPANY NAME

ADDRESS

CITY   STATE   ZIP

                                                        ( )
E-MAIL ADDRESS   PHONE NUMBER

U.S. and Canada addresses only. Fill in information above and mail postage-free.
Please mail only the bottom half of this page.

**For information about Microsoft Press®
products, visit our Web site at
mspress.microsoft.com**

Microsoft·Press